STUDY GUIDE

TO ACCOMPANY

ECONOMICS

PRINCIPLES AND POLICY

EIGHTH EDITION

CRAIG SWAN
University of Minnesota

WILLIAM J. BAUMOL
C.V. Starr Center for Applied Economics
New York University

ALAN S. BLINDER
Princeton University

THE DRYDEN PRESS
A DIVISION OF HARCOURT COLLEGE PUBLISHERS
FORT WORTH   PHILADELPHIA   SAN DIEGO   NEW YORK   AUSTIN   ORLANDO   SAN ANTONIO
TORONTO   MONTREAL   LONDON   SYDNEY   TOKYO

TABLE OF CONTENTS

PREFACE

INTRODUCTION

This study guide is designed to be used with *Economics: Principles and Policy*, Eighth Edition, by William J. Baumol and Alan S. Blinder. This guide is not a substitute for the basic textbook; rather, experience has shown that conscientious use of a supplement such as this guide can lead to greater learning and understanding of the course material. It might also improve your grade.

The chapters in this book parallel those in *Economics: Principles and Policy*, Eighth Edition. Each chapter here is a review of the material covered in the textbook chapters. You should first read and study each chapter in the textbook and then use the corresponding chapter in this book. "Use" is the correct verb, as chapters in this book are designed for your *active* participation.

The material with which you will be working is organized into the following elements.

LEARNING OBJECTIVES

Each chapter starts with a set of behavioral learning objectives. These objectives indicate the things you should be able to do upon completing each chapter.

IMPORTANT TERMS AND CONCEPTS

As one of the learning objectives for each chapter states, you should be able to define, understand, and use correctly the terms and concepts that are listed in this section. They parallel the important terms and concepts listed at the end of the text chapter. Being able to *define* these terms is likely to be important for your grade. But to really *understand* what they mean, rather than to temporarily memorize their definition, is even better. The ultimate test of your understanding will be your ability to *use correctly* the terms and concepts in real life situations.

CHAPTER REVIEW

Each review has a summary discussion of the major points of each chapter. The reviews are designed to be used actively. Frequently, you will need to supply the appropriate missing term or to choose between pairs of alternate words. Some of the missing words are quite specific and can be found in the list of important terms and concepts. At other times, the answers are less clear-cut, as the following hypothetical example illustrates: "If people expect inflation at higher rates than before, nominal interest rates are likely to _____." Any of the following would be correct answers: increase, rise, go up. In cases like this, do not get concerned if the answer you choose is different from the one in the back of the book.

IMPORTANT TERMS AND CONCEPTS QUIZ

Each chapter contains an important terms and concepts quiz to help you review important terms and concepts. Match each term with the most appropriate definition.

BASIC EXERCISE

Most chapters have one or more exercises that are designed for you to use as a check on your understanding of a basic principle discussed in the chapter. Many of the exercises use simple arithmetic or geometry. While getting the correct answers is one measure of understanding, do not mistake the arithmetic manipulations for the economic content of the problems. A hand calculator or microcomputer spreadsheet may make the arithmetic less burdensome.

SELF-TEST FOR UNDERSTANDING

Each chapter has a set of multiple choice and true-false questions for you to use as a further check on your understanding. It is important to know not only the correct answers but also why the other answers are wrong. When considering the true-false questions especially, be sure you understand why the false statements are false. Answers for the Self-Tests are in the back of this guide.

APPENDIX

Many chapters in the text contain an appendix, which generally is designed to supplement the chapter content with material that is either a bit more difficult or offers further exposition of a particular economic concept. In some cases, the review material for the appendix parallels that for the chapter, including learning objectives, important terms and concepts, and so forth. On other cases, the appendix material is reviewed here in the form of an additional exercise designed to illustrate the principals discussed in the appendix.

SUPPLEMENTARY EXERCISE

Many chapters end with a supplementary exercise, which may be either an additional mathematical exercise or some suggestions that allow you to use what you have learned in real-world situations. Some exercises use more advanced mathematics. Since many of these exercises review Basic Exercise material, they illustrate how economists use mathematics and are included for students with appropriate background in mathematics. The mathematics are a means to an end and not an end in themselves. It is most important to understand the economic principles that underlie the Basic Exercise, something that does not depend upon advanced mathematics.

ECONOMICS IN ACTION

Most chapters include a brief example, often from recent newspapers or magazines. Each example has been chosen to show how economic concepts and ideas can help one understand real world problems and issues.

ECONOMICS ONLINE

Many chapters include one or more World Wide Web addresses that you can use to access current information or for additional information.
    There is also a homepage for the textbook:

www.dryden.com/econ/baumol

STUDY QUESTIONS

Each chapter ends with a short list of study questions. Working with friends on these questions is a useful way to review chapter material and should help on examinations.

NOTE FROM THE AUTHOR

Being introduced to economics for the first time should be exciting and fun. For many, it is likely to be hard work, but hard work does not have to be dull and uninteresting. Do not look for a pat set of answers with universal applicability. Economics does not offer answers but rather a way of looking at the world and thinking systematically about issues. As the English economist John Maynard Keynes said:

> The theory of economics does not furnish a body of settled conclusions immediately applicable to policy. It is a method rather than a doctrine, an apparatus of the mind, a technique of thinking, which helps its possessor to draw correct conclusions.

Bertrand Russell, the distinguished British philosopher and mathematician, had considered studying economics but decided it was too easy. The Nobel prize-winning physicist, Max Planck, also considered studying economics but decided it was too hard. Whether, like Russell, you find economics easy or, like Planck, you find it hard, I trust that with the use of this guide you will find it relevant and exciting!

The preparation of this guide would not have been possible without the help and contributions of many others. I especially want to acknowledge the contributions of Dr. Marianne Felton of Indiana University, Southeast, Jack Stecher, Jenita Dumond and my wife, Janet.

Craig Swan

CHAPTER

WHAT IS ECONOMICS?

LEARNING OBJECTIVES

After completing this chapter, you should be able to:

■ explain the role of abstraction, or simplification, in economic theory.

■ explain the role of theory as a guide to understanding real-world phenomena.

■ explain why correlation need not imply causation.

■ explain why imperfect information and value judgments will always mean that economics cannot provide definitive answers to all social problems.

■ CHAPTER REVIEW

Chapter 1 has two objectives: It introduces the types of problems that concern economists, offering a set of important ideas for Beyond the Final Exam, and it discusses the methods of economic analysis, in particular the role of theory in economics.

Problems discussed in the first part of the chapter have been chosen to illustrate basic economic issues to be remembered beyond the final exam. You should not only read this material now, but reexamine the list at the end of the course. Understanding the economic principles that underlie these basic issues is the real final examination in economics.

The methods of economic inquiry are best described as "eclectic," meaning they are drawn from many sources according to their usefulness to the subject matter. Economists borrow from other social sciences to theorize about human behavior. They borrow from mathematics to express theories concisely. And they borrow from statistics to make inferences from real-world data about hypotheses suggested by economic theory.

Economists are interested in understanding human behavior not only for its own sake, but for the policy implications of this knowledge. How can we know what to expect from changes resulting from public policy or business decisions unless we understand how markets work and why people behave the way they do? Consider the ideas discussed in the first part of this chapter. Each derives from economic theory. As you will learn, each idea also offers insight into actual experience and is an important guide to evaluating future changes.

As in other scientific disciplines, theory in economics is an abstraction, or simplification, of innumerable complex relationships in the real world. When thinking about some aspects of behavior, say a family's spending decisions or why the price of wheat fluctuates so much, economists will develop a model that attempts to explain the behavior under examination. Elements of the model derive from economic theory. Economists study the model to see what hypotheses, or predictions, it suggests. These can then be checked against real-world data. An economist's model will typically be built not with hammer and nails, but with pencil, paper, and computers. The appropriate degree of abstraction for an economic model is determined, to a large extent, by the problem at hand and is not something that can be specified in advance for all problems.

Economists believe they can make an important contribution to resolving many important social issues. It is hoped that by the time you finish this course, you will agree with this belief. At the same time, you should realize that economics offers a way of looking at questions rather than a comprehensive set of answers to all questions. Economists will always have differences of opinion on final policy recommendations because of incomplete _____ and different _____ (1) judgments.

IMPORTANT TERMS AND CONCEPTS QUIZ ■

Choose the best definition for each of the following terms.

1. _____ Voluntary exchange

2. _____ Opportunity cost

3. _____ Comparative advantage

4. _____ Externalities

5. _____ Marginal analysis

6. _____ Marginal costs

7. _____ Abstraction

8. _____ Theory

9. _____ Correlation

10. _____ Model

11. _____ Productivity

a. Additional cost incurred by a one-unit increase in output.

b. When people and nations concentrate on activities they do best compared to each other.

c. Ignoring many details to focus on essential parts of a problem.

d. Two variables change simultaneously, whether or not a causal relation exists.

e. Effects on third parties that are not part of an economic transaction.

f. Trade in which both parties are willing participants.

g. Evaluation of the impact of changes

h. Output per hour of work.

i. Deliberate simplification of relationships to explain how those relationships work.

j. Value of the next best alternative.

k. Simplified version of some aspect of the economy.

l. Cost per unit produced.

■ **BASIC EXERCISE**

Each statement or vignette below illustrate one of the 12 important Ideas for Beyond the Final Exam. Which statement goes with which idea?

_____ 1. Both parties gain in a voluntary exchange.

_____ 2. Opportunity cost is the correct measure of cost.

_____ 3. Attempts to fight market forces often backfire or have unintended consequences.

_____ 4. Nations can gain from trade by exploiting their comparative advantage.

_____ 5. Good decisions typically require marginal analysis.

_____ 6. The adverse impact of externalities can often be repaired by market methods.

_____ 7. Personal services are subject to a cost disease that drives their prices inexorably higher.

_____ 8. There is a tradeoff between efficiency and equality. Many policies that promote one damage the other.

_____ 9. In the short run, tradeoff policymakers face a trade-off between inflation and unemployment.

_____10. Inflation distorts many economic measurements.

_____11. Budget deficits may or may not be harmful depending on the their size and circumstance.

_____12. In the long run, productivity is almost the only thing that matters for a society's material well-being.

A. On June 2, 1999, Northwest Airlines offered a last minute roundtrip cybersaver fare between Minneapolis and Los Angeles of $179. This fare required travelers to fly on Saturday, June 5, and return the following Monday or Tuesday. AT the same time the regular unrestricted fare was over $1,000 and the two week, advance purchase Saturday stay-over fare was around $300. Economists would argue that, properly counted, Northwest was more than covering costs on the $179 passengers.

B. "We trade because we can get more of the goods and services we value by devoting our energies to what we can do well and using the proceeds to purchase what others are good at making (or doing)."

I.M. Destler, "Trade Policy at a Crossroads," *Brookings Review*, Winter 1999

C. Writing in December of 1996, Robert Kuttner argued that a constitutional amendment requiring a balanced federal budget would be "fiscal overkill." In recessions federal outlays operate as an automatic stabilizer, increasing as private spending declines. "A constitutional amendment mandating budget balance would throw that process into reverse."

"A Balanced Budget Amendment Could Unbalance the Economy," Robert Kuttner, *Business Week*, December 2, 1996

D. In New York individuals who need a passport at the last minute have to pay a $35 fee for rush service and often spend most of a day waiting in line. Others pay up to $150 extra for someone else to stand on-line for them. "If six hours of your time is worth more than $150, you're going to be prepared to use one of these services," said George Brokaw, a New York investment banker.

"Speeding Up a Passport," *The New York Times*, June 6, 1999.

E. Commenting on the economy in July 1998, Alan Greenspan, Chairman of the Board of Governors of the Federal Reserve System said ". . . the extent to which strong growth and high labor force utilization have been joined with low inflation over an extended period is . . . exceptional . . . With labor markets very tight and domestic final demand retaining considerable momentum, the risks of a pickup in inflation remain significant . . . [T]he impending constraint from domestic labor markets could bind more abruptly than it has to date, intensifying inflation pressures."

Testimony of Alan Greenspan, Chairman of the Federal Reserve Board of Governors Before the Committee on Banking, Housing, and Urban Affairs, U.S. Senate, July 21, 1998

F. Third graders Jennifer and Jolene trade sandwiches at lunch because each prefers what the other's mother fixed.

G. Robert Arnold and Robert Dennis argue that the impact of the growth in labor productivity since the beginning of this century has been astounding. Not only has output per worker increased over sevenfold, but "the typical workday and typical workweek shrank . . . the share of family income required to meet the bare necessities was cut in half . . . and goods that were once considered luxuries came within reach of the middle class."

"Perspectives on productivity growth," *Business Economics*, April 1, 1999 .

H. Since 1960, prices of commodities have risen a little over fourfold while the price of services have risen over seven-and-one-half fold. In particular the price of medical care has risen by over twelve-and-one-half fold.

1999 Economic Report of the President, Table B-62.

I. A study of sixteen American cities found that advertised rents for vacant units were higher in cities with rent control than cities without rent control. In cities without rent control, advertised rents are distributed almost evenly above and below median rents as measured by the U.S. Bureau of the Census. In cities with rent control, "most available units are priced well above the median. In other words, inhabitants in cities without rent control have a far easier time finding moderately priced rental units than do inhabitants in rent-controlled cities."

William Tucker, "Rent control drives out affordable housing." *USA Today* (Magazine), July 1998.

J. "There is great comprehension today that ambitious redistribution policies will reduce either economic efficiency or economic growth, or both, because of undesired behavioral adjustment of work, savings, investment, and entrepreneurship."

Assar Lindbeck, "How Can Economic Policy Strike a Balance Between Economic Efficiency and Income Equality," in *Income Inequality: Issues and Policy Options*, A symposium sponsored by the Federal Reserve Bank of Kansas City, August 27–28, 1998. Available on line at www.kc.frb.org/publicat/sympos/1998/sym98prg.htm

K. Under EPA's Acid Rain Program, fossil fuel-fired power plants are allotted SO_2 emission allowances that allow them to emit one ton of SO_2. Utilities with surplus allowances may sell them to utilities whose emissions levels exceed their allowances.

L. Writing in the spring of 1998, Rob Norton argued that although the Federal Reserve had not changed interest rates they had tightened monetary policy. Norton said "real interest rates—short term rates less inflation—have been rising sharply over the past year, as inflation has continued to wither away . . . real rates are higher than they've been since the last recession, meaning that the Fed has in effect been tightening monetary policy" even as it appeared to be making no changes.

"Is the Fed really asleep?," *Fortune*, April 27, 1998.

SELF-TESTS FOR UNDERSTANDING ■

TEST A

Circle the most appropriate answer.

1. Most economists believe that exchange
    a. is likely to be considered mutually advantageous to both parties when it is voluntary.
    b. only takes place when one side can extract a profit from the other.
    c. usually makes both parties worse off.
    d. is best when strictly regulated by the government.

2. Economists define opportunity cost as
    a. the money price of goods and services.
    b. the lowest price you can bargain for.
    c. the value of the next best alternative.
    d. the time you must spend when shopping.

3. Most economists believe that attempts to set prices by decree
    a. will work best in the long run.
    b. are likely to create significant new problems.
    c. are the only way to establish fair prices.
    d. have a history of practical effectiveness.

4. Marginal analysis is concerned with the study of
    a. buying stocks and bonds on credit.
    b. those groups that operate on the margins of the market economy.
    c. changes, such as the increase in cost when output increases.
    d. an engineer's fudge factor for possible errors.

5. When the actions of some economic agents impose cost on others, for example, the polluting smoke of a factory or power plant,
    a. market mechanisms may exist that can help remedy the situation.
    b. the only answer is government regulation.
    c. there is very little one can do; such is the price of progress.
    d. it is always best to close down the offending action.

6. The cost disease of personal services
    a. could be eliminated if only the government would regulate prices.
    b. would be eliminated if everyone practiced safe sex.
    c. is only an excuse for the government's inability to control its own spending.
    d. refers to the impact of differential rates of growth productivity between the manufacturing and service sectors of the economy.

7. Most economists believe that policies to reduce inflation
    a. have never been successful.
    b. will never be adopted in democracies.
    c. normally require a higher rate of unemployment.
    d. have an immediate and lasting impact.

8. In addition to interest rates, information about _____ is necessary to investigate the real cost of borrowing and lending.
    a. the inflation rate
    b. exchange rates
    c. the unemployment rate
    d. marginal cost

9. Economic analysis shows that federal budget deficits
    a. are a significant burden on future generations.
    b. are really of no concern.
    c. produce an impact that will depend on particular circumstances.
    d. are, in reality, usually beneficial.

10. Economic analysis suggests that
    a. policies that promote the highest rate of economic growth unambiguously improve the distribution of income.
    b. policies to increase equality may reduce output.
    c. incentives for work and savings have almost no impact on people's behavior.
    d. there is no trade-off between the size of the economic pie and how the pie is divided.

11. With respect to international trade,
    a. a country can gain only if its neighbors lose.
    b. countries should try to be self-sufficient of all goods.
    c. only those countries with the highest productivity levels will gain.
    d. a country can gain by producing those goods in which it has a comparative advantage.

12. Small differences in the productivity growth rate
    a. make little difference, even over periods as long as a century.
    b. can compound into significant differences.
    c. can be safely ignored by citizens and politicians.
    d. will lead only to small differences in the standard of living between countries.

TEST B

Circle T or F for true or false.

T F   1. Economic models are no good unless they include all of the detail that characterizes the real world.

T F   2. Material in this text will reveal the true answer to many important social problems.

T F   3. Opportunity cost is measured by considering the best alternative forgone.

T F   4. Economists' policy prescriptions differ because of incomplete information and different value judgments.

T F   5. Theory and practical policy have nothing to do with each other.

T F   6. If two variables are correlated, we can be certain that one causes the other.

T F   7. The best economic models all use the same degree of abstraction.

T F   8. An economist tests a hypothesis when she deliberately simplifies the nature of relationships in order to explain cause and effect.

T F   9. In any transaction one party must always gain at the expense of the other.

T F 10. The dollars one must pay is the best measure of the cost of any decision.

T F 11. We would all be better off if the government regulated more markets.

T F 12. The most productive economies would be better off if they did not trade with other nations and tried to produce everything they need by themselves.

T F 13. No business should ever sell its output at a price that does not cover full cost.

T F 14. Since pollution problems are often seen as a market shortcoming, market methods cannot help correct the problem.

T F 15. Economics suggests that the increasing cost of public service reflects only the greed of public employees.

T F 16. Policies to lower unemployment usually reduce the rate of inflation at the same time.

T F 17. The real cost of borrowing is higher when high interest rates are associated with high rates of inflation than when they are not.

T F 18. Balancing the federal government's budget is always better for the economy than a budget deficit.

T F 19. There is no tradeoff between policies that increase output and those that equalize income.

T F 20. Over the long run, it makes little difference whether productivity grows at 1 percent or 2 percent per year.

SUPPLEMENTARY EXERCISE   ■

The following suggested readings offer an excellent introduction to the ideas and lives of economists past and present:

1. *The Worldly Philosophers: The Lives, Times & Ideas of the Great Economic Thinkers*, 6th ed., by Robert L. Heilbroner (Touchstone Books, 1987).

2. *Lives of the Laureates*, 3rd edition, edited by William Breit and Roger W. Spencer (MIT Press, 1995). This is a collection of recollections by 13 winners of the Nobel Prize in Economics.

ECONOMICS IN ACTION

PLAY BALL

Are baseball players overpaid? Does it make sense to pay someone over $10 million to play what is, after all, just a game? Haven't baseball salaries gotten out of hand? Even after adjusting for inflation, Babe Ruth's highest salary is estimated to have been about $700,000. Why are players today paid so much, and does it make economic sense?

Writing in *Scientific American*, Paul Wallich and Elizabeth Corcoran explain the difference in salaries using the concepts of opportunity cost and marginal analysis, ideas used extensively by economists. Under the reserve clause, in effect from 1903 until the mid-1970s, a baseball player who did not like his contract had little choice other than retiring from baseball. Players were not free to bargain with other teams. After the introduction of free agency, baseball players could sell their services to the team with the best offer.

Gerald Scully, in his book *The Business of Major League Baseball*, used statistical techniques to see how hitting and pitching help determine a team's winning percentage and how a team's revenue relates to its record and the size of the market in which it plays. He then estimated how adding a particular player might add to a team's performance and hence its revenue.

Using data from the late 1980s, Scully found that the performance of selected superstars increased team revenues by $2 million to $3 million, numbers consistent with the highest salaries at the time. Using data from the late 1960s, he estimates that superstars increased team revenues by $600,000 to $1 million and noted that the highest salaries were only $100,000 to $125,000.

1. How would marginal analysis help a team determine how much it should offer a free agent?

2. How does the concept of opportunity cost help explain baseball salaries? What was the opportunity cost of a baseball player's time under the reserve clause? How did free agency change the opportunity cost for a player deciding whether to stay with a team or move to a new team?

SOURCES: Paul Wallich and Elizabeth Corcoran, "The MBAs of Summer," *Scientific American* (June 1992): p. 120. Gerald W. Scully, *The Business of Major League Baseball* (Chicago: University of Chicago Press, 1989).

STUDY QUESTIONS

1. Explain the relationships between theories, models, and hypotheses.

2. Why are theories necessary for understanding the causal links between economic variables? Why can't the facts speak for themselves?

3. Many trace the establishment of economics as a field of study to the publication of Adam Smith's *Wealth of Nations* in 1776. Why, after more than 200 years, do so many questions remain?

ECONOMICS ONLINE

Find out about the current and former Nobel Prize winners in Economics at this site maintained by the Nobel Prize committee. There are easy links to the Nobel Prize in Economics from this site:

www.nobel.se

The Minneapolis Federal Reserve Bank regularly publishes interviews with economists in its quarterly publication *The Region*. The December 1994 interview is with Alan Blinder. You can read these interviews on line at

woodrow.mpls.frb.fed.us/pubs/region/int.html

THE USE AND MISUSE OF GRAPHS

LEARNING OBJECTIVES

After completing this chapter, you should be able to:

■ interpret various graphs:

   ■ use a two-variable graph to determine what combinations of variables go together.

   ■ use a three-variable graph to determine what combinations of the X and Y variables are consistent with the same value for the Z variable.

■ construct two-variable and three-variable graphs.

■ compute the slope of a straight line and explain what it measures.

■ explain how to compute the slope of a curved line.

■ explain how a 45-degree line can divide a graph into two regions, one in which the Y variable exceeds the X variable, and another in which the X variable exceeds the Y variable.

■ explain the implications of the pitfalls of time series graphs:

   ■ failure to adjust for changes in prices and/or population.

Important Terms and Concepts

VARIABLE

TWO-VARIABLE DIAGRAM

HORIZONTAL AND VERTICAL AXES

ORIGIN (OF A GRAPH)

SLOPE OF A STRAIGHT (OR CURVED) LINE

NEGATIVE, POSITIVE, ZERO, AND INFINITE SLOPE

TANGENT TO A CURVE

Y-INTERCEPT

RAY THROUGH THE ORIGIN, OR RAY 45-DEGREE LINE

45⁰ LINE

CONTOUR MAP

PRODUCTON INDIFFERENCE MAP

TIME SERIES GRAPH

INFLATION

DEFLATION BY A PRICE INDEX

REAL GDP

- the use of short time periods with unique features.

- omitting the origin.

- the use of different units to measure the same variable.

■ CHAPTER REVIEW

Economists like to draw pictures, primarily *graphs*. Your textbook and this study guide will make extensive use of graphs. There is nothing very difficult about graphs, but understanding them from the beginning will help you avoid mistakes later on.

All the graphs we will use start with two straight lines, one on the bottom and one on the left side. These edges of the graph will usually have labels to indicate what is being measured in both the vertical and horizontal directions. The line on the bottom is called the (horizontal/vertical) axis, and the

(1)   line running up the side is called the _____ axis. The point at which the two lines meet is called the _____. The variable measured along the horizontal axis is often called the X variable, while the term Y variable is often used to refer to the variable measured along the vertical axis.

Figure 2-1 is a two-variable diagram plotting expenditures on alcoholic beverages and ministers' salaries. Does this graph imply that wealthier clergymen drink more, or does it suggest that more drinking in general is increasing the demand for, and hence the salaries of, clergymen? Most likely neither interpretation is correct; just because you can plot two variables does not mean that one caused the other.

Many two-variable diagrams encountered in introductory economics use *straight lines*, primarily for simplicity. An important characteristic of a straight line is its slope, measured by comparing differences between two points. To calculate the slope of a straight line, divide the (horizontal/vertical) change by the corresponding _____ change as you move to the right along the line. The change between any two points can be used to compute the slope because the slope of a straight line is _____. If the straight line shows that both

FIGURE 2-1   **Ministers' Salaries and Expenditures on Alcohol**

(2)

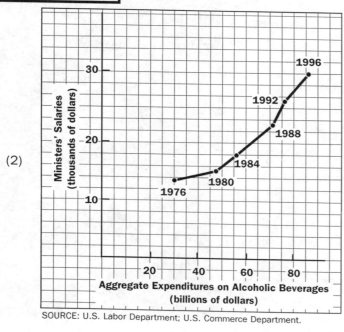

SOURCE: U.S. Labor Department; U.S. Commerce Department.

the horizontal and vertical variables increase together, then the line is said to have a (<u>positive/negative</u>)

slope; that is, as we move to the right, the line slopes (<u>up/down</u>). If one variable decreases as the other vari-

able increases, the line is said to have a _____ slope. A line with a zero slope shows

_____ change in the Y variable as the X variable changes.

A special type of straight line passes through the origin of a graph. This is called a _____   (3)

through the origin. Its slope is measured the same as the slope of any other straight line. A special type

of ray is one that connects all points where the vertical and horizontal variables are equal. If the ver-

tical and horizontal variables are measured in the same units, then this line has a slope of +1 and is

called the _____ line.

Like straight lines, curved lines also have slopes, but the slope of a curved line is not constant. We

measure the slope of a curved line at any point by the slope of the one straight line that just touches,

or is _____ to, the line at that point.   (4)

A special type of graph is used by economists as well as cartographers. Such a graph can represent

three dimensions on a diagram with only two axes by the use of _____ lines. A tradi-   (5)

tional application of such a graph in economics is a diagram that measures inputs along the horizon-

tal and vertical axes and then uses contour lines to show what different combinations of inputs can be

used to produce the same amount of output.

As illustrated in the text, economists make extensive use of time series graphs. These are two vari-

able graphs with time measured along the (<u>horizontal/vertical</u>) axis and one or more variables of inter-   (6)

est measured along the _____ axis. Time series graphs are an effective way to convey a

lot of information, but they also can be misleading if misused either inadvertently or deliberately.

When making or interpreting time series graphs you should be aware of the following pitfalls:

- ■ Failing to adjust for inflation or population growth can give a misleading impression of
  growth.

- ■ Showing only a brief period of time and/or one with an atypical beginning or ending can give
  a distorted impression of actual experience.

- ■ Omitting the origin can give an exaggerated impression of changes.

- ■ Changing the units of measurement, say from pounds to ounces or dollars to pennies, can
  make a graph arbitrarily steeper or flatter.

■ IMPORTANT TERMS AND CONCEPTS QUIZ

Choose the best definition for each of the following terms.

1. _____ Variable
2. _____ Two-variable diagram
3. _____ Horizontal axis
4. _____ Vertical axis
5. _____ Origin
6. _____ Slope
7. _____ Negative slope
8. _____ Positive slope
9. _____ Zero slope
10. _____ Infinite slope
11. _____ Tangent to a curve
12. _____ Y-intercept
13. _____ Ray
14. _____ 45-degree line
15. _____ Contour map
16. _____ Production indifference map
17. _____ Time series graph
18. _____ Inflation
19. _____ Deflation by a price index
20. _____ Real GDP

a. Graph of how a variable changes over time.

b. Vertical line segment.

c. Straight line, touching a curve at a point without cutting the curve.

d. A sustained increase in prices.

e. Straight line emanating from the origin.

f. Object whose magnitude is measured by a number.

g. Simultaneous representation of the magnitudes of two variables.

h. A two variable diagram in whcih time is measured on the horixotnal axis.

i. Straight line through the origin with a slope of +1.

j. Point at which a straight line cuts the vertical axis.

k. Line that goes down, moving from left to right.

l. Using data on prices to adjust for inflation.

m. The side of a graph.

n. Two-dimensional representation of three variables.

o. Ratio of vertical change to corresponding horizontal change.

p. Line that rises, moving from left to right.

q. The bottom line of a graph.

r. Point where both axes meet and where both variables are zero.

s. Value of all newly produced goods and services, evalued in dollars of constant purchasing power.

t. Line that neither rises nor falls, moving from left to right.

u. A graph showing different combinations of two inputs necessary to produce a given level of output.

READING GRAPHS

These exercises are designed to give practice working with two-variable diagrams.

1. **Understanding a Demand Curve**
   The demand curve in Figure 2-2 represents the demand for new Ph.D. economists.
   a. What quantity would colleges and universities demand if they have to pay a salary of $54,000?
   _____

   b. What does the graph indicate would happen to the quantity demanded if salaries fall to $42,000? The quantity demanded would (_increase/decrease_) to _____.

   c. What would happen to the quantity demanded if salaries were $60,000? It would (_increase/decrease_) to _____.

   d. What is the slope of the demand curve? _____.

   e. Explain how the slope of the demand curve provides information about the change in the number of new Ph.D. economists demanded as salary changes.

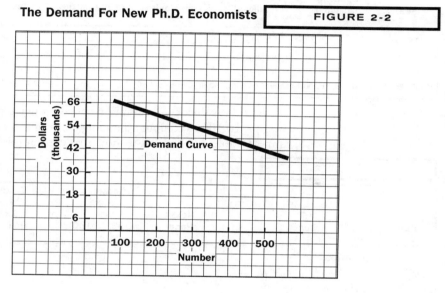

The Demand For New Ph.D. Economists | **FIGURE 2-2**

2. **Understanding a 45-degree Line**
   Figure 2-3 shows data on grade point averages for Valerie and her friends. Overall averages are measured along the horizontal axis while GPAs for courses in economics are measured along the vertical axis. Figure 2-3 also includes a 45-degree line.
   a. How many individuals have higher overall GPAs than economics GPAs? _____

   b. How many individuals do better in economics courses than in their other courses? _____

   c. If all of Valerie's friends had their best grades in economics courses, all of the points in Figure 2-3 would lie (_above/below_) the 45-degree line.

   d. If all of the points in Figure 2-3 were below the 45-degree line, we could conclude that Valerie and her friends did better in (_economics/non-economics_) courses.

Grade Point Averages | **FIGURE 2-3**

3. **Growth Trends**

a. Look at Table 2-1, which has data on personal consumption expenditures. The data show that over the thirty eight years from 1960 to 1998 aggregate personal consumption expenditures increased more than seventeenfold (5,810.2/ 332.2 = 17.5). Do you agree that on average individuals in 1998 are able to buy 17.5 times as many goods and services as they could in 1960?

TABLE 2-1	Personal Income After Taxes				
Year	Aggregate Personal Consumption Spending (billions)	Population (millions)	Consumption Spending per Capita	Price Index (1992 = 100)	Real Consumption Spending per Capita (1992 prices)
1960	332.2	180,671	_____	23.19	_____
1998	5,810.2	270,290	_____	112.70	_____

SOURCE: 1999 Economic Report of the President, Tables B-1, B-7, B-34

b. For each year in Table 2-1 divide aggregate consumption spending by the corresponding population to compute consumption spending per capita rather than aggregate spending. Rather than a nineteenfold increase, per capita consumption spending in 1998 was only _____ times its 1960 level.

c. For each year divide consumption spending per capita by the corresponding price index and multiply by 100 to compute spending per capita in constant prices. The figures in the last column of Table 2-1 will tell us how real consumption spending per capita (expressed in 1992 prices) has changed since 1960. In 1998, per capita real consumption spending was _____ times its 1960 level.

TABLE 2-2				
Year	Concert	Ticket Price	Consumer Price Index (1998 = 100)	Ticket Price in 1995 Dollars
1965	Beatles	$3.50	19.3	$_____
1971	The Band, Muddy Waters, John Sebastian, Paul Butterfield Blues Band	$8.00	24.8	$_____
1976	Fleetwood Mac, Jeff Beck	$9.00	34.9	$_____
1978	Eagles, Steve Miller	$10.00	40.0	$_____
1982	The Who	$16.00	59.2	$_____
1983	Simon and Garfunkel	$20.00	61.1	$_____
1985	Bruce Springsteen	$17.50	66.0	$_____
1986	Bob Dylan, Grateful Dead	$20.00	67.2	$_____
1988	Pink Floyd	$22.50	72.6	$_____
1989	Rolling Stones	$28.50	76.1	$_____
1993	Paul McCartney	$32.50	88.7	$_____
1995	Elton John	$35.50	93.5	$_____
1996	Rod Stewart	$34.50	96.3	$_____
1997	Fleetwood Mac	$47.50	98.5	$_____
1998	Garth Brooks	$21.25	100.0	$_____

SOURCE: *Minneapolis StarTribune,* May 21, 1993; 1999 Economic Report of the President; Stephanie Hanson, Target Center.

4. **Rock Concerts: Adjusting for Inflation**
Who paid more to attend their favorite rock/country concert, you or your parents? Table 2-2 has data on ticket prices of stadium rock concerts. Use the data on consumer prices to adjust ticket prices for inflation and express prices for earlier years in 1995 dollars. (Divide each ticket price by the value of the price index and multiply by 100.)

5. **Choice of Time Periods**
In 1960, John F. Kennedy campaigned on a promise to get the country moving, including more rapid economic growth. When Kennedy was elected president the unemployment rate was rising as the economy was slipping into a recession. Many observers were claiming that for a variety of "structural" reasons the United States was entering an era of permanently higher unemployment. A major piece of evidence used to support this line of thinking was the rising succession of lowest unemployment rates in each postwar business expansion up to the early 1960s. The data are presented here, in Figure 2-4, together with a trend line connecting the succession of lowest unemployment rates. Use the data in Figure 2-4 to extend the time series graph and to check the accuracy of this argument. If the graph were restricted to data from 1968 to 1983, what would a similar trend line over this period show? What could one conclude from such a trend line?

Rate of Unemployment

FIGURE 2-4

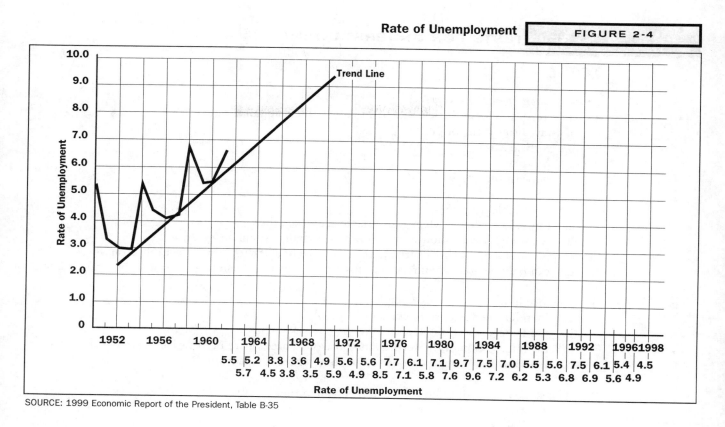

1952	1956	1960	1964	1968	1972	1976	1980	1984	1988	1992	19961998
		5.5	5.2	3.8	3.6	4.9	5.6	5.6	7.7	6.1	7.1	9.7	7.5	7.0	5.5	5.6	7.5	6.1	5.4	4.5
		5.7	4.5	3.8	3.5	5.9	4.9	8.5	7.1	5.8	7.6	9.6	7.2	6.2	5.3	6.8	6.9	5.6	4.9

Rate of Unemployment

SOURCE: 1999 Economic Report of the President, Table B-35

6. **Dangers of Omitting the Origin**

A quick looks at Figure 2-5a suggests that in early February 1999 stocks lost all their value. Table 2-3 contains data on stock prices as measured by the Dow Jones Index. Plot this data in Figure 2-5b. Which figure gives the more accurate representation of the change in stock prices and why?

Stock Prices—February 1999

TABLE 2-3

Date	Stock Price (Dow Jones Index)
Feb 3	9,366.81
Feb 4	9,304.50
Feb 5	9,304.24
Feb 8	9,291.11
Feb 9	9,133.03

Stock Prices - February 1999

FIGURE 2-5

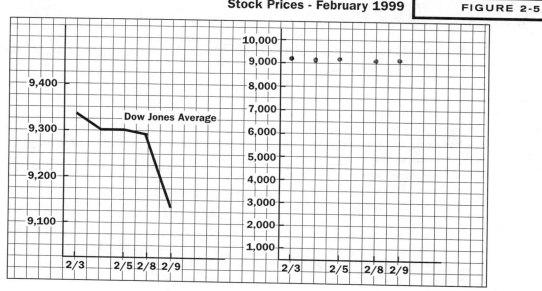

■   **SELF TESTS FOR UNDERSTANDING**

TEST A

Circle the most appropriate answer.

1. The vertical line on the left side of a two-variable diagram is called the
   a. ray through the origin.
   b. vertical axis.
   c. X axis.
   d. slope of the graph.

2. A two-variable diagram
   a. can only be drawn when one variable causes another.
   b. is a useful way to show how two variables change simultaneously.
   c. is a useful way of summarizing the influence of all factors that affect the Y variable.
   d. can only be used when relationships between variables can be represented by straight lines.

3. The origin of a two-variable graph is
   a. found in the lower right corner of a graph.
   b. the same as the Y-intercept.
   c. the intersection of the vertical and horizontal axes where both variables are equal to zero.
   d. found by following the slope to the point where it equals zero.

4. The slope of a straight line is found by dividing the
   a. Y variable by the X variable.
   b. vertical axis by the horizontal axis.
   c. largest value of the Y variable by the smallest value of the X variable.
   d. vertical change by the corresponding horizontal change.

5. The slope of a straight line
   a. is the same at all points along the line.
   b. increases moving to the right.
   c. will be zero when the X variable equals zero.
   d. is always positive.

6. If a straight line has a positive slope, then we know that
   a. it runs uphill, moving to the right.
   b. the slope of the line will be greater than that of a 45-degree line.
   c. it must also have a positive Y-intercept.
   d. it will reach its maximum value when its slope is zero.

7. Referring to parts (a), (b), (c), and (d) of Figure 2-6, determine which line has a(n)
   a. positive slope _____
   b. negative slope _____
   c. zero slope _____
   d. infinite slope _____

8. Referring to Figure 2-7, determine at which point(s) the curved line has a(n)
   a. positive slope   _____ _____ _____
   b. negative slope   _____ _____ _____
   c. zero slope   _____ _____ _____
   d. infinite slope   _____ _____ _____

FIGURE 2-6

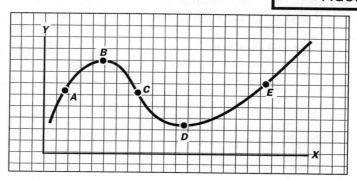

FIGURE 2-7

9. If when $X = 5$, $Y = 16$ and when $X = 8$, $Y = 10$, then the
   a. line connecting X and Y has a positive slope.
   b. line connecting X and Y is a ray through the origin.
   c. slope of the line connecting X and Y is +6.
   d. slope of the line connecting X and Y is –2.

10. The slope of a curved line is
    a. the same at all points on the line.
    b. found by dividing the Y variable by the X variable.
    c. found by determining the slope of a straight line tangent to the curved line at the point of interest.
    d. always positive.

11. If a curved line is in the shape of a hill, then the point of zero slope will occur at the
    a. origin of the line.
    b. highest point of the line.
    c. Y-intercept of the line.
    d. point where a ray from the origin intercepts the line.

12. The Y-intercept is
    a. the same as the origin of a graph.
    b. the point where a line cuts the Y axis.
    c. usually equal to the X-intercept.
    d. equal to the reciprocal of the slope of a straight line.

13. If the Y-intercept of a straight line is equal to zero, then this line is called
    a. the opportunity cost of a graph.
    b. a ray through the origin.
    c. the 45-degree line.
    d. the X axis.

14. A ray is
    a.   any straight line with a slope of +1.
    b.   any line, straight or curved, that passes through the origin of a graph.
    c.   a straight line with a positive Y-intercept.
    d.   a straight line that passes through the origin.

15. If the X and Y variables are measured in the same units, a 45-degree line will
    a.   have a positive Y-intercept.
    b.   have a negative slope.
    c.   show all points where X and Y are equal.
    d.   be steeper than the Y axis.

16. If X and Y are measured in the same units, and we consider a point that lies below a 45-degree line, then we know that for the X and Y combination associated with this point,
    a.   the X variable is greater than the Y variable.
    b.   a line from the origin through this point will be a ray and will have a slope greater than +1.
    c.   the Y variable is greater than the X variable.
    d.   the slope of the point is less than 1.

17. Referring to parts (a), (b), (c), and (d) of Figure 2-8, determine which part(s) show a ray through the origin.
    a.   (b)
    b.   (a) and (c)
    c.   (a) and (d)
    d.   (c) and (d)

FIGURE 2-8

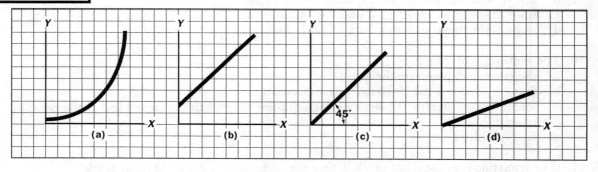

18. If in part (d) of Figure 2-8, the Y variable changes by 2 units when the X variable changes by 5 units, then the slope of the line is
    a.   .4 = (2/5).
    b.   2.5 = (5/2).
    c.   10 = (2 + 3 + 5).
    d.   Insufficient information to compute.

19. If two straight lines have the same slope, then they
    a.   must also have the same Y-intercept.
    b.   will show the same change in Y for similar changes in X.
    c.   will both pass through the origin.
    d.   are said to be complements.

20. A contour map
    a.   is always better than a two-variable diagram.
    b.   is a way of collapsing three variables into a two-variable diagram.
    c.   shows how the Y variable changes when the X variable is held constant.
    d.   is only of relevance to geographers.

TEST B

Circle T or F for true or false.

T F 1. The line along the bottom of a two-variable graph is called the vertical axis.

T F 2. The slope of a line measures the value of the Y variable when the X variable is equal to zero.

T F 3. The slope of a straight line is the same at all points on the line.

T F 4. A negative slope means that the Y variable decreases when the X variable increases.

T F 5. The slope of a curved line cannot be measured.

T F 6. A straight line that has a Y-intercept of zero is also called a ray through the origin.

T F 7. All rays through the origin have the same slope.

T F 8. If X and Y are measured in the same units, then a 45-degree line is a ray through the origin with a slope of +1.

T F 9. If X and Y are measured in the same units, then any point above a 45-degree line is a point at which the Y variable is greater than the X variable.

T F 10. A contour map is a way to show the relationship between two variables in three dimensions.

SUPPLEMENTARY EXERCISE   ■

Table 2-4 reports data on tuition and required fees at four-year universities. How do increases in tuition and fees compare to the increase in prices in general and increases in income? You can adjust the data on nominal tuition and fees by dividing it by the price index. (Remember to multiply by 100.) An increase in real tuition and fees would indicate that this element of the cost of college has increased faster than prices in general. Once you have computed tuition and fees in terms of 1987 purchasing power, divide these figures by real per capita income to see how tuition and fees have changed relative to real income per capita.

At most schools tuition and fees increase every year. How have these recent increases compared to inflation and increases in personal income? Use the reference to Table 2-4 to update these figures. What has happened to tuition and fees at the college or university you attend? The appropriate office at your institution should be able to provide current and historical data on tuition and fees.

Tuition and Required Fees | **TABLE 2-4**

Year	4-Year Universities Tuition and Fees Public	Private	Price Index (1992 = 100)	Real Income per Capita
1970–71	$ 478	$ 1,980	30.16	$12,203
1980–81	$ 915	$ 4,275	76.61	$14,966
1990–91	$2,159	$11,379	94.87	$17.853
1995–96	$3,151	$15,605	108.66	$18,815

SOURCE: *Digest of Education Statistics,* 1997, National Center for Education Statistics, U.S. Department of Education, Table 301; *1999 Economic Report of the President,* Tables B-7 and B-3.1.

CHAPTER

3

THE ECONOMY: MYTH AND REALITY

LEARNING OBJECTIVES

After completing this chapter, you should be able to:

■ explain the difference between inputs and outputs.

■ explain why total output of the American economy is larger than that of other nations.

■ explain why real GDP per capita is a better measure of living standards than GDP.

■ explain the difference between a closed and an open economy.

■ describe the broad changes in American work experience: Who goes to work outside the home? What sorts of jobs do they hold? What sorts of goods and services do they produce?

■ describe who gets what proportion of national income.

■ describe the role of government in the American economy.

Important Terms and Concepts

FACTORS OF PRODUCTION (INPUTS)

OUTPUTS

GROSS DOMESTIC PRODUCT (GDP)

REAL GDP PER CAPITA

OPEN ECONOMY

CLOSED ECONOMY

RECESSION

PRODUCTIVITY

TRANSFER PAYMENTS

PROGRESSIVE TAX

MIXED ECONOMY

■ CHAPTER REVIEW

This chapter offers an introduction to and overview of the American economy. The money value of

total output of the American economy is usually measured by something called gross

(1)   _____   _____   or   _____   for

short. American GDP is so large because of the size of the work force and the _____

of American workers. Other countries, for example China and India, have larger populations, but the

productivity of their workers does not compare with that of American workers.

Why is the American economy so productive? It is useful to view an economic system as a social

(2)   mechanism that organizes (inputs/outputs) to produce _____. Many believe that the pro-

ductivity of the American economy is a reflection of business competition fostered by the extensive use

of _____ markets and _____ enterprise.

No economy is self-sufficient. All economies trade with each other, although their reliance on trade

varies. The average of exports and imports as a percentage of GDP is often used as a measure of the

(3)   degree to which an economy can be called _____ or _____. Compared to other

industrialized countries, the United States would look like a(n) (closed/open) economy. Both exports

and imports have increased substantially since World War II and are now about 12 percent of

American GDP.

Because it uses money values to add up different types of outputs, i.e., food, clothes, cars, medical

services, and new houses, GDP will increase when prices increase even if there is no change in pro-

(4)   duction. A sustained increase in prices on average is referred to as _____ . A time

series graph of American GDP since World War II shows significant growth. As with all time series

graphs, one needs to be careful about exactly how the variable of interest is measured. If one is inter-

ested in consumption possibilities, it is best to correct for inflation by looking at GDP measured in

dollars of constant purchasing power or _____ GDP. It may also be useful to adjust real

GDP by the growth in population for a measure of GDP _____ _____. Adjusting for

inflation and population growth still shows a doubling of per capita real GDP over the past 40 years.

While the time series graph of real GDP for the United States shows significant growth since

World War II, it has not been continual growth. There have been periods when total output declined.

These periods are called _____ . How the government should respond during or in   (5)

anticipation of a period of recession continues to spark controversy.

Organizing inputs, also called _____ of production , is a central issue that any economy   (6)

must address. For the most part, output in the United States is produced by private firms that com-

pete in free markets. Most economists believe that having to meet the competition is an important rea-

son why the American economy is so productive. Inputs include labor, capital (e.g., machinery and

buildings), and natural resources. It is the revenue from selling output that creates income for these

factors of production.

In the United States the largest share of income accrues to which factor of production?

_____. The income earned by those who put up the money to buy buildings and machin-   (7)

ery comes in the form of interest and profits. Together, these two forms of income receive about

_____ cents of each sales dollar. Most Americans work in (<u>manufacturing/service</u>) industries.

The discussion in the text lists five roles for government:

    1)   To provide certain goods and services.

    2)   To raise taxes to finance its operations.

    3)   To redistribute income.

    4)   To regulate business.

    5)   To enforce the rules of business and society, including property rights.

The size of the American government relative to GDP is (<u>small/large</u>) compared to most other   (8)

industrialized countries. This comparison and any other list does not say whether particular actions

are best done by the government or by the private economy. Are there legitimate unmet needs that

should be addressed by government, or is government already too big? Much of the material in sub-

sequent chapters is designed to help you understand what markets do well and what they do poorly. It

is hoped that a better understanding of the insights from economic analysis will help you decide where

you would draw the line between markets and government.

■   **IMPORTANT TERMS AND CONCEPTS QUIZ**

Choose the best definition for each of the following terms.

1. _____ Inputs (factors of production)

2. _____ Outputs

3. _____ Gross domestic product (GDP)

4. _____ Real GDP per capita

5. _____ Open economy

6. _____ Closed economy

7. _____ Recession

8. _____ Productivity

9. _____ Transfer payments

10. _____ Progressive tax

11. _____ Mixed economy

a. Money value of all goods and services produced in a year.

b. Economy with public influence over the workings of free markets.

c. A sustained increase in the average level of prices.

d. Money that individuals receive from the government as grants.

e. Economy in which exports and imports are small relative to GDP.

f. Total output for the economy divided by population.

g. A period when real GDP declines.

h. Labor, machinery, buildings, and natural resources used to produce

i. Goods and services desired by consumers.

j. International trade is a large proportion of GDP.

k. Ouput per worker.

l. The proportion of income paid as taxes increases as income increases.

■   **BASIC EXERCISES**

THE MORE THINGS CHANGE, THE MORE THEY ARE THE SAME—OR NOT?

Chapter 3 was a quick introduction to the structure of the American economy. These questions ask you to consider how some things may have changed over the past forty years.

1. What do Americans buy? Complete the missing column in Table 3-1 to see how consumption spending has changed. Do these changes surprise you? What do you think explains them? You can find more detail about consumption spending at

TABLE 3-1	Composition of Consumption Spending			
	1960		**1998**	
	Spending ($ billions)	**Proportion**	**Spending ($billions)**	**Proportion**
Durables[a]	43.3	_____	724.7	_____
Non Durables[b]	152.9	_____	1,662.4	_____
Services[c]	136.0	_____	3,420.8	_____
Total	332.2		5,807.9	

[a] e.g., automobiles, furniture
[b] e.g., food, clothing, gasoline
[c] e.g., housing, medical care, entertainment, education

SOURCE: *1999 Economic Report of the President*, Table B-1.

www.bea.doc.gov/bea/dn1.htm

Composition of Federal Government Spending

TABLE 3-2

	1960		1998	
	Spending ($ billions)	Proportion	Spending ($ billions)	Proportion
National Defense	48.1	_____	268.5	16%
Health	0.8	_____	324.2	20%
Pensions and Income Security	19.0	_____	612.4	37%
Interest	6.9	_____	243.4	15%
All Other	17.4	_____	20.4	13%
Total	92.2		1,652.5	100%

SOURCE: *1999 Economic Report of the President,* Table B-80.

2. How has the spending of the federal government changed? Complete the missing column in Table 3-2 to see. Do these changes surprise you? What do you think explains them?

Labor Force Participation: 1998

TABLE 3-3

	Men			Women		
Age	Labor Force[a]	Population	Participation Rate[b]	Labor Force[a]	Population	Participation Rate[b]
16-18	1,728	4,059	_____	1,607	3,835	_____
18-20	2,516	3,909	_____	2,405	3,840	_____
20-24	7,221	8,804	_____	6,418	8,790	_____
25-35	17,796	19,094	_____	15,017	19,683	_____
35-45	20,242	21,857	_____	17,294	22,442	_____
45-55	14,963	16,773	_____	13,405	17,600	_____
55-65	7,253	10,649	_____	5,962	11,646	_____
65 & over	2,240	13,613	_____	1,607	18,625	_____

SOURCE: Bureau of Labor Statistics, *Employment and Earning,* January 1999

[a] Labor Force = people working plus those looking for work
[b] Labor Force Participation Rate = Labor Force/Population

3. Who's going to work outside the home now? The labor force participation rate is an important measure of labor markets. It is computed by looking at the number of people working or looking for work as a proportion of total population. This measure excludes those who are retired and those who are not looking for paid work. Figure 3-1 shows labor force participation by men and women of various ages in 1950. Complete the missing columns in Table 3-3 to compute labor force participation rates for 1998 and then plot your results in Figure 3-1 to see how labor force participation has changed since 1950. Are you surprised by the differences for

Labor Force Participation: 1950 and 1998

FIGURE 3-1

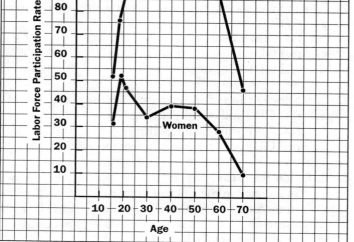

men and women? Do the changes over time surprise you? What do you think explains these differences?

■   **SELF-TESTS FOR UNDERSTANDING**

TEST A

Circle the most appropriate answer.

1. Which of the following help to explain why output of the American economy is as high as it is? (There may be more than one correct answer to this question.)
   a. The size of the labor force.
   b. The amount of money provided by the government.
   c. Business regulation.
   d. The productivity of American workers.

2. Total output of the United States economy
   a. is slightly less than that of Japan.
   b. is comparable to that of other industrialized countries.
   c. exceeds that of other national economies.
   d. is among the lowest for industrialized countries.

3. Many economists believe that the success of the American economy reflects, in part, our reliance on (There may be more than one correct answer.)
   a. regulation.
   b. private enterprise.
   c. free markets.
   d. nationalization.

4. Gross domestic product measures
   a. consumer spending.
   b. the vulgarness of many consumer goods.
   c. unpaid economic activity that takes place inside households.
   d. the money value of all the goods and services produced in an economy in a year.

5. Gross domestic product per capita refers to
   a. GDP per person (GDP/population).
   b. GDP times population (GDP × population).
   c. GDP per worker (GDP/employment).
   d. GDP measured in dollars of constant purchasing power.

6. The average standard of living over time is best measured by
   a. GDP.
   b. GDP per capita.
   c. real GDP.
   d. real GDP per capita.

7. If the price of everything increases, but the production of specific goods and services is unchanged,
   a. real GDP will actually decline.
   b. real GDP will remain unchanged.
   c. real GDP will increase as prices increase.

8. Inflation refers to
   a. an increase in the stock of money.
   b. an increase in the price of any single commodity.
   c. a sustained increase in the average level of prices.
   d. an increase in GDP.

9. The term *recession* refers to
   a. a period of inflation.
   b. a period of above-average economic growth.
   c. reductions in government spending designed to reduce the deficit.
   d. a period when real GDP declines.

10. When referring to inputs, the term *capital* refers to
    a. money business firms need to borrow.
    b. the importance of a firm's head office.
    c. machines and buildings used to produce output.
    d. all of a firm's factors of production.

11. Which of the following would not be classified as an input?
    a. A farmer's time to grow wheat.
    b. The farmer's tractor.
    c. The farmer's land.
    d. The bread that is made from the wheat.

12. The majority of American workers work for
    a. manufacturing companies.
    b. the federal government.
    c. state and local governments.
    d. firms that produce a variety of services, including retail and wholesale trade.

13. When businesses pay factors of production, which of the following gets the largest share of income?
    a. profits
    b. labor
    c. interest
    d. the government (taxes)

14. There are about
    a. 270 thousand business firms or one for every 1,000 people.
    b. 1.35 million business firms or one for every 200 people.
    c. 5.4 million business firms or one for every 50 people.
    d. 22 million business firms or one for every 12 people.

15. When Americans buy goods produced abroad, _____ increase.
    a. exports
    b. taxes
    c. transfer payments
    d. imports

16. When Americans are able to sell goods to foreigners, this adds to
    a. exports.
    b. taxes.
    c. transfer payments.
    d. imports.

17. Consumer spending accounts for _____ of American GDP.
    a. about a third
    b. about half
    c. about two-thirds
    d. about three-quarters

18. National defense accounts for _____ of federal government spending.
    a. less than a fifth
    b. about a third
    c. about half
    d. about two-thirds

19. For the most part, the United States has chosen to let markets determine pre-tax income and then uses taxes and _____ to reduce income inequalities.
    a. tariffs
    b. inflation
    c. transfer payments
    d. government production

20. Compared to other industrialized countries, taxes as a percent of GDP in the United States are
    a. among the lowest.
    b. about the same as most other industrialized countries.
    c. among the highest.

TEST B

Circle T or F for true or false.

T F 1. An economic system is a social mechanism that organizes inputs to produce outputs.

T F 2. Since World War II, American real GDP has increased every year without interruption.

T F 3. As inflation has been relatively minor in the United States, there is little need to adjust economic data for changes in the price level.

T F 4. The American economy is a more open economy than other industrialized economies.

T F 5. The American economy relies on free markets and private enterprise to a greater extent than most other industrialized economies.

T F 6. During a recession, unemployment usually increases.

T F 7. Government production accounts for more than half of American GDP.

T F 8. Women hold more than half of the jobs outside the home.

T F 9. Most American workers still produce goods rather than services.

T F 10. Labor gets most of the income generated in the United States.

■   ECONOMICS IN ACTION

THE PROPER ROLE FOR GOVERNMENT

How far should the government go when regulating business? If the government is to provide some goods and services, what principles determine which goods and services? How far should the government go in redistributing income?

Noted economist Milton Friedman has consistently argued for a limited role for government. In a widely publicized PBS series, Friedman and his wife, Rose, advocated four principles as tests of the appropriate business of government. National defense, domestic police and justice, the provision of goods and services in the limited cases where markets do not work well, and protection for citizens who cannot protect themselves (e.g., children) define the Friedmans' four principles. These principles, especially the third, could be seen as justifying a wide range of government action. The Friedmans are as concerned with government failures as with market failures. They note that once started, government initiatives are rarely stopped. In their view the burden of proof should be on the proponents of government action.

The Friedmans argue that government should be organized to maximize individual "freedom to choose as individuals, as families, as members of voluntary groups." They endorse the view of Adam Smith that as long as individuals do not violate the laws of justice, they should be free to pursue their own interests and that competitive markets rather than government regulation are usually the most effective forms of social organization. "We can shape our institutions. Physical and human characteristics limit the alternatives available to us. But none prevents us, if we will, from building a society that relies primarily on voluntary cooperation to organize both economic and other activity, a society that preserves and expands human freedom, that keeps government in its place, keeping it our servant and not letting it become our master."[1]

The equally renowned John Kenneth Galbraith, on the other hand, argues that increasing affluence has led to an imbalance between private and public goods. Goods and services that are marketable to individuals allow private producers to accumulate the financial resources that give them control of labor, capital, and raw materials. Sophisticated advertising creates and sustains demand for private goods, generating more income and profits. This affluence of the private sector is in marked contrast to the poverty of the public sector. Galbraith argues that society needs a balance between private and public goods but that the pernicious effects of advertising that creates the demand that sustains the production of private goods gives rise to a serious imbalance. One result is an increasing demand for private goods and services to protect individuals from the poverty of public goods and services, such as elaborate alarm systems and private guards to counteract the lack of police.

How much increase in public spending is necessary to redress the balance? Galbraith will only say that the distance is considerable. "When we arrive, the opulence of our private consumption will no longer be in contrast with the poverty of our schools, the unloveliness and congestion of our cities, our inability to get to work without a struggle, and the social disorder that is associated with imbalance . . . the precise point of balance will never be defined. This will be of comfort only to those who believe that any failure of definition can be made to score decisively against the larger idea."[2]

1. How would you define the proper role of government? Where would you draw the line between those activities best left to individual initiative and markets and those that are the appropriate business of government?

STUDY QUESTIONS ■

1. What is the difference between inputs and outputs? Is steel an input or an output? What about the steel used to build factories compared to the steel used in home appliances?

2. How can output of the American economy be greater than that of countries like China and India with larger populations?

3. What measure(s) of economic activity would you use to compare living standards, either over time for a single country or between countries at a point in time? Why?

4. What does the historical record show regarding the growth in real GDP and real GDP per capita in the United States?

5. What is meant by a closed or an open economy? How would you characterize the United States?

---

[1]Milton and Rose Friedman, *Free to Choose: A Personal Statement*, Harcourt Brace Jovanovich, 1980.
[2]John Kenneth Galbraith, *The Affluent Society*, Houghton Mifflin, 1958.

6. In the United States, who works outside the home for wages and salary and what types of jobs do they hold?

7. How is income in the United States distributed among factors of production?

8. How does the role of government in the American economy compare with that of other industrialized countries?

■   **ECONOMICS ONLINE**

The *Statistical Abstract of the United States* is a good place to begin a statistical profile of the United States.

www.census.gov/statab/www/

It is often useful to compare the United States to other countries. Information about the major industrialized countries can be found from the homepage for the Organization for Economic Cooperation and Development (OECD).

www.oecd.org

The *CIA World Factbook* is a useful summary of information about lots of countries. It is available on-line.

www.odci.gov/cia/publications/factbook

SCARCITY AND CHOICE: *THE* ECONOMIC PROBLEM

LEARNING OBJECTIVES

After completing this chapter, you should be able to:

■ explain why the true cost of any decision is its opportunity cost.

■ explain the link between market prices and opportunity costs.

■ explain why the scarcity of goods and services (outputs) must be attributed to a scarcity of resources, or inputs, used in production processes.

■ draw a production possibilities frontier for a firm or for the economy.

■ explain how the production possibilities frontier contains information about the opportunity cost of changing output combinations.

■ explain why specialized resources mean that a firm's or an economy's production possibilities frontier is likely to bow outward.

■ explain how the shape of the production possibilities frontier illustrates the principle of increasing costs.

■ explain how an economy can shift its production possibilities frontier.

Important Terms and Concepts

RESOURCES

SCARCITY

CHOICE

RATIONAL DECISION

OPPORTUNITY COST

OUTPUTS

INPUTS (MEANS OF PRODUCTION)

PRODUCTION POSSIBILITIES FRONTIER

ALLOCATION OF RESOURCES

PRINCIPLE OF INCREASING COSTS

ECONOMIC GROWTH

CONSUMPTION GOODS

CAPITAL GOODS

EFFICIENCY

SPECIALIZATION

DIVISION OF LABOR

COMPARATIVE ADVANTAGE

EXCHANGE

MARKET SYSTEM

THREE COORDINATION TASKS

■ explain why production efficiency requires that an economy produce on, rather than inside, its production possibilities frontier.

■ describe the three coordination tasks that every economy must confront.

■ explain why specialization and division of labor are likely to require the use of markets.

■ describe how a market economy solves the three coordination tasks.

■ explain how both parties gain from voluntary exchange even if no new goods are produced.

■ describe how the allocation of tasks by the principle of comparative advantage increases the total output of all parties.

■ CHAPTER REVIEW

"You can't always get what you want"—Mick Jagger

Even rock stars whose income and wealth are beyond comprehension understand that scarcity and the resulting necessity to make choices are fundamental concerns of economics.[1] This chapter is an introduction to these issues, although they have already been implicitly introduced in many of the 12 ideas for Beyond the Final Exam, and will reappear throughout the text.

(1)   The importance of *choice* starts with the fact that virtually all resources are _____. Most people's desires exceed their incomes, and, thus, everyone makes buying choices all the time. Similarly, firms, educational institutions, and government agencies make choices between what kinds of outputs to produce and what combination of inputs to use. An economist studying the use of inputs for the overall economy is studying the allocation of resources.

What is a good way to make choices? The obvious answer is to consider the alternatives.

(2)   Economists call these forgone alternatives the _____ _____ of a decision. Imagine it is the night before the first midterm in Introductory Economics, which will cover Chapters 1–6, and here you are only on Chapter 4. A friend suggests a night at the movies and even offers to buy your ticket so "it won't cost you anything." Do you agree? What will you be giving up?

At first the idea of choices for the economy may sound strange. It may be easiest to imagine such choices being made by bureaucrats in a centrally planned economy. Even though there is no central planning bureau for the U.S. economy, it is useful to think of opportunities available to the American

_____

[1]Before he was a rock star, Mick Jagger studied economics at the London School of Economics.

economy. The opportunities selected result from the combined spending and production decisions of all citizens, firms, and governmental units, decisions coordinated by our reliance on markets.

The *production possibilities frontier* is a useful diagram for representing the choices available to a firm or an economy. The frontier will tend to slope downward to the right because resources are (scarce/specialized). The frontier will tend to bow out because most resources are   (3)

_____. For any single year the resources available to an economy—the number of workers, factories, and machines, and the state of technology—are essentially fixed. Over time, an economy can increase its resources if it produces (more/fewer) consumption goods and _____ capital goods. Similarly, technological advancements are more likely if an economy devotes (more/fewer) resources to research and development. In terms of a frontier showing possible combinations of consumption and capital goods, the true cost of faster economic growth is given by the forgone output of _____ goods.

Opportunity cost is the best measure of the true cost of any decision. For a single firm or an economy as a whole, with choices represented by a production possibilities frontier, the opportunity cost of changing the composition of output can be measured by the _____ of the produc-   (4)
tion possibilities frontier.

As an economy produces more and more of one good, say automobiles, the opportunity cost of further increases is likely to (increase/decrease). This change in opportunity cost illustrates the principle   (5)
of _____ cost and is a result of the fact that most resources are (scarce/specialized).

For given amounts of all but one good, the production possibilities frontier for an economy measures the maximum amount of the remaining good that can be produced. Thus the production possibilities frontier defines maximum outputs or efficient production. There is, of course, no guarantee that the economy will operate on its frontier. If there is unemployment, then the economy is operating (on/inside) the frontier. If a firm or economy operates inside its production possibilities frontier, it is said to be _____; that is, with the same resources the firm or the economy   (6)
could have produced more of some commodities. Assigning inputs to the wrong or inappropriate tasks will also result in production inefficiency. Assigning tasks according to the principle of comparative advantage helps to achieve economic efficiency.

All economies must answer three questions:

1.   How can we use resources efficiently to operate on the production possibilities frontier?

2.   What combinations of output shall we produce: that is, where on the frontier shall we produce?

3.   To whom shall we distribute what is produced?

The American economy answers these questions through the use of markets and prices. If markets

(7)   are functioning well, then money prices (<u>will/will not</u>) be a reliable guide to opportunity costs.

Problems arise when markets do not function well and when items do not have explicit price tags.

IMPORTANT TERMS AND CONCEPTS QUIZ ■

Choose the best definition for each of the following terms.

1. _____ Resources
2. _____ Scarcity
3. _____ Choice
4. _____ Rational decision
5. _____ Opportunity cost
6. _____ Outputs.
7. _____ Inputs
8. _____ Production possibilities frontier
9. _____ Allocation of resources
10. _____ Principle of increasing costs
11. _____ Consumption goods
12. _____ Capital goods
13. _____ Economic growth
14. _____ Efficiency
15. _____ Specialization
16. _____ Division of labor
17. _____ Comparative advantage
18. _____ Exchange
19. _____ Market system
20. _____ Three coordination tasks

a. Resources used in production process.

b. Produced goods used to produce other goods in the future.

c. System in which allocation decisions are made in accordance with centralized direction.

d. Breaking tasks into smaller jobs

e. Outward shift of the production possibilities frontier.

f. Decision on how to divide scarce resources among different uses.

g. Instruments used to create the goods and services people desire.

h. By focusing efforts on one task a worker becomes more adept at that job.

i. Situation in which the amount of an item available is less than people want.

j. Goods and services that firms produce.

k. System in which decisions on resource allocation come from independent decisions of consumers and producers.

l. Absence of waste.

m. Forgone value of the next best alternative.

n. Decision made from a set of alternatives.

o. System in which people can trade with others.

p. Item available for immediate use by households.

q. Tendency for the opportunity cost of an additional unit of output to rise as production increases.

r. A decision that best serves the decision maker's objectives.

s. Graph of combinations of goods that can be produced with available inputs and technology.

t. Decisions on what goods to produce, how to produce them, and how to distribute them.

u. Ability to produce goods less inefficiently than other producers.

■ BASIC EXERCISES

These exercises are designed to explore more fully some of the implications of the production possibilities frontier for an economy.

1. Figure 4-1 shows the production possibilities frontier (PPF) for the economy of Adirondack, which produces consumption and capital goods, here called bread and computers.

FIGURE 4-1   **Production Possibilities Frontier**

a. If all resources are devoted to the production of bread, Adirondack can produce _____ loaves of bread. In order to produce 1,000 computers, the opportunity cost in terms of bread is _____ loaves. To produce another 1,000 computers, the opportunity cost (<u>rises/falls</u>) to _____ loaves. As long as the PPF continues to curve downward, the opportunity costs of increased computer output will (<u>continue to rise/start to fall</u>). These changes are the result, not of scarce resources per se, but of _____ resources. (You might try drawing a PPF on the assumption that all resources are equally productive in the production of both outputs. Can you convince yourself that it should be a straight line?)

b. Find the output combination of 2,500 computers and 320,000 loaves on Figure 4-1. Label this point A. Is it an attainable combination for Adirondack? Label the output combination 1,500 computers and 400,000 loaves B. Is this combination attainable

Finally, label the output combination 1,000 computers and 520,000 loaves C. Is this combination attainable? We can conclude that the attainable output combinations for Adirondack are (<u>on/inside/outside</u>) the production possibilities frontier. Among the obtainable output combinations, efficient points of production are located (<u>on/inside/outside</u>) the production possibilities frontier.

c. An output combination is inefficient if it is possible to produce more of one or both goods. Which, if any, of the output combinations identified in question b is an inefficient combination? _____. Show that this point is inefficient by shading in all attainable points indicating more of one or both goods.

2. Figure 4-2 shows a PPF that is applicable for two identical economies, Catskill and Adirondack. The only difference is that Catskill produces 2,500 computers and 280,000 loaves of bread, point D, and Adirondack produces 2,000 computers and 400,000 loaves of bread, point E. Remember that computers stand for all capital goods and that the production of capital goods adds to the productive resources of an economy.

a. The production of capital goods this year should cause the PPF for both economies to shift out next year. Figure 4-3 shows the new and initial PPFs for Adirondack following

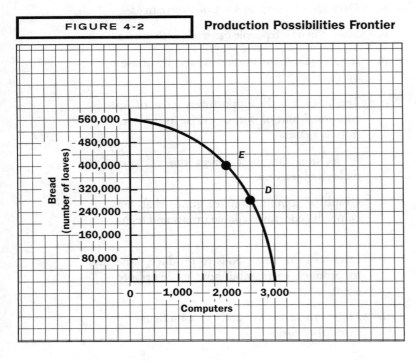

FIGURE 4-2   **Production Possibilities Frontier**

the production of 2,000 computers. Note that the new PPF lies outside the initial PPF. Draw the new PPF for Catskill. Has the PPF for Catskill shifted by more or less than that of Adirondack? Why?

b. Describe how you would measure the cost of growth for the economy with the higher rate of economic growth.

Production Possibilities Frontier | FIGURE 4-3

SELF-TESTS FOR UNDERSTANDING ■

TEST A

Circle the most appropriate answer.

1. Economists define opportunity cost as
   a. the dollar price of goods and services.
   b. the hidden cost imposed by inflation.
   c. the value of the next best alternative use that is not chosen.
   d. the time spent shopping.

2. The position of an economy's production possibilities frontier is determined by all but which one of the following?
   a. The size of the labor force.
   b. Labor skills and training.
   c. The amount of consumption goods the economy can produce.
   d. Current technology.

3. A firm's production possibilities frontier shows
   a. the best combination of output for a firm to produce.
   b. its plans for increasing production over time.
   c. the architectural drawings of its most productive plant.
   d. different combinations of goods it can produce with available resources and technology.

4. An efficient economy utilizes all available resources and produces the _____ output its technology permits.
   a. minimum amount of
   b. best combination of
   c. one combination of
   d. maximum amount of

5. The fact that resources are scarce implies that the production possibilities frontier will
   a. have a negative slope.
   b. be a straight line.
   c. shift out over time.
   d. bow out from the origin.

6. Which of the following statements implies that production possibilities frontiers are likely to be curved, rather than straight, lines?
   a. Ultimately all resources are scarce.
   b. Most resources are more productive in certain uses than in others.
   c. Unemployment is a more serious problem for some social groups than for others.
   d. Economists are notoriously poor at drawing straight lines.

7. The set of attainable points for a firm that produces two goods is given by
   a. all points on the production possibilities frontier.
   b. all points inside the production possibilities frontier.
   c. all points on or inside the production possibilities frontier.
   d. none of the above.

8. If an economy is operating efficiently, it will be producing
   a. inside its production possibilities frontier.
   b. on its production possibilities frontier.
   c. outside its production possibilities frontier.
   d. the maximum amount of necessities and the minimum amount of luxuries.

9. The principle of increasing cost is consistent with a _____ production possibilities frontier.
   a. straight-line
   b. bowed-in
   c. shifting
   d. bowed-out

10. The inability of the economy to produce as much as everyone would like is ultimately a reflection of
    a. a lack of money in the economy.
    b. congressional gridlock.
    c. the inability of a market economy to perform the necessary coordination tasks.
    d. a limited amount of productive resources.

11. The process of economic growth will be accompanied by
    a. a steeper production possibilities frontier.
    b. a production possibilities frontier that has shifted out.
    c. a smaller share of output devoted to government spending.
    d. an increase in the birth rate.

12. When, in Figure 4-1, the production of bread is increased from 280,000 loaves to 400,000 loaves, the opportunity cost in terms of reduced output of computers is
    a. 0.
    b. 500.
    c. 2,000.
    d. 2,500.

13. Which of the following implies a shift in the production possibilities frontier for a shoe firm?
    a. Raising all prices by 10 percent.
    b. Borrowing money to hire more workers and buying more machines.
    c. Changing the composition output toward more women's shoes and fewer men's shoes.
    d. Expanding the advertising budget.

14. Consider a production possibilities frontier showing alternative combinations of corn and computers that can be produced in Cimonoce, a small island in the South Pacific. The opportunity cost of more computers can be measured by
    a. the slope of the production possibilities frontier.
    b. the X-intercept of the production possibilities frontier.
    c. the Y-intercept of the production possibilities frontier.
    d. the area under the production possibilities frontier.

15. Which one of the following situations reflects a shift of the economy's production possibilities frontier?
    a. The proportion of labor devoted to the production of agricultural products has declined from 21 percent in 1929 to less than 3 percent in 1990.
    b. Total real output for the U.S. economy in 1999 was about nine times greater than in 1929.
    c. Between 1990 and 1991 total real output of the U.S. economy declined by $35 billion as the unemployment rate rose from 5.5 percent to 6.7 percent.
    d. In 1980 the inflation rate was about 13.5 percent.

16. Which of the following would not shift an economy's production possibilities frontier?
    a. A doubling of the labor force.
    b. A doubling of the number of machines.
    c. A doubling of the money supply.
    d. More advanced technology.

17. A rational decision is one that
    a. will win a majority if put to a vote.
    b. is supported unanimously.
    c. best serves the objectives of the decision maker.
    d. is supported by *The New York Times*.

18. If exchange is voluntary,
    a. there can be mutual gain even if no new goods are produced.
    b. one party will always get the better of the other.
    c. there can be mutual gain only if new goods are produced as a result of the trade.
    d. there can be mutual gain only if the government regulates retail trade.

19. All but which one of the following are examples of waste and inefficiency?
    a. Employment discrimination against women and people of color.
    b. Operating on an economy's production possibilities frontier.
    c. High levels of unemployment.
    d. Quotas that limit the educational opportunities of particular ethnic groups.

20. The three coordination tasks that all economies must perform
    a. can only be done by a central planning bureau.
    b. can only be done by markets.
    c. can only be done inefficiently.
    d. can be done by planning bureaus or markets.

TEST B

Circle T or F for true or false.

T F 1. There can never be any real scarcity of manufactured goods, as we can always produce more.

T F 2. Market prices are always a good measure of opportunity cost.

T F 3. The principle of increasing costs is a reflection of the fact that most productive resources tend to be best at producing a limited number of things.

T F 4. An economy can shift its production possibilities frontier outward by the process of economic growth.

T F 5. Because they have the power to tax, governments do not need to make choices.

T   F   6. The existence of specialized resources means that a firm's production possibilities frontier will be a straight line.

T   F   7. The existence of widespread unemployment means that an economy is operating inside its production possibilities frontier.

T   F   8. An economy using its resources efficiently is operating on its production possibilities frontier.

T   F   9. Because they are nonprofit organizations, colleges and universities do not have to make choices.

T   F   10. A sudden increase in the number of dollar bills will shift the economy's production possibilities frontier.

■ SUPPLEMENTARY EXERCISES

1.   **The Cost of College**

Those of you paying your way through college may not need to be reminded that the opportunity cost of lost wages is an important part of the cost of education. You can estimate the cost of your education as follows: Estimate what you could earn if instead of attending classes and studying you used those hours to work. Add in the direct outlays on tuition, books, and any differential living expenses incurred because you go to school. (Why only differential and not your total living expenses?)

2.   **The Cost of Children**

Bob and Jane both took Sociology 1 last year. As part of the course they were asked to compute the cost of raising a child. Bob estimated the cost at $180,000, an average of $6,000 a year in increased family expenditures for the first 12 years, then $8,000 a year for the next six years, and finally four years of college at $15,000 per year. Jane also was enrolled in Economics 1. She estimated the cost at $360,000. She started with all the same outlays that Bob did but also included $30,000 a year for six years as the opportunity cost of the parent who stayed at home to care for the child. Which calculation better reflects the cost of raising a child? What would be the cost of a second child?

3.   Consider an economy with a production possibilities frontier between cars (C) and tanks (T) given by

$$C = 6L^{.5}K^{.5} - 0.3T^2$$

where L is the size of the labor force (50,000 people) and K is the number of machines, also 50,000.
   a.   What is the maximum number of cars that can be produced? Call this number of cars C^*. The maximum number of tanks? Call this number of tanks T^*.
   b.   Draw a PPF graph.
   c.   Is this frontier consistent with the principle of increasing costs?
   d.   Is the output combination ($1/2C^*$, $1/2T^*$) attainable? Is the output combination ($1/2C^*$, $1/2T^*$) efficient? Why or why not?
   e.   What is the opportunity cost of more tanks when 10 tanks are produced? 50 tanks? 200 tanks?
   f.   Find a mathematical expression for the opportunity cost of tanks in terms of cars. Is this mathematical expression consistent with the principle of increasing cost?
   g.   Draw the new PPF if the labor force and the number of machines both increase by 10 percent. Where does this frontier lie relative to the original frontier?

4. The Cost of Economic Growth

If you have access to a microcomputer, you might try programming this small recursive model to investigate the cost of economic growth. You could either try writing your own program in BASIC or some other programming language, or you could use a spreadsheet program. Some programming hints are given at the end of the problem.

Imagine an economy that produces bundles of consumption goods C, and investment goods, I, with the help of labor, L, and machines, M, that exist at the beginning of the year. The production of consumption and investment goods is described by equation (1)

(1) $C + I = L^{.75}M^{.25}$

Some machines wear out each year. The number of machines at the beginning of the next year is equal to 92 percent of the machines at the beginning of the year plus investment during the year, or $.92M + I$. The number of machines will be constant when investment is just sufficient to replace the 8 percent that wear out each year. If investment is greater, then the number of machines will increase, and the economy's production possibilities frontier will shift out.

This economy has 10,000 laborers, $L = 10,000$, and originally there are 20,000 machines, $M = 20,000$.

a. Verify that if $I = 1,600$, output and consumption will be constant.
b. What happens to output and consumption over time if I increases by 25 percent to 2,000?
c. In question b you should find that consumption initially declines as some output is diverted from consumption to investment. However, over time, the output of consumption goods should increase and eventually surpass its earlier value found in a. If an increase in investment from 1,600 to 2,000 is a good thing, what about an increase from 2,000 to 2,400? How does the eventual increase in consumption following the increase in the production of investment goods from 2,000 to 2,400 compare with what you found in b?
d. Can there ever be too much investment? Try additional increases in investment and watch what happens to the eventual level of consumption. Can you explain what is going on?

Programming Hints   Columns in a spreadsheet would correspond to the following equations where subscripts refer to time periods. Note that equations for I and C are the same for all periods. Following the initial period you will need to be sure that your expression for the number of machines incorporates the subtraction of machines that have worn out and the addition of new machines from the production of investment goods. You will probably want to set your program or spreadsheet to run for about 100 periods. You can investigate the effect of higher and lower levels of investment by changing the value for I.

$M_t = 20,000$ $\qquad\qquad\qquad\qquad$ $t = 1$

$I_t = 1,600$ $\qquad\qquad\qquad\qquad$ $t = 1, 2, \ldots$

$C_t = (10,000)^{.75} \times (M_t)^{.25} - I_t$ $\qquad$ $t = 1, 2, \ldots$

$M_t = .92 \times M_{t-1} + I_{t-1}$ $\qquad\qquad$ $t = 2, 3, \ldots$

ECONOMICS IN ACTION ■

In 1971 the Brookings Institution published the first of a sequence of studies of the President's budget proposal called *Setting National Priorities*. The following is from the introduction to the first study.

The United States budget is not the document of an executive whose decisions are law, nor of a prime minister whose party must support him or bring down the government. It is, rather, a set of proposals to the Congress for action on appropriations and tax measures. Precisely because it must advocate the course recommended by the President, the budget cannot emphasize the difficulty of the choices made. It records the President's decisions, but it does not identify the close ones. Alternatives that were serious contenders for adoption but were finally rejected are seldom if ever mentioned. In some cases, programs generally recognized as ineffective or of low priority are debated but finally left unchanged because all participants in the debate realize how few are the lances a President can afford to break against politically impregnable targets. Thus, the budget is a document designed to persuade an independent Congress rather than to analyze policy alternatives.

The following pages seek to illuminate some of the President's budgetary choices for 1971. The study will (1) identify the major choices in fiscal policy and in specific expenditure programs; (2) consider some of the available alternatives and the reasoning behind the choices actually proposed; (3) discuss, by way of example, several federal programs that continue to be supported despite attempts by several administrations to alter or eliminate them; and (4) project to fiscal 1975 the revenue yield of existing tax laws and the expenditure consequences of current and proposed programs in order to estimate the likely size of the "fiscal dividends" over the next four years. The 1971 budget is the first in history to present longer-term projections. The projections offered in this study are spelled out in somewhat greater detail than those presented in the budget and include a range of alternatives that would depend on budgetary policies adopted in coming years.

The purpose of the study is to contribute to informed discussion of the budget, not to propose a different budget. It *examines* alternatives; it does not *recommend* alternatives. Its aim is to show the difficulty of making choices in a complex and uncertain world, not to criticize those who had to make them.

1. What sort of information would you need if you had to make decisions about defense spending or the structure of a national health insurance plan?

2. Are you likely to find the information for these and other decisions in the President's budget?

3. If not, what is the role of the President's budget?

SOURCE: From *Setting National Priorities. The 1971 Budget,* Charles L. Schultze, et al., The Brookings Institution et al. (Washington, D.C. 1970): p. 4.

■ STUDY QUESTIONS

1. How do markets help an economy address the three coordination tasks of deciding "how," "what," and "to whom"?

2. What do economists mean by opportunity cost and why do they say it is the true measure of the cost of any decision?

3. Explain when market prices are likely to be a good measure of opportunity cost and when they are not.

4. What are the factors that determine the location of a country's production possibilities frontier?

5. What is the difference between resources being scarce and resources being specialized? What are the implications of scarcity and specialization for the production possibilities frontier?

6. How do specialization and the division of labor enhance economic efficiency? Why do they require a system of exchange?

7. How can an economy choose to grow faster, and how can you use a production possibilities frontier to measure the cost of faster growth?

8. What is the difference between attainable points of production and efficient points of production? (It may be easiest to illustrate your answer using a diagram of a production possibilities frontier. Be sure that you can define and identify those points that are attainable and those points that are efficient.)

9. What is meant by the principle of comparative advantage? What does it imply for individuals and economies?

SUPPLY AND DEMAND: AN INITIAL LOOK

LEARNING OBJECTIVES

After completing this chapter, you should be able to:

- explain why the quantity demanded and the quantity supplied are not fixed numbers but rather depend upon a number of factors including price.

- draw a demand curve, given appropriate information from a demand schedule of possible prices and the associated quantity demanded.

- draw a supply curve, given appropriate information from a supply schedule of possible prices and the associated quantity supplied.

- explain why demand curves usually slope downward and supply curves usually slope upward.

- determine the equilibrium price and quantity, given a demand curve and a supply curve.

- explain what forces tend to move market prices and quantities toward their equilibrium values.

- list major factors that will affect the quantity demanded by shifting the demand curve.

- list major factors that will affect the quantity supplied by shifting the supply curve.

Important Terms and Concepts

QUANTITY DEMANDED

DEMAND SCHEDULE

DEMAND CURVE

QUANTITY SUPPLIED

SUPPLY SCHEDULE

SUPPLY CURVE

SUPPLY-DEMAND DIAGRAM

SHORTAGE

SURPLUS

EQUILIBRIUM PRICE AND QUANTITY

EQUILIBRIUM

LAW OF SUPPLY AND DEMAND

SHIFTS IN (VERSUS) MOVEMENTS ALONG SUPPLY AND DEMAND CURVES

PRICE CEILING

PRICE FLOOR

■ distinguish between a shift in and a movement along either the demand or supply curve.

■ analyze the impact on prices and quantities of shifts in the demand curve, supply curve, or both.

■ explain why sellers are unlikely to be able to pass on the full increase in excise or sales taxes.

■ distinguish between price ceilings and price floors.

■ explain the likely consequences of government interference with market-determined prices.

■   CHAPTER REVIEW

Along with scarcity and the need for choice, *demand and supply analysis* is a fundamental idea that pervades all of economics. After studying this chapter, look back at the Ideas for Beyond the Final Exam in Chapter 1 and see how many concern the "law" of supply and demand.

Economists use a *demand curve* as a summary of the factors influencing people's demand for different commodities. A demand curve shows how, during a specified period, the quantity demanded of

(1)   some good changes as the _____ of that good changes, holding all other determinants of demand constant. A demand curve usually has a (negative/positive) slope, indicating that as the price of a good declines, people will demand (more/less) of it. A particular quantity demanded is represented by a point on the demand curve. The change in the quantity demanded as price changes is a (shift in/movement along) the demand curve. Quantity demanded is also influenced by other factors, such as consumer incomes and tastes, population and the prices of related goods. Changes in any of these factors will result in a (shift in/movement along) the demand curve. Remember, a demand curve is defined for a particular period—a week, a month, or a year.

Economists use a *supply curve* to summarize the factors influencing producers' decisions. Like the

(2)   demand curve, the supply curve is a relationship between quantity and _____. Supply curves usually have a (negative/positive) slope, indicating that at higher prices producers will be willing to supply (more/less) of the good in question. Like quantity demanded, quantity supplied is also influenced by factors other than price. The size of the industry, the state of technology, the prices of inputs, and the price of related outputs are important determinants. Changes in any of these factors will change the quantity supplied and can be represented by a (shift in/movement along) the supply curve.

Demand and supply curves are hypothetical constructs that answer what-if questions. For example, the supply curve answers the question, "What quantity of milk would be supplied if its price were $10 a gallon?" At this point it is not fair to ask whether anyone would buy milk at that price. Information about the quantity demanded is given by the _____ curve, which answers the ques-   (3)

tion, "What quantity would be demanded if its price were $10 a gallon?" The viability of a price of

$10 will be determined when we consider both curves simultaneously.

Figure 5-1 shows a demand and supply curve for stereo sets. The market outcome will be a price

of $_____ and a quantity of _____. If the price is $400, then the quantity demanded will be   (4)

(<u>less/more</u>) than the quantity supplied. In particular, from Figure 5-1 we can see that at a price of $400,

producers will supply _____ sets while consumers will demand _____ sets. This imbalance is a

(<u>shortage/surplus</u>) and will lead to a(n)

(<u>increase/reduction</u>) in price as invento-

ries start piling up and suppliers compete

for sales. If, instead, the price of stereo

sets is only $200, there will be a (<u>short-</u>

<u>age/surplus</u>) as the quantity (<u>demand-</u>

<u>ed/supplied</u>) exceeds the quantity

_____ . Price is apt to

(<u>decrease/increase</u>) as consumers scram-

Demand and Supply: Stereos | **FIGURE 5-1**

ble for a limited number of stereos at what appear to be bargain prices.

These forces working to raise or lower prices will continue until price and quantity settle down at

values given by the _____ of the demand and supply curves. At this point, barring   (5)

outside changes that would shift either curve, there will be no further tendency for change. Market-

determined price and quantity are then said to be in _____. This price and quanti-

ty combination is the only one in which consumers demand exactly what producers supply. There are

no frustrated consumers or producers. However, equilibrium price and quantity will change if any-

thing happens to shift either the demand or supply curves. The Basic Exercise in this chapter asks you

to examine a number of shifts in demand and supply curves.

Often factors affect demand but not supply, and vice versa. For example, changes in consumer

incomes and tastes will shift the (<u>demand/supply</u>) curve but not the _____ curve.   (6)

Following a shift in the demand curve, price must change to re-establish equilibrium. The change in

price will lead to a (<u>shift in/movement along</u>) the supply curve until equilibrium is re-established at the intersection of the new demand curve and the original supply curve.[1] Similarly a change in technology or the price of inputs will shift the _____ curve but not the _____ curve. Equilibrium will be re-established as the price change induced by the shift in the supply curve leads to a movement along the _____ curve to the new intersection.

In many cases governments intervene in the market mechanism in an attempt to control prices. Some price controls dictate a particular price; other controls set maximum or minimum prices. A *price*

(7)   *ceiling* is a (<u>maximum/minimum</u>) legal price, typically below the market-determined equilibrium price. Examples of price ceilings include rent controls and usury laws. A *price floor* sets a _____ legal price. To be effective, the price floor would have to be above the equilibrium price. Price floors are often used in agricultural programs.

In general, economists argue that interferences with the market mechanism are likely to have a number of undesirable features. Price controls will almost surely lead to a misallocation of resources, as it is unlikely legislated prices will equal opportunity cost. If there are a large number of suppliers,

(8)   price controls will be (<u>hard/easy</u>) to monitor and evasion will be hard to police. In order to prevent the breakdown of price controls, governments quite likely find it necessary to introduce a large number of _____ _____. The enforcement of price controls can provide opportunities for favoritism and corruption. If all of this is not enough, price controls are almost certain to produce groups with a monetary stake in preserving controls. Another form of inefficiency involves the use of time and resources to evade effective controls.

(9)   Price ceilings have a history of persistent (<u>shortages/surpluses</u>) and the development of black markets. Prices in the illegal market are likely to be greater than those that would have prevailed in a free market, with substantial income going to those whose only business is circumventing the controls. Over a longer period of time new investment is likely to (<u>decrease/increase</u>) as controlled prices reduce the profitability of investment in the industry.

Firms try to get around effective price floors by offering nonprice inducements for consumers to buy from them rather than from someone else. (Remember that effective price floors result in excess

---

[1] If following an increase in consumer income the increase in price were sufficiently large to induce an increase in the size of the industry, the supply curve would shift. However, such an change would take some time. The analysis here focuses on immediate or short run impacts.

supply.) These nonprice inducements are apt to be less preferred by consumers than would a general reduction in prices. Price floors will also result in inefficiencies as high-cost firms are protected from failing by artificially (high/low) prices. (10)

IMPORTANT TERMS AND CONCEPTS QUIZ ■

Choose the best definition for each of the following terms.

1. _____ Quantity supplied

2. _____ Quantity demanded

3. _____ Demand schedule

4. _____ Demand curve

5. _____ Supply schedule

6. _____ Supply curve

7. _____ Supply-demand diagram

8. _____ Shortage

9. _____ Surplus

10. _____ Equilibrium

11. _____ Equilibrium price and quantity

12. _____ Shifts in supply or demand curves

13. _____ Movement along a supply or demand curve

14. _____ Price ceiling

15. _____ Price floor

16. _____ Law of supply and demand

a. Observation that in a free market, price tends to a level where quantity supplied equals quantity demanded.

b. Legal minimum price that may be charged.

c. Graph depicting how quantity demanded changes as price changes.

d. Change in price causing a change in quantity supplied or demanded.

e. Number of units consumers want to buy at a given price.

f. Price/quantity pair at which quantity demanded equals quantity supplied.

g. Table depicting how the quantity demanded change as price changess

h. Situation in which there are no inherent forces producing change.

i. Table depicting how quantity supplied changes as price changes.

j. Legal maximum price that may be charged.

k. Number of units producers want to sell at a given price.

l. Table depicting the changes in both quantity demanded and quantity supplied as price changes.

m. Change in a variable other than price that affects quantity supplied or demanded.

n. Excess of quantity supplied over quantity demanded.

o. Graph depicting the changes in both quantity supplied and quantity demanded as price changes.

p. Excess of quantity demanded over quantity supplied.

q. Graph depicting how quantity supplied changes as price changes.

■ BASIC EXERCISES

These exercises ask you to analyze the impact of changes in factors that affect demand and supply.

1. a. Table 5-1 has data on the quantity of candy bars that would be demanded and supplied at various prices. Use the data to draw the demand curve and the supply curve for candy bars in Figure 5-2.
   b. From the information given in Table 5-1 and represented in Figure 5-2, the equilibrium price is _____ cents and the equilibrium quantity is _____.
   c. Now assume that increases in income and population mean the demand curve has shifted. Assume the shift is such that, at each price, the quantity demanded has increased by 300 candy bars. Draw the new demand curve. At the new equilibrium, price has (increased/decreased) to _____ cents, and quantity has (increased/decreased) to _____ million candy bars. Note that the change in the equilibrium quantity is (less/more) than the shift in the demand curve. Can you explain why?
   d. Next assume that Congress imposes a tax of 15 cents on every candy bar sold. As sellers must now pay the government 15 cents for each candy bar sold, the tax can be modeled as a 15 cent upward shift in the supply curve. This tax-induced shift in the supply curve will (increase/decrease) the equilibrium price and _____ the equilibrium quantity. Draw this new supply curve in Figure 5-2. Using the demand curve you drew in part c, above, the new equilibrium price following the imposition of the candy tax will be _____ cents and the equilibrium quantity will be _____ million candy bars. Compared to the equilibrium price you identified in part c, the increase in the market price of candy bars is (less than / equal to / more than) the new tax.

2. Figure 5-3 shows the demand and supply of chicken. Use Figure 5-3 while you fill in Table 5-2 to trace the effects of various events on the equilibrium price and quantity.

TABLE 5-1	Demand and Supply Schedules for Candy Bars	
Quantity Demanded	Price per Bar	Quantity Supplied
1,200	35	1,050
1,100	40	1,100
900	50	1,200
800	55	1,250
700	60	1,300

FIGURE 5-2   **Demand and Supply: Candy Bars**

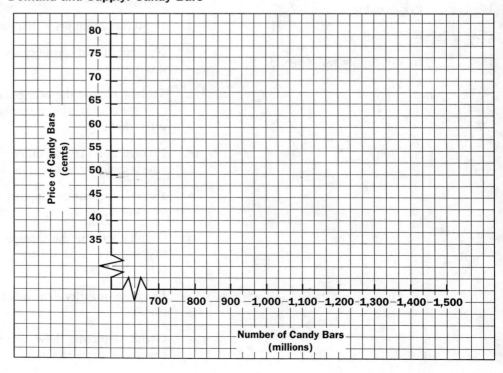

TABLE 5-2				
Event	**Which curve shifts?**	**Is the direction left or right?**	**Does the equilibrium price rise or fall?**	**Does the equilibrium quantity rise or fall?**
a. A sharp increase in the price of beef leads many consumers to switch from beef to chicken.				
b. A bumper grain crop cuts the cost of chicken feed in half.				
c. Extraordinarily cold weather destroys a significant number of chickens.				
d. A sudden interest in Eastern religions converts many chicken eaters to vegetarians.				

TABLE 5-3

	Quantity Demanded	**Quantity Supplied**	**Shortage or Surplus**
a. Price ceiling = $18			
b. Price ceiling = $9			
c. Price floor = $15			
d. Price floor = $6			

3. Figure 5-4 shows the demand and supply of compact discs. Complete Table 5-3 to examine the impact of price ceilings and price floors. What conclusion can you draw about when ceilings and floors will affect market outcomes?

Demand and Supply: Chicken   FIGURE 5-3

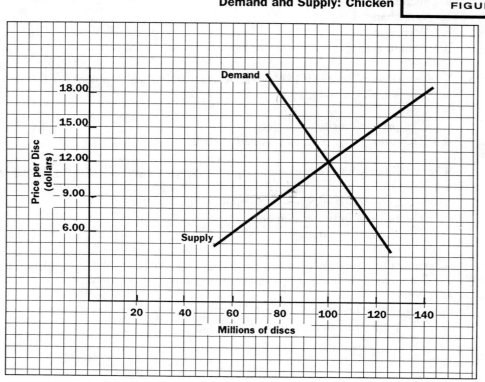

Demand and Supply: Chicken   FIGURE 5-4

■   **SELF-TESTS FOR UNDERSTANDING**

TEST A

Circle the most appropriate answer.

1. A demand curve is a graph showing how the quantity demanded changes when _____ changes.
   a. consumer income
   b. population
   c. price
   d. the price of closely related goods

2. The slope of a demand curve is usually _____, indicating that as price declines the quantity demanded increases.
   a. negative
   b. positive
   c. infinite
   d. zero

3. Quantity demanded is likely to depend upon all but which one of the following?
   a. Consumer tastes.
   b. Consumer income.
   c. Price.
   d. The size of the industry producing the good in question.

4. A supply curve is a graphical representation of information in a(n)
   a. demand schedule.
   b. equilibrium.
   c. supply schedule.
   d. balance sheet.

5. If price decreases, the quantity supplied usually
   a. increases.
   b. is unchanged.
   c. decreases.
   d. goes to zero.

6. The entire supply curve is likely to shift when all but which one of the following change?
   a. The size of the industry.
   b. Price.
   c. The price of important inputs.
   d. Technology that reduces production costs.

7. There will likely be a movement along a fixed supply curve if which one of the following changes?
   a. Price.
   b. Technology that reduces production costs.
   c. The price of important inputs.
   d. The size of the industry.

8. There will be a movement along the demand curve when which one of the following changes?
   a. The size of the industry producing the good.
   b. Population.
   c. Consumer incomes.
   d. The price of related goods.

9. Graphically, the equilibrium price and quantity in a free market will be given by
    a.   the *Y*-axis intercept of the demand curve.
    b.   the *X*-axis intercept of the supply curve.
    c.   the point of maximum vertical difference between the demand and supply curves.
    d.   the intersection of the demand and supply curves.

10. When the demand curve shifts to the right, which of the following is likely to occur?
    a.   Equilibrium price rises and equilibrium quantity declines.
    b.   Equilibrium price rises and equilibrium quantity rises.
    c.   Equilibrium price declines and equilibrium quantity rises.
    d.   Equilibrium price declines and equilibrium quantity declines.

11. If equilibrium price and quantity both decrease, it is likely that
    a.   the supply curve has shifted to the right.
    b.   the demand curve has shifted to the right.
    c.   the demand curve has shifted to the left.
    d.   the supply curve has shifted to the left.

12. A shift in the demand curve for sailboats resulting from a general increase in incomes will lead to
    a.   higher prices.
    b.   lower prices.
    c.   a shift in the supply curve.
    d.   lower output.

13. Which of the following is likely to result in a shift in the supply curve for dresses? (There may be more than one correct answer.)
    a.   An increase in consumer incomes.
    b.   An increase in tariffs that forces manufacturers to import cotton cloth at higher prices.
    c.   An increase in dress prices.
    d.   Higher prices for skirts, pants, and blouses.

14. From an initial equilibrium, which of the following changes will lead to a shift in the supply curve for Chevrolets?
    a.   Import restrictions on Japanese cars.
    b.   New environmental protection measures that raise the cost of producing steel.
    c.   A decrease in the price of Fords.
    d.   Increases in the cost of gasoline.

15. If the price of oil, a close substitute for coal, increases, then
    a.   the supply curve for coal will shift to the right.
    b.   the demand curve for coal will shift to the right.
    c.   the equilibrium price and quantity of coal will not change.
    d.   the quantity of coal demanded will decline.

16. If the price of shoes is initially above the equilibrium value, which of the following is likely to occur?
    a.   Stores' inventories will decrease as consumers buy more shoes than shoe companies produce.
    b.   The demand curve for shoes will shift in response to higher prices.
    c.   Shoe stores and companies likely will reduce prices in order to increase sales, leading to a lower equilibrium price.
    d.   Equilibrium will be re-established at the original price as the supply curve shifts to the left.

17. An new tax on backpacks that shifts the supply curve should increase the market price of backpacks
    a. not at all.
    b. by less than the increase in the tax.
    c. by an amount equal to the increase in the tax.
    d. by more than the increase in the tax.

18. Binding price floors are likely to
    a. lead to a reduction in the volume of transactions, as we move along the demand curve, above the equilibrium price to the higher price floor.
    b. result in increased sales as suppliers react to higher prices.
    c. lead to shortages.
    d. be effective only if they are set at levels below the market equilibrium level.

19. Effective price ceilings are likely to
    a. result in surpluses.
    b. increase the volume of transactions as we move along the demand curve.
    c. increase production as producers respond to higher consumer demand at the low ceiling price.
    d. result in the development of black markets.

20. A surplus results when
    a. the quantity demanded exceeds the quantity supplied.
    b. the quantity supplied exceeds the quantity demanded.
    c. the demand curve shifts to the right.
    d. effective price ceilings are imposed.

TEST B

Circle T or F for true or false.

T   F   1. The Law of Supply and Demand was passed by Congress in 1776.

T   F   2. The demand curve for hamburgers is a graph showing the quantity of hamburgers that would be demanded during a specified period at each possible price.

T   F   3. The slope of the supply curve indicates the increase in price necessary to get producers to increase output.

T   F   4. An increase in consumer income will shift both the supply and demand curves.

T   F   5. Both demand and supply curves usually have positive slopes.

T   F   6. If at a particular price the quantity supplied exceeds the quantity demanded, then price is likely to fall as suppliers compete for sales.

T   F   7. Equilibrium price and quantity are determined by the intersection of the demand and supply curves.

T   F   8. Since equilibrium is defined as a situation with no inherent forces producing change, the equilibrium price and quantity will not change following an increase in consumer income.

T   F   9. A change in the price of important inputs will change the quantity supplied but will not shift the supply curve.

T   F   10. Increases in commodity specific taxes typically lead to equal increases in market prices.

T   F   11. When binding, price ceilings are likely to result in the development of black markets.

T   F   12. Price controls, whether floors or ceilings, likely will increase the volume of transactions from what it would be without controls.

T   F   13. An effective price ceiling is normally accompanied by shortages.

T   F   14. An effective price floor is also normally accompanied by shortages.

T   F   15. An increase in both the market price and quantity of beef following an increase in consumer incomes proves that demand curves do not always have a negative slope.

SUPPLEMENTARY EXERCISE

Imagine that the demand curve for tomatoes can be represented as:

$$Q = 1,000 - 250P.$$

The supply curve is a bit trickier. Farmers must make planting decisions on what they anticipate prices to be. Once they have made these decisions, there is little room for increases or decreases in the quantity supplied. Except for disastrously low prices, it will almost certainly pay a farmer to harvest and market his tomatoes. Assuming that farmers forecast price on the basis of the price last period, we can represent the supply curve for tomatoes as:

$$Q = 200 + 150P_{-1},$$

where P_{-1}, refers to price in the previous period. Initial equilibrium price and quantity of tomatoes are $2 and 500, respectively. Verify that at this price the quantity supplied is equal to the quantity demanded. (Equilibrium implies the same price in each period.)

Now assume that an increase in income has shifted the demand curve to:

$$Q = 1,400 - 250P.$$

Starting with the initial equilibrium price, trace the evolution of price and quantity over time. Do prices and quantities seem to be approaching some sort of equilibrium? If so, what? You might try programming this example on a microcomputer or simulating it with a spreadsheet program. What happens if the slope of the demand and/or supply curve changes?

Ask your instructor about cobweb models. Do you think looking at last period's price is a good way to forecast prices?

ECONOMICS IN ACTION

HEY, BUDDY . . .

Scalping tickets—selling tickets at whatever the market will bear rather than at face value—is illegal in a number of states, including New York City. In 1992 the high demand for tickets to a retrospective exhibition of Henri Matisse at the Museum of Modern Art prompted renewed interest in the economic effects of scalping. Admission to the exhibition was by special ticket. By the time the exhibit opened, all advance sale tickets had been sold. A limited number of tickets were available each day. Art lovers had to wait in line for up to two hours early in the morning to purchase these tickets at $12.50 each. Tickets also were available without the wait at $20 to $50 from scalpers who evaded the police. The Monet retrospective exhibit at the Art Institute in Chicago in 1995 attracted such interest that scalpers were reported to be getting $100 for tickets with a face value of $10.

Scalpers also do a lively business at the Super Bowl, the Final Four of the NCAA basketball playoffs and other major sporting and entertainment events. Why don't museums, the National Football League and the NCAA simply raise the price of tickets? Some argue that these organizations, along with other businesses, are concerned with "goodwill." Even if higher profits could be earned from higher ticket prices, it might come by sacrificing profits over the long run as goodwill is replaced by ill will and a growing lack of consumer interest.

Some economists view scalpers as providing a service to those who have not planned ahead or do not wish to stand in line. They point out that other businesses, such as airlines, charge a hefty price for last-minute purchases.

It is often argued that scalping should be illegal, as it makes events unaffordable for the average person. Others wonder whether the average person ever gets tickets to such events and, if she does, whether she might not prefer the option of selling her tickets at a handsome profit.

The following two-tier price system has been proposed by some economists. First a limited number of tickets would be sold at lower prices to those willing to stand in line or enter a lottery. Then the remaining tickets would be sold at whatever price the market will bear.

1. Who is harmed when scalping is illegal? Who would be harmed if scalping were legal?
2. Would you expect legalizing scalping to affect the price of tickets from scalpers? Why?
3. Evaluate the pros and cons of a two-tier system.

SOURCE: "Tickets: Supply Meets Demand on Sidewalk," *The New York Times*, December 26, 1992.

■ STUDY QUESTIONS

1. Why do economists argue that neither quantity demanded nor quantity supplied is likely to be a fixed number?

2. What adjustment mechanisms are likely to ensure that free-market prices move toward their equilibrium values given by the intersection of the demand and supply curves?

3. Why are changes in all of the supply determinants, except price, said to shift the entire supply curve while changes in price are said to give rise to a movement along a fixed supply curve?

4. How do factors that shift the supply curve give rise to a movement along a given demand curve?

5. What are the important factors that help to determine the quantity demanded? the quantity supplied?

6. Why do economists expect that an increase in a tax on a specific commodity will not lead to an equal increase in market prices?

7. If price cannot adjust, say due to an effective price ceiling, what factors will likely allocate the quantity supplied among consumers?

8. Consider the demand for a necessity (for example, food), and the demand for a luxury (for example, home hot tubs). For which good would you expect the quantity demanded to show a greater response to changes in price? Why? For which good would you expect the demand curve to be steeper? Why? For which good would you expect the demand curve to show a greater shift in response to changes in consumer income? Why?

CONSUMER CHOICE: INDIVIDUAL AND MARKET DEMAND

LEARNING OBJECTIVES

After completing this chapter, you should be able to:

■ distinguish between total and marginal utility.

■ explain how the law of diminishing marginal utility can be used to derive an optimal purchase rule.

■ explain how the optimal purchase rule can be used to derive a demand curve.

■ explain how the concept of consumer surplus helps explain why mutual gain arises from voluntary exchange.

■ explain the role of marginal utility as a guide to maximizing consumer surplus.

■ explain what economists mean by inferior goods.

■ derive a market demand curve given information on individual demand curves.

■ explain why a market demand curve can have a negative slope even if individual demand curves do not.

This chapter discusses economic models of consumer choice. These models are what lie behind the negatively sloped demand curves we encountered in Chapter 5. The appendix to the chapter discusses indifference curve analysis, which is a more sophisticated treatment of the same material. This chapter is also an introduction to *marginal analysis,* an extremely powerful tool of economic analysis.

Economists derive implications for individual demand curves by starting with assumptions about individual behavior. One relatively innocent assumption should be sufficient. It concerns consumer preferences and is called the "law" of diminishing marginal utility. Perhaps we should first start with utility.

The term *utility* refers to the benefits people derive from consuming goods and services. Actual utility is unique to each one of us and thus is incapable of being measured. To get around the measurement problem, we will use the term *total utility* to refer to the maximum amount a consumer will pay for a given quantity of the commodity. (It should be obvious that this amount will differ from person to another. For an individual consumer, total utility will be influenced by her income and preferences.) Rather than focusing on total utility, however, economists have found it useful to pay attention to the additional amount of money that a consumer would pay for one more unit of the commodity, or

(1)   _____ utility, measured in money terms. (Marginal utility (<u>will/will not</u>) also be influenced by a person's income and preferences.) The law of diminishing marginal utility is a hypothesis about consumer preferences. It says that normally additional units of any commodity provide less and less satisfaction. As a result, the additional amount a consumer will pay for an additional unit of some commodity will (<u>increase/decrease</u>) the more units she is already consuming.

The law of diminishing marginal utility can be used as a guide to optimal commodity purchases. Optimal purchases are ones that maximize the difference between total utility and total expenditures

(2)   on a commodity. This difference is called _____ surplus.[1] Our optimal purchase rule says that an individual consumer should buy additional units of a commodity as long as the marginal utility of the additional units exceeds the _____ of the commodity. If marginal utility

---

[1] There is a geometric interpretation of consumer's surplus. As the demand curve is the curve of marginal utility, the area under the demand curve equals total utility. If a consumer can buy as much as he wants at market prices, total expenditures are price times the quantity purchased. The difference between total utility and total expenditure is consumer's surplus and can be represented as the area under the demand curve and above the horizontal line drawn at the market price. For a straight line demand curve consumer's surplus is a triangle. This triangle is analogous to the shaded bars of Figure 6-3 in the text.

exceeds price, the addition to total utility from consuming one more unit will be (<u>greater/less</u>) than the addition to total spending, and consumer's surplus will (<u>increase/decrease</u>).

This notion of optimal purchases and purchasing more until marginal utility falls below price is all well and good for a single commodity, but couldn't a consumer run out of income before she has considered optimal purchases of all goods and services? When one looks at demand curves commodity by commodity, this seems a real possibility. But remember that utility and demand are influenced by income and preferences. Total utility measures what people are willing to pay, given their preferences, their income, and the prices of other goods, not what they desire. As Mick Jagger and the Rolling Stones said, "You can't always get what you want." The appendix to this chapter shows geometrically how total income constrains the demand for individual commodities.

With our optimal purchase rule it is easy to derive an individual demand curve. A demand curve shows the quantity demanded at different prices, holding all other things constant. (Look back at Chapter 5 if necessary.) To derive an individual demand curve we confront our consumer with different prices and see how the quantity demanded changes. Our optimal purchase rule tells us that she will purchase more units as long as the marginal utility is (<u>greater/less</u>) than the price of the unit. She   (3) will stop when the two are equal. If we now lower the price, we know that she will again try to equate price and (<u>marginal/total</u>) utility, which she does by considering buying (<u>more/less</u>). Thus, as price goes down the quantity demanded tends to go (<u>down/up</u>), and this individual demand curve has a (<u>positive/negative</u>) slope.

Income also affects an individual's demand for various commodities. We saw in Chapter 5 that a change in income will mean a (<u>shift in/movement along</u>) the demand curve. In terms of the concepts of this chapter, a change in income will influence how much a person would spend to buy various commodities; that is, a change in income will influence total and marginal _____. Following   (4) a change in income, we could again conduct our demand curve experiment, and it would not be surprising if the resulting demand curve had shifted. An increase in income will typically mean an increase in the demand for most commodities, but occasionally the demand for some commodity decreases following an increase in income. Commodities whose demand decreases when income increases are called _____ goods. For example, if potatoes were an inferior good, then increased income would lead our consumer to demand (<u>fewer/more</u>) potatoes.

Individual demand curves are a critical building block to market demand curves. If people determine their own demands without regard to the purchases of others, then we can derive the market

(5)   demand curve by the (<u>horizontal/vertical</u>) summation of individual demand curves. For each price we simply add up the individual quantities demanded. If individual demand curves each have a negative slope, the market demand curve must have a _____ slope. Even if individual demand curves are vertical, that is, individuals purchase only a fixed quantity, the market demand curve is still likely to have a negative slope as long as lower prices attract new consumers and higher prices drive some consumers away.

■   IMPORTANT TERMS AND CONCEPTS QUIZ

Choose the best definition for each of the following terms.

1. _____ Marginal analysis

2. _____ Total utility

3. _____ Marginal utility

4. _____ "Law" of diminishing marginal utility

5. _____ Consumer's surplus

6. _____ Inferior goods

7. _____ Market demand curve

a.   Horizontal summation of individual demand curves.

b.   Difference between total utility and total expenditures for a given quantity of some commodity

c.   Observation that additional units of a given commodity generally have decreasing value for a consumer.

d.   Evaluation of the effects of small changes.

e.   Maximum amount of money a consumer will pay for an additional unit of some commodity.

f.   Quantity demanded increases when consumer real income rises.

g.   Quantity demanded declines when consumer real income rises.

h.   Maximum amount of money a consumer will give in exchange for a quantity of some commodity.

■   BASIC EXERCISES

These exercises review how we use the law of diminishing marginal utility to derive a negatively sloped demand curve.

1.   Table 6-1 presents data on Dolores' evaluation of different quantities of dresses.
     a.   Use these data to compute the marginal utility of each dress.
     b.   The optimal purchase rule says to buy more dresses as long as the marginal utility of the next dress exceeds the price of the dress. According to this rule, how many dresses should Dolores buy if they cost

$90 each? _____
$60 each? _____
$40 each? _____

c. Now, fill in columns 3, 5, and 7 of Table 6-2 to compute the difference between total utility and total expenditures for each price. What quantity maximizes the difference between total utility and total expenditures when price equals
$90? _____
$60? _____
$40? _____

Dresses	Total Utility	Marginal Utility
1	$110	$ _____
2	$210	$ _____
3	$290	$ _____
4	$360	$ _____
5	$410	$ _____
6	$440	$ _____
7	$460	$ _____

TABLE 6-1

d. The text defines total utility as the maximum amount Dolores would pay for various quantities of dresses. The difference between what she would be willing to pay and what she has to pay is called _____ surplus. How do the quantities determined using the optimal purchase rule in question b compare with those determined by maximizing consumer surplus in question c?

TABLE 6-2

Dresses	Price = $90 Total Expenditure	Difference* (Consumer's Surplus)	Price = $60 Total Expenditure	Difference* (Consumer's Surplus)	Price = $40 Total Expenditure	Difference* (Consumer's Surplus)
1	$ 90	_____	$ 60	_____	$ 40	_____
2	180	_____	120	_____	80	_____
3	270	_____	180	_____	120	_____
4	360	_____	240	_____	160	_____
5	450	_____	300	_____	200	_____
6	540	_____	360	_____	240	_____
7	630	_____	420	_____	280	_____

*Differences between total utility and total expenditures

e. Use the information in Table 6-1 to plot Dolores' demand curve for dresses in Figure 6-1. Is your demand curve consistent with your answers to questions b and c? (It should be.)

2. Consider the following information about Joel's total utility for CD purchases:

Number of CDs	Total Utility
1	$25
2	$45
3	$63
4	$78
5	$90
6	$100
7	$106
8	$110

a. What marginal utility is associated with the purchase of the third CD? _____

b. What is Joel's consumer's surplus if he purchases 3 CDs at $11 apiece? _____

c. What would happen to Joel's consumer's surplus if he purchased a fourth CD at $11?
_____

Demand for Dresses   **FIGURE 6-1**

    d. How many CDs should Joel buy when they cost $11 apiece? _____

    e. What is Joel's consumer's surplus at the optimal number of record purchases? _____

    f. If the CDs go on sale and their price drops to $8, how many CDs do you expect Joel to buy? Why? _____

■ SELF-TESTS FOR UNDERSTANDING

TEST A

Circle the most appropriate answer.

1. The total utility of any commodity bundle
    a. should be the same for all individuals.
    b. is defined as the maximum amount a consumer will spend for the bundle.
    c. will equal expenditures on the commodity in question.
    d. is not likely to change even if a consumer's income changes.

2. Total utility will increase as long as
    a. marginal utility is positive.
    b. marginal utility is greater than price.
    c. the good in question is not an inferior good.
    d. consumer's surplus is positive.

3. The law of diminishing marginal utility
    a. implies that total utility declines as a consumer buys more of any good.
    b. is an important psychological premise that helps explain why all demand curves must have a negative slope.
    c. must hold for every commodity and every individual.
    d. says that increments to total utility will decrease as an individual consumes more of a commodity.

4. Rick is willing to spend up to $200 for one ski trip this winter and up to $300 for two trips. The marginal utility of the second trip to Rick is
    a. $100.
    b. $200.
    c. $300.
    d. $500.

5. The optimal purchase rule says that consumers should maximize
    a. total utility.
    b. the difference between total utility and consumer's surplus.
    c. marginal utility.
    d. the difference between total utility and total expenditures on the good in question.

6. The optimal purchase rule says that to maximize the difference between total utility, measured in money terms, and total expenditures a consumer should purchase additional units
    a. as long as total utility is increasing.
    b. until marginal utility equals zero.
    c. as long as marginal utility exceeds price.
    d. until marginal utility equals total utility.

7. Consumer's surplus refers to the
    a. money a consumer has left over at the end of the month.
    b. accumulation of garbage that could be, but is not, recycled.
    c. difference between total expenditures and what a consumer would have been willing to pay for the same purchases.
    d. the pleasure a consumer takes when he finds an especially good deal.

8. Consumer's surplus will increase as long as the marginal utility of each additional purchase is
   a. positive.
   b. increasing.
   c. greater than total utility.
   d. greater than the price of the commodity.

9. If consumers act to maximize consumer's surplus, price will be closely related to
   a. total utility.
   b. average utility.
   c. marginal utility.
   d. consumer's surplus.

10. On a demand curve diagram, consumer's surplus is equal to the
    a. *Y*-axis intercept of the demand curve.
    b. the market price.
    c. the areas between the demand curve and the horizontal line indicating the market price.
    d. the slope of the demand curve.

11. The law of diminishing marginal utility implies that individual demand curves will typically
    a. have a negative slope.
    b. show no response to a change in price.
    c. slope up and to the right.
    d. have a positive slope.

12. A downward sloping demand curve means that the quantity demanded will
    a. not change when price changes.
    b. increase when price falls.
    c. increase when price rises.
    d. increase when income increases.

13. Scarcity raises _____ utility but lowers _____.
    a. total; price
    b. marginal; price
    c. marginal; total utility
    d. total; marginal utility

14. The diamond-water paradox indicates that
    a. contrary to economists' assumptions, consumers are really irrational.
    b. price is more closely related to marginal utility than to total utility.
    c. water is an inferior good.
    d. the demand for diamonds is very elastic.

15. The effect of an increase in income on quantity demanded
    a. is always positive.
    b. may be positive or negative.
    c. is positive for necessities and negative for luxuries.
    d. depends on the price elasticity of demand.

16. When economists say that some commodity is an inferior good, they are referring to the impact of
    a. a change in price on the quantity demanded.
    b. an increase in the quantity consumed on total utility.
    c. an increase in the quantity consumed on marginal utility.
    d. a change in income on the quantity demanded.

17. The term *inferior good* refers to goods
    a. made with substandard materials.
    b. that economists dislike.
    c. for which the quantity demanded declines when real income increases.
    d. advertised in the *National Enquirer*.

18. The opportunity cost of a purchase _____ its money cost.
    a. is always less than
    b. is always equal to
    c. is always greater than
    d. may be greater or less than

19. Market demand curves can be constructed by
    a. the vertical summation of individual demand curves.
    b. varying the number of people in the market.
    c. charging different people different prices and observing their behavior.
    d. the horizontal summation of individual demand curves.

20. A market demand curve will have a negative slope (there may be more than one correct answer)
    a. if all individual demand curves are downward sloping.
    b. only if the good is question is an inferior good.
    c. even if individual demands are not affected by price, but a lower price attracts new buyers.
    d. if a higher price increases the quantity demanded.

TEST B

Circle T or F for true or false.

T   F   1. The term *marginal utility* refers to the amount of dollars that consumers will pay for a particular commodity bundle.

T   F   2. If the law of diminishing marginal utility holds for pizza, then the demand curve for pizza should have a negative slope.

T   F   3. If a consumer is interested in maximizing the difference between total utility and expenditures, it is optimal to consume more of a commodity as long as the marginal utility of additional units exceeds the market price.

T   F   4. Consumer's surplus is defined as the difference between price and marginal utility.

T   F   5. Maximizing the difference between total utility and total expenditures is the same as maximizing consumer's surplus.

T   F   6. The term *inferior good* refers to those commodities that economists do not like.

T   F   7. If the quantity of ramen demanded decreases when income increases, we can conclude that ramen is an inferior good.

T   F   8. If a consumer is rational, he will never buy an inferior good.

T   F   9. The opportunity cost of making a purchase is always equal to the money cost of the good being bought.

T   F   10. A market demand curve can have a negative slope only if all individual demand curves have a negative slope.

APPENDIX: INDIFFERENCE CURVE ANALYSIS

LEARNING OBJECTIVES

After completing this appendix, you should be able to:

■ draw a budget line, given data on prices and money income.

■ explain why economists usually make four assumptions about indifference curves: (1) higher is better, (2) they never intersect, (2) they have a negative slope, and (3) they are bowed in toward the origin.

■ explain why higher indifference curves are preferred to lower indifference curves.

■ determine optimal commodity bundle(s) for a consumer, given a budget line and a set of indifference curves.

■ explain why, if indifference curves are smooth and bowed in to the origin, the optimal commodity bundle is the one for which the marginal rate of substitution equals the ratio of commodity prices.

■ use indifference curve analysis to derive a demand curve, that is, show the change in the quantity demanded of a good as its price changes.

■ use indifference curve analysis to analyze the impact on commodity demands of a change in income.

Important Terms and Concepts

BUDGET LINE

INDIFFERENCE CURVES

MARGINAL RATE OF SUBSTITUTION

SLOPE OF AN INDIFFERENCE CURVE

SLOPE OF A BUDGET LINE

■   **APPENDIX REVIEW**

Indifference curve analysis is a more rigorous treatment of the material covered in Chapter 6. As the appendix shows, we can study consumer choices by confronting a consumer's desires or preferences, indicated by indifference curves, with a consumer's opportunities, indicated by a budget line. This approach clearly shows how total purchases are constrained by income.

The budget line represents all possible combinations of commodities that a consumer can buy, given her income. The arithmetic of a budget line for two commodities shows that it is a

(1)   (straight/curved) line with a (positive/negative) slope. An increase in money income will produce a change in the (intercept/slope) of the budget line. A change in the price of either commodity will mean a change in the _____ of the budget line. The slope of the budget line is equal to the ratio of the prices of the two commodities. (The price of the commodity measured along the horizontal axis goes on top.)

The budget line indicates only all the different ways a consumer could spend her income. In order to figure out what consumption bundle is best for her, we must examine her own personal preferences.

(2)   Economists use the concept of _____ curves to summarize an individual's preferences. These curves are derived from a person's ranking of alternative commodity bundles. For two commodities, a single indifference curve is a line connecting all possible combinations (bundles) of the two commodities between which our consumer is _____. From the assumption that more is better, we can deduce (1) that higher indifference curves (are/are not) preferred to lower indifference curves, (2) that indifference curves (never/often) intersect, and (3) that indifference curves will have a (positive/negative) slope.

(3)   Indifference curves are usually assumed to be curved lines that are bowed (in/out). The slope of an indifference curve indicates the terms of trade between commodities that our consumer is indifferent about. For a given reduction in one commodity the slope tells us how much (more/less) of the other commodity is necessary to keep our consumer as well off as before. The slope of the indifference curve is also known as the marginal rate of _____. If indifference curves are bowed in, or convex to the origin, the marginal rate of substitution (increases/decreases) as we move from left to right along a given indifference curve. This change in the marginal rate of substitution is

a psychological premise similar to our earlier assumption about declining marginal utility, and it is what makes the indifference curves convex to the origin.

We can now determine optimal consumer choices. The optimal choice is the commodity bundle that makes our consumer as satisfied as possible, given her opportunities. In this case, opportunities are represented by the _____ line, and the evaluation of alternative commodity   (4) bundles is given by the _____ curves. The best choice is the commodity bundle that puts our consumer on her (<u>highest/lowest</u>) possible indifference curve. This consumption bundle is indicated by the indifference curve that is just tangent to the _____ _____.

From the definition of the slope of a curved line (Chapter 2) we know that at the point of tangency the slope of the associated indifference curve will equal the slope of the budget line. Since the slope of the budget line is given by the ratio of the prices of the two goods, we know that at the optimal decision the slope of the indifference curve, or the marginal rate of substitution, will equal the ratio of prices.

The marginal rate of substitution tells how our consumer *is willing* to trade goods, and the price ratio tells us how she *can* trade goods in the market by buying more of one good and less of the other. If these two trading ratios are different, our consumer can make herself better off by changing her purchases. It is only when the two trading ratios are equal that her opportunities for gain have been eliminated.

Once you master the logic and mechanics of indifference curve analysis, you can use it to investigate the impact on demand of changes in price or incomes. A change in either income or prices will shift the _____ _____. It is the resulting change in the optimal com-   (5) modity bundle that helps trace out a movement along the demand curve in the case of a change in prices, and the shift in the demand curve, in the case of a change in income.

Choose the best definition for each of the following terms.

1. _____ Budget line

2. _____ Indifference curves

3. _____ Marginal rate of substitution

4. _____ Slope of budget line

a. Maximum amount of one commodity a consumer will give up for an extra unit of another commodity.

b. Lines connecting all combinations of commodities on a consumer's utility function.

c. Line showing all possible combinations of two commodities a consumer can purchase given prices and the consumer's income.

d. Lines connecting all combinations of commodities that a consumer finds equally desirable.

e. Ratio of commodity prices.

■   **BASIC EXERCISES**

These problems are designed to review the logic of the rule for optimal consumer choice using indifference curve analysis, which says that a consumer should choose the commodity bundle associated with the point of tangency between the budget line and the highest indifference curve.

1. Figure 6-2 shows Gloria's set of indifference curves between books and hamburgers.
    a. Gloria has an income of $120 that she will spend on books and hamburgers. Hamburgers cost $3 each and paperback books $6 each. Draw the budget line in Figure 6-2 that constrains Gloria's choices. (You might first compute the maximum number of hamburgers Gloria can buy; then determine the maximum number of books, then connect these points with a straight line.)
    b. How many hamburgers will Gloria buy? _____
        How many books will she buy? _____
    In Figure 6-2, label this combination B for best choice. (If you drew the budget line correctly, this point should lie on indifference curve I_3.)

    c. The combination of 30 hamburgers and five books, point Z, is obviously not a better choice, as it lies on a lower indifference curve. Assume that Gloria tentatively chooses point Z and is considering whether this choice is best. If you put a ruler along indifference curve I_2, you should be able to verify that at point Z the marginal rate of substitution of hamburgers for books is 3. This means that Gloria is willing to give up _____ hamburgers in order to be able to buy one more book. (You can check this by noting that the combination of 27 hamburgers and six books is on the same indifference curve.)[1] However, since books cost only $6 while hamburgers cost $3, Gloria has only to give up _____ hamburgers in order to buy one book. This is clearly a good deal for Gloria, and

[2] Most indifference curves do not have straight-line segments. The straight-line segment is used for convenience; the general argument is still correct.

she will reduce her consumption of hamburgers in order to buy more books; that is, she will move down the budget line away from point Z.

d. Consider point W, on indifference curve I_1. Think about the trade-off Gloria would accept as given by the slope of her indifference curve and the trade-off available in the market as given by the slope of the budget line. Explain why Gloria will be better off moving to the left along the budget line away from point W.

e. Arguments similar to those in c and d indicate that for smooth indifference curves as in Figure 6-2, the optimal consumer choice cannot involve a commodity bundle for which the marginal rate of substitution differs from the ratio of market prices. The conclusion is that the optimal decision must be the commodity bundle for which the marginal rate of substitution _____ .

Sharon's Indifference Curves   **FIGURE 6-3**

2. Figure 6-3 assumes that Sharon spends all of her income on pizza and baseball tickets. The budget line P_1B_1 reflects Sharon's initial income and market prices for pizza and baseball tickets. Her preferences are shown by the curved indifference curves. Initially, Sharon chooses to consume at point X.

a. Change in income. Where will Sharon consume following a change in income that shifts the budget line to P_2B_2? _____ Is either good an inferior good? How do you know?

b. Change in price. Where will Sharon consume following a reduction in the price of pizzas that shifts the budget line from P_1B_1 to P_3B_1?

SELF-TESTS FOR UNDERSTANDING ■

TEST A

Circle the most appropriate answer.

1. The budget line
    a. determines an individual's optimal consumption bundle.
    b. will not shift at all if prices of both commodities increase and income is unchanged.
    c. determines an individual's possible consumption bundles.
    d. is a straight line whose slope is given by the rate of inflation.

2. The slope of the budget line
    a. is equal to the marginal rate of substitution.
    b. depends upon a consumer's income.
    c. is determined by commodity prices.
    d. should be positive.

3. Following an increase in income,
    a. a consumer's indifference curves will shift.
    b. the slope of the budget line will increase.
    c. individual commodity demand curves will not shift.
    d. the budget line will shift in a parallel fashion.

4. A change in the price of one good will
    a. lead to a parallel shift of the budget line.
    b. shift the indifference curves in closer to the origin.
    c. change the slope of the budget line.
    d. have no effect on either the budget line or indifference curves.

5. A set of indifference curves is
    a. usually assumed to have a positive slope.
    b. used by economists to represent a person's preferences among different commodity bundles.
    c. the same for everyone.

6. The marginal rate of substitution refers to the slope of
    a. an individual's demand curve.
    b. the budget line.
    c. the market demand curve.
    d. indifference curves.

7. The slope of an indifference curve
    a. is constant if the indifference curve is convex to the origin.
    b. always equals the slope of the budget line.
    c. indicates what commodity trades an individual would be indifferent about.

8. The assumption that more is preferred to less is sufficient to prove all but which one of the following?
    a. Indifference curves never intersect.
    b. Indifference curves bow in toward the origin.
    c. Higher indifference curves are preferred to lower ones.
    d. Indifference curves have a negative slope.

9. If when choosing between beer and pretzels, a consumer is always willing to trade one beer for one bag of pretzels, the resulting indifference curve will
    a. still bow in toward the origin.
    b. be a straight line.
    c. bow out away from the origin.

10. On an indifference curve diagram, optimal purchases are given by
    a. the point where the budget line intersects the Y axis.
    b. the intersection of a ray from the origin and the budget line.
    c. the highest indifference curve that is attainable given the budget line.
    d. any indifference curve that crosses the budget line.

11. The optimal purchases from question 10 occurs where
    a. the substitution effect just equals the income effect.
    b. all goods are inferior goods.
    c. demand curves begin to slope up.
    d. at the point of tangency between the highest indifference curve and the budget line.

12. If an indifference curve is tangent to the budget line, then the marginal rate of substitution is
    a. less than the ratio of prices.
    b. just equal to the ratio of prices.
    c. greater than the ratio of prices.
    d. zero.

13. On an indifference curve diagram an increase in the price of one commodity will
   a. cause the resulting budget line to lie inside the original budget line.
   b. lead a consumer to choose a new commodity bundle, but one that is on the same indifference curve.
   c. shift consumer preferences.
   d. have no effect on the demand for either commodity.

TEST B

Circle T or F for true or false.

T F 1. The budget line is a curved line, convex to the origin.

T F 2. A change in the price of one commodity will change the slope of the budget line.

T F 3. A change in income will also change the slope of the budget line.

T F 4. The assumption that consumers prefer more to less is sufficient to establish that indifference curves will be convex to the origin.

T F 5. The slope of indifference curves at any point is given by the ratio of commodity prices.

T F 6. The slope of an indifference curve is also called the marginal rate of substitution.

T F 7. Optimal decision making implies that a consumer should never choose a commodity bundle for which the marginal rate of substitution equals the ratio of market prices.

T F 8. Indifference curve analysis shows that consumers should be indifferent about all the commodity bundles along the budget line, e.g., consumers should be indifferent as between points Y and Z in Figure 6-3.

T F 9. Indifference curve analysis shows us that the demand for all goods is interrelated in the sense that changes in the price of one good can affect the demand for other goods.

T F 10. Indifference curve analysis suggests that a doubling of all prices and a doubling of income will not change optimal consumption bundles.

SUPPLEMENTARY EXERCISE ■

Consider a consumer whose total utility can be represented as

$$U = (F + 12)(C + 20)$$

where F = quantity of food, C = quantity of clothing, and U = the arbitrary level of utility associated with a particular indifference curve. (A different value for U will imply a different indifference curve.)

1. Draw a typical indifference curve. (Try $U = 7840$.)

2. Can you derive an expression for the demand for food? For clothing? (Try using the equation for the budget line and what you know about optimal consumer choice to derive an equation that expresses F or C as a function of prices and income. The particular form of these demand curves comes from the mathematical specification of the indifference curves. A different specification of the indifference curves would lead to a different demand function.)

3. If food costs $1.50, clothing $3, and income is $300, what combination of food and clothing will maximize utility?

4. Assume the price of food rises to $2. Now what combination of food and clothing maximizes utility?

5. Assume income increases to $330. What happens to the demand for food and clothing? Is either good an inferior good?

■ ECONOMICS IN ACTION

DRIP, DRIP, DRIP

In spite of recent very wet winters, drought is a consistent threat to Californians. A year or two of below-average rain and snowfall can seriously deplete the state's reservoirs. As the effects of a water shortage become progressively more severe, there is discussion of various schemes for water rationing, but typically these schemes do not involve using prices to ration water. Most water districts set price to cover cost and do not think very much about price as a variable that might limit demand when drought limits supply.

A typical sequence of events will start with a campaign to encourage voluntary reduction in water usage. As drought persists, many areas establish quotas for water usage, usually based on family size, with stiff increases in price for water consumption in excess of the quota. (The dashed line in Figure 6-4 illustrates such a "quota—high price" scheme. The dashed line indicates the total water bill. The price per gallon is given by the slope of the line.)

The "quota—high price" scheme offers a strong incentive to limit water consumption to the basic quota, but there is little monetary incentive to reduce water consumption below the quota. In 1977 economist Milton Friedman suggested that rather than impose quotas with high prices for excess consumption, water districts should charge a very high price for all water consumption, with a rebate to consumers with especially low water consumption. (See *Newsweek*, March 21, 1977.)

The solid line in Figure 6-4 illustrates a possible "high price—rebate" scheme. To ensure that a water district has enough money to cover its fixed costs, the position and/or slope of the solid line could be adjusted. Parallel shifts of the solid line would affect the maximum rebate and the no-charge point, but not the price of a gallon of water. Shifts in the slope would change the price. For example, pivoting the solid line on point A would change both the price and the maximum rebate, while leaving the cost of the basic quota unchanged.

Ross and Judy live in San Francisco. During 1976, in response to the growing concern about water conservation, they voluntarily cut their water consumption significantly below the quotas established by other water districts. The San Francisco rationing scheme, adopted in early 1977, mandated that all San Francisco residents reduce their consumption below 1976 levels by the same percentage. When drought returned to California in the mid-80s, Ross and Judy were heard telling their friends that they were using all the water they could to increase their base use.

1. What advice would you give to a water district facing a drought? How much reliance should be placed on campaigns for voluntary reductions? How much reliance should be placed on prices? If prices, what sort of scheme would you recommend and why—a quota with high price scheme, a high price with rebate scheme or something else? Do you think price affects people's demand for water? What about businesses, government, and farmers?

FIGURE 6-4	Water Bill

STUDY QUESTIONS ■

1. What is the difference between total and marginal utility?

2. How is it that total utility can increase while marginal utility decreases?

3. Why do economists expect a close relation between price and *marginal* utility rather than total utility?

4. How does the difference between total and marginal utility resolve the diamond–water paradox?

5. What is the logic behind the optimal purchase rule?

6. Why does the law of diminishing marginal utility imply that demand curves are likely to have a negative slope?

7. How do we know that purchasing more of a commodity as long as marginal utility exceeds prices will also maximize consumer surplus?

8. How can there be mutual gain from voluntary trade even when no new goods are produced?

9. Economists have a particular definition of inferior goods that does not refer to the quality of product directly but may be correlated with quality. What is the economist's definition of an inferior good?

10. How can one derive a market demand curve from individual demand curves?

DEMAND AND ELASTICITY

LEARNING OBJECTIVES

After completing this chapter, you should be able to:

■ compute the elasticity of demand, given data from a demand curve.

■ describe how various factors affect the elasticity of demand.

■ explain why the price elasticity of demand is a better measure of the price sensitivity of demand than the slope of the demand curve.

■ explain how the impact of a change in price on total revenue and consumer expenditures depends on the price elasticity of demand.

■ explain how the concept of cross elasticity of demand relates to the concepts of substitutes and complements.

■ explain how factors other than price can affect the quantity demanded.

The material in this chapter offers an intensive look at demand curves. Demand curves provide important information for analyzing business decisions, market structures, and public policies.

An important property of demand curves is the responsiveness of demand to a change in price. If a firm raises its price, how big a sales drop is likely? If a firm lowers its price, how large an increase in sales will there be?

To avoid problems with changing units, economists find it useful to measure these changes as percentages. If, for a given change in price, we divide the percentage change in the quantity demanded by the percentage change in the price producing the change in quantity and ignore the negative sign, we

(1)   have just computed the price _____ of _____. Remember, this calculation ignores minus signs and uses the *average* price and quantity to compute percentage changes.

It is useful to know the elasticity properties of certain, special types of demand curves. If the demand curve is truly a vertical line, then there is no change in the quantity demanded following any change

(2)   in price, and the elasticity of demand is _____. (No demand curve is likely to be vertical for all prices, but it may be for some.) The other extreme is a perfectly horizontal demand curve where a small change in price produces a very large change in the quantity demanded. Such a demand curve implies that if price declines, even just a little, the quantity demanded will be infinite, while if the price rises, even a little, the quantity demanded will fall to zero. In this case a very small percentage change in price produces a very large percentage change in the quantity demanded, and the price elasticity of demand is, in the limit, _____. The price elasticity of demand along a negatively sloped straight-line demand curve (is constant/changes). One of the Basic Exercises illustrates just this point.

A demand curve with a price elasticity of demand greater than 1.0 is commonly called

(3)   _____ while demand curves with a price elasticity of demand less than 1.0 are called _____. If the price elasticity of demand is exactly 1.0 the demand curve is said to be a _____ _____ demand curve.

Some simple arithmetic, not economics, can show the connection between the price elasticity of demand and the change in total consumer expenditure (or, equivalently, the change in sales revenue) following a change in price. We know that total expenditures or revenues are simply price times quantity, or

Consumer expenditures = Sales revenues = $p \times q$.

A decrease in price will increase quantity as we move along a given demand curve. Whether total revenue increases clearly depends on whether the increase in quantity is big enough to outweigh the decline in price. (Remember the old saying: "We lose a little on each sale but make it up on volume.")

Again, it is mathematics, not economics, that tells us the percentage change in total expenditures or revenue is equal to the sum of the percentage change in price and the percentage change in quantity.[1]

| Percentage change in sales revenues | = | Percentage change in price | + | Percentage change in quantity |

Remember that as we move along a given demand curve, a positive change in price will lead to a negative change in quantity, and vice versa.

If the absolute value of the percentage change in quantity is equal to the absolute value of the percentage change in price, then total revenue (will/will not) change following a change in price. In this case, the price elasticity of demand is equal to _____.

When the elasticity of demand is greater than 1, the absolute value of the percentage change in quantity will be (greater/less) than the percentage change in price. In this case, an increase in price that reduces the quantity demanded will (decrease/increase) total revenue, and a reduction in price that increases the quantity demanded will (decrease/increase) total revenue. Opposite conclusions apply when the price elasticity of demand is less than 1.0. In this case the percentage change in quantity will be (greater/less) than the percentage change in price. An increase in price that reduces the quantity demanded will (decrease/increase) total revenue, and a reduction in price that increases the quantity demanded will (decrease/increase) total revenue.

(4)

(5)

The price elasticity of demand refers to the impact on the quantity demanded of a change in a commodity's price. A related elasticity concept compares the change in the quantity demanded of one good with a change in the price of another good. This quotient is called the _____ elasticity of demand. In this case we must keep track of any negative signs.

(6)

Some goods, such as knives and forks, film and cameras, are usually demanded together. Such pairs are called _____ and are likely to have a (positive/negative) cross elasticity of

(7)

---

[1]This result is strictly true only for very small changes in p and q. Total revenue always equals $p \times q$, but this simple way of calculating the percentage change in total revenue is only true for small changes.

demand. For example a decline in the price of cameras is likely to (decrease/increase) the demand for film. That is, following a decline in the price of cameras, the demand curve for film will likely shift to the (left/right).

(8)   Other goods, such as different brands of toothpaste, are probably close _____ and are likely to have a _____ cross elasticity of demand. What is the likely impact on the demand for Colgate toothpaste of a change in the price of Crest? A decrease in the price of Crest toothpaste would likely (decrease/increase) the demand for Colgate toothpaste. Alternatively, one could say that a decrease in the price of Crest will likely shift the Colgate demand curve to the (left/right).

The price of a commodity is not the only variable influencing demand. Changes in other factors, say, advertising, consumers' income, tastes, and, as we just saw, the price of a close substitute or com-

(9)   plement, will mean a (shift in/movement along) a demand curve drawn against price. Finally, remember that a demand curve refers only to a particular period of time.

■ IMPORTANT TERMS AND CONCEPTS QUIZ

Choose the best definition for each of the following terms.

1. _____ Price elasticity of demand

2. _____ Elastic demand curve

3. _____ Inelastic demand curve

4. _____ Unit-elastic demand curve

5. _____ Complements

6. _____ Substitutes

7. _____ Cross elasticity of demand

8. _____ Shift in demand curve.

a. Ratio of percent change in quantity demanded of one product to the percent change in the price of another.

b. A change in price leads to a less than proportionate change in quantity demanded.

c. Good for which an increase in price leads to higher demand.

d. An increase in price of one good decreases the demand for the other.

e. A change in price leads to a more than proportionate change in quantity demanded.

f. Ratio of percent change in quantity demanded to percent change in price.

g. A change in price accompanied by an equal proportionate change in quantity demanded.

h. An increase in the price of one good increases the demand for the other.

i. Change in the quantity demanded due to a change in any determinant of demand except price.

BASIC EXERCISES ■

These exercises offer practice in calculating and interpreting price elasticities of demand.

1. **The Price Elasticity of Demand**
   a. Table 7-1 has data on possible prices and the associated demand for schmoos and gizmos. Use these data to plot the demand curves in Figures 7-1 and 7-2. Looking at these demand curves, which curve looks more elastic? More inelastic?
   b. Now use the data in Table 7-1 to calculate the elasticity of demand for schmoos for a change in price from $60 to $50.[2] It is

   _____.

   c. Use the same data to calculate the elasticity of demand for gizmos for a change in price from $1 to 50 cents. It is

   _____.

   d. For these changes, which demand curve is more elastic? In fact, if you look closely at the underlying data for both curves—for example, by computing the total revenue—you will see that for both curves the elasticity of demand is

   _____.

TABLE 7-1			
Demand for Schmoos		Demand for Gizmos	
Price (dollars)	Quantity	Price (dollars)	Quantity
60	200	2.00	2,000
50	240	1.25	3,200
48	250	1.00	4,000
40	300	0.50	8,000

Demand for Schmoos | FIGURE 7-1 |

Demand for Gizmos | FIGURE 7-2 |

---

[2]Remember to use the average of the two prices or quantities when computing each percentage change. For example, compute the elasticity of demand when the price changes from $60 to $50 as [40/220] ÷ [10/55].

TABLE 7-2	Demand for Jeans					
Price (dollars)	Quantity Demanded	Percentage Change Price	Percentage Change Quantity	Elasticity of Demand	Total Revenue	
40	15,000					
36	18,000	———	———	———	———	
32	21,000	———	———	———	———	
28	24,000	———	———	———	———	
24	27,000	———	———	———	———	

FIGURE 7-3   Demand for Jeans

2. The Price Elasticity of Straight-Line Demand Curves

Table 7-2 contains data on possible prices and the associated quantity of demand for jeans in Collegetown. Plot this demand curve in Figure 7-3. It is a (curved/straight) line.

a. Using the data in Table 7-2, compute the elasticity of demand for each change in price.[3] What general conclusion can you draw about the elasticity of demand along a straight-line demand curve? The elasticity of demand (increases/decreases) as one moves down and to the right along a straight-line demand curve.

b. Use the same data to compute total revenue for each price-quantity pair in Table 7-2. Compare the change in total revenue to the elasticity of demand. What conclusion can you draw about this relationship?

■ SELF-TESTS FOR UNDERSTANDING

TEST A

Circle the most appropriate answer.

1. Looking just at the demand curve, the price responsiveness of demand is given by
   a. the Y-intercept.
   b. the slope of the demand curve.
   c. the slope of a ray from the origin to a point on the demand curve.
   d. the product of price times quantity.

2. If when price increases the quantity demanded declines, we know that
   a. the demand curve has a negative slope.
   b. the price elasticity of demand is less than 1.0.
   c. total sales revenue will increase.
   d. total sales revenue will decrease.

---

[3] Remember to use the average of the two prices and quantities. For a change in price from $40 to $36 compute the elasticity of demand as 3,000/16,500 ÷ 4/38.

3. The price elasticity of demand is defined as the _____ change in the quantity demanded divided by the _____ change in price.
   a. percentage; absolute
   b. absolute; absolute
   c. percentage; percentage
   d. absolute; percentage

4. If the price elasticity of demand is less than 1.0, then for a 10 percent change in price the quantity demanded will change by
   a. less than 10 percent.
   b. exactly 10 percent.
   c. more than 10 percent.
   d. There is not enough information.

5. If the units in which the quantity demanded is measured are changed, say from pounds to ounces, then the price elasticity of demand will
   a. decrease.
   b. increase.
   c. be unaffected.
   d. increase by a factor of 16.

6. If a 10 percent price increase leads to a 12 percent decline in the quantity demanded, the price elasticity of demand is
   a. $(10 \div 12) = .83$.
   b. $(12 \div 10) = 1.2$.
   c. $(12 - 10) = 2$.
   d. $(12 + 10) = 22$.

7. If the elasticity of demand is equal to 1.0, then a change in price leads to
   a. no change in the quantity demanded.
   b. a reduction in total revenue.
   c. a shift in the demand curve.
   d. an equal (ignoring any negative signs), proportionate change in the quantity demanded.

8. If the elasticity of demand is greater than 1.0, a reduction in price will
   a. decrease total sales revenue.
   b. leave total sales revenue unchanged.
   c. increase total sales revenue.
   d. lead to a reduction in the quantity demanded.

9. Sales revenue will not change following an increase in price if
   a. the price elasticity of demand is equal to 1.0.
   b. the demand curve is a straight line.
   c. the cross elasticity of demand is positive.
   d. the quantity demanded doesn't change.

10. If the demand for apples is inelastic, apple producers could increase total revenue by
    a. decreasing price.
    b. increasing price.
    c. changing price will not affect total revenue.

11. If a 20 percent decrease in the price of long-distance phone calls leads to a 35 percent increase in the quantity of calls demanded, we can conclude that the demand for phone calls is
    a. elastic.
    b. inelastic.
    c. unit elastic.

12. From the data given above, what would happen to total revenue following a 20 percent decrease in the price of long-distance phone calls? It would
    a. decrease.
    b. increase.
    c. remain the same.

13. Angelita manufactures artificial valves used in open-heart surgery. She is contemplating increasing prices. Total revenue will decrease unless the demand for valves is
    a. elastic.
    b. inelastic.
    c. unit elastic.

14. Goods that are usually used together are said to be
    a. complements.
    b. inelastic.
    c. spin-offs.
    d. substitutes.

15. If goods are substitutes, then the cross elasticity of demand is likely to be
    a. equal to 1.0.
    b. negative.
    c. positive.
    d. zero.

16. The cross elasticity of demand between frozen pizza and home-delivered pizza would be computed as the percentage change in the quantity of frozen pizza demanded divided by
    a. the percentage change in the price of frozen pizza.
    b. the percentage change in the quantity of home-delivery pizza demanded.
    c. the percentage change in the price of home-delivery pizza.
    d. the change in the price of mozzarella cheese.

17. If, following an increase in the price of schmoos, the quantity demanded of gizmos declined, we would conclude that
    a. the demand for gizmos is inelastic.
    b. gizmos and schmoos are substitutes.
    c. gizmos and schmoos are complements.
    d. schmoos are likely to be a luxury good.

18. If the cross elasticity of demand between two goods is positive, we would conclude that the two goods are
    a. substitutes.
    b. complements.
    c. necessities.
    d. both likely to have inelastic demand curves.

19. If the price of Sony 90-minute audio tapes increases, the demand curve for JVC audio tapes is likely to
    a. shift to the right.
    b. shift to the left.
    c. be unchanged.
    d. become vertical.

20. If skis and boots are complements, then which one of the following statements is false?
    a. A reduction in the price of skis is likely to increase the sales of boots.
    b. Revenue from ski sales will increase following a reduction in the price of ski boots.
    c. An increase in the price of boots will likely reduce the sales of skis.
    d. The cross elasticity of demand between skis and boots will likely be positive.

21. The income elasticity of demand is measured as the percentage change in
    a. price divided by the percentage change in income.
    b. the quantity demanded divided by the percentage change in income that changes demand.
    c. income divided by the change in demand.
    d. income divided by the percentage change in price.

TEST B

Circle T or F for true or false.

T F 1. The price elasticity of demand is defined as the change in quantity divided by the change in price.

T F 2. The elasticity of demand will be the same at all points along a straight-line demand curve.

T F 3. A vertical demand curve would have a price elasticity of zero.

T F 4. A demand curve is elastic if, following a decrease in price, the quantity demanded increases.

T F 5. If demand is inelastic, an increase in price will actually increase the quantity demanded.

T F 6. If the demand for airplane travel is elastic, then a reduction in the price of airline tickets will increase total expenditures on airplane trips.

T F 7. If two goods are substitutes, then an increase in the price of one good is likely to reduce the demand for the other good.

T F 8. The cross elasticity of demand between complements is normally negative.

T F 9. If sales of Whoppers at Burger King increase following an increase in the price of Big Macs at McDonald's, we can conclude that Whoppers and Big Macs are complements.

T F 10. The price elasticity of demand for Chevrolets is likely to be greater than that for cars as a whole.

T F 11. A demand curve will shift to the left following an increase in price of a close complement.

T F 12. An increase in consumer income will shift the demand curve for most goods to the left.

T F 13. The income elasticity of demand is defined as the percentage change in income divided by the percentage change in price.

T F 14. Plotting price and quantity for a period of months or years is a good way to estimate a demand curve.

APPENDIX: STATISTICAL ANALYSIS OF DEMAND RELATIONSHIPS

BASIC EXERCISES

Completing these exercises should help underscore the necessity and difficulty of distinguishing between a demand curve and observations on price and quantity that are determined by the intersection of demand and supply curves.

TABLE 7-3			
	Year	Quantity (millions of pounds)	Price (dollars per pound)
	1970	2,356	0.65
	1971	2,490	0.67
	1972	2,757	0.71
	1973	2,891	0.84
	1974	3,077	0.97
	1975	3,017	1.04
	1976	3,423	1.16
	1977	3,577	1.19
	1978	3,794	1.30
	1979	3,888	1.41
	1980	4,149	1.56

SOURCE: Computed from *Survey of Current Business*, various issues.

1. Consider the data on cheese consumption and prices for the period 1970 to 1980 in Table 7-3. Plot these data on piece of graph paper. What does this graph say about the demand for cheese? Why?

2. Assume that the demand for hand-held calculators depends on consumer income and price as follows:

$$Q^D = -110 + 0.2Y - 5P$$

where

Q^D = quantity demanded (thousands),

Y = consumer income (millions), and

P = price (dollars).

Supply is assumed to be determined as follows:

$$Q^S = 50 + 15P$$

where Q^S = quantity supplied (thousands).
   a.   Compute the equilibrium price and quantity for 1996, 1997, and 1998, given that consumer income was as follows:

Year	Consumer Income
1996	$3,000
1997	3,100
1998	3,200

Plot these price-quantity pairs for each year on a two-variable diagram. Are these points a good estimate of the demand curve? Why? Why not?
   b.   Assume now that the supply curve for calculators shifts each year in response to technical advances in the production process. To capture these technical advances, we need a new supply curve for each year as follows:
   1996 $Q^S = 50 + 15P$
   1997 $Q^S = 100 + 15P$
   1998 $Q^S = 300 + 15P$
Compute and plot equilibrium price and quantity for each year. (Remember to include the effect of the change in consumer income in the demand curve.) Are these points a good estimate of the demand curve? Why? Why not?

ECONOMICS IN ACTION ■

1. Howard Grant operates a movie theater in New Jersey, just across the Hudson River from New York. He used to show the most recently released movies at a ticket price of $6.50. He was especially discouraged when attendance dropped to 212 people over a full weekend. He then changed the format of his theater to show still current but previously released movies, and he reduced his ticket price to $1. Weekend attendance jumped to 3,782 people. (*The New York Times*, March 20, 1992)

   a. Using the numbers above, what is the elasticity of demand for movies at Mr. Grant's theater?

   b. What is likely to happen to Mr. Grant's attendance if other theaters adopt his format and lower their prices?

2. In the late spring of 1992 Northwest Airlines offered a promotional fare advertised as parents fly free with children. The program cut airline fares in half for family travel. American Airlines, which had unsuccessfully tried earlier to reduce the number of special promotional airfares, responded by halving all fares purchased seven days in advance. To avoid the anger of passengers who had bought tickets earlier, the airlines agreed that these passengers could reticket at the new, lower fares. Not surprisingly, airlines and travel agents were swamped with calls. At one point, new bookings were so heavy that some airline executives were reported saying that total sales revenue might not drop "because of the extraordinary high response." (*The New York Times*, June 2, 1992)

   a. What would the price elasticity of demand for air travel have to be if these airline executives were correct?

   b. How would we know whether the reduction in ticket prices did double the demand for air travel? Consider the following. In the summer of 1991, June through September, travel on domestic airlines totaled 120 billion passenger miles. In 1992, summer travel totaled 134.5 billion passenger miles. Discuss the relevance of this information for an evaluation of the impact of the reduction in airfares.

STUDY QUESTIONS ■

1. Why is elasticity measured as the ratio of percentage changes and not just as the ratio of the change in quantity demanded to the change in price?

2. What is the logic behind the statement in the text that the demand for narrowly defined commodities, for example a particular brand of clothing, is more elastic than the demand for broadly defined commodities, that is, all clothing?

3. Which is likely to be larger and why, the price elasticity of demand for luxuries or the price elasticity of demand for necessities?

4. What is meant by the terms "perfectly elastic" and "perfectly inelastic"? What do these demand curves look like and why?

5. How does the elasticity of demand help determine whether a change in price will raise or lower total sales revenue?

6. If a government is interested in increasing revenue, will it want to impose tariffs or sales taxes on goods with a high or low price elasticity of demand? Why?

7. What is the cross elasticity of demand and how does its numerical value help to determine whether goods are complements or substitutes?

8. Consider the demand for pretzels. Why does the change in the price of a complement, say, beer, or the change in the price of a close substitute, say, potato chips, lead to shifts in the demand curve for pretzels rather than a movement along the curve? What exactly is the nature of the shifts?

PRODUCTION, INPUTS, AND COST: BUILDING BLOCKS FOR SUPPLY ANALYSIS

LEARNING OBJECTIVES

After completing this chapter, you should be able to:

■ describe the difference between the short run and long run.

■ compute the average and marginal physical product for a single input given total output at different input levels.

■ explain the "law" of diminishing marginal returns.

■ compute the marginal revenue product for additional units of some input given information on the marginal physical product of the input and the price of the output.

■ explain why a profit-maximizing firm will expand the use of each input until its marginal revenue product equals the price of the input.

■ explain why the law of diminishing returns implies that a profit-maximizing firm will use less of an input following a price increase.

■ explain the importance of opportunity cost when distinguishing between total cost and total expenditure.

■ explain the difference between fixed and variable costs.

■ explain why fixed costs, administrative problems of large organizations, and the law of diminishing returns imply that the short-run average cost curve is usually U-shaped.

■ explain how to determine the long-run average cost curve from a set of short-run average cost curves.

■ show how information on a firm's production function allows you to investigate the substitutability of inputs.

■ explain how and why the ratio of input prices and the ratio of marginal physical products is relevant to the optimal choice of input combinations.

■ explain how total costs—and hence average costs—can be computed given information on the production function and input prices.

■ determine whether a particular production function shows increasing, decreasing, or constant returns to scale, given data on output and on various input combinations.

■ explain the relationship between returns to scale and the long-run average cost curve.

■ distinguish between diminishing returns to increases of a single productive input and economies of scale when all inputs change.

■ explain the difference between analytical and historical cost curves.

■ CHAPTER REVIEW

In this chapter we will make extensive use of the concept of marginal analysis as a guide to optimal decision making. We will see how marginal analysis can help a firm make optimal decisions about the use of production inputs and how these decisions can be used to derive cost curves. In Chapter 6 we saw how marginal analysis helps to understand optimal consumer decisions. We use it here in an analogous way to understand optimal firm decisions about the use of inputs.

This chapter introduces a potentially bewildering array of curves and concepts—marginal physical product, marginal revenue product, fixed costs, variable costs, long run, short run. All of these curves and concepts relate to each other and underlie optimal firm decisions. Spending time now to get these relationships clear will save you time in later chapters and the night before the exam.

In deciding whether to use an additional unit of some input, say, hiring more workers, a firm should look at the contribution of the additional workers to both total revenue and total cost. If the increase in

(1) revenue exceeds the increase in cost, then profits will (increase/decrease). The increase in revenue comes from producing and selling additional units of output. Economists call the amount of additional output from the use of one more unit of input the *marginal* (physical/revenue) product of the input. For a firm selling its output at a constant price, the increase in revenue comes from multiplying the

additional output by the price at which it can be sold. Economists call this the marginal

_____ product.

Consider a small firm that faces fixed market prices for its production inputs. Common sense tells

us that a profit-maximizing firm should use additional units of any input if the addition to total rev-

enue exceeds the addition to total cost. Another way of saying the same thing is that the firm should

consider using more of an input as long as the marginal (<u>physical/revenue</u>) product exceeds the price   (2)

of the input. A firm has clearly gone too far if additions to revenue are less than additions to cost. Thus

a profit-maximizing firm should expand the use of any factor until the marginal revenue product

equals the _____ of the input.

If the price of an input is constant, firms will use more and more units of this input until the mar-

ginal revenue product falls to a point where it equals the input price. As a result, firms will usually

expand the use of any input past any region of increasing marginal returns and into the region of

decreasing returns to the one input.

So far we have talked about the optimal use of only one input. What if production involves trade-

offs between more than one input? Our rule holds true for more than one input. The idea is to adjust

the use of all inputs until the marginal physical product divided by the input price is equal for all

inputs. In symbols, assuming the use of two inputs A and B, we have

$$MPP_A/P_A = MPP_B/P_B$$

as the condition for an optimal input combination. Either fraction shows how output will change per

dollar spent on that input. When the fraction is high, one gets a lot of output per dollar spent. A low

fraction means less output per dollar spent. If this ratio were initially high for input B and low for input

A, a firm would want to use (<u>less/more</u>) of input B and _____ of input A. Making these adjust-   (3)

ments should (<u>increase/reduce</u>) the MPP of input B and _____ the MPP of input A, mov-

ing the fractions toward the equality necessary for the optimal input combination.

What about our original result that we should adjust the use of a single input until marginal rev-

enue product equals the price of the input? Is it still valid when there is more than one input? Yes.

Remember that for input A, $MRP_A = MPP_A \times P_{OUTPUT}$. Following our earlier rule, we would adjust

the use of input A until $P_A = MRP_A$ or until $P_A = MPP_A \times P_{OUTPUT}$. The use of input B also should be adjusted until $P_B = \text{MPP}_B \times P_{OUTPUT}$. A little multiplication and division should show that when the prices of inputs and output are constant, making these adjustments individually also results in the optimal input combination.[1]

If the price of an input changes, it is natural to expect the firm's optimal input combination to change.

(4)   Specifically, it is natural to expect that a profit-maximizing firm will (<u>reduce/increase</u>) the use of any factor whose price has risen. Changing the quantity of one input will typically affect the marginal physical product of other inputs. As a result, a firm will want to rethink its use of all inputs following a change in price of any one input. It is quite likely that following an increase in the price of one input, a profit-maximizing firm will decide to use relatively (<u>less/more</u>) of the more expensive input and relatively _____ of the inputs with unchanged prices.

The relationship between inputs and outputs has been formalized by economists into something that measures the maximum amount of output that can be produced from any specified combination

(5)   of inputs given current technology, or, for short, the _____ function. Information about the marginal physical product for a single factor comes from this function. (The appendix to this chapter discusses a geometrical representation of a production function through the use of a contour-line diagram.) The concept of a production function is also useful in separating what happens if we increase the use of all factors or of just one factor. If all inputs are increased by the same percentage amount, then the percentage increase in output is used to indicate the degree of economies of scale. If output increases by more than the common percentage increase in all inputs, the production function exhibits _____ returns to scale. If output increases by less, there are _____ returns to scale, and if output increases by the same percentage, we would say that returns to scale are _____.

Information from the production function can be used to construct cost curves for a firm. Over a very short time horizon, previous commitments may limit a firm's ability to adjust all inputs. These commitments often imply that at least one input is predetermined and cannot be adjusted immediately. Imagine a farmer with a five-year lease on a parcel of land and unable to rent additional land. The interval of time

(6)   over which *none* of a firm's fixed commitments can be adjusted is called the (<u>long/short</u>) run.

---

[1] For input A, we can write our condition for optimal input use as $\text{MPP}_A \times P_{output} = P_A$. Dividing both sides of this equality by MPP_A we see that $P_{OUTPUT} = P_A/\text{MPP}_A$. Similar results hold for input B. That is, setting MRP_B equal to the price of input B also sets $P_{OUTPUT} = P_B/\text{MPP}_B$. Since both fractions are equal to the price of output, they are equal to each other and their reciprocals are also equal, that is if $P_A/\text{MPP}_A = P_B/\text{MPP}_B$ then $\text{MPP}_A/P_A = \text{MPP}_B/P_B$, our condition for the optimal input combination.

The total cost of producing each level of output in the short run can be computed with the help of the production function, input prices and any relevant opportunity costs. We will be interested only in minimum total costs for every level of output. We first use what we know about optimal factor use to determine the most efficient combination of variable inputs. We can then compute minimum total cost. As an example, assume that production requires two inputs, one of which is fixed in the short run. To compute total cost, the firm must first use the production function to see what amount of the variable input is necessary to produce different levels of output. Then it can compute total cost for each level of output by multiplying the quantity of the fixed input and the optimal quantity of the variable input by their prices, remembering relevant opportunity costs, and adding the results. After computing total cost, the firm can compute average cost by dividing total cost by the associated level of _____.

To compute marginal cost the firm must examine how (<u>average/total</u>) cost changes when output changes.   (7)

The period of time over which a firm can adjust all its fixed commitments is called the _____ _____. Long-run cost curves can be derived by either of two equivalent methods. One procedure would first derive short-run cost curves for each possible amount of the fixed input.   (8) The long-run cost curve is then determined by joining the _____ segments of the short-run cost curves. An alternative and equivalent method would treat both factors as variable. One would first use the production function and input prices to determine the optimal level of both inputs to produce every level of output. Total cost for each output level can then be computed by multiplying optimal input levels by their respective prices and adding the results. Average and marginal cost are then easily computed.

Since in the long run all factors can be changed, the shape of the long-run average cost curve is related to economies of scale. Constant returns to scale imply that a doubling of output requires twice as much of all inputs. In this case, total costs also double and average cost (<u>falls/is unchanged/rises</u>). Increasing returns to scale mean that twice the output can be produced with (<u>more/less</u>) than twice the inputs and average cost will (<u>fall/rise</u>). With decreasing returns to scale, twice the output requires   (9) _____ than twice the inputs and average cost _____.

We've covered a lot of ground and a lot of curves. You may want to take a deep breath before a quick review. The production function contains the basic technical information about inputs and output. From this information we can derive total physical product and marginal physical product for a single input. By itself the technical information is not sufficient to determine the minimum cost combination of inputs. Knowing the price of output will let us compute marginal revenue product for each input. Comparing marginal revenue product with input prices will then determine the optimal input quantities. Optimal input quantities in turn, determine (minimum) total cost for alternative levels of output. Once we know total cost, we can easily compute average and marginal cost. In the short run, there may be fixed costs. In the long run, all inputs, and hence all costs, are variable. In either run, the same optimizing principles apply.

■ IMPORTANT TERMS AND CONCEPTS QUIZ

Choose the best definition for each of the following terms.

1. _____ Total physical product

2. _____ Average physical product

3. _____ Marginal physical product

4. _____ Marginal revenue product

5. _____ Fixed costs

6. _____ Variable costs

7. _____ Short run

8. _____ Long run

9. _____ Production function

10. _____ Returns to scale

11. _____ Economies of scale

a. A graph showing how average cost has changed over time.

b. Costs which do not change when output rises or falls.

c. Increase in output greater than the proportionate increase in all inputs.

d. Period of time long enough for all of a firm's commitments to end.

e. Dollar value of output produced by an extra unit of input.

f. Graph of output generated by various quantities of one input, holding other inputs fixed.

g. Total output divided by total quantity of input.

h. Maximum amount of product obtainable from any specified combination of inputs, given the current state of knowledge.

i. Increase in output that results from an additional unit of a given input, holding all other inputs constant.

j. Relation of percentage change in output to proportionate change in all inputs.

k. Period of time during which some of a firm's commitments will not have ended.

l. Costs that change as the level of production changes.

BASIC EXERCISES

These questions review the concept of a production function and optimal input decisions.

Megan and Jamie have invested in Greenacre Farms to grow cornbeans. Since they both work in the city, they will need to hire workers for the farm. Table 8-1 has data on various input combinations and the resulting output of cornbeans.

1. Using the data in Table 8-1, draw on Figure 8-1 the relationship between total output and labor input for 100 acres of land.

   What is the region of increasing marginal returns? _____

   What is the region of decreasing marginal returns? _____

   What is the region of negative marginal returns? _____

Total Output of Cornbeans (thousands of tons)   **TABLE 8-1**

Number of Workers		1	2	3	4	5	6
Acres	100	1	4	6	7	6	4
of	200	2	6	9.5	12	13	12
Land	300	3	7.5	11	14	16	17

Marginal Physical Product of Labor

		1	2	3	4	5	6
Acres	100	___	___	___	___	___	___
of	200	___	___	___	___	___	___
Land	300	___	___	___	___	___	___

Marginal Revenue Product of Labor

		1	2	3	4	5	6
200 Acres of Land		___	___	___	___	___	___

2. Use Figure 8-1 to draw the relationship between total output and labor input, assuming the use of 200 acres of land. Identify the regions of increasing, decreasing, and negative returns.

   Do the same assuming 300 acres of land. How does the output-labor curve, i.e., the curve of total physical product, shift when more land is used?

3. Fill in the middle part of Table 8-1 by computing the marginal physical product of each worker. Check to see that the regions of increasing, diminishing, and negative returns that you identified above correspond to information about the marginal physical product of labor. (The marginal physical product of labor is equal to the slope of the total physical

Output of Cornbeans   **FIGURE 8-1**

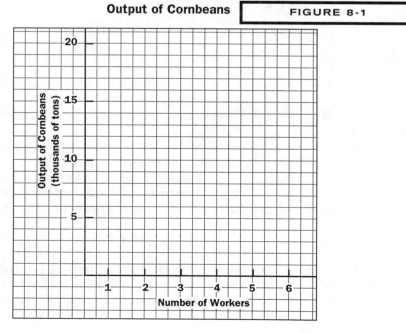

product curve. Check to see that your entries for each row in the middle of Table 8-1 equal the slope of the relevant total product curve in Figure 8-1.)

4. Your answers to questions 1, 2, and 3 should confirm that the production function for cornbeans eventually shows decreasing returns to labor for all three potential farm sizes. (What about returns to the increased use of land for a fixed amount of labor?)

5. Now consider the following pairs of inputs (acres, workers) and indicate for each whether economies of scale are increasing, decreasing, or constant.

Economies of Scale

(100, 1) to (200, 2) _____
(100, 2) to (200, 4) _____
(100, 3) to (200, 6) _____
(200, 2) to (300, 3) _____
(200, 4) to (300, 6) _____

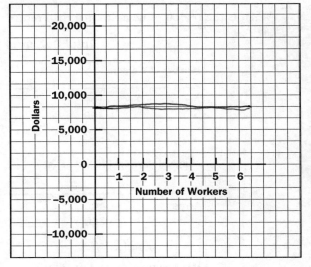

FIGURE 8-2   **Marginal Revenue Product**

6. Assume that cornbeans can be sold for $5 a ton and that Greenacre Farms has 200 acres of land. Calculate the marginal revenue product of labor for 200 acres of land in the bottom part of Table 8-1. Plot the marginal revenue product in Figure 8-2. Hired help costs $8,000 for a growing season. Draw a horizontal line in Figure 8-2 at $8,000 to indicate the price of labor. How many workers should Megan and Jamie hire? _____. At the level of labor input you just determined, what is the difference between the proceeds from selling cornbeans (output) and labor costs? _____ (Check to see that your labor input choice maximizes this difference by considering the use of one more or one fewer worker.)

■   SELF-TESTS FOR UNDERSTANDING

TEST A

Circle the most appropriate answer.
1. A graph of total physical product shows how output changes as
    a. all inputs are increased simultaneously.
    b. the firm adopts new technologies.
    c. the scale of production varies.
    d. one input is increased, holding all others constant.

2. For a production process that uses just one input, average physical product is found by
    a. graphing total output against the number of units of input.
    b. computing the change in output for a unit change in input.
    c. dividing total output by the number of units of input.
    d. multiplying the number of units of input by their cost.

3. The "law" of diminishing marginal returns
    a. says that eventually the marginal physical product of any input must become negative.
    b. applies to only a simultaneous increase in all inputs.
    c. can only be true for a production function with decreasing returns to scale.
    d. refers to what happens to output as only one factor is increased, all other inputs being held constant.

4. Marginal physical product refers to
    a. the increased revenue from employing an additional worker.
    b. the change in total output from a one-unit increase in a variable input.
    c. total output divided by total input.
    d. total output divided by total cost.

5. When looking at the curve for total physical product, the region of diminishing marginal returns is given by the region where marginal physical product is
    a. negative.
    b. positive.
    c. positive and increasing.
    d. positive and decreasing.

6. Consider the following data on workers and output.

Workers	1	2	3	4	5
Output	10	25	35	42	40

    Where do diminishing marginal returns to workers begin to set in?
    a. After the first worker.
    b. After the second worker.
    c. After the third worker.
    d. After the fourth worker.

7. For a production process that uses just one input, a firm should expand output as long as
    a. marginal revenue product is greater than the price of the input.
    b. marginal physical product is positive.
    c. average cost is declining.
    d. marginal physical product is greater than average physical product.

8. The rule for optimal input use implies that a firm should use additional units of an input until
    a. average cost equals the price of the input.
    b. marginal physical product is maximized.
    c. marginal revenue product equals the price of the input.
    d. increasing returns to scale are exhausted.

9. A change in fixed costs affects
    a. marginal physical product of the variable input.
    b. average physical product of the variable input.
    c. marginal cost associated with changes in the variable input.
    d. average cost associated with changes in total output.

10. In the short run, decisions to vary the amount of output will affect all but which one of the following?
    a. fixed costs
    b. variable costs
    c. marginal physical product
    d. average costs

11. As output increases, average fixed costs
    a. first decline and then increase.
    b. decrease continuously.
    c. are constant.
    d. increase more or less continuously.

12. As output increases, average total costs typically
    a. first decline and then increase.
    b. decrease continuously.
    c. are constant.
    d. increase more or less continuously.

13. A change in which of the following will *not* shift the short-run average cost curve?
    a. The price of output.
    b. The price of inputs.
    c. The quantity of fixed factors.
    d. The marginal physical product of variable inputs.

14. The term *economies of scale* refers to
    a. the change over time in average cost as firms grow larger.
    b. the percentage change in the marginal revenue product divided by the percentage change of the associated input.
    c. the increase in output when only one input is increased.
    d. what happens to total output following a simultaneous and equal percentage increase in all inputs.

15. If all inputs are doubled and output more than doubles, one would say that the production relationship
    a. shows decreasing returns to scale.
    b. shows constant returns to scale.
    c. shows increasing returns to scale.
    d. violates the "law" of diminishing returns.

16. In the long run,
    a. inputs are likely to be less substitutable than in the short run.
    b. all production functions will exhibit constant returns to scale.
    c. a firm is assumed to be able to make adjustments in all its fixed commitments.
    d. average cost must decline.

17. The optimal choice of input combinations
    a. is a purely technological decision, unaffected by input prices, and better left to engineers than economists.
    b. can be determined by looking at information on the marginal physical product and price of various inputs.
    c. will always be the same in both the short and long run.
    d. is likely to include more of an input if its price rises and if other input prices are unchanged.

18. Assume that on a small farm with 10 workers, the hiring of an eleventh worker actually lowers total output. Which of the following statements is not necessarily true?
    a. The marginal physical product of the last worker is negative.
    b. The marginal revenue product of the last worker is negative.
    c. A profit-maximizing firm would never hire the 11th worker.
    d. The production function shows decreasing returns to scale.

19. Marginal revenue product (MRP) is equal to
    a. MPP/P_{OUTPUT}.
    b. $MPP \times P_{OUTPUT}$.
    c. P_{OUTPUT}/MPP.
    d. $MPP \times P_{INPUT}$.

20. The ratio of a productive input's marginal physical product (MPP) to its price is a measure of the
    a. marginal cost of expanding output.
    b. average cost of expanding output.
    c. efficiency of production.
    d. increase in output from spending an extra dollar on this input.

21. To maximize profits, firms should increase the use of inputs with _____ ratios of MPP to price and reduce the use of inputs with _____ ratios of MPP to price.
    a. high; low
    b. low; high

Test B

Circle T or F for true or false.

T   F   1. The "law" of diminishing returns says that economies of scale can never be increasing.

T   F   2. The marginal physical product of an input refers to the increase in output associated with an additional unit of that input when all other inputs are held constant.

T   F   3. The marginal revenue product measures the total revenue that a firm will have at different use levels of a particular input.

T   F   4. If a production function shows increasing returns to scale from the additional use of all inputs, it violates the "law" of diminishing returns.

T   F   5. If a production function shows decreasing returns to scale, it is likely that long-run average costs will be increasing.

T   F   6. The short run is defined as any time less than six months.

T   F   7. The curve of average fixed cost is usually U-shaped.

T   F   8. Long-run cost curves will always lie above short-run cost curves.

T   F   9. Inputs are likely to be more substitutable in the long run than in the short run.

T   F   10. Historical data on costs and output is a good guide to the relevant cost curves for a firm's current decisions.

APPENDIX: PRODUCTION INDIFFERENCE CURVES

LEARNING OBJECTIVES

After completing this appendix, you should be able to:

■ describe how diminishing returns to a single factor help determine the shape of a typical production indifference curve.

■ determine what input combination will minimize costs for a given level of output, given information about production indifference curves and input prices.

■ explain how a firm's expansion path helps determine (minimum) total cost for every possible output level.

■ use a production indifference curve to explain how a change in the price of one productive factor can affect the least cost combination of inputs.

Important Terms and Concepts

PRODUCTION INDIFFERENCE CURVE

BUDGET LINE

EXPANSION PATH

■   **APPENDIX REVIEW**

A set of *production indifference curves* (or isoquants) is a geometrical device that can be used to represent a production function involving two inputs and one output. The horizontal and vertical axes are used to measure quantities of each input. A line connecting all input combinations capable of producing the

(1)   same amount of output is called the _____ _____ curve. Each separate curve represents a particular output level. Higher curves will mean (<u>more/less</u>) output.

(2)   Production indifference curves will usually have a (<u>negative/positive</u>) slope as a reduction in the use of one input must be compensated for by an increase in the use of the other input. Production indifference curves (<u>will/will not</u>) bow in toward the origin. This last property follows from the "law" of

_____ _____ returns. Production indifference curves (<u>do/do not</u>) cross.

Production indifference curves tell a firm what alternative combinations of inputs it could use to produce the same amount of output. An optimizing firm should *not* be indifferent to these alternatives. To determine the least costly combination of inputs, the firm will need to know the price of each input. From this information the firm can construct a budget line showing combinations of inputs that can

(3)   be purchased for the same total cost. The budget line is a (<u>curved/straight</u>) line. The slope of the budget line is given by the ratio of input prices. The price of the input measured on the (<u>horizontal/vertical</u>) axis goes on the top of the ratio. The intercept on each axis comes from dividing the total budget by the price of input measured on that axis.

To minimize cost for a given level of output, the firm chooses that combination of inputs lying on

(4)   the (<u>highest/lowest</u>) budget line consistent with the given level of output. For smooth and convex production indifference curves, the least costly input combination is given by the point of tangency between the budget line and the relevant production indifference curve. A change in the price of either input will change the slope of the budget line and result in a new optimal input combination. It is now easy to see that an increase in the price of one input will typically lead firms to use (<u>less/more</u>) of that input and _____ of the input whose price has not changed.

The procedure described in the previous paragraph will determine the optimal input combination to minimize cost for a given output target. Using the same procedure to find the lowest cost input combination for different levels of output defines the firm's _____ path. It also allows us   (5)

to compute total cost for any level of output. At this point, division and subtraction will allow us to

compute average and marginal cost. What level of output maximizes profits is considered in the next

chapter.

Is the solution to the question of optimal input combinations in this appendix consistent with the earlier discussion about the ratio of input prices and marginal physical products? Yes. Although it may not be

immediately obvious, the slope of the production indifference curve equals the ratio of marginal physical

products. When we choose the optimal input combination from the point of tangency where the slope of

the production indifference curve equals the slope of the budget line, we set the ratio of marginal products equal to the ratio of input prices. In symbols, assuming that our two inputs are A and B, choosing the

point of tangency between the production indifference curve and the budget line means that

$$\text{MPP}_A/\text{MPP}_B = P_A/P_B$$

Some multiplication and division[2] allows us to rewrite this expression as

$$\text{MPP}_A/P_A = \text{MPP}_B/P_B$$

our earlier condition for the optimal use of inputs.

IMPORTANT TERMS AND CONCEPTS QUIZ ■

Choose the best definition for each of the following terms.

1. _____ Production indifference curve

2. _____ Budget line

3. _____ Expansion path

a. Locus of firm's cost-minimizing input levels for different output levels.

b. Graph showing how total output varies as one input is increased.

c. Graph depicting all combinations of input quantities that yield a given level of output.

d. Representation of equally costly input combinations.

BASIC EXERCISES ■

Figure 8-3 shows a production indifference curve for producing 6,000 tons of cornbeans. This curve is derived from data given in Table 8-1.

1. (Read all of this question before answering.) If land can be rented at $65 an acre a year and if labor costs are $8,000 a worker, what is the least cost combination for producing 6,000 tons of cornbeans? Restrict your answer to the dots in Figure 8-3 that correspond to data in Table 8-1.

---

[2] Multiply both sides of the expression by MRP_B and divide each side by P_A.

FIGURE 8-3   **Production Indifference Curves**

_____ acres and _____ workers.

If land rents for $125 a year and labor costs $8,000 a worker, what is the least cost input combination for producing 6,000 tons of cornbeans?

_____ acres and _____ workers.

Remember that the ratio of input prices determines the slope of the budget line. For a given set of input prices draw the budget lines that pass through each of the possible input combinations. Remember that for a given set of input prices these lines should be parallel and the least cost combination is given by the lowest budget line. Can you explain why?

2. From your answer to the previous question, you know that if the cost of using land is relatively low, the least cost input combination will use more land with a smaller number of workers. You also know that if the cost of using land rises enough, an optimizing farmer would be induced to use less land and more workers. What is the rental price of land that just tips the balance away from the input combination of 200 acres and two workers to the combination of 100 acres and three workers?

$ _____ .

The answer to this question comes from "rotating" a budget line around the outside of the production indifference curve. For given input prices, find the lowest budget line that just touches the production indifference curve. This point will show the lowest cost-input combination. As one input price changes, the slope of the budget line will change and the lowest cost-budget line rotates around the outside of the production indifference curve. If the price of land is low, the input combination of 200 acres and two workers will be on the lowest budget line. As the price of land rises, the slope of the budget line becomes flatter, and there will come a point where suddenly the input combination of 100 acres and three workers is on the lowest budget line.

■ SELF-TESTS FOR UNDERSTANDING

TEST A

Circle the most appropriate answer.

1. A production indifference curve shows
   a. different levels of output that can be produced with a given amount of inputs.
   b. levels of output about which producers should be indifferent.
   c. what changes in one input are necessary to keep the marginal physical product of a second input constant.
   d. what input combinations can be used to produce a given output.

2. Which of the following properties is *not* true of production indifference curves?
   a. They have a negative slope.
   b. Their slope is always equal to the ratio of input prices.
   c. They bow in toward the origin because of the "law" of diminishing returns.
   d. The amount of output is the same for all points on the production indifference curve.

3. A single budget line shows
   a. how total cost varies when the level of output changes.
   b. how production costs vary when the price of inputs changes.
   c. what different combinations of inputs can be purchased with a fixed budget.
   d. how production costs have changed over time.

4. The budget line
   a. has a positive slope.
   b. will shift in a parallel fashion in response to an increase in the price of one input.
   c. is a straight line with a negative slope reflecting relative input prices.
   d. will have a different slope following an equal percentage change in the price of all inputs.

5. The optimal input combination for a given level of output is determined by
   a. the *Y*-axis intercept of the budget line.
   b. the point where marginal utility is equal to price.
   c. the point of tangency between the lowest budget line and the relevant production indifference curve.
   d. where the relevant production indifference curve intersects the budget line.

6. Using budget lines to determine the optimal input combination for every possible level of output traces out
   a. the total physical product curve.
   b. a firm's expansion path.
   c. marginal revenue product.
   d. a firm's average cost curve.

7. When the price of one input increases, the
   a. budget line will shift out in parallel fashion.
   b. budget line will shift in toward the origin in parallel fashion.
   c. slope of the budget line will change.
   d. production indifference curves will shift.

8. If production requires two inputs, labor and capital, and the price of both doubles,
   a. the slope of the budget line will double.
   b. production indifference curves will become steeper.
   c. the marginal physical product of the more expensive input will decline.
   d. the slope of the budget line and the least costly input combination do not change.

9. Which one of the following will not occur after a reduction in the price of one input?
   a. The budget line will shift in such a way that a fixed production budget can now buy more of the cheaper input.
   b. The optimal input combination for a given level of output is likely to involve the use of more of the cheaper input.
   c. The minimum total cost for producing a given level of output will fall.
   d. Each production indifference curve will show a parallel shift.

TEST B

Circle T or F for true or false.

T   F   1. Production indifference curves have a positive slope because higher output usually requires more of both inputs.

T   F   2. Typically, a production indifference curve will bow in at the middle because of the "law" of diminishing returns.

T   F   3. A firm minimizes cost for any level of output by choosing the input combination given by the tangency of the budget line to the production indifference curve.

T   F   4. An increase in the price of either input will make the budget line steeper.

T   F   5. If production requires the use of two inputs, x_1 and x_2, a change in the price of x_1 will never affect the optimal use of x_2.

T   F   6. A change in the price of output will change the cost-minimizing input combination for a given level of output.

T   F   7. For given input prices, the tangencies of production indifference curves with alternative budget lines trace out a firm's expansion path.

■   SUPPLEMENTARY EXERCISES

Assume that the production of widgets (W) requires labor (L) and machines (M) and can be represented by the production function[3]

$$W = L^{1/2} M^{1/2}.$$

1. Draw a production indifference curve for the production of 500,000 widgets.

2. L measures labor hours and M measures machine hours. In the long run, both machine and labor hours are variable. If machine hours cost $48 and labor hours cost $12, what is the cost-minimizing number of labor and machine hours to produce 500,000 widgets? (Whether it is profitable to produce 500,000 widgets depends on the price of widgets.)

3. Assume that the firm has 125 machines capable of supplying 250,000 machine hours and that labor hours are the only variable input.
    a. Draw a picture of total output as a function of the number of labor hours.
    b. Use the production function to derive an expression for the marginal physical product of labor conditional on the 250,000 machine hours. Draw a picture of this function. What, if any, is the connection between your pictures of total output and marginal physical product?
    c. Divide your picture of the marginal physical product into regions of increasing, decreasing, and negative marginal returns to labor. (Note: Not all areas of need exist.)
    d. If the price of widgets is $50 and the price of labor is $12 per hour, what is the optimal number of labor hours that the firm should use? How many widgets will the firm produce?

4. Graph the expansion path for this production function on the assumption that labor hours cost $12 and machine hours cost $48.

5. Are returns to scale in the production of widgets constant, increasing, or decreasing?

■   STUDY QUESTIONS

1. What is the difference between diminishing marginal returns and negative marginal returns?

2. Why does the discussion of optimal input use focus on marginal revenue product and not average revenue product?

3. What is the relation between marginal physical product and marginal revenue product?

---

[3]This particular mathematical representation of a production function is called the Cobb-Douglas production function. Cobb was a mathematician. Douglas was an economist at The University of Chicago, president of the American Economic Association, and United States senator from Illinois from 1948 to 1966. You might enjoy reading the comments by Albert Rees and Paul Samuelson about Douglas and his work in the *Journal of Political Economy*, October 1979, Part 1.

4. Why is it optimal for a firm to use more of an input as long as marginal revenue product is greater than the price of the input?

5. What is the difference between fixed and variable cost?

6. Why do economists typically use a U-shaped curve to represent an average cost curve?

7. What is the difference between the short run and the long run?

8. If a firm's production function shows increasing returns to scale, what will its long-run average cost curve look like and why?

9. Why isn't a firm's long-run average cost curve found by connecting the minimum points of its short-run average cost curves?

10. Consider a production function that involves the input of two factors. For each factor individually, increases in inputs lead to diminishing returns. However, when both inputs are increased simultaneously, there are increasing returns to scale. Can this be possible? Explain how.

11. If output can be produced with varying quantities of different inputs, how can a firm figure out the cost-minimizing input combination?

12. Is data on how average cost has evolved over time appropriate to analyze the cost implications of different output levels today? Why or why not?

OUTPUT, PRICE, AND PROFIT: THE IMPORTANCE OF MARGINAL ANALYSIS

Important Terms and Concepts

PROFIT MAXIMIZATION

OPTIMAL DECISION

TOTAL PROFIT

ECONOMIC PROFIT

TOTAL REVENUE (TR)

AVERAGE REVENUE (AR)

MARGINAL REVENUE (MR)

MARGINAL ANALYSIS

MARGINAL PROFIT

LEARNING OBJECTIVES

After completing this chapter, you should be able to:

■ explain why a firm can make a decision about output or price, but not usually about both.

■ explain why the demand curve is the curve of average revenue.

■ calculate total and marginal revenue from data on the demand curve.

■ calculate average and marginal cost from data on total cost.

■ use data on costs and revenues to compute the level of output that maximizes profits.

■ explain why the point of maximum profit cannot be associated with a positive or negative marginal profit.

■ explain why comparing marginal revenue and marginal cost is equivalent to looking at marginal profit.

■ explain why profit is maximized only when marginal revenue is (approximately) equal to marginal cost.

■ explain how and why an economist's definition of profit differs from that of an accountant.

■ explain how selling at a price above marginal cost can increase profits even if the price is below average cost.

CHAPTER REVIEW

This is the last of four building block chapters that explore what lies behind the demand and supply curves introduced in Chapter 5. As with Chapters 6 and 8, this chapter makes extensive use of marginal analysis, one of the most important tools an economist has. In this chapter marginal analysis is used to help decide how much output a firm should produce to maximize its profits.

While marginal analysis is a powerful tool for business decision making, it is applicable in many nonbusiness situations as well. For example, how much should the government spend to clean up the environment? Or a related question: To clean up our lakes and rivers, should the government require all industries and towns to reduce their discharges by an equal percentage, or is there a more efficient alternative? As discussed in Chapter 22, marginal analysis can help answer these questions.

You may already have had more experience with marginal analysis than you realize. Have you ever had to pay federal income taxes? If so, you might dig out your records and make two calculations. Your

(1) total taxes divided by your total income would be your (average/marginal) tax rate. Now assume that you had $100 more income. Figure out how much more taxes you would have owed. This increase in taxes divided by the $100 additional income would be your (average/marginal) tax rate.

Your grade point average is another example of the distinction between marginal and average. If you want to raise your overall GPA, what sorts of grades do you need? The grades you earn this semester are the marginal contribution to your overall grade average. Similarly, a baseball player's batting record for a single game is a marginal measure when compared with his season's batting average.[1]

In whatever context, marginal analysis focuses on the effect of changes. For business output decisions, marginal analysis looks at the effect on costs, revenues, and profits as output changes. The

(2) change in total cost from changing output by one unit is called _____ cost. The change in total revenue from producing and selling one more unit is _____ revenue. Marginal profit is the change in total _____ as output expands by one unit. Because profits equal

---

[1]One could take the position that each time at bat, rather than a whole game, is the real marginal measure. On this view, the marginal measure is either 1.000 (a hit) or 0.000 (no hit). Consistent with Rule 4 in the Appendix to this chapter, every hit increases a player's overall batting average and every at bat without a hit lowers one's overall batting average.

revenue minus costs, marginal profit equals marginal _____ minus marginal

_____ .

Economists usually assume that business firms are interested in maximizing (average/marginal/total) profit. This assumption need not be true for all firms, but economists have (3) found that models based on this assumption provide useful insights into actual events. (Refer back to the discussion in Chapter 1 about the role of abstraction in theory.) Economists are interested in marginal profit, not as an end in itself, but because marginal profit is an extremely useful guide to maximizing total profit.

It should be common sense that any firm interested in maximizing profit will want to expand output as long as the increase in total revenue exceeds the increase in total costs. If the increase in revenue is less than the increase in cost, the firm has gone too far. Rather than looking at total revenue and total cost, we could just as easily look at the changes in revenue and cost as output changes. An increase in output will add to profits if the increase in revenue is greater than the increase in costs. An economist might make the same point by saying that an increase in output will add to profits if (marginal/average) revenue exceeds (marginal/average) cost. We could also say that an increase in out- (4) put will add to total profits as long as marginal profits are (positive/zero/negative). Total profits will stop rising when marginal profits fail to _____, that is, when marginal revenue

_____ marginal cost.

■ IMPORTANT TERMS AND CONCEPTS QUIZ

Choose the best definition for each of the following terms.

1. _____ Profit maximization

2. _____ Optimal decision

3. _____ Total profit

4. _____ Economic profit

5. _____ Total Revenue

6. _____ Average revenue

7. _____ Marginal revenue

8. _____ Marginal analysis

9. _____ Marginal Profit

a. Net earnings minus a firm's opportunity cost of capital.

b. Total revenue divided by quantity of output.

c. Decision rules that look at the impact of changes.

d. Amount firm must spend to produce a given quantity of output.

e. Difference between total revenue and total costs.

f. Best outcome for the decision maker.

g. Addition to profit from producing an additional unit of output.

h. Level of output where revenue minus cost is greatest.

i. Price of output times quantity sold.

j. Addition to total revenue when producing one more unit of output.

■ BASIC EXERCISES

1. **Wanda's Widget Company**
   This exercise is designed to review the use of marginal revenue and marginal cost as a guide to maximizing profits.

| TABLE 9-1 | **Wanda's Widget Company** |

Marginal Revenue	Total Revenue	Demand Curve Price (dollars)	Output	Total Cost (dollars)	Marginal Cost	Total Profits
_____	3,500	3,500	1	2,000	_____	_____
_____	6,600	3,300	2	3,000	_____	_____
_____	9,300	3,100	3	4,100	_____	_____
_____	11,600	2,900	4	5,300	_____	_____
_____	13,500	2,700	5	6,900	_____	_____
_____	15,000	2,500	6	8,900	_____	_____
_____	16,100	2,300	7	11,100	_____	_____
_____	16,800	2,100	8	13,400	_____	_____
_____	17,100	1,900	9	15,800	_____	_____
_____	17,000	1,700	10	18,300	_____	_____

a.   Table 9-1 has data on demand for widgets from Wanda's Widget Company as well as data on production costs. Total revenue and total cost are plotted in the top panel of Figure 9-1. Fill in the column on total profits by subtracting total cost from total revenue. Plot the data on total profit in the second panel of Figure 9-1. Looking just at your graph of total profit, what output level maximizes total profits?

b.   Complete Table 9-1 by computing marginal cost and marginal revenue. Plot these series in the bottom panel of Figure 9-1. Marginal revenue exceeds marginal cost up to what level of output? _____ Looking just at your graph of marginal cost and marginal revenue, what output level maximizes total profits? Is this the same answer as above?

c.   Figure 9-2 plots the average cost of producing widgets. Use the data on the demand curve from Table 9-1 to plot the curve of average revenue in Figure 9-2. Using the profit-maximizing level of output determined above, find the profit-maximizing price on the demand curve: Draw the rectangle for total revenue and shade it lightly with positively sloped lines. Using the average cost curve, draw the rectangle for total cost and shade it lightly with

Cost and Revenue Curves   **FIGURE 9-1**

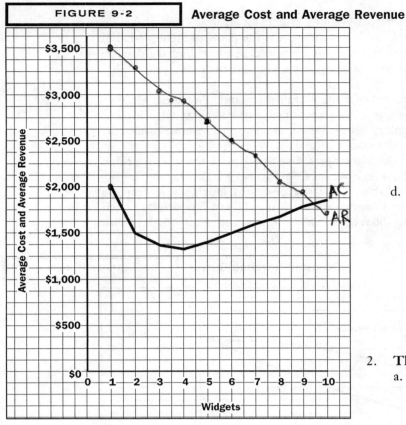

FIGURE 9-2   **Average Cost and Average Revenue**

negatively sloped lines. This rectangle should overlap a part of the rectangle for total revenue. The non-overlapped part of the total revenue rectangle is a measure of total (cost/profit/revenue). Maximizing total profit maximizes the size of this rectangle. It (does/does not) maximize the difference between average revenue and average cost. It (does/does not) imply that output should increase whenever average revenue, i.e., price, exceeds average cost.

d. (Optional) Assume now that there is an increase in the fixed costs Wanda must pay. Specifically assume that all of the entries in the column for total cost in Table 9-1 are now $3,000 higher. Write out a new version of Table 9-1 to determine the profit-maximizing level of output following the increase in fixed costs. What happens to total profits? Consider Figure 9-1. For each panel explain which curve(s) shift and why.

2. **The Geometry of Marginal Revenue**

a. Figure 9-3 shows the demand curve for Medalist bicycles. Draw a rectangle for total revenue on the assumption that 55,000 bicycles are sold. Lightly shade this rectangle with horizontal lines.

b. Assume now that 70,000 bicycles are sold rather than 55,000. Draw a rectangle for total revenue at this higher level of sales. Lightly shade this rectangle with vertical lines.

If you have drawn and shaded the rectangles correctly, you should have a large, cross-hatched rectangle and two smaller rectangles: a horizontal rectangle on the top of the cross-hatched rectangle and a vertical rectangle on the right side. The vertical rectangle represents revenue from additional sales at the new lower price. This rectangle (is/is not) a complete measure of marginal revenue. It measures the receipts of additional sales but neglects the drop in revenue from the reduction in price that was necessary to expand sales in the first place. The reduction in revenue on previous units is represented by the _____ rectangle. The geometric representation of marginal revenue is the (vertical/horizontal) rectangle minus the _____ rectangle.

FIGURE 9-3   **The Demand for Medalist Bicycles**

SELF-TESTS FOR UNDERSTANDING ■

TEST A

Circle the most appropriate answer.

1. The logic of the demand curve says that business firms can choose
   a. both the level of output and the level of prices.
   b. the level of output or the level of prices but not both.
   c. to sell whatever quantity they want at whatever price.
   d. only those levels of output where marginal cost equals marginal revenue.

2. The assumption of profit maximization is
   a. likely to be true for all firms.
   b. the same as the assumption of satisficing.
   c. a useful abstraction that gives sharp insights.
   d. the best description of what firms actually do.

3. Total profit is equal to
   a. average revenue minus average cost.
   b. marginal revenue minus marginal cost.
   c. total revenue minus total cost.
   d. zero when marginal cost equals marginal revenue.

4. Marginal profit is
   a. the difference between total revenue and total cost.
   b. only positive at the profit-maximizing output level.
   c. another term for the return on an owner's own time and resources.
   d. the change in profit when output increases by one unit.

5. Marginal cost equals
   a. total cost divided by total output.
   b. the change in total cost associated with an additional unit of output.
   c. the change in average cost.
   d. the slope of the average cost curve.

6. Average cost is found by
   a. dividing total cost by output.
   b. multiplying marginal cost by output.
   c. looking at how total cost changes when output changes.
   d. considering how price changes with quantity along the demand curve.

7. If total costs are increasing then
   a. marginal cost must also be increasing.
   b. marginal cost must be positive.
   c. average cost must be greater than marginal costs.
   d. average cost must be increasing.

8. The demand curve is the curve of
   a. total revenue.
   b. marginal revenue.
   c. variable revenue.
   d. average revenue.

9. Marginal revenue to a firm is
   a. the same as the demand curve for the firm's output.
   b. found by dividing price by output.
   c. found by dividing output by price.
   d. the change in revenue associated with an additional unit of output.

10. When output increases by one unit, marginal revenue will typically be
    a. less than the new lower price.
    b. equal to the new lower price.
    c. greater than the new lower price.

11. Marginal profit equals the difference between
    a. total revenue and total cost.
    b. average revenue and average cost.
    c. marginal revenue and marginal cost.
    d. the demand curve and the marginal cost curve.

12. As long as total revenue is greater than total cost,
    a. marginal profit must be positive.
    b. total profit must be increasing.
    c. total profit will be positive.
    d. marginal revenue will be greater than marginal cost.

13. If marginal revenue is greater than marginal cost, then a firm interested in maximizing profits should probably
    a. reduce output.
    b. expand output.
    c. leave output unchanged.

14. To maximize profits a firm should produce where
    a. marginal cost is minimized.
    b. average cost is minimized.
    c. marginal revenue equals marginal cost.
    d. marginal revenue is maximized.

15. If a firm has chosen an output level that maximizes profits, then at this level
    a. marginal profits are also maximized.
    b. average cost is minimized.
    c. further increases in output will involve negative marginal profits.
    d. the difference between average revenue and average cost is maximized.

16. Once a firm has determined the output level that maximizes profits, it can determine the profit-maximizing price from
    a. the demand curve.
    b. setting its usual markup on average cost.
    c. adding marginal cost to marginal revenue.
    d. adding marginal cost to average cost.

17. Producing where marginal revenue equals marginal cost is the same as producing where
    a. average cost is minimized.
    b. total profit is maximized.
    c. average cost equals average revenue.
    d. marginal profit is maximized.

18. An economist's definition of profit differs from that of an accountant because
    a. the economist is only interested in marginal cost and marginal revenue.
    b. the economist includes the opportunity cost of owner-supplied inputs in total cost.
    c. accountants cannot maximize.
    d. economists cannot add or subtract correctly.

19. If accounting profits are zero, it is likely that economic profits are
    a. negative.
    b. also zero.
    c. positive.

20. If marginal revenue is less than average cost, a firm
    a. should reduce output; it loses the additional revenue but saves more in cost.
    b. must be losing money.
    c. should consider a temporary shutdown.
    d. can still increase profits if marginal revenue exceeds marginal cost.

TEST B

Circle T or F for true or false.

T F 1. Business firms can decide both the price and quantity of their output.

T F 2. Firms always make optimal decisions.

T F 3. The demand curve for a firm's product is also the firm's marginal revenue curve.

T F 4. Marginal revenue is simply the price of the last unit sold.

T F 6. An output decision will generally not maximize profits unless it corresponds to a zero marginal profit.

T F 6. Marginal profit will be zero when marginal revenue equals marginal cost.

T F 7. An economist's measure of profit would typically be smaller than an accountant's.

T F 8. A reduction in fixed costs should lead a firm to increase output.

T F 9. As long as average revenue exceeds average cost, a firm is making profits and should increase output.

T F 10. It never pays to sell below average cost.

APPENDIX: THE RELATIONSHIPS AMONG TOTAL, AVERAGE, AND MARGINAL DATA

BASIC EXERCISES

These questions are designed to help review the relationships between total, average, and marginal measures described in the appendix to Chapter 9.

TABLE 9-2	Heather's Batting			
Game	At-bats	Hits	Daily Batting Average	Season Batting Average
1	4	2	.500	.500
2	4	2	.500	.500
3	4	1	.250	.417
4	3	1	.333	.400
5	4	3	.750	.474
6	3	1	.333	.455
7	6	2	.333	.429
8	3	0	.000	.387
9	4	2	.500	.400
10	5	2	.400	.400

1. Table 9-2 contains information on Heather's first ten games with the college softball team. The table includes her batting performance for each game, a marginal measure, as well as her season average updated to include the results of each game. Answer the following questions to see if the marginal data, Heather's daily batting record, is consistent with the average data, her season batting average. It may be useful to first plot both the marginal and average data in Figure 9-4.

a. According to Rule 3, the marginal and average records should be equal on the first day of the season. Is this the case?

b. According to Rule 4, if the marginal data are equal to the average, the average should be unchanged. Check to see if this is always the case.

c. According to Rule 4, if the marginal data are less than the average, the average should decline. Check to see if this is always the case.

d. According to Rule 4, if the marginal data are greater than the average, the average should increase. Check to see if this is always the case.

2. a. Explain what is wrong with both of the illustrations in Figure 9-5.

b. For part (a) of Figure 9-5, assume that the total profit curve is correct and draw an appropriate marginal profit curve.

c. For part (b) of Figure 9-5, assume that the average cost curve is correct and draw an appropriate marginal cost curve.

FIGURE 9-4   Heather's Batting Average

FIGURE 9-5

SUPPLEMENTARY EXERCISES ■

MATHEMATICAL EXAMPLES OF PROFIT MAXIMIZATION

1. The demand for Acme stereos is

    $$Q = 1,200 - 4P$$

    where Q represents output measured in thousands of sets and P represents price. The total cost of producing stereos is given by

    $$TC = 16,000 + 120Q - .4Q^2 + .002Q^3.$$

    a. What are Acme's fixed costs? *16,000*
    b. What mathematical expression describes average costs? Marginal costs?
    c. Plot average cost and marginal cost. Does your marginal cost curve go through the minimum point of your average cost curve?
    d. Use the information from the demand curve to derive a mathematical expression for marginal revenue.
    e. On the same graph as in c draw the demand curve (the average revenue curve) and the marginal revenue curve.
    f. What does your graph suggest about the profit-maximizing level of output?
    g. Does your answer in f coincide with a direct mathematical solution for Q when MR = MC? It should. (To answer this question you will need to set the expressions you derived for marginal revenue and marginal cost equal and solve the resulting equation for Q.)
    h. What is Acme's maximum profit?
    i. Shade in the portion of your graph that represents maximum profit.
    j. What if fixed cost were $20,000? How, if at all, do your answers to b, c, d, g, and h change?

2. Consider the mathematical representation of the production of widgets in the Supplementary Exercise to Chapter 7.
    Assume the demand for widgets is given by

    $$W = 2,500,000 - 25,000 \, P_W$$

    where P_W = price of widgets.
    a. If a firm can purchase labor services at $12 per hour and machines can be rented at $48 per hour, what is the marginal cost of increases in output? What is the profit-maximizing level of output? What is the market price of widgets?
    b. Assume now that the firm owns 100 machines that supply 200,000 machine hours and that the firm can purchase labor at a cost of $12 per hour. Derive an expression for marginal cost and determine the profit-maximizing level of output on the assumption that the number of machines is fixed at 100. What is the market price of widgets?

3. **Profit Maximization and the Elasticity of Demand**

    A profit-maximizing firm will not try to produce so much output that it is operating in the inelastic portion of its demand curve. Why not? What about the firm producing stereos and widgets in problems 1 and 2 above? What is the elasticity of demand at the profit-maximizing point of output?

ECONOMICS IN ACTION ■

FAIR TRADE, FREE TRADE, AND MARGINAL COST

American trade laws, like those of many other countries, include anti-dumping provisions. Foreign producers are not supposed to have access to American markets if they sell their output at unfairly low prices. The concern is that a foreign producer might drive American competitors out of business and then be in a position to act as a monopolist, raising prices and restricting output. Such actions are sometimes called ruinous competition.

Complaints about dumping by foreign firms are typically initiated by American producers, not consumers, and investigated by an office of the U.S. government. If a complaint is found to have cause, the government can impose anti-dumping tariffs on specific foreign manufacturers that are intended to establish prices that reflect "fair value," that is, raise prices to a level sufficient to cover fully allocated costs plus a normal profit. Recent examples involve imports of computer chips and steel.

Fully allocated cost is another term for the average cost of purchased inputs, including labor. Normal profit refers to the opportunity cost of the investment by a firm's owners. (As we have seen, economists include both measures when they talk of average cost.)

1. Are there conditions under which domestic producers would willingly sell output for less than "fair value," that is, less than average cost? (For example, from an initial position of equilibrium, how might a domestic producer respond to a temporary shift of the demand curve to the left during a recession?)

2. How does one distinguish possible ruinous competition from normal market fluctuations and the natural tendency of all producers to exploit opportunities to limit competition? Should foreign producers be prohibited from behavior that domestic producers are likely to engage in on a regular basis?

SOURCE: "Cement Shoes for Venezuela," Peter Passell, *New York Times*, September 25, 1991. "Thriving Steel Industry Needs No Import Curb, Experts Say; Trade: House vote illustrates lure of protectionism. Production last year was second highest in history"; Donald W. Nauss, *Los Angeles Times;* March 22, 1999.

■   STUDY QUESTIONS

1. Why can't firms sell as much output as they want at whatever price they want?

2. The condition for profit maximization is stated in terms of marginal revenue and marginal cost. What would happen to total profits if instead a firm produced where average revenue equaled average cost?

3. Why isn't marginal revenue equal to the price of the last unit sold?

4. Why is the demand curve also the curve of average revenue?

5. Why is it better to produce where marginal profit is zero rather than at some point where marginal profit is greater than zero?

6. What are the differences between profits as measured by an economist and profits as measured by an accountant? Which is likely to be larger? Why?

7. Should a firm raise or lower its price following an increase in fixed costs? Why?

8. How can it be rational for a firm to continue producing if the price it receives is less than the (average) cost of production?

THE FIRM AND THE INDUSTRY UNDER PERFECT COMPETITION

LEARNING OBJECTIVES

After completing this chapter, you should be able to:

■ describe the conditions that distinguish perfect competition from other market structures.

■ explain why the study of perfect competition can be profitable even if few industries satisfy the conditions of perfect competition exactly.

■ explain why under perfect competition the firm faces a horizontal demand curve while the industry faces a downward-sloping demand curve.

■ explain the relation of price, average revenue, and marginal revenue as seen by individual firms under perfect competition.

■ find the profit-maximizing output level for a perfectly competitive firm given information on the firm's marginal cost curve and the market price for its output.

■ explain why a perfectly competitive firm's short-run supply curve is the portion of its marginal cost curve that is above average variable costs.

Important Terms and Concepts

MARKET

PERFECT COMPETITION

PURE MONOPOLY

MONOPOLISTIC COMPETITION

OLIGOPOLY

PRICE TAKER

HORIZONTAL DEMAND CURVE

SHORT-RUN EQUILIBRIUM

VARIABLE COST

FIRM'S SUPPLY CURVE

INDUSTRY SUPPLY CURVE

LONG-RUN EQUILIBRIUM

OPPORTUNITY COST

ECONOMIC PROFIT

■ derive an industry's short-run supply curve given information on the supply curves for individual firms.

■ use the concept of opportunity cost to reconcile economic and accounting profits.

■ explain how freedom of entry and exit imply that in the long run firms operating under perfect competition will earn zero economic profit.

■ explain why the long-run supply curve for a competitive industry is given by the industry's long-run average cost curve.

■ explain how perfect competition implies the efficient production of goods and services.

■ CHAPTER REVIEW

This chapter uses the concepts developed in earlier chapters to study in more detail the supply decisions of firms. The discussion also adds important material about market structures. The decisions of individual firms depend not only upon their production functions and cost curves, but also upon the type of market structure the firm faces. Among other things, different market structures have important implications for demand conditions that firms face. This chapter focuses on the abstraction of the market structure of perfect competition. Later chapters will investigate other market structures—monopolistic competition, oligopoly, and pure monopoly.

Perfect competition is distinguished from other market structures by four conditions:

(1)   1.   (<u>Few/Many</u>) buyers and sellers.

2.   (<u>Differentiated/Identical</u>) product.

3.   (<u>Easy/Difficult</u>) entry and exit.

4.   (<u>Perfect/Imperfect</u>) information.

Conditions 1, 2, and 4 imply that the actions of individual buyers and sellers (<u>do/do not</u>) affect the market price for the identical product. Condition 3 implies that the number of firms can easily expand or contract and leads to the condition that long-run equilibrium will be characterized by (<u>positive/zero/negative</u>) economic profits.

An important first step to analyzing the firm's decisions in a particular market structure is to be careful about what the market structure implies for the firm's demand curve and its marginal revenue. Let us first consider the short-run supply decision of an individual firm under perfect competition. Since the actions of this firm will not affect the market price, the firm can sell as much or as little as it wants

(2)   at the prevailing market price. Alternatively, we may say that the firm faces a (<u>horizontal/vertical</u>)

demand curve. In Chapter 9 we saw that the demand curve is also the curve of average revenue. If the demand curve is horizontal, then besides being the curve of average revenue it is also the curve of _____ revenue. (Remember the picture of marginal revenue in the Basic Exercise of the previous chapter. If the demand curve is horizontal, there is no horizontal rectangle to subtract.) As we saw in Chapter 9, the firm maximizes profits by producing where MC = MR. Under perfect competition, MR = P, thus under perfect competition the firm should produce where MC = MR = P.

We can now derive the short-run supply curve for the firm by imagining that the firm faces a variety of possible prices and considering what output the firm would supply at each price. These price-output pairs will define the firm's short-run supply curve. For many possible prices, short-run supply will be given by the intersection of price and the (<u>average/marginal</u>) cost curve. If price drops below   (3) the minimum of the average total cost curve, the MC = P rule maximizes profits by minimizing _____. Even if price is less than average total cost, the firm should continue to produce as long as price exceeds average _____ cost. If the firm decides to produce nothing it still must cover its fixed costs. As long as price exceeds average variable cost, there will be something left over to help cover these costs. Putting all of this together, we can conclude that under perfect competition a firm's short-run supply curve is given by the portion of the _____ _____ curve above average _____ cost.

The industry short-run supply curve is given by the (<u>horizontal/vertical</u>) summation of individual   (4) firms' supply curves. Market price, the variable so crucial to individual firms' decisions, will be given by the intersection of the market _____ and _____ curves. In the short run, the number of firms in the industry is fixed; and the short-run industry supply curve will come from the supply decisions of existing firms.

In the long run, there will be more (fewer) firms if the short-run equilibrium involves economic profits (losses). For example, if general market returns are around 8 percent and investments in the firm show a return of 6 percent, an economist would conclude that the firm has an economic (<u>loss/profit</u>) of _____ percent. In this case, by investing elsewhere and earning 8 percent, the firm's   (5) owners would be (<u>better/worse</u>) off. The 8 percent is the _____ cost of capital to the firm and it is an important part of costs as counted by the economist. Thus, economists focus on economic profits as the indicator of entry or exit rather than on accounting profits. The condition of long-run equilibrium that (accounting/economic) profits be zero is consistent with _____ profits equal to general market rates of return.

As firms enter or leave, the industry short-run supply curve will shift appropriately, price will adjust as we move along the industry demand curve, and industry long-run equilibrium will be achieved when there are no further incentives for entry or exit. Figure 10-1(a) illustrates a firm in a perfectly competitive industry. Figure 10-1(b) shows the industry demand and supply. The illustrated firm will be

(6)   making economic (profits/losses). Shade in the appropriate rectangle showing economic profits or losses. There will be an incentive for some firms to (enter/leave) the industry. As the number of firms in the industry changes, the supply curve in Figure 10-1(b) will shift to the (right/left) and price will (rise/fall). If the cost curves in Figure 10-1(a) are representative of long-run costs for all current and potential firms in the industry, long-run equilibrium will involve a price of $_____. Note that at all times our representative firm is producing where $MC = P$. But in the long-run equilibrium, $MC = P$ = minimum _____ _____ _____ cost. It is this last condition that explains the efficiency of perfectly competitive markets.

| FIGURE 10-1 | **Competitive Market Equilibrium** |

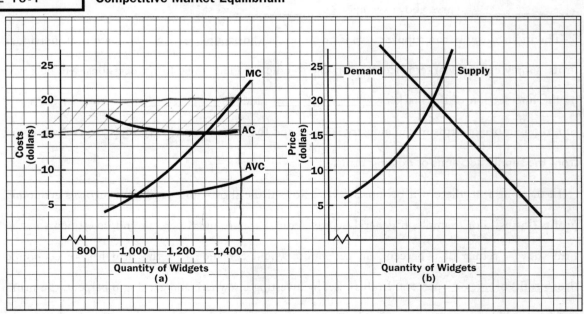

IMPORTANT TERMS AND CONCEPTS QUIZ ■

Choose the best definition for each of the following terms.

1. _____ Market

2. _____ Perfect competition

3. _____ Pure monopoly

4. _____ Monopolistic competition

5. _____ Oligopoly

6. _____ Price taker

7. _____ Horizontal demand curve

8. _____ Variable cost

9. _____ Firm's supply curve

10. _____ Industry supply curve

11. _____ Short-run equilibrium

12. _____ Long-run equilibrium

13. _____ Economic profit

a. Industry composed of a few large rival firms.

b. The part of the marginal cost curve that exceeds average variable cost.

c. Industry with only one supplier.

d. Return to an owner's investment in her firm in excess of the return on alternative investments.

e. Single buyer in a market.

f. Demand curve as seen by firms in a perfectly competitive industry.

g. Set of buyers and sellers whose actions affect the price of some commodity.

h. Market price that provides no incentive for firms to enter or leave the industry.

i. Horizontal sum of supply curves for each firm in the industry.

j. Costs that depend upon the production level.

k. Agent or firm too small to affect the market price.

l. Market price that differs from minimum long-run average cost.

m. Many small firms selling an identical product.

n. Many small firms selling slightly differentiated products.

BASIC EXERCISE ■

This exercise is designed to explore the short-run supply curve for a firm under perfect competition.

Assume that widgets are produced by perfectly competitive firms. The data in Table 10-1 are consistent with Figure 10-1 and are for a representative widget firm. Although not listed separately in Table 10-1, producing widgets involves fixed costs of $10,140.

1. If the price of widgets is $19.10, what is the profit-maximizing level of output? _____

TABLE 10-1	Costs of Producing Widgets		
Quantity	Average Cost (dollars)	Average Variable Cost (dollars)	Marginal Cost (dollars)
900	17.67	6.40	4.60
1,000	16.44	6.30	6.30
1,100	15.62	6.40	8.60
1,200	15.15	6.70	11.50
1,300	15.00	7.20	15.00
1,400	15.14	7.90	19.10
1,500	15.56	8.80	23.80

What are economic profits at this level of output? $ _____ Check that this level of output maximizes profits by calculating profits for output levels 100 units higher and lower.

Economic profits at higher output = $ _____

Economic profits at lower output = $ _____

2. What is the profit-maximizing level of output if the price of widgets falls to $11.50, below all values for average cost? _____. What are economic profits at this level of output? $ _____ Again check that this level of output maximizes profits or minimizes losses by considering output levels 100 units higher, 100 units lower, and no production.

Economic losses at higher output = $ _____

Economic losses at lower output = $ _____

Economic losses at zero output = $ _____

3. If the price of widgets is $6.00, what is the profit-maximizing level of output? Why?

_____

4. What general conclusion can you draw about the short-run supply curve for a firm operating under conditions of perfect competition?

_____

_____

5. Note that in question 1, when the market price was assumed to be $19.10, the profit-maximizing level of output was at a point where price exceeded both average cost and average variable cost. Remembering that under perfect competition a firm can sell as much output as it wants at the given market price, why isn't it profitable for the firm to produce even more when price exceeds average costs?

6. If many firms can produce widgets with the same cost functions, what is the long-run equilibrium price of widgets? $ _____. What is the associated level of production for the representative firm?

_____

■ SELF-TESTS FOR UNDERSTANDING

TEST A

Circle the most appropriate answer.

1. Which of the following is inconsistent with perfect competition?
   a. Perfect information about products.
   b. One firm producing many products.
   c. Freedom of entry.
   d. Freedom of exit.

2. If production is limited to a few large firms, the resulting market structure is called
   a. perfect competition.
   b. monopolistic competition.
   c. oligopoly.
   d. pure monopoly.

3. If a firm can sell any amount of output without affecting price, we say that the demand curve for this firm is
   a. horizontal.
   b. inelastic.
   c. equal to the marginal cost curve.
   d. indeterminate.

4. Which one of the following is not true under perfect competition?
   a. The firm's demand curve is horizontal.
   b. The firm's demand curve is also the curve of average revenue.
   c. The firm's demand curve is also the curve of marginal revenue.
   d. The firm's demand curve is inelastic.

5. If a firm's demand curve is horizontal, marginal revenue equals
   a. average cost.
   b. marginal cost.
   c. average revenue.
   d. minimum long-run average cost.

6. If a firm's demand curve is horizontal, the firm should produce
   a. as much output as it can.
   b. more output as long as price exceeds average variable cost.
   c. at the point where marginal cost equals price.
   d. at the minimum of its long-run average cost curve.

7. Under perfect competition, a profit-maximizing firm should shut down when price falls below
   a. average cost.
   b. average variable cost.
   c. marginal cost.
   d. fixed costs.

8. The short-run supply curve for a firm under perfect competition is the portion of the firm's marginal cost curve that is above the
   a. average total cost curve.
   b. average fixed cost curve.
   c. average variable cost curve.
   d. minimum of the marginal cost curve.

9. Under perfect competition, industry supply in the short run is given by
   a. the intersection of market demand and average cost.
   b. the horizontal sum of firms' short-run supply curves.
   c. the horizontal sum of firms' average cost curves.
   d. a fixed markup over average variable cost.

10. Which of the following is not a characteristic of long-run equilibrium under perfect competition?
    a. Production where $P = MC$.
    b. Zero accounting profits.
    c. Zero economic profits.
    d. Production where P = minimum average cost.

11. Which of the following explains why in the long run economic profits in a perfectly competitive industry will equal zero?
    a. The assumption of perfect information.
    b. The elasticity of market demand.
    c. The ease of entry and exit by new and existing firms.
    d. The existence of fixed costs that must be covered in the long run.

12. When economic profits equal zero, we know that accounting profits will
    a. also be zero.
    b. likely understate economic profits.
    c. be at their minimum.
    d. equal the opportunity cost of an owner's investment in her firm.

13. In long-run equilibrium under perfect competition, all but which one of the following are equal to price?
    a. Average cost.
    b. Marginal cost.
    c. Marginal revenue.
    d. Fixed cost.

14. Under perfect competition, price will equal average cost
    a. in the short run.
    b. in the long run.
    c. in both the short and long run.
    d. never.

15. Under perfect competition, firms will produce where MC = P
    a. in the short run.
    b. in the long run.
    c. in both the short and long run.
    d. never.

16. Under perfect competition, price is determined by the intersection of the industry supply and demand curves
    a. in the short run.
    b. in the long run.
    c. in both the short and long run.
    d. never.

17. Under perfect competition, the industry's long run supply curve is
    a. horizontal.
    b. its long-run average cost curve.
    c. its long-run average variable cost curve.
    d. its long-run fixed cost curve.

18. Economic profits will be positive as long as
    a. price equals marginal cost.
    b. price is greater than average variable cost.
    c. price is greater than average fixed cost.
    d. price is greater than average cost.

19. Imagine that pencils are produced by firms with U-shaped average costs under conditions of perfect competition. Concern about the quality of education has increased government spending on education and disturbed the original long-run equilibrium by shifting the demand curve for pencils to the right. Which one of the following is not a likely response?
    a. Pencil prices rise initially in response to the increase in demand.
    b. Existing firms are likely to earn positive economic profits in the short run.
    c. Existing firms in the industry expand output to the point where average cost equals the new, higher price.
    d. New firms are likely to enter the industry in response to earnings above the opportunity cost of capital.

20. Widgets are produced by perfectly competitive firms. The demand curve for widgets has a negative slope. A technological innovation dramatically reduces average and marginal costs for current and potential widget manufacturers. All but which one of the following will occur?
    a. The quantity supplied increases in the short run.
    b. The price of widgets declines in the short run.
    c. Economic profits increase in the short run.
    d. Economic profits will be positive in the long run.

TEST B

Circle T or F for true or false.

T   F   1. Perfect competition is characterized by many firms producing similar but not identical products.

T   F   2. Under perfect competition, firms maximize profits by always producing at the minimum of their average cost.

T   F   3. Freedom of entry and exit are really unnecessary for the existence of perfect competition.

T   F   4. Under perfect competition a firm is always guaranteed to earn positive economic profits if it produces where $MC = P$.

T   F   5. Under perfect competition, the demand curve facing the industry is horizontal.

T   F   6. A competitive firm should always expand output as long as price exceeds average cost.

T   F   7. The firm's short-run supply curve is given by the portion of its marginal cost curve with a positive slope.

T   F   8. In long-run equilibrium, perfectly competitive firms will show positive accounting profits but zero economic profits.

T   F   9. If price is less than average cost, a firm is always better off shutting down.

T   F   10. Perfect competition is studied because a very large number of markets satisfy the conditions for perfect competition.

SUPPLEMENTARY EXERCISES ■

Consider a firm with the following total cost curve:

$$TC = 10{,}140 + .00001Q^3 - .02Q^2 + 16.3Q$$

where Q is output. (This cost curve is consistent with the Basic Exercise.)

1. Derive equations for the firm's
   a. average cost.
   b. average variable cost.
   c. marginal cost.

2. Draw a picture showing these various measures of cost as a function of output.

3. Verify that the marginal cost curve goes through the bottom of the average cost curve and the average variable cost curve.

4. Assume this firm operates in a perfectly competitive market. Derive a mathematical expression for the firm's supply curve.

ECONOMICS IN ACTION

THREE RS AND ONE C?

The quality of education in public schools and what to do about it has become a major issue in election campaigns for everything from local school boards to President of the United States. Declining test scores, mathematical abilities that appear to rank among the lowest in the world, drugs and violence at school are all common stories in newspapers. A recent report about education in America viewed the situation with such alarm that it was entitled "A Nation at Risk." Everything from smaller classes and higher pay for teachers to more computers and mandatory standardized tests have been proposed. Some, like English Professor E. D. Hirsch, have developed elaborate curricular proposals they would like to see adopted.

Some argue that spending more money or requiring extensive testing within the present structure of public schools will make little difference. They see schools as too bureaucratic and too involved in politics to be responsive to the concerns of individual parents or children. A solution favored by some would introduce market competition into primary and secondary schooling. In its most radical form these proposals would abolish public schools, take the money currently spent on schooling, divide it by the number of students, and give every parent of school-age children a voucher for this amount to be spent at the school of their choice. A school's revenue would depend upon its ability to attract and enroll students. Advocates of these plans argue that as schools compete for students the quality of education will increase, and likely without increased spending. Money currently spent on bloated bureaucracies would be channeled to direct instruction. Bad schools would fail to attract students while innovations that increase learning would spread as they were copied by competing schools.

Opponents of voucher systems argue that the market is an inappropriate solution to the problems of public schools. They argue that goods are allocated in markets according to the ability of customers to pay while schooling should not be. Private schools look like a panacea because they can be selective about whom they admit. Taking the best students, they leave public schools, especially large urban schools, with a disproportionate number of students with serious emotional and learning disabilities. Over time a voucher system might also lead to a widening gap between socioeconomic groups as continuing concerns about the level of public spending brings budgetary pressures to reduce the size of vouchers. Wealthy families would have the resources to supplement the voucher; poor households would not. The result would be a two-track schooling system that belies the traditional American commitment to equal opportunity for all.

1. Is the market an appropriate institution for the delivery of primary and secondary education? What are the conditions for the efficiency of competitive markets? Are they likely to apply in this case? Do equity considerations argue for public schools or market competition?

STUDY QUESTIONS

1. What conditions are necessary for perfect competition?

2. Which of these conditions helps to ensure that in the long run economic profits are driven to zero? Explain.

3. How can firms in a perfectly competitive industry face a horizontal demand curve when the demand curve for the industry is sloping downward?

4. Explain the difference between average and marginal cost. Which is relevant for the short-run supply decisions of firms in a perfectly competitive industry? Why?

5. How can it be profitable for a firm to stay in business if price is less than average cost?

6. Often firms think that if they raise their price just a bit they might lose a few customers but make enough from those who remain to increase profits. Why wouldn't a firm in a perfectly competitive industry do the same thing? What about reducing price just a bit in an effort to attract more customers?

7. What is meant by the efficient production of commodities and how is it fostered by market forces under perfect competition?

8. The discussion of equilibrium makes a distinction between the short run and the long run. What is it that is different between the short run and the long run for firms and for an industry of perfectly competitive firms?

9. If long-run equilibrium yields zero economic profits, why do any firms stay in a perfectly competitive industry?

CHAPTER

11

THE PRICE SYSTEM AND THE CASE FOR FREE MARKETS

Important Terms and Concepts

EFFICIENT ALLOCATION OF RESOURCES

COORDINATION TASKS:

    SELECTING OUTPUT

    PLANNING PRODUCTION

    DISTRIBUTION OF GOODS

LAISSEZ-FAIRE

INPUT-OUTPUT ANALYSIS

P = MU REQUIREMENT OF CONSUMER EQUILIBRIUM

MC = P REQUIREMENT OF PERFECT COMPETITION

MC = MU EFFICIENCY REQUIREMENT

LEARNING OBJECTIVES

After completing this chapter, you should be able to:

■ list the three coordination tasks that must be solved by any system of resource allocation.

■ explain the difference between an efficient and inefficient allocation of resources.

■ explain how competitive markets, in which all producers and consumers respond to common market prices, can allocate resources efficiently.

■ describe situations in which price increases may be in society's best interest.

■ explain how prices play a critical role in determining both the allocation of resources and the distribution of income.

■ describe the conditions under which an inefficient allocation of resources might be preferred to an efficient allocation.

■   **CHAPTER REVIEW**

This chapter discusses how prices work to allocate resources and how they affect the efficiency of the economy. In particular, it is shown that in a competitive economy, the self-serving actions of utility-maximizing individuals and profit-maximizing firms can lead to an efficient allocation of the economy's resources. The complete, rigorous proof of this proposition is usually discussed only in graduate courses in economic theory and involves the use of some fairly advanced mathematics. This chapter offers a simpler introduction to this material.

The efficiency implications of a laissez-faire, competitive economy are important reasons why economists have great respect for the workings of the price system. But the proof of this abstract proposition is not a proof that we should dismantle the federal government and that all markets should be unregulated. The proposition refers to the efficiency of a perfectly competitive economy. Many aspects

(1)   of the American economy (are/are not) consistent with the requirements for a competitive economy. The implications of these real-world imperfections are the subject of Chapters 12–19. Also, efficiency is not the only way to judge the workings of an economy. Notions of fairness, or equity, are also important and may at times lead to a preference for less efficient, but fairer, nonmarket procedures.

Sometimes proposals to change prices for efficiency reasons are opposed because of their potentially adverse impact on a particular group. For example, higher taxes on energy to foster conservation and the development of alternative energy sources to reduce our dependence on foreign energy are often opposed because they will increase the cost of living for poor households. These equity considerations are an important part of any final decision. However, many economists argue that it is preferable to address the issue of income distribution through general taxes or transfers rather than by limiting changes in prices that promote efficiency. For example, changes in income tax credits, personal exemptions or the standard deduction could be used to provide protection to lower income households while letting higher energy prices provide an incentive for all households to reduce their use of energy.

(2)   All economies must answer three questions. First there is the question of _____ output: How much of each type of good and service should be produced? Next, there is the question of _____ production: How should various productive inputs be allocated among the millions of firms and plants in order to meet the original output decisions? Finally, there is the

question of the _____ of products: How are the available goods and services to be divided among consumers? How do we evaluate the job that an economy does in answering these questions? Economists typically use two yardsticks: efficiency and equity. This chapter concentrates on efficiency.

Economic efficiency is an important but relatively abstract concept. If by redistributing the commodities that are produced we can make everyone better off in his or her own estimation, we would say that the initial allocation of commodities (<u>was/was not</u>) efficient. It is only when there are no more   (3) opportunities to make some individuals better off while not worsening the situation of others that economists would characterize the economy as _____.

There are usually many efficient allocations of resources. For example, each point on an economy's production possibilities frontier is (<u>efficient/inefficient</u>) in terms of the production of output. If an   (4) economy is operating on this frontier, it is impossible to increase the output of one good without _____ the output of one or more other goods.

Let us consider in more detail how a competitive economy achieves efficiency in the selection of output. (The Supplementary Exercises to this chapter discuss efficiency in production and output distribution.) Efficiency in the selection of output requires that, for the quantity produced, the marginal _____ of the last unit to consumers must equal the marginal _____ of   (5) producers.

Why is this condition necessary for an efficient output selection? Remember that the definition of efficiency refers to consumers' evaluations of their own well-being, an evaluation that economists assume consumers are making when they maximize the difference between total utility and spending. If the marginal utility of some good exceeds the marginal cost of producing more units, then the production of at least one more unit of output will result in a net (<u>increase/decrease</u>) in consumer well-   (6) being. Consumers benefit by the increase in their utility while the cost to society of additional production is given by the marginal _____. If marginal utility exceeds marginal cost, the benefit to consumers from increased production will be (<u>greater/less</u>) than the cost to society, and the initial output selection (<u>is/is not</u>) efficient. It is only when marginal utility (<u>exceeds/equals/is less than</u>) marginal cost that there are no more opportunities for net gains.

It is one of the beauties of a competitive economy that utility-maximizing individuals and profit-maximizing firms will, while pursuing their own self-interests, make decisions that result in marginal utility being equal to marginal cost. Our optimal purchase rule of Chapter 6 showed that utility-maximizing consumers will purchase additional units until the marginal utility of the last unit con-

(7)   sumed equals the _____ of the commodity. The discussion in Chapter 9 showed that profit-maximizing   firms   will   equate   marginal   revenue   and   _____

_____. The discussion in Chapter 10 showed that for a firm under perfect competition, marginal revenue is equal to _____. Thus a profit-maximizing firm under perfect competition, producing where marginal cost equals marginal revenue, will be producing where the marginal cost of the last unit produced equals the _____ of the commodity.

(8)   To summarize, utility-maximizing consumers set marginal _____ equal to price, and profit-maximizing competitive firms set marginal _____ equal to price. The result is that marginal utility (<u>exceeds/equals/is less than</u>) marginal cost, our condition for efficiency in the selection of output.

A centrally planned economy would attempt to answer the three basic questions of output selection, production planning, and product distribution by direct decree, without the use of prices. Often in these economies decisions about output selection were made with little attention to individual consumer preferences. More weight was typically given to the planners' preferences for such things as increased production of steel and electricity, although periodic newspaper accounts of a readjustment of production goals in response to consumer unrest and the final collapse of central planning in Eastern Europe and the former Soviet Union showed that even planners cannot forget entirely about consumers.

Once decisions about output levels have been made, a central planner must be sure that productive inputs are allocated to ensure that the production goals can in fact be achieved. One type of analysis that takes account of the interindustry flows of inputs necessary for the production of goods for final

(9)   use is _____ - _____ analysis. A major limitation of this analysis is the enormity and complexity of the sets of equations. It is a major conceptual advantage that the price system in a competitive economy does not require that this information be centralized.

IMPORTANT TERMS AND CONCEPTS QUIZ ■

Choose the best definition for each of the following terms.

1. _____ Efficient allocation of resources

2. _____ Selecting output

3. _____ Planning production

4. _____ Distribution of output

5. _____ Laissez-faire

6. _____ Input-output analysis

a. Decisions on what quantities of each input to use to produce each good.

b. Technique of simultaneously solving equations that link necessary inputs to output for all industries.

c. Situation that takes advantage of every opportunity to make some individuals better off without harming others.

d. Situation in which one person's welfare can be improved without injury to anyone else.

e. Decisions on the division of output among consumers.

f. Decisions on how much of each commodity to produce.

g. Minimal interference with the workings of the free market.

BASIC EXERCISES ■

This problem is designed to illustrate the logic of the rule for efficiency in output selection. Discussion in the chapter indicated that efficiency in the selection of output requires that marginal utility equals marginal cost for all commodities. If not, it is possible, by changing the selection of output, to improve consumers' well-being.

Consider an economy's production of shirts. Assume that at the current level of shirt output, the marginal utility of shirts is $25 and the marginal cost is $15.

1. The production of one more shirt will increase total utility by $ _____. The production of one more shirt will cost society $ _____.

2. In Chapter 6 we saw that utility-maximizing consumers will maximize the difference between total utility and total spending. This difference equals the money value of their well-being. Looking at the change in utility and assuming that the price of shirts is equal to their marginal cost of $15, we can see that the production of one more shirt will increase consumer well-being by $ _____. Efficiency in the production of shirts requires (more/fewer) shirts.

3. What if the marginal utility of an additional shirt is $15 and the marginal cost is $18? Then the production of an additional shirt will (increase/decrease) consumer well-being by $ _____ and efficiency in the production of shirts will call for (more/fewer) shirts.

4. If the marginal cost of additional shirts is constant at $18, then in order that there be no opportunity for a change in the production of shirts to increase consumer well-being, enough shirts should be produced so that the marginal utility of an additional shirt is $ _____.

TEST A

Circle the most appropriate answer.

1. For any economy that uses the price system, which of the following is not necessarily true?
    a. Prices play an important role in shaping the allocation of resources.
    b. Prices play an important role in shaping the distribution of income and wealth.
    c. Prices will reflect consumer preference and income.
    d. Prices of necessities will be low, and prices of luxuries will be high.

2. The price system distributes goods and services on the basis of income and
    a. scarcity.
    b. consumer preferences.
    c. education.
    d. planner preferences.

3. The three basic coordination tasks for resource allocation that economies may solve by markets or planning include all but which one of the following?
    a. The distribution of output among consumers.
    b. How much of different goods to produce.
    c. The allocation of available resources to the production of different goods.
    d. The amount of money that the government will print.

4. The use of prices to allocate goods among consumers means that
    a. all consumers will be able to buy an equal share of all outputs.
    b. the resulting allocation must necessarily be inefficient.
    c. wealthy consumers will be able to command a greater amount of output.
    d. there must be persistent inflation in order to choke off consumer excess demand.

5. Prices in competitive markets affect all but which one of the following?
    a. The allocation of inputs among competing producers.
    b. The allocation of output among consumers.
    c. The distribution of income.
    d. The location of the production possibilities frontier.

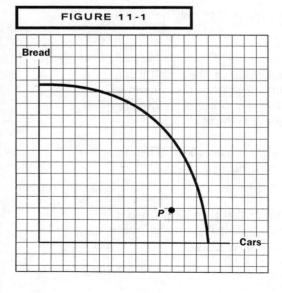

FIGURE 11-1

6. Consider the production possibilities frontier shown in Figure 11-1. Efficiency in production is given by
    a. all of the points inside the frontier.
    b. all of the points on or inside the frontier.
    c. all of the points on the frontier.
    d. the point of equal output of all goods.

7. Consider production at point *P* in Figure 11-1. If the economy produces at point *P*, one would say that output selection is
    a. efficient.
    b. inefficient.
    c. efficient or inefficient depending upon consumers' preferences.

8. Under conditions of perfect competition, firms will choose to produce the quantity of output such that
    a. MC = MU.
    b. MU = *P*.
    c. MC = *P*.
    d. MRP = *P*.

9. In competitive markets consumers will demand particular commodities up to the point where
   a. MU = MC.
   b. MU = P.
   c. MC = P.
   d. MU = Zero.

10. The condition for optimal output selection is
    a. MC = P.
    b. MC = MU.
    c. MRP = P.
    d. MU = P.

11. Competitive markets can meet the criterion for efficiency in production planning
    a. through the use of input-output tables.
    b. only after the Congress approves the president's budget proposal.
    c. automatically.
    d. less efficiently than centrally planned economies.

12. If the marginal utility of color television sets is $400 and the marginal cost is $300, then efficiency in output selection requires that the production of color television sets should
    a. increase.
    b. decrease.
    c. neither increase nor decrease.

13. The change in the production of color television sets from question 12 will likely
    a. increase marginal cost and marginal utility.
    b. increase marginal cost and decrease marginal utility.
    c. decrease marginal cost and marginal utility.
    d. decrease marginal cost and increase marginal utility.

14. An efficient allocation of resources
    a. will always be fair.
    b. is the best allocation possible.
    c. means the economy is operating somewhere on its production opportunity frontier.
    d. is always better than an inefficient allocation.

15. Leon does not now own a motorcycle. He would pay up to $2,000 for one. Motorcycles produced by competitive firms in long-run equilibrium, earning zero economic profit, cost $4,000 to produce. Which of the following is false?
    a. Leon is not likely to buy a motorcycle.
    b. Since Leon's marginal utility is less than the marginal cost of production, there would be a social gain if direct government controls reduced the production of motorcycles.
    c. The marginal utility of a motorcycle to someone must be at least $4,000.

16. If resources have been allocated in a way that meets the requirements of economic efficiency, then we know that
    a. output is being produced in accordance with the preferences of the Council of Economic Advisers.
    b. production occurs at a point inside the economy's production possibilities frontier.
    c. there is no reallocation of resources that can make some individuals better off without making others worse off.
    d. the marginal cost of producing every commodity has been minimized.

TEST B

Circle T or F for true or false.

T   F   1. The term *laissez-faire* refers to an economy with minimal economic regulation by government.

T   F   2. If resources are being allocated efficiently, we know that there is no better allocation possible.

T   F   3. Efficient resource allocation always requires the intervention of a central planner to set prices correctly.

T   F   4. Efficiency in the selection of output requires that the marginal utility of every commodity be equal to its marginal cost.

T   F   5. An unregulated competitive economy is incapable of seeing that appropriate efficiency conditions are achieved for all commodities.

T   F   6. Input-output analysis is a mathematical tool to aid in the distribution of output among consumers without using the price system.

T   F   7. Charging higher prices on public transportation during rush hours can be an example of using the price system to increase efficiency.

T   F   8. Considerations of fairness may sometimes lead a society to prefer an inefficient allocation to an efficient one.

T   F   9. Efficiency in the distribution of goods implies that everyone will get an equal share of all goods.

T   F   10. Competitive markets promote efficiency in output selection because both firms and consumers respond to the same price.

■ SUPPLEMENTARY EXERCISES

The first two exercises illustrate the implications of the rules for efficiency in the allocation of output among consumers and in the allocation of productive inputs.

1. **Efficiency in the Distribution of Output Among Consumers**

    The rule for efficiency in the distribution of output among consumers is that every consumer must have the same marginal utility for every commodity. If not, it would be possible to redistribute output among consumers in a way that makes at least one person better off without harming anyone else.

    Imagine that Todd and Nicole both consume steaks and pizzas. The initial allocation of steak and pizza has resulted in the following marginal utilities:

    Marginal Utility

	Todd	Nicole
Steaks	$9	$6
Pizzas	4	4

a. Is the condition for efficiency in the distribution of output satisfied? _____ If not, there should be some, possibly many, reallocations of output that will increase either Todd's or Nicole's total utility (or both) without reducing total utility for the other.

b. Imagine that Nicole gives Todd one steak in exchange for two pizzas. On net, considering the full effects of the trade, what is the change in Todd's utility? (<u>increase/decrease</u>) $ _____ Nicole's utility? (<u>increase/decrease</u>) $ _____ An implication of the utility changes of the real-location is that the initial allocation was (<u>efficient/inefficient</u>).

c. How do competitive markets work to ensure that uncoordinated individual demands will satisfy the condition for efficiency in the distribution of output among consumers?

2. **Efficiency in Production Planning**

The rule for efficiency in Production Planning says that if two inputs, labor and land, are both used to produce two outputs, then inputs should be assigned to each output until the ratio of marginal physical product for two inputs is the same in all uses. If not, it will be possible to reallocate resources and increase the production of at least one commodity without decreasing the production of other commodities.

a. We know from Chapter 8 that this condition will be automatically satisfied under perfect competition for profit-maximizing firms that can buy inputs at given prices. Perhaps less clear is that if this condition is not satisfied, then it would be possible to reallocate inputs among firms and produce more total output—with the same amount of inputs. Consider the following table showing the initial marginal physical products of land and labor in the production of corn and tomatoes. Note that the ratio of marginal physical products in the production of corn (120/40) is less than the ratio in the production of tomatoes (1,200/200).

**Marginal Physical Product of Labor and Land
In the Production of Corn and Tomatoes**

	Corn (bushels)	Tomatoes (pounds)
Labor (person)	120	1,200
Land (acre)	40	200

Consider the reallocation of one worker from corn production to tomato production. As a result of this reallocation of labor, the production of corn will fall by _____ bushels and the production of tomatoes will rise by _____ pounds. Now consider moving four acres of land from tomato production to corn production. As a result of the reallocation of land, the production of corn will rise by _____ bushels and the production of tomatoes will fall by _____ pounds. Counting the reallocation of both land and labor, the production of corn changes by _____ bushels and the production of tomatoes changes by _____ pounds.

b. How do competitive markets work to ensure that the uncoordinated decisions of firms satisfy the condition for efficiency in the allocation of productive inputs?

Efficiency in the selection of inputs helps to achieve efficiency in the choice of outputs. We have seen that efficiency in the selection of outputs requires that $MU = MC$. In competitive markets, $MU = MC$ because utility-maximizing individuals see to it that $MU = P$. The discussion below shows how efficiency in the selection of inputs helps to insure that competitive firms produce where $MC = P$.

We saw in Chapter 8 that our rule for optimal use of inputs could also be expressed in terms of marginal revenue product. Using symbols, our optimal input rule says

$$P_Q \times MPP_X = P_X$$

where P_Q is the product price, P_X is the input price, and MPP_X is the marginal physical product of input X in the production of Q. If we divide both sides of the equation by MPP_X we get

$$P_Q = P_X/MPP_X$$

Note that P_X/MPP_X is the marginal cost of producing more output by using more of input X. If we buy one more unit of input X, we spend P_X and get MPP_X more units of output at a cost of P_X/MPP_X per unit of additional output. A profit-maximizing firm will use the optimal input rule for all its inputs. Thus, the marginal cost of an output expansion by the use of any single input, of the many that a firm may use, will be equal to the marginal cost from the additional use of any other input.

3. Go to the library and look up information about the most recent input-output table for the U.S. economy. (Information about input-output tables can be found in the *Survey of Current Business*, a monthly publication of the U.S. Commerce Department. Every five years information from a number of economic censuses is used to construct detailed input-output tables for about 500 industries and commodities. Input-output tables for 1992 were published in the November and December 1997 issues of the *Survey of Current Business*.)

There are several input-output tables. One table indicates which industries use which commodities. Another table indicates which industries produce which commodities. The table of direct requirements shows what direct inputs are necessary per unit of output of each industry. The table of direct and indirect requirements solves all the input-output relationships and shows how the output of every industry must adjust in order to increase the output of any one industry. It is this table that takes account of such indirect requirements as increased electricity to make more steel in order to increase the output of cars.

   a. How many separate pieces of information do these input-output tables contain? How long do you think it would take to construct such a table? How long do you think it would take you to solve all the interrelationships and produce a table of direct and indirect requirements?

   b. Which industries produce mainly for final uses and which produce mainly intermediate outputs, that is, inputs for other industries?

   c. The November 1969 *Survey of Current Business* contains data for the 1963 input-output table. Compare these data to the most recent table you can find. Pick one or two favorite industries and see how total and direct requirements have changed over time. If you are a planner concerned with the year 2010, how should you determine what input-output requirements are relevant?

■ ECONOMICS IN ACTION

HI-HO, HI-HO, IT'S OFF TO WORK WE GO

It's not only bridges that get congested. On Sunday morning, additional cars do not seem to interfere with the traffic flow on most urban highway systems, but on Monday morning each additional driver adds to congestion, makes every other driver's commute take longer, and seems to turn many highways into linear parking lots.

The highway and road systems of most large cities seem to be a clear case of too many vehicles and too few roads. Yet building more roads seems only to increase the traffic without solving the problem. Economist Kenneth A. Small, writing in *The Brookings Review*, Spring 1993, talks of a reservoir of potential drivers, deterred from driving by existing congestion, who quickly fill up new roads as they are completed. Small is skeptical that policies such as campaigns to promote ride-sharing, mass transit, staggered work hours, or high-occupancy-vehicle lanes will have more than a temporary impact on urban congestion. Are there market mechanisms that would improve the situation? Small believes there are, specifically congestion pricing—"charging motorists a very high premium for using the most popular roads during peak hours."

Small argues that congestion pricing provides an incentive for drivers to consider alternative routes, alternative times, and/or alternative means of transportation. The other policies listed above focus on only a subset of travelers while providing no incentive for the vast majority of drivers to change their behavior. While no one likes paying tolls, not many of us like being stuck in traffic, either.

To be successful, Small argues that congestion pricing must impose tolls that vary widely by time of day and are sufficiently high at peak demand to have a measurable impact. Although not its primary purpose, Small believes congestion pricing also would improve air quality by reducing both the volume of traffic and the higher emissions associated with congestion.

Small is concerned that congestion prices might be a burden for lower income families and argues that a portion of the revenues collected should be used in ways that benefit low-income households. Using the Los Angeles region as an example, Small suggested a congestion price of 15 cents a mile or $66 a month for a commuter with a 20-mile round trip commute each day. He estimated net revenues of around $3 billion a year and proposed using one-third for reimbursements to travelers through an employee commuting allowance and fuel tax reduction; another third for reductions of the portion of sales and property taxes that subsidize highways and transportation; and the remaining third for improvements to transportation services, including mass transit and critical highway projects.

What is your evaluation of Small's proposal?

STUDY QUESTIONS

1. What are the three coordination tasks that must be solved by any system of resource allocation?

2. Why is the determination of efficient allocations a largely technical exercise with many potential solutions rather than a method for determining the best allocation for the economy?

3. Why isn't point P in Figure 11-1 an example of efficiency in output selection? Starting at point P, show what other possible points of production dominate point P in terms of efficiency considerations. Is there only one such point or a set of points? If a set, how can there be more than one?

4. Is it ever possible that society would be better off with higher rather than lower prices? Explain.

5. Should an economy always prefer an efficient allocation to an inefficient allocation? Explain.

6. How can a price system (market mechanism) hope to solve the large number of coordination decisions that are included in the mathematics of an input-output table for the entire economy?

MONOPOLY

LEARNING OBJECTIVES

After completing this chapter, you should be able to:

- explain why for a monopolist marginal revenue is less than price.

- calculate a monopolist's profit-maximizing price and output, given information on costs and demand.

- explain why, unlike with a competitive firm, there is no supply curve for a monopolist.

- describe what factors allow a particular monopoly to persist.

- explain why a monopolist will receive positive economic profits in both the short and long runs.

- explain how a monopoly can give rise to an inefficient allocation of resources.

- describe why a monopolist's demand and cost curves may differ from those of a comparable competitive industry.

- show how price discrimination can increase a monopolist's profit.

- explain why a monopolist cannot pass on all of any pollution charge or other increase in cost.

Important Terms and Concepts

PURE MONOPOLY

BARRIERS TO ENTRY

PATENTS

NATURAL MONOPOLY

MONOPOLY PROFITS

INEFFICIENCY OF MONOPOLY

PRICE DISCRIMINATION

■ CHAPTER REVIEW

In Chapter 10 we studied the decisions of firms operating in markets characterized as perfect competition, that is, markets with lots of firms competing to produce and sell one good. Chapter 8 considered optimal firm decisions and Chapter 11 considered the implications of these decisions for the effi-

(1)   ciency of resource allocation. This chapter will consider a pure monopoly, a market with (one/many) firm(s) producing a single good with (no/lots of) close substitutes. Not only is there no competition at the moment, but the entry and survival of potential competitors is extremely unlikely. The essence of a pure monopoly is one producer without effective competition.

A pure monopoly may arise for one of two broad reasons. If the technology of large-scale production enables one firm to produce enough to satisfy the whole market at lower average costs than a

(2)   number of smaller firms can, the result is a _____ monopoly. Legal restrictions such as exclusive licensing or patents; advantages the monopolist acquires for himself, such as control of a vital input or technical superiority; or special risks faced by potential entrants who must spend large amounts on factories or advertising before realizing any revenue can also create a pure monopoly. All of these factors would deter potential competitors and are called _____ to

_____.

The study of a pure monopoly often starts by assuming that some enterprising entrepreneur is able to monopolize a previously competitive industry. It is also traditional to assume that the monopolist initially faces the previous industry demand curve and operates with the same cost curves.

Under pure competition, individual firms face demand curves that are horizontal; that is, any firm can sell as much as it wants at the market price. A monopolist will face the industry demand curve with

(3)   a (positive/negative/zero) slope. The monopolist who wants to sell more must (raise/lower) her price. A monopolist who raises her price will find that sales (decrease/do not change/increase).

The monopolist maximizes profit just like any other profit-maximizing firm; that is, the monopolist

(4)   chooses the output level at which (marginal/average) cost equals (marginal/average) revenue. Now the only trick is to figure out what the relevant cost and revenue curves look like. Marginal cost comes from the monopolist's total costs in exactly the same way that it does for anyone else. The tricky part is marginal revenue. Marginal revenue is the addition to total revenue from producing and selling one more unit. Under

perfect competition, the actions of an individual firm have no effect on the market price and marginal revenue equals _____. But with a monopolist, quantity decisions do affect price and marginal revenue (is/is not) equal to price.

Remember from Chapter 9 that the demand curve is the curve of (average/total) revenue. From Rule 4 in the Appendix to Chapter 9 we know that when average revenue is declining, marginal revenue will be (less/more) than average revenue. In other words, for the monopolist with a downward-sloping demand curve, the curve of marginal revenue will lie (above/below) the curve of average revenue. (Remember the geometry of marginal revenue in the Basic Exercise to Chapter 9 in the Study Guide.) A similar use of Rule 4 indicates that when average cost is rising, the marginal cost curve will lie _____ the average cost curve. (5)

Once we have used the marginal cost and marginal revenue curves to compute the monopolist's profit-maximizing output level, we can use the (demand/supply) curve to figure out what price she should charge. We know that since the curve of marginal revenue lies below the demand curve, the monopolist's market price will be (greater/less) than both marginal revenue and marginal cost. We also know that if average cost is rising, average cost will be (greater/less) than marginal cost and hence also (greater/less) than the market price given by the demand curve. Thus, for a profit-maximizing monopolist, operating at a level where average cost is rising, price will be greater than average cost and the monopolist will receive positive economic profits. Since, by definition, the monopolist is the only supplier, new firms (will/will not) arise to compete away these profits. Compared with results under pure competition, the monopolist's profit-maximizing behavior will result in a (higher/lower) price and a (higher/lower) level of output in both the short and long run. (If average costs are not rising, the long-run viability of the monopolist requires that price exceed average cost.) (6)

In Chapter 11 we saw that pure competition leads to an efficient allocation of resources. Efficient resource allocation requires that the marginal utility (MU) of each commodity equal its marginal cost (MC). Optimal consumer decisions lead to the result that MU equals _____. Under perfect competition, optimal firm decisions imply that MC equals _____. The upshot is clearly that under pure competition MU equals MC. With a pure monopoly as outlined above—that is, with the same demand and cost curves—we know that while consumers will continue to equate MU and P, the (7) monopolist will equate MC to _____ _____ , which is (greater/less) than *P*. The result is that with a pure monopoly, MU is (greater/less) than MC. Increased quantity of the monopolized commodity would yield marginal benefits, measured by MU, that are (less than/the same as/greater than) marginal costs. In this sense the monopoly leads to an inefficient allocation of resources.

It is important to note that in the discussion above we assumed that the monopolist faces demand and cost curves that are the same as those of the previously competitive industry. However, several factors could shift these curves following a change in market structure. Advertising might shift demand and cost curves. Savings from centralizing various operations and avoiding duplication might shift the

(8)   cost curves (up/down). Greater inefficiencies from greater size would have the opposite effect. Particular results will depend upon particular circumstances.

Why do we say there is no supply curve for a monopolist? Remember that the supply curve shows the relationship between each possible market price and the quantity supplied. Under pure competition a firm takes price as given and then decides how much to produce, knowing that its individual

(9)   quantity decision (will/will not) affect the market price. The firm's supply curve comes from considering its reaction to possible prices. But the monopolist (does/does not) take price as given. The monopolist is interested in trading off the revenue implications of different price-quantity combinations, as shown by the demand curve, against the cost implications of producing those different amounts. The monopolist chooses the one quantity that maximizes profits and receives the price given by the point on the demand curve consistent with the quantity. The monopolist is a price (maker/taker).

IMPORTANT TERMS AND CONCEPTS QUIZ ■

Choose the best definition for the following terms.

1. _____ Pure monopoly

2. _____ Barriers to entry

3. _____ Patents

4. _____ Natural monopoly

5. _____ Monopoly profits

6. _____ Price discrimination

a. Impediments preventing potential rivals from entering an industry.

b. Industry in which advantages of large-scale production enable a single firm to supply the market demand at a lower average cost than a number of smaller firms could.

c. Industry with a single buyer for the entire market.

d. Charging different prices to different customers when the cost of supplying customers is the same.

e. Industry with single supplier of a product for which there are no close substitutes.

f. Economic profits that persist in the long run.

g. Accounting profits that do not disappear in the long run.

h. Temporary government grants of exclusive production rights to product's inventors.

BASIC EXERCISES ■

These exercises are designed to offer practice in computing the profit-maximizing quantity and price for a monopolist.

1. Mario has a monopoly in the production of widgets. Table 12-1 contains data on the demand for widgets and the cost of producing them. Use this data to compute Mario's profit-maximizing quantity and the associated price.

   TABLE 12-1

Quantity	Average Revenue (Price)	Average Cost
12	$9,500	$7,068.00
13	9,300	6,957.00
14	9,100	6,894.00
15	8,900	6,869.40
16	8,700	6,876.00

   a. One way is to consider columns 2 and 5 of Table 12-3. Choose the output level that maximizes the difference. That level of output is _____ widgets.

   b. The second way is to fill in columns 3 and 4 of Table 12-3 by computing marginal revenue and marginal cost. Mario could maximize profits by increasing production as long as marginal _____ exceeds marginal _____ widgets. In this case, Mario maximizes profits by producing _____ widgets.

   c. To maximize profits Mario should charge a price of $ _____.

   d. What is Mario's profit? _____

TABLE 12-2

Quantity	Average Revenue (Price)	Average Cost
12	$9,500	$8,068.00
13	9,300	7,957.00
14	9,100	7,894.00
15	8,900	7,869.40
16	8,700	7,876.00

TABLE 12-3

(1) Quantity	(2) Total Revenue	(3) Marginal Revenue	(4) Marginal Cost	(5) Total Cost
12	$144,000	6900 / 23,100	-5625	$84,816
13	120,900	-6500	-6075	90,441
14	127,400	-6100	-6525	96,516
15	133,500	-5700	-6975	103,041
16	139,200			110,016

TABLE 12-4

(1) Quantity	(2) Total Revenue	(3) Marginal Revenue	(4) Marginal Cost	(5) Total Cost
12	114,000	6900	6625	96,816
13	120,900	6500	7075	103,441
14	127,400	6100	7525	110,516
15	133,500	5700	7975	118,041
16	139,200			126,016

e. Unfortunately, the production of widgets involves significant pollution, and the government has imposed a pollution charge that costs Mario $1,000 a widget. Table 12-2 contains the original data on demand along with the new average cost data that reflect the $1,000 a widget pollution charge.

f. Use Table 12-4 to compute the new profit-maximizing output level. Mario's new profit-maximizing output level is _____ and the associated price is $ _____.

g. How much pollution tax does Mario pay? $ _____. Note that while the pollution charge is $1,000 a widget, Mario's profit-maximizing price increases by only $ _____. Why doesn't Mario simply raise his price by the full $1,000?

h. What is the new level of profits? $_____.

i. (Optional) Your answer should indicate that the pollution tax has reduced both the output of widgets and the associated volume of pollution. What would have happened if, instead of a per-unit tax, the government had simply fined Mario $13,000 for polluting and imposed no further charges? Compared with the initial situation, what happens to Mario's profit-maximizing level of output, the associated level of pollution output, and actual profits with this lump-sum pollution charge? (When answering this question be sure you are working with the correct cost curves. Adjust Table 12-3, remembering that at each output level, total costs will now be $13,000 higher than the entries in column 5.)

2. This exercise illustrates how a monopolist may be able to increase her profits by engaging in price discrimination. Table 12-5 contains data on the demand for snow tires in Centerville and Middletown. Centerville does not get much snow, and the demand for snow tires is quite elastic. Middletown is smaller, and gets more snow; it should not be surprising that the demand for snow tires in Middletown is less elastic than in Centerville. Snow tires are supplied to both cities by a monopolist who can produce tires with a fixed cost of $2,500,000 and a constant marginal cost of $10 a tire.

a. Assume that the monopolist charges the same price in both towns. Use the data on total demand to compute the monopolist's profit-maximizing level of output and price. First compute total revenue in order to compute marginal revenue per tire by dividing the change in total revenue by the change in output. Then compare marginal revenue to the monopolist's marginal cost of $10 to determine the profit-maximizing level of output.

Price? $ _____

Output? _____

Profits? $ _____

TABLE 12-5

Price	Quantity Demanded Centerville	Quantity Demanded Middletown	Total Demand	Total Revenue	Marginal Revenue
$48	10,000	40,000	50,000	2,400,000	
45	25,000	43,750	68,750	3,093,750	693,750 ÷ 18,750 = $37
42	40,000	47,500	87,500	3,675,000	581,250 ÷ 18,750 = $31
39	55,000	51,250	106,250	4,143,750	468,750 = $25
36	70,000	55,000	125,000	4,500,000	356,250 = $19
33	85,000	58,750	143,750	4,743,750	243,750 = $13
30	100,000	62,500	162,500	4,875,000	131,250 = $7
27	115,000	66,250	181,250	4,893,750	18,750 = $1

b. Assume now that the monopolist is able to charge different prices in the towns; that is, she is a price discriminator. Can the monopolist increase her profits by charging different prices? Complete Table 12-6 to answer this question.
Profit-maximizing price in Centerville: $ _____
Profit-maximizing price in Middletown: $ _____
Quantity of snow tires in Centerville: _____
Quantity of snow tires in Middletown: _____
Total Profits: $ _____

c. In which town did the monopolist raise the price? In which town did she lower the price? The monopolist should charge a higher price in the town with the lower elasticity of demand. Can you explain why? Is that the case here?

TABLE 12-6

Price	Centerville Total Revenue	Centerville Marginal Revenue	Middletown Total Revenue	Middletown Marginal Revenue
$48	480,000		1,920,000	43
45	1,125,000	$43	1,968,750	$13
42	1,680,000	$37	1,995,000	$7
39	2,145,000	$31	1,998,750	$1
36	2,520,000	$25	1,980,000	$ -5
33	2,805,000	$19	1,938,750	$ -11
30	3,000,000	$15	1,875,000	$ -17
27	3,105,000	$7	1,788,750	$ -23

■   **SELF-TESTS FOR UNDERSTANDING**

TEST A

Circle the most appropriate answer.

1. Pure monopoly is characterized by
   a. many firms producing slightly different products.
   b. many firms producing slightly different products that are close substitutes.
   c. such a small number of firms that each must figure out how the others will respond to its own actions.
   d. one firm, with no competitors, producing a product with no close substitutes.

2. Which one of the following is *not* likely to lead to a monopoly?
   a. Patents.
   b. Control of the sole source of an important commodity.
   c. A commodity with many close substitutes.
   d. Significant increasing returns to scale.

3. A natural monopoly arises when
   a. natural resources are an important input.
   b. there are significant cost advantages to large-scale production.
   c. the government prohibits entry.
   d. patents protect a firm's technology.

4. Which of the following is not an example of a barrier to entry?
   a. Patents that give exclusive rights to production.
   b. The existence of large fixed costs before one can begin production.
   c. A legal charter that grants its holder the right to be the sole supplier.
   d. A simple production process with constant average cost and no fixed costs.

5. Which of the following is likely to represent a monopoly?
   a. The largest department store in town.
   b. The University of Iowa, which is the largest employer in Iowa City.
   c. The local TV cable company, which operates under an exclusive contract from the city.
   d. Amtrak.

6. If in order to sell more, a firm must reduce the price on all units sold, we can conclude that the firm's demand curve
   a. has a positive slope.
   b. is horizontal.
   c. slopes down and to the right.
   d is vertical.

7. Under the conditions of question 6, we know that marginal revenue will
   a. be less than average revenue.
   b. equal average revenue.
   c. exceed average revenue.
   d. always equal marginal cost.

8. If average costs are increasing, marginal cost will be
   a. less than average cost.
   b. equal to average cost.
   c. greater than average cost.
   d. There's insufficient information to determine whether marginal cost will be above or below average cost.

9. A monopolist maximizes profit by producing where
   a. marginal cost equals marginal revenue.
   b. marginal cost equals marginal utility.
   c. average cost equals average revenue.
   d. the difference between average cost and average revenue is greatest.

10. Once a monopolist has determined the profit-maximizing level of output, the price she should charge is given by
    a. the curve of marginal revenue.
    b. the curve of marginal cost.
    c. the curve of average cost.
    d. the curve of average revenue.

11. A monopolist's profits are found by multiplying the quantity produced by the difference between
    a. marginal cost and marginal revenue.
    b. marginal cost and average revenue.
    c. average cost and average revenue.
    d. average cost and marginal revenue.

12. A monopolist's economic profits will
    a. be competed away in the long run.
    b. be driven to the opportunity cost of capital.
    c. persist in the long run.
    d. be limited by usury laws.

13. Because a monopolist is a price maker, it is typically said that he has
    a. an inelastic demand curve.
    b. no demand curve.
    c. no supply curve.
    d. an upward-sloping demand curve.

14. An entrepreneur who monopolizes a previously competitive industry and now faces the same demand curve and produces with the same cost function will typically maximize profits by
    a. forcing consumers to buy more at a higher price.
    b. producing less but charging a higher price.
    c. increasing volume.
    d. lowering both output and price.

15. Pollution charges or other taxes that are levied on each unit of output will lead to a shift in all but which one of the following?
    a. Marginal cost.
    b. Marginal revenue.
    c. Average cost.
    d. Total cost.

16. A monopolist cannot simply pass on any increase in average cost because
    a. marginal cost exceeds average cost.
    b. the average cost curve often has a positive slope.
    c. the demand curve for the output is typically downward sloping.
    d. of concerns about excessive profiteering.

17. An increase in a monopolist's average cost will lead to a(n)
    a. increase in price by the same amount, as the monopolist passes on the price increase.
    b. increase in price only if marginal cost also increases.
    c. decrease in price as the monopolist needs to sell more in order to cover increased costs.
    d. increase in price only if the elasticity of demand is less than 1.0.

18. Some argue that because they control the whole market and can thus garner all of the benefits, monopolies are more likely to foster innovations. Statistical evidence
    a. confirms this argument.
    b. suggests exactly the reverse.
    c. lacks a firm conclusion.

19. An increase in a monopolist's fixed cost will
    a. reduce the profit-maximizing level of output.
    b. not affect the profit-maximizing level of output.
    c. increase the profit-maximizing level of output as the monopolist needs to sell more to cover costs.

20. If marginal cost is greater than zero, we know that a monopolist will produce where the elasticity of demand is
    a. greater than unity.
    b. equal to unity.
    c. less than unity.

TEST B

Circle T or F for true or false.

T F 1. A pure monopoly results when only a few firms supply a particular commodity for which there are no close substitutes.

T F 2. Significant increasing returns to scale, which reduce average costs as output expands, may result in a natural monopoly.

T F 3. A pure monopolist can earn positive economic profits only in the long run.

T F 4. An entrepreneur who successfully monopolizes a competitive industry will face a horizontal demand curve just like each of the previous competitive firms.

T F 5. A monopolist maximizes profits by producing at the point at which marginal cost equals marginal revenue.

T F 6. If in a monopolistic industry, demand and cost curves are identical to a comparable competitive industry, and the demand curve slopes downward while the average cost curve slopes upward, then the monopolist's price will always exceed the competitive industry's price, but the monopolist's output will be larger.

T F 7. A monopolist has a greater incentive to advertise than does an individual firm under pure competition.

T F 8. When market price is greater than average cost, a monopolist can always increase profits by producing more.

T F 9. A monopolist will be able to increase price by the full amount of any per-unit tax, such as a per-unit pollution charge.

T F 10. A firm operating under conditions of pure competition will not be able to pass on any of a per-unit pollution tax and must therefore pay the whole tax out of reduced profits.

SUPPLEMENTARY EXERCISES ■

1. The demand curve for the first problem in the Basic Exercise is

    $$Q = 59.5 - .005P.$$

    The total cost curve is

    $$TC = 52,416 + 225Q^2.$$

    a. Derive mathematical expressions for total revenue, marginal revenue, average cost, and marginal cost.
    b. Plot the demand, marginal revenue, average cost, and marginal cost curves.
    c. Use your expressions for marginal revenue and marginal cost to solve for the profit-maximizing level of output. Is your answer consistent with your graph in part b and your answer to the Basic Exercise?
    d. What is the impact of the per-unit pollution tax and the fixed-charge pollution tax on your expressions for total, average, and marginal cost? Do differences here help explain the impact of these taxes on the profit-maximizing level of output?

2. Why is (a) the correct answer to question 20 in Test A? (You might want to refer back to Chapter 7.)

ECONOMICS IN ACTION ■

THE HIGH COST OF NEW DRUGS

Debate over health-care reform at the beginning of the Clinton Administration focused attention on the pricing policies of drug companies. On March 28, 1993, *The New York Times* reported that Tacrine, the first drug to treat Alzheimer's disease, had recently been recommended by an advisory panel of the Food and Drug Administration. Industry observers were expecting Tacrine would cost more than $1,000 a year even though it was not effective for most patients. What explains such high prices for this and other new drugs?

Some point to the high cost of drug research, and the fact that most new ideas are not successful, as justification for the high cost of drugs. Pharmaceutical manufacturers argue that drugs save money, as even expensive drugs are often cheaper than hospitalization or surgery.

Regulating drug prices to allow manufacturers a reasonable rate of return while recognizing the significant research and development costs a company incurs—that is, setting prices on the basis of cost-plus pricing—has been advocated by some. Others are concerned that this approach may only subsidize and encourage wasteful and mediocre research. Sam Peltzman, a professor of economics at the University of Chicago, argues that one should not be surprised by high prices. Patents mean that drug companies enjoy a ten-year monopoly. As Peltzman puts it, "These companies are not charities—they are charging what the market will allow."

Are there other solutions? Peltzman has advocated limiting patent monopolies to five years. Others argue that the concept of managed competition, under which patients are organized into large groups to bargain with drug companies and other health providers, is necessary for patients to get the best price. Some are less optimistic that patients, even if organized into large groups, will be successful in bargaining with drug companies who hold a monopoly position unless patients are willing to refuse drug treatments that cost too much.

1. How would you determine a fair price for new drugs?

2. What would it take to enforce your concept of fair prices and what side effects are likely to be associated with enforcement?

3. What do you think explains the high price of new drugs?

■   STUDY QUESTIONS

1. Who has the greater incentive to advertise and why, a firm in a purely competitive industry or a monopolist?

2. Why are barriers to entry important for the preservation of a monopolist's monopoly?

3. What is the difference between a price taker and a price maker? Which description is relevant for a monopolist?

4. Why do economists argue that monopoly leads to an inefficient allocation of resources?

5. Are there conditions under which society might benefit from a monopoly? Explain.

6. What is meant by the term "price discrimination"?

7. How can a monopolist increase profits by engaging in price discrimination?

8. Will price discrimination always raise prices for customers?

9. Why doesn't a monopolist simply raise her price by the full cost of things like pollution charges?

10. If both monopolists and competitive firms produce where marginal revenue equals marginal cost, why are the results of a competitive industry and a monopolized industry different?

Important Terms and Concepts

MONOPOLISTIC COMPETITION

EXCESS CAPACITY THEOREM

OLIGOPOLY

OLIGOPOLISTIC INTERDEPENDENCE

CARTEL

PRICE LEADERSHIP

SALES MAXIMIZATION

KINKED DEMAND CURVE

STICKY PRICE

GAME THEORY

PRICE WAR

MAXIMIN CRITERION

NASH EQUILIBRIUM

PRISONERS' DILEMMA

REPEATED GAMES

CREDIBLE THREAT

PERFECTLY CONTESTABLE MARKETS

BETWEEN COMPETITION AND MONOPOLY

LEARNING OBJECTIVES

After completing this chapter, you should be able to:

■ compare the four conditions that define monopolistic competition with those of perfect competition.

■ explain why and how the long-run equilibrium of a firm under monopolistic competition differs from that of a firm under pure competition.

■ explain why firms under monopolistic competition earn zero profit in the long run even though they face a downward-sloping demand curve.

■ explain why monopolistic competitors are said to have excess capacity.

■ explain why it is so difficult to make a formal analysis of an oligopolistic market structure.

■ describe briefly the alternative approaches to modeling oligopolistic behavior.

■ explain why most economists believe it is difficult to maintain the discipline necessary to sustain a cartel.

■ use marginal cost and marginal revenue curves to derive the implications for price and quantity of sales maximization as opposed to profit maximization.

- ■ use marginal cost and marginal revenue curves to explain how a kinked demand curve can imply sticky prices.

- ■ use the maximin criterion to determine the final outcome in a game-theory setting.

- ■ explain how the concept of contestable markets means that even in an industry with few firms, no firm will earn long-run profits in excess of the opportunity cost of capital, and inefficient firms will not survive if entry and exit is costless.

■ CHAPTER REVIEW

Pure competition and pure monopoly are the polar examples of market structure most easily analyzed in textbooks. Actual markets tend more toward *monopolistic competition* and *oligopoly*, which are the subjects of this chapter. It is harder to model firm behavior in these market structures, especially in the case of oligopoly. However, profit maximization remains a dominant characteristic of most firms and marginal cost and marginal revenue curves still are important tools when analyzing the decisions firms make.

(1)   A market structure in which there are numerous participants, freedom of entry and exit, perfect information, and product heterogeneity is referred to as _____ competition. Because each seller is able to partially differentiate his product, individual firms will face a demand curve with a (negative/positive/zero) slope. At each point in time, profit-maximizing firms will try to produce at the output level where _____ equals _____. The assumption of freedom of entry and exit implies that in the long run under monopolistic competition firms will earn (negative/positive/zero) economic profit. If an individual firm is earning positive economic profits, the (entry/exit) of new firms will shift the demand curve down (and may raise costs) until the demand curve is just tangent to the (average/marginal) cost curve.

(2)   A market structure with only a few firms producing a similar or identical product, and in which some firms are very large, is called a(n) _____. Formal analysis of such market structures is difficult for when considering the decisions of one firm, one must also take into account the possible reactions of competitors. No single model describes all the possible outcomes under oligopoly, and economists have found it useful to consider a number of possible models and outcomes. If firms in an oligopolistic market band together and act like a single profit-maximizing monopolist, the resulting group is called a _____. If most firms look to pricing decisions made by a dominant firm, economists refer to the outcome as one of _____ _____.

Oligopolistic firms tend to be large corporations with professional managers. Some argue that managers are likely to be more interested in maximizing total revenue than in maximizing profits. This outcome is more likely if the compensation of managers depends more upon the size of the firm than upon its profitability. A firm interested in maximizing sales revenue will increase output until marginal revenue equals _____. Compared with profit maximization, sales maximization will mean a (higher/lower) price and a _____ quantity. (3)

Another traditional element of the analysis of oligopoly is the concept of a kinked demand curve. Such a demand curve comes from assuming that your competitors (will/will not) match any decrease in your price but (will/will not) match any increase in your price. As a result, there is a gap in the (marginal/average) revenue curve, and profit-maximizing prices may not change unless there is a significant shift in the marginal _____ curve. (4)

Game theory has been fruitfully used in the study of oligopolistic behavior by a number of economists. Game theory involves listing the possible outcomes of your moves and your opponents' countermoves in a(n) _____ matrix and then choosing an appropriate _____. (5)
If firms choose a strategy that protects them against the worst possible outcome, they are choosing a _____ strategy. If firms choose strategies to maximize payoffs assuming competitors stick to their announced strategies, the result is called a _____ equilibrium. In repeated games, _____ becomes important and may lead to higher long-run profits. Threats are likely to be most effective if they are _____.

The concept of perfectly contestable markets suggests that even oligopolists may be limited in their ability to earn monopolistic profits. The crucial condition for perfect contestability is that _____ and _____ are costless and unimpeded. In such a case, competitors would get into and out of the market whenever profits exceeded the _____ _____ of _____. While no market may be perfectly contestable, the extent to which markets are contestable will limit the ability of firms to charge monopolistic prices. (6)

■ IMPORTANT TERMS AND CONCEPTS QUIZ

Choose the best definition for each of the following terms.

1. _____ Monopolistic competition

2. _____ Excess capacity theorem

3. _____ Oligopoly

4. _____ Cartel

5. _____ Price leadership

6. _____ Sales maximization

7. _____ Kinked demand curve

8. _____ Game theory

9. _____ Price War

10. _____ Maximin criterion

11. _____ Nash equilibrium

12. _____ Prisoners' Dilemma

13. _____ Repeated game

14. _____ Credible threat

15. _____ Perfectly contestable markets

a. Group of sellers who join together to control production, sales, and price.

b. Industry with a single purchaser.

c. Notion that under monopolistic competition firms will tend to produce at less than minimum average cost.

d. Market in which entry and exit are costless and unimpeded.

e. Mathematical analysis of the behavior of competing firms involving strategic interactions.

f. Threat that would not harm threatener if carried out.

g. Many firms selling slightly different products.

h. Selecting the strategy that yields the maximum profit, assuming your opponent tries to damage you as much as possible.

i. Situation where one firm sets the price and other firms follow.

j. Situations that are played out again and again.

k. Situation where price declines are matched by competitors while price increases are not.

l. Best result when one assumes their opponent will stick to their chosen strategy.

m. Industry composed of a few large rival firms.

n. Expanding output to the point where marginal revenue equals zero.

o. Operating independently, players choose strategies that lead to a worse outcome than would be chosen if players could coordinate strategies.

p. Selling at a lower price than your competitor without regard to cost.

BASIC EXERCISES ■

These problems explore several important issues in the analysis of monopolistic competition and oligopoly.

TABLE 13-1

Quantity	Average Revenue	Average Cost	Total Revenue	Total Cost	Total Profit
600	$19	$21.67	$11,400	$13,002	$–1,602
800	17	17.50	13,600	14,000	–400
1,000	15	15.00	15,000	15,000	0
1,200	13	13.33	15,600	15,996	–396
1,400	11	12.14	15,400	16,996	–1,596

1. Our discussion of monopolistic competition argued that long-run equilibrium implies the firm's demand curve will be tangent to its average cost curve. We have also argued that profit maximization requires that marginal revenue equal marginal cost (or, alternatively, that firms should expand output as long as marginal revenue exceeds marginal cost). How do we know that marginal revenue equals marginal cost at the quantity given by the tangency between the demand curve and the average cost curve?

   a. Table 13-1 contains data on weekly costs and revenue for Alice's restaurant. Average revenue and average cost are plotted in Figure 13-1. Note that the demand curve is tangent to the average cost curve. Plot total profits in the left half of Figure 13-1. What output level maximizes profits? *1,000*

   b. Use the data in Table 13-1 to compute marginal revenue and marginal cost in Table 13-2. According to Table 13-2, what level of output maximizes profits? Why?

TABLE 13-2

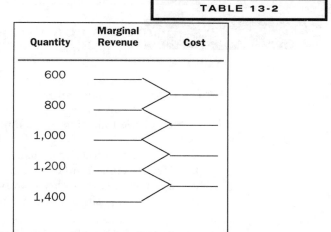

Quantity	Marginal Revenue	Cost
600		
800		
1,000		
1,200		
1,400		

Alice's Restaurant   **FIGURE 13-1**

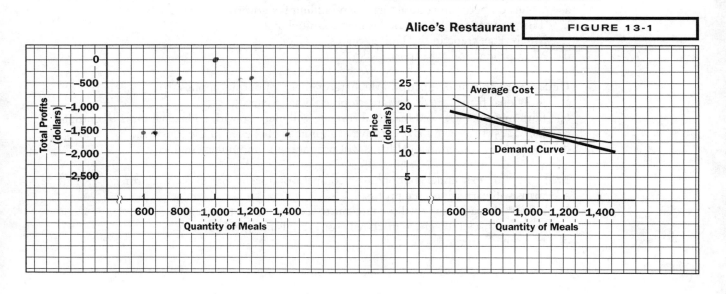

FIGURE 13-2   **Kinked Demand Curve**

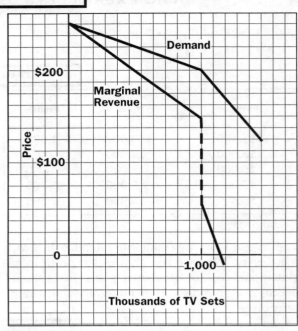

2. Figure 13-2 shows the kinked demand curve for a profit-maximizing firm that produces TV sets in an oligopolistic situation.

   a. What is the profit-maximizing level of output and the corresponding price if TVs can be produced at a marginal cost of $100?

      Quantity _____

      Price _____

   b. Assume that marginal cost increases by 40 percent to $140 per TV. Describe what happens to the profit-maximizing levels of price and quantity following this increase in marginal cost. _____

   c. What increase in marginal cost is necessary to induce a change in behavior on the part of this oligopolist and why? _____

   d. What decrease in marginal cost is necessary to induce a change in behavior on the part of this oligopolist and why? _____

■ SELF-TESTS FOR UNDERSTANDING

TEST A

Circle the most appropriate answer.

1. Which of the following is the important difference between perfect and monopolistic competition?
   a. Few sellers rather than many.
   b. Heterogeneous rather than homogeneous product.
   c. Barriers to entry rather than freedom of entry.
   d. Long-run positive economic profits rather than zero economic profits.

2. Monopolistic competition would be most appropriate when describing which of the following?
   a. Collusion between contractors when bidding for government contracts.
   b. The production of automobiles in the United States.
   c. Much retail trade in the United States.
   d. Most production for export.

3. Under monopolistic competition the heterogeneity of output implies that
   a. individual firms face downward-sloping demand curves.
   b. both marginal cost and marginal revenue will increase with additional units of output.
   c. individual firms can make positive economic profits even in the long run.
   d. in the long run, individual firms will produce at minimum average cost.

4. Free entry and exit under monopolistic competition means that in the long run
   a. firms will earn economic profits.
   b. a firm's demand curve will be tangent to its average cost curve.
   c. a firm will operate where marginal cost exceeds marginal revenue.
   d. only one firm can survive.

5. Under monopolistic competition firms are likely to produce
   a. to the left of the point of minimum average cost.
   b. at the point of minimum average cost.
   c. to the right of the point of minimum average cost.

6. Which of the following is most likely an example of monopolistic competition?
   a. The airline industry.
   b. Restaurants in Denver.
   c. Competition between automobile manufacturers.
   d. Cable television in Atlanta.

7. Which of the following characterizes a firm's short-run equilibrium under monopolistic competition?
   a. Production where average cost equals price.
   b. Production at minimum average cost.
   c. Production where marginal revenue equals marginal cost.
   d. Zero economic profits.

8. Which of the following does not characterize a firm's long-run equilibrium under monopolistic competition?
   a. Production where average cost equals price.
   b. Production at minimum average cost.
   c. Production where marginal revenue equals marginal cost.
   d. Zero economic profits.

9. If long-run economic profits are zero, we know that firms are producing where
   a. marginal cost equals marginal revenue.
   b. marginal revenue equals average cost.
   c. marginal cost equals price.
   d. average cost equals price.

10. The situation where a few large firms produce similar products is referred to as
    a. monopolistic competition.
    b. an oligopoly.
    c. contestable markets.
    d. price leadership.

11. Oligopoly may be associated with all but which one of the following?
    a. Price leadership.
    b. Collusive behavior.
    c. Advertising.
    d. Lots of firms.

12. If oligopolistic firms get together to carve up the market and act like a monopolist, the result is called a
    a. cabal.
    b. contestable market.
    c. cartel.
    d. natural monopoly.

13. A firm interested in maximizing sales revenue will produce at a point where
    a. marginal revenue equals marginal cost.
    b. average cost is minimized.
    c. marginal revenue equals zero.
    d. average revenue equals average cost.

14. A firm that maximizes sales revenues instead of profits will charge
    a.   a higher price.
    b.   a lower price.
    c.   the same price but will advertise more.

15. Game theory may be especially useful in analyzing a firm's behavior under conditions of
    a.   pure competition.
    b.   monopolistic competition.
    c.   oligopoly.
    d.   pure monopoly.

16. The term *payoff matrix* refers to
    a.   bribes paid by cartels.
    b.   the structure of winnings in an office pool on the NCAA basketball championship.
    c.   the set of possible outcomes in a game theory situation.
    d.   players' shares in the NFL playoffs.

17. The term *kinked demand curve* refers to
    a.   economists' inability to draw straight lines.
    b.   the demand for X-rated movies.
    c.   industries with substantial economies of scale.
    d.   a situation where competitors match price decreases but not price increases.

18. If a firm faces a kinked demand curve, the demand curve for price increases will likely
    a.   be steeper than for price decreases.
    b.   have a positive slope.
    c.   be more elastic than for price decreases.
    d.   be less elastic than for price decreases.

19. Markets can be perfectly contestable if
    a.   products are identical.
    b.   entry and exit is free and easy.
    c.   only two firms are bidding against each other.
    d.   long-run economic profits are zero.

20. All but which one of the following market structures are likely to result in a misallocation of resources?
    a.   Perfect competition.
    b.   Monopolistic competition.
    c.   Oligopoly.
    d.   Monopoly.

TEST B

Circle T or F for true or false.

T   F   1. Firms that operate under conditions of oligopoly are likely to engage in lots of advertising.

T   F   2. Heterogeneity of output is an important feature of monopolistic competition.

T   F   3. Under monopolistic competition, freedom of entry and exit will guarantee that a firm always earns a zero economic profit, in both the short run and the long run.

T   F   4. Under monopolistic competition, marginal revenue equals marginal cost in the short run but not in the long run.

T   F   5. There would be an unambiguous social gain if in a market with monopolistic competition some firms were forced by regulation to stop producing.

T   F   6. Oligopoly is characterized by a small number of firms, some very large, producing an identical or similar product.

T   F   7. Arrangements such as price leadership and tacit collusion can be important in oligopolistic markets.

T   F   8. A firm that maximizes sales revenue will typically charge a higher price than a firm that maximizes profits.

T   F   9. An oligopolist facing a kinked demand curve will see a more elastic demand curve for price increases than for price decreases.

T   F   10. Perfectly contestable markets are only possible when there are a large number of competing firms.

SUPPLEMENTARY EXERCISES ■

1. The equations below for demand and total cost underlie the first problem in the Basic Exercises. Use these equations to derive explicit expressions for marginal cost, marginal revenue, and average cost. Now solve for the level of output that maximizes profits. Compare your answer with the results you obtained in the Basic Exercises.

$$Q = 2500 - 100P \text{ (demand curve)}$$

$$TC = 10,000 + 5Q \text{ (total cost curve)}$$

where Q = total quantity, P = price, and TC = total cost.

2. This problem illustrates the difference between maximizing profits and maximizing sales. Demand and total cost are given by the equations below.

Demand

$$Q = 16,000 - 200P$$

Total Cost

$$TC = .00000015625Q^3 - .003125Q^2 + 40.625Q$$

a) If the firm maximizes profits, what are output, price, and profits?
b) If the firm maximizes sales revenue, what are output, price, and profits?
c) Is it true that maximizing sales revenue involves a higher quantity, lower price, and lower profits?

3. For an interesting discussion of apparent tacit collusion in practice and how academic research along with the resulting publicity changed behavior, see "Policy Watch: Did Nasdaq Market Makers Implicitly Collude?" William G. Christie and Paul H. Schultz, *Journal of Economic Perspectives* (Vol. 9, Number 3) Summer 1995, pp. 199–208. Figure 1 is a dramatic piece of evidence.

ECONOMICS IN ACTION ■

New planes and the 1990 recession left airlines in the United States with more seats than passengers. Fierce price competition to fill seats resulted in large reported losses that continued for several years. In the spring of 1992, Robert Crandall, president of American Airlines, introduced a fare structure that was intended to limit the number of low-priced tickets that airlines had been offering. *The New York Times* described Crandall's announcement as an attempt "to discipline the industry and the business traveler by curbing the use of discount fares and other loopholes" (May 29, 1992). Seven weeks later when Northwest Airlines tried offering half-priced tickets to families, American responded with a general two-for-one offer that was matched by other airlines. The result was a bargain for travelers and continued red ink for airlines.

In the winter of 1993, Northwest Airlines tried again, offering discounts of 20 to 40 percent to groups of two to four travelers when they purchased 14-day advance tickets. When these discounts were matched by Delta and American, Northwest withdrew its fare reductions and also rescinded a fare increase that was to have been implemented following the availability of the discount fares. Michael Levine, Northwest's executive vice-president for marketing, said, "Unfortunately, competitive response eliminated the possibility of realizing the revenue enhancement that we and the industry need. Our competitors choose to broaden our offer and risk industry pricing havoc" (*Minneapolis Star Tribune*).

1. How do the concepts of price leadership and a kinked demand curve help to explain:
   a. The fare structure that American Airlines tried to introduce in 1992?
   b. The response by other airlines to meet or exceed the price reductions offered by Northwest in 1992 and 1993?
   c. Northwest's decision to abandon its previously announced fare increase in 1993?

■ STUDY QUESTIONS

1. How does monopolistic competition differ from perfect competition?

2. What is meant by the notion that monopolistic competition leads to excess capacity?

3. "As monopolistic competition leads to excess capacity, there will be an unambiguous social gain if government regulation reduces the number of firms and eliminates the excess capacity." Do you agree or disagree? Why?

4. What difference would it make if a firm acts to maximize profits or to maximize sales?

5. As a cartel is assumed to act to maximize profits, why do economists believe that cartels are difficult to establish and tend to self-destruct?

6. How can a kinked demand curve help explain price stickiness in an oligopolistic setting?

7. "Even if there are few firms in a market, the power of these firms to charge high prices will be limited if markets are contestable." Why is free and easy exit as important to contestable markets as free and easy entry?

8. What is the maximin criterion for choosing among strategies in a game theory setting?

9. Why is reputation an important element in repeated games?

14

THE MARKET MECHANISM: SHORTCOMINGS AND REMEDIES

Important Terms and Concepts

OPPORTUNITY COST

RESOURCE MISALLOCATION

PRODUCTION POSSIBILITIES FRONTIER

EXTERNALITIES (DETRIMENTAL AND BENEFICIAL)

MARGINAL SOCIAL COST (MSC)

MARGINAL PRIVATE COST (MPC)

PUBLIC GOODS

PRIVATE GOODS

DEPLETABILITY

EXCLUDABILITY

IRREVERSIBLE DECISIONS

COST DISEASE OF PERSONAL SERVICES

ASYMMETRIC INFORMATION

PRINCIPALS

AGENTS

RENT SEEKING

MORAL HAZARD

LEARNING OBJECTIVES

After completing this chapter, you should be able to:

■ list the major shortcomings of free markets.

■ explain why detrimental externalities mean that marginal private costs will understate marginal social costs.

■ explain why the existence of externalities, whether beneficial or detrimental, will result in an inefficient allocation of resources.

■ describe the important characteristics of public goods.

■ explain why these characteristics mean that private profit-maximizing firms will not supply public goods.

■ explain why some people believe that free markets are unlikely to result in an appropriate allocation of resources between the present and the future.

■ explain how uneven productivity growth results in the cost disease of personal services.

■   **CHAPTER REVIEW**

This chapter lists seven issues often seen as shortcomings of unregulated markets. Some have been discussed in previous chapters, and several others will receive a more complete treatment later. The discussion here focuses on four of the seven: externalities, public goods, the trade-off between present and future consumption, and the cost disease of personal services.

The material in Chapter 4 introduced the concept of an economy's *production possibilities frontier.* We saw that the slope of the frontier measured how much the output of one commodity must decrease in order to increase the production of another commodity. In other words, the slope of the production

(1)   possibilities frontier measures the _____ cost of increasing the output of any one commodity.

Chapter 11 explained how a market economy can lead to an *efficient allocation of resources;* that is, one where marginal utilities and marginal costs are equal. If the marginal utility of the last unit of some good is not equal to the marginal cost of producing that last unit, the result is a *misallocation of resources.* The virtue of competitive markets is that firms maximize profits by producing where price equals

(2)   _____, and individuals maximize by consuming where price equals _____ _____. Thus, our condition for an efficient allocation is automatically satisfied. An economy that satisfies all of the assumptions necessary for perfect competition will automatically result in an efficient allocation of resources. The economy will operate (<u>on/inside</u>) the production possibilities frontier.

Many of the reasons mentioned at the beginning of the chapter may imply that an economy may not satisfy the conditions for perfect competition. In this case the wrong prices may get established, leading to an inefficient allocation of resources. If price is greater than marginal cost, the economy will

(3)   tend to produce too (<u>much/little</u>) of a good to maximize consumer benefits. There may be a case for government intervention to help establish prices that will lead to an efficient allocation.

EXTERNALITIES

Many economic activities impose incidental burdens or benefits on other individuals for which there

(4)   is no compensation. These sorts of activities are said to involve _____. If an activity, such as pollution, harms others and there is no compensation, we say that there are

_____ externalities. If an activity benefits others who do not pay for the benefits they receive, we say that there are _____ externalities.

Externalities imply that many activities are likely to have private benefits and costs that are different from social benefits and costs. In the case of detrimental externalities, social costs will be (higher/lower) than private costs, while in the case of beneficial externalities, social benefits will be _____ than private benefits. (5)

Private profit-maximizing firms will base their production decisions on (private/social) costs. If there are detrimental externalities, the result will be an (efficient/inefficient) use of resources. From a social viewpoint, too (much/little) of the commodity in question will be produced. In the case of beneficial externalities, unregulated markets are likely to produce (less/more) output than is socially desirable. Schemes for taxes and subsidies are, in principle, capable of adjusting private costs and benefits to more adequately reflect social costs and benefits. (6)

PUBLIC GOODS

Most goods provided by private profit-maximizing firms have two primary characteristics. The first is that the more of a good you use, the less there is for someone else. This characteristic is called _____. The second is that you must pay for goods in order to use them. This characteristic is called _____. Goods that have neither of these characteristics are called _____ goods. Things like national defense, police protection, beautiful parks, and clean streets are examples of such goods. (7)

Once public goods are provided to one individual, their benefits cannot easily be restricted to just a few people. It is (difficult/easy) to exclude nonpayers. As a result, it is difficult to get individuals to pay for the goods they can enjoy for free when someone else is paying for them. This is sometimes referred to as the free-_____ problem. (8)

Besides the problem of lack of excludability, one person's use of public goods, such as enjoying a park, does not usually deplete the supply for others. In technical language, the marginal cost of serving additional users is _____. This contrasts with private goods, where providing additional units of output does require additional resources and does entail a positive marginal cost. An efficient allocation of resources requires that price equal marginal social cost. The clear implication is that (9) from an efficiency standpoint, public goods should be priced at _____ and one should not

be surprised if profit-maximizing firms fail to provide public goods.

PRESENT AND FUTURE CONSUMPTION

The productive use of resources is time-specific. Loafing today will not make tomorrow twice as long.

A machine that is idle one day does not mean that twice as many machine hours will be available the

next day. While the use of resources is time-specific, the consumption of output is not. Output can be

saved, either directly by adding to inventories in warehouses or indirectly by building plants and

machines that increase future production possibilities. Thus, an economy does have the ability to

transfer consumption through time by acts of saving and investment.

The rate of interest is an important determinant of how much investment will take place. A num-

ber of observers have questioned whether the private economy will result in interest rates and invest-

ment spending that are socially optimal. In the real world, monetary and fiscal policies can be used to

manipulate interest rates and will, hence, influence investment in ways that may not correspond to the

best plans for the future. Some observers, such as the English economist A. G. Pigou, have argued that

people are simply shortsighted when it comes to saving for the future.

Individual investment projects often entail great risk for the individual investors but little risk for

(10)   society. Bankruptcy may wipe out an investor's financial investment, but it (does/does not) destroy

buildings and machines. These capital goods will still be around for others to use. It has been argued

that the high individual risk will result in a level of investment that is (less/more) than socially optimal.

(11)   Many decisions, such as damming a canyon, are essentially _____, and

some people are concerned that unregulated market decisions in these cases do not adequately repre-

sent the interests of future generations. These arguments suggest that even competitive markets may

result in inappropriate decisions about saving and investments.

COST DISEASE OF PERSONAL SERVICES

Many services—doctor visits, education, police protection—require mainly labor input and offer

(12)   (limited/substantial) opportunities for increases in labor productivity. By contrast, increasing mecha-

nization and technological innovations have resulted in substantial increases in labor productivity in the production of many commodities. Increased labor productivity has led to higher wages for workers in these industries. Since workers can move among occupations, the wages of teachers, nurses and police, for example, have had to increase to remain competitive with opportunities in other jobs. In manufacturing industries, increased labor productivity helps offset the cost pressures from higher wages. In service industries there are limited opportunities for increases in labor productivity to help contain cost pressures. The result is that many personal services have become more expensive over time because of the uneven pattern of increases in labor productivity. Increases in productivity always make an economy better off in the sense that it can now produce more of all goods, including personal services. But at the same time, society will find that lagging productivity in service industries means that the cost of these services has increased. Concerns about controlling costs may be misdirected if the major problem is the natural market response to differential productivity growth.

■ IMPORTANT TERMS AND CONCEPTS QUIZ

Choose the best definition for each of the following terms.

1. _____ Opportunity cost

2. _____ Resource misallocation

3. _____ Production possibilities frontier

4. _____ Externalities

5. _____ Marginal private cost

6. _____ Marginal social cost

7. _____ Public good

8. _____ Private good

9. _____ Depletability

10. _____ Excludability

11. _____ Cost disease of personal services

12. _____ Asymmetric information

13. _____ Principals

14. _____ Agents

15. _____ Rent seeking

16. _____ Moral hazard

a. Tendency of clients who have the lowest risks to be the most likely insurance customers.

b. Results of activities that provide incidental harm or benefit to others.

c. Tendency of the real cost of services to increase because of difficulty of increasing productivity.

d. Decision makers who delegate their power to others.

e. Graph depicting the combinations of various goods that can be produced with available resources and existing technology.

f. Commodity or service whose benefits are not depleted by an additional user and for which it is difficult to exclude people from enjoying its benefits.

g. Unproductive activity in pursuit of profit.

h. Utility of a change in output differs from its opportunity cost.

i. Parties to a transaction know different things about the item to be exchanged.

j. Marginal private cost plus costs imposed on others.

k. Commodity or service whose benefits are depleted by an additional user and for which people are excluded from its benefits unless they pay.

l. The ability to keep someone who does not pay from enjoying a commodity.

m. Tendency of insurance to encourage risk taking.

n. Share of marginal cost for an activity that those who engage in the activity pay.

o. Those to whom decision-making authority is delegated.

p. Commodity is used up when consumed.

q. Forgone value of next best alternative that is not chosen.

This exercise is designed to illustrate the cost disease of personal services.

Table 14-1 has spaces to compute the costs of producing both widgets and police services; both are assumed to be produced with only labor input. (Wages for police officers and for workers in the widget factory are assumed to be equal, as individuals can choose between these occupations.)

1. Fill in the missing spaces in the first column to determine the cost per widget of producing 240,000 widgets and the cost per hour of 200,000 hours of police services.

2. The first entry in the second column assumes that labor productivity in the production of widgets has risen by 4.17 percent. The earnings of widget workers and police officers are assumed to increase by the same percentage as productivity. Now fill in the rest of the second column. What has happened to the average cost of producing one widget? What about the cost of producing one hour of police services?

3. The first entry in column 3 assumes that the growth in average labor productivity continues for another 10 years. Again, the growth in earnings is assumed to match the growth in productivity. Fill in the rest of column 3. What is the increase in the cost of producing one widget? _____. What about the cost of one hour of police services? _____.

4. One way to hold the line on police costs is to refuse to increase salaries for police officers. Another way is to reduce the number of police officers. What are the long-run implications of both these policies?

TABLE 14-1

Costs of Producing 240,000 Widgets

	(1)	(2)	(3)
Widgets per worker	1,920	2,000	3,000
Number of workers[a]	125	_____	_____
Annual earnings per worker	$21,120	$22,000	$33,000
Total labor costs (total cost)	_____	_____	_____
Cost per widget	_____	_____	_____

Costs of Producing 200,000 Hours of Police Services

	(1)	(2)	(3)
Hours per police officer	2,000	2,000	2,000
Number of police officers[b]	100	_____	_____
Annual earnings per police officer	$21,120	$22,000	$33,000
Total labor cost (total cost)	_____	_____	_____
Cost per hour of police services	_____	_____	_____

[a]240,000 ÷ widgets per worker
[b]200,000 ÷ hours per police officer

■ SELF-TESTS FOR UNDERSTANDING

TEST A

Circle the most appropriate answer.

1. The condition for efficient resource allocation is
   a. MC = MR.
   b. *P* = Average Revenue.
   c. MU = MC.
   d. MU = Price.

2. Which of the following is a clear indicator of a misallocation of resources?
   a. Barney and Michelle, who subscribe to *Gourmet* magazine, despair over the increasing number of fast-food outlets.
   b. In the long run, farmer Fran makes zero economic profit.
   c. After careful study, economists have concluded that the economy of Arcadia is operating at a point inside its production possibilities frontier.
   d. The latest census survey indicates that the top 10 percent of the income distribution has an average income that is more than 12 times that of the bottom 10 percent.

3. The term *externalities* is used by economists to describe
   a. economic decisions by foreign governments.
   b. occupants of extraterrestrial spaceships.
   c. all economic activity that takes place outside the classroom.
   d. activities that impose costs or benefits on third parties.

4. Economists expect profit-maximizing competitive firms to expand production as long as price exceeds
   a. marginal social cost.
   b. marginal utility.
   c. marginal private cost.
   d. average cost.

5. Which of the following is an externality?
   a. Imperfect information.
   b. Your pride in the new stereo system you just purchased at a bargain price.
   c. Natural monopolies, such as the local electric utility.
   d. The new road built for the NASA tracking station that has substantially reduced transportation costs for local farmers.

6. A detrimental externality arises when
   a. the actions of a firm provide unintended benefits for third parties.
   b. having bought insurance, Jason figures he doesn't need to buy as sturdy a bike lock.
   c. a firm's managers cannot be closely monitored by stockholders.
   d. the actions of a firm impose costs on families living near the firm's plants.

7. In the presence of detrimental externalities, marginal private cost is usually
   a. less than marginal social cost.
   b. equal to marginal social cost.
   c. greater than marginal social cost.

8. Economists argue that if the production of paper is associated with detrimental externalities, a free market will likely
   a. produce more paper than is socially desirable.
   b. produce less paper than is socially desirable.
   c. produce the socially optimal quantity of paper in spite of the detrimental externality.

9. If the production of gizmos involves beneficial externalities, then it is likely that
    a. marginal private benefits are less than marginal social benefits.
    b. a free market will produce too many gizmos.
    c. a tax on the production of gizmos will lead to a more efficient allocation.
    d. the use of gizmos does not involve depletion.

10. Economists define public goods as
    a. all things the government spends money on.
    b. economic activities that impose costs or benefits on third parties.
    c. goods and services that many people can enjoy at the same time and from which it is difficult to exclude potential customers who do not want to pay.
    d. goods and services that should receive public subsidy such as improved health care and better housing for poor families.

11. Economists expect that profit-maximizing firms in competitive markets will produce _____ public goods.
    a. too few
    b. too many
    c. about the right quantity
    d. no

12. For a pure public good, the marginal cost of serving an additional user is equal to
    a. marginal social cost.
    b. marginal private cost.
    c. zero.
    d. marginal utility.

13. Which of the following does not have the characteristics of a public good?
    a. Clean rivers.
    b. Visits to the doctor.
    c. Police and fire protection.
    d. Unscrambled radio and television signals.

14. The "free-rider" problem refers to
    a. the difficulty of stopping kids from sneaking onto the local merry-go-round.
    b. the difficulty of getting people to voluntarily contribute to pay for public goods.
    c. using subsidies to encourage the production of goods with beneficial externalities.
    d. increasing problems with hitchhikers on the interstate highways.

15. Which of the following is *not* an argument that free markets will result in an inappropriate amount of saving and investment?
    a. Investment projects are often riskier to individuals than to the community.
    b. During periods of inflation, nominal interest rates will rise to incorporate expectations of continuing inflation.
    c. Due to "defective telescopic faculties," people do not give enough consideration to the future.
    d. Many decisions concerning natural resources are made without enough consideration given to their irreversible consequences.

16. Which of the following explains the cost disease of personal services?
    a. The supply effects of price controls, such as rent control.
    b. The existence of monopoly elements in the economy.
    c. Detrimental externalities.
    d. The uneven prospects for improved labor productivity in different sectors of the economy.

17. Which of the following is *not* likely to suffer from the cost disease of personal services?
    a. Individual piano lessons.
    b. The production of television sets.
    c. Small liberal arts colleges that maintain an unchanged student-faculty ratio.
    d. Orchestras and symphonies.

18. Which of the following is an example of rent seeking?
    a. The efforts of lobbyists to get Congress to restrict the import of foreign steel.
    b. Cleon's efforts to find an inexpensive apartment before school starts.
    c. The hours Juan and Ramona spend working in their own restaurant.
    d. The time and effort Julie spends studying to be a doctor.

19. As used by economists, the term *moral hazard* refers to the
    a. temptations of large cities on impressionable teenagers.
    b. state of much television programming.
    c. tendency of insurance to make people less concerned about risky behavior.
    d. widespread incidence of sexually transmitted diseases among single men and women.

20. Decisions by company managers that make their own lives more comfortable at the cost of reducing stockholder profits are examples of
    a. moral hazards.
    b. principal-agent problems.
    c. detrimental externalities.
    d. public goods.

TEST B

Circle T or F for true or false.

T   F   1. An unregulated market economy would never have business cycles.

T   F   2. Externalities, whether beneficial or detrimental, imply that marginal social cost is always less than marginal private cost.

T   F   3. An activity that causes damage to someone else and for which there is no compensation is said to involve a detrimental externality.

T   F   4. A beneficial externality is likely to result in marginal private benefits exceeding marginal social benefits.

T   F   5. Economists define public goods as anything for which the government spends money.

T   F   6. The fact that it is difficult to restrict the use of public goods to those who are willing to pay is the problem of depletability.

T   F   7. The provision of public goods is complicated by the "free-rider" problem.

T   F   8. The fact that public goods are not depleted by use implies that the marginal cost of providing the goods to one more consumer is zero.

T   F   9. The interest rate plays an important role in the allocation of resources between the present and the future, because it affects the profitability of investment projects.

T   F   10. Many investment projects will entail less risk for the individual investor than for the community as a whole.

1. Consider the economy of Beethovia, which produces two goods: widgets and music recitals. Widgets are manufactured with capital and labor according to the following production function:

$$W = 60L^{1/2} K^{1/2},$$

where L = number of workers producing widgets and K = number of machines. Music recitals are labor intensive and produced according to the following production function:

$$M = 50 \times L.$$

Initially there are 40,000 workers in Beethovia, meaning that the sum of labor allocated to the production of widgets or recitals cannot exceed 40,000, and there are 22,500 machines, or K = 22,500.

a. Draw the production possibilities frontier for Beethovia showing the trade-off between the production of widgets and recitals. (It is probably easiest to arbitrarily fix the number of recitals and then calculate the maximum production of widgets with the remaining labor and all the machines.)

b. Competitive markets have resulted in 39,601 widget workers and 399 musicians. At this allocation, what is the marginal product and average product of labor in the production of widgets? In the production of recitals?

c. Saving and investment by the people of Beethovia have increased the number of machines to 28,900. At the initial allocation of labor, but with the new number of machines, what is the marginal and average product of labor in the production of widgets? What has happened to the productivity of workers in the production of recitals?

d. What has happened to the opportunity cost of music recitals; that is, what is the new slope of the production possibilities frontier at the allocation specified in question b? To answer this question, either draw a new production possibilities frontier or derive a mathematical expression for the slope of the frontier.

e. If you have answered question d correctly, you should have determined that the cost of recitals has increased. Recitals suffer from the cost disease of personal services. At the same time, how can you show that the increase in productivity has made Beethovia unambiguously richer?

2. Go to the library or bookstore and get a copy of *Encounters with the Archdruid* (New York: Farrar, Straus and Giroux, 1971) by John McPhee. The book reports on three encounters between David Brower, who was president of the Sierra Club, and other individuals who want to dam the Colorado River, build a copper mine in the Cascades, and develop Hilton Head Island. Many think that McPhee's description of the raft trip down the Colorado River with Brower and Floyd Dominy, who was head of the Bureau of Reclamation, is especially good.

a. Whose position do you favor?

b. Is Brower always right? Is he ever right?

STANDARDS OR TAXES?

In 1975, after the first increase in oil prices, the Energy Policy and Conservation Act mandated minimum corporate average fuel economy (CAFE) standards for new passenger cars sold in the United States. Originally established at 18.5 miles per gallon (mpg) for 1978, the CAFE standards are now 27.5 mpg for cars and 20.7 mpg for light trucks, a category that includes sport utility vehicles. Under the original policy, CAFE standards were to increase still further to reduce American dependency on foreign oil. Increases are now proposed to help reduce carbon dioxide emissions. However since the mid-1990s Congress has frozen CAFE standards.

Writing in *The Journal of Economic Perspectives*, Spring 1992, economist Robert Crandall compared the efficiency of CAFE standards with that of a fuel tax. Crandall noted that cars consume 55 percent of motor vehicle fuel and account for about 13 percent of carbon dioxide emissions. New cars make up about 7 percent of all cars on the road and account for 9 percent of passenger car miles driven. As petroleum is used for things other than motor vehicle fuels, Crandall estimated that new cars account for about 2 percent of annual petroleum consumption.

He argued that while CAFE standards will eventually improve the fuel efficiency of cars, they have some perverse effects in the short run. By increasing the cost of new cars, higher CAFE standards induce some drivers to hold on to their less efficient older cars. By lowering the marginal cost of driving, higher CAFE standards might increase the number of miles driven by new car owners. In contrast, a fuel tax has opposite effects. It provides an incentive to get rid of older, less efficient cars for newer cars while increasing the marginal cost of driving for all drivers. Crandall argued that a fuel tax also has the edge on safety considerations as it leads to a greater reduction in total miles driven and induces less vehicle downsizing than higher CAFE standards. While some worry about the impact of higher gasoline taxes on the poor, Crandall cited research that suggested automatic adjustment of transfer payments to increases in the consumer price index may offset higher gasoline taxes for poor households.

CAFE standards were originally preferred by legislators because their cost is hidden in the price of new cars. An increased gasoline tax would have been quite visible. Crandall cited a study by Charles River Associates that estimated it would take a tax of 25 cents a gallon to match the fuel savings of a 40 mpg CAFE standard. If the tax were to be levied on all petroleum consumption, the study by Charles River Associates estimates that it need only have been about 10 cents to induce an equivalent reduction in petroleum use. Crandall estimated that CAFE standards would cost about 7 to 10 times as much as a broad-based petroleum tax to achieve the same reduction in oil consumption.

1. Which would you favor to reduce oil consumption, higher CAFE standards or higher gasoline taxes? Which do you think would be more effective? Which do you think is fairer? Why? Do you think that reducing oil consumption should be a national priority?

■ STUDY QUESTIONS

1. Why do economists argue that externalities, whether beneficial or detrimental, are likely to lead to a misallocation of resources?

2. Why does a free market tend to overproduce goods with detrimental externalities?

3. Why does a free market tend to underproduce goods with beneficial externalities?

4. How can the price system help correct the problems of externalities?

5. What are the distinguishing characteristics of a public good as compared with a private good?

6. Why can't we leave the provision of public goods to profit-maximizing firms?

7. Do you believe that unregulated private markets will save too little or too much? Why?

8. Colleges and universities have been urged to hold tuition increases under the inflation rate. What does the concept of the cost disease of personal services suggest would happen if such a policy were followed for the next 10 years?

9. What is rent seeking behavior and why do people engage in it?

10. Is direct government regulation the appropriate response to all market failures?

THE MICROECONOMICS OF INNOVATION: PRIME ENGINE OF GROWTH

LEARNING OBJECTIVES

After completing this chapter, you should be able to:

■ explain the importance of innovations for economic growth.

■ explain the difference between process and product innovation.

■ explain the difference between basic and applied research.

■ explain how the concepts of marginal cost and marginal revenue can help a firm determine how much to spend on research and development

■ describe some of the arrangements firms might use to control the risk associated with specific R&D projects.

■ describe the three growth creating properties of innovations.

■ evaluate the arguments about whether free economies invest enough in R&D and describe the role of patents in dealing with this issue.

■ analyze the impact of process innovations on price and output.

Important Terms and Concepts

INNOVATION

CAPITALISM

INDUSTRIAL REVOLUTION

RESEARCH AND DEVELOPMENT (R&D)

TECHNOLOGY TRADING

RATCHET

PATENT

BASIC RESEARCH

APPLIED RESEARCH

PRODUCT INNOVATION

PROCESS INNOVATION

■   **CHAPTER REVIEW**

This chapter reviews some of the microeconomic forces behind the process of innovation. Up to the Industrial Revolution, economic growth as we know it today hardly existed. Many products and processes at the beginning of the 18th century would have been familiar to Roman citizens. The past 200 years however, have seen a dramatic change. Labor at the beginning of the 21st century is about

(1)   _____times more productivity that at the beginning of the 19th century. In America in 1800 close to 90 percent of the worked force was employed on farms. Now less than 3 percent is. What explains this dramatic increase in labor productivity and why have capitalist economies been so successful at it?

Major factors responsible for the growth in labor productivity include education and experience of the labor force, investment in plant and equipment, and the almost continuous development and intro-

(2)   duction of new products and production processes or _____. Today it seems that competition between firms in innovation is as important as price competition.

Research and development activities are organized expenditures by firms to develop new products and processes. That is rather than leaving innovation to chance, firms make clear decisions to invest in innovation. R&D budgets are like other business decisions and can be analyzed using the tools and concepts we have developed in earlier chapters. One cannot guarantee that every dollar spent on R&D will lead to major breakthroughs, so to some extent, a firm's R&D efforts are like choosing a portfolio of stocks. There are likely to be benefits in diversification and the returns from broad based efforts may be more predictable than the returns to specific projects. As with other business decisions, firms should expand R&D expenditures as long as the expected marginal returns are greater than the mar-

(3)   ginal _____.

Specific innovations often lead to patents that give a firm a monopoly on the new product or process for a period of time. Other firms will try to imitate successful innovations or may be willing to pay fees for the use of important innovations. So while specific innovations may be wildly profitable, the returns to innovation as a whole do not appear to offer above normal profits, a result that should not

(4)   be surprising under conditions of free _____.

Why is innovation such an important part of capitalist economies? Why has innovation become such an important part of competition? Some have suggested that the kinked revenue model is an important part of the explanation. If a firm does not keep up with the competition in terms of the attractiveness of its products or the efficiency of its production processes, it will lose out. As a result, a firm that spends less on R&D runs the risk of not keeping up. There is little inventive to spend more than the average, as your competitors will only match your efforts. However, when someone's efforts have made an important difference, competitors need to increase their R&D spending to keep up. The process works like a ratchet that helps to sustain R&D spending.

Innovations have important impacts for the economy as a whole. There are three important characteristics of innovations. 1) Many innovations enlarge the range of choices for consumers and producers, that is they create _____ change. 2) Many innovations have characteristics of public goods in that the use of new production process by one firm that lowers cost does not preclude its use by other firms. 3) Many innovations have an accelerator like feature as they allow the economy to grow faster by permitting firms to produce more with the same resources or to produce more valuable products. A constant rate of innovation should lead to a sustained rate of growth in output.   (5)

Do firms spend enough on innovation? Those who are concerned that firms spend too little point out that most innovations have beneficial externalities, that is new and enhanced products and production processes offers significant benefits to lots of people in terms of better commodities and lower prices. As a result the social benefits to innovation may exceed the private returns and profit maximizing firms may stop short of a social optimum. The patent system is an attempt to overcome this problem as its provides exclusive monopoly or licensing rights for a period of time. Competitive pressures to match the innovative efforts of competitors also works to increase spending on innovations.

Individual R&D projects can be quite risky. For example, it has been estimated that only 6 to 7 percent of new products make it to market. Large firms can begin to reduce the risk of R&D by sponsoring numerous projects. Firms can also enter into arrangements to share the innovations of other firms through technology _____ and cross _____ of   (6) patents.

Do consumer benefits from innovation? Product innovations mean new or enhanced products but at what cost? Process innovations that lower the marginal cost of production should mean an unambiguous gain for consumers through (<u>higher/lower</u>) output and _____ prices.

■ IMPORTANT TERMS AND CONCEPTS QUIZ

Choose the best definition for each of the following terms.

1. _____ Product innovation
2. _____ Process innovation
3. _____ Capitalism
4. _____ Industrial Revolution
5. _____ Research and development
6. _____ Technology trading
7. _____ Ratchet
8. _____ Patent
9. _____ Basic research
10. _____ Applied research

a. Research on scientific knowledge and general principles.

b. Implementing new ways of production.

c. Production processes controlled by private firms with minimal government control.

d. Introduction of new or major modification of existing products.

e. Growth in economic output.

f. Limited term monopoly on the use of new innovation.

g. Shared use of technological innovations among firms.

h. Research on specific products or processes.

i. Permits increases but prevents decreases.

j. New technologies that spurred economic growth in England toward the end of the 18th century.

k. Organized efforts to invent new and improve existing products and processes.

■ BASIC EXERCISE

DOES IT REALLY MATTER?

Why all the fuss about innovation? Can a one percent difference in the rate of economic growth make all that much difference? Press the multiplication key on your calculator 100 times or use a microcomputer or financial calculator to complete Table 15-1 to see if the rate of economic growth will make any difference for your great grand children?

TABLE 15-1   The Impact of Differences in Economic Growth on GDP per Capita

Year	Growth Rate of GDP Per Capita				
	0%	0.5%	1.0%	1.5%	2.0%
2000	$31,000	$31,000	$31,000	$31,000	$31,000
2100	_____	_____	_____	_____	_____

SELF-TESTS FOR UNDERSTANDING   ■

TEST A

Circle the most appropriate answer.

1. Over the past 200 years, labor productivity has
    a. doubled.
    b. increased 10 fold.
    c. increased 20 fold.
    d. increased 100 fold.

2. The Industrial Revolution started in
    a. Russia.
    b. the United States.
    c. England.
    d. Germany.

3. For the 1500 years before the Industrial Revolution, economic growth in Europe
    a. was actually negative.
    b. was close to zero.
    c. averaged 2.5 percent per year.
    d. resulted in labor that was 20 times more productive than in Roman times.

4. Which of the following is not usually cited as an important sources of growth in labor productivity?
    a. innovations.
    b. education and experience of the workforce
    c. investment in factories and machine tools.
    d. government regulation.

5. What type of economy has shown the strongest record of innovation and growth?
    a. Socialist economies.
    b. Soviet style central planning.
    c. Capitalist economies.
    d. Feudalism.

6. The text argues that which two of the following have played especially crucial roles in the ability of capitalist economies to sustain high rates of innovation?
    a. The encouragement of cartels in key sectors of the economy.
    b. The use of innovation as a way of competing with rivals.
    c. Targeted investments by the government in key sectors of the economy.
    d. Markets that are free from tight regulation and limiting customs.

7. Firms should expand spending on R&D as long as
    a. the average revenue from all of a firms innovations exceeds average cost.
    b. the marginal revenue from expected innovations exceeds marginal cost.
    c. the results are patentable.
    d. it is on applied rather than basic research.

8. Under conditions of free entry one would expect that the returns to innovation as a whole would be
    a. very high.
    b. equal to market average rates of return.
    c. zero.
    d. negative.

9. Which is an example of a process innovation?
    a. A university researcher identifies the electrical properties of a new synthetic material.
    b. A chemist for DuPont discovers a new fabric
    c. A partnership between a history and computer science student results in a new computer-based action game set in 16th century Japan.
    d. An engineer for Ford discovers a new way of rust proofing car bodies that saves $150 per car.

10. Which is an example of a product innovation?
    a. Post-it notes.
    b. A government grant to a researcher who is studying polymer chemistry.
    c. Boeing reorganizes its production line to enhance worker productivity.
    d. Einstein's theory of relativity.

11. Which is an example of a basic research?
    a. New methods for making stronger sheets of glass for larger windows.
    b. New designs from Ralph Lauren.
    c. The development of an artificial kidney.
    d. The discovery of DNA.

12. Which of the following is most likely to support basic research?
    a. The National Association of Manufacturers.
    b. Microsoft.
    c. The federal government.
    d. Ford Motor Company.

13. The term "technology trading"
    a. refers to the venture capitalists who specialize in funding high-tech start up companies.
    b. refers to the export and import of high tech capital goods.
    c. was coined by the stock broker who first sold shares of IBM.
    d. is a way that firms can try and managed the risk of research and development.

14. Which of the following is an example of technology trading?
    a. Eli Whitney left England for America with the plans for the cotton gin in his head.
    b. Two companies agree to share innovations.
    c. Jane is employed to reverse engineer the latest innovation from her firm's major competitors.
    d. Federal government support of basic research in university laboratories.

15. Patents are
    a. an annual award from the government given to the person who makes the most significant innovation each year.
    b. the name of the latest super-star rock group.
    c. a slang term for shiny shoes.
    d. a legal right that restricts the use of a new invention or innovation to its discoverer or those to whom she gives permission, usually in exchange for a fee.

16. The kinked revenue model helps to explain
    a. the returns to innovation.
    b. product innovations rather than process innovations.
    c. why firms tend to match R&D spending of their competitors.
    d. why profit maximizing firms are likely to favor applied research over basic research.

17. An innovation that increases the variety of products available for consumer would be an example of
    a. basic research.
    b. the public good nature of many innovations.
    c. the cumulative effect of many innovations.
    d. the accelerator impact of many innovations.

18. In the United States, R&D spending is
    a. about 22 percent of GDP.
    b. about 2.2 percent of GDP.
    c. about 0.22 percent of GDP.
    d. only conducted by the federal government.

19. An unchanging rate of innovation
    a. will be insufficient to prevent declines in GDP.
    b. will mean an unchanging GDP.
    c. is an example of the public good nature of innovation.
    d. should result in steady growth in the economy's output.

20. A process innovation that leads to a downward shift in a monopolist's marginal cost curve should
    a. lower price and lower output.
    b. lower price and increase output.
    c. increase price and increase output.
    d. increase price and lower output.

TEST B

Circle T or F for true or false.

T   F   1. Labor today is not much more productive than it was 200 years ago.

T   F   2. There is little reason to expect that capitalist economies will be more successful at innovation than centrally planned economies.

T   F   3. Innovation is a major source of economic growth.

T   F   4. The kinked revenue model of innovation works like a ratchet to sustain the level of R&D spending.

T   F   5. Firms can reduce the risk associated with R&D efforts by engaging in technology trading.

T   F   6. The development of a new or improved production process is an example of basic, not applied, research.

T   F   7. The concept of externalities has little relevance for the analysis of the impact of innovations.

T   F   8. Profit maximizing firms are likely to devote more resources to applied research than basic research.

T   F   9. A steady stream of innovations should lead to continual growth of output.

T   F   10. Process innovations should lower price and increase output, even for monopolists.

ECONOMICS IN ACTION ∎

IS A NEW ERA DAWNING?

From 1948 to 1973 the productivity of American labor increased at an annual rate of over two percent per year. After 1973, the rate of increase of labor productivity plummeted to around one percent per year. Since 1996 the growth in productivity has rebounded to about two percent per year. While it is not unusual for the growth of productivity to increase near the beginning of a business cycle recovery, this increase has come late in the expansion that started in March 1991.

Some economy watches wonder whether experience since 1996 signals a new period of higher productivity growth, one that looks more like the period from 1948 to 1973 rather than the period from 1973 to 1996. If so, what explains the increase in the growth of productivity?

A number of observers point to the widespread use of computers and information technology as responsible for the increase in the growth of productivity. By 1998 information technology equipment accounted for over half of total spending on business equipment. If the widespread use of computers is responsible for the higher growth in productivity, why has it taken so long? Microcomputers began to appear in offices about 20 years ago while mainframe computers that support remote terminals have been available for over thirty years.

Economist Paul David would not be surprised at the time it has taken for the introduction of computers to be reflected in faster growth of productivity. In a paper published in 1990, he pointed out that although the electric motor was first introduced In the early 1880s, it was not until the 1920s that it began to generate discernible increases in productivity. Not only did it take time for the use of electric motors to become widespread, but it also took time for businesses to reorganize work in a way that made full use of the advantages offered by the electric motor. According to David, "The process takes longer than people think, but I still believe that we will get a revival of productivity growth led by the spread of computing."

While many observers are hopeful that we are now seeing the returns to the significant investments in information technology equipment, others are not so sure. The are concerned that the increasing importance of services in the economy provides less opportunity for productivity enhancing innovations. Stephen Roach argues that "Paul David's electric motor has nothing to do with the knowledge-intensive process of work in a service economy." Paul Strassman wonders if much of the spending on computers is only an economic arms race that had been inspired by misguided management theories.

What has happened to the growth in labor productivity since 1998? How important do you believe investments in information technology have been?

SOURCE: Steve Lohr, "Computer Age Gains Respect of Economists," *The New York Times,* April 4, 1999.

■   STUDY QUESTIONS

1. Why do capitalist economies have a better record of innovation that planned economies?

2. What is the difference between basic and applied research? Which is more likely to be done by profit maximizing firms? Why?

3. What is the difference between process and product innovation? Are these examples of basic or applied research?

4. What is meant by the kinked revenue model of spending on innovation?

5. How can firms control the risk associated with specific R&D projects?

6. What is meant by the public good aspect of innovations?

7. What is meant by the accelerator property of innovations?

8. Does the American economy spend enough on research and development?

9. Should the government spend any money on research and development? If so, should it favor one type of research over another? Why?

REAL FIRMS AND THEIR FINANCING: STOCKS AND BONDS

LEARNING OBJECTIVES

After completing this chapter, you should be able to:

■ explain the major advantages and disadvantages of alternative forms of business organization.

■ explain why investors in common stock are not penalized in the form of lower rates of return from the double taxation of corporate dividends.

■ explain how double taxation can affect the business investment decisions of corporations and may lead to inefficient resource allocation.

■ explain the advantages of plowback as a source of funds to a corporation.

■ explain why bond prices fall when interest rates go up and vice versa.

■ explain how the use of stocks or bonds shifts risk between a corporation and financial investors.

■ describe how portfolio diversification can reduce the risk faced by a financial investor.

Important Terms and Concepts

PROPRIETORSHIP

UNLIMITED LIABILITY

PARTNERSHIP

CORPORATION

LIMITED LIABILITY

DOUBLE TAXATION

COMMON STOCK

BOND

PLOWBACK OR RETAINED EARNINGS

PORTFOLIO DIVERSIFICATION

STOCK MARKET INDEX

INDEX FUND

STOCK EXCHANGES

TAKEOVERS

SPECULATION

RANDOM WALK

■ explain why the stock market is of critical importance to the financing of corporations even though new stock issues account for only a small proportion of new funds raised by corporations.

■ discuss the advantages and disadvantages of corporate takeovers.

■ discuss the role of speculation both in the economy and in the securities markets.

■ CHAPTER REVIEW

This chapter explores the advantages and disadvantages of alternative legal forms of business organization. Special attention is given to the different ways in which corporations raise funds and to the markets on which corporate securities are traded.

(1)   A business owned and operated by an individual is called a _____. This is by far the most common form of business organization in the United States. When a firm's ownership and decision making are shared by a fixed number of individuals, the business is called a _____. Another form of business organization is one in which the firm has the legal status of a fictional individual and is owned by a large number of stockholders and run by an elected board of directors and officers. This form of organization is called a _____. A major advantage here is that stockholders, the legal owners of the business, are not liable for the firm's debts. Having _____ liability makes it possible for corporations to raise very large sums of money in the pursuit of profits.

A corporation that raises funds by selling shares of ownership and offering a stake in profits is issu-

(2)   ing (stock/bonds). If a corporation issues securities that promise to pay fixed sums as interest and principal, it is issuing _____. Corporations can also borrow directly from large financial institutions, such as banks or insurance companies. The most common way of raising funds is to directly reinvest part of a corporation's profits. This method of raising funds is called _____. Corporations typically prefer to use plowback to finance corporate investments as it avoids the cost and scrutiny that accompany new issues of stocks and bonds.

Assuming a firm does not become bankrupt, a bond that is held to maturity offers the bondholder a fixed stream of payments. Investing in stock promises dividend payments and stock prices that

(3)   (are/are not) known at the time of purchase. The greater uncertainty of dividends and stock prices as compared to bond payments leads many investors to conclude that stocks are (more/less) risky than

bonds. From the viewpoint of a firm, (bonds/stocks) are more risky, because a failure to (meet bond payments/pay dividends) can force bankruptcy.

This comparison understates the riskiness to individual investors of investing in bonds. If a bond must be sold before maturity and interest rates have changed, the market price of the bond will also change. If interest rates have risen, previously issued bonds with low coupon payments will look less attractive unless their price (rises/falls). Holders of these bonds will suffer a (gain/loss). Conversely, if (4) interest rates have fallen, competition for existing bonds with high coupon payments will (increase/decrease) the price of previously issued bonds.

Shares of stock offer investors returns in the form of dividend payments and/or changes in the stock price. Investors have the option of buying shares of only one company or shares of several companies. Buying shares of several companies is an example of _____. Institutional (5) investors who use computers to make automatic trading decisions are engaging in _____ trading. One assumes control of an existing corporation by buying a sufficient number of current shares of stock. When such an action is contested, it is called a _____ battle and can be an effective way to remove incompetent management. There is concern that these struggles lead to wasteful and costly actions on both sides.

Stocks and bonds are traded in markets that sometimes have a specific location, such as the New York Stock Exchange, but they are also traded by dealers and brokers who keep track, by telephone or computer, of the latest price changes. New stock issues (are/are not) usually sold through established (6) exchanges. Two important functions served by established exchanges include (1) reducing the _____ of stock ownership by providing a secondary market in existing shares and (2) determining the current price of a company's stock. In the latter role, established exchanges help allocate the economy's resources to those firms that, in the market's judgment, are expected to make the most profitable use of those resources.

Speculators are not much different from most investors who hope to profit from increases in stock prices. From a general perspective, speculation serves two important functions. First, it can help decrease price fluctuations. Buying at low prices in anticipation of being able to sell next year at high prices will, in fact, make prices today (higher/lower) than they otherwise would be and will also make (7) prices next year _____ than they otherwise would be. The second function of speculation is that it can provide _____ for those who want to avoid taking risks. Commodity speculators will agree now on a price to be paid for buying crops next year, thus insuring a farmer against the adverse effects of a decrease in price. Other speculators may agree now on a price at which to sell crops next year to a milling company, thus insuring the miller against the adverse effects of an increase in price.

The behavior of individual stock prices has long fascinated investors. Much time and effort is spent trying to forecast price movements. Some investors look at things like a firm's earnings and its current stock price; others plot recent stock prices and try to discover laws of motion in their graphs. Economists have also studied the changes in individual stock prices. Much of this research supports the conclusion that changes in stock prices are essentially unpredictable; that is, they look like a

(8)   _____ _____. Such a result could arise because of essentially random waves of buying and selling as investors try to outguess each other. It could also arise from investors' careful study and analysis of individual companies, study that is so complete that all anticipated events are fully reflected in current stock prices. The expectation today of higher profits tomorrow raises stock prices (<u>today/tomorrow</u>). In this view, changes in stock prices can only reflect currently unanticipated events, events that will likely look like random events. This viewpoint has been formalized in the hypothesis of "efficient markets." Much advanced research in financial economics is concerned with testing this hypothesis.

IMPORTANT TERMS AND CONCEPTS QUIZ ■

Choose the best definition for each of the following terms.

1. _____ Proprietorship

2. _____ Unlimited liability

3. _____ Partnership

4. _____ Corporation

5. _____ Limited liability

6. _____ Double taxation

7. _____ Common stock

8. _____ Bond

9. _____ Retained earnings (plowback)

10. _____ Portfolio diversification

11. _____ Stock market index

12. _____ Index fund

13. _____ Takeovers

14. _____ Stock exchange

15. _____ Speculation

16. _____ Random walk

a. Change in variable is completely unpredictable.

b. Legal obligation to repay company debts only with money owners have already invested in the firm.

c. Purchase of risky assets in anticipation of favorable price changes.

d. Corporation's promise to pay a fixed sum at maturity plus annual interest.

e. Firm owned by an individual.

f. Portion of a corporation's profits that management returns to shareholders.

g. An average of the price of a large set of stocks.

h. Holding a number and variety of stocks, bonds, and other assets in an attempt to find offsetting risks.

i. A group of individuals not currently in control of a firm buys enough stock to gain control.

j. Legal obligation to repay company's debts with whatever resources owners may have.

k. Piece of paper that gives holder a share of ownership in a company.

l. Firm owned by a fixed number of individuals.

m. Portion of a corporation's profits that management decides to keep and reinvest.

n. Firm owned by stockholders, with the legal status of a fictitious individual.

o. Taxes on corporate profits before distribution to shareholders and taxes on dividends received by shareholders.

p. Organized market for trading corporate shares.

q. An investment fund that buys the stocks in a particular stock index.

■ **BASIC EXERCISES**

1. **Double Taxation**

This exercise is designed to illustrate how market forces adjust stock prices to reflect alternative yields available to investors and to ensure that the returns to shareholders are not reduced by the double taxation of corporate profits.

The XYZ Corporation earns $80 million in profits and pays $28 million in profits tax to the government, leaving $52 million that is paid out as a $4 dividend on each of 13 million shares of stock. (XYZ does not plowback any of its after-tax profits.) Investors in XYZ stock have the option of investing in corporate bonds and earning a return of 10 percent on which they will have to pay income taxes, just as they must pay taxes on dividend income.

Stock Price	Dividend Before Taxes	Dividend Yield (col. 2 ÷ col. 1)
$ 25	$4	_____
40	4	_____
64	4	_____
100	4	_____

a. Fill in the blank column to compute the dividend yield on a share of XYZ stock at various prices.
b. Assume that the XYZ dividend has always been $4 and is expected to remain $4. Further, since XYZ does not plowback any of its after-tax profits, the price of XYZ stock is not expected to change. If investors require the same return on shares of XYZ stock as they do on corporate bonds, what will be the price of XYZ stock? _____ Do investors in XYZ stock receive a lower rate of return because of the double taxation of corporate income—once as corporate profits and then again as dividends? Why or why not?
c. What is likely to happen to the price of XYZ stock if the interest rate on corporate bonds rises to 16 percent? Falls to 6.25 percent?
d. Suddenly and unexpectedly, the president of XYZ announces that oil has been discovered on company property. The revenues from this discovery will double profits for the foreseeable future. Furthermore, XYZ announces that starting next year and continuing into the future, the dividend per share will also double to $8. Why will the price of XYZ stock rise immediately rather than waiting until next year when higher dividend payments start?
e. If everyone believes that dividends on XYZ stock will double beginning next year, and if alternative investments continue to yield 10 percent, what is the likely new stock price? Why?

2. **Portfolio Diversification**

This exercise is meant to illustrate the principle of diversification. Assume you invested $10,000 on December 31, 1997, and sold your holdings one year later on December 30, 1998. Tables 16-1 and 16-2 contain data for some of the most heavily traded stocks in 1998. Table 16-1 shows the results of dividing your investment among each of 10 stocks, $1,000 in each. The entries in Table 16-2 assume that your $10,000 was invested in just one company. Column (1) shows the number of shares purchased on December 31, 1997. Column (2) reports stock prices on December 30, 1998.
a. Column (3) has spaces for the value of your stock holdings on December 30, 1998. Complete this column in both tables by multiplying stock prices on December 30, 1998, by the number of shares; that is, multiply each entry in column (2) by the corresponding entry in column (1).
b. Complete column (5) by adding the dividends you received in 1998, column (4), to the value of your stock holdings in column (3). Column (5) shows the total return, dividends plus the change in stock prices. Be sure to sum all of the entries in column (5) for Table 16-1.
c. Each entry in column (5), Table 16-2, shows how you would have done had you invested all of the $10,000 in the stock of just one company. The sum for column (5), Table 16-1, shows the results of a ten-stock portfolio. How do your results illustrate the link between portfolio diversification and risk?

TABLE 16-1

Company	(1) Number of Shares If Investing $1,000 12/31/97	(2) Price per Share on 12/31/98	(3) Value of Shares on 12/30/98 (1) × (2)	(4) Dividends Received during 1998	(5) Gross Returns (3) + (4)
AT&T	16.31	$ 75.75	_____	86.12	_____
Boeing	20.43	32.63	_____	45.77	_____
Cendant	29.09	19.31	_____	0.00	_____
Citigroup	18.56	49.69	_____	53.46	_____
General Electric	12.06	102.00	_____	67.54	_____
IBM	9.56	184.38	_____	33.64	_____
Iomega	80.40	7.31	_____	0.00	_____
Lucent Technology	25.04	109.94	_____	8.01	_____
Micron	38.55	50.56	_____	0.00	_____
Walt Disney	30.30	30.00	_____	25.45	_____
Total Portfolio*					_____

TABLE 16-2

Company	(1) Number of Shares If Investing $10,000 12/31/97	(2) Price per Share on 12/31/98	(3) Value of Shares on 12/30/98 (1) × (2)	(4) Dividends Received during 1998	(5) Gross Returns* (3) + (4)
AT&T	163.10	$ 75.75	_____	861.16	_____
Boeing	204.34	32.63	_____	457.73	_____
Cendant	290.91	19.31	_____	0.00	_____
Citigroup	185.61	49.69	_____	534.57	_____
General Electric	120.60	102.00	_____	675.37	_____
IBM	95.58	184.38	_____	336.44	_____
Iomega	804.02	7.31	_____	0.00	_____
Lucent Technology	250.39	109.94	_____	80.13	_____
Micron	385.54	50.56	_____	0.00	_____
Walt Disney	303.03	30.00	_____	254.55	_____

*Net Returns = Gross Returns − $10,000
 Rate of Return = (Gross Returns/$10,000) − 1

SELF-TESTS FOR UNDERSTANDING

TEST A

Circle the most appropriate answer.

1. Most business firms are
   a. corporations.
   b. proprietorships.
   c. partnerships.
   d. financed by issuing stock.

2. What form of business accounts for the largest share of output?
    a. Corporations.
    b. Franchises
    c. Partnerships.
    d. Proprietorships.

3. Which one of the following is *not* true of proprietorships?
    a. The proprietor has complete and full personal control of the business.
    b. The proprietor has limited liability for the debts of the business.
    c. Income is only taxed once.
    d. Few legal complications exist.

4. Disadvantages of partnerships include all but which one of the following?
    a. Unlimited liability of partners for the debts of the partnership.
    b. Pooling of the resources and expertise of partners.
    c. Potential difficulty of getting partners to agree on important issues.
    d. Legal difficulties associated with changes in partners.

5. What form of business offers owners limited liability for the debts of the business?
    a. Corporations.
    b. Partnerships.
    c. Proprietorships.

6. In which form of business is income subject to double taxation?
    a. Proprietorship.
    b. Partnership.
    c. Corporation.

7. Ways in which corporations can raise money include all but which one of the following?
    a. Issuing shares of stock.
    b. Borrowing money in the form of bonds.
    c. The reinvestment, or plowback, of profits.
    d. Paying dividends.

8. Which of the following is the most important source of new funds for corporations?
    a. New stock issues.
    b. Corporate bonds.
    c. Retained earnings (i.e., plowback).
    d. Bank loans.

9. Why do economists expect that corporations will ignore business opportunities offering profitable but limited returns?
    a. The difficulty of getting agreement from millions of owners.
    b. The double taxation of corporate income.
    c. Limited liability for stockholders.
    d. Corporate managers will be more concerned with their welfare than that of the stockholders.

10. If held to maturity and there is no risk of bankruptcy, bonds offer investors
    a. greater returns because interest payments as opposed to dividend payments are not subject to double taxation.
    b. unknown interest payments that will fluctuate with profits.
    c. returns that are usually greater than those available from stocks.
    d. known interest payments.

11. A decrease in interest rates will tend to _____ the price of existing bonds.
    a. increase
    b. lower
    c. have no effect on

12. Emerson purchased a newly issued General Electric bond several years ago with coupon payments offering an interest rate of 10 percent. Since then, market interest rates on similar bonds have fallen to 6 percent. Which of the following is true?
    a. The market value of the bonds that Emerson bought will have increased from the price he paid.
    b. If held to maturity and General Electric does not default, Emerson will earn 6 percent on his investment.
    c. Anyone purchasing such bonds today at their current market price and holding them to maturity can expect to earn 10 percent on the investment.
    d. If Emerson sold his bonds today at their current market price, he would have to sell them for less than he paid.

13. Five million shares of stock are outstanding in XYZ Corporation. If the price of XYZ stock rises by $1, then
    a. XYZ Corporation will have $5 million more to invest or use to pay higher dividends.
    b. existing shareholders will benefit by $1 a share.
    c. investors who hold XYZ bonds will have suffered a capital loss.
    d. XYZ Corporation will owe federal tax on the increased stock price.

14. A limit order specifies
    a. the number of shares you will buy at the prevailing market price.
    b. trading between bonds and stocks.
    c. the price at which you are willing to buy or sell shares of stock.
    d. the time at which you are willing to buy or sell shares of stock.

15. Program trading refers to
    a. a systematic plan for building an investment portfolio.
    b. individuals who purchase stocks recommended by individuals appearing on the television program *Wall Street Week*.
    c. the use of computers to design and execute buying and selling of stocks.
    d. the activities of market specialists.

16. Which of the following $100,000 investments offers the most diversification?
    a. $100,000 of Kodak stock.
    b. $100,000 of Sears stock.
    c. $100,000 of Du Pont stock.
    d. $100,000 of Shell Oil stock.
    e. $25,000 invested in each of the following: Kodak, Sears, Du Pont, and Shell Oil.

17. The important economic functions of organized stock exchanges include all but which one of the following?
    a. Offering investors insurance against the risk of changes in stock prices.
    b. Reducing the risk of purchasing stock by offering investors a place to sell their shares should they need the funds for some other purpose.
    c. Helping allocate the economy's resources, since companies with high current stock prices will find it easier to raise additional funds to pursue investment opportunities.

18. If Maxine is to be a successful speculator she must
    a.   buy during a period of excess supply and sell during a period of excess supply.
    b.   buy during a period of excess supply and sell during a period of excess demand.
    c.   buy during a period of excess demand and sell during a period of excess demand.
    d.   buy during a period of excess demand and sell during a period of excess supply.

19. Advantages to existing stockholders from takeovers can include all but which one of the following?
    a.   The elimination of incompetent management.
    b.   Increasing the price of an undervalued company.
    c.   A greater chance that low earnings will grow to match their potential.
    d.   The time and effort of top management in responding to the takeover bid.

20. To say that stock prices follow a random walk is to say that
    a.   stock prices are easily predicted given information about past prices.
    b.   the predictions of stock analysts are uniformly better than those of individual investors.
    c.   day-to-day changes in stock prices are essentially unpredictable.
    d.   over the long run, individual investors will only lose money by buying stocks.

TEST B

Circle T or F for true or false.

T   F   1. Corporations, while constituting a minority of the number of business organizations, are the most important form of organization when measured by total sales.

T   F   2. When measured by the number of firms, proprietorships are the most common form of business organization in the United States.

T   F   3. The double taxation of corporate income—once as corporate profits and again as dividends—means that investors in the stock market must settle for a lower rate of return on stocks.

T   F   4. Assuming no bankruptcy, a corporate bond is a riskless investment even if the bond must be sold before maturity.

T   F   5. Any individual who wants to buy or sell shares of stock can do so by walking onto the floor of the New York Stock Exchange and announcing her intentions.

T   F   6. Whenever a share of Xerox stock is sold on the New York Stock Exchange, Xerox gets the proceeds.

T   F   7. A corporation that decides to issue stock will typically offer the shares initially through one of the regional stock exchanges.

T   F   8. Established stock exchanges, such as the New York Stock Exchange, are really just a form of legalized gambling and serve no social function.

T   F   9. The finding that stock prices follow a random walk implies that investing in stock is essentially a gamble.

T   F   10. Profitable speculation involves buying high and selling low.

SUPPLEMENTARY EXERCISES ■

1. Stocks and Bonds

Consult the financial page of any newspaper that lists bonds. Find the listing for several regular bonds of corporations with a similar maturity date sometime past 2010. Write down their coupon rate, current yield, and market price. Also note stock prices for the same companies. After three months, again check the stock prices and the current yield and price of the bonds. Note if any increase (or decrease) in the current yield is matched by an opposite movement in the bond price. Had you actually bought these bonds, would you now have a gain or loss? What if you had bought shares of stock? Have all or most of the bond prices moved together? Have all the stock prices moved together? (It would not be surprising if the prices of bonds of different corporations rose or fell together. Stock prices are less likely to change together. Can you explain why?)

2. Bond Prices and Interest Rates

The market price of a $1,000 bond paying interest once a year can be calculated by computing the present value of future payments:

$$\text{Price} = \sum_{t=1}^{N} \frac{INT}{(1 + i)^t} + \frac{1000}{(1 + i)^N}$$

where Price = market price, i = market interest rate, N = number of years to maturity, and INT = annual interest payment.

It may be easiest to complete the following exercises if you have access to a microcomputer or sophisticated hand calculator.

a. Show that if INT = $80 and i = .08, the market price of this bond will be $1,000 for all values of N.

b. Now vary i, holding INT constant at $80 and N constant at 25 years. Note how the price of a bond issued with a coupon payment of $80 changes as market interest rates change. You should find that price is less than $1,000 when i is greater than .08 and price is greater than $1,000 when i is less than .08.

c. Choose a particular value for i, say .06, and calculate the difference in price from the original $1,000 as N varies from one year to 25 years. Remember to keep INT = 80. You should find that the difference in price is greater as N gets larger; that is, longer term bonds show a greater change in price for a given change in interest rates. Can you explain why?

ECONOMICS IN ACTION ■

BULLISH OR BEARISH?

Were internet stocks overvalued in early 1999? It certainly seemed plausible. When it first offered stock, Priceline.com, an internet company that allows customers to offer low bids for airline tickets if they can be flexible about their travel plans, saw its stock price rise fourfold to an implied market value for the company of $9.8 billion, larger than the combined market value of United, Continental and Northwest Airlines. This for a company that lost $114 million on sales of $35 million. Amazon.com was another high flying internet stock that had yet to earn a profit. At one point it was estimated that Amazon lost 29 cents on every dollar of sales.

Writing in *The Wall Street Journal* Jermey Siegel, Professor of Finance at the Wharton School, argued that internet stocks were overvalued while David Alger argued they were not. Siegel likened the rise in internet stock prices to the 16th century tulip bulb mania in Holland and the boom in land sales in Florida in the 1920s. He pointed out that while technology stocks in the 1960s and 1970s saw dramatic increases in their stock prices, all of these early technology companies, IBM, Xerox, Digital Equipment, Texas Instruments, Kodak and Polaroid, underperformed the S&P 500 (a popular broad based stock index) over the next 25 years.

American Online (AOL) was one stock about which Siegel was especially skeptical. The price of its stock put it near the top 10 of American companies in terms of market value while profits and sales ranked AOL 311th and 415th. In early 1999 AOL's market value was about $15,000 per subscriber, over 50 times the annual subscription fee. Siegel observed that this valuation assumed that AOL would be able to generate substantial revenues by selling additional services or merchandise to its subscribers. He was skeptical, arguing that profit margins from selling on the web were not likely to be all that different from other industries.

David Alger, CEO of Fred Alger, a New York based investment firm, argued that while internet stock prices may seem high, conventional valuation standards should not apply. According to Alger, "the Internet is more than just an industry. It is a revolution in communication and commerce." He argued that because internet companies do not have large investments in bricks and mortar, there is the potential for large margins in electronic distribution. Unlike conventional retailers, physical facilities do not have to be duplicated to serve more customers. As a result, Alger argued, it is possible to expand service with little increase in costs and to earn significant revenue from advertising. In addition, internet retailers are currently spending large sums on advertising and marketing ($26 per sale as compared to $2.50 for conventional retailers according to one estimate). Alger expected these costs to be trimmed significantly as on-line merchandising matures. He argued that growth stock valuations depends upon three issues: the growth in earnings, the stability of this growth, and the excitement factor. Alger was excited about the growth potential of electronic commerce over the Internet, especially inter-firm transactions which he expected to increase over six fold in four years.

What has happened to the value of Internet stocks since April 1999? What do you think will happen to these stocks in the future? Which market structure is most appropriate for doing business on the web: perfect competition, monopolistic competition, oligopoly, monopoly? Why? What do these different models say about future profit prospects?

SOURCE: Jeremy J. Siegel, "Are Internet Stock Overvalued? Are They Ever," *The Wall Street Journal,* April 19, 1999. David D. Alger, "Big Profits are in Store From the Online Revolution," *The Wall Street Journal,* April 26, 1999. Laurence Zuckerman, "The Long Reach of Internet Stock Mania." *The New York Times,* April 7, 1999. Peter de Jonge, "Riding the Wild, Perilous Waters of Amazon.com," *The New York Times,* March 14, 1999.

■   STUDY QUESTIONS

1.   The text points out that although a small percentage of business firms, corporations account for a much larger percentage of business sales and output. This difference arises because the biggest firms are corporations. Why are the biggest firms corporations?

2.   How can it be that investors in stock are not penalized by the double taxation of income to corporations?

3.   Why is most business investment financed by plowback or retained earnings rather than by new stock issues or bonds?

4.   What explains the inverse relationship between market interest rates and bond prices?

5.   Why is it often said that bonds are riskier than stocks to a corporation but stocks are riskier than bonds for investors?

6.   Why do economists argue that portfolio diversification reduces the risk of investing in stocks?

7.   What is the difference between a limit order and a marker order?

8.   What is the difference between a stock market index and an index fund.

9.   What is the economic role of the stock market if new stock issues are seldom used to finance business investment?

10. Many people would like to regulate speculators on the belief that they are greedy predators who profit only on the misfortune of others. Why do economists often disagree with this assessment?

ECONOMICS ONLINE ■

1. There are now lots of ways to follow stocks, bonds and mutual funds on the web. Many mutual funds and stock exchanges have their own homepage. Here are some popular sites that give access to these other sites

   CBS Marketwatch

   cbs.marketwatch.com/news/newsroom.htx

   CNN Financial

   cnnfn.com

   Bloomberg

   www.bloomberg.com

   USA Today

   www.usatoday.com/money

   Yahoo

   dir.yahoo.com/business_and_economy/finance_and_investment

2. The Securities and Exchange Commission regulates trading in stocks and bonds. See what they are up to at their homepage. You might want to investigate EDGAR, the SEC's electronic database of corporate reports.

   www.sec.gov

CHAPTER

17

PRICING THE FACTORS OF PRODUCTION

LEARNING OBJECTIVES

After completing this chapter, you should be able to:

■ explain why the demand curve for a factor of production is the downward-sloping portion of its marginal revenue product curve.

■ explain why the demand for inputs is a derived demand.

■ distinguish between investment and capital.

■ explain how changes in interest rates may affect the profitability of specific investment decisions and hence the demand for funds.

■ explain who gains, who loses, and why, under an effective usury ceiling.

■ distinguish between land rents and economic rents.

■ identify input units that receive economic rent, given supply curves of various slopes.

■ explain why the fact that apartment buildings need to be maintained and that they can be reproduced at close to constant cost implies that, in the long run, rent control measures are likely to be self-defeating.

■ explain why, in the real world, profits are likely to offer returns in excess of the interest rate.

■ explain how the concept of economic rent is relevant to issues concerning the taxation of profits.

■ CHAPTER REVIEW

This chapter initiates the discussion of input prices by considering what determines the rental price of money, the rental price of land, and the income of entrepreneurs. If this material is combined with the material in the next chapter on wages—the rental price for labor services—and later material on the price of natural resources, we have a complete theory of income distribution based on marginal

(1) _____. This chapter and the next build upon our earlier discussion of optimal input use by firms. We saw earlier that the demand for factors of production can be derived from profit-maximizing considerations. A firm should be willing to pay for labor, land, natural resources, and so forth because it can use these factors to produce and sell output. As we have learned, the demand curve for a particular factor of production is simply the downward-sloping portion of the marginal _____ product curve.

INTEREST

Interest rates adjust to balance the demand for funds by borrowers and the supply of funds from

(2) lenders. The demand curve for funds has a (<u>negative/positive</u>) slope, indicating that at lower interest people will want to borrow (<u>less/more</u>). The supply curve of funds is most likely to have a (<u>negative/positive</u>) slope, indicating that a (<u>higher/lower</u>) interest rate is necessary to induce lenders to increase the supply of loans. An effective usury ceiling would impose an interest rate (<u>above/below</u>) the market clearing rate as determined by the intersection of the demand and supply curves.

The demand for funds for business borrowing derives from a consideration of the profitability of investment projects. In earlier chapters we talked about capital and labor as factors of production. Investment projects add to the stock of capital. The profitability of investment projects is another way of referring to the marginal revenue product of more capital. The profitability of investment projects is complicated because most projects require dollar outlays immediately while offering returns in the future. To evaluate the profitability of an investment we need some way of comparing current and future dollars. Economists and business people compare future and present dollars through a process called _____. As explained in the appendix to this chapter, this process relies on interest rate calculations. Higher interest rates will mean that (<u>fewer/more</u>) investment projects will be profitable. Thus higher interest rates will be associated with a (<u>higher/lower</u>) quantity of funds demanded and imply a negatively sloped demand curve for business borrowing.

RENT

When considering the notion of rent, remember that economists use the term in a special way different from everyday usage. Most of the rent that you may pay for an apartment (<u>is/is not</u>) economic rent.   (3)
Economic rent refers to the earnings of a factor of production that exceed the minimum amount necessary to keep that factor in its current employment.

If the supply curve of some factor, such as land, is really vertical, it means that the factor would be willing to work for as little as nothing. It also means that it is impossible to duplicate this factor at any cost; otherwise, a high enough price would induce an increase in supply, and the supply curve would not be vertical. In the case of a vertical supply curve, (<u>some/all</u>) of any market price would be economic   (4)
rent. If the supply curve of some factor is a horizontal line, the market price will reflect exactly what is necessary to induce any supply. In this case an economist would say that the factor receives _____ economic rent.

An upward-sloping supply curve means that higher prices will induce an increase in supply, but there will be some units of supply that would have been present at lower prices. In this case (<u>most/all</u>)   (5)
units of the factor will receive economic rent. In fact, it is only the marginal unit, the unit on the supply curve at the market equilibrium price, that earns no economic rent. The market price is as high as it is to induce this last unit to supply itself. All other units would have been available at a lower price, and thus (<u>part/all</u>) of their earnings are economic rent. Land is a traditional input to use when talking about rent, but remember that land is not the only factor to earn economic rent. Anyone who would stay in a particular job for less pay, because he or she likes the work or the location, or for any other reason, (<u>is/is not</u>) earning some economic rent.

When considering land rentals it is clear that not all land is the same: Some parcels are more productive or better located than others. Economists would expect that land rentals, the price for using a piece of land for a period of time, will adjust to reflect these differences. More productive land that produces the same output at lower cost will receive a (higher/lower) land rent. In equilibrium, rents should adjust so that the cost of producing the same quantity of output, including land rents, will be

(6)   _____ on all parcels of land. If not, there is a clear incentive to use the land with lower total cost. This incentive to switch parcels increases the rent on the originally (low/high)-cost piece of land and decreases rent on the other pieces of land. The process stops only when land rentals have adjusted to again equate total cost.

As with any other productive factor, an increase in the demand for goods produced with land will (decrease/increase) the demand for land. Poor quality land, whose use was unprofitable at lower output prices, will now become profitable to use. Thus, more land will be used, and land rents will again

(7)   adjust to equalize the costs of production on all parcels. As a result, the rent on previously used, higher quality land will (increase/decrease). An additional part of the response to increased land demand is likely to be (more/less) intensive use of existing land.

PROFIT

Profits are a residual item after revenues have been used to pay other costs—labor, material inputs, interest on borrowed funds, and taxes. Profits also represent the return on equity investments in a firm.[1] In a world of perfect certainty, capitalists should expect the profits on their investments to offer a return just equal to the interest rate. The rate of interest would be the opportunity cost of their equity investment in the firm. Any higher return would be competed away. Any lower return would lead some funds to be invested elsewhere in the pursuit of returns at least equal to the interest rate. (Remember that in simple competitive markets, economic profits equal zero in long-run equilibrium.)

In the real world, investments are not certain. Many business investments look like uncertain gambles. If entrepreneurs dislike taking risks, then profits will have to offer them the expectation of returns that are (greater/less) than the rate of interest. Profits that are the result of monopoly power would be (greater/less) than the interest rate. Finally, successful (innovation/invention) will often give an entre-

(8)   preneur temporary monopoly profits and lead to a rate of profit that is (greater/less) than the interest

---

[1]Equity refers here to the amount of their own money the owners have invested in their company. Specifically, if they dissolved the company and paid off its creditors, the amount left over is their equity.

rate. The effects of taxing profits will depend upon whether profits are mostly economic rents or mostly a necessary return to attract entrepreneurial talent.

IMPORTANT TERMS AND CONCEPTS QUIZ ■

Choose the best definition for the following terms.

1. _____ Factors of production

2. _____ Entrepreneurship

3. _____ Marginal productivity principle

4. _____ Marginal physical product

5. _____ Marginal revenue product

6. _____ Investment

7. _____ Capital

8. _____ Interest

9. _____ Discounting

10. _____ Usury law

11. _____ Marginal land

12. _____ Economic rent

13. _____ Economic profit

14. _____ Invention

15. _____ Innovation

a. Payment to a factor of production in excess of the minimum amount necessary to keep the factor in its present employment.

b. Additional units of a given input add diminishing amounts to total output.

c. Starting firms, introducing innovations, and taking the necessary risks in seeking business opportunities.

d. Change in sales revenue from selling the marginal physical product of an additional unit of input.

e. Flow of resources into the production of new capital.

f. Act of generating a new idea.

g. Inputs used in the production process.

h. Payment for the use of funds.

i. Land on the borderline of being used.

j. Profit-maximizing firm should hire that quantity of an input at which marginal revenue product equals the price of the input.

k. Using interest rates to determine the present worth of a sum of money receivable or payable at a future date.

l. Act of putting a new idea into practical use.

m. Increase in output from a one-unit increase in a given input.

n. Stock of plant and equipment from past investment.

o. Maximum legally permissible interest rate.

p. Total revenue minus total cost including the opportunity cost of owner supplied inputs.

■ BASIC EXERCISE

This exercise is designed to illustrate how differences in land rents reflect differences in productivity.

This summer Darlene can work as a checker at the local grocery store for as many hours as she wants, earning $8 an hour. She also is considering raising flowers for sale on one of two plots of land. The sunny plot has good soil, and Darlene estimates that if she worked 40 hours a week she could earn $400 a week raising flowers on this land. The second plot is marginal land available for free. It would require the use of fertilizer and special mulches to raise the same quantity of flowers. Darlene estimates these extra costs would total $30 a week.

1. Calculate Darlene's profit from using the marginal plot of land on the assumption that it is available at zero rent. Do not forget to include the opportunity cost of Darlene's own work as an element of cost.

2. If Darlene's estimate of the increased cost of using the marginal land is typical of other uses, what market rent would you expect will be charged for the use of the sunny plot and why?

3. Explain why the profit that Darlene could earn from using the marginal plot of land limits the rent the owner of the sunny plot will be able to charge.

■ SELF-TESTS FOR UNDERSTANDING

TEST A

Circle the most appropriate answer.

1. Economists argue that the demand for factors of production is
    a. an applied demand.
    b. insensitive to changes in the price of factors.
    c. best represented as an upward-sloping curve.
    d. a derived demand.

2. Profit-maximizing firms will use more of a productive factor as long as the price of the factor is less than its
    a. marginal revenue product.
    b. marginal cost.
    c. marginal physical product.
    d. average product.

3. The demand curve for productive factors is the downward-sloping portion of the relevant
    a. marginal physical product curve.
    b. marginal cost curve.
    c. marginal revenue product curve.
    d. average cost curve.

4. If the price of widgets increases,
    a. we should see a movement along the demand curves for factors producing widgets.
    b. there should be a shift in the demand curves for factors producing widgets.
    c. the best guess is that there will be little change in the demand for factors producing widgets.
    d. the demand curves for factors producing widgets should shift to the left.

5. The concept of discounting suggests that when compared with a dollar next year, a dollar today is worth
    a. less.
    b. the same.
    c. more.

6. If interest rates increase, the difference in the value of $100 today compared with $100 next year will
    a. decrease.
    b. be unchanged.
    c. increase.
    d. be impossible to determine.

7. Firms produce output using land, labor, exhaustible resources, entrepreneurship, and
    a. capital.
    b. investment.
    c. interest.
    d. economic rent.

8. Firms undertake _____ to add to the stock of _____.
    a. innovation; invention
    b. discounting; investment
    c. investment; capital
    d. capital; investment

9. Which of the following is an example of investment as opposed to capital?
    a. The fleet of 747s owned by American Airlines.
    b. Julia's purchase of 100 shares of Xerox stock.
    c. The five apartment buildings owned by Ralph.
    d. The new warehouse that Norma will have built this year.

10. Economists expect that land rents will
    a. adjust to equalize total costs of production across different parcels of land.
    b. mean that more productive parcels of land receive higher rents.
    c. result in more intensive use of more productive parcels of land.
    d. all of the above.

11. Parcel of land B can be used to raise corn at a cost of $50,000. The same amount of corn can be raised on parcel P for $75,000. An economist would expect the rent on parcel B to exceed that on parcel P by
    a. $25,000.
    b. $50,000.
    c. $75,000.
    d. $125,000.

12. Marginal land refers to land that
    a. is most productive for growing any given crop.
    b. is on the borderline of being used in productive activity.
    c. earns economic rent.
    d. borders interstate highways in rural areas.

13. The term *economic rent* refers to
    a. any rent paid by someone as part of an economic transaction.
    b. rent paid by economists for their apartments.
    c. earnings by factors of production greater than they would settle for.
    d. land rents.

14. If the supply curve for some factor of production can be represented as a horizontal line, an economist would say that _____ of the income earned by this factor is economic rent.
    a. none
    b. some
    c. all

15. An input will earn pure economic rent if the supply curve for the input is
    a. horizontal.
    b. upward sloping.
    c. vertical.

16. Which of the following individuals are earning economic rent?
    a. Ruth, who says, "If this job paid any less I'd quit; it wouldn't be worth the hassle."
    b. Sergio, who says, "This job is so interesting I'd work here even for a lot less."
    c. Nick, whose purchase of an apartment building should bring him a return equal to the interest rate.
    d. Sophia, who is expecting a substantial profit from her investment in the manufacture of solar energy panels to compensate her for the risks she is taking.

17. Rent seeking refers to
    a. efforts of college students to find apartments each fall.
    b. the use of productive resources in the pursuit of political opportunities for profits.
    c. attempts to get departments within a company to pay for space they occupy.
    d. a landlord's efforts to collect from deadbeat tenants.

18. In a world of competitive firms with no uncertainty or risk, economists expect that the profit rate will be
    a. less than the rate of interest.
    b. equal to the rate of interest.
    c. higher than the rate of interest.

19. Monopoly power, whether permanent or temporary, means that profits will be
    a. less than the rate of interest.
    b. equal to the rate of interest.
    c. higher than the rate of interest.

20. Higher taxes on profits will have little impact if
    a. profits are mostly economic rent.
    b. profits are equal to nominal interest rates.
    c. profits are growing.
    d. the supply curve for entrepreneurial talent is horizontal.

TEST B

Circle T or F for true or false.

T   F   1. The demand curve for a factor of production is identical to its curve of marginal physical productivity.

T   F   2. Interest rates represent the market price for the use of funds.

T   F   3. Discounting means using the rate of interest to compare future and present dollars.

T   F   4. The factories that the Ford Motor Company uses to produce cars are an example of capital rather than investment.

T   F   5. According to economists, only land earns economic rent.

T   F   6. Inputs available in perfectly elastic supply will earn no economic rent.

T   F   7. The rent on any piece of land will equal the difference between production costs on that piece of land and production costs on the next-best available piece of land.

T   F   8. The law of diminishing returns implies that an increase in the demand for land will actually reduce the rent paid on most parcels of land.

T   F   9. The reason that most rent-control laws have adverse effects in the long run is that the long-run supply of structures, as opposed to land, is likely to be quite elastic.

T   F   10. Economic theory proves that the rate of profits must equal the rate of interest.

APPENDIX: DISCOUNTING AND PRESENT VALUE

Important Terms and Concepts

DISCOUNTING

PRESENT VALUE

LEARNING OBJECTIVE

After completing the exercises below, you should be able to appreciate how discounting, or present value, calculations can help when considering investment decisions.

IMPORTANT TERMS AND CONCEPTS QUIZ ■

Choose the best definition for the following term.

1. _____ Present value

    a. The current value of dollars to be received or paid at various dates in the future.

    b. Future worth of a sum of money receivable or payable at the present date.

BASIC EXERCISES ■

1. **Discounting and Investment Decision**

Eric has an opportunity to purchase a machine to make gyros. The machine cost $4,000 and is expected to last two years. After other expenses, Eric expects to this investment to return $2,000 next year and $2,500 in two years. Is it a good investment?

    a. Fill in the column of Table 17-1 to compute the present value of costs and returns on the assumption that Eric uses his own $4,000 and the interest rate is 10 percent.

    b. Add up the present value of the returns and compare this sum with the present value of the cost. Which is greater? _____. If the interest rate is 10 percent, should Eric purchase the machine? _____.

    c. Assume now that the interest rate is 5 percent. Fill in the relevant column of the table to compute the present value of the returns at an interest rate of 5 percent.

    d. Sum the present value of the returns and compare this sum with the present value of the costs. Which is greater? _____. If the interest rate is 5 percent, should Eric purchase the machine? _____

TABLE 17-1	Eric's Gyro Machine

Time	Item	Amount	Present Value* 5 percent	Present Value* 10 percent
Now	Cost	$4,000	_____	_____
One year	Return	2,000	_____	_____
Two years	Return	2,500	_____	_____
		Present value of all returns	_____	_____
		Net present value of project	_____	_____

*Present value = dollars in n years $\div$ $(1 + i)^n$ = (dollars in the nth year) divided by (1 plus the rate of interest multiplied by itself n times)

TABLE 17-2	Can Eric Do As Well by Investing $4,000 at the Rate of Interest?

	Interest Rate 5 percent	Interest Rate 10 percent
1. Initial deposit	$4,000	$4,000
2. Interest after one year (5 percent and 10 percent of line 1)	_____	_____
3. Balance after one year (line 1 plus line 2)	_____	_____
4. Withdrawal after one year*	$2,000	$2,000
5. New balance (line 3 minus line 4)	_____	_____
6. Interest during second year (5 percent and 10 percent of line 5)	_____	_____
7. Balance after second year (line 5 plus line 6)	_____	_____

Compare line 7 with the $2,500 Eric would have received in the second year if he had bought the gyro machine. Line 7 should be greater (less) if the net present value of the project in Table 17-1 is negative (positive). That is, if the net present value of the project is negative (positive), Eric will do better (worse) by making a financial investment at the given rate of interest.

*This $2,000 matches the return after one year from the gyro investment.

e.   The decision rule discussed in the text, and the one you should have used when answering questions b and d, compares the present value of future returns to the present value of costs. If the present value of the returns exceeds the present value of the cost, it means that Eric can do better by undertaking the investment than by investing in financial assets that yield the rate of interest we used to compute the present values. If the present value of the returns is less than the present value of the costs, it means that Eric would do better with a financial investment. You can verify that this is the case by filling in the missing parts of Table 17-2 for interest rates of 5 and 10 percent.

f.   What if Eric had to borrow the money? Would the same sorts of calculations be sufficient to help you decide whether he should borrow the money? The answer is yes. The reason is that while figuring the present value of the returns, you are accounting for interest payments whether Eric has the money or not. If he does not have the money, he will need to pay a lender. Even if he does have the money he will need to "pay" himself as much as he might have earned in some other investment. That is, he will need to meet the opportunity cost of his own money. Fill in the missing parts of Table 17-3, which has been constructed to illustrate just this point.

To summarize:

a.   Present value calculations use interest rates to transform dollars in the future into their equivalent today.

b.   Comparing the present value of returns and costs is a good way to evaluate investment opportunities.

c.   Comparing the present value of returns and costs is a good procedure whether you have to borrow the money or not, assuming that you can borrow or lend at the same rate of interest you are using in your present value calculations.

What If Eric Had to Borrow the $4,000?

TABLE 17-3

	Interest Rate	
	5 percent	10 percent
1. Amount borrowed	$4,000	$4,000
2. Interest due at end of first year	$ 200	$ 400
3. Cash flow from investment	$2,000	$2,000
4. Net cash flow after interest payment (line 3 minus line 2)	_____	_____
5. Interest earned during second year by investing net cash flow (5 percent and 10 percent of line 4)	_____	_____
6. Cash flow from investment	$2,500	$2,500
7. Total at end of second year (line 4 plus line 5 plus line 6)	_____	_____
8. Interest due at end of second year	$ 200	$ 400
9. Loan repayment	$4,000	$4,000
10. Net (line 7 minus line 8 and line 9)	_____	_____

The crucial question is whether the gyro investment offers any return after paying back the loan with interest. Any dollars left over are pure profit for Eric since he did not invest any of his own money. It should be true that Eric will have a positive (negative) net if the present value of returns is greater (less) than the present value of costs. Is it?

(The entries on line 10 are dollars in the second year. What is the present value of these dollars? How do these present values compare with the net present values calculated in Table 17-1 above?)

d. If the present value of returns equals the present value of costs, an investment opportunity offers the same return as investing at the rate of interest.

e. If the present value of returns exceeds the present value of costs, an investment opportunity offers a greater return than investing at the rate of interest.

f. If the present value of returns is less than the present value of costs, an investment opportunity offers a worse return than investing at the rate of interest.

2. **When Is $1,000,000 Not $1,000,000?**

On Wednesday, April 14, 1993, Don Calhoun earned $1,000,000 for about 5 seconds of work. Or did he? After reluctantly accompanying a friend to a basketball game between the Chicago Bulls and Miami Heat, Mr. Calhoun was chosen at random from the audience. Standing at one free-throw line, he was given one shot at the basket at the other end of the court. His baseball-like hurl was all net.

Like most state lotteries, the million dollars that Mr. Calhoun received was not $1,000,000 immediately, rather it was a commitment to pay $50,000 a year for 20 years. What is the cost of Mr. Calhoun's $1,000,000 to the restaurant and soft-drink sponsors of the long free-throw contest (or their insurance company)? Why is it less than $1,000,000?

SUPPLEMENTARY EXERCISE   ∎

CAN YOU SHARE IN MONOPOLY PROFITS?

Assume that the major oil companies are able to exercise considerable monopoly power and, as a result, earn substantial monopoly profits on their investments, far in excess of the interest rate. Can you share these profits and earn the same high rate of return by buying oil company stocks?

What determines the price of oil company stocks? An economist would expect the market price to be close to the present value of the future returns from owning the stock, that is, close to the present value of expected future dividends and capital gains. Thus if dividends are high because of huge monopoly profits, the price of the stock will be _____. If huge monopoly profits and the resulting future dividends were known for sure, what rate of return do you think you could earn by buying oil company stocks? Just who does earn those monopoly profits?

■ ECONOMICS IN ACTION

NICE WORK IF YOU CAN GET IT

A number of observers have charged that compensation for executives of American corporations is excessive. Certainly the compensation received by some individuals has been eye-catching, notably the $569.8 million that Michael Eisner, chairman and CEO of Walt Disney Co., realized in 1998. The $220.16 million that Sanford I. Weill, CEO of Travelers Group Inc., realized seems puny only by comparison. Critics charge that since executives sit on each other's boards of directors they are hardly the ones to be trusted when it comes to setting each other's compensation.

In the 1980s direct salary payments were a major part of executive compensation. Since then stock options have become increasingly important and now account for over half of executive compensation at large companies.[2] Stock options give an individual the right to purchase stock at an earlier agreed upon price. This price is called the exercise price of the option. If a company does well and its stock price increases, there may be a substantial difference between the stock price and the option price. The increasing importance of stock options in executive compensation reflects three factors: legislation authored by U.S. Representative Martin Sabo (D-Minnesota) to limit the ability of corporations to deduct salary payments from taxable income; criticism that compensation bore little relation to performance; and changes in tax laws that tax capital gains at lower rates than salary.

Writing in *The Wall Street Journal* in 1999, Alfred Rappaport, professor emeritus, Kellogg Graduate School of Management, Northwestern University, argues that the current structure of stock options is not efficient. Just as a rising tide raises all boats, a rising stock market means stock price increases that have nothing to do with the performance or leadership of individual CEOs. Rappaport argues that much of the rise in stock values in the late 1990s was related to declines in interest rates and inflation, factors that bore no relation to the contributions of an individual CEO. Citing a survey by LEK Consulting, Rappaport notes that over 60 percent of stock options granted over the past six years were for below average performance, that is the increase in the price of stock of these companies was less than the increase in broad market averages. Rappaport argues that the exercise price of stock options should be linked to an index of the stock of a company's competitor. In this way, options would have value only if the company's stock outperformed its competitors.

SOURCE: Alfred Rappaport, "Stock Options that Don't Reward Laggards," *The Wall Street Journal*, March 30, 1999. "Executive Pay," *The Wall Street Journal*, April 8, 1999.

1. *Forbes* magazine conducts an annual survey of executive compensation. What does the most recent survey show? Is executive compensation excessive?

2. What sorts of incentives and rewards for executive performance are in the best interests of stockholders? of the economy?

3. Should there be limits on executive compensation? If so, what and why? What would be the effect on incentives of different limits?

4. What do you think of Rappaport's idea to link the exercise price of stock options to a relevant stock price index?

■ STUDY QUESTIONS

1. What does it mean to say that the demand for a factor of production is a derived demand?

2. Why is the demand curve for a factor of production the downward-sloping portion of the factor's curve of marginal revenue product?

---

[2]Stock options are not restricted just to top executives. Startup companies often offer stock options to attract employees.

3. What is the difference between investment and capital?

4. How does discounting help a firm determine the profitability of investment projects?

5. How is the profitability of investment projects affected when interest rates change?

6. What is the definition of economic rent?

7. Why isn't the rent you pay for an apartment economic rent?

8. What is meant by the statement in the text that almost all employees earn some economic rent?

9. What explains differences in rent for different parcels of land?

10. Why doesn't competition work to limit profits to the rate of interest?

11. What is the difference between invention and innovation?

ECONOMICS ONLINE ■

You can get information on executive compensation on-line from *Forbes* magazine.

www.forbes.com

The AFL-CIO maintains a web page to track executive compensation.

www.aflcio.org/paywatch/index.htm

How do the very rich today compare with their historical counterparts? Looking just at dollars, Bill Gates has wealth that far exceeds that of Rockefeller, Carnegie and Mellon, but the American economy is far larger in 1999 than it was in 1899. Writing in *American Heritage*, Michael Klepper and Robert Gunther rank the 40 wealthiest Americans by comparing their wealth to the size of the economy. Bill Gates is not first on this list. Who is?

www.americanheritage.com/98/oct/40index.htm

LABOR: THE HUMAN INPUT

LEARNING OBJECTIVES

After completing this chapter, you should be able to:

■ explain how income and substitution effects influence the slope of the supply curve of labor.

■ discuss recent trends in American labor markets..

■ explain how the demand for labor is derived from a firm's profit-maximizing decisions about the use of factors of production.

■ use demand and supply curves to determine the equilibrium wage and employment in a competitive labor market.

■ describe the impact of labor saving innovations on wages.

■ explain why wages for some individuals contain substantial economic rent.

■ discuss the factors that help explain why wages differ among individuals.

■ discuss how human capital theory explains the observed correlation between more education and higher wages.

Important Terms and Concepts

MINIMUM WAGE LAW

INCOME AND SUBSTITUTION EFFECTS

BACKWARD-BENDING SUPPLY CURVE

ECONOMIC RENT

INVESTMENTS IN HUMAN CAPITAL

HUMAN CAPITAL THEORY

DUAL LABOR MARKETS

UNION

TAFT-HARTLEY ACT (1947)

CLOSED SHOP

UNION SHOP

MONOPSONY

BILATERAL MONOPOLY

COLLECTIVE BARGAINING

MEDIATION

ARBITRATION

■ discuss some of the alternative views of the role of education.

■ describe the history of unions and major labor legislation in the United States.

■ use demand and supply curves to describe labor unions' possible alternative goals.

■ describe the strategies a union might follow to increase wages.

■ distinguish between a monopsonist and a monopolist.

■ describe the differences between arbitration and mediation.

■ CHAPTER REVIEW

In a competitive market without minimum wages or unions, wages and employment––the price and quantity of labor services—will be determined by the interaction of the demand for and the supply of labor services and can be analyzed with tools that should now be familiar—demand and supply curves.

The supply of labor comes from individual decisions to work. Individual decisions to supply work are simultaneously decisions to forgo leisure. Thus, a decision to supply less labor is simultaneously a

(1)   decision to demand _____. At higher wages, the same number of working hours will mean a larger income. If leisure is not an inferior good, people are apt to demand (more/less) leisure as their income increases. This suggests that the supply of labor might (increase/decrease) as wages increase. This is called the (income/substitution) effect of higher wages, but it is only part of the story.

Higher wages also increase the opportunity cost of an hour of leisure. As a result we expect that as

(2)   wages increase the substitution effect will lead people to work (more/less). The ultimate effect of increased wages comes from the sum of the income and substitution effects. Statistical evidence suggests that at low wages the _____ effect predominates and labor supply (increases/decreases) with an increase in wages, while at high wages the two effects tend to (enhance/offset) each other. The response of individuals to a change in wages, the income and substitution effects, helps determine the slope of the labor supply curve. Other factors, such as the size of the available working population and nonmonetary aspects of many jobs, help determine the _____ of the labor supply curve. The strength of the (income/substitution) effect is important for an understanding of the historical evidence on real wages and average weekly hours in the United States.

The demand for labor comes from the decisions of firms to use labor as one of many factors of production. Labor services are valuable because they add to output and, businesses hope, to profits. Thus the demand for labor is a derived demand. The discussion in earlier chapters of how a profit-maximizing firm makes optimal decisions about the use of factors of production showed that a firm should use more of any factor as long as the addition to revenue exceeds the addition to cost or, in technical terms, as long as the marginal revenue product of the factor is greater than the marginal cost of the factor. A firm's demand curve for labor is determined by its curve of marginal revenue product. The curve has a negative slope because of the law of diminishing marginal returns.

In competitive markets, equilibrium wages and employment are determined by the intersection of the market demand and supply curves, which come from the horizontal summation of firms' demand curves and individuals' supply curves. Any factor that shifts either curve will change equilibrium wages and employment. For example, an increase in the demand for a firm's output or a technological innovation that increases the productivity of labor should shift the (<u>demand/supply</u>) curve and lead to (3) (<u>higher/lower</u>) wages, employment, or both. It is often argued that labor saving innovations eliminate jobs as the same output can be produced with fewer workers. Yet these innovations also increase the productivity of workers and shift a country's production possibilities frontier. As long as macroeconomic policy works to match aggregate demand with a country's aggregate supply potential, innovations should, over time, work to increase real wages.

Wages will differ for a number of reasons. Differences in abilities and work effort will affect individual wages. Differing amounts of other factors of production would also be expected to affect the marginal physical product of labor and hence wages. If individual skills are not easily duplicated, as may be the case for star athletes or performers, wages will be high as they contain significant economic rents. If skills are easily duplicated, one would expect that competition in the form of entry would work to keep wages in line with the costs of acquiring skills.

Education and wages are positively correlated—people with more education typically earn higher wages. Human capital theory views these higher wages as the return from investments in human capital—that is, the time, money, and effort spent on schooling and training. Other theories hold that rather than enhancing skills, schooling only sorts workers by their innate abilities, helping employers identify those who will be most productive. Theories of dual labor markets argue that schooling sorts workers into good and bad jobs. In the primary labor market with good jobs, education

(4)   (<u>does/does not</u>) enhance the skills and wages of workers. In the secondary labor market, workers (<u>do/do not</u>) have an incentive to invest in their own skills.

In some cases the market determination of wages and employment is affected by a legal floor on

(5)   wage rates, or a(n) _____ wage. Chapter 5 discussed the effects of price floors. We saw there that an effective minimum wage (one above the competitive market wage) should reduce employment as firms move backward and to the left along their demand curves for labor. While this effect is clear in theory, statistical evidence of the impact of minimum wage laws on the level of employment is controversial.

Currently, about 14 percent of American workers belong to a union. The development of unions in America can be traced back just over 100 years. Significant union gains were made during the 1930s with the passage of the Wagner, or National Labor Relations Act, which guaranteed workers the right to form unions and established the National Labor Relations Board to ensure that these rights were

(6)   not violated. Some union practices were declared illegal by the _____ - _____ Act, passed in 1947. Union membership as a proportion of the labor force has been declining since the 1950s. No one is quite sure why. The shift from manufacturing to service industries, changing preferences of American workers, and the threat of foreign competition have been suggested as possible explanations.

In some labor markets, unions are the only supplier of labor services; that is, they are a

(7)   (<u>monopolist/monopsonist</u>). As such, they face a trade-off between wages and employment just as a monopoly supplier of widgets faces a trade-off between price and output. Geometrically, a union, as a monopolist, can choose any point on the relevant _____ curve for labor. The trade-off between wages and employment comes because the demand curve for labor has a negative slope. A union might be able to raise both wages and employment if it can shift the demand curve for labor to the (<u>right/left</u>). Increasing the demand for union-made products or featherbedding and other restrictive work practices will have the desired impact on the demand for union labor. (In terms of efforts to increase wages and income, do not limit your conception of unions to the AFL-CIO or to the Teamsters. Many professional organizations attempt to enhance the income of their members, often by limiting supply.) Efforts to increase productivity are an alternative way to increase the demand for labor.

Sometimes a union, as a monopolistic supplier of labor, faces a single buyer of labor services. When one buyer constitutes the entire market demand, the buyer is called a _____. (8) Both monopolists and monopsonists realize that their decisions about quantity of labor must at the same time affect _____. Monopolists who want to sell more must accept a (higher/lower) price, and monopsonists who want to buy more must pay a _____ price. If a monopsonist faces a monopolist, then the whole market has only _____ participants. The technical term for this situation is _____ monopoly. Each will consider the actions of the other, and, as for oligopoly, the outcome is difficult to predict.

When union and management sit down to decide the terms and conditions of employment, they are engaging in _____ _____. This process establishes not (9) only wages but also fringe benefits, overtime premiums, grievance procedures, and a host of other details. If both sides cannot come to an agreement and wish to avoid a strike, they may agree to _____ or _____. If labor and management call on the services of someone to help them reach an agreement but with no power to enforce a settlement, this person is called a(n) _____. If she listens to the arguments of both sides and then also makes the final decisions, she is called a(n) _____.

■ IMPORTANT TERMS AND CONCEPTS QUIZ

Choose the most appropriate definition for each of the following terms.

1. _____ Minimum wage law

2. _____ Income effect (of higher wages)

3. _____ Substitution effect (of higher wages)

4. _____ Backward-bending supply curve of labor

5. _____ Human capital theory

6. _____ Dual labor markets

7. _____ Union

8. _____ Taft-Hartley Act

9. _____ Closed shop

10. _____ Union shop

11. _____ Monopsony

12. _____ Bilateral monopoly

13. _____ Collective bargaining

14. _____ Mediation

15. _____ Arbitration

a. All workers must join the union.

b. Reduction in supply of labor as wages increase.

c. Legal floor on wages for all workers.

d. Viewing education as an investment in a person's earning potential.

e. Market composed of a single seller and a single buyer.

f. Organization of workers to negotiate with employers over wages and other terms and conditions of employment.

g. Market situation in which there is only one producer.

h. Impact on demand for increased leisure from higher income when wages increase.

i. Intervention of an impartial individual who is empowered to impose binding decisions on unresolved issues.

j. Market situation in which there is only one buyer.

k. Law that limited closed shops and allowed states to ban union shops.

l. Increased opportunity cost of leisure as wages increase.

m. Hiring only union members.

n. Discussions between labor and management to determine wages and other conditions of employment.

o. Intervention of an impartial observer who attempts to hasten the bargaining process.

p. Notion that there are mainly two types of jobs: those offering opportunities for acquisition of skills and promotions, and "dead-end jobs."

BASIC EXERCISES ■

This problem illustrates the determination of wages and employment in both a competitive market and a market monopolized by a labor union.

Tony runs a small company, Bearpaw Boots, that manufactures hiking boots. Table 18-1 shows output per month for different quantities of labor.

1. Fill in the third column by using the data in the second column to compute the marginal physical product of each additional worker.

2. Tony can sell boots for $60 a pair. Each boot contains $20 worth of leather, leaving $40 for wages or profits. As Tony has a small firm, the price of boots is unaffected by the quantity that he sells. Fill in the fourth column by computing the marginal revenue products of each worker. Be sure to use the $40 net figure rather than the $60 gross.

3. Tony wants to maximize profits. How many workers should he employ if monthly wages are $1,100? _____

4. Show that your answer to question 3 maximizes profits by computing total profits for one more and for one less worker.

5. Figure 18-1 shows the supply of bootmakers for the entire industry. Assume there are 100 competitive firms just like Tony's. Using your data on the marginal revenue product for a typical firm, plot the market demand for bootmakers. What is the equilibrium market wage and employment? $_____ and _____. At the equilibrium market wage, how many workers should Tony employ?_____ What are Tony's profits? _____.

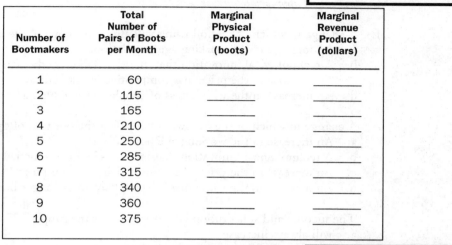

Output Figures for Bearpaw Boots

TABLE 18-1

Number of Bootmakers	Total Number of Pairs of Boots per Month	Marginal Physical Product (boots)	Marginal Revenue Product (dollars)
1	60	_____	_____
2	115	_____	_____
3	165	_____	_____
4	210	_____	_____
5	250	_____	_____
6	285	_____	_____
7	315	_____	_____
8	340	_____	_____
9	360	_____	_____
10	375	_____	_____

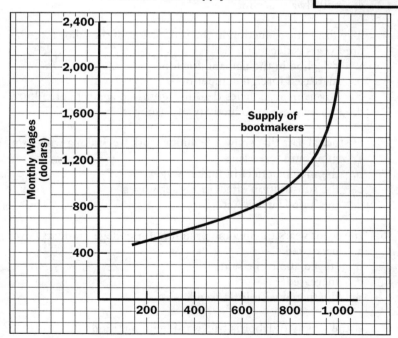

Demand and Supply: Bootmakers   **FIGURE 18-1**

6. Assume now that the IAB, the International Association of Bootmakers, has been successful in unionizing bootmakers. In order to evaluate possible alternative goals, the union has asked you to use your knowledge of the industry demand curve to answer the following questions:
   a. If union membership is limited to 400 persons, what is the maximum monthly wage the union can get from employers? $_____

b. If the union wage is set at $700 a month, what is the maximum amount of employment? $_____

c. What wage and employment combination will maximize total wage payments? $_____

■ SELF-TESTS FOR UNDERSTANDING

TEST A
Circle the most appropriate answer.

1. A change in which of the following will affect the slope of the labor supply curve?
    a. An increase in the working age population.
    b. A technological innovation that increases labor productivity.
    c. An increase in the price of a competitive firm's output.
    d. An increase in the willingness of people to trade higher money incomes for more leisure.

2. A change in which of the following will affect the position of the labor supply curve?
    a. An increase in the working age population.
    b. A technological innovation that increases labor productivity.
    c. An increase in the price of a competitive firm's output.
    d. An increase in the willingness of people to work longer hours in return for higher wages.

3. The income and substitution effects mean that the supply of labor _____ when wages increase.
    a. will always increase
    b. may rise or fall
    c. will always decline

4. The dramatic reduction in the proportion of the labor force in agriculture over the past two hundred years reflects
    a. a decline in the demand for food.
    b. increased foreign competition.
    c. government policies that discriminated against agriculture.
    d. the increased productivity of farm workers.

5. Historical data that show a declining work week along with rising real wages are probably reflecting
    a. minimum wage laws.
    b. the income effect of higher wages.
    c. the substitution effect of higher wages.
    d. the Taft-Hartley Act.

6. In recent years the income premium for college graduates over high school graduates has
    a   narrowed.
    b. stayed about the same.
    c. increased.
    d. fluctuated with little trend.

7. If the supply of labor is backward bending, then
    a. we're probably talking about manual labor.
    b. even higher wages are needed to increase supply.
    c. the income effect is greater than the substitution effect.
    d. the incentive to work more hours when wages are higher is outweighing the income effect of higher wages.

8. The demand for labor is the downward-sloping portion of the _____ curve for labor.
    a. marginal physical product
    b. marginal revenue product
    c. marginal cost
    d. average revenue

9. A change in which of the following will affect the demand for labor by affecting the marginal physical product of labor?
   a. The demand for a firm's output.
   b. The amount of other factors of production per worker.
   c. The supply of labor.
   d. The minimum wage.

10. A change in which of the following will affect the demand for labor by affecting the marginal revenue product of labor?
    a. The demand for a firm's output.
    b. Union militancy.
    c. The supply of labor.
    d. The minimum wage.

11. Wages are likely to contain a large component of economic rent when
    a. significant training is involved in learning valuable skills.
    b. schooling works only to sort individuals into good or bad jobs.
    c. minimum wage laws are effective.
    d. valuable skills are virtually impossible to duplicate.

12. The supply curve for schmoos is upward sloping. An increase in the demand for schmoos (the demand curve shifts to the right) will lead to all but which one of the following?
    a. The price of schmoos increases.
    b. The marginal physical product of labor schedule shifts upward.
    c. The marginal revenue product of labor schedule shifts upward.
    d. The demand curve for labor to produce schmoos shifts upward.
    e. Employment and/or wages increase in the schmoo industry.

13. The theory of human capital says that
    a. individuals can repair their own bodies with artificial parts, just like machines.
    b. soon all work will be done by robots.
    c. individual decisions to seek training and new skills can be modeled in the same way as ordinary investment decisions, involving present costs in the expectation of future returns.
    d. slavery in the United States was doomed because it was uneconomical.

14. Human capital theory explains the correlation between education and wages as the result of
    a. learning in school that enhances productivity.
    b. sorting by social class.
    c. the dual labor market.
    d. the growing influence of white collar unions.

15. What percent of American workers belong to unions?
    a. 56 percent.
    b. 33 percent.
    c. 14 percent.
    d. 9 percent.

16. In contrast with unions in Europe and Japan, unions in America
    a. are much more political.
    b. have resulted in almost twice the level of strike activity found in any other country.
    c. involve a smaller percentage of the labor force than in most countries.
    d. have been less adversarial than unions in Japan.

17. The Taft-Hartley Act
    a. permitted states to ban union shops.
    b. legalized closed shops.
    c. created the National Labor Relations Board.
    d. increased the minimum wage.

18. A single union that controls the supply of labor to many small firms is a
    a. socialist.
    b. monopsonist.
    c. oligopolist.
    d. monopolist.

19. Unless a union can shift the demand curve for labor, it can increase wages only if it is willing to
    a. strike.
    b. accept lower employment.
    c. submit to binding arbitration.
    d. engage in a secondary boycott.

20. Which of the following are examples of
    mediation?_____
    arbitration?_____
    strike?_____
    featherbedding?_____
    union shop?_____
    closed shop?_____
    a. Public school teachers and the local school board, unable to reach agreement, consent to accept the determination of a three-person board.
    b. Anyone may seek work at the local meat-packing plant, but once employed she must join the union.
    c. In an attempt to avert a steel strike, the Secretary of Labor helps the United Steelworkers and the steel companies to resolve their differences.
    d. The United Mine Workers start picketing after contract negotiations fail.
    e. Union rules require that two janitors must be present whenever the local school building is open in the evening, even if there is only enough work for one.
    f. Only union members can work on the production line at the local factory.

TEST B

Circle T or F for true or false.

T   F   1. Information on the marginal revenue product of labor can be used to derive a firm's demand for labor.

T   F   2. The law of diminishing returns implies that the demand curve for labor will have a negative slope.

T   F   3. The income effect of higher wages suggests that the supply of labor schedule may have a positively sloped portion.

T   F   4. An increase in wages that increases the quantity of labor supplied is represented as a shift in the supply curve.

T   F   5. When skills are easily duplicated, a large portion of wages will be economic rent.

T   F   6. If a labor union has complete control over the supply of a particular type of labor, it is a monopsonist.

T   F   7. A market with a single buyer and a single seller is called an oligopoly.

T   F   8. In general there is no conflict between union attempts to maximize wages for current union members and attempts to provide employment for the largest possible number of workers.

T   F   9. Statistical evidence suggests that unions have been successful in raising wages by 50 to 100 percent above their competitive level.

T   F   10. If a union and employer, unable to reach agreement on a new contract, agree to accept the decision of an impartial third party, they have agreed to settle their differences by arbitration.

SUPPLEMENTARY EXERCISES ■

1. **Wages and Employment Under Monopsony**

This problem is designed to show how monopoly elements in labor markets, either a monopsonist firm or a monopolist union, can affect wages and employment.

Assume that Bearpaw Boots (the subject of the Basic Exercise for the chapter) is located in a small, isolated town in northern Maine and is the sole employer of bootmakers. Tony still sells his boots in a competitive market for a net price of $40. Table 18-2 contains data on what wages Tony must pay to get various numbers of employees.

a. Use the data in the first two columns of Table 18-2 to plot the supply curve of labor in Figure 18-2. Use the data on the marginal revenue product computed in Table 18-1 to plot the demand curve for labor in Figure 18-2. These curves intersect where wages are $ _____ and the number of employees is _____.

b. Will Tony pay the wage you determined in question a? Remember, Tony is the only employer of bootmakers in town. As he employs additional workers, he must pay a higher wage not only to each new employee but also to all existing employees. Thus the marginal cost of an additional

Supply of Bootmakers in a Small, Isolated Town   TABLE 18-2

Number of Bootmakers	Monthly Wage (dollars)	Total Labor Cost[a] (dollars)	Marginal Labor Cost[b] (dollars)
1	300	_____	_____
2	400	_____	_____
3	500	_____	_____
4	600	_____	_____
5	700	_____	_____
6	800	_____	_____
7	900	_____	_____
8	1,000	_____	_____
9	1,100	_____	_____
10	1,200	_____	_____

[a] Total Labor Cost = (Number of bootmakers) × (Monthly Wage)

[b] Marginal Labor Cost = change in Total Labor Cost. For example, when employing 2 workers rather than 1, Total Labor Cost changes by $500.

Demand and Supply: Bootmakers   FIGURE 18-2

worker is (greater/less) than the wage. Fill in the remaining columns of Table 18-2 to compute Tony's marginal labor costs.

c. Plot the figures on marginal labor costs in Figure 18-2.

d. Tony should increase employment as long as the marginal revenue of additional workers exceeds the marginal cost. Using this logic, Tony's profit-maximizing level of employment is _____ workers.

e. While the curve of marginal labor cost is critical for Tony's calculation of the profit-maximizing level of employment, it is the supply curve for labor that tells Tony how much he must offer workers. What is the lowest wage that Tony must offer in order to attract the profit-maximizing number of workers? $ _____

f. What are Tony's profits (net revenue minus total wages)? _____
(Check to be sure that this level of employment maximizes profits by considering what happens if Tony hires one more or one fewer worker.)

g. If Tony were forced to pay a minimum wage of $1,100 a month, what would happen to wages and employment?

h. Would a union necessarily force the minimum wage solution to question g on Tony? Why or why not?

ECONOMICS IN ACTION

9 TO 5 OR 9 TO 9?

Beginning in the early 1990s, average overtime for factory workers began to rise. While some increase in average overtime is to be expected during a business recovery, recent levels of overtime hours have been at historically high levels. ("Fewer Jobs Filled as Factories Rely on Overtime Pay," *The New York Times*, May 16, 1993.) Why has there been such an increase in overtime work when overtime pay is 50 percent more expensive than straight wages?

Many workers welcome the opportunity to work overtime, and many companies find it the most profitable way to expand production, especially when they are not sure whether demand for their products will remain high. The rising cost of fringe benefits—health insurance, unemployment compensation, retirement, social security—is also cited as an important factor that leads companies to prefer expanding overtime to hiring new workers. For example, paying overtime may cost more in terms of salary but does not typically add to a company's health insurance costs the way hiring new workers would. By 1993 these extra costs amounted to 28 percent of a typical worker's wages. James Waters of Towers Perrin, a personnel consulting firm, put the matter somewhat differently when he said, "Benefit costs, including health costs, are a major factor, but there is more concern about all the costs of recruiting people, training them, carrying them until they become fully productive, and then the cost of firing them if production slacks off."

Overtime is quite common in manufacturing where workers are generally highly skilled and the hiring of new workers takes time and effort for recruitment and training. In contrast, the work force for retail sales and food industries is less skilled with more extensive use of part-time workers and contract workers without benefits. The result has been less overtime and more new hires in service sectors than in manufacturing.

1. Firms can increase employment by hiring new workers or increasing hours for their current workers. How is a firm likely to choose between these options when, in addition to hourly wages and fringe benefits, there is a significant fixed cost to hiring new workers?

2. Consider each of the following elements of labor compensation: wages, social security taxes, retirement contributions, health insurance benefits, training costs, costs of hiring and firing. Which vary directly with the number of hours worked and which operate like fixed costs, that is, which vary with the number of workers and which with the number of hours worked?

STUDY QUESTIONS

1. Why does the income effect of an increase in wages tend to reduce the supply of labor when wages increase?

2. Why does the substitution effect of an increase in wages tend to increase the supply of labor when wages increase?

3. How can distinguishing between the income and substitution effects of an increase in wages help one understand the historical record of increasing real wages and a declining workweek?

4. What explains the demand for labor?

5. When will wages contain significant economic rent?

6. Demand and supply analysis seems to suggest that there should be a single wage, yet there is significant variation in the wages individuals receive. What other factors explain the difference in wages among individuals? Which of these factors can be seen as factors affecting the demand and supply curves and which cannot?

7. What is human capital theory and how might it explain differences in wages?

8. What would you expect to happen if the minimum wage is increased? Why?

9. Economists often argue that a union can only raise wages by accepting a reduction in employment. When does a union face this sort of trade-off and what might it do to try and increase both employment and wages?

10. What is the difference between mediation and arbitration? Is one better than the other? Why?

11. Is the introduction of labor saving technological innovations good or bad for workers? for the economy? Why?

ECONOMICS ONLINE

What's up at the AFL-CIO? Find out by checking their homepage.

www.aflcio.org/home.htm

Does it pay to go to college? This web site has historical data on income and educational attainment for men, women, Blacks, Whites, and Hispanics. See for yourself.

www.census.gov/population/socdemo/education/tablea-03.txt

The School of Industrial Labor Relations at Cornell University maintains a web site with lots of labor market links.

http://workindex.com

POVERTY, INEQUALITY, AND DISCRIMINATION

LEARNING OBJECTIVES

After completing this chapter, you should be able to:

■ discuss some of the facts of poverty and income distribution.

■ describe the implications of the use of absolute or relative concepts of poverty.

■ explain what a Lorenz curve is.

■ draw a Lorenz curve, given data on population and income.

■ describe what factors account for differences in incomes, how some of these factors reflect voluntary choices, and why these factors make identifying economic discrimination so difficult.

■ explain how competition can minimize some forms of discrimination but not others.

■ explain why the trade-off between equality and efficiency implies that the optimal distribution of income will involve some inequality.

■ explain the concept of a negative income tax and how it affects work incentives.

■ explain why, if implementing a negative income tax program, policymakers can only choose two of the following three parameters: guaranteed level of income, tax rate, and break-even level of income.

■ describe the controversy surrounding programs for affirmative action.

■ CHAPTER REVIEW

Discussions of poverty in America usually focus on the number of families below the poverty line. In

(1)   1997 this dividing line was about $_____ a year for a family of four. It is adjusted every year

for changes in prices. Since the yearly adjustment reflects only prices and not general increases in real

income, the poverty line is a(n) (absolute/relative) concept of poverty rather than a(n)

_____ concept.

The facts about the distribution of income can be presented in a number of different ways.

(2)   Economists often use a form of graphical representation called a(n) _____ curve. To

construct such a curve, one first orders families or individuals by income, lowest to highest. Then the

cumulative percentage of total income is plotted against the cumulative percentage of families (or indi-

viduals). The Lorenz curve starts at the origin, where zero percent of families have _____ per-

cent of income. Perfect equality in the distribution of income would result in a Lorenz curve that coin-

cided with the _____ line. In real economies, with inequality in the distribution of income, the

Lorenz curve lies (above/below) the 45-degree line. (Can you convince yourself that the Lorenz curve

never crosses the 45-degree line?) From 1950 to 1970 there was a slight trend toward greater

(equality/inequality) while the period since 1970 has seen a trend toward greater _____.

U.S. income data show that in 1997, families with incomes above $80,000 were in the top 20 per-

cent of the income distribution, while families with incomes below approximately $20,000 were in the

(3)   bottom 20 percent. The top 20 percent of families received _____ percent of income while the

bottom 20 percent received _____ percent.

Why do incomes differ? The list of reasons is long and includes differences in abilities, intensity of

work, risk taking, wage differentials for unpleasant or hazardous tasks, schooling and training, work

experience, inherited wealth, luck, and discrimination. Some of the reasons for differences in incomes

represent voluntary choices by individuals to work harder, take more risks, or accept unpleasant work

in order to earn higher incomes. Measures to equalize incomes may adversely affect the work effort of

(4)   these individuals. In more technical terms, efforts for greater equality may reduce _____.

This important trade-off does not mean that all efforts to increase equality should be abandoned. It

does mean that efforts to increase equality have a price and should not be pushed beyond the point where the marginal gains from further equality are worth less than the marginal loss from reduced efficiency. Exactly where this point is reached is the subject of continuing political debate.

The trade-off between equality and efficiency also suggests that in the fight for greater equality one should choose policies with small rather than large effects on efficiency. Economists argue that many welfare programs have been inefficient. One important reason is the relatively large reduction in benefits for each additional dollar of earned income. These high implicit marginal tax rates (increase/decrease) the incentive for increased work effort on the part of welfare recipients who are able to work.   (5)

Many economists favor replacing the current welfare system with a negative income tax, that is, a system of direct cash grants tied to income levels and linked to the tax system. These schemes usually start with a minimum guaranteed level of income and a tax rate that specifies the (increase/decrease)   (6) in the cash grant for every dollar increase in income. A low tax rate will retain significant work incentives; however, a low tax rate also means that grants continue until income is quite high. The point where payments from the government stop and payments to the government start is called the _____ level of income. A negative income tax with a low marginal tax rate can offer significantly better work incentives to those currently receiving welfare, but there will be (positive/negative) work incentives for those not now on welfare but who become eligible for grants. Recent negative income tax experiments have investigated the size of these negative work incentives and found them to be (large/small).

Economic discrimination is defined as a situation in which equivalent factors of production receive _____ payments for equal contributions to output. Average differences in income   (7) between large social groups, such as men and women or blacks and whites, (are/are not) sufficient proof of economic discrimination. These average differences tend to (overstate/understate) the amount of economic discrimination. To accurately measure the impact of possible discrimination, we must first correct for the factors listed above that could create differences in income without implying economic discrimination. Some factors, such as schooling, are tricky. For instance, differences in wages associated with differences in schooling would not imply any discrimination if everyone has had an equal opportunity for the same amount of schooling. But it is unclear whether observed differences in schooling represent voluntary choices or another form of discrimination.

Public policy makes it illegal to discriminate, but the evidence concerning what constitutes discrimination is subject to dispute as are policies to promote affirmative action. Competitive markets can

(8)   work to decrease some forms of discrimination, especially discrimination by (employers/employees).

■ IMPORTANT TERMS AND CONCEPTS QUIZ

Choose the most appropriate definition for each of the following terms.

1. _____ Poverty line

2. _____ Lorenz curve

3. _____ Economic discrimination

4. _____ Statistical discrimination

5. _____ Affirmative action

6. _____ TANF

7. _____ Negative income tax

8. _____ Food stamps

a. Amount of income below which a family is considered "poor."

b. Active efforts to recruit and hire members of underrepresented groups.

c. Graph depicting the distribution of income.

d. Income share of poorest quartile of income distribution.

e. Time limited welfare assistance.

f. Income-conditioned cash grants available to all families as an entitlement.

g. Estimating a worker's productivity as low solely because that worker belongs to some group.

h. Stamps that allow families to buy food at subsidized prices.

i. Equivalent factors of production receive unequal pay for equal contributions to output.

■ BASIC EXERCISE

This problem illustrates the high marginal tax rates that often result from combining welfare programs. The numbers in this problem do not come from any specific welfare program but illustrate many.

Imagine a welfare system that offers a family of four the following forms of public support.

■ General assistance in the form of a basic grant of $300 a month. The first $50 of earned income every month is assumed to be for work-related expenses and does not reduce benefits. After that, benefits are reduced by 50 cents for every dollar of earned income.

■ Food stamps that offer the family $3,000 a year but require payments equal to 25 percent of gross wage earnings.

TABLE 19-1

(1) Earned Income	(2) Social Security and Income Taxes*	(3) General Assistance	(4) Food Stamps	(5) Medicaid Subsidy	(6) Housing Subsidy	(7) Net Income (1) − (2) + (3) + (4) + (5) + (6)
0	0	3,600	3,000	2,000	4,400	_____
600**	−194	3,600	2,850	2,000	4,250	_____
7,799	−2,523	1	1050	2,000	3,350	_____
7,800	−2,523	0	1050	0	3,350	_____
9,400	−3,037	0	650	0	2,950	_____
12,000	−2,838	0	0	0	2,300	_____
12,300	−2,815	0	0	0	2,225	_____
17,900	−1,205	0	0	0	835	_____
21,200	239	0	0	0	0	_____
30,095	4,132	0	0	0	0	_____
35,000	5,243	0	0	0	0	_____

*Income taxes include earned income credit at 1998 tax rates.
**Assume $50 a month.

■ Medicaid benefits of $2,000 a year. The family is assumed to receive these benefits as long as it is eligible for general assistance.

■ Housing subsidy that gives the family an apartment worth $4,800 a year in rent. The family must contribute 25 percent of its net income toward rent. Net income is determined as gross wage earnings plus general assistance minus $500 for each dependent.

1. Fill in column 7 of Table 19-1 by computing net income after taxes and after welfare payments for the different levels of earned income.

2. Use the data in columns 1 and 7 to plot net income against earned income in Figure 19-1 on page 230. Plot each pair of points and then connect successive pairs with a straight line. What does the graph suggest about work incentives under these programs?

3. Use the data in Table 19-1 to complete Table 19-2, computing the implicit marginal tax rates that this family faces as it earns income. What is the relationship between the implicit marginal tax rates you computed in Table 19-2 and the

TABLE 19-2

(1) Earned Income (dollars)	(2) Change in Earned Income (dollars)	(3) Net Income (Table 19-1, Column 7) (dollars)	(4) Change in Net Income (dollars)	(5) "Implicit Taxes" (2) – (4) (dollars)	(6) Implicit Marginal Tax Rate (5) 4 (2) (percent)
0					
600	600				
7,799	7,199				
7,800	1				
9,400	1,600				
12,000	2,600				
12,300	300				
17,900	5,600				
21,200	3,300				
30,095	8,895				
35,000	4,905				

Income Before and After Subsidy Programs

FIGURE 19-1

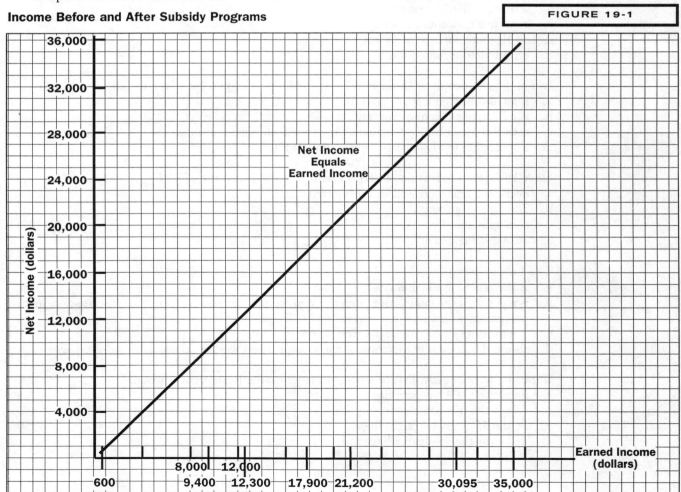

slope of the graph in Figure 19-1? (How do these marginal rates compare with marginal rates under the positive portion of federal income taxes which ranged from 15 percent to 39.6 percent in 1998?)

4. One could reduce the implicit marginal tax rate by lowering the rate at which benefits are reduced under any of the programs. To investigate the impact of such reductions, construct a new version of Table 19-1 in which general assistance payments are reduced by only 25 cents for every dollar reduction in income, and the food stamp subsidy is reduced by only 10 cents. What happens to the magnitude of the subsidy payments at each level of income? What happens to the break-even levels of income for each program, that is, to the level of income when a family is no longer eligible? What would happen to total public outlays for these programs?

■ SELF-TESTS FOR UNDERSTANDING

TEST A

Circle the most appropriate answer.

1. The facts on income distribution in the United States show
    a. a substantial move toward equality over the last 30 years.
    b. that the richest 20 percent of families receive about 80 percent of the total income.
    c. that the poorest 20 percent of families receive less than 2 percent of income.
    d. a Lorenz curve that sags below the 45-degree line.

2. The poverty line computed by the government, estimated to be $16,400 in 1997, is an example of
    a. statistical discrimination.
    b. a relative concept of poverty.
    c. an absolute concept of poverty.
    d. economic discrimination.

3. Defining poor people as those who fall in the bottom 20 percent of the income distribution
    a. is an absolute concept of poverty.
    b. is a relative concept of poverty.
    c. means that continued economic growth will eliminate poverty.
    d. implies that the Lorenz curve is a straight line.

4. Since 1980, the proportion of persons with incomes below the official poverty line
    a. decreased and increased with little trend.
    b. decreased significantly.
    c. rose substantially.
    d. has stayed constant.

5. The Lorenz curve
    a. is the same for all countries.
    b. is a graph of the cumulative percentage of families (or persons) and the associated cumulative percentage of income they receive.
    c. is a measure of economic discrimination.
    d. shows the growth in income one might expect as a worker accumulates work experience.

6. If income were equally divided among all families, the Lorenz curve would
    a. lie above the 45-degree line.
    b. follow the horizontal axis.
    c. be the 45-degree straight line.
    d. lie below the 45-degree line.

7. If there were no economic discrimination, the Lorenz curve would
   a. lie above the 45-degree line.
   b. follow the horizontal axis.
   c. be the 45-degree straight line.
   d. lie below the 45-degree line.

8. Compared with other industrial countries, data on the distribution of income in the United States show
   a. more inequality than most other countries.
   b. about the same degree of inequality.
   c. much more equality.

9. In 1997, the richest 20 percent of families received about _____ percent of total income.
   a. 20 percent
   b. 32 percent
   c. 47 percent
   d. 50 percent

10. In 1997, the poorest 20 percent of families received _____ percent of total income.
    a. less than 2 percent
    b. about 4 percent
    c. about 10 percent
    d. about 20 percent

11. In 1997, families with an income above _____ were in the top 20 percent of the income distribution.
    a. $40,000
    b. $80,000
    c. $120,000
    d. $200,000

12. Consider a negative income tax scheme with a guaranteed minimum income of $8,000 for a family of four and a tax rate of 50 percent. The break-even level of income would be
    a. $4,000.
    b. $8,000.
    c. $12,000.
    d. $16,000.

13. If the Vincents earn $8,000 in wages, their total income after including the negative income tax will be
    a. $4,000.
    b. $8,000.
    c. $12,000.
    d. $16,000.

14. Reducing the tax rate while retaining the same minimum guarantee will
    a. reduce the break-even level of income.
    b. leave the break-even level of income unchanged.
    c. increase the break-even level of income.
    d. there's too little information to know.

15. If a negative income tax system is to be financed within a given budget, then a reduction in the negative tax rate to increase work incentives
    a. must be offset by a reduction in the minimum guaranteed level of income.
    b. needs no change in the minimum guaranteed level of income.
    c. must be offset by an increase in the minimum guaranteed level of income.

16. Choose all of the actions that would reduce the break-even level of income.
    a. Lower the minimum guarantee level.
    b. Lower the tax rate on earned income.
    c. Increase the minimum guarantee level.
    d. Increase the tax rate on earned income.

17. If two individuals with similar productivity receive different pay for the same work, one would call this evidence of
    a. economic discrimination.
    b. prejudice.
    c. statistical discrimination.
    d. luck.

18. All but which one of the following could give rise to differences in income without implying discrimination?
    a. Schooling.
    b. Ability.
    c. Compensating wage differential for night work.
    d. Intensity of work effort.

19. Which of the following would be an example of economic discrimination?
    a. Census data show that, on average, women earn less than men.
    b. Nurses earn less than doctors.
    c. Over the period 1980 to 1990, plumbers and electricians received larger percentage wage increases than did college professors.
    d. A careful study showing that among blacks and whites with identical education, work experience, productivity, and motivation, blacks earn less than whites.

20. Competitive markets work to erode what type of discrimination?
    a. Discrimination by employees.
    b. Discrimination by employers.
    c. Statistical discrimination.

TEST B

Circle T or F for true or false.

T   F   1. Continued economic growth is capable of eliminating poverty as measured by an absolute standard, but not as measured by a relative standard.

T   F   2. U.S. data show no change in poverty since 1960 as measured by the proportion of persons below the poverty line.

T   F   3. In the United States, the 20 percent of families that are poorest receive about 20 percent of total income.

T   F   4. Perfect equality in the distribution of income would result in a Lorenz curve that lies on the 45-degree line.

T   F   5. The optimal amount of inequality is a poverty rate of 10 percent.

T   F   6. The fact that women, white or black, have lower average incomes than men, is sufficient proof of economic discrimination.

T   F   7. Competitive markets can help reduce discrimination by employees.

T   F   8. In the absence of monopolies, unregulated markets would result in an equal distribution of income.

T   F   9. Some differences in income reflect voluntary choices, such as decisions to work more hours or to take early retirement.

T   F 10. The federal personal income tax system has substantially reduced the degree of income inequality in the United States.

SUPPLEMENTARY EXERCISES ■

1. Table 19-3 shows data on the distribution of income for 10 Organization for Economic Cooperation and Development (OECD) countries. Which countries have the greatest equality in the distribution of income? You might try drawing a Lorenz curve for several countries to help you decide. For example, consider Finland and the United States. Use one large piece of graph paper to draw a Lorenz curve for both countries. In which country is income distributed more equally? What about Switzerland and the United States?

Percentage of Income Received by Population Decines

TABLE 19-3

| | Year | Population Deciles | | | | | | | | | |
		1st	2nd	3rd	4th	5th	6th	7th	8th	9th	10th
Australia	1985	2.9	4.8	6.0	7.3	8.4	9.6	11.2	12.8	15.3	21.7
Canada	1987	2.8	5.0	6.3	7.4	8.6	9.7	10.9	12.6	15.1	21.6
Finland	1987	4.5	6.3	7.3	8.3	9.2	10.0	11.0	12.0	13.6	17.8
France	1984	3.0	5.3	6.3	7.2	8.1	9.2	10.4	12.1	14.7	23.7
Germany	1984	4.0	5.8	6.8	7.6	8.7	9.6	10.7	12.1	14.1	20.6
Italy	1986	3.1	4.9	5.9	6.8	8.0	9.3	10.7	12.5	15.0	23.8
Sweden	1987	3.3	6.2	7.4	8.4	9.3	10.2	11.1	12.3	13.7	18.1
Switzerland	1982	2.8	5.2	6.1	6.9	8.0	8.8	9.9	11.2	13.6	27.5
United Kingdom	1986	2.5	5.0	6.0	7.0	8.2	9.5	10.9	12.7	15.3	22.9
United States	1986	1.9	3.8	5.5	6.8	8.2	9.5	11.2	13.3	16.1	23.7

Compare these data on income distribution for industrialized countries with similar data for lower-income developing countries. *World Development Report*, published annually by the World Bank, reports data on income distribution for a large number of countries.

SOURCE: Anthony B. Atkinson, Lee Rainwater, and Timothy M. Smeeding, "Income Distribution in OECD Countries: Evidence from the Luxembourg Income Study," *Social Policy Studies*, No. 18, (OECD 1995) Table 4-3.

2. Following is a suggested list of additional readings on three important topics covered in this chapter.

On the general issue of trade-offs between increased equality and reduced efficiency, read Arthur Okun's *Equality and Efficiency: The Big Trade-off*, published by the Brookings Institution, 1975. This important book is the source of the "leaky bucket" analogy used in the text.

For an excellent discussion of how existing welfare schemes confront poor people with "economic choices no rational person would want to make," read *Why Is Welfare So Hard to Reform?* by Henry J. Aaron, published by the Brookings Institution, 1973. The book was written following the Nixon administration's attempt to implement a negative income tax.

Martin Anderson's book, *Welfare: The Political Economy of Welfare Reform in the United States*, Hoover Institution Press, 1978, argued that existing welfare programs have essentially eliminated poverty as a critical social issue. Anderson served for a while as one of President Reagan's White House aides for domestic policy. More recent data on the impact of noncash benefits can be found in *The Statistical Abstract of the United States.*

3.   Women now account for more than 45 percent of the American labor force. Economic issues concerning the role of women in the labor force are examined by Claudia Goldin in *Understanding the Gender Gap: An Economic History of American Women*, Oxford University Press, 1990.

4.   Investigate the details of welfare programs in the city or county in which you live. Use this information to construct your own version of Table 19-1.

■   ECONOMICS IN ACTION

EMPLOYMENT, WAGES, AND POVERTY

The economic expansion from 1982 to 1990 was the second longest in U.S. history. Poverty rates declined but not by as much as one would have expected from experience during the 1960s. Experience during the expansion of the 1990s has been similar to that of the 1980s, while the incidence of poverty declined, the decline was less than one might have expected. Why was economic expansion less effective in reducing poverty in the 1980s and 1990s than in the 1960s?

Economist Rebecca Blank studied the expansion of the 1980s and considered a number of explanations. For example, census data on the incidence of poverty focus on cash income. There was a substantial expansion of in-kind transfer programs between the 1960s and the 1980s, food stamps, housing subsidies, and Medicaid being the primary examples. Might these changes explain differences in the 1980s as compared with the 1960s? Blank is skeptical. While the level of in-kind transfers was higher in the 1980s and measures of poverty that include in-kind transfer were thus lower than measures that count only cash incomes, she can find little evidence of any substantial increase in these programs over the 1980s. Including in-kind transfers makes little difference in the decline in the poverty rate during the 1980s. Other possibilities that Blank investigates include changes in the regional location of the poor, changes in public assistance programs, and changes in the types of families that are poor. In all cases, she concludes that these factors were either unimportant or too small to explain why the reduction in the poverty rate over the 1980s lagged experience of the 1960s.

What does explain the difference? Blank points to the decline in the real wages of low-wage workers as explaining why economic growth was less effective in reducing poverty. According to Blank, "The primary reason why the poor 'catch up' in economic booms is expanded employment opportunities. The incidence of unemployment, non-employment, and part-time employment is heavily skewed toward the bottom of the income distribution; when employment grows it is the unemployed, the non-employed, and part-time employed who are most able to take advantage of that growth." Blank found that economic growth in the 1980s did lead to increased economic opportunities for low-income families. If anything, employment and weeks of work for low-income families expanded more rapidly in the 1980s than in the 1960s. However, the increased hours of work were largely offset by declines in real wages. Blank's findings are consistent with information from the 1990 Census that showed a widening differential in the earnings of college graduates compared with high school graduates and dropouts.

What explains the decline in the real wages of low-wage workers? Blank does not offer a particular reason but points to the work of other researchers that suggests a combination of factors including "changes in unionization, changes in technology, changes in international markets... and changes in the relative supply of more and less skilled workers relative to a rapidly growing demand for labor market skills by employers."[1]

1.   What do you think explains why the economic expansions of the 1980s and 1990s did not result in a larger decline in the poverty rate?

[1]Rebecca M. Blank, "Why Were Poverty Rates So High in the 1980s?" *Poverty and Prosperity in the USA in the Late Twentieth Century*, D. B. Papadimitriou and E. N. Wolff, eds. (New York: St. Martin's Press, 1993), pp. 21–55. In the spring of 1999 Professor Blank was on leave from Northwestern University to serve as a member of the President's Council of Economic Advisers.

2. What are the implications for public policy?

1. What do you believe has happened to the degree of inequality in the distribution of income in the United States over the past decade? Why?

2. Which is the most meaningful measure of poverty, an absolute standard or a relative standard? Why?

3. What is a Lorenz curve and how does it provide information about the distribution of income?

4. Differences in income may be related to a number of factors. What factors reflect voluntary choices and what factors might reflect economic discrimination?

5. What is the difference between statistical discrimination and economic discrimination? Does statistical discrimination always lead to economic discrimination? Is economic discrimination always the result of statistical discrimination?

6. Competitive market forces can be counted on to help reduce some forms of discrimination but not others. When will market forces work to eliminate discrimination and when might additional measures be needed?

7. What is meant by the optimal degree of inequality? Why isn't it zero?

8. How does a negative income tax improve work incentives as compared with a system of overlapping poverty programs?

9. If one labels defines poverty as the poorest 20 percent of the population, then the poor will always be with us. What if one defines poverty as incomes that are less than 50 percent of median income. Under this definition it is necessarily true that the poor will always be with us? If not, what would it take to eliminate poverty?

LIMITING MARKET POWER: REGULATION AND ANTITRUST

LEARNING OBJECTIVES

After completing this chapter, you should be able to:

■ describe the major purposes of regulation.

■ identify the major regulatory agencies and the industries they regulate(d).

■ discuss the major arguments for and against bigness per se.

■ critically evaluate the arguments supporting regulation.

■ explain why marginal cost pricing may be infeasible in an industry with significant economies of scale.

■ explain why allowing a firm to earn profits equal to the opportunity cost of its capital provides little incentive for increased efficiency.

■ summarize recent experience under deregulation of several industries.

■ explain the major features of each of the major antitrust laws.

■ describe how concentration ratios in the United States have changed.

Important Terms and Concepts

REGULATION

ANTITRUST POLICY

MONOPOLY POWER

ECONOMIES OF SCALE

ECONOMIES OF SCOPE

BOTTLENECK FACILITY

PARITY-PRICING PRINCIPLE

CROSS-SUBSIDIZATION

MARGINAL VS. AVERAGE COST PRICING

RAMSEY PRICING RULE

PRICE CAP

REGULATORY LAG

DEREGULATION

RULE OF REASON

CONCENTRATION OF INDUSTRY

CONCENTRATION RATIOS

PREDATORY PRICING

BUNDLING

MERGERS

HORIZONTAL MERGERS

- describe how concentration may or may not be related to market power.

- describe the evidence about the effectiveness of mergers.

- describe what is meant by predatory pricing and how might one identify it.

- explain how antitrust laws can be used to thwart competition.

CHAPTER REVIEW

Economists and others have long argued whether bigness per se is good or bad. Opponents contend that the flow of wealth to firms with significant market power is socially undesirable and should be restrained; profit-maximizing monopolists are likely to lead to a misallocation of resources as they pro-

(1) duce (<u>more/less</u>) output than is socially desirable; and large firms with significant market power have little inducement for _____.

Proponents counter that large firms are necessary for successful innovation. They maintain that

(2) many big firms, because of (<u>increasing/decreasing</u>) returns to scale, can yield benefits to the public as a result of the associated (<u>reduction/increase</u>) in unit cost that accompanies large-scale production. To break up these firms into smaller units would (<u>increase/decrease</u>) costs. The United States has chosen to deal with potential monopolies through the use of regulation and antitrust policy.

REGULATION

Regulatory procedures have been adopted for a number of reasons including:

1. To regulate the actions of natural monopolies in industries where economies of

(3)   _____ and economies of _____ mean that free competition between a large number of suppliers (<u>is/is not</u>) sustainable.

2. To support competition by insuring access to _____ facilities that are necessary for firms to be able to compete.

3. To ensure service at reasonable prices to isolated areas. It is argued that regulation is necessary so that suppliers can offset (<u>above/below</u>)-cost prices in isolated areas with (<u>above/below</u>)-cost prices elsewhere and thus be protected from competitors who concentrate only on the profitable markets.

Regulation of prices is a very complicated undertaking. Established to prevent abuses of monopoly such as charging prices that are "too high," the regulatory agencies have, in many cases, actually raised prices. In these cases, regulation preserves the shadow of competition only by protecting (<u>high/low</u>)- (4)

cost, inefficient firms. Economists typically argue for the use of marginal cost as a more appropriate

basis for regulated prices.

The application of marginal cost pricing is difficult in an industry with significant economies of

scale. In this case, average cost will (<u>decline/increase</u>) as output increases. When average cost declines, (5)

marginal cost is (<u>greater/less</u>) than average cost and setting price equal to marginal cost will mean

(<u>losses/profits</u>). One response would set price equal to average cost or use tax revenues for subsidies.

In these cases economists and some regulators have urged use of the Ramsey Pricing Rule, under

which the excess of price over marginal cost depends upon the elasticity of _____.

Sometimes regulation limits overall profitability rather than prices. For example, a firm's rate of

return might be limited to 10 percent. While such regulation might seem to limit the ability of firms

to exercise monopoly power, it also (<u>enhances/reduces</u>) the incentive for firms to be efficient. In the (6)

absence of profit regulation, successful efforts to reduce costs will be rewarded with higher profits. If

profits are regulated, there is less incentive to seek out the most efficient means of production. The

term *regulatory lag* has been coined to describe the drawn-out regulatory process. Some suggest that

this process itself offers one of the few incentives for efficiency and innovation, since it actually builds

in some penalty for (<u>efficiency/inefficiency</u>) and some reward for _____. A variant of

this notion would predetermine price ceilings and leave firms free to earn higher profits through even

greater efficiency.

Experience with deregulation, especially in airline, transportation, and telephone service, is now

close to two decades old, and a number of trends have emerged.

1. Adjusted for inflation, prices have generally declined.

2. Local airline service has not suffered, as was feared, due to the establishment of specialized
    commuter airlines.

3. New firms have entered previously regulated industries, although not all have survived.

4. Unions in previously regulated industries have been under significant pressure to reduce
    wages and adjust work rules.

5. Mergers have increased the average size of the largest firms.

Items 4 and 5 need careful interpretation. To the extent that regulation allowed firms to easily pass on increased labor costs, unions will find the bargaining position of firms now subject to competitive market pressures much tougher. Mergers are understandable if regulation was originally concentrated on industries with economies of scale. In addition there are continuing concerns about the quality of service and safety in deregulated industries.

ANTITRUST POLICY

Antitrust policy is designed to control the growth of monopolies and prevent undesirable behavior from powerful firms. The history of antitrust legislation in the United States starts with the

(7) _____ Act, enacted in 1890. This act declared illegal any actions in restraint of trade and any attempts to monopolize trade.

The next important pieces of legislation were both enacted in 1914. The Federal Trade

(8) Commission Act established the Federal Trade Commission, and the _____ Act prohibited a number of practices, including preferential prices to some buyers that were not based on cost differences, known as _____ _____; requirements that buyers purchase not only what they want but also other goods exclusively from the same seller, called _____ contracts; having the same individuals serve as directors of two or more competing firms, or _____ _____; and the purchasing of a competitor's stock if that acquisition tended to reduce competition. Court decisions in antitrust cases have focused on the rule of _____ which says that size per se (is/is not) illegal; rather, the focus should be on firm conduct.

(9) Reducing your price to destroy your rivals and become a monopolist is called _____ _____. Economists argue that a price below average cost (is/is not) by itself evidence of predatory pricing. Remember that setting price below average cost may maximize profits by minimizing losses. Only if price is below marginal or average _____ cost might there be evidence of predatory pricing. Even then the courts have held that there must be evidence that such prices were adopted to harm rival firms and that the predatory firm could subsequently raise prices to monopoly levels.

There is no perfect measure of how concentrated an industry is. One widely used gauge looks at the percent of industry output accounted for by the four largest firms. This measure is called a four-firm _____ ratio. In this century, concentration ratios in the United States have (10) shown (<u>much/little</u>) change.

A firm can grow bigger by expanding its own factories or building new ones. A firm can also become bigger by buying up other firms. Combining two firms into one is a _____. (11) Mergers between competitors are called _____ mergers. Mergers may be pursued to gain monopoly power, but mergers may also be initiated in hope of increased efficiency. Evidence on the efficiency of past mergers is somewhat mixed although studies of recent mergers have reported important productivity improvements.

■ IMPORTANT TERMS AND CONCEPTS QUIZ

Choose the most appropriate definition for each of the following terms.

1. _____ Regulation
2. _____ Antitrust policy
3. _____ Monopoly power
4. _____ Economies of scale
5. _____ Economies of scope
6. _____ Bottleneck facility
7. _____ Parity-pricing principle
8. _____ Cross-subsidization
9. _____ Ramsey pricing rule
10. _____ Regulatory lag
11. _____ Price cap
12. _____ Rule of reason
13. _____ Concentration ratio
14. _____ Predatory pricing
15. _____ Bundling
16. _____ Horizontal merger

a. Losses on one product balanced by profits on another.

b. Principle that, in a multiproduct, regulated firm where price must exceed marginal cost for the firm to break even, the ratio of price to marginal cost should be highest for the products with the lowest demand elasticities.

c. Legal restrictions or controls on business decisions of firms.

d. Pricing to destroy rivals.

e. Size per se is not illegal, rather the focus of antitrust efforts should be on objectionable actions.

f. Joining firms that produce similar products into a single firm.

g. Percentage of an industry's output produced by the largest firms.

h. Temporary monopoly for the initial use of an innovation.

i. Common facility, e.g., bridge or local telephone wires, that must be used by rivals if competition is to be viable.

j. Delays in considering requests for price changes.

k. Policies designed to control growth of monopoly and to prevent powerful firms from engaging in "anti-competitive" practices.

l. Savings acquired through increases in quantities produced.

m. Pre-assigned price ceilings that decline in future years in anticipation of future productivity growth.

n. Ability of a firm to affect the price of its output for its own benefit.

o. Savings acquired through simultaneous production of different products.

p. Price of bottleneck facility should be no higher than a firm in a perfectly contestable market would charge.

q. Discounts to customers who buy a set of products as a group.

BASIC EXERCISES ■

1. **Economies of Scale**

   This exercise illustrates the difficulty of marginal cost pricing when average cost declines.

   Imagine that the efficient provision of telephone calls in a medium-sized city involves an initial
   investment of $100 million financed by borrowing at 6.75 percent and
   variable cost of 15 cents
   a phone call. The phone
   company's annual fixed
   cost would be $6.75 million (6.75 percent of
   $100 million).

   a. Use this information about costs to
   plot marginal cost
   and average total
   cost in Figure 20-1.
   (Use the $6.75 million figure for annual fixed cost.)

   b. Assume that regulators set price at 15
   cents, the level of
   marginal cost. What
   is the firm's profit
   position if 60 million calls a year are
   demanded at that
   price? 90 million?
   150 million?

   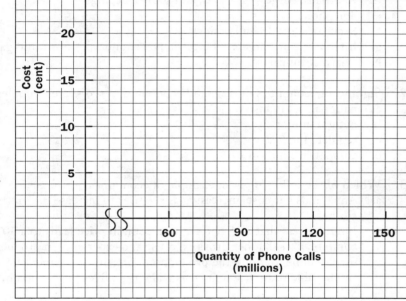

   Cost Curves | **FIGURE 20-1**

   c. Is setting price
   equal to marginal cost a viable option in this case? Why or why not?

2. **Predatory Pricing**

   Michelle owns a company that manufactures Yuk, a gooey substance that drips down the wall in
   a horrible mess but can be peeled off without damaging paint or wallpaper. While Michelle
   thought that Yuk would appeal to grade school children she has found that her strongest market
   is college students. Michelle is concerned about plans by a rival firm to introduce Splat, a similar
   product. Yuk can be produced with a fixed cost of $50,000 and a variable cost of 75¢ a pound.
   Michelle hopes to produce and sell 100,000 pounds of Yuk at an average cost of $1.25 a pound.

   a. If average variable cost is taken as an indicator of predatory pricing, how far could Michelle
   lower her price without fear of losing a court case over possible predatory pricing?

   b. As argued in Chapter 9, while it can be "profitable" for firms to continue production even if
   price is less than average cost, once price has dropped below average variable cost, the firm
   would be better off shutting down production. The discussion in this chapter suggested that
   predatory pricing requires a firm to set price below average variable cost. How can it ever be
   in Michelle's or any company's interest to sell at a price below average variable cost?

■   **SELF-TESTS FOR UNDERSTANDING**

TEST A

Circle the most appropriate answer.

1. Match each of these regulatory agencies with the appropriate industries from the list below.
    Federal Communications Commission (FCC)   _____
    Federal Energy Regulatory Commission (FERC)   _____
    Federal Reserve   _____
    Securities and Exchange Commission (SEC)   _____
    a. Banking
    b. Automobile manufacturers
    c. Broadcasting and telecommunications
    d. Railroads, barges, pipelines, and some trucking
    e. Telephone
    f. Securities (stocks and bonds)
    g. Interstate transmission of electric power and sales of natural gas
    h. Pharmaceuticals

2. Significant economies of scale and economies of scope are examples of a
    a. nationalized industry.
    b. natural monopoly.
    c. regulated industry.
    d. competitive industry.

3. Which of the following is an example of economies of scale?
    a. Anna finds her costs increasing as she tries to increase the production of her custom designed clothes.
    b. Jim discovers that a 15 percent reduction in price leads to a 30 percent increase in sales.
    c. Sarah realizes that her firm's expertise and experience in producing specialized medical equipment will be useful in the production of testing equipment for physicists.
    d. Intel is able to reduce unit costs when it doubles production of computer chips.

4. Which of the following is an example of economies of scope?
    a. An increase in circulation for the *Daily Planet* would involve only printing costs and require no increase in the editorial staff.
    b. Ramona and Ricardo have invested their wealth in a portfolio of stocks, bonds, and real estate.
    c. In an effort to keep production lines busy all year, Arctic Enterprises produces a variety of small-engine home and garden tools in addition to its successful line of snowblowers.
    d. Ma Bell formerly used profits from long-distance calls to reduce monthly charges for local phone service.

5. The term *cross subsidy* refers to
    a. an angry firm that does not receive a subsidy.
    b. higher prices on some products that help to cover costs on other products.
    c. congressional subsidies for agriculture.
    d. the financing of Christian churches.

6. Regulation has promoted cross-subsidization as a way of
    a. dealing with universal service to isolated, high-cost locations.
    b. protecting the economy.
    c. promoting efficiencies from synergetic business combinations.
    d. addressing the effects of self-destructive competition.

7. If regulators want existing firms to engage in extensive cross-subsidization they
   a. should encourage entry of new firms.
   b. will need to pursue privatization as a long-run strategy.
   c. will need to restrict entry.
   d. prevent firms from taking advantage of economies of scale.

8. Marginal cost pricing is not feasible in industries characterized by
   a. an elastic demand curve.
   b. constant returns to scale.
   c. rising average costs.
   d. significant economies of scale.

9. According to the Ramsey rule, the ratio of price to marginal cost should be largest for those products with the
   a. largest fully distributed costs.
   b. largest income elasticity of demand.
   c. smallest price elasticity of demand.
   d. largest stand-alone costs.

10. The term *regulatory lag* refers to
    a. the time it takes people to respond to a change in prices.
    b. the long time it may take for a change in regulated prices to be approved.
    c. the slowness of moves to deregulation.
    d. the delay that occurs on many long-distance phone calls.

11. The term *price caps* refers to
    a. price floors.
    b. price ceilings that are adjusted in anticipation of future efficiencies.
    c. limits on a firm's overall profits.
    d. attempts to control inflationary increases in prices.

12. To serve customers, competitors must sometimes share a common facility, often owned by one of the competitors. This common facility is called a(n)
    a. essential link.
    b. keystone facility.
    c. marginal unit.
    d. bottleneck facility.

13. Regarding the Sherman Act, which of the following is not true?
    a. It prohibited contracts, combinations, and conspiracies in restraint of trade.
    b. It prohibited acts that attempt monopolization of trade.
    c. It declared any firm with 50 percent of an industry's output to be an illegal monopoly.
    d. It prohibited price fixing.

14. The Clayton Act prohibits all but which one of the following?
    a. The direct purchase of a competitor's assets.
    b. Tying contracts.
    c. Price discrimination.
    d. Interlocking directorates.

15. The rule of reason said that
   a. reasonable people could determine what levels of concentration ratios imply excessive market power.
   b. reasonable prices, even if fixed by competing firms, were not illegal.
   c. size is illegal only if acquired or maintained through objectionable overt acts that tend to monopolize trade.
   d. it is reasonable to prosecute a firm under the Sherman Act when it controls an excessive proportion of industry output.

16. Tying contracts
   a. require purchasing firms to sign long-term exclusive purchase agreements.
   b. are often used by companies that sell rope and string.
   c. require retailers to tie their sales price to a manufacturer's suggested price.
   d. require buyers of one good to also buy other goods from the same seller.

17. If a firm lowers its price below average variable cost to drive out rivals, it is said to be engaging in
   a. predatory pricing.
   b. price discrimination.
   c. tying contracts.
   d. tacit collusion.

18. A horizontal merger occurs when
   a. one firm buys another.
   b. a supplier buys one of its customers.
   c. a firm buys one of its competitors.
   d. a successful antitrust case forces a large firm to spin off competing divisions.

19. If an industry is composed of 10 firms, each the same size, then the four-firm concentration ratio would be
   a. 4.
   b. 10.
   c. 40.
   d. 100.

20. Studies of concentration and market power conclude that
   a. any increase in concentration ratios tends to increase prices.
   b. contestable markets are the most susceptible to the exercise of market power.
   c. no correlation exists between concentration and the use of market power.
   d. whether increases in concentration will allow firms to exercise more market power depends upon whether other factors favor collusion.

TEST B

Circle T or F for true or false.

T   F   1. Regulators are exclusively concerned with getting regulated industries to lower prices.

T   F   2. The term *economies of scope* refers to the reduction in average costs that come from large-scale production.

T   F   3. Fair-rate-of-return regulations—that is, price controls that allow firms in an industry to earn profits sufficient to cover the opportunity cost of their capital—offer strong incentives for efficiency and innovation.

T   F   4. The term *regulatory lag* refers to the lag between actual regulatory practice and the conventional wisdom as to the best practice.

T F 5. In the absence of regulation, firms required to provide service to isolated communities at high cost might find their more profitable low-cost markets taken over by competitors through a process called cream-skimming.

T F 6. The Sherman Act outlawed actions in restraint of trade and monopolization of trade.

T F 7. A manufacturing firm that merges with its supplier is engaging in a horizontal merger.

T F 8. Actual evidence on four-firm concentration ratios indicates a significant increase in concentration of American business over the last 95 years.

T F 9. Evidence clearly shows that any increase in concentration leads to an increase in market power.

T F 10. Research by economists suggests that only the largest firms can afford to engage in research and development.

SUPPLEMENTARY EXERCISE ■

The two lists in Table 20-1 identify the 25 largest industrial firms in the United States in 1929 and 1955, ranked by assets. The list for 1955 comes from the first *Fortune*[1] list of the 500 largest industrial companies. The list for 1929 comes from work by two economists, Norman Collins and Lee Preston.[2]

See if you can list the largest firms today. Then look up the most recent list of the *Fortune* 500. It is usually in the May issue of *Fortune* and can be found on the web at http://cgi.pathfinder.com/fortune/fortune500. Beginning in 1995 the *Fortune* list was modified to include the 500 largest corporations, not just the 500 largest industrial corporations. In the 1995 listing, Wal-Mart appeared as the fourth largest corporation. Of the original 500 industrial firms included in the 1955 list, only 116 appear in the 1995 list. How many of the corporations listed above are still in the top 25 or even the top 500? How many corporations have slipped in ranking? How many have gained?

In 1955 the companies listed above had sales that totaled $46.8 billion. Their sales equaled 12 percent of GDP. What are comparable figures today?

Fortune also publishes a list of the 500 largest corporations in the world. How big are the biggest American firms when compared to their international competition?

TABLE 20-1

1929	Rank	1955
U.S. Steel	1	Standard Oil (N.J.)
Standard Oil (N.J.)	2	General Motors
General Motors	3	U.S. Steel
Bethlehem Steel	4	Du Pont
Anaconda	5	Mobil Oil
Ford Motor Company	6	Standard Oil (Ind.)
Mobil Oil	7	Gulf Oil
Standard Oil (Ind.)	8	Texaco
Gulf Oil	9	General Electric
Shell Oil	10	Standard Oil (Cal.)
Texaco	11	Bethlehem Steel
Standard Oil (Cal.)	12	Westinghouse
Du Pont	13	Union Carbide
General Electric	14	Sinclair Oil
Armour	15	Phillips Petroleum
Sinclair Oil	16	Western Electric
Allied Chemical	17	Cities Service
International Harvester	18	Shell Oil
Western Electric	19	Chrysler
Union Oil	20	International Harvester
Union Carbide	21	Alcoa
Swift	22	Anaconda
Kennecott Copper	23	American Tobacco
International Paper	24	Republic Steel
Republic Steel	25	Kennecott Copper

---

[1]*Fortune*, July 1956, Supplement, page 2. Reprinted with permission.
[2]Norman R. Collins and Lee E. Preston, "The Size Structure of the Largest Industrial Firms, 1901–1958," *American Economic Review*, vol. 51, Number 5, December 1961, pages 986–1011.

■   ECONOMICS IN ACTION

PREDATORY PRICING

In May 1999 the federal government filed an antitrust suit accusing American Airlines of engaging in predatory pricing. The Justice Department reported, after an 18 month investigation, that company documents entitled "Dallas-Ft. Worth Low Cost Carriers Strategy," showed that American had deliberately incurred short-term losses to eliminate three low cost competitors—Vanguard Airlines, Sun Jet International and Western Pacific—from the Dallas-Fort Worth airport. The Justice Department suit cited internal memos that said American "would like to 'drive [Vanguard] from the market' and 'get [Western Pacific] out.'"

According to Joel Klein, head of the Justice Department's antitrust division, "American adopted a predatory responsive strategy, saturating the market in which the startup carriers had begun service with as much new, low-fare service of its own as was necessary to drive out the start-ups." In announcing the suit, the Justice Department released the following data which they said illustrated how American Airlines implemented a policy of predatory pricing.

Average nonstop one-way fare	Colorado Springs	Kansas City	Wichita, KA
Before competition	$158	$113	$110
With competition	$88	$83	$57
Post-competition	$133	$125	$96
Average number of passengers per month			
Before competition	3,723	22,423	4,465
With competition	19,909	31,228	11,246
Post-competition	9,237	23,460	8,540

American, which controls about 70 percent of scheduled seats out of Dallas-Fort Worth, was willing to risk losing money to drive out the three actual competitors and to discourage future potential competitors. According to the Justice Department, American's dominant position at the airport would allow it to earn back any losses by exercising market power.

American Airline officials rejected the argument that it had engaged in predatory pricing or flooded the market with extra flights. They called the suit sour grapes on the part of airlines that had been unable to compete successfully and said there was nothing illegal about "tough talk." Spokesperson Chris Chiames argued that American simply matched the competition with regard to price and added flights when the lower prices attracted additional customers. "It would have a chilling effect on the marketplace if companies felt they could not match prices of competitors," said Chiames.

A major issue is whether the new prices were below variable cost. American asserted they were not while the Justice Department argued that they were below American's established measures of acceptable profits and thus predatory.

Seasoned court observers said it would be difficult for the government to win its case, citing a 1986 decision in which the Supreme Court said, "Cutting prices in order to increase business often is the very essence of competition." Mistaken conclusions of predatory pricing "chill the very conduct the antitrust laws are designed to protect."

What is the current status of the lawsuit? Has the government proven that American priced flights below cost and that American had plausible means for recouping losses? Or is American right and is the law suit just a way for competitors to win in court what they could not win in the marketplace?

SOURCES: Stephen Labaton and Laurence Zuckerman, "Airline is Accused of Illegal Pricing: U.S. Says American Was Trying to Drive Out Competitors," *The New York Times*, May 14, 1999. Laurence Zuckerman, "Airline Suit: 70's Revival in Antitrust," *The New York Times*, May 15, 1999. Anna Wilde Matthews and Scott McCartney, "U.S. Sues American Sir in Antitrust Case, *The Wall Street Journal*, May 14, 1999.

■   STUDY QUESTIONS

1.   What is the difference between economies of scale and economies of scope?

2.   Why do regulators often work to increase rather than limit prices?

3. What is meant by the term *cross-subsidy?*

4. Why aren't prices based on marginal cost a feasible alternative in cases of natural monopolies arising from economies of scale?

5. How can regulatory lags provide incentives for efficiency?

6. What is your evaluation of the American experience with deregulation?

7. Why regulate at all? Why not let the free market work without regulation?

8. How are concentration ratios measured?

9. Has American business become more or less concentrated over the last 50 years?

10. What does the evidence suggest about increasing concentration and the use of market power?

11. Consider antitrust policy that divided the largest firms whenever the four-firm concentration ratio in any industry exceeded 50 percent. Would such a policy be good for the country? Why? Why not?

12. Should American antitrust laws include an explicit exclusion for cooperative research and development activities? Why?

13. How effective do you believe American antitrust laws have been?

ECONOMICS ONLINE

The Antitrust Division of the U.S. Department of Justice maintains its own homepage. During the Microsoft trial, the division posted its own court submissions at this site.

www.usdoj.gov/atr

Concentration ratios for many industries from the 1992 Economic Census are posted at this site. Concentration ratios are calculated for the largest 4, 8, 20, and 50 companies. Similar information from the 1997 Economic Census may be available now or should be available shortly from the U.S. Census Bureau.

www.census.gov/epcd/www/concentration.html

TAXATION AND RESOURCE ALLOCATION

LEARNING OBJECTIVES

After completing this chapter, you should be able to:

- distinguish between progressive, proportional, and regressive tax systems.

- describe the major taxes levied by the federal, state, and local governments and identify which are direct taxes and which are indirect taxes.

- explain why the payroll tax is regressive.

- explain what issues make the financing of social security controversial.

- explain the concept of fiscal federalism.

- contrast various concepts of fair or equitable taxation.

- explain the difference between the burden and the excess burden of a tax.

- explain how changes in economic behavior can enable individuals to shift the burden of a tax, that is, explain what is wrong with the flypaper theory of tax incidence.

- explain what factors influence how the burden of a tax will be shared by consumers and suppliers.

- explain how some taxes can lead to efficiency gains, not losses.

Important Terms and Concepts

PROGRESSIVE, PROPORTIONAL, AND REGRESSIVE TAXES

AVERAGE AND MARGINAL TAX RATES

DIRECT AND INDIRECT TAXES

PERSONAL INCOME TAX

PAYROLL TAX

CORPORATE INCOME TAX

EXCISE TAX

TAX LOOPHOLES

SOCIAL SECURITY SYSTEM

PROPERTY TAX

FISCAL FEDERALISM

HORIZONTAL AND VERTICAL EQUITY

ABILITY-TO-PAY PRINCIPLE

BENEFITS PRINCIPLE OF TAXATION

ECONOMIC EFFICIENCY

BURDEN OF A TAX

EXCESS BURDEN

INCIDENCE OF A TAX

FLYPAPER THEORY OF INCIDENCE

TAX SHIFTING

■ CHAPTER REVIEW

This chapter concentrates on taxes: What taxes are collected in America and what economic effects they have. Few people like paying taxes. In fact, many people make adjustments in their behavior to reduce the taxes they must pay. These adjustments are an important part of the economic impact of taxes, an aspect often overlooked in popular discussions.

Taxes are levied by federal, state, and local governments. For the most part, federal taxes tend to be

(1)   (direct/indirect) taxes, while state and local governments rely more on _____ taxes. The largest revenue raiser for the federal government is the _____ _____ tax. Next in line in terms of revenue raised is the _____ tax. Other important federal taxes include the _____ income tax and excise taxes.

When talking about income tax systems it is important to distinguish between *average* and *marginal* tax

(2)   rates. The fraction of total income paid as income taxes is the (average/marginal) tax rate, while the fraction of each additional dollar of income paid as taxes is the _____ tax rate. If the average tax rate increases with income, the tax system is called _____. If the average tax rate stays constant for all levels of income, the tax system is said to be _____, while if the average tax rate falls as income increases, the result is a _____ tax system. Changes under the Tax Reform Act of 1986 reduced marginal income tax rates and enhanced the efficiency of the U.S. federal personal income tax by closing a number of loopholes.

(3)   The social security system is financed by (income/payroll) taxes. These taxes are considered (regressive/progressive) because they (do/do not) apply to all sources of income and because, except for taxes to support Medicare, after a certain level of income the marginal tax rate becomes _____. Social security benefits do not work like private pension funds, because benefits are not limited by individual contributions.

The social security system has been able to offer retired people good benefits for two reasons: (1) Real wages and incomes of those currently employed have shown substantial growth; and (2) the number of working people has been large relative to the number of retired individuals. The continued operation of both these factors has been called into question by the slowdown in the growth of real wages and population. Recent adjustments in both taxes and benefits have attempted to solve the problem by accumulating a surplus in the social security trust fund to pay future benefits. However, these adjustments do not appear to be sufficient for a permanent solution.

The major state and local taxes, _____ taxes, and _____ taxes, are indi- (4)
rect taxes. In the aggregate, state income taxes raise a smaller percentage of state revenues, but their importance is growing. In addition to the taxes raised by state governments, there is a system of transfers from the federal to state governments called fiscal _____.

Economists use their dual criteria of equity and efficiency to judge taxes. When talking about the fairness of a tax, we are talking about _____. Various criteria have been advanced to (5)
judge the fairness of a particular tax. The principle that equally situated individuals should pay equal taxes is referred to as _____ equity. The principle that differentially situated individuals should be taxed in ways that society deems fair is referred to as _____ equity. The ability-to-pay principle is an example of _____ equity. Rather than looking at the income and wealth of families, there is an alternative approach to taxation that says people should pay in proportion to what they get from public services. This principle for taxation is called the _____ principle. User fees for a variety of public services, such as garbage collection, the use of parks, and street cleaning, are an example of the _____ principle.

Efficiency is the other criterion that economists use to judge taxes. Almost all taxes cause some inefficiency. The amount of money that would make an individual as well off with a tax as she was without the tax is called the _____ of the tax. Sometimes it just equals the tax payment an indi- (6)
vidual makes, but more generally it is (greater/less) than an individual's tax payment. The difference between the total burden and tax payments is called the _____ _____. The reason that tax payments typically understate the total burden of a tax is that the existence of the tax will often induce a change in behavior. Measuring only the taxes paid (does/does not) take account of the loss of satisfaction resulting from the induced change in behavior. The excess burden is the measure of the inefficiency of a particular tax. Thus the principle of efficiency in taxation calls for using taxes that raise the same revenue but with the (largest/smallest) excess burden. That is, the principle of efficiency calls for using taxes that induce the smallest changes in behavior.

Often taxes will affect even those people who do not pay them. Imagine that the government imposes a $50 excise tax on bicycles, paid by consumers at the time of purchase. Even though paid by consumers,

FIGURE 21-1   **Demand and Supply: Bicycles**

it may be easiest to examine the impact of this tax by viewing it as a shift in the supply curve, as illustrated in Figure 21-1. Consumers do not care why the price of bicycles has increased; there is no reason for their demand curve to shift. The change in price from the new tax will lead to a movement along the demand curve. Suppliers collect the tax for the government and are concerned with what is left over after taxes in order to pay their suppliers and cover their labor cost and the opportunity cost of their capital. How suppliers will respond to the after-tax price is given by the original supply curve. The price that consumers must pay comes from adding the excise tax onto the original supply curve and is given by the dashed line in Figure 21-1.

Looking at Figure 21-1 we see that compared with the original equilibrium, the new equilibrium

(7)   involves a (<u>higher/lower</u>) price to consumers, a (<u>higher/lower</u>) price to suppliers, and a (<u>larger/smaller</u>) quantity of bicycles produced. It would not be surprising if the change in supply resulted in unemployed bicycle workers, lower wages for employed bicycle workers, and fewer bicycle firms. None of these workers or firms paid the tax, yet all were affected by it.

In the bicycle example, as consumers adjusted to the new tax, they shifted part of the burden onto others. The question of how the burden of taxes is divided among different groups is the question of

(8)   tax _____. At first glance it might appear that the burden of the tax is borne entirely by consumers who pay it at the time of sale. The notion that the burden of the tax rests with those who pay the tax is called the _____ theory of tax incidence. As the bicycle example makes clear, if consumers change their behavior as a result of the tax, they may succeed in _____ part of the burden of the tax.

The study of tax incidence suggests that the incidence of excise or sales taxes depends on the slopes

(9)   of both the _____ and _____ curves. Payroll taxes, such as social security taxes, are like an excise tax on labor services. Statistical work suggests that for most workers the supply of labor services is relatively (<u>elastic/inelastic</u>) with respect to wage rates, which in turn suggests that (<u>workers/firms</u>) rather than _____ bear most of the burden of the payroll tax.

IMPORTANT TERMS AND CONCEPTS QUIZ ■

Choose the most appropriate definition for each of the following terms.

1. _____ Progressive tax

2. _____ Proportional tax

3. _____ Regressive tax

4. _____ Average tax rate

5. _____ Marginal tax rate

6. _____ Direct taxes

7. _____ Indirect taxes

8. _____ Excise tax

9. _____ Tax loophole

10. _____ Fiscal federalism

11. _____ Horizontal equity

12. _____ Vertical equity

13. _____ Ability-to-pay principle

14. _____ Benefits principle of taxation

15. _____ Burden of a tax

16. _____ Excess burden

17. _____ Incidence of a tax

18. _____ Flypaper theory of incidence

19. _____ Tax shifting

a. Provision in the tax code that reduces taxes below statutory rates if certain conditions are met.

b. Average tax rate increases with income.

c. People who derive benefits from a government-provided service should pay the taxes to support it.

d. Amount an individual would have to receive to make her as well off with the tax as she was without it.

e. Allocation of the burden of a tax to specific groups.

f. Frequency with which a tax is levied.

g. Taxes levied on people.

h. Equally situated individuals should be taxed equally.

i. Average tax rate falls as income rises.

j. Notion that the burden of a tax is borne by those who pay it.

k. Sales tax on a specific commodity.

l. Situation where economic reactions to a tax mean others bear part of the burden of the tax.

m. System of grants from one level of government to the next.

n. Ratio of taxes to income.

o. Wealthier people should pay higher taxes.

p. Average tax rate is the same at all income levels.

q. Amount by which the burden of a tax exceeds the tax paid.

r. Fraction of each additional dollar of income that is paid in taxes.

s. Taxes levied on specific economic activities.

t. Differently situated individuals should be taxed differently in a way society deems fair.

■ BASIC EXERCISE

This exercise is designed to illustrate how the incidence of an excise tax depends on the elasticity (slope) of the demand and supply curves.

TABLE 21-1	Demand For and Supply of Running Shoes				
Demand (millions of pairs)		Price (dollars)		Supply (millions of pairs)	
(1)	(2)		(3)	(4)	
68	53.0	30	38	48.00	
65	52.5	32	40	48.33	
62	52.0	34	42	48.67	
59	51.5	36	44	49.00	
56	51.0	38	46	49.33	
53	50.5	40	48	49.67	
50	50.0	42	50	50.00	
47	49.5	44	52	50.33	
44	49.0	46	54	50.67	
41	48.5	48	56	51.00	
38	48.0	50	58	51.33	
35	47.5	52	60	51.67	
32	47.0	54	62	52.00	

1. Table 21-1 has data on the demand and supply of running shoes. Plot the demand curve from column 1 and the supply curve from column 3 in Figure 21-2.

2. Determine the initial equilibrium price and quantity of running shoes.

   Price $ _____

   Quantity _____

3. Now assume that in a fit of pique, non-running legislators impose a fitness tax of $10 on each pair of shoes. Draw the new supply curve by shifting the original supply curve by the magnitude of the excise tax. The new equilibrium price is $ _____ and the new equilibrium quantity is _____.

4. How much more do consumers, who continue to buy running shoes, pay? $ _____. How does this increase in price compare with the excise tax of $10?

5. What is likely to happen to employment, wages, and profits in the running-shoe industry?

6. On Figure 21-3, plot the demand curve from column 2 and supply curve from column 3 of Table 21-1. Comparing Figures 21-2 and 21-3, we have the same supply curve but different demand curves. Both figures should show the same initial equilibrium price and quantity.

7. At the initial equilibrium price and quantity, which demand curve is more elastic? _____. (Review the appropriate material in Chapter 8 if you do not remember how to compute the price elasticity of a demand curve. Remember this distinction when it comes to comparing results.)

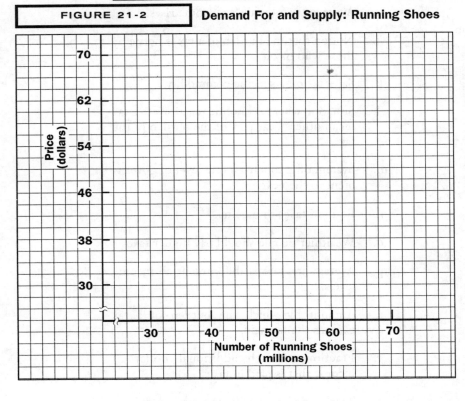

| FIGURE 21-2 | Demand For and Supply: Running Shoes |

Price (dollars)

70
62
54
46
38
30

30   40   50   60   70

Number of Running Shoes (millions)

8. Now analyze the impact of the imposition of the same excise tax of $10 per pair of running shoes using Figure 21-3. The new equilibrium price is $ _____ and the new equilibrium quantity _____. In which case, Figure 21-2 or Figure 21-3, does the equilibrium price of running shoes rise the most? In which case are the volume of employment and the level of wages likely to fall the least? From this comparison we can conclude that the more inelastic the demand curve, the more the burden of an excise tax will be borne by _____.

9. Use information on demand from either column 1 or 2 and the two supply curves in columns 3 and 4 in Table 21-1 to analyze how the incidence of the tax is affected as the elasticity of supply changes.

Demand For and Supply: Running Shoes   **FIGURE 21-3**

SELF-TESTS FOR UNDERSTANDING ■

TEST A

Circle the most appropriate answer.

1. In the United States since 1950, federal taxes as a proportion of GDP have
   a. declined.
   b. fluctuated but shown little trend.
   c. increased dramatically.

2. In the United States, state and local taxes as a percentage of GDP have
   a. declined since 1960.
   b. shown virtually no change over the last 60 years.
   c. increased from 1945 to the early 1970s and shown little trend since then.

3. For the most part the federal government relies on _____ taxes while state and local governments rely on _____ taxes.
   a. excise; property
   b. sales; income
   c. property; sales
   d. direct; indirect

4. Direct taxes are levied on
   a. specific economic activities.
   b. reproducible property.
   c. people.
   d. the value added at each stage of production.

5. Which of the following is an indirect tax?
   a. Income taxes.
   b. Inheritance taxes.
   c. Head taxes.
   d. Sales taxes.

6. Fiscal federalism refers to
   a. Alexander Hamilton's plan for assuming the debts of the individual states.
   b. federal government control of state and local spending.
   c. grants from one level of government to another.
   d. the balance between taxes paid to the federal government and the value of federal contracts received, measured on a state-by-state basis.

7. If income taxes are progressive, then the average tax rate
   a. decreases as income increases.
   b. is unchanged as income increases.
   c. increases as income increases.
   d. Insufficient information to determine.

8. If income taxes are progressive, then the marginal tax rate
   a. decreases as income increases.
   b. is unchanged as income increases.
   c. increases as income increases.
   d. Insufficient information to determine.

9. Christopher earned $20,000 last year and paid 10 percent or $2,000 in income taxes. His marginal income tax rate is 15 percent. If his income rises by $5,000 this year to $25,000, his income taxes will go up by
   a. less than $500.
   b. $500.
   c. more than $500.
   In fact, Christopher will have to pay an additional $ _____ in income taxes.

10. The Abbotts have an income of $20,000 a year and pay $2,000 a year in income taxes. The Beards have an income of $40,000 a year and pay $5,000 a year in income taxes. From this information we can conclude that this tax system
    a. is regressive.
    b. is proportional.
    c. is progressive.
    d. satisfies the benefits principle of taxation.

11. The ability-to-pay principle of taxation is an example of
    a. horizontal equity.
    b. vertical equity.
    c. the benefits principle.
    d. fiscal federalism.

12. If two families are identical in all respects, the principle of horizontal equity says that
    a. both families should pay more income taxes than other families with less income.
    b. both families should pay the same income tax.
    c. both families should have a lower average tax rate than a richer family.
    d. income taxes are, from a social viewpoint, a more appropriate form of taxation than are payroll taxes.

13. Which of the following is an example of the benefits principle of taxation?
    a. Excise taxes on expensive jewelry.
    b. Higher property taxes as a percent of market value for more expensive homes.
    c. Special assessments on homeowners in proportion to their street frontage to help pay for repairs to curbs and gutters.
    d. Social security taxes.

14. The burden of a tax is defined as
    a. revenue raised minus the cost of collection.
    b. the proportion of taxes paid by individuals rather than corporations.
    c. the amount of money that would make a taxpayer as well off as he was before the tax was introduced.
    d. revenue raised plus the cost of collection.

15. The burden of most taxes is _____ the revenue raised.
    a. less than
    b. equal to
    c. greater than

16. The excess burden of a tax is
    a. the cost of collecting the tax.
    b. a measure of the inefficiency of the tax.
    c. best measured by the amount of complaining done by taxpayers.
    d. highest when the tax induces the least change in behavior.

17. A sales tax on which of the following will involve a small excess burden?
    a. A tax on a commodity with a zero price elasticity of demand.
    b. A tax on a commodity with a very high elasticity of demand.
    c. A tax on a commodity consumed primarily by poor families.
    d. A tax on a commodity consumed primarily by rich families.

18. The flypaper theory of tax incidence
    a. is a shorthand reference to such sticky issues as the appropriate degree of progressivity in the personal income tax.
    b. implies that if a tax induces changes in economic behavior, part of the burden of the tax may be shifted to other economic agents.
    c. is usually right regarding who bears the burden of a tax.
    d. says that the burden of a tax is borne by those who pay the tax.

19. Tax loopholes typically introduce new inefficiencies and _____ the progressivity of the income tax.
    a. reduce
    b. have little effect on
    c. increase

20. The Tax Reform Act of 1986
    a. reduced marginal tax rates.
    b. introduced significant loopholes.
    c. increased personal income taxes in order to reduce corporate taxes.
    d. is generally conceded to have worsened the efficiency of the American tax system.

TEST B

Circle T or F for true or false.

T   F   1. Over the past 40 years federal government taxes have taken an ever-increasing share of the GDP.

T   F   2. Federal payroll taxes are a more important source of revenue than the federal corporate income tax.

T   F   3. State personal income taxes are an example of a direct, as opposed to indirect, tax.

T   F   4. State taxes are primarily indirect taxes.

T   F   5. The principle of horizontal equity says that equally situated individuals should be taxed equally.

T   F   6. The ability-to-pay principle says that people who derive benefits from a particular public service should pay the taxes to finance it.

T   F   7. The burden of a tax is normally less than the revenue raised by the tax.

T   F   8. If a tax does not induce a change in economic behavior, then there is no excess burden.

T   F   9. The flypaper theory of incidence is correct in regards to social security taxes.

T   F   10. The concept of excess burden proves that taxes can never improve efficiency.

■ SUPPLEMENTARY EXERCISES

1. How Flat Is the Flat Tax?

Most flat tax proposals have a basic exemption after which all income is taxed at the same rate. Proposals differ in the magnitude of the basic exemption, the tax rate to be used after that, whether some forms of income might be excluded from taxation or whether some deductions would be allowed. (See Economics in Action below for a discussion of this last point.) Economists distinguish between marginal and average tax rates. Complete Table 21-2 to compute the marginal and average tax rates taxpayers might face at different levels of income. Assume that every family is allowed a basic exemption of $25,000 on which no taxes are owed and after that, every dollar of additional income generates a tax liability of 20 cents. That is, the flat rate after the basic exemption is 20 percent.

TABLE 21-2   **Marginal and Average Tax Rates under a Flat Tax**

Income	Total Taxes	Average Tax Rate[a]	Marginal Tax Rate[b]
$25,000	_____	_____	
$30,000	_____	_____	_____
$40,000	_____	_____	_____
$50,000	_____	_____	_____
$100,000	_____	_____	_____
$200,000	_____	_____	_____

[a]Average tax rate = (Total taxes) ÷ Income
[b]Marginal tax rate = (Change in taxes) ÷ (Change in income)

2. Revenue Maximizing Cigarette Taxes

In the spring of 1993 there was considerable discussion of a possible increase in the federal tax on cigarettes. Some saw an increase as a cash cow to finance medical care reform or to help reduce the federal deficit. If interested in maximizing the amount of revenue, one would need to be careful not to raise the tax so high that demand fell too much and tax revenues actually declined.

Writing separately in *The New York Times* in June of 1993, economists Jeffrey Harris and Michael Grossman offered dramatically different estimates of the demand elasticity. Drawing on Canadian experience, Harris suggested that the price elasticity of demand for cigarettes was around 0.25. He estimated that a $2 increase in cigarette taxes would raise an additional $28 billion in revenue each year. Grossman argued that because of the addictive properties of smoking, the response to a change in price would be small in the short run but much larger in the long run.

The following straight-line demand curves are approximations of the Harris estimate and Grossman's long-run demand curve. Both of these demand curves have been constructed to mimic actual price and quantity data for 1992 when 24.9 billion packs of cigarettes were sold in the United States at an average price of $2 a pack that included a tax of $.24.

Harris: $Q = 30.80 - 2.95 \, (P + T)$

Grossman: $Q = 46.72 - 10.91 \, (P + T)$

a. Verify that when $P + T = 2$ each demand curve is consistent with the 1992 quantity and price combination.
b. For each estimate of the demand curve and on the assumption that the supply curve for cigarettes is horizontal at a net-of-tax price of $1.76 a pack, i.e., P = 1.76, what tax maximizes tax revenues? (If you have access to a spreadsheet program on a microcomputer you might set up a small example that calculates the quantity demanded and tax revenues at different taxes. Alternatively, after writing down the expression for total tax revenues, you could differentiate the expression to find the value of T that maximizes revenue.)
c. What is the price elasticity of demand for each demand curve? For which estimate of demand, the estimate with the high or low elasticity, is the revenue maximizing tax highest? Why?
d. Actual tax revenues will depend upon the price elasticity of supply as well as the price elasticity of demand. Question b assumed that the price elasticity of supply was infinite. What would happen to the incidence of any increase in taxes if the price elasticity of supply were zero or somewhere in between?

ECONOMICS IN ACTION ■

A PERSON'S MORTGAGE IS HER TAX DEDUCTION

While a person's home may or may not be a castle, her mortgage is likely to yield a handsome tax deduction. Under current law, taxpayers may deduct from taxable income mortgage interest on up to $1 million of mortgage debt they have used to acquire and improve first or second homes and interest on up to $100,000 of home-equity loans regardless of the purpose of the loan. No other consumer interest is deductible. Whether it is in an individual's best interest to take the mortgage interest deduction depends upon the magnitude of his mortgage interest and other deductions vis-à-vis the standard deduction. For example, in 1998, a family could itemize deductions or take a standard deduction of $7,100. If a family's deductions, including mortgage interest, totaled less than $7,100, then it made more sense to use the standard deduction. While roughly 64 percent of households are homeowners and, of these, a bit less than 60 percent have a mortgage, only 28 percent of taxpayers take the mortgage interest deduction. For the others, using the standard deduction rather than itemizing is preferable.

Not surprisingly, higher income taxpayers with larger homes and larger mortgages derive the largest benefit from the mortgage interest deduction. Peter Dreier, a professor of public policy at Occidental College in Los Angeles, estimates that 44 percent of the tax benefits associated with the mortgage interest deduction go to the richest 5 percent of taxpayers, those making over $100,000 a year in income. Professor Dreier estimates that the tax savings for these rich taxpayers is about $22 billion annually, an amount that is roughly the same as government spending on subsidized housing for the poor.

The popularity of the mortgage interest deduction is such that a number of prominent flat tax proposals would retain the deduction while attempting to eliminate other deductions and loopholes. For example, in early 1996 Republican candidates for president were divided on this issue. According to *The New York Times*, only Malcolm Forbes Jr. wanted to eliminate the mortgage interest deduction, Pat Buchanan wanted to retain it, while Senators Bob Dole and Phil Gramm had managed to avoid taking a hard position one way or the other.

What explains this popularity when only a minority of taxpayers use the deduction each year and the benefits go disproportionately to rich taxpayers? Counting only those who use the deduction in a single year understates the constituency who supports the deduction. Many homeowners took advantage of the mortgage interest deduction when they first bought their home. Sellers and potential homeowners see the deduction as an important part of a buyer's financial planning. Some argue that public policy should support homeownership and that the mortgage interest deduction does just that. Others argue that one could achieve the same objective with a tax credit rather than a tax deduction and that a tax credit would be fairer.[1] Stricter limits on the magnitude of mortgage interest that could be deducted have also been proposed. States with the highest house prices, for example, California, New York, Connecticut, and New Jersey, would be most affected by such a change.

There is concern that elimination of the mortgage interest deduction would disrupt housing markets causing the price of many homes to decline. Estimates of such effects vary, but most analysts agree that the largest adjustments would occur for the most expensive homes. Should the deduction be eliminated suddenly, the Mortgage Bankers Association projects an increase in mortgage defaults. Economists who argue in favor of elimination of the mortgage interest deduction see it as part of a broader strategy of tax reform. They are concerned that the favorable tax treatment of mortgage interest has distorted investment away from business capital toward houses, in particular, housing for the rich. Alvin Rabushka, an early advocate of a flat tax system, has argued that if the flat tax exempts interest income, there would be no adjustment in house prices. One might also note that not all countries allow homeowners to deduct mortgage interest. For example, levels of homeownership are high in Canada and Australia, two countries without mortgage interest deduction.

1. Should anything be done about the mortgage interest deduction? Should it be eliminated? Should stricter limits be adopted? Should it be turned into a tax credit?

2. If a decision were made to eliminate or change the mortgage interest deduction, what would you expect to happen to house prices and the affordability of housing? What provisions, if any, should be made for homeowners who purchased homes believing that the mortgage interest deduction would not be changed?

SOURCE: "The Pitfall in the Flat Tax, Republicans Tiptoe Around the Mortgage Deduction," *The New York Times*, January 12, 1996. Alvin Rabushka, "Flat Tax Lite," *The New York Times*, January 23, 1996.

■   STUDY QUESTIONS

1. Should income taxes be progressive or proportional? Explain your reasoning.

2. Without changing the level of spending, should your state increase income taxes in order to reduce sales taxes or increase sales taxes to reduce income taxes? Why?

3. Why do economists consider the social security tax to be regressive?

4. In the final analysis, who pays the social security tax, workers or firms?

5. What is fiscal federalism?

6. What is the difference between horizontal and vertical equity?

7. If a progressive income tax meets social concerns about vertical equity, can it also satisfy concerns about horizontal equity? Explain.

---

[1] Assume that two families each pay $1,000 mortgage interest. A tax credit of 20 percent would reduce the taxes of both families by $200. In contrast the value of a deduction depends upon a family's marginal tax rate which in turn depends upon its income. For example, in 1998 the value of a $1,000 deduction to a family earning $35,000 was $150 while the same $1,000 deduction would save $396 for a rich family paying the highest marginal tax rate.

8. What is the difference between the benefits principle of taxation and the concept of ability to pay?

9. Why do economists say that the burden of a tax is usually greater than the revenue raised by the tax?

10. Is it true that the more elastic the demand curve, the smaller the amount of any sales tax that consumers will pay? Explain.

11. Should the United States move to a flat tax system?

ECONOMICS ONLINE ■

Get your tax forms and find data about the federal tax system from the IRS homepage.

www.irs.ustreas.gov/prod/cover.html

Should states use tax incentives as a way to attract businesses? Does the country as a whole benefit from this sort of activity or is this just a way for companies to minimize their taxes by playing off states against each other? Examine these questions at a web site maintained by the Federal Reserve Bank of Minneapolis:

woodrow.mpls.frb.fed.us/sylloge/econwar/index.html

EXTERNALITIES, THE ENVIRONMENT, AND NATURAL RESOURCES

Important Terms and Concepts

EXTERNALITY

DIRECT CONTROLS

POLLUTION CHARGES (TAXES ON EMISSIONS)

SUBSIDIES FOR REDUCED EMISSIONS

EMISSIONS PERMITS

KNOWN RESERVES

ORGANIZATION OF PETROLEUM EXPORTING COUNTRIES (OPEC)

PARADOX OF GROWING RESERVES OF FINITE RESOURCES

LEARNING OBJECTIVES

After completing this chapter, you should be able to:

■ explain why, in most cases, it is impossible to reduce pollution to zero.

■ explain why unrestricted competitive markets are likely to result in a socially unacceptable level of pollution.

■ explain why it is unlikely that profit-maximizing private firms can be expected to clean up the environment.

■ describe the major approaches to limiting pollution.

■ compare the advantages and disadvantages of using taxes and permits to control pollution.

■ explain why, under perfect competition and negligible extraction costs, the price of depletable resources would be expected to rise at the rate of interest.

■ explain how and why actual prices of depletable resources have behaved differently over most of the twentieth century.

■ describe the three virtues of rising prices for scarce resources.

■ explain why known reserves for many resources have not tended to fall over time.

■ ## ■   CHAPTER REVIEW

This chapter explores the economics of environmental protection and resource conservation, with emphasis on the strengths and weaknesses of a market economy in dealing with both issues.

ENVIRONMENTAL PROTECTION

Pollution is one example of instances in which unregulated markets will fail to achieve an efficient allocation of resources. Typically, pollution imposes little or no cost on the polluter, yet it imposes costs

(1) on others. In the language of economists, pollution is an example of a detrimental _____. Pollution happens because individuals, firms, and government agencies use the air, land, and waterways as free dumping grounds for their waste. Economists believe that if there is a high cost to using these public resources, then the volume of pollution will (increase/decrease) because people will be more careful about producing wastes and/or they will choose less costly alternatives for waste disposal. One way to make the use of public resources costly is to impose (taxes/subsidies) in direct proportion to the volume of pollution emitted. This is an example of using the price system to clean up the environment.

(2) Many government policies have relied on voluntarism and direct _____. Economists, though, are skeptical of relying on voluntary cooperation as a long-range solution. Cleaning up the environment is costly, and firms that voluntarily incur these costs are likely to be undersold by less public-spirited competitors.

A government ruling that mandates an equal percentage reduction in pollution activity by all polluters is an example of a direct control. Economists argue that since the costs of reducing pollution are apt to vary among polluters, an equal percentage reduction by all polluters is likely to be

(3) (efficient/inefficient) compared with other alternatives, such as emissions taxes. From a social viewpoint, unequal reductions in pollution will be (less/more) efficient, as it is likely to cost less for some firms to reduce pollution.

(4) Faced with an emissions tax, firms will reduce pollution until the (marginal/average) cost of further reductions exceeds the tax. Firms that continue to pollute pay the tax; other firms will pay for pollution-control devices. All firms will choose the least costly alternative. The sale or auction of emission

permits also generates a market price that firms must pay if they pollute. One advantage of emission permits is that by controlling the number of permits, there may be greater control over the final volume of pollution.

While economists have a strong preference for market-based approaches to reducing pollution, there may be cases where one needs to rely on voluntarism or direct control. For example, when conditions have changed suddenly and action must be taken quickly, there may not be time to implement a program of pollution taxes or emission permits; if monitoring pollution is not possible or prohibitively expensive, direct controls may be a preferable alternative; and society may also prefer to ban especially dangerous activities.

RESOURCE CONSERVATION

Some resources, such as trees and fish, are called renewable resources. As long as breeding stocks are not destroyed, these resources will replenish themselves. The rest of this chapter concentrates on non-renewable or depletable resources such as minerals and oil. In this case there is no reproduction, although in some cases there may be recycling.

Many observers have voiced concern that the world is running out of natural resources. They allege that soon the quantity of resources supplied will not be able to keep up with the quantity of resources demanded and that the result will be massive shortages and chaos. Yet, in a free market we know that the quantity demanded (can/can never) exceed the quantity supplied, because demand and supply will   (5)
always be brought into equilibrium by adjustments in _____. This fundamental mechanism of free markets, first discussed in Chapter 5, is as applicable to the supply and demand of scarce resources as it is to any other commodity.

Harold Hotelling first described the special behavior of the prices of depletable resources in free markets. He argued that if the costs of extraction are negligible, the price of depletable resources must rise at a rate equal to the rate of _____. This result follows from relatively simple consid-   (6)
erations. Assets held in the form of bank deposits or bonds earn interest for their owners. Owners of natural resource reserves expect their asset—the reserves—to earn a similar risk-adjusted return. If increases in the price of future resources offer a less attractive return than do interest rates, resource owners will sell their resources and put the money in the bank. This action decreases the current price

of resources. There will be a continuing incentive to sell, with downward pressure on current resource prices, until the return from holding resources again provides a return competitive with other investment alternatives. Similarly, if the future return from holding resources is expected to be extremely high, more investors will want to buy resource inventories, (increasing/decreasing) current prices. These pressures will continue until holding resource inventories again offers a risk-adjusted return comparable to that of other investment alternatives.

(7)   This theory suggests that the prices of depletable resources should show a rising trend at a rate equal to the rate of _____. The unexpected discovery of resource reserves or new methods of manufacturing that economize on the use of resources, technological progress that reduces the cost of extraction, and government attempts at price controls can all make prices behave differently. Data on known reserves, rather than declining as implied in the literal interpretation of a nonrenewable resource, have typically shown slight increases. These increases in reserves reflect the workings of the price system as the pressure for higher prices has induced new exploration and made the use of high-cost deposits profitable. It is important to remember that pressure for higher prices is what equates demand and supply, avoids chaos, and facilitates the adjustment to alternative technologies.

Many economists see increasing prices for depletable resources as an important virtue of free markets. Increasing prices help to deal with the problem of declining reserves in three important ways:

(8)   1.   Increasing prices (encourage/discourage) consumption and waste and provide a(n) (disincentive/incentive) for conservation on the part of consumers.

2.   Increasing prices (encourage/discourage) more efficient use of scarce resources in the production of commodities.

3.   Increasing prices provide a(n) (disincentive/incentive) for technological innovation and the use of substitutes as well as (encouraging/discouraging) additional exploration and the exploitation of high-cost sources of supply.

IMPORTANT TERMS AND CONCEPTS QUIZ ■

Choose the most appropriate definition for each of the following terms.

1. _____ Externality

2. _____ Direct controls

3. _____ Pollution charges

4. _____ Emissions permit

5. _____ Known reserves

6. _____ Organization of Petroleum Exporting Countries

a. Cartel of oil-rich nations that has attempted to control oil markets.

b. Monetary incentives and penalties used to make polluting financially unattractive.

c. Fees paid to polluting firms in exchange for reductions in pollution.

d. Result of activities that affect other people, without corresponding compensation.

e. Authorization to pollute up to a specified level.

f. Legal limits on pollution emissions or performance specifications for polluting activities.

g. Amount of a resource that can be extracted economically based on existing technology and already discovered sources.

BASIC EXERCISES ■

POLLUTION TAXES

This exercise examines the implications of alternative pollution taxes.

Assume that plastic trash bags are produced in a market that is best characterized as one of perfect competition. Manufacturers have long used local rivers as convenient dumping grounds for their industrial wastes. Figure 22-1 plots the average cost of producing trash bags. These data are applicable for each firm.

a. In the absence of pollution-control measures, what is the long-run equilibrium price of plastic bags? $_____. What is the long-run equilibrium level of output for each firm? _____. (To answer this question you may want to review the material in Chapter 10 about long-run equilibrium under perfect competition.)

b. The amount of pollution discharge is directly proportional to the number of bags produced. Assume that the government imposes a pollution charge of 5 cents per bag. Draw in the new average cost curve on Figure 22-1. Will there be an increase, a decrease, or no change in each of the following as a result of the pollution charge? (Assume for now that

Long-Run Average Cost Curve   FIGURE 22-1

there is no pollution-control technology, that each firm must pay the tax, and that the demand for plastic bags declines as price rises.)

Industry output _____

Price_____

Number of firms in the industry _____

Average cost curve for each firm _____

Output level of each firm _____

Total pollution _____

c. Assume that pollution-control equipment becomes available. This equipment will eliminate 75 percent of pollution at an average cost of 4 cents per bag. Explain why no firm will adopt the pollution-control equipment if the pollution charge is unchanged at 5 cents a bag. (Assume that the cost of the control equipment is all variable cost at 4 cents per bag and that there is no fixed-cost component.)

d. Assume now that the tax is shifted to the volume of emissions, not to the number of bags produced, and that it is equivalent to 5 cents a bag if no pollution-control equipment is installed. Will any firm purchase the pollution-control equipment?

e. With the emissions tax at a rate equivalent to 5 cents per bag, to what rate must the cost of pollution control decline before firms will use it? If the cost of pollution control is constant at 4 cents, to what rate must the tax increase to induce firms to install the pollution-control equipment?

f. Assume now that the costs of reducing pollution are not identical for all firms. For simplicity, assume that there are two types of firms, low-cost pollution-control firms and high-cost pollution-control firms. The low-cost firms can eliminate pollution at costs lower than the emissions tax but the high-cost firms cannot. What is the result of imposing an emissions tax? What will happen to total industry output? Will any firms leave the industry? If so, which ones, the high-cost or the low-cost firms? Why?

ENERGY AND TAXES

a. Table 22-1 contains data on real output and energy consumption for the U.S. economy. Use these data to compute the use of energy per thousand dollars of GDP.

TABLE 22-1

Year	Real GDP (billions of 1987 $)	Energy Consumption (quadrillion BTUs)	Energy Consumption per $1,000 GDP (thousands of BTUs)	Year	Real GDP (billions of 1987 $)	Energy Consumption (quadrillion BTUs)	Energy Consumption per $1,000 GDP (thousands of BTUs)
1970	3,397.6	66.43	_____	1984	5,140.1	74.14	_____
1971	3,510.0	67.89	_____	1985	5,323.5	73.98	_____
1972	3,702.3	71.26	_____	1986	5,487.7	74.30	_____
1973	3,916.3	74.28	_____	1987	5,649.5	76.89	_____
1974	3,891.2	72.54	_____	1988	5,865.2	80.22	_____
1975	3,873.9	70.55	_____	1989	6,062.0	81.35	_____
1976	4,082.9	74.36	_____	1990	6,136.3	84.12	_____
1977	4,273.6	76.29	_____	1991	6,079.4	84.03	_____
1978	4,503.0	78.09	_____	1992	6,244.4	85.55	_____
1979	4,630.6	78.90	_____	1993	6,389.6	87.37	_____
1980	4,615.0	76.96	_____	1994	6,610.7	89.25	_____
1981	4,270.7	73.99	_____	1995	6,761.7	90.86	_____
1982	4,620.3	70.85	_____	1996	6,994.8	93.87	_____
1983	4,803.7	70.52	_____	1997	7,269.8	94.21	_____

SOURCES: GDP and prices: *Economic Report of the President*, 1999, Table B-2 and B-60; Energy consumption: Department of Energy, http://www.eia.doe.gov/pub/energy.overview/aer/aer0105.txt (April 25, 1999).

Energy Prices and Consumption | FIGURE 22-2

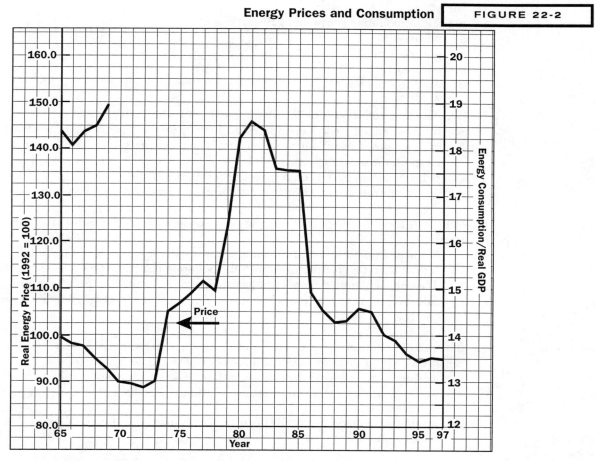

b. Figure 22-2 shows real energy prices, i.e., energy prices divided by the consumer price index. Complete Figure 22-2 by plotting the data on energy consumption per thousand dollars of GDP. Use this graph to discuss the pattern of energy consumption over the last 25 years.

SELF-TESTS FOR UNDERSTANDING ■

TEST A

Circle the most appropriate answer.

1. Which of the following suggests that, except for recycling, all economic activity results in a disposal problem?
    a. The edifice complex.
    b. The law of conservation of energy and matter.
    c. Emissions permits.
    d. Externalities.

2. Which of the following countries has avoided significant pollution problems?
    a. China.
    b. Russia.
    c. The United States.
    d. Poland.
    e. None of the above.

3. Economists view pollution as a textbook example of
    a. public goods.
    b. externalities.
    c. increasing returns to scale.
    d. the evils of monopoly.

4. Significant pollution is caused by the actions of
    a. business.
    b. government.
    c. consumers.
    d. All of the above.

5. The fact that pollution is often a detrimental externality suggests that
    a. cleaning up the environment must be done by direct government expenditures.
    b. without government intervention, profit-maximizing private firms cannot be expected to clean up the environment.
    c. public agencies have been responsible for most pollution.
    d. direct controls are superior to other forms of government intervention.

6. Which of the following is not an example of using financial incentives to clean up the environment?
    a. Mandated pollution-control equipment in an attempt to reduce automobile emissions.
    b. A graduated tax that increases with the polluting characteristics of each automobile engine.
    c. The sale of a limited number of permits to control emissions into Lake Erie.
    d. Allowing firms to buy and sell emission rights originally assigned under a program of direct controls.

7. The use of pollution charges as a means of cleaning up the environment
    a. is the predominant form of pollution control in the United States.
    b. is likely to be more efficient than a system of direct controls.
    c. would be most appropriate in situations calling for sudden action, such as a serious smog condition.
    d. would have exactly the same effects on the volume of pollution as do subsidies for pollution-control equipment.

8. As a strategy to control pollution, voluntarism
    a. is the best long-run strategy.
    b. may be the only practical alternative in cases where surveillance is impractical.
    c. should be the most effective alternative.
    d. has significant efficiency advantages as compared with pollution taxes.

9. Economists typically argue that _____ are likely to be most effective in reducing pollution over the long run.
    a. direct controls
    b. taxes on emissions
    c. voluntary programs
    d. specifications as to allowable equipment and/or procedures

10. Pollution charges are likely to be more efficient than direct controls because
    a. most of the reduction in pollution will be done by those who can implement reductions at low cost.
    b. everyone will be forced to show the same percentage reduction in pollution.
    c. no one likes paying taxes.
    d. pollution is a detrimental externality.

11. Compared with a system of direct controls, pollution charges
    a. are basically a "carrot" approach, relying on everyone's voluntary cooperation.
    b. are likely to lead to an equal percentage reduction in emissions from all pollution sources.
    c. will not reduce pollution, as firms will simply pass on these costs to their consumers with no impact on output levels.
    d. offer an incentive for continually reducing emissions, rather than reducing them just to some mandated level.

12. Harold Hotelling argued that, in competitive markets, even if extraction costs are negligible, the price of depletable resources will rise at a rate equal to the rate of
    a. inflation.
    b. unemployment.
    c. interest.
    d. growth of real income.

13. Which one of the following would be expected to reduce the price of a natural resource?
    a. The establishment of an effective producer cartel.
    b. The discovery of previously unknown reserves.
    c. An increase in the rate of inflation.
    d. An increase in GDP.

14. The quantity demanded of a scarce resource can exceed the quantity supplied
    a. if there is a sudden surge in demand.
    b. as economic growth increases demand.
    c. if monopolistic suppliers withhold supply.
    d. only if something prevents prices from adjusting.

15. Which of the following reflects a movement along the demand curve for energy?
    a. Reductions in the use of energy induced by higher prices.
    b. The development of new lower-cost extraction procedures.
    c. Increased demand from increases in GDP.
    d. The building of manufacturing capacity to extract oil from shale.

16. The record of resource prices in the twentieth century shows
    a. most have increased in line with the Hotelling principle.
    b. most have shown even greater increases in price.
    c. little trend in the real price of many resources.
    d. a steady trend toward lower real prices for all resources.

17. Rising resource prices can be a virtue as they provide an incentive for all but which one of the following?
    a. Increased waste.
    b. Increased use of substitutes.
    c. Increased conservation.
    d. Increased innovation.

18. Data for 1950–1980 suggest that the known reserves of some natural resources
    a. declined.
    b. remained roughly constant.
    c. actually increased.

19. Measured relative to total output, i.e., GDP, the use of energy in the United States is now
    a. about as high as it has ever been.
    b. about the same as it has been for the last 20 years.
    c. significantly lower than it was 20 years ago.

20. Effective price ceilings for natural resources would likely
    a. provide an increased incentive for further exploration.
    b. shift the demand curve to the left.
    c. induce consumers to conserve.
    d. lead to resource shortages.

TEST B

Circle T or F for true or false.

T   F   1. Pollution has been a serious problem only since World War II.

T   F   2. Only capitalist economies suffer from extensive pollution.

T   F   3. When considering public policies to limit discharges of wastes into a river basin, an equal percentage reduction by all polluters is likely to be the most economically efficient policy.

T   F   4. Pollution charges imposed on monopolist firms will have no effect on the volume of their polluting activity, because they will simply pass on the higher costs in the form of higher prices.

T   F   5. Efficiency considerations strongly suggest that society should spend enough to reduce all pollution to zero.

T   F   6. If left unchecked, the free-market mechanism will cause the demand for natural resources to exceed supply.

T   F   7. For much of the twentieth century the relative prices of most natural resources have shown dramatic increases.

T   F   8. Hotelling argued that, in free markets and with constant extraction costs, the price of natural resources will rise at the rate of inflation.

T   F   9. The unexpected discovery of resource deposits would reduce prices and delay the onset of the Hotelling pricing principle.

T   F 10. Rising prices can help control resource depletion as they induce firms and households to conserve.

■ SUPPLEMENTARY EXERCISES

POLLUTION AND PRICES

Can a producer simply pass on to her customers any pollution charge imposed on her? This numerical example expands upon the problem in the Basic Exercise.

Consider the production of plastic bags, which cause pollution in direct proportion to the volume of production. The demand for bags is given by

$$Q = 2,600 - 40P$$

where Q is measured in millions of bags and P is measured in cents.

1. Assume that plastic bags are produced by a monopolist at a cost of \$.15 a bag; that is,

$$TC = .15 \times Q.$$

Plot the demand, marginal revenue, average cost, and marginal cost curves on a piece of graph paper. What is the monopolist's profit-maximizing level of output, the associated price, and her profits?

2. The government now imposes a pollution tax of 5 cents a bag, that is, TC = .20 × Q. What happens to output, prices, and profits if the monopolist simply raises her price by 5 cents? Can she do better by charging a different price? If so, what is that price, the associated quantity, and the new level of profits?

3. Assume now that bags are produced by identical small firms under conditions of perfect competition. Each firm produces bags with average cost given by

$$AC = .4(Q - 10)^2 + 15.$$

What is the long-run market equilibrium price and quantity? How many firms are in the industry? How many bags does each firm produce?

4. Again the government imposes a pollution tax of 5 cents a bag on each producer. What happens in the short run when there are still the same number of bag producers? What about the long run? How many firms will produce how many bags at what price?

ECONOMICS IN ACTION ■

HEAVY METAL

It seems like we cannot pick up a newspaper without reading about some impending ecological disaster or some resource that is about to disappear. The late economist Julian Simon was an outspoken critic of such doomsday forecasts. He argued that our ancestors faced similar apparent disasters and, with some effort, overcame them. In many cases this involved learning how to use new metals or new sources of energy. According to Simon, the ultimate resource is human ingenuity. He was fond of quoting Henry George: "Both the jayhawk and the man eat chickens, but the more jayhawks, the fewer the chickens, while the more men, the more chickens."

In 1980 Simon issued a challenge to those predicting disaster. He argued that if resources were becoming increasingly scarce, their real price should increase. Simon offered the following $1,000 bet: Pick any resources and any future date. On that date, look to see if resource prices have risen by more or less than inflation. If prices were to rise by more than inflation, Simon would pay. If prices had not risen as fast as inflation, Simon would collect.

Simon's challenge was accepted in October 1980 by Paul Ehrlich, author of *Population Bomb*, along with John Harte and John Holdren. They chose five metals: chrome, copper, nickel, tin, and tungsten. On paper, they spent $200 on each metal, buying 51.28 pounds of chrome, 196.56 pounds of copper, 65.32 pounds of nickel, 229.16 pounds of tin, and 13.64 pounds of tungsten. The bet was to look at the inflation-adjusted price of this market basket of metal in October 1990. If, after adjusting for inflation, the market basket of metal cost more than $1,000, Simon would pay Ehrlich, Harte and Holdren the difference from $1,000. On the other hand, if the total cost were less than $1,000, Ehrlich, Harte and Holdren owed Simon the difference.

The controversy was renewed in the spring of 1995 when, writing in the *San Francisco Chronicle*, Simon again offered to accept a bet, this time on "any trend pertaining to human welfare." Paul Ehrlich and Stephen Schneider responded by offering a package bet on 15 measures including average global temperature, the concentration of tropospheric ozone, emissions of sulfur dioxide in Asia, and biodiversity. Simon rejected their offer arguing that their measures would have only indirect effects on people. Simon preferred more direct measures such as life expectancy or the trend in deaths from skin cancer.

1. Who do you think won the original bet? What was the magnitude of the payoff?

2. What has happened to the prices of the five metals since 1990? (Remember you will need to correct for inflation as the bet concerned relative prices.)

3. If, today, you could choose either side of the original bet, with the outcome to be determined in the year 2010, which would you take and why?

4. What about the most recent set of proposed wagers? What has happened to Ehrlich's and Schneider's preferred measures? What has happened to Simon's preferred measures? Which do you think is a more reasonable proposal? Which side would you take? (Remember to check your wager against actual results in ten years.)

■ STUDY QUESTIONS

1. What do economists mean when they say pollution is an externality?

2. Why do unregulated competitive markets tend to produce more pollution than is socially desirable?

3. Would it be a good idea to reduce all pollution to zero?

4. Why do you think business firms prefer government regulation to voluntary compliance with pollution standards?

5. Why do economists argue that emission taxes are a more efficient means of reducing pollution than direct controls?

6. What is the Hotelling principle of resource pricing?

7. Is the history of resource prices over the twentieth century consistent with the Hotelling principle?

8. Under what circumstances can the quantity demanded of a depletable resource exceed the quantity supplied?

9. What are the three virtues of rising prices for natural resources?

10. Why haven't reserves for many resources been falling over time as use of these resources continues to grow every year?

■ ECONOMICS ONLINE

Lots of information on energy production, consumption and prices is available from the U.S. Department of Energy

www.eia.doe.gov

THE REALM OF MACROECONOMICS

LEARNING OBJECTIVES

After completing this chapter, you should be able to:

■ explain the difference between microeconomics and macroeconomics.

■ determine whether particular problems are within the realm of microeconomics or macroeconomics.

■ describe the role of economic aggregates in macroeconomics.

■ explain how supply-demand analysis can be used to study inflation, recessions, and stabilization policy.

■ distinguish between real and nominal GDP.

■ explain how GDP is a measure of economic production, not economic well-being.

■ characterize, in general terms, the movement in prices and output over the last 130 years.

■ use aggregate demand and supply curves to explain how stabilization policy addresses problems of unemployment and inflation.

■   **CHAPTER REVIEW**

Economic theory is traditionally split into two parts, microeconomics and macroeconomics. If one

(1)   studies the behavior of individual decision-making units, one is studying _____. If

one studies the behavior of entire economies, one is studying _____. This chapter

is an introduction to macroeconomics.

The American economy is made up of millions of firms, hundreds of millions of individuals, and

innumerable different goods and services. Since it would be impossible to list each of these firms, indi-

viduals, and commodities, economists have found it useful to use certain overall averages or aggregates.

The concept of *domestic product* is an example. If we concentrate on macroeconomic aggregates, we

ignore much of the micro detail; whereas by concentrating on the micro detail, we may miss the big pic-

ture. The two forms of analysis are not substitutes; rather, they can be usefully employed together.

(Remember the map analogy in Chapter 1 of the text.) It has been argued that only successful macro-

economic policy leads to a situation in which the study of microeconomics is important, and vice versa.

Supply and demand analysis is a fundamental tool of both micro and macro theory. In microeco-

nomics one looks at the supply and demand for individual commodities, while in macroeconomics one

studies aggregate supply and aggregate demand. The intersection of the demand and supply curves in

(2)   microeconomics determines equilibrium _____ and _____ . In

macroeconomics the intersection of the aggregate demand and supply curves determines the price

level and aggregate output, or the gross _____ _____.

(3)   A sustained increase in the price level would be called _____, whereas a sus-

tained decrease would be called _____. Because of long-term growth factors,

domestic product in the U.S. economy usually increases every year. Periods when real domestic prod-

uct declines are referred to as _____. With an unchanged aggregate supply curve,

an outward (rightward) shift of the aggregate demand curve would lead to (<u>higher/lower</u>) prices and

(<u>higher/lower</u>) output. Higher prices would also result if the aggregate supply curve shifted to the

(<u>left/right</u>), but, this time, higher prices would be associated with a(n) (<u>increase/decrease</u>) in output.

Such a combination of rising prices and declining output is called _____. If both

curves shift to the right at the same rate, then it is possible to have increased output without inflation.

Gross domestic product is defined as the sum of the _____ values of all   (4)

_____ goods and services produced in the domestic economy during a year.

Because GDP counts only production in the domestic economy it (<u>excludes/includes</u>) the foreign

operations of American firms and _____ the activities of foreign firms and

workers operating in the United States. For the most part GDP includes only those newly produced

goods and services that are traded in markets. Illegal activities, the underground economy, and unpaid

housework are all examples of economic activity that (<u>are/are not</u>) included in GDP.

To measure GDP, economists and national income statisticians use prices to add up the different

kinds of output. If one uses today's prices, the result is (<u>nominal/real</u>) GDP. If one values output by   (5)

prices from some base period, one gets _____ GDP. Which is the better measure of

changes in output? (<u>Nominal/Real</u>) GDP. If all prices rise and all outputs are unchanged,

(<u>nominal/real</u>) GDP will increase while _____ GDP will not.

It is important to remember that GDP is a measure of production; it (<u>is/is not</u>) a measure of eco-   (6)

nomic well-being. The economic activity necessary to recover from a natural disaster such as an earth-

quake or hurricane is likely to (<u>decrease/increase</u>) GDP while _____ people's sense of

well-being. Similarly, goods and services used to clean up the environment mean a (<u>larger/smaller</u>)

GDP but are likely to reflect a (<u>higher/lower</u>) sense of well-being.

If you look at a long period of American history, you will see that there have been periods when

both output and prices have risen and fallen. The long-term trend for output is (<u>up/down</u>). The over-   (7)

all trend for prices (<u>depends/does not depend</u>) upon the period you are reviewing. Up until World

War II, prices rose and fell whereas since 1945, prices seem only to have _____.

The government would like to keep output growing, thus avoiding recession; at the same time, it

would like to keep prices from rising, thus avoiding (<u>inflation/deflation</u>). Attempts to do just this are   (8)

called _____ policy. The American government has been formally committed to

such policies only since the end of World War II. A look at Figures 23-4 and 23-5 in the text suggests

that since 1950 stabilization policy has done a good job of avoiding _____ but not

of avoiding _____. Chapter 34 discusses why this result is not surprising; that is,

why, if one concentrates on maintaining high levels of employment and output, the result is likely to

be higher prices.

■ IMPORTANT TERMS AND CONCEPTS QUIZ

Choose the best definition for each of the following terms.

1. _____ Microeconomics

2. _____ Macroeconomics

3. _____ Aggregation

4. _____ Aggregate demand curve

5. _____ Aggregate supply curve

6. _____ Inflation

7. _____ Deflation

8. _____ Recession

9. _____ Gross domestic product (GDP)

10. _____ Nominal GDP

11. _____ Real GDP

12. _____ Final goods and services

13. _____ Intermediate goods

14. _____ Stagflation

15. _____ Stabilization policy

16. _____ Unemployment

a. Period of expansion in an economy's total output.

b. Period of decline in an economy's total output.

c. Inflation occurring while the economy is growing slowly or in a recession.

d. Gross domestic product calculated at current price levels.

e. People willing to work but without jobs.

f. Government programs designed to prevent or shorten recessions and to counteract inflation.

g. Products purchased by their ultimate users.

h. Study of behavior of an entire economy.

i. Combining individual markets into a single, overall market.

j. Gross domestic product calculated using prices from some agreed-upon base year.

k. Products purchased for resale or for their use in producing other products.

l. Sustained decrease in general price level.

m. Graph of quantity of domestic product demanded at each possible price level.

n. Sum of money values of all final goods and services produced in the domestic economy within the year.

o. Graph of quantity of domestic product produced at each possible price level.

p. Study of individual decision-making units.

q. Sustained increase in general price level.

BASIC EXERCISES

These exercises use the aggregate demand-aggregate supply diagram to review a few basic concepts.

1. Figure 23-1 has four panels. The solid lines indicate the initial situation, and the dashed lines indicate a shift in one or both curves.
   a. Which diagram(s) suggest(s) a period, or periods, of inflation? _____
   b. Which diagram(s) suggest(s) a period, or periods, of deflation? _____
      (Have prices in the U.S. economy ever declined in the twentieth century? If so, when? _____
   c. Which diagram(s) illustrate(s) growth in real output with stable prices? _____
   d. Which diagram(s) illustrate(s) stagflation? _____

2. Stabilization policy involves changes in government policies designed to shorten recessions and stabilize prices. For reasons examined in later chapters, stabilization policies have their initial and primary effect on the aggregate demand curve. For the cases listed below explain how stabilization policy can reestablish the initial levels of output and prices. Do this by indicating the appropriate shift in the aggregate demand curve. (The exact policies that will achieve these shifts will be described in detail in Chapters 29 through 34.)
   a. Inflation [diagram (d)]
   b. Recession [diagram (b)]
   c. Consider diagram (c), the case of stagnation. If the government is restricted to policies that shift the aggregate demand curve, what will happen to output if the government adopts policies to combat inflation and restore the original price level? What happens to prices if the government is committed to maintaining the original level of output?

3. Table 23-1 contains data on output and prices in a hypothetical economy that produces only fast food.
   a. Calculate the money value of the production of hamburgers, shakes, and fries by multiplying price and quantity. Sum these results to calculate nominal gross domestic product (GDP) for each year.
   b. What is the percentage increase in nominal GDP from 1998 to 1999? _____

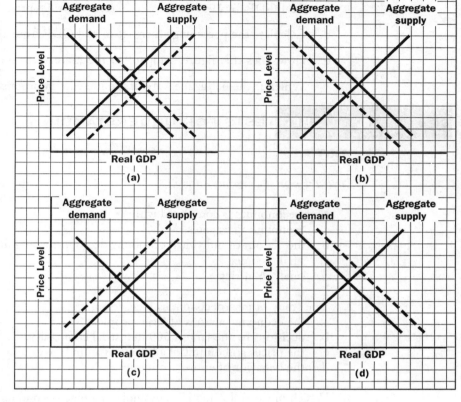

Aggregate Demand and Aggregate Supply   FIGURE 23-1

TABLE 23-1

	1998			1999		
	Price (1)	Quantity (2)	Nominal Value (3)	Price (4)	Quantity (5)	Nominal Value (6)
Hamburgers	$2.00	300	_____	$2.80	310	_____
Shakes	1.00	300	_____	1.30	320	_____
Fries	0.75	300	_____	0.90	330	_____
	Nominal GDP		_____	Nominal GDP		_____

c. Use 1998 prices to compute real GDP for 1999 based on 1998 prices.

Value of 1999 hamburger production using 1998 prices   _____

Value of 1999 shake production using 1998 prices   _____

Value of 1999 fries production using 1998 prices   _____

Real GDP for 1999 (expressed in terms of 1998 prices)   _____

d. Calculate the percentage increase in real GDP from 1998 to 1999.   _____

e. How does this figure compare to the increase in nominal GDP calculated in question b?

Which is the better measure of the increase in production?   _____

■ SELF-TESTS FOR UNDERSTANDING

TEST A

Circle the most appropriate answer.

1. Microeconomics is concerned with
   a. economic aggregates.
   b. the actions of individual economic decision-making units.
   c. small people.
   d. small countries.

2. The study of macroeconomics focuses on
   a. the economic actions of large people.
   b. decisions by the largest 500 industrial companies.
   c. the prices and output of all firms in an industry.
   d. the behavior of entire economies.

3. Which of the following is an example of a macroeconomic aggregate?
   a. The national output of Haiti.
   b. The total output of General Motors.
   c. Employment at Wal-Mart.
   d. The price of unleaded gas.

4. The aggregate demand curve shows
   a. the history of real GDP over the recent past.
   b. alternative levels of domestic output that policymakers might choose.
   c. how the quantity of domestic product demanded changes with changes in the price level.
   d. the demand for goods and services by the federal government.

5. The graph showing how the quantity of output produced by all firms depends upon the price level is called the
   a. aggregate supply curve.
   b. Phillips curve.
   c. production possibilities frontier.
   d. economy's aggregate indifference curve.

6. GDP measures the sum of money values of
   a. all goods sold in the domestic economy during the past year.
   b. all final goods and services produced in the domestic economy during the past year.
   c. attendance at all the worst movies during the past year.
   d. all payments to household domestic help during the past year.

7. GDP is designed to be a measure of
    a. economic activity conducted through organized markets.
    b. national well-being.
    c. all economic activity during the preceding year.
    d. all economic transactions involving checks or cash during the preceding year.

8. Using today's prices to aggregate all final output in the economy will yield
    a. nominal GDP.
    b. real GDP.
    c. the cost of living.
    d. GDP in constant dollars.

9. Real GDP is computed by valuing output at
    a. manufacturers' costs.
    b. current prices.
    c. prices from an agreed-upon base year.
    d. last year's rate of inflation.

10. Which of the following would not be included in GDP for 2000?
    a. The production of refrigerators in 2000.
    b. The government's purchase of paper clips produced in 2000.
    c. Consumer expenditures on haircuts in 2000.
    d. General Motors' expenditures on steel for producing Cadillacs in 2000.

11. Which of the following would not be part of GDP for 1999?
    a. Stacey's purchase of a 1999 Pontiac.
    b. Tanya's purchase of the latest computer produced by Apple.
    c. Ramon's expenditures on new furniture for his apartment.
    d. Jamal's purchase of a guitar originally used by John Lennon in 1965.

12. Which of the following is counted by the GDP statisticians?
    a. Jerita's purchase of Boeing stock from Walter.
    b. Your spending on tuition and fees for this year.
    c. Durwood's winnings from his bookie.
    d. The value of Yvonne's volunteer time at her daughter's school.

13. Which of the following will be measured as an increase in GDP but need not reflect an increase in economic well-being?
    a. Expenditures to clean up a major oil spill in Prince William Sound.
    b. The value of the time Roland spends painting his own house.
    c. The cost of new medical care that reduces infant mortality.
    d. Earnings of numbers runners in Chicago.

14. In 1974 nominal GDP was $1.459 trillion. In 1975 nominal GDP increased to $1.768 trillion. On the basis of just this information, which of the following statements is true?
    a. Total output of the American economy was greater in 1975 than in 1974.
    b. The whole increase in nominal GDP was the result of inflation.
    c. Actual output increased by 8.50 percent.
       $[(1.598 - 1.473) \div (1.473)] = .085$
    d. It is impossible to determine what happened to prices and output from data on nominal GDP alone.

15. A recession is likely to occur if
    a. unemployment is falling.
    b. the aggregate supply curve shifts to the right.
    c. the increase in nominal GDP exceeds the increase in real GDP.
    d. the aggregate demand curve shifts to the left.

16. Inflation is defined as a period of
    a. rising nominal GDP.
    b. generally rising prices.
    c. falling real GDP.
    d. falling unemployment.

17. Which of the following conditions will result in stagflation?
    a. The aggregate demand curve shifts to the right.
    b. The aggregate demand curve shifts to the left.
    c. The aggregate supply curve shifts to the right.
    d. The aggregate supply curve shifts to the left.

18. Stabilization policy refers to actions by the government to
    a. keep real GDP from rising.
    b. minimize changes in government regulation.
    c. prevent recessions and fight inflation.
    d. equalize the rate of unemployment and inflation.

19. In the period following World War II, the historical record shows
    a. more frequent and more severe recessionary dips in real output than before World War II.
    b. an economy that appears to be more inflation prone.
    c. little if any increase in real GDP.
    d. little increase in the price level.

20. Successful stabilization policy to reduce inflation would shift
    a. the aggregate supply curve to the left.
    b. the burden of taxes from individuals to corporations.
    c. the aggregate demand curve to the left.
    d. decision making about monetary policy to the Congress.

TEST B

Circle T or F for true or false.

T F 1. A study of the economy of Luxembourg would be an example of microeconomics.

T F 2. GDP is an example of a macroeconomic aggregate.

T F 3. An increase in nominal GDP necessarily implies an increase in real GDP.

T F 4. Changes in real GDP are a better measure of changes in national output than changes in nominal GDP.

T F 5. Deflation can occur only as a result of shifts in the aggregate supply curve.

T F 6. Even during the Great Depression of the 1930s prices did not decline.

T F 7. On the eve of World War II, national output, or real GDP, was not much greater than at the end of the Civil War.

T F 8. Stagflation refers to the simultaneous occurrence of rising prices and little if any increase in output.

T F 9. Stabilization policy refers to attempts by the government to influence both prices and output by shifting the aggregate demand curve.

T F 10. Stabilization policy to combat a recession would call for policies that shift the aggregate demand curve to the left.

ECONOMICS IN ACTION ■

LEADING INDICATORS AND TURNING POINTS

The text describes recessions as a period of decline in GDP. This is also the definition that is used by many media commentators. The beginnings and ends of recessions are actually determined by a group of economists associated with the National Bureau of Economic Research. They look at a broader range of measures of economic activity than just GDP. Much controversy surrounded the dating of the 1990–91 recession. The following is taken from a report by Professor Robert Hall, Stanford University, chairman of the NBER Business Cycle Dating Committee, written in late 1991. The Committee had agreed on a date for the beginning of the recession but had not yet agreed upon when the recession ended. Using Figure 23-2 how would you date the beginning and end of the recession? The Committee's decisions are reported in the answers section of the

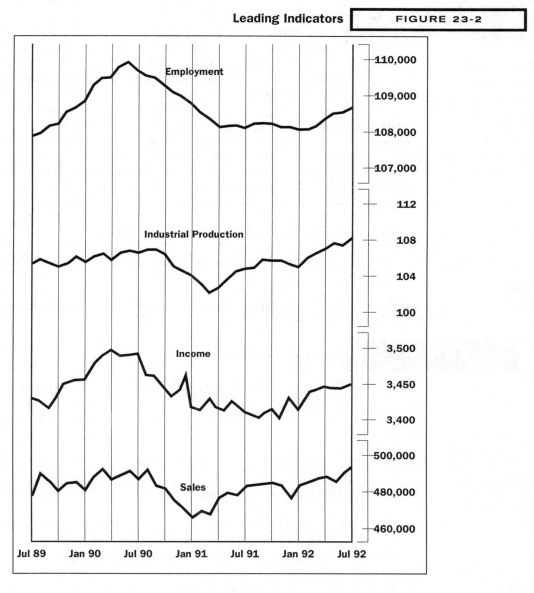

Leading Indicators   FIGURE 23-2

Study Guide, but make your own determination before looking at their decision.

In April 1991, the NBER's Business Cycle Dating Committee determined that a recession had started _____. [Figure 23-2] shows the data that most strongly influenced the committee: real personal income less transfers, real sales in manufacturing and trade, nonagricultural employment (because 1990 was a census year, the committee looked at private nonagricultural employment, and nonagricultural employment minus census workers), and industrial production. The figure shows the basic problem of dating a business cycle: that different cyclical indicators have different turning points.

The U.S. economy in 1990 reflected the combined influence of two different forces. One was a very broad slowdown starting in the spring. The other was a sharp contraction in industries (automobile and others) following the spike in oil prices in August. The result was an unusual combination of leading employment and lagging industrial production. The peak date was a reasonable compromise. It embodied the notion that breadth, or dispersion, is an important characteristic of a recession. When measures that span all sectors of the economy—income and employment—peak earlier, the fact that goods production stayed strong for [several] months should not control the date of the recession.

[Figure 23-2] also shows some of the challenges that faced the NBER Business Cycle Dating Committee in determining the date of the trough in economic activity. First, the figure makes it completely clear that any such determination in the near future would be quite premature. Should the economy begin to contract again, it is a distinct possibility that the trough would occur in late 1991 or 1992. A trough date cannot be assigned until activity has reached a sufficiently high level that a contraction would be a new recession, not a continuation of the existing one.

Economist James Tobin has argued that the traditional approach to dating business cycles is misguided in that it assumes that any increase in economic activity signals the end of a recession. Tobin notes that in a growing economy, output and employment have to increase simply to keep pace with a growing population. He prefers growth-oriented dating and definitions of business cycles, recoveries, and recessions. In this view, any time the growth of output and employment failed to match the growth in the potential output would be candidates to be called recession or growth-recession.

1. How would you date the 1990–91 recession? Why?

2. Do you think the definition of recessions should be growth-oriented as advocated by Tobin? Why?

SOURCES: *NBER Reporter* (National Bureau of Economic Research, Winter 1991/92), pp. 1–3; James Tobin, "Comments," *Brookings Papers on Economic Activity,* 1993:1, pp. 200–208.

STUDY QUESTIONS

1. Why is GDP, a measure of domestic production, not a good measure of national well-being?

2. Why does GDP exclude the sales of existing goods and assets such as used college textbooks and existing homes?

3. Why does GDP include only final goods and exclude intermediate goods?

4. Which is the better measure of the change in domestic output, nominal GDP or real GDP? Why?

5. Should measures of GDP include estimates of non-market economic activity? Why?

6. How can stabilization policy help to reduce unemployment? Inflation?

7. If stabilization policy has the strongest and most immediate impact on aggregate demand, what are the implications for prices when the government wants to reduce unemployment? What are the implications for unemployment when the government wants to reduce prices?

8. What might account for the differences in the American economy's record of economic growth and inflation after 1950 as compared with the period before World War II?

ECONOMICS ONLINE

You can get current information on a number of economic indicators from a number of web sites:
Economic Indicators, a monthly publication prepared by the Council of Economic Advisers for the Joint Economic Committee.

http://www.gpo.ucop.edu/catalog/econind.html

White House Economic Statistics Briefing Room

> http://www2.whitehouse.gov/fsbr/esbr.html

Bureau of Labor Statistics (U.S. Department of Labor)

> http://www.bls.gov/eag.table.html

Bureau of Economic Analysis (U.S. Department of Commerce)

> http://www.bea.doc.gov

U.S. Census Economic Briefing Room

> http://www.census.gov/cgi-bin/briefroom/BriefRm

THE GOALS OF MACROECONOMIC POLICY

LEARNING OBJECTIVES

After completing this chapter, you should be able to:

■ summarize arguments in favor of and opposed to higher rates of economic growth.

■ distinguish between alternative measures of economic growth.

■ explain how potential GDP is estimated and how growth in potential GDP is related to an economy's growth potential.

■ explain why growth in labor productivity is the major determinant of the growth in living standards.

■ explain how economists use the concept of potential GDP to measure the economic cost of unemployment.

■ describe how the Bureau of Labor Statistics measures the number of unemployed and in what ways this number may be an overestimate or an underestimate of the unemployment level.

Important Terms and Concepts

ECONOMIC GROWTH

UNEMPLOYMENT RATE

POTENTIAL GDP

LABOR FORCE

LABOR PRODUCTIVITY

GDP PER CAPITA

PRODUCTIVITY SLOWDOWN

DISCOURAGED WORKERS

FRICTIONAL UNEMPLOYMENT

STRUCTURAL UNEMPLOYMENT

CYCLICAL UNEMPLOYMENT

FULL EMPLOYMENT

UNEMPLOYMENT INSURANCE

PURCHASING POWER

REAL WAGE

RELATIVE PRICES

REDISTRIBUTION BY INFLATION

REAL RATE OF INTEREST

NOMINAL RATE OF INTEREST

CAPITAL GAIN

EXPECTED RATE OF INFLATION

■ explain the differences between frictional, structural, and cyclical unemployment.

■ summarize the debate over how much unemployment is consistent with full employment.

■ explain why unemployment insurance only spreads the financial burden of unemployment that individuals would otherwise face, but does not eliminate the economic cost of unemployment.

■ distinguish between real and mythical costs of inflation.

■ explain how the concept of real wages suggests that inflation has not systematically eroded the purchasing power of wages.

■ distinguish between changes in prices that reflect a change in relative prices and changes that reflect general inflation.

■ distinguish between real and nominal rates of interest.

■ describe how the difference between real and nominal rates of interest is related to expectations about the rate of inflation.

■ explain how the taxation of nominal magnitudes can mean that, during a period of inflation, savers and investors will receive a reduced real return after taxes.

■ explain why and how usury ceilings, based on nominal interest rates, can have undesirable impacts during periods of rapid inflation.

■ distinguish between low and high inflation.

■ explain why the variability of inflation is important to an understanding of the cost of inflation.

■ CHAPTER REVIEW

This chapter is an introduction to three important issues at the heart of the formulation of macro-economic policy: economic growth, unemployment and inflation.

ECONOMIC GROWTH

The tools of economics cannot help you determine whether an economy should grow faster or slower; they can, however, identify the sources of growth and the consequences of more or less growth. In particular, a number of economists oppose zero economic growth on the grounds that a move in this direction would require extensive government controls and may seriously hamper efforts to eliminate poverty and to protect the environment. Solutions to these last two problems are likely to require more rather than fewer resources. Many feel that it is easier to reach a political agreement to devote resources to problems of poverty and the environment if total output is expanding rather than if it is not growing.

The growth in labor productivity is the major determinant of material well-being or living standards over long periods of time. Growth in labor productivity explains why, on the average, your parents are wealthier than their parents and their parents' parents. Continued growth in labor productivity will mean that your children and their children will be wealthier than you. This chapter looks at factors affecting economic growth.

Discussions of productivity usually focus on labor productivity, which is defined as the amount of output per unit of labor input. For a firm producing a single output, measuring labor productivity per hour is a simple matter of dividing output by total labor hours. For the American economy as a whole, labor productivity is measured as real GDP divided by total labor hours. An increase in labor productivity means that (more/less) output can be produced with the same number of labor hours. If aggregate output were unchanged, an increase in labor productivity would mean (more/less) unemploy-   (1) ment. But remember that total output and the unemployment rate are determined by the intersection of the aggregate _____ and aggregate _____ curves. An increase in productivity means that the production possibilities frontier has shifted (out/in); that is, the aggregate supply curve has shifted to the (left/right) and there has been a(n) (increase/decrease) in potential GDP. It is macroeconomic policy that helps to determine whether we take advantage of new possibilities.

What makes labor more or less productive? While there are many factors, certainly the intensity of work, the quality of training, the availability of more and better equipment, and the level of technology are important factors. Sustained growth in labor productivity (is/is not) a relatively new phenom-   (2) enon, tracing back about (2,000/200) years. The following word equation shows why growth in labor productivity is the basic determinant of living standards or output per capita:

$$\frac{\text{Total output}}{\text{Total population}} = \frac{\text{Total output}}{\text{Total hours worked}} \times \frac{\text{Total hours worked}}{\text{Number of workers}} \times \frac{\text{Number of workers}}{\text{Total population}}$$

The expression on the left of the equal sign is output per capita. The first expression on the right side of the equal sign is labor productivity. The second and third expressions measure the number of hours a typical worker works and the proportion of the population that works. (This last term is sometimes referred to as the employment ratio.) Notice that two of the numerators and denominators on the right-hand side of the equal sign can be canceled, establishing the equality of the expression. If the number of hours per worker does not change and the proportion of the population that works is constant—that is, if the second and third terms on the right-hand side do not change—then the only way that output or GDP per capita can increase is if labor productivity increases. If hours per worker decline, then increases in labor productivity will imply a smaller increase in output per capita. Much of the difference between the growth in labor productivity and the growth in output per capita over the past 100 years can be accounted for by the decline in the number of hours worked each year by a typical worker. Over the past 25 years there has been a sharp increase in the employment ratio, a change that is related to the increased labor force participation of women along with the changing age structure of the population as baby boomers finished school and began working. These latter changes can be important for several decades but are unlikely to be sustained over a century or two. Thus in the long run, changes in GDP per capita will be dominated by changes in labor productivity.

UNEMPLOYMENT

Unemployment has two sorts of costs. The personal costs include not only the lost income for individuals out of work, but also the loss of work experience and the psychic costs of involuntary idleness. The economic costs for the nation as a whole can be measured by the output of goods and services that might have been produced by those who are unemployed.

(3) Economists have attempted to measure the economic cost of unemployment by estimating what output would have been at full employment. These figures are estimates of (potential/actual) GDP. The economic cost of unemployment is the difference between potential GDP and _____

_____ .

Unemployment statistics come from a monthly survey by the Bureau of Labor Statistics. People are asked if they have a job. If they answer no, they are asked if they are laid off from a job they expect to return to, are actively looking for work, or are not looking for work. From these answers government statisticians derive estimates of employment, unemployment, and the labor force. These numbers are not above criticism. When unemployment rates are high, some people give up looking for work because they believe that looking for work is not worth the effort. These people are called

(4) _____ workers. An increase in the number of people who have given up looking for work means a(n) (increase/decrease) in the amount of statistical unemployment and is an important reason why some observers feel that the official unemployment statistics (understate/overstate) the

problem of unemployment. All part-time workers are counted as employed. If part-time work is involuntary and these individuals would prefer full-time work, official unemployment statistics will (<u>understate/overstate</u>) the problem of unemployment. If liberal unemployment compensation induces people to call themselves unemployed even if they have no intention of looking for work then official statistics will (<u>overstate/understate</u>) unemployment.

Some unemployment occurs naturally from the normal workings of labor markets, as people initially look for jobs, improve their own skills, look for better jobs, move to new locations, and so forth. Such unemployment is called _____ unemployment and involves people who are temporarily without a job more or less voluntarily. Full employment would not eliminate this kind of unemployment. Full employment would eliminate unemployment that is due to a decline in the economy's total production; that is, at full employment there would be no _____ unemployment. Unemployment may also occur because people's skills are no longer in demand due to automation or massive changes in production. This type of unemployment is called _____ unemployment.   (5)

How do we determine how much unemployment is consistent with full employment or, more succinctly, what is the full employment rate of unemployment? In the early 1960s President Kennedy argued that the United States should aim for an employment rate of 4 percent. During the 1970s it was argued that the increasing number of young workers in the labor force increased the percentage of (<u>cyclical/frictional/structural</u>) unemployment and (<u>decreased/increased</u>) the full employment rate of unemployment. Some argued that more generous unemployment compensation had increased the incentive for people to say they were looking for work, when they really were not, a change that would increase the full employment rate of unemployment. Finally, many economists base their estimate of the full employment rate of unemployment on their evaluation of the links between unemployment and inflation. Experience in recent years suggests that the full employment of unemployment is (<u>higher/lower</u>) than estimates of the 1970s and 1980s.   (6)

Unemployment insurance can help ease the burden of unemployment for individual families, but it (<u>can/cannot</u>) protect society against the lost output that the unemployed might have produced. Employing these people in the future does not bring back the hours of employment that have already   (7) been missed. Unemployment compensation provides (<u>complete/partial</u>) protection for (<u>all/some</u>) unemployed workers.

INFLATION

There are important and valid reasons why people are concerned about continuing inflation. Nevertheless, quite a few popular arguments against inflation turn out to be based on misunderstandings. Many people worry that a high rate of inflation reduces their standard of living, or their

(8)   (<u>real/nominal</u>) income. But the facts show that periods of high inflation are usually accompanied by equally large if not larger increases in wages. For most workers, the real standard of living, or the change in wages adjusted for the change in prices, continues to increase, even during periods of rapid inflation. A worker whose wages double when prices double is able to consume (<u>more/less/the same</u>) goods and services (<u>than/as</u>) before the rise in prices and wages. In this case one would say that real wages (<u>increased/were unchanged/decreased</u>).

(9)   During inflationary periods most prices increase at (<u>the same/different</u>) rates. As a result, goods and services with smaller than average price increases become relatively (<u>more/less</u>) expensive than they were before. Analogously, goods and services with larger than average price increases become relatively _____ expensive. Relative prices change all the time, during both inflationary and noninflationary periods. Changes in relative prices usually reflect shifts in demand and/or supply curves or various forms of government interventions. It is inaccurate to blame inflation for an increase in relative prices.

But inflation does have real effects. One important effect is the redistribution of wealth between borrowers and lenders in inflationary periods. If lenders expect higher prices in the future they will

(10)   demand (<u>higher/lower</u>) interest rates to compensate them for the loss of purchasing power of the future dollars used to repay loans. Economists have thus found it useful to distinguish between nominal and real interest rates. If one looks at interest rates only in terms of the dollars that borrowers must pay lenders, one is looking at _____ interest rates. If one looks at interest rates in terms of the purchasing power the borrower will pay the lender, one is looking at _____ interest rates. During periods of inflation it is usual for nominal interest rates to incorporate expectations of inflation. There need be no unexpected redistribution of income between borrowers and lenders if actual inflation matches the expectations of inflation embodied in nominal interest rates.

If a change in the rate of inflation is accurately foreseen, and if nominal interest rates are correctly adjusted to reflect the change in expected inflation, then nominal interest rates (will/will not) change **(11)** while real interest rates will (also change/be unchanged). More typically, expectations of inflation are incorrect, in which case inflation will result in a redistribution of wealth between borrowers and lenders. Who gains and who loses will depend on whether the adjustment of nominal interest rates is too large or too small. Lenders lose when the adjustment of nominal interest rates is too (large/small) and borrowers lose when the adjustment is too _____. The tax treatment of interest payments and capital gains can have a substantial impact on the real after-tax rate of return. Problems here reflect the fact that the tax system, originally designed for a world of no inflation, focuses on (nominal/real) interest rates.

Legal ceilings on interest charges for different types of loans are called _____ ceil- **(12)** ings. These ceilings are almost universally written in terms of (nominal/real) interest rates rather than _____ interest rates. During periods of rapid inflation, (nominal/real) interest rates may rise, bumping into usury ceilings, while _____ interest rates may show little if any change. The result will be frustrated borrowers and lenders and reduced levels of economic activity in the affected areas.

Over the long run, small unexpected differences in the rate of inflation can compound to create large differences in profits and losses. Since most business investments depend on long-term contracts, this area of economic activity may suffer during periods of high inflation. The difficulty of making long-term contracts is a real cost of inflation.

Inflation that proceeds at a fairly moderate and steady pace may pose few problems for an economy, but inflation that progresses at high, sometimes accelerating, and often variable rates imposes significant social and economic costs. There is no simple borderline between the two. In different countries or in different periods of time, the dividing line will vary considerably.

■ IMPORTANT TERMS AND CONCEPTS QUIZ

Choose the best definition for each of the following terms.

1. _____ Economic growth

2. _____ Labor productivity

3. _____ GDP per capita

4. _____ Unemployment rate

5. _____ Potential GDP

6. _____ Labor force

7. _____ Discouraged workers

8. _____ Frictional unemployment

9. _____ Structural unemployment

10. _____ Cyclical unemployment

11. _____ Unemployment insurance

12. _____ Purchasing power

13. _____ Real wage

14. _____ Relative prices

15. _____ Real rate of interest

16. _____ Nominal rate of interest

17. _____ Capital gain

a. Difference between an asset's selling price and its original cost.

b. Number of people holding or seeking jobs

c. Output per unit of labor input.

d. Government transfer payments to eligible workers if unemployed.

e. Percentage of labor force unemployed.

f. Interest payments, in percentage terms, measured in dollars.

g. Total output divided by population.

h. Unemployed people who cease looking for work, believing that no jobs are available.

i. Unemployment attributable to decline in economy's total production.

j. Unemployment due to normal workings of the labor market.

k. Legal maximum interest rate.

l. Interest payment, in percentage terms, measured in terms of purchasing power.

m. Volume of goods and services that money wage will buy.

n. Unemployment due to changes in nature of economy.

o. Price of an item in terms of some other item.

p. Volume of goods and services that a sum of money will buy.

q. Level of real output attainable if all resources were fully employed.

r. Increase in total output.

1. **Lower Growth in Productivity or Lower Level of Productivity?**

    This exercise investigates whether a decline in the growth of labor productivity results in a decline in the level of productivity. Assume that labor productivity is originally $13.71 per hour, and that it grows at an annual rate of 2.8 percent for 25 years, and 1.1 percent for the next 25 years.
    a. What is labor productivity at the end of the first 25 years? $ _____
    b. What is labor productivity at the end of the next 25 years? $ _____
    c. Does the decline in the rate of growth of productivity lead to a decline in the level of productivity?
    d. What happens to GDP per capita over the same 50 years if average hours per week decline from 40.0 to 34.6 and the proportion of the population that is employed increases from 40.8 percent to 48.6 percent?

2. **Who Gains and Loses from an Adjustment of Nominal Interest Rates?**

    This problem is designed to illustrate how the adjustment of nominal interest rates, when it is an accurate reflection of future inflation, can leave the real costs and returns to borrowers and lenders unchanged. For simplicity this problem ignores taxes.

    Angela Abbott has a manufacturing firm. After paying other costs she expects a cash flow of $10 million, out of which she must pay the principal and interest on a $5 million loan. If prices are unchanged and if the interest rate is 5 percent, Angela expects a nominal and real profit of $4,750,000. This result is shown in the first column of Table 24-1.

    The next three columns reflect three possible alternatives. The second column shows the consequences of unexpected inflation of 10 percent. In the third column, nominal interest rates have adjusted in expectation of an inflation of 10 percent, which actually occurs. And in the last column, nominal interest rates reflect the consequences of expecting a higher rate of inflation than actually occurs.
    a. Fill in the missing figures in the second column. Compare the real returns to both Angela and her lender with those of the noninflationary situation in column 1. Who gains and who loses when there is unexpected inflation?
    b. Fill in the missing figures in the third column. This is the case in which nominal interest rates have adjusted appropriately. (The approximation is to add the rate of inflation, 10 percent, to the rate of interest in the noninflationary situation, 5 percent. The extra 0.5 percent comes

Angela's Cash Flow | **TABLE 24-1**

	(1)	(2)	(3)	(4)
1. Price level	1.00	1.10	1.10	1.10
2. Sales revenue minus labor and materials costs*	10,000,000	11,000,000	11,000,000	11,000,000
3. Principal repayment	5,000,000	5,000,000	5,000,000	5,000,000
4. Interest rate	0.05	0.05	0.155	0.20
5. Interest payment [(4) × (3)]	250,000	_____	_____	_____
6. Total nominal payment to lender [(3) + (5)]	5,250,000	_____	_____	_____
7. Real payment to lender [(6) ÷ (1)]	5,250,000	_____	_____	_____
8. Nominal profits [(2) − (6)]	4,750,000	_____	_____	_____
9. Real profits [(8) ÷ (1)]	4,750,000	_____	_____	_____

*Inflation of 10 percent is assumed to increase sales revenue, labor costs, and materials costs by 10 percent each. As a result, the difference between sales revenue and labor plus material costs also increases by 10 percent in columns 2, 3, and 4.

from a more complex and complete adjustment.) Compare the real returns in rows 7 and 9 with the comparable figures in column 1. Who gains and who loses now?

   c. Fill in the missing figures in column 4, where interest rates have adjusted in anticipation of a rate of inflation higher than the rate that actually occurs. Who gains and who loses when inflation turns out to be less than expected?

3. **When Are High Interest Rates Really Low?**

Let R = nominal interest rate,
π = actual rate of inflation, and
r = real rate of interest.

It is usual to estimate actual real interest rates as $r = R - \pi$. Consider the data in Table 24-2. Column 1 shows data on nominal interest rates on one-year government securities issued in December of each year from 1970 through 1994. Column 2 shows the rate of inflation over the same period, December to December, as measured by the consumer price index. (For example, the rate of inflation reported for 1970 is from December 1970 to December 1971, the same period for which a holder of the government security earned interest.)

   a. Complete column 3 by subtracting the rate of inflation from the nominal rate of interest to compute the real rate of interest.

   b. The nominal interest rates from column 1 are plotted in Figure 24-2. Plot the real interest rates you calculated in column 3 in Figure 24-2.

   c. Were actual real rates ever negative? If so, how can this be?

   d. When were interest rates higher, 1977, 1987, or 1997?

This exercise has made use of data on actual inflation to estimate actual real interest rates. Remember that when individuals decide to borrow or lend they typically know the nominal interest rate they will receive or have to pay, but they cannot know what the real interest rate will turn out to be, as that will depend upon future inflation. Thus decisions to borrow and lend will be strongly influenced by

| TABLE 24-2 | **Nominal Interest Rates and Inflation** |

	Nominal Interest Rate on 1-Year Government Securities (December)	Rate of Inflation (December to December)	Real Interest Rate
1970	5.00%	3.3%	_____ %
1971	4.61%	3.4%	_____ %
1972	5.52%	8.7%	_____ %
1973	7.27%	12.3%	_____ %
1974	7.31%	6.9%	_____ %
1975	6.60%	4.9%	_____ %
1976	4.89%	6.7%	_____ %
1977	6.96%	9.0%	_____ %
1978	10.30%	13.3%	_____ %
1979	11.98%	12.5%	_____ %
1980	14.88%	8.9%	_____ %
1981	12.85%	3.8%	_____ %
1982	8.91%	3.8%	_____ %
1983	10.11%	3.9%	_____ %
1984	9.33%	3.8%	_____ %
1985	7.67%	1.1%	_____ %
1986	5.87%	4.4%	_____ %
1987	7.17%	4.4%	_____ %
1988	8.99%	4.6%	_____ %
1989	7.72%	6.1%	_____ %
1990	7.05%	3.1%	_____ %
1991	4.38%	2.9%	_____ %
1992	3.71%	2.7%	_____ %
1993	3.61%	2.7%	_____ %
1994	7.14%	2.5%	_____ %
1995	5.31%	3.3 %	_____ %
1996	5.47%	1.7%	_____ %
1997	5.53%	1.6%	_____ %

SOURCES: Federal Reserve, Bureau of Labor Statistics.

expectations of inflation and the corresponding expectations for real interest rates.

Interest Rates   FIGURE 24-2

SELF-TESTS FOR UNDERSTANDING ■

TEST A

Circle the most appropriate answer.

1. Labor productivity is defined as
    a. output per capita.
    b. GDP divided by population.
    c. the growth in output per worker.
    d. output per unit of labor input.

2. A country's standard of living is usually measured as
    a. GDP per capita.
    b. output per worker.
    c. the growth in GDP.
    d. output per unit of labor input.

3. Which of the following would not explain differences in labor productivity between countries?
    a. The amount of capital per worker.
    b. The level of technology.
    c. The size of the labor force.
    d. The amount of training received by workers.

4. Indicate which examples go with which concepts.
    a. An older, unemployed telephone operator replaced by new, computerized switching machines.
    b. An unemployed college senior looking for her first job.
    c. A former construction worker who has given up looking for work because of a belief that no one is hiring.
    d. An unemployed retail clerk who is laid off because of declining sales associated with a general business recession.
    frictional unemployment _____
    structural unemployment _____
    cyclical unemployment _____
    discouraged worker _____

5. Which of the following factors implies that official statistics may understate the magnitude of the problem of unemployment? (There may be more than one correct answer.)
   a. Discouraged workers.
   b. The loss of expected overtime work.
   c. Generous unemployment benefits.
   d. Involuntary part-time work.

6. Which of the following people are eligible for unemployment compensation?
   a. A mechanic for Ford Motor Company laid off because of declining auto sales.
   b. A housewife seeking paid work after six years spent at home with two small children.
   c. A college senior looking for his first job.
   d. An engineer who quits to find a better job.

7. Which one of the following groups experiences the highest rate of unemployment?
   a. Married men.
   b. College graduates.
   c. Teenage workers.
   d. Adult nonwhite workers.

8. The measure of output that the economy could produce with the full employment of all people and factories is called
   a. real GDP.
   b. potential GDP.
   c. nominal GDP.
   d. expected GDP.

9. The difference between potential GDP and actual GDP is a reflection of
   a. frictional unemployment.
   b. cyclical unemployment.
   c. usury laws.
   d. nominal interest rates.

10. In 1998 unemployment insurance provided benefits to about _____ of the unemployed.
    a. one-quarter
    b. one-third
    c. one-half
    d. all

11. Unemployment insurance
    a. eliminates the cost of unemployment to the economy as a whole.
    b. means that no unemployed worker need suffer a decline in his or her standard of living.
    c. helps to protect insured individuals by spreading the cost.
    d. must be paid back by the unemployed once they find a new job.

12. The real rate of interest relevant for a lender about to lend money is measured as the
    a. nominal interest rate divided by the rate of inflation.
    b. nominal interest rate minus the expected rate of inflation.
    c. rate of inflation minus the nominal interest rate.
    d. the increase in nominal GDP divided by the rate of increase in prices.

13. A nominal interest rate of 10 percent and inflationary expectations of 4 percent imply a real interest rate of _____ percent.
    a. 4
    b. 6
    c. 10
    d. 14

14. If suddenly everyone expects a higher rate of inflation, economists would expect nominal interest rates to
   a. rise.
   b. fall.
   c. stay unchanged.

15. If inflation is unexpected, there is apt to be a redistribution of wealth from
   a. borrowers to lenders.
   b. lenders to borrowers.
   c. rich to poor.
   d. poor to rich.

16. Usury laws are designed to limit
   a. increases in nominal wages.
   b. real interest rates.
   c. the rate of inflation.
   d. nominal interest rates.

17. With overall inflation at 5 percent, if the price of jeans increases by 7 percent and the price of hand calculators declines by 3 percent, we would say that
   a. the relative price of jeans has increased.
   b. calculators are now less expensive in terms of jeans.
   c. both a and b are correct.
   d. the relative price of calculators has increased.

18. Assume that in a world without inflation, interest rates are 4 percent and 25 percent of interest income must be paid to the government in taxes. (That is, the after-tax real return to lenders is 3 percent.) Assume now that inflation is expected to be and turns out to be 4 percent. Assume further that nominal interest rates increase to 8 percent in line with expectations of inflation at 4 percent. With taxes based on nominal income, what is the after-tax real return when nominal interest rates increase to 8 percent?
   a. Less than 3 percent.
   b. Unchanged at 3 percent.
   c. More than 3 percent.

19. If your wages go up by 10 percent when prices go up by 7 percent, the increase in your real wage is about _____ percent.
   a. 3
   b. 7
   c. 10
   d. 17

20. The historical evidence suggests that in periods with high rates of inflation, nominal wages
   a. increase at about the same rate as before.
   b. increase at much lower rates than inflation.
   c. also increase at high rates.
   d. remain unchanged.

TEST B

Circle T or F for true or false.

T   F   1. Long term, it makes little difference whether productivity grows at 1 percent per year or at 3 percent per year.

T F 2. There is clear evidence of a long-term decline in the productivity of American manufacturing workers.

T F 3. In periods of high unemployment the only people whose incomes are reduced are those who are out of work.

T F 4. The official unemployment statistics are adjusted to include those people with part-time jobs who are looking for full-timework.

T F 5. Unemployment insurance protects society against lost output from unemployment.

T F 6. Potential GDP is an estimate of the maximum possible output our economy could produce under conditions similar to wartime.

T F 7. Most economists agree that full employment should be defined as an unemployment rate of zero.

T F 8. Inflation does not redistribute wealth between borrowers and lenders because nominal interest rates are automatically adjusted to reflect actual inflation.

T F 9. The historical record shows that low inflation will always lead to high inflation.

T F 10. Predictable inflation is likely to impose less cost than unpredictable inflation.

Important Terms and Concepts

INDEX NUMBER

INDEX NUMBER PROBLEM

CONSUMER PRICE INDEX

DEFLATING BY A PRICE INDEX

GDP DEFLATOR

APPENDIX: HOW STATISTICIANS MEASURE INFLATION

LEARNING OBJECTIVES

After completing this appendix, you should be able to:

■ construct a price index from data on prices and the composition of the market basket in the base year.

■ use a price index to compute real measures of economic activity by deflating the corresponding nominal measures.

■ use a price index to compute the rate of inflation from one period to the next.

■ explain how the market baskets differ for the Consumer Price Index and the GDP deflator.

IMPORTANT TERMS AND CONCEPTS QUIZ ■

Choose the best definition for each of the following terms.

1. _____ Index number

2. _____ Consumer Price Index

3. _____ Deflating

4. _____ GDP deflator

5. _____ Index number problem

a. Dividing a nominal magnitude by a price index to express the magnitude in constant purchasing power.

b. Magnitude of some variable relative to its magnitude in the base period.

c. Price index obtained by dividing nominal GDP by real GDP.

d. Measure of price level based on the spending of urban households.

e. Average change in consumer prices.

f. Differences between consumption patterns of actual families and the market basket used for a price index.

BASIC EXERCISES ■

The following exercise should help you review the material on price indexes presented in the appendix to Chapter 24.

Table 24-3 presents data on expenditures and prices for a hypothetical family that buys only food and clothing. We see that in 1997 this family spent $5,000 on food at $2 per unit of food, and $10,000 on clothing at $25 per unit. Note that between 1997 and 1998, dollar expenditures by this family increased by 15.65 percent, rising from $15,000 to $17,348. Is this family able to consume 15.65 percent more of everything? Clearly not, since prices have risen. How much inflation has there been on average? What is the increase in real income for this family? These are the sorts of questions that a good price index can help you answer.

Hypothetical Prices and Expenditures   **TABLE 24-3**

Year	Food Price	Food Expenditures	Clothing Price	Clothing Expenditures	Total Expenditures
1997	$2.00	$5,000	$25.00	$10,000	$15,000
1998	$2.36	$5,900	$26.50	$11,448	$17,348

1. Use the data in Table 24-3 to construct a family price index (FPI) using 1997 as the base year.
   a. Divide expenditures by price to find the quantities of each good purchased in 1997. This is the base-period market basket.
      Quantity of food _____
      Quantity of clothing _____
   b. Use 1998 prices to find out how much the base-period market basket would cost at 1998 prices.
      1998 cost of 1997 market basket _____
   c. Divide the 1998 cost of the base-period market basket by the 1997 cost of the same market basket and multiply by 100 to compute the value of the FPI for 1998.
      FPI for 1998 _____
   d. Convince yourself that if you repeat steps b and c using 1997 prices you will get an answer of 100 for the value of the FPI for 1997.
   e. Estimate inflation by computing the percentage change in your price index from 1997 to 1998.
      Inflation between 1997 and 1998 _____

    f. Divide total dollar expenditures in 1998 by the 1998 FPI and multiply by 100 to deflate 1998 nominal expenditures.

        Real expenditures in 1998 (1997 prices) _____

        Percentage change in real expenditures 1997 to 1998 _____

        Remember the following points about price indexes:

- Most price indexes, like the Consumer Price Index, are computed by pricing a standard market basket of goods in subsequent periods.
- A price index can be used to measure inflation and to deflate nominal values to adjust for inflation.
- Different price indexes, such as the Consumer Price Index and the GDP deflator, will show slightly different measures of inflation because they use different market baskets.

2. (Optional) Compute a new FPI using 1998 as the base period rather than 1997. Now the value of your price index for 1998 will be 100 and the price index for 1997 will be something less than 100. Does this index give the same measure of inflation as the index with 1997 as the base period? Do not be surprised if it does not. Can you explain why they differ?

■ SUPPLEMENTARY EXERCISES

1. Table 24-4 contains data on consumer prices for seven countries. Try to answer each of the following questions or explain why the information in Table 24-4 is insufficient to answer the question.

TABLE 24-4	Index of Consumer Prices (1982–1984 = 100)					
	Canada	**France**	**Germany**	**Italy**	**Japan**	**United Kingdom**	**United States**
1970	35.1	28.8	52.8	17.1	38.5	21.8	38.8
1980	76.1	72.3	86.7	63.2	90.9	78.5	82.4
1990	135.5	133.0	112.2	159.6	111.4	148.2	130.7
1997	156.3	153.2	137.8	215.7	121.3	185.0	160.5

SOURCE: Economic Report of the President, 1999 Table B-108.

a. In 1970 which country had the lowest prices?

b. In 1997 which country had the highest prices?

c. Over the period 1970 to 1997, which country experienced the most inflation as measured by the percentage change in the consumer price index? Which country experienced the least inflation?

2. Go to the library to document the current unemployment situation of different workers. *Employment and Earnings* is published monthly by the Bureau of Labor Statistics. It contains detailed data on employment and unemployment by age, sex, and race of workers. *The Economic Report of the President*, issued annually, is a good source for historic data.

■ ECONOMICS IN ACTION

HOW TO MEASURE INFLATION

Does the Consumer Price Index (CPI) overstate inflation? If so, by how much? In the late 1990s these questions were of more than academic interest. They became an important part of discussions about how to balance the federal budget. A number of federal programs, most notably social security payments and income tax brackets, are adjusted annually in step with increases in the CPI. If the CPI overstates inflation, these adjustments have been too generous in the sense that federal government spending is larger and revenues are smaller than they otherwise would be.

    The impact of adjusting the CPI adjustment is not small. The Congressional Budget Office estimated that if, starting in 1996, CPI adjustments each year were one percentage point lower, then over seven years, tax revenues would total almost $100 billion more and spending would total about $180 billion less.

    In 1995, while looking for ways to eliminate the deficit, the Senate Finance Committee asked a panel of prominent economists, headed by Michael Boskin, an economist at Stanford University and former Chairman of the Council of Economic Advisers, to study this issue and make a recommendation to the

Committee. The panel reported in the fall of 1995. It concluded that the CPI has overstated inflation by 1.5 percent per year in the past and, in the absence of changes, will overstate inflation by about 1 percent per year in the future. The panel's report was promptly followed by proposals to adjust the CPI adjustments in spending and taxes accordingly. While there is widespread support for the position that the CPI has overstated inflation, there was disagreement about the magnitude of any overstatement and thus the appropriateness of the 1 percent adjustment recommended by the panel.

If the CPI has overstated inflation, the implications are broader than the federal government's deficit as David Wessel discussed in *The Wall Street Journal*.[1] For example, if inflation has been overstated, then trends in real wages are not "quite as gloomy as frequently cited statistics suggest." It also means that inflation had been closer to zero than many realized.

1. Do you think that the CPI has overstated inflation? If so by how much? A good place to begin to look for answers is "The Anatomy of Price Change," a series of articles in the December 1993 issue of the *Monthly Labor Review*. See also "A Better CPI," Alison Wallace and Brian Motley, *Federal Reserve Bank of San Francisco Economic Letter*, February 5, 1999 (http://www.frbsf.org/econrsrch/wklyltr/wklyltr99/el99-05.html).

STUDY QUESTIONS ■

1. What is the difference between measures of labor productivity and output per capita?

2. Why is the growth of labor productivity so important for the growth in standards of living?

3. What factors are important for growth in labor productivity?

4. Is it possible for the growth in a country's standard of living to exceed the growth in labor productivity? If so, how, and is it likely that such a difference could be sustained over a long period of time?

5. Why doesn't unemployment insurance eliminate the cost of unemployment for the economy as a whole?

6. Consider the following numbers for two hypothetical months:

	Month 1	Month 2
Employed	92	91
Unemployed	8	7
Not in the Labor Force	60	62
Rate of Unemployment	8.0%	7.1%

How might the concept of discouraged workers be relevant for explaining why the decline in employment is associated with a decline in the unemployment rate?

7. Do you believe the official rate of unemployment overstates or understates the seriousness of unemployment? Why?

8. Which concepts of unemployment—frictional, structural, and cyclical—are relevant when considering the full employment rate of unemployment? Why?

9. What rate of unemployment is an appropriate target for macroeconomic policy?

10. When does an increase in the price of textbooks reflect a change in relative prices and when does it reflect inflation?

11. During a period of inflation which is likely to be higher, nominal or real interest rates? Why?

12. Do you agree or disagree with the argument that the taxation of interest and capital gains should be based on real returns rather than nominal returns? Why?

13. Which is likely to have more adverse effects, steady or variable inflation? Why?

■ **ECONOMICS ONLINE**

The latest press release on the rate of unemployment can be found here.

http://www.bls.gov/newsrelease/empsit.toc.htm

The CPI has its own homepage. You can access historical data as well as the latest press release from this site.

http://stats.bls.gov/cpihome.htm

The Boskin Commission Report can be found at

http://199.173.225.3/history/reports/boskinrpt.html

INCOME AND SPENDING: THE POWERFUL CONSUMER

Important Terms and Concepts

AGGREGATE DEMAND

CONSUMER EXPENDITURE (C)

INVESTMENT SPENDING (I)

GOVERNMENT PURCHASES (G)

NET EXPORTS (X – IM)

C + I + G + (X – IM)

NATIONAL INCOME

DISPOSABLE INCOME (DI)

CIRCULAR FLOW DIAGRAM

TRANSFER PAYMENTS

SCATTER DIAGRAM

CONSUMPTION FUNCTION

MARGINAL PROPENSITY TO CONSUME (MPC)

MOVEMENTS ALONG VERSUS SHIFTS OF THE CONSUMPTION FUNCTION

MONEY FIXED ASSETS

TEMPORARY VERSUS PERMANENT TAX CHANGES

LEARNING OBJECTIVES

After completing this chapter, you should be able to:

■ distinguish between spending, output, and income.

■ describe what spending categories make up aggregate demand.

■ distinguish between investment spending as a part of aggregate demand and as financial investment.

■ explain why, except for some technical complications, national product and national income are necessarily equal.

■ explain how disposable income differs from national income.

■ derive a consumption function given data on consumption and disposable income.

■ compute the marginal propensity to consume at various levels of income.

■ explain why the marginal propensity to consume is equal to the slope of the consumption function.

■ distinguish between factors that result in a *movement along* the consumption function and factors that result in a *shift* of the function.

■ explain why consumption spending is affected by a change in the level of prices even if real income is unchanged.

■ describe why permanent and temporary changes in taxes of the same magnitude would be expected to have different impacts on consumption spending.

■ CHAPTER REVIEW

This chapter introduces two key concepts that economists use when discussing the determination of an economy's output: *aggregate demand* and the *consumption function*. These basic concepts will be fundamental to the material in later chapters.

The total amount that all consumers, business firms, government agencies, and foreigners are willing to spend on goods and services produced by the domestic economy is called aggregate

(1) _____. Economists typically divide this sum into four components: consumption expenditures, investment spending, government purchases, and net exports. Food, clothing, movies, and hamburgers are examples of (<u>consumption/investment/government</u>) expenditures. New factories, office buildings, machinery, and houses would be examples of _____ spending. Red tape, bombers, filing cabinets, and the services of bureaucrats are examples of _____ purchases. American wheat and tractors sold abroad are examples of (<u>exports/imports</u>), and American purchases of French wines, Canadian paper, and Mexican oil are examples of _____. The difference between exports and imports is called _____ _____. Economists use national income accounts to keep track of these components of demand. The appendix to this chapter provides an introduction to these accounts.

There is a close analogy between the demand for a single product and aggregate demand. As seen in the study of consumer demand in microeconomics, economists argue that demand should be seen as a schedule showing how the quantity demanded depends upon a number of factors, including price. In later chapters we will see that aggregate demand is also a schedule showing how the demand by everyone for newly produced goods and services is affected by a variety of factors, including the overall level of prices or, for short, the price level.

Two other concepts that are closely related to aggregate demand are *national product* and *national*

(2) *income*. National product is simply the output of the economy. National income is the (<u>before/after</u>)-

tax income of all the individuals in the economy. Disposable income is the income of individuals after

_____ have been paid and any _____ payments from the government

have been counted. The circular flow diagram shows that national product and national income are

two ways of measuring the same thing: Producing goods and selling them results in income for the

owners and employees of firms.

Economists use the concept of a *consumption function* to organize the determinants of consumption

expenditures. Specifically, the consumption function is the relation between aggregate real consump-

tion expenditures and aggregate real disposable income, holding all other determinants of consumer

spending constant. Higher disposable income leads to (<u>more/less</u>) consumption spending. A change in   (3)

disposable income leads to a (<u>shift in/movement along</u>) the consumption function. A change in one of

the other factors that affect consumer spending, such as wealth, the level of prices, the rate of infla-

tion, real interest rates, or expectations of future income, leads to a _____ _____ the con-

sumption function. (Two, more technical, aspects of the consumption function, the *marginal propensi-*

ty to consume and the *average propensity to consume*, are considered more fully in the Basic Exercise sec-

tion of this chapter.)

An increase in the price level affects consumption spending and is an important reason why aggre-

gate demand, _____ + _____ + _____ + _____ − _____, is a schedule. If prices are higher   (4)

we expect (<u>more/less</u>) consumption spending. Consumption spending changes because the value of

many consumer assets is fixed in money terms, and an increase in the price level will

(<u>increase/decrease</u>) the purchasing power of these assets. It is important to remember that higher

prices will lead to lower real consumption expenditures even if real disposable income is constant. A

doubling of all prices will also double wages, the price for an hour of labor services. If wages and prices

both double, there is no change in the purchasing power of labor income, but there is a loss to con-

sumers from the decline in the purchasing power of their money fixed assets. It is this latter decline

that leads to a shift in the consumption function in response to a change in the price level.

Separately from the level of prices, the rate of inflation may also affect consumption spending. On the

one hand, the notion that one should buy now, before prices increase still further, suggests that inflation

stimulates consumption spending. On the other hand, the notion that one may have to save more in

order to meet higher prices tomorrow, suggests that inflation depresses consumption spending. For rates of inflation experienced in the United States there is no clear evidence as to which tendency is greater. Economists have also found it difficult to detect a large impact on consumption spending from changes in real interest rates. While a higher real interest rate provides an increased incentive to save more, it also means that one can reach a given dollar target with less savings.

(5)   A change in income taxes changes disposable income immediately. The consumption function, then, tells us how a change in disposable income will affect consumption spending. For example, a reduction in income taxes would (<u>increase/decrease</u>) disposable income. After computing the change in disposable income, one could estimate the initial impact on consumption spending by multiplying the change in disposable income by the (<u>marginal/average</u>) propensity to consume. A permanent increase in taxes would be expected to have a (<u>larger/smaller</u>) effect on consumption expenditures than a temporary tax increase of the same magnitude because the permanent increase changes consumers' long-run income prospects by (<u>more/less</u>) than the temporary increase. The same argument works in reverse and implies that temporary tax changes have a (<u>larger/smaller</u>) impact on consumption expenditures than do permanent tax changes. One must also remember that while it may be easy to calculate the movement along the consumption function from a change in taxes, other factors influencing consumption are likely to be changing at the same time making it difficult to predict the final change in consumption spending.

IMPORTANT TERMS AND CONCEPTS QUIZ ▪

Choose the best definition for each of the following terms.

1. _____ Aggregate demand

2. _____ Consumer expenditure (*C*)

3. _____ Investment spending (*I*)

4. _____ Government purchases (*G*)

5. _____ Net exports (*X – IM*)

6. _____ National income

7. _____ Disposable income (*DI*)

8. _____ Transfer payments

9. _____ Consumption function

10. _____ Marginal propensity to consume

11. _____ Movement along the consumption function

12. _____ Shift of the consumption function

13. _____ Money fixed asset

a. Relation between aggregate real consumption expenditures and aggregate real disposable income.

b. Income of individuals after taxes and transfer payments.

c. Purchases of newly produced goods and services by all levels of government.

d. Total amount spent by consumers on newly produced goods and services.

e. Change in consumption due to a change in disposable income.

f. Gross national product divided by price level.

g. Total amount consumers, firms, government agencies and foreigners are willing to spend on final goods.

h. Total spending by firms on new plants and equipment and by consumers on new homes.

i. Change in consumption divided by change in disposable income.

j. Asset whose value is fixed in terms of dollars.

k. Exports minus imports.

l. Total before-tax earnings of all individuals in economy.

m. Change in consumption due to a change in any factor affecting consumption other than disposable income.

n. Government grants to individuals.

BASIC EXERCISES ▪

Note that the first three problems are based on income and consumption data for individual families rather than aggregate income and consumption. Along with the fourth problem, they will give you practice using and understanding the MPC.

1. Table 25-1 reports some data on disposable income and consumption.

FIGURE 25-1   Consumption Function

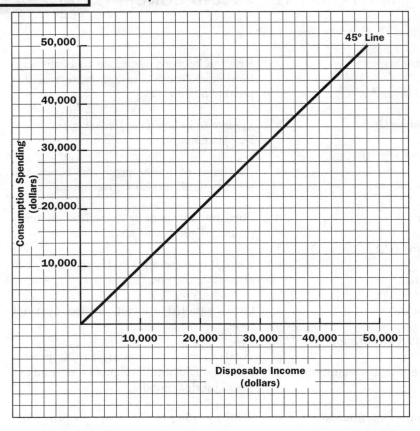

a. For each change in disposable income compute the marginal propensity to consume by dividing the change in _____ by the change in _____.

b. The average propensity to consume is defined as the ratio of consumption expenditures to disposable income or APC = $C \div DI$. For example, when disposable income is $10,000 the average propensity to consume is .90 = $9,000 ÷ $10,000. Use the data on disposable income and consumption to fill in the column for the APC. Use the data on the changes in disposable income and consumption spending to fill in the column for the APC.

TABLE 25-1   Personal Income After Taxes

Average Propensity to Consume	Disposable Income	Change in Disposable Income	Marginal Propensity to Consume	Change in Consumption Expenditures	Consumption Expenditures
_____	$10,000				$9,000
		$10,000	_____	$7,500	
_____	$20,000				$16,500
		$10,000	_____	$7,500	
_____	$30,000				$24,000
		$10,000	_____	$7,500	
_____	$40,000				$31,500
		$10,000	_____	$7,500	
_____	$50,000				$39,000

c. Are the average and marginal propensities equal? Do the differences surprise you? Can you explain them? Perhaps steps d to f will help.

d. Use the graph of Figure 25-1 to draw the consumption function consistent with the data in Table 25-1. (Locate each income-consumption data pair and then draw a line connecting the points.)

e. The MPC is represented by what part of your graph?

f. The APC can be represented by the slope of a ray from the origin to a point on the consumption function. Remember the slope of any straight line, including a ray, is the vertical change over the horizontal change. When measured from the origin, the vertical change of a ray to a point on the consumption function is C and the horizontal change is DI. Thus the slope of the ray, ($C \div DI$), is the APC. Draw rays to represent the APC for incomes of $10,000 and $50,000. How does the slope of your rays change as income increases? Is this change consistent with changes in the APC you calculated in step c?

2. Imagine an economy made up of 100 families each earning $10,000, and 100 families each earning $50,000. Each family consumes according to the consumption function described in Table 25-1.
   a. Fill in the following:
   Consumption of a family earning $10,000   _____
   Consumption of a family earning $50,000   _____
   Aggregate consumption of all 200 families   _____
   b. What is the APC of the richer families?   _____
   What is the APC of the poorer families?   _____
   c. Randy argues that since the lower-income families are spending a greater proportion of their income than the higher-income families, a redistribution of income from high- to low-income families will increase total consumption expenditures. Test Randy's assertion by assuming that the government takes $5,000 from each high-income family and gives it to each low-income family, and that all families adjust their consumption in line with the consumption function described in Table 25-1. Then fill in the following:
   Consumption of a family with $15,000 income   _____
   Consumption of a family with $45,000 income   _____
   Aggregate consumption of all 200 families   _____
   d. Explain why in this example aggregate consumption is unaffected by the redistribution of income.

3. (Optional) Use the data in Table 25-1 to compute an algebraic expression for the consumption function.

   Consumption = _____ + 0. _____ × (disposable income)

4. The lower line in Figure 25-2 shows the location of the consumption function of Baulmovia in 1997. In 1997 Baulmovian disposable income was $4.0 trillion and consumption spending was $3.5 trillion. In 1998 there was a significant surge in consumer confidence that shifted the consumption function to the higher line in Figure 25-2. In 1998 Baulmovian disposable income was $4.5 trillion and consumption spending was $4.05 trillion.

   Consider an estimate of MPC by looking at the change in consumption spending and the change in disposable income from 1997 to 1998.

Consumption Functions For 1997 and 1998   **FIGURE 25-2**

   a. What is this estimate of MPC? _____
   b. How does this estimate of MPC compare to the slope of either consumption function? Explain any differences.

■   **SELF-TESTS FOR UNDERSTANDING**

TEST A

Circle the most appropriate answer.

1. Which of the following is not a part of aggregate demand?
    a. Consumption expenditures.
    b. National income.
    c. Net exports.
    d. Investment expenditures.

2. When thinking about aggregate demand, economists use the term *investment* to refer to all except which one of the following?
    a. The newly built house that Roberta just bought.
    b. The stock in General Electric that Ralph bought with his summer earnings.
    c. The new factory that is being built on the edge of town.
    d. The new machinery that Sherry bought to start her own company.

3. Which of the following would be an example of a government transfer payment?
    a. Wages paid to government bureaucrats.
    b. A tax refund for excess withholding.
    c. The purchase of paper clips by a government agency.
    d. Social security payments.

4. In a circular flow diagram all but which one of the following would be depicted as an injection into the stream of spending?
    a. The Defense Department's purchase of a new airplane.
    b. Joyce and Jim's purchase of an existing house.
    c. Alice's spending to rebuild her restaurant after the fire.
    d. The new microcomputers that Elaine's company bought for all its top management.

5. National income refers to
    a. the income of consumers after taxes.
    b. the sum of everyone's before-tax income.
    c. employee wage and salary payments.
    d. the income of federal government employee.

6. Disposable income is equal to the income of individuals after
    a. subtracting taxes.
    b. adding transfer payments.
    c. adding taxes to transfer payments.
    d. subtracting taxes and adding transfer payments.

7. A graphical representation of how consumption spending varies with changes in disposable income is called the
    a. aggregate demand curve.
    b. income-expenditure schedule.
    c. consumption function.
    d. Phillips curve.

8. A change in which one of the following would be associated with a movement along the consumption function?
    a. Current disposable income.
    b. Wealth.
    c. The price level.
    d. Expected future incomes.

9. A change in all but which one of the following would be associated with a shift in the consumption function?
   a. Wealth.
   b. Interest rates.
   c. Current disposable income.
   d. The price level.

10. A consumption function is an example of a
    a. time series graph.
    b. two-variable diagram.
    c. contour diagram.

11. If an increase in prices is matched by an increase in wages and salaries such that there is no change in real disposable income, then
    a. there should be no effect on consumption spending.
    b. the increase in prices will lead to a movement along the consumption function.
    c. one should expect MPC to decline.
    d. the impact of the change in prices on the purchasing power of money fixed assets should lead to a shift in the consumption function.

12. The impact of a change in real disposable income on consumption spending can be represented as a
    a. movement along a given consumption function.
    b. a shift in the consumption function.
    c. a shift in MPC.
    d. a change in the price level.

13. MPC refers to
    a. Y-axis is intercept of the consumption function.
    b. the slope of the consumption function.
    c. the ratio of consumption spending to income.
    d. the slope of a ray from the origin to a point on the consumption function.

14. If MPC is 0.7, then a $100 billion change in disposable income will be associated with what change in consumption spending?
    a. $20 billion.
    b. $30 billion.
    c. $70 billion.
    d. $100 billion.

15. If a $100 billion increase in disposable income results in a $75 billion increase in consumption spending, then MPC is
    a. 0.25
    b. 0.50
    c. 0.75
    d. 1.0

16. If MPC is 0.80, what decrease in taxes will initially increase consumption spending by $16 billion?
    a. $12.8 billion.
    b. $16 billion.
    c. $20 billion.
    d. $64 billion.

17. If consumption spending declines by $45 billion when disposable income declines by $50 billion, what is MPC?
    a. 0.9
    b. 0.1
    c. -0.1
    d. -0.9

18. If MPC is 0.8, a $100 billion change in the wealth of consumers will lead to
    a. a $100 billion change in consumption spending.
    b. an $80 billion change in consumption spending.
    c. a movement along the consumption function.
    d. a shift in the entire consumption function.

19. An increase in real interest rates
    a. always leads to a decrease in consumption spending as it provides an increased incentive for greater saving.
    b. can be modeled as a movement along the consumption function.
    c. always leads to an increase in consumption spending as the higher interest rate allows savers to reach fixed objectives with smaller savings.
    d. does not appear to have influenced consumption spending very much one way or the other.

20. Which type of tax change would be expected to have the largest impact on consumption spending?
    a. The one-time tax rebate of 1975.
    b. The tax surcharge of 1969.
    c. The permanent reduction in tax rates of 1981.
    d. A reduction in tax withholding "to get money into the hands of consumers" that is enacted with no change in taxes due at the end of the year.

TEST B

Circle T or F for true or false.

T   F   1. Aggregate demand is the aggregate of individual household consumption decisions.

T   F   2. The consumption function reflects the close relationship between consumption spending and national output.

T   F   3. Disposable income equals national income minus taxes.

T   F   4. A change in consumption divided by the change in disposable income that produced the change in consumption is called the marginal propensity to consume.

T   F   5. An increase in the level of prices is likely to reduce consumption expenditures.

T   F   6. The effect of a change in the level of prices on consumption would be viewed graphically as a shift in the consumption function.

T   F   7. By increasing household wealth, a big increase in the stock market is likely to lead to a movement along the consumption function.

T   F   8. The magnitude of the impact of a change in taxes on consumption expenditures is likely to depend on whether consumers view the change in taxes as permanent or temporary.

T   F   9. A temporary decrease in taxes is likely to have a smaller impact on consumption than will a permanent decrease.

T   F   10. The initial impact of a change in income taxes on consumption spending can be calculated by multiplying the change in disposable income by MPC.

APPENDIX: NATIONAL INCOME ACCOUNTING

LEARNING OBJECTIVES

After completing this appendix, you should be able to:

■ describe the three alternative ways of measuring GDP
and explain why, except for bookkeeping or statistical
errors, they give the same answer.

■ explain why national income accounting treats government purchases of goods and services differently from
government transfer payments.

■ explain the difference in theory and practice between
the following macro measurements: GDP, NDP, and
national income.

Important Terms and Concepts

NATIONAL INCOME ACCOUNTING

GROSS DOMESTIC PRODUCT (GDP)

GROSS PRIVATE DOMESTIC INVESTMENT

GOVERNMENT PURCHASES

TRANSFER PAYMENTS

NET EXPORTS

NATIONAL INCOME

NET DOMESTIC PRODUCT (NDP)

NET NATIONAL PRODUCT (NNP)

DEPRECIATION

VALUE ADDED

■   **APPENDIX REVIEW**

Although included in an appendix, this material on national income accounting deserves special treatment. When working through this material, do not lose sight of the forest for the trees. The forest is composed of broad income concepts, such as gross domestic product (GDP), net domestic product (NDP), and national income, what each of these concepts measures and how they relate to one another. This appendix is an introduction to the forest rather than to each individual tree.

The national income accounts measure economic activity: the production of goods and services and the incomes that are generated as a result. Accurate measurement of production and income is an important prerequisite to attempts to understand and control the economy. National income accounts are centered around measurement of gross domestic product (GDP). Consumption (C), investment (I), government purchases of goods and services (G), and net exports ($X - IM$) are parts of GDP. Other concepts, such as net domestic product (NDP) and national income, are alternative measures of total economic activity.

(1)   GDP is defined as the sum of the money values of all _____ goods and services that are (produced/sold) during a specified period of time. Economists use money values or market prices to add up the very different types of output that make up GDP. Two of the three exceptions mentioned in the appendix—government output and inventories—arise because some production is not sold on markets.

The emphasis on final goods and services is important, because it avoids double counting of intermediate goods. (The need to avoid double counting is also the key to why the three alternative ways of measuring GDP are conceptually equivalent.) The third part of the definition says that GDP is a statement of production, not sales. It is only production that creates new goods available for consumption or investment. Thus GDP, as a measure of production, is the appropriate measure of how much new consumption or investment our economy can enjoy.

There are three ways to measure GDP. Perhaps the simplest way to measure GDP is to add up the purchases of newly produced final goods and services by private individuals and firms—for consumption and investment—and by the government. For the United States in 1998, this sum of $C + I + G + (X - IM)$ was estimated to be about $8.65 trillion.

Net exports are (<u>imports/exports</u>) minus _____. We must add exports to $C + I + G$ (2)

because, even though bought by foreigners, exports are American products and GDP is a measure of

total production in the United States. We subtract imports because C and I and G include spending

on imports, and we want a measure that reflects only those goods and services (<u>purchased/produced</u>)

in the United States. In 1998, $C + I + G + (X - IM)$ totaled about \$8.5 trillion.

All of a firm's sales receipts eventually end up as income for someone, directly in the case of work-

ers, creditors, and firm owners, and indirectly in the case of payments to suppliers, who in turn use

this money to pay their workers, creditors, and so forth. Thus, instead of measuring GDP as purchases

of final goods and services, we could equivalently add up all incomes earned in the production of goods

and services. This sum of factor incomes is also called national _____ and is the second   (3)

way to measure GDP. It is conceptually similar to GDP but differs for U.S. national income accounts

because of three items. Indirect business taxes are included in market prices paid by consumers but

(<u>do/do not</u>) result in income for any factor of production as they are immediately collected by the gov-

ernment. National income plus indirect business taxes is equal to NNP or _____

_____ product, which is almost, but not quite, equal to GDP. Adjusting for income that

Americans receive from business activities abroad and for income that foreigners receive for business

activities in the United States gives us net domestic product. The difference between NDP and GDP

is _____ and, conceptually, refers to the portion of current total production that is

used to replace those parts of the capital stock that have deteriorated as a result of current production.

If GDP were all one edible good, we could eat NDP while maintaining our productive capacity.

Eating GDP would reduce our productive capacity as we would not be replacing worn-out plants and

machines.

To measure GDP as the money value of final goods and services, one would start by collecting sales

data for final goods. The second way of measuring GDP, total factor incomes, would start with the

collection of income data from firms and individuals. The third way of measuring GDP looks at the

difference between a firm's sales receipts and its purchases from other firms. This difference, also

called a firm's _____ _____, is the amount of money a firm has to pay the   (4)

factors of production that it has employed, including the profits firm owners pay themselves. Thus,

the sum of total value added in the economy is the third way to measure GDP.

■   IMPORTANT TERMS AND CONCEPTS QUIZ

Choose the best definition for each of the following terms.

1. _____ National income accounting

2. _____ Net domestic product

3. _____ Depreciation

4. _____ Value added

a. Bookkeeping and measurement system for national economic data.

b. Value of an economy's capital used up during a year.

c. Revenue from sale of product minus amount paid for goods and services purchased from other firms.

d. Loss on value of business assets from inflation.

e. GDP minus depreciation.

■   BASIC EXERCISES

These problems are designed to give you practice in understanding alternative ways of measuring GDP.

1. Consider the following two-firm economy. Firm A is a mining company that does not make purchases from firm B. Firm A sells all its output to firm B, which uses the output of Firm A to make consumption goods that it sells

	Firm A	Firm B
Total sales	$500	$1,700
Wages	400	800
Profits	100	400
Purchases from other firms	0	500

     a. What are the total sales for the economy? $ _____
     b. What is the total value of sales for final uses? $ _____
     c. What is the total of all factor incomes? $ _____
     d. What is value added for firm A? $ _____
     e. What is value added for firm B? $ _____
     f. What is the total value added of both firms? $ _____
     g. What is GDP? $ _____
     h. What is national income? $ _____

2. Table 25-3 contains information on a three-firm economy. Firm A sells only to other firms. Firm B has both an industrial and a household division. Firm C sells only to final consumers. Note also that production by firm C was greater than sales, thus the entry showing the addition to inventories. Simple addition shows that the sum of factor incomes, in this case wages and profits, is equal to $4,700. Answer the following questions to see if the two other ways of measuring GDP give the same answer. The tricky part of this question is the treatment of production that has not been sold, but added to inventories. You may want to review the discussion of inventories in the appendix before answering the following questions.
     a. Calculate value added for each firm and the sum of value added for all firms.
        Value Added, firm A   _____
        Value Added, firm B   _____

Value Added, firm C _____

Sum _____

b. GDP is defined as the production of newly produced final goods and services. It is typically calculated by summing sales of newly produced final goods and services. Calculate sales for final use for each firm and the sum for all firms.

Sales for final use, firm A _____

Sales for final use, firm B _____

Sales for final use, firm C _____

Sum _____

TABLE 25-3			
	Firm A	**Firm B**	**Firm C**
Total Sales	$1,000	$2,500	$3,000
Sales to firm B	$400		
Sales to firm C	$600	$1,000	
Sales to consumers		$1,500	$3,000
Change in inventories			$200
Wages	$750	$1,800	$1,200
Profits	$250	$300	$400

SELF-TESTS FOR UNDERSTANDING ∎

TEST A

Circle the most appropriate answers.

1. GDP is
   a. the sum of all sales in the economy.
   b. the sum of all purchases in the economy.
   c. the sum of money value of all newly produced final goods and services produced during a year.
   d. equal to $C + I + G + X + IM$.

2. Conceptually, GDP can be measured by all but which one of the following?
   a. Add up all factor payments by firms in the economy.
   b. Add up all purchases of final goods and services, $C + I + G + (X - IM)$.
   c. Add up total sales of all firms in the economy.
   d. Add up value added for all firms in the economy.

3. When measuring GDP, money values are for the most part determined by
   a. the cost of production.
   b. market prices.
   c. estimates prepared by national income accountants who work for the U.S. Commerce Department.
   d. banks and eastern money interests.

4. Which of the following is not valued at market prices when computing GDP?
   a. Imports.
   b. Investment.
   c. Government output.
   d. Exports.

5. Which of the following would add to this year's GDP?
   a. Jim purchases a new copy of the Baumol Blinder textbook for this course.
   b. Michelle purchases a used copy of the Baumol Blinder textbook for this course.
   c. Susan purchases 100 shares of GM stock.
   d. Steve sells his three-year-old car.

6. Which of the following transactions represents the sale of a final good as opposed to sale of an intermediate good?
   a. Farmer Jones sells her peaches to the Good Food Packing and Canning Company.
   b. Good Food sells a load of canned peaches to Smith Brothers Distributors.
   c. Smith Brothers sells the load of canned peaches to Irving's Supermarket.
   d. You buy a can of peaches at Irving's.

7. Which of the following events results in an addition to gross private domestic investment?
   a. Managers of the Good Earth, a newly formed food co-op, buy a used refrigerator case for their store.
   b. Sony's office in Tokyo buys a new IBM computer.
   c. The U.S. Air Force purchases a new plane for the president.
   d. United Airlines purchases 20 new planes so it can expand its service.

8. Gross private domestic investment includes all but which one of the following?
   a. The new home purchased by Kimberly and Jason.
   b. Ryan's purchase of a used fax machine for his new business.
   c. The increase in the inventory of newly produced but unsold cars.
   d. The construction of a new plant to manufacture microchips for Intel.

9. When measuring GDP, government purchases include all but which one of the following?
   a. Salaries paid to members of Congress.
   b. Newly produced red tape purchased by government agencies.
   c. Social security payments to older Americans.
   d. Concrete for new highway construction.

10. If net exports are negative it means that
    a. the national income accountant made a mistake.
    b. exports are greater than imports.
    c. Americans are consuming too many foreign goods.
    d. imports are greater than exports.

11. Which accounts for the largest proportion of national income?
    a. Profits.
    b. Employee compensation.
    c. Rents.
    d. Interest.

12. In the national income accounts, transfer payments are
    a. part of NDP but not GDP.
    b. included in G, government purchases of goods and services.
    c. added to wages when computing national income.
    d. not a direct component of GDP, and are reflected in GDP only when they influence consumption spending.

13. Which of the following adds to consumption spending as measured by the national income accountants?
    a. Howard buys a used CD at Play It Again Sam.
    b. Rachel builds a new store to house her business.
    c. Tyrone buys three new suits when he gets a job as a marketing representative.
    d. Hilary sells the computer she bought when she first came to campus four years ago.

14. Which of the following is not part of the difference between GDP and national income?
    a. Depreciation.
    b. Indirect business taxes.
    c. Profits.
    d. Income earned by Americans from foreign business activities.

15. Depreciation explains the difference between
    a. GDP and NDP.
    b. NDP and National Income.
    c. GDP and National Income.
    d. savings and investment.

16. Value added by a single firm is measured as total sales revenue
    a. minus factor payments.
    b. plus indirect business taxes.
    c. plus depreciation.
    d. minus the purchase of intermediate goods.

17. Additions to inventory
    a. add to next year's GDP when the goods are actually sold.
    b. are simply ignored when calculating GDP.
    c. add to current GDP.
    d. are priced at zero since they have not been sold.

18. In measuring GDP, government outputs are
    a. appropriately valued at zero.
    b. valued by estimates of their market prices.
    c. valued at the cost of inputs needed to produce them.

19. If net national product equals $5 trillion and indirect business taxes are $300 billion, then national income would equal
    a. $5.3 trillion.
    b. $5 trillion.
    c. $4.7 trillion.
    d. Insufficient information to determine national income.

20. NDP is
    a. always greater than GDP.
    b. considered by many economists to be a more meaningful measure of the nation's economic output than is GDP.
    c. conceptually superior to GDP because it excludes the output of environmental "bads."
    d. measured by subtracting indirect business taxes from GDP.

TEST B

Circle T or F for true or false.

T   F   1. GDP is designed to be a measure of economic well-being, not a measure of economic production.

T   F   2. If you measured GDP by adding up total sales in the economy, you would be double or triple counting many intermediate goods.

T   F   3. Production that is not sold but is instead added to inventories is not counted in GDP.

T   F   4. If GM started its own steel company rather than continuing to buy steel from independent steel companies, GDP would be lower because intrafirm transfers are not part of GDP but all interfirm sales are.

T   F   5. Since the output of government agencies is not sold on markets, it is not included in GDP.

T   F   6. Value added is the difference between what a firm sells its output for and the cost of its own purchases from other firms.

T   F   7. The difference between GDP and NDP is net exports.

T   F   8. Adding up value added for all firms will underestimate GDP as it ignores the production of intermediate goods.

T   F   9. Corporate profits are the largest component of national income.

T   F   10. The sum of value added for all firms in the economy is equal to the sum of all factor incomes—wages, interest, rents, and profits.

SUPPLEMENTARY EXERCISES

1. Consider the following nonlinear, consumption function.

   $C = 100 \sqrt{DI}$.

   Restricting yourself to positive values for disposable income, graph this function. What happens to MPC as income increases? Can you find an explicit expression for MPC as a function of income? (A knowledge of simple calculus will be helpful.) Use this new consumption function to re-answer Basic Exercise question 2 about income redistribution. Does your answer change? If so, why?

   What is the savings function that goes with this consumption function? Does MPC + MPS = 1? Does APC + APS = 1?

2. GDP accounts are often criticized for being an inadequate measure of general welfare or well-being. It is easy to think of situations where GDP increases but the country is worse off. Rebuilding after a major earthquake or hurricane is a specific example. A recent article that attracted significant attention along this line was "If the GDP Is Up, Why Is America Down?" by Clifford Cobb, Ted Halstead, and Jonathon Rowe (*Atlantic Monthly*, October 1995, pp. 59–78). Others argue that GDP is but one gauge of the economy; it was never meant to be a measure of economic well being; and attempts to make it so will only compromise what it does best. It has been argued that just as a car's dashboard includes a speedometer and odometer, along with a gas gauge and other gauges for temperature, oil pressure, a car's electrical system, and perhaps engine speed, economists should use a battery of gauges for the economy.

   You might want to look at the article by Cobb, Halstead, and Rowe. It is available online at

   http://www.theatlantic.com/atlantic/election/connection/ecbig/gdp.htm.

   Do you agree with them that GDP should be overhauled or not?

ECONOMICS IN ACTION

DO TAX INCENTIVES INCREASE SAVINGS?

A number of specialized programs to increase household savings were introduced during the 1980s. One of the most controversial was the Individual Retirement Account or IRA. Under rules adopted in 1981, all employees could make a tax-deductible $2,000 contribution to an IRA. Previously, IRAs had been limited to individuals without an employer-provided pension plan. Not only did an IRA contribution reduce one's immediate taxable income by $2,000 but interest earnings on IRAs were tax free until the time of withdrawal.[1] In exchange for these advantages, withdrawals before the age of 59-1/2 were subject to substantial tax penalties. Since regular savings can only be done with after-tax, not pre-tax, dollars and the interest earnings of regular savings are taxed on a year by year basis, IRAs offered

---

[1]Each wage earner could contribute up to $2,000. A family with two working spouses could thus contribute $4,000. There was also a provision for a $250 contribution for a non-working spouse. Taxes on the $2,000 contribution and accumulated interest earnings would be assessed and due at the time of withdrawal. In 1998 Roth IRAs, named for Senator William Roth (R-Del), were introduced. Contributions to a Roth IRA require the use of after tax dollars but all future tax earnings are tax free. By contrast, the earnings of most financial investments are taxed every year.

taxpayers significant advantages and were heavily promoted by banks and other financial institutions. It was hoped that IRAs would lead to a significant increase in household savings.

Why were IRA accounts controversial? There were several reasons. For one, the advantages of an IRA depended upon one's marginal tax rate. An IRA postponed rather than reduced taxes, but being able to use that money until taxes were due could offer a significant benefit, especially to wealthy taxpayers with high marginal tax rates. For example, a $2,000 IRA contribution in 1982 by the wealthiest taxpayers reduced 1982 income taxes by $1,000, while the same contribution by a low-income family would have reduced 1982 taxes by only $220.

A second area of controversy was whether IRAs would actually increase savings or only lead households to change the way they saved. That is, were people being given tax breaks for doing what they would have done anyway or would people save more? A related concern was that the money for opening an IRA could come from an existing taxable savings account. If so, there might be only a shuffling of financial assets for tax advantages rather than any increase in savings. These concerns plus the continuing decline in personal savings as a proportion of disposable income led Congress to restructure and limit the tax advantages of IRAs in 1986.

What does the evidence show about the effectiveness of IRAs? Work by economists Harvey Galper and Charles Byce showed that wealthier taxpayers were more likely to make an IRA contribution and were more likely to make the largest possible contribution. At the same time, a substantial proportion of moderate-income taxpayers making IRA contributions were making the maximum possible contribution. In a series of papers, economists James Poterba, Steven Venti, and David Wise examined the savings behavior of households. They found a great deal of variability. Some households are thrifty while others appear to be spendthrifts. Poterba, Venti, and Wise argued the introduction of IRAs resulted in a net increase in saving as the restrictions on IRAs and the special feelings many people have about retirement savings made them poor substitutes for other forms of savings.

Other economists were skeptical that IRAs or other tax advantaged savings schemes had increased personal savings very much. These economists noted that households could be divided into serious and non-serious savers. For many "serious savers," the $2,000 IRA contribution was likely to be only a part of what the household would have saved anyway. As of early 1999 there was still no consensus among economists as to the efficacy of these programs.

1. Should the United States use expanded tax incentives to induce households to increase their own savings? If so, how would you structure such a program? How does your program provide incentives for new savings and not just an advantage for asset adjustments in pursuit of tax advantages?

SOURCES: Harvey, Galper, and Charles Byce, "IRAs: Facts and Figures," *Tax Notes,* June 2, 1986; David A. Wise, "Do Retirement Saving Programs Increase Savings?" *NBER Reporter,* Fall 1995; Eric M. Engen, William G. Gale, and John Karl Scholz, "Do Saving Incentives Work?" *Brookings Papers on Economic Activity,* 1994:1.

STUDY QUESTIONS ■

1. What are the four major components of GDP? (Why are imports subtracted when everything else is added?)

2. What is the difference between national income and disposable income?

3. How is MPC different from the proportion of disposable income that is spent on consumption?

4. MPC can be represented by what part of the consumption function?

5. Why would a change in the price level or in expected future incomes lead to a shift in the consumption function rather than a movement along the function?

6. If planning a reduction in income taxes to increase consumption spending by $200 billion, what difference would it make if MPC were 0.75 or 0.90? Would you expect any differences if the reduction in taxes were to be permanent or temporary? Why?

7. Why is knowledge of the consumption function sufficient for one to be able to describe the savings function for an economy?

8. What are the different ways one can measure GDP?

9. Economists often use national income or GDP interchangeably as a measure of the level of aggregate economic activity. What is the difference between national income and GDP?

■ ECONOMICS ONLINE

Check here for the most recent estimates of GDP.

http://www.bea.doc.gov/bea/rels.htm

The Economic Report of the President is issued every year in early February. The Report includes extensive tables with historical data on macroeconomic activity including Gross Domestic Product and its components. Since 1996 the Report has been available online. Use the following URL and scroll down to Economic Report of the President.

http://www.gpo.ucop.edu/catalog

DEMAND-SIDE EQUILIBRIUM: UNEMPLOYMENT OR INFLATION?

LEARNING OBJECTIVES

After completing this chapter, you should be able to:

■ describe some of the major determinants of investment spending by firms and explain which of these determinants can be directly affected by government action.

■ describe how income and prices, both American and foreign, affect exports and imports.

■ draw an expenditure schedule, given information about consumption spending, investment spending, government purchases, and net exports.

■ determine the equilibrium level of income on the demand side and explain why the level of income tends toward its equilibrium value.

■ describe how a change in the price level affects the expenditure schedule and the equilibrium level of income on the demand side.

■ describe how the impact of a change in prices on the expenditure schedule can be used to derive the aggregate demand curve.

■ explain why equilibrium GDP can be above or below the full employment level of GDP.

Important Terms and Concepts

INVESTMENT (*I*)

NET EXPORTS (*X − IM*)

EQUILIBRIUM LEVEL OF GDP

EXPENDITURE SCHEDULE

INDUCED INVESTMENT

$Y = C + I + G + (X − IM)$

INCOME-EXPENDITURE (OR 45° LINE) DIAGRAM

AGGREGATE DEMAND CURVE

FULL-EMPLOYMENT LEVEL OF GDP (OR POTENTIAL GDP)

RECESSIONARY GAP

INFLATIONARY GAP

COORDINATION OF SAVING AND INVESTMENT

COORDINATION FAILURE

■ CHAPTER REVIEW

This chapter is the introduction to explicit models of income determination. The model discussed in this chapter is relatively simple and is not meant to be taken literally. Do not be put off by the simplicity of the model or its lack of realism. Careful study now will pay future dividends in terms of easier understanding of later chapters, in which both the mechanics and policy implications of more complicated models are described.

The central focus of this chapter is on the concept of the *equilibrium level of income and output.* (You may want to review the material in the previous chapter on the equality of national income and national output.) The models discussed in this chapter show us how spending decisions are reconciled with production decisions of firms to determine the equilibrium level of GDP on the demand side.

When considering the determination of the equilibrium level of GDP, it is important to distinguish between output and income on the one hand and total spending on the other hand. If total spending exceeds current production, firms will find that their inventories are decreasing. They are then likely

(1) to take steps to (<u>decrease/increase</u>) production and output. Analogously, if total spending is less than current output, firms are likely to find their inventories _____, and they are likely to take steps to _____ production.

The concept of equilibrium refers to a situation in which producers and consumers are satisfied with things the way they are and see no reason to change their behavior. Thus the equilibrium level of GDP must be a level of GDP at which firms have no reason to increase or decrease output; that is, at

(2) the equilibrium level of GDP, total spending will be (<u>less than/equal to/greater </u>than) output. The determination of the equilibrium level of output thus reduces to

1. describing how total spending changes as output (and income) changes, and

2. finding the one level of output (and income) at which total spending equals output.

In the simplified model discussed in this chapter, there are four components to total spending: consumption, investment, government purchases, and net exports. The preceding chapter discussed the important role that income plays as a determinant of consumption expenditures. There is no such central factor influencing investment expenditures. Instead, investment expenditures are influenced by a variety of factors, including business people's expectations about the future, the rate of growth of demand as measured against existing capacity, technology and product innovation, interest rates, and tax factors. If any of these factors change, investment spending is likely to change.

Net exports are the difference between exports and imports, specifically _____ minus   (3)

_____. Exports reflect foreign demand for American production and imports come from American demand for foreign goods and services. It should not be surprising that both are influenced by income and prices. The tricky part is keeping straight whose income influences which demand and how changes in American and foreign prices influence net exports.

The income-expenditure diagram is a useful tool for analyzing the determination of the equilibrium level of output. Output (and income) is measured along the (horizontal/vertical) axis, and spending is   (4)

measured on the _____ axis. To find the equilibrium level of output and income we need to know how total spending changes as output (and income) change, and we need to know where total spending equals output. The relationship between total spending, $C + I + G + (X - IM)$, and income is given by the *expenditure schedule*. The 45-degree line shows all possible points of equilibrium. The one place where spending is equal to output is given by the _____ of the expenditure schedule and the 45-degree line. This is the equilibrium level of output because it is the only level of output where total spending is equal to output. At any other level of output, total spending will not be equal to output. (You should be sure that you understand why the economy tends to move to the equilibrium level of output rather than getting stuck at a level of income and output where total spending is either larger or smaller than output. Consider what happens to business inventories when spending is greater or less than output. Do not get confused between this tendency to move to the equilibrium level of output on the income-expenditure diagram and the real possibility that the economy can end up at a point away from full employment.)

Any particular expenditure schedule relates total spending to income for a given level of prices. If prices change, total spending will change, even for the same level of real income. In particular, a higher price level is apt to mean (more/less) consumption spending because of the decline in the purchas-   (5)

ing power of the money assets of consumers. A change in the price level will also affect net exports. Specifically higher prices (increase/reduce) exports and _____ imports as our goods are (less/more) price competitive vis-á-vis foreign goods. These changes in consumption spending and net exports will lead to a (downward/upward) shift in the expenditure schedule and a new equilibrium of income that is (<u>higher/lower</u>) than before. In the opposite case, a lower price level would (<u>increase/decrease</u>) consumption spending and _____ net exports. The result will be a (<u>higher/lower</u>) equilibrium level of income. The relationship between the price level and the equilibrium level of income given by the income-expenditure diagram is called the *aggregate demand curve*.

The aggregate demand curve is derived from the income-expenditure diagram and, from the view-

(6)   point of demand, shows how the equilibrium level of income changes when the _____ _____ changes. The qualifier "from the viewpoint of demand" is important. Complete determination of the equilibrium level of income/output and the equilibrium price level comes from the interaction of the aggregate demand and aggregate supply curves.

At this point we are considering only the demand side of the economy. Nothing that has been said so far implies that, with regard to demand, the equilibrium level of output must equal the full-employment level of output. It may be larger or it may be smaller. It all depends upon the strength of aggregate demand. In particular if savings plans at full employment are greater than investment plans,

(7)   spending will be (<u>less/more</u>) than full employment output and equilibrium on the demand side will result in a _____ gap. The importance of savings and investment plans in determining equilibrium means that recessions and inflation can be seen as failures of coordination. If the equilibrium level of output exceeds the full-employment level of output, the difference is called a(n) _____ gap.

IMPORTANT TERMS AND CONCEPTS QUIZ ■

Choose the best definition for each of the following.

1. _____ Investment

2. _____ Net exports

3. _____ Equilibrium level of GDP

4. _____ Expenditure schedule

5. _____ Induced investment

6. _____ Income-expenditure diagram

7. _____ Aggregate demand curve

8. _____ Recessionary gap

9. _____ Inflationary gap

10. _____ Potential GDP

11. _____ Coordination failure.

a. Graph of quantity of national product demanded at each possible price level.

b. Line showing relationship between GDP and total spending.

c. Full-employment level of GDP.

d. Spending on new plant, new equipment, new houses, and additions to inventories.

e. When equilibrium GDP exceeds full-employment GDP.

f. Level of output where aggregate demand equals total production.

g. Investment spending that changes with changes in GDP.

h. Table or graph showing how saving depends on consumption.

i. When full-employment GDP exceeds equilibrium GDP.

j. Two-variable graph that allows plotting of total real expenditures against real income.

k. Savings plans at full employment differ from investment plans at full employment.

l. Exports minus imports.

BASIC EXERCISES ■

These exercises are designed to give you practice with manipulations on the income-expenditure diagram. They are based on data for income (output), consumption spending, investment spending, government purchases, and net exports given in Table 26-1.

TABLE 26-1

(Price Level = 100)

National Income (Output) Y	Taxes T	Disposable Income DI	Consumption Spending C	Investment Spending I	Government Purchases G	Exports X	Imports IM	Total Spending
5,600	700	4,900	4,300	900	800	500	600	_____
5,800	700	5,100	4,400	900	800	500	600	_____
6,000	700	5,300	4,500	900	800	500	600	_____
6,200	700	5,500	4,600	900	800	500	600	_____
6,400	700	5,700	4,700	900	800	500	600	_____
6,600	700	5,900	4,800	900	800	500	600	_____

FIGURE 26-1   Expenditure Schedule

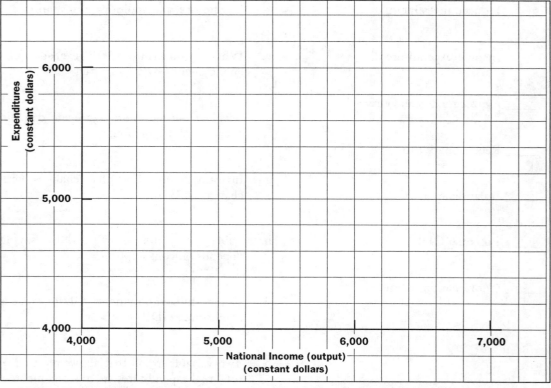

1. This exercise shows you how the expenditure schedule is derived and how it helps to determine the equilibrium level of income. For this exercise it is assumed that prices are constant with the price level having a value of 100.

   a. Use the data on consumption spending and income to show how consumption spending varies with income in Figure 26-1.

   b. Add investment spending to the line drawn in Figure 26-1 to show how consumption plus investment spending varies with income.

   c. Now draw the expenditure schedule by adding G and $(X - IM)$ to the line drawn in step b.

   d. Next, draw a line representing all the points where total spending and income could be equal. (This is the 45-degree line. Do you know why?)

   e. The 45-degree line represents all the points that *could be* the equilibrium level of income. Now circle the one point that is the equilibrium level of income. What is the equilibrium level of income on your graph?

   f. Check your answer by filling in the Total Spending column in Table 26-1 to see where total spending equals income. You should get the same answer from Table 26-1 as you do from the graph.

g. Why isn't the equilibrium level of output $5,800 billion? If for some reason national output and income started out at $5,800 billion, what forces would tend to move the economy toward the equilibrium you determined in questions e and f?

h. Using the data in Table 26-1 and assuming that the full-employment level of output income is $6,000 billion, is there an inflationary or recessionary gap? How large is the gap? If the full-employment level of income were $6,500 billion, how large would the inflationary or recessionary gap be?

i. Assume now that an increase in business confidence leads to an increased level of investment spending. Specifically, assume that investment spending rises to $1,000 billion at all levels of national income. As a result of this shift, what happens to each of the following?
    ■ The expenditure schedule.
    ■ The equilibrium level of income.
    ■ Consumption spending at the new equilibrium level of income.
    (You can either draw a new expenditure schedule or complete a new version of Table 26-1 that reflects the higher level of investment spending.)

2. This exercise explores the implications of changes in the price level. It is designed to show how a change in the price level implies a shift in the expenditure schedule and can be used to derive the aggregate demand curve.

a. The data in Table 26-1 assumed that prices were constant with the price level at a value of 100. Mark the point in Figure 26-2 that shows the price level of 100 and the equilibrium level of income you found when answering questions e and f of Exercise 1.

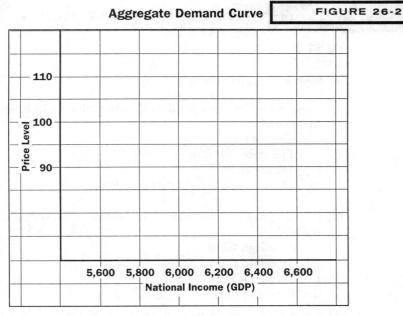

Aggregate Demand Curve | **FIGURE 26-2**

b. Economic research has determined that if prices rose to 110, consumption spending and net exports would decline by a total of $100 billion at every level of real income. Table 26-2 shows the relevant information. Each entry in the column for a price level of 110 should be 100 less than the values you calculated for total spending in question 1.f. What is the new equilibrium level of income on the income-expenditure diagram with this higher price level? Mark the point in Figure 26-2 that shows the price level of 110 and this new equilibrium level of income.

c. This same research determined that if prices fell to 90, consumption spending and net exports would increase over amounts shown in Table 26-1 by a total of $100 billion at every level of real income. What is the new equilibrium level of income on the income-expenditure diagram for this lower price level? Mark the point in Figure 26-2 that shows the price level of 90 and this new equilibrium level of income.

TABLE 26-2

Real Income (Output)	Total Spending (Price Level = 90)	Total Spending (Price Level = 110)
5,600	6,000	5,800
5,800	6,100	5,900
6,000	6,200	6,000
6,200	6,300	6,100
6,400	6,400	6,200
6,600	6,500	6,300

    d.   The points you have marked in Figure 26-2 help to trace what curve?

    e.   Connect these points to verify that your curve has a (<u>negative/positive</u>) slope.

3.   Question 1.i. asked you to consider the impact of an increase in investment spending. We saw then that an increase in investment spending shifts the expenditure schedule and leads to a new equilibrium on the income-expenditure diagram. What about the aggregate demand curve? Assume that the increase in business confidence means that investment spending rises to $1,000 regardless of the level of income or the price level. Table 26-3 contains information on total spending that includes the increase in investment spending. Use this information to plot the new aggregate demand curve in Figure 26-2 following the increase in investment spending. How does the new aggregate demand curve compare to the one you derived in question 2?

TABLE 26-3	**Real Income and Total Spending**		
When Investment Spending =$1,000			
Real Income (Output)	**Total Spending (Price Level = 90)**	**Total Spending (Price Level = 100)**	**Total Spending (Price Level = 110)**
5,600	6,100	6,000	5,900
5,800	6,200	6,100	6,000
6,000	6,300	6,200	6,100
6,200	6,400	6,300	6,200
6,400	6,500	6,400	6,300
6,600	6,600	6,500	6,400

■ SELF-TESTS FOR UNDERSTANDING

TEST A

Circle the most appropriate answer.

1.   Government policies can directly affect all but which one of the following determinants of investment spending?

    a.   Interest rates.

    b.   The state of business confidence.

    c.   Tax incentives.

    d.   The overall state of aggregate demand.

2.   The demand for imports into the United States is directly affected by all but which one of the following?

    a.   American GDP

    b.   American prices

    c.   Foreign GDP

    d.   Foreign prices

3.   The demand for American exports is directly affected by all but which one of the following?

    a.   American GDP

    b.   American prices

    c.   Foreign GDP

    d.   Foreign prices

4.   On balance, net exports are likely to _____ when domestic income increases.

    a.   decrease

    b.   remain unchanged

    c.   increase

5.   Of production, income and spending, _____ and _____ are always equal while _____ equals the other two only in equilibrium.

    a.   spending and income; production

    b.   production and spending; income

    c.   income and production; spending

6. The expenditure schedule is a relationship between
   a. the equilibrium level of national income and prices.
   b. consumption spending and national income.
   c. total spending and national income.
   d. consumption spending and prices.

7. The expenditure schedule is derived by showing how which of the following vary with income? (There may be more than one correct answer.)
   a. *C* - consumption
   b. *DI* - disposable income
   c *G* - government purchases
   d. *I* - investment spending
   e. *IM* - imports
   f. *T* - taxes
   g. *X* - exports

8. If investment spending were now higher at all levels of income, the expenditure schedule would
   a. shift down.
   b. show no change.
   c. shift up.

9. An increase in the demand for exports will cause
   a. the expenditure schedule to shift up.
   b. no change in the expenditure schedule.
   c. the expenditure schedule to shift down.

10. A reduction in purchases of goods and services by the government will cause
    a. the expenditure schedule to shift up.
    b. no change in the expenditure schedule.
    c. the expenditure schedule to shift down.

11. Induced investment means the expenditure schedule
    a. is flatter than before.
    b. shifts up.
    c. shifts down.
    d. is steeper than before.

12. In the income-expenditure diagram, the equilibrium level of output is given by the intersection of the expenditure schedule and the
    a. consumption function.
    b. aggregate demand curve.
    c. 45-degree line.
    d. level of full-employment output.

13. When total spending is less than output,
    a. inventories are likely to be increasing.
    b. inventories are likely to be decreasing.
    c. there will be a shift in the expenditure schedule.
    d. firms are likely to raise prices.

14. When total spending is equal to output,
    a. the resulting level of output is called the full-employment level of output.
    b. the level of income is given by the intersection of the expenditure schedule and the 45-degree line.
    c. there is never an inflationary gap.
    d. the expenditure schedule and the aggregate demand curve coincide.

15. At the equilibrium level of income which one of the following is not necessarily true?
    a. The expenditure schedule will intersect the 45-degree line.
    b. There will be no unexpected changes in business inventories.
    c. There will be no unemployment.
    d. The equilibrium level of output and the price level will together determine one point on the aggregate demand curve.

16. If, at the full-employment level of income, consumers' savings plans are equal to firms' investment plans, then
    a. the equilibrium level of income will be equal to the full-employment level of income.
    b. there will be an inflationary gap.
    c. firms will find their inventories increasing.
    d. the economy will be producing less than potential output.

17. There is a recessionary gap when the equilibrium level of income
    a. is less than potential GDP.
    b. is equal to the full-employment level of GDP.
    c. is greater than potential GDP.

18. A lower price level will _____ the equilibrium level of income on the income-expenditure diagram.
    a. decrease
    b. not affect
    c. increase

19. The aggregate demand curve is a relationship between the price level and
    a. consumption spending.
    b. the equilibrium level of income on the income-expenditure diagram.
    c. full-employment GDP.
    d. the interest rate.

20. A lower price level will lead to which of the following? (There may be more than one correct answer.)
    a. An increase in exports.
    b. A shift in the consumption function.
    c. A shift in the expenditure schedule.
    d. A shift in the aggregate demand curve.

TEST B

Circle T or F for true or false.

T   F   1. It is an easy task for government policymakers to influence the state of business confidence.

T   F   2. The expenditure schedule refers to a relationship between total spending and the level of output (and income).

T   F   3. The equilibrium level of GDP never equals the full-employment level of GDP.

T   F   4. If total spending exceeds national output, the resulting decrease in inventories should lead firms to reduce the level of output and production.

T   F   5. The intersection of the expenditure schedule and the 45-degree line determines one point on the aggregate demand curve.

T   F   6. The vertical difference between the 45-degree line and the aggregate demand curve is called the inflationary gap.

T   F   7. The term *recessionary gap* refers to a situation in which the equilibrium level of GDP is less than the full-employment level of GDP.

T   F   8. Because consumers usually invest their savings at financial institutions, there can be no difference between desired savings and desired investment for the economy.

T   F   9. An increase in the level of prices, through its impact on consumption spending and net exports, will lead to a movement along the expenditure schedule.

T   F   10. The aggregate demand curve refers to a relationship between the equilibrium level of income and the price level.

APPENDIX: THE SIMPLE ALGEBRA OF INCOME DETERMINATION

BASIC EXERCISES

This exercise is meant to illustrate the material in the Appendix to Chapter 26. If we are willing to use algebra we can use equations rather than graphs or tables to determine the equilibrium level of output. If we have done all our work accurately, we should get the same answer regardless of whether we use graphs, tables, or algebra.

The following equations are consistent with the numbers in Table 26-1:

(1) C = $1850 + 0.5\ DI$
(2) DI = $Y - T$
(3) T = 700
(4) I = 900
(5) G = 800
(6) X = 500
(7) IM = 600
(8) Y = $C + I + G + (X - IM)$

1. Equation 1 is the consumption function. It shows how consumption spending changes with changes in disposable income. To derive the expenditure schedule we need to figure out how spending changes with changes in national income. Start by substituting equations 2 and 3 for disposable income and taxes into equation 1 to see how C varies with Y.

    (9) $C = \underline{\hspace{1.5cm}} + \underline{\hspace{1.5cm}}\ Y.$

2. Now use equation 9, along with equations 4, 5, 6, and 7, to show how total spending varies with Y.

    (10) $C + I + G + (X - IM) = \underline{\hspace{1.5cm}} + \underline{\hspace{1.5cm}}\ Y.$

3. To find the one level of income where spending equals output (and income), substitute the right-hand side of equation 10 for the right-hand side of equation 8 and solve for the equilibrium level of Y.

    $Y = \underline{\hspace{2cm}}$

    Equation 10 is the expenditure schedule. Equation 8 is the 45-degree line. Substituting the right-hand side of equation 10 for the right-hand side of equation 8 is the algebraic way of finding the intersection of these two lines.

■   ECONOMICS IN ACTION

MILITARY SPENDING AND AGGREGATE DEMAND

Some critics on the left argue that America's economic strength is dependent upon large military outlays. These critics point out that the periods of lowest unemployment over the past 50 years have tended to be periods of war—World War II, Korea, and Vietnam. They also argue that the years of economic expansion under Presidents Reagan and Bush were associated with a substantial increase in defense spending and that unemployment in the early 1990s was aggravated by defense-related layoffs.

Others are not so sure, arguing that employment will be determined by the level of aggregate demand relative to potential output. Defense spending increases aggregate demand and employment, but so does any other type of spending. While increased military spending has been associated with periods of full employment, this does not mean that only military spending can result in low rates of unemployment. Increases in other types of spending, public or private, also increase employment and lower unemployment. In this view, the historical correlation between defense spending and full employment may really reflect politics, not economics. That is, it may have been easier to organize the political commitment for high levels of defense spending than for high levels of non-defense spending.

When evaluating these arguments, it is also instructive to look at data. World War II saw the most dramatic increase in defense spending when measured as a proportion of GDP. From about 3 percent in 1940, defense spending climbed to over 40 percent of GDP by 1943. The Korean conflict saw an increase in defense spending from less than 5 percent of GDP to just over 13 percent in two years. The Vietnam increase in defense spending was substantially smaller, less than 2 percent of GDP. It began after a four-year period when both the unemployment rate and defense as a proportion of GDP had been falling. The increase in defense spending under President Reagan actually started in 1979 under President Carter and was a bit smaller than the Vietnam increase. Furthermore, as in the immediate pre-Vietnam period, the unemployment rate continued to decline even after the growth in defense budgets stopped. From 1987 to 1989, the unemployment rate declined from 6.1 percent to 5.2 percent as real defense spending declined by 4 percent. More recently the rate of unemployment fell from 7.5 percent in 1992 to 4.5 percent in 1998 while real spending on national defense measured in 1992 dollars declined by almost 20 percent from $376 billion to $302 billion.

To argue that full employment is not dependent upon high levels of defense spending does not imply that changes in defense spending will not affect aggregate demand and employment. In the absence of offsetting changes, increases in defense spending would add to aggregate demand while decreases would subtract. The closing of a military base and the termination of defense contracts will typically have an immediate and significant impact on particular communities and states. A number of observers have argued that planned reductions in military spending should have been accompanied by special government financed adjustment assistance for the individuals and communities suddenly without jobs. Others argued that job losses from defense cutbacks should be treated no differently than job losses from any other cause. That is, individuals and communities should be eligible for the same assistance they would receive for any job loss but should not receive special treatment.

1. Are concerns about full employment an appropriate argument in support of high levels of defense spending?

2. Should there be special assistance for individuals and communities who are affected by base closings and the cancellation of military contracts?

You might want to look at the following articles about defense conversion: Jurgen Brauer and John T. Marlin, "Converting Resources from Military to Non-Military Uses," *The Journal of Economic Perspectives* (Vol. 6, Number 4), Fall 1992, pp. 145-164. Michelle R. Garfinkel, "The Economic Consequences of Reducing Military Spending," *Review*, Federal Reserve Bank of St. Louis (November/December 1990), pp. 47-58.

■   STUDY QUESTIONS

1. Why is investment spending so volatile? Does the volatility of investment mean that policy changes by the government have no impact on investment?

2. "Exports will change with changes in foreign but not domestic income. They will also change if foreign or domestic prices change." How can it be that exports respond to domestic prices but not domestic income?

3. How do imports respond to changes in domestic income, foreign income, domestic prices, and foreign prices?

4. The expenditure schedule shows how total spending changes with domestic income. What categories of spending does the expenditure schedule need to include?

5. What would happen to the expenditure schedule if the marginal propensity to consume were larger or smaller? Why?

6. What would happen to the expenditure schedule if there were a change in any of the following: investment spending, government purchases of goods and services, exports, or imports?

7. What would happen to the expenditure schedule if investment spending or imports increased as national income increases?

8. According to the text, equilibrium occurs at the intersection of the expenditure schedule and the 45-degree line. Why there? What prevents points to the left or right of the intersection from also being points of equilibrium?

9. Why do we say the expenditure schedule is drawn for a given level of prices?

10. What happens to the expenditure schedule if prices increase or if they decrease?

11. Plotting different price levels and the corresponding equilibrium level of income from the income-expenditure diagram results in what curve?

CHANGES ON THE DEMAND SIDE: MULTIPLIER ANALYSIS

LEARNING OBJECTIVES

After completing this chapter, you should be able to:

■ explain why any autonomous increases in expenditures will have a multiplier effect on GDP.

■ calculate the value of the multiplier in specific examples.

■ explain how and why the value of the multiplier would change if MPC changed.

■ explain why the multiplier expression, $1/(1 - MPC)$, is oversimplified.

■ explain the difference between an autonomous and an induced increase in consumption expenditures.

■ explain how and why economic booms and recessions tend to be transmitted across national boundaries.

■ explain why an increase in savings may be good for an individual but bad for the economy as a whole.

■ describe how any change in autonomous spending leads to a shift in the aggregate demand curve.

■ CHAPTER REVIEW

The main topic of this chapter is the *multiplier*. It is a fundamental concept in economics, which is why a whole chapter is devoted to explaining how it works. The multiplier has already played an important but unheralded role in the preceding chapter, so if you paid close attention then you should have an easier time grasping the concept of multiplier analysis presented here.

The idea of the multiplier is that a change in autonomous spending by one sector of the economy (1) will change the equilibrium level of income by (<u>more than/the same as/less than</u>) the change in autonomous spending. We have been studying the determination of the equilibrium level of income in the income-expenditure diagram. Multiplier analysis investigates changes in the equilibrium level of income when the expenditure schedule shifts. In this chapter we will be concerned with parallel shifts in the expenditure schedule which are represented graphically as a change in the vertical axis intercept of the expenditure schedule. A parallel shift in the expenditure schedule shows the same change in spending at all levels of income and is thus a change in (<u>autonomous/induced</u>) spending. Spending that changes when income changes, such as the response of consumption spending to a change in income, is called an _____ change.

Multiplier analysis shows that the equilibrium level of GDP changes by a multiple of the change in autonomous spending, which is where the term "multiplier" comes from. The basic reason for this multiplier result is relatively simple: Increased spending by one sector of the economy means increased sales receipts for other sectors of the economy. Higher sales receipts will show up in bigger paychecks, or profits, or both; in short, higher income for some people. These higher incomes will then induce more consumer spending, which in turn will result in still higher incomes and more consumption spending by others, and so on and so on.

You may be wondering at this point whether the multiplier is finite or whether income will increase without limit. Another way of looking at this question is to ask what determines the value of the multiplier. There are several alternative, but equally good, ways of answering this question. In the text the value is determined by summing the increments to spending and income that follow from the original autonomous change in spending. When consumption is the only induced spending, the oversimplified (2) multiplier expression turns out to be 1/(1 –_____).

Here is an alternative derivation of the same result. We know that in equilibrium national output, or income, will equal total spending:

$$Y = C + I + G + (X - IM).$$

Now assume that there is an autonomous increase in investment spending which induces subsequent increases in consumption spending. At the new equilibrium, we know that the change in the equilibrium level of national output must equal the change in total spending. If net exports and government purchases are the same at all levels of income, the change in total spending will have two parts. One is the autonomous change in investment spending and the other is the induced change in consumption spending. We know that

| Change in equilibrium level of income | = | Autonomous change in investment spending | + | Induced change in _____ _____ | (3) |

It is possible to represent this symbolically. Let ΔY represent the change in the equilibrium level of income and ΔI represent the autonomous change in investment spending. What about the induced change in consumption spending? The discussion of the consumption function in Chapter 25 told us that consumption spending will change as disposable _____ changes. Further, with the (4) use of the concept of the marginal propensity to consume, we can represent the change in consumption spending as the product of the change in disposable income multiplied by the _____. When taxes are constant, disposable income changes dollar for dollar whenever GDP or Y changes. We can represent the induced change in consumption spending as $\Delta DI \times MPC$. When taxes do not vary with income, $\Delta DI = \Delta Y$ and we can represent the change in consumption as $\Delta Y \times MPC$. If we substitute all these symbols for the words above, we see that

$$\Delta Y = \Delta I + (\Delta Y \times MPC).$$

We can now solve this equation for the change in income by moving all terms in ΔY to the left-hand side of the equation:

$$\Delta Y - (\Delta Y \times MPC) = \Delta I.$$

If we factor out the ΔY we can rewrite the expression as

$$\Delta Y(1 - MPC) = \Delta I.$$

We can now solve for ΔY by dividing both sides of the equation by $(1 - \text{MPC})$.

$$\Delta Y = \frac{1}{1 - \text{MPC}} \Delta I.$$

Therefore we find that

Change in				**Autonomous**
equilibrium level	**=**	**Multiplier**	**×**	**change in**
of income				**investment spending**

Would our calculation of the multiplier be any different if we considered a change in net exports or an autonomous change in consumption spending? The Basic Exercises to this chapter are designed to help answer this question.

Although our derivation was different, the multiplier expression we just identified, $1 / (1 - \text{MPC})$, is the same as the one in the text and is subject to the same limitations.[1] That is, this expression is over-

(5) simplified. There are four important reasons why real world multipliers will be (<u>smaller/larger</u>) than our formula. These reasons are related to the effects of _____, international _____, _____ taxes, and the _____ system.

The simplified multiplier expression we derived above is applicable when analyzing a shift in the expenditure schedule in the 45-degree line diagram. As such, this expression assumes that prices

(6) (<u>do/do not</u>) change. In the preceding chapter we saw that the income-expenditure diagram is only a building-block on the way to the aggregate demand curve. (Even the aggregate demand curve is only part of the story. For a complete analysis we need to consider both the aggregate demand and the aggregate _____ curves.) To complete our analysis on the demand side, we need to see how our multiplier analysis affects the aggregate demand curve. The multiplier analysis we have done by using the income-expenditure diagram shows us that if prices are constant, the equilibrium level of income will change following any change in (<u>autonomous/induced</u>) spending. This result is true at all price levels and implies that a shift in the expenditure schedule following a change in autonomous

---

[1]A somewhat more general expression for the multiplier is 1/(1 – slope of the expenditure schedule). The multiplier is based on summing the rounds of spending induced by an autonomous increase in spending. In the model of this chapter only consumption spending changes as income changes. As taxes are a fixed amount, every dollar change in national income is also a dollar change in disposable income which induces a change in consumption spending determined by the MPC. In this case consumption spending goes up by MPC for every dollar increase in national income and the slope of the expenditure schedule is equal to the MPC. Appendix B examines what happens when imports vary with income. We will see then that the slope of the expenditure schedule is flatter and the multiplier is smaller.

spending leads to a (<u>movement along/shift in</u>) the aggregate demand curve. In fact, it leads to a (<u>horizontal/vertical</u>) shift in the aggregate demand curve. The magnitude of the shift can be computed with the help of the multiplier, as shown in Figure 27-5.

IMPORTANT TERMS AND CONCEPTS QUIZ ■

Choose the best definition for each of the following terms.

1. _____ Multiplier

2. _____ Induced increase in consumption

3. _____ Autonomous increase in consumption

4. _____ Paradox of thrift

a. Increase in consumer spending due to an increase in disposable income.

b. Attempts to increase savings that cause national income to fall with little net impact on savings.

c. Ratio of change in spending to change in equilibrium GDP.

d. Ratio of change in equilibrium GDP to change in autonomous spending that causes GDP to change.

e. Increase in consumer spending not due to increased incomes.

BASIC EXERCISES ■

These exercises are designed to illustrate the concepts of the multiplier and the paradox of thrift.

1. **The Multiplier**
   a. Using the data in Table 27-1, fill in the values for total spending and then find the equilibrium level of income.

TABLE 27-1

Constant Prices

Income (Output) Y	Taxes T	Disposable Income DI	Consumption Spending C	Investment Spending I	Government Purchases G	Exports X	Imports IM	Total Spending $C + I + G + (X - IM)$
5,500	800	4,700	4,100	800	850	500	650	_____
5,750	800	4,950	4,300	800	850	500	650	_____
6,000	800	5,200	4,500	800	850	500	650	_____
6,250	800	5,450	4,700	800	850	500	650	_____
6,500	800	5,700	4,900	800	850	500	650	_____
6,750	800	5,950	5,100	800	850	500	650	_____
7,000	800	6,200	5,300	800	850	500	650	_____

TABLE 27-2

Constant Prices

Income (Output) Y	Taxes T	Disposable Income DI	Consumption Spending C	Investment Spending I	Government Purchases G	Exports X	Imports IM	Total Spending C + I + G + (X − IM)
5,500	800	4,700	4,100	900	850	500	650	_____
5,750	800	4,950	4,300	900	850	500	650	_____
6,000	800	5,200	4,500	900	850	500	650	_____
6,250	800	5,450	4,700	900	850	500	650	_____
6,500	800	5,700	4,900	900	850	500	650	_____
6,750	800	5,950	5,100	900	850	500	650	_____
7,000	800	6,200	5,300	900	850	500	650	_____

b. Table 27-2 has a similar set of data except that investment spending has risen by $100 billion. Find the equilibrium level of income after the rise in investment spending.

c. What is the change in the equilibrium level of income following the increase in investment spending? _____

d. What is the value of the multiplier for this increase in autonomous investment spending? _____ (Remember that the multiplier is defined as the ratio of the change in the _____ _____ of _____ divided by the change in _____ _____ that produced the change in income.)

e. Now let us verify that the value of the multiplier that you found in question d is the same as the simplified formula 1/(1 − MPC). To do this we will first need to calculate the MPC for the economy in Table 27-1. Write the value of the MPC here: _____. (If you do not remember how to calculate the MPC, review the discussion of the consumption function in the textbook and in this study guide.)

f. Now calculate the value of the multiplier from the oversimplified formula 1/(1 − MPC). Write your answer here: _____.

g. (Optional) The multiplier can also be calculated as

$$\frac{1}{(1 - \text{slope of the expenditure schedule})}.$$

The slope of the expenditure schedule tells us how total spending changes when income changes. Calculate the slope of the expenditure schedule by dividing any of the changes in the last column of Table 27-1 or Table 27-2 by the corresponding change in income in the first column. What is the slope of the expenditure schedule and how is it related to the MPC and the multiplier?

2. **International Trade**

Assume that an increase in income abroad has increased the demand for exports by $100 billion. Table 27-3 shows consumption spending, investment spending, and net exports following this increase in foreign demand.

a. What is the new equilibrium level of domestic income following the increase in net exports? _____

b. What is the change in the equilibrium level of income from its equilibrium in Table 27-2? _____

c. What is the multiplier for the change in the equilibrium level of income following the $100 billion increase in net exports, and how does it compare to the multiplier computed earlier for a change in investment spending? _____

TABLE 27-3

Constant Prices

Income (Output) Y	Taxes T	Disposable Income DI	Consumption Spending C	Investment Spending I	Government Purchases G	Exports X	Imports IM	Total Spending C + I + G + (X − IM)
5,500	800	4,700	4,100	900	850	600	650	_____
5,750	800	4,950	4,300	900	850	600	650	_____
6,000	800	5,200	4,500	900	850	600	650	_____
6,250	800	5,450	4,700	900	850	600	650	_____
6,500	800	5,700	4,900	900	850	600	650	_____
6,750	800	5,950	5,100	900	850	600	650	_____
7,000	800	6,200	5,300	900	850	600	650	_____

TABLE 27-4

Constant Prices

Income (Output) Y	Taxes T	Disposable Income DI	Consumption Spending C	Investment Spending I	Government Purchases G	Exports X	Imports IM	Total Spending C + I + G + (X − IM)
5,500	800	4,700	4,050	900	850	600	650	_____
5,750	800	4,950	4,250	900	850	600	650	_____
6,000	800	5,200	4,450	900	850	600	650	_____
6,250	800	5,450	4,650	900	850	600	650	_____
6,500	800	5,700	4,850	900	850	600	650	_____
6,750	800	5,950	5,050	900	850	600	650	_____
7,000	800	6,200	6,250	900	850	600	650	_____

3. **The Paradox of Thrift**

Assume now that in the aggregate all consumers suddenly decided to save $50 billion more than they have been saving at every level of income. If people want to save more it means they must consume _____.

This change is an (<u>autonomous/induced</u>) change in savings and consumption. Table 27-4 shows the new values for consumption spending following the increased desire to save. Notice that the numbers for consumption spending in Table 27-4 are all $50 billion less than the numbers in the earlier tables, while investment spending and net exports are unchanged from Table 27-3.

a. Using the data in Table 27-4, find the new equilibrium level of income.
b. What is the change in the equilibrium level of income compared with Table 27-3? _____
c. At this point we can conclude that if consumer saving shows an autonomous increase while investment spending and net exports are unchanged, then the equilibrium level of income will (<u>rise/fall</u>).
d. The multiplier for this change is _____.
e. How does this multiplier compare with the multiplier you computed for the increase in investment spending?
f. Why is the specific numerical value you have calculated likely to be an overstatement of the multiplier response of a real economy to a change in investment spending, net exports, or saving?

■   SELF-TESTS FOR UNDERSTANDING

TEST A

Circle the most appropriate answer.

1. The multiplier is defined as the ratio of the change in
    a. autonomous spending divided by the change in consumption expenditures.
    b. the equilibrium level of income divided by the increase in consumption spending.
    c. the equilibrium level of income divided by the change in autonomous spending that produced the change in income.
    d. consumption spending divided by the change in autonomous spending.

2. The multiplier shows that
    a. any increase in induced spending will be a multiple of the increase in income.
    b. an autonomous increase in spending will increase income by a multiple of the increase in autonomous spending.
    c. to influence income, any change in autonomous spending must be a multiple of the induced changes in spending.
    d. an induced change in spending will lead to a multiple increase in income.

3. The oversimplified multiplier formula is
    a. 1/MPC.
    b. 1/(MPC − 1)
    c. MPC × (1 − MPC)
    d. 1/(1 − MPC)

4. The secret behind the multiplier is
    a. the government's printing press.
    b. understanding that an autonomous increase in investment spending leads to an autonomous increase in consumption spending.
    c. understanding that any increase in autonomous spending induces additional increases in spending as income increases.
    d. the gnomes of Zurich.

5. Actual multipliers will be less than theoretical multipliers because of which of the following? (There may be more than one correct answer.)
    a. Inflation.
    b. Accounting practices.
    c. International trade.
    d. The government deficit.
    e. Income taxes.
    f. Price controls.
    g. The financial system.

6. An autonomous change in spending can be modeled as
    a. a horizontal shift in the expenditure schedule.
    b. a tilt in the slope of the expenditure schedule.
    c. a vertical shift in the expenditure schedule.
    d. an increase in MPC.

7. Which one of the following is not the beginning of a multiplier process?
    a. An autonomous increase in net exports.
    b. An induced increase in consumption spending.
    c. An autonomous increase in investment spending.
    d. An autonomous increase in savings.

8. The multiplier will be largest for which type of change?
   a. An increase in investment spending.
   b. An autonomous decrease in consumption spending.
   c. A decrease in exports.
   d. An increase in government purchases.
   e. The multiplier should be similar for all changes.

9. If MPC were 0.6 and prices did not change, the multiplier would be
   a. $1/0.6 = 1.67$.
   b. 0.6.
   c. $1/(1 - 0.6) = 2.5$.
   d. $1/(1 + 0.6) = 0.63$.

10. If MPC were 0.7 instead of 0.6, the textbook multiplier would be
    a. smaller than in question 9.
    b. the same as in question 9.
    c. larger than in question 9.

11. The textbook multiplier would be largest if MPC were
    a. 0.73.
    b. 0.89.
    c. 0.45.
    d. 0.67.

12. When compared with changes in investment spending, the multiplier associated with autonomous changes in consumption spending will be
    a. smaller.
    b. about the same.
    c. larger.

13. A boom in Japan would likely lead to an increased demand for which of the following: (There may be more than one correct answer.)
    a. Japanese exports.
    b. American exports.
    c. American imports.
    d. Japanese imports.

14. If a $100 billion increase in exports led to a $300 billion increase in GDP, we could conclude that the multiplier is
    a. 1.
    b. 2.
    c. 3.
    d. 4.

15. An increase in which of the following will not lead to an increase in GDP?
    a. Investment spending.
    b. Government purchases of goods and services.
    c. Exports.
    d. Imports.

16. The multiplier is useful in calculating
    a. the slope of the consumption function.
    b. the horizontal shift in the aggregate demand curve following an increase in autonomous spending.
    c. the vertical shift of the expenditure schedule following a change in autonomous spending.
    d. the shift of the consumption function following an increase in autonomous spending.

17. The multiplier response following an increase in exports would have what impact on the aggregate demand curve?
    a. Horizontal shift to the left.
    b. No impact.
    c. Horizontal shift to the right.

18. The multiplier response following a decrease in investment spending would have what impact on the aggregate demand curve?
    a. Horizontal shift to the left.
    b. No impact.
    c. Horizontal shift to the right.

19. An autonomous increase in savings
    a. is necessarily accompanied by an increase in consumption spending.
    b. will shift the expenditure schedule down.
    c. will not affect the level of income as neither the aggregate demand nor the aggregate supply curve will shift.
    d. shifts the aggregate demand curve to the right.

20. When compared with increases in autonomous spending, multiplier responses to decreases in autonomous spending are likely to be
    a. smaller.
    b. about the same.
    c. larger.
    d. zero.

TEST B

Circle T or F for true or false.

T F 1. The multiplier is defined as the ratio of a change in autonomous spending divided by the resulting change in the equilibrium level of income.

T F 2. Multiplier responses mean that the equilibrium level of national income is likely to change by less than any change in autonomous spending.

T F 3. Multiplier increases illustrated on the income-expenditure diagram are based on the assumption that prices do not change.

T F 4. Actual multiplier responses to changes in autonomous spending are likely to be less than that suggested by the formula $1/(1 - MPC)$.

T F 5. If income increases because of an autonomous increase in investment spending, the resulting increase in consumption spending is called an induced increase.

T F 6. An autonomous increase in savings by all consumers will immediately lead to a higher level of real GDP, as resources are freed for higher levels of investment.

T F 7. The multiplier for autonomous increases in investment spending is always greater than the multiplier for autonomous increases in consumption spending.

T F 8. An increase in European income that resulted in an increased demand for American exports would have no effect on the equilibrium level of American income.

T F 9. The multiplier works for increases in autonomous spending, but because of price and wage rigidities the multiplier is irrelevant when we examine decreases in autonomous spending.

T   F   10. The impact of a shift in the aggregate demand curve on prices and real output will depend
            upon the slope of the aggregate supply curve.

APPENDIX A: THE SIMPLE ALGEBRA OF THE MULTIPLIER

BASIC EXERCISES ■

The following exercises are meant to give you practice working with the algebraic representation of
the multiplier found in Appendix A.

1. The consumption function can be represented as $C = a + b \Delta DI$. In this economy $\Delta DI = Y - T$.
   Substitute the expression for disposable income into the consumption function and then substitute the consumption function into the following in order to solve for the equilibrium level of
   national income: $Y = C + I + G + (X - IM)$. What is the resulting expression for national
   income? Identify the multiplier in your expression.

2. An change in autonomous spending would be a change in a, I, G, X, or IM. What does your equation for national income (Y) indicate will happen if the intercept of the consumption function, a,
   or any of the other components of autonomous spending change?

APPENDIX B: THE MULTIPLIER WITH VARIABLE IMPORTS

BASIC EXERCISES ■

The following exercises are meant to illustrate the major point of Appendix B: When the demand for
imports increases with domestic GDP, the multiplier will be smaller.

1. Table 27-5 is similar to Table 27-1 except that imports increase with income. Compute total spending to verify that the equilibrium level of income in Table 27-5 is the same as in Table 27-1.

TABLE 27-5

Constant Prices

Income (Output) Y	Taxes T	Disposable Income DI	Consumption Spending C	Investment Spending I	Government Purchases G	Exports X	Imports IM	Total Spending C + I + G + (X – IM)
5,500	800	4,700	4,100	800	850	500	625.0	_____
5,750	800	4,950	4,300	800	850	500	637.5	_____
6,000	800	5,200	4,500	800	850	500	650.0	_____
6,250	800	5,450	4,700	800	850	500	662.5	_____
6,500	800	5,700	4,900	800	850	500	675.0	_____
6,750	800	5,950	5,100	800	850	500	687.5	_____
7,000	800	6,200	5,300	800	850	500	700.0	_____

TABLE 27-6

Constant Prices

Income (Output) Y	Taxes T	Disposable Income DI	Consumption Spending C	Investment Spending I	Government Purchases G	Exports X	Imports IM	Total Spending C + I + G + (X – IM)
5,500	800	4,700	4,100	925	850	500	625.0	_____
5,750	800	4,950	4,300	925	850	500	637.5	_____
6,000	800	5,200	4,500	925	850	500	650.0	_____
6,250	800	5,450	4,700	925	850	500	662.5	_____
6,500	800	5,700	4,900	925	850	500	675.0	_____
6,750	800	5,950	5,100	925	850	500	687.5	_____
7,000	800	6,200	5,300	925	850	500	700.0	_____

2. Table 27-6 is based on the assumption that investment spending has increased by $125. The new equilibrium level of income is _____.

3. We calculate the multiplier as before: the change in the equilibrium level of income divided by the change that changed income. Now the multiplier is _____.

4. Explain any difference between this multiplier and the one you calculated for Table 27-2.

■ SUPPLEMENTARY EXERCISES

1. In 1963 the President's Council of Economic Advisers was considering how large a tax cut would be necessary to return the economy to full employment. These economists estimated that actual output was about $30 billion to $35 billion less than potential, or full-employment, output. That is, they wanted a tax cut that would increase output by $30 billion to $35 billion, yet they recommended a tax cut of only $13 billion, to be divided between consumers ($10 billion) and businesses ($3 billion). How could these economists expect that total spending could rise by $30 billion to $35 billion when taxes were only reduced by $13 billion? Even if consumers and businesses spent the whole reduction in taxes, spending would only rise by $13 billion, not nearly enough to return the economy to full employment. What is wrong with this line of reasoning?

2. Use the data in Table 27-1 and a piece of graph paper to draw the income-expenditure diagram.
    a. Show how the expenditure schedule shifts as a result of the increase in investment spending in Basic Exercise 1b. Does your graph give you the same result as Basic Exercise 1c?
    b. Show how the expenditure schedule shifts following the increase in net exports in Basic Exercise 2. How does the new equilibrium level of income, and hence the multiplier, on your graph compare to your answers in the Basic Exercise?
    c. Show how the expenditure schedule shifts after the increase in savings described in Basic Exercise 3. How does your graph compare with your answer to Basic Exercise 3c?

3. If you have access to a computer, try programming or using a spreadsheet to simulate the following model to investigate the dynamics of the multiplier.

    Assume that consumption spending responds to income with a one-period lag as follows:

    $$C = 340 + 0.8DI\,(-1)$$

    where C is consumption and DI is disposable income. Other important elements of the model are:

$DI = Y - T$
$T = 800$
$I = 800$
$G = 850$
$X = 500$
$IM = 650$

a. Confirm that the equilibrium level of income is 6,000. That is, if income last period was 6,000, then total spending, $C + I + G + (X - IM)$, will equal 6,000 this period.

b. Now assume that investment spending increases by 100. Assuming that consumption responds with the one-period lag, simulate your model to investigate how the change in investment spending affects income over time. Does the level of income appear to converge to a new equilibrium value? What is that value? What is the multiplier for the change in investment spending? How does the multiplier from your simulation compare to the over-simplified formula of $1/(1 - MPC)$?

c. Investigate the impact of increases and decreases in net exports. Investigate the impact of a change in government purchases. Investigate the impact of autonomous changes in consumption spending, that is, a change in the constant term of the consumption function. How would you model an autonomous change in savings?

d. What happens if the MPC changes? You will need first to determine the initial equilibrium level of income for given levels of investment spending, net exports, and autonomous consumption spending. Then simulate your model to see how the change in the MPC affects the multiplier.

e. What happens to the multiplier if imports vary with income? Rather than assuming that imports are constant as above, assume that imports vary with income as follows:

$$IM = 350 + .05Y(-1).$$

Now simulate various changes in autonomous spending to see what happens to the multiplier.

ECONOMICS IN ACTION ■

AUTONOMOUS AND INDUCED CHANGES IN CONSUMPTION SPENDING

The multiplier shows how an autonomous increase in spending, through its impact on income, induces additional spending. The final result is that the equilibrium level of income increases by more than, or by a multiple of, the original autonomous change. We have also seen the close link between disposable income and consumption spending. Indeed, the induced changes in consumption spending are a critical part of the multiplier process.

Can changes in consumption spending ever initiate multiplier changes or are they only a part of a process that must be initiated by some other element of spending? To answer this question one must distinguish between factors that shift the consumption function and factors that lead to a movement along the consumption function. As a particular example, let's consider material from the 1998 Report of the Council of Economic Advisers.

Early each year, the President's Council of Economic Advisers issues its annual report. The council's report is published along with the Economic Report of the President. The volume's statistical appendix reports numerous data series that measure the macroeconomic performance of the economy. The council's report itself includes commentary on recent developments, a forecast for the upcoming year, and a detailed study of two or three topics of interest. The report is a mixture of politics and economic analysis as it is, in part, a brief for the policies of the president.

The January 1998 Report commented on the strong performance of the American economy in 1997 and noted that while there was strong growth in disposable income, consumer spending increased even faster.

Both aggregate statistics and consumer surveys painted an exceptionally favorable picture of the economic circumstances of American households in 1997. The tight labor market that led to a 24-year-low in the unemployment rate also lured enough new workers into the labor market to set an all-time record for the labor force participation rate. The combination of healthy wage growth and increasing employment helped push real disposable personal income up a solid 3 percent over the year. Despite the stock market volatility witnessed in the second half of the year, at year's end all major market indexes remained sharply above their levels at the end of 1996, representing a substantial boost to household net worth. Largely reflecting this combination of favorable circumstances and the low inflation rate, consumer sentiment reached record highs in early summer and remained near those levels for the rest of the year. Growing income and wealth together with buoyant sentiment led to a 3.8 percent rate of spending growth over the four quarters of 1997—outpacing even the robust growth of disposable income.

The report cites three factors to explain the growth in consumer spending: growth in income, growth in household wealth and increasingly optimistic consumers.

1. Which of these factors reflect a movement along an unchanged consumption function and which reflect a shift in the consumption function? Which would initiate a multiplier process and which would be part of the multiplier response to an autonomous change in spending?

2. What does the most recent Report say about autonomous and induced elements of consumption spending and other categories of spending?

SOURCE: *Economic Report of the President,* January 1998 (Washington, D.C.: United States Government Printing Office.)

■   STUDY QUESTIONS

1. Looking just at the expenditure schedule, how can you represent a change in autonomous spending? A change in induced spending?

2. How can it be that a change in autonomous spending results in an even larger change in the equilibrium level of income?

3. What happens to the value of the multiplier if the MPC is larger? Smaller? Why?

4. What are the four shortcomings of the multiplier formula $1/(1 - MPC)$?

5. Do these shortcomings mean that the formula overstates or understates the likely value of the multiplier?

6. What is the mechanism by which a recession in Europe may lead to a decline in output in the United States?

7. If an increase in savings is good for an individual, how can it be bad for a nation as a whole? (Explain the reasoning behind the paradox of thrift.)

8. How would results differ if an autonomous increase in savings were matched by an increase in investment spending, as contrasted with the situation where savings increase without any increase in investment spending?

9. What is the relation between the multiplier analysis on the income-expenditure diagram following an autonomous change in spending and the resulting shift of the aggregate demand curve?

SUPPLY-SIDE EQUILIBRIUM: UNEMPLOYMENT *AND* INFLATION?

LEARNING OBJECTIVES

After completing this chapter, you should be able to:

■ describe how the aggregate supply curve is derived from an analysis of business costs and why it slopes upward.

■ distinguish between factors that will lead to a movement along or a shift in the aggregate supply curve.

■ use a graph depicting both the aggregate demand curve and the aggregate supply curve to determine the price level and the equilibrium level of real GDP.

■ use the same graph as above to analyze how factors that shift either the aggregate demand curve or the aggregate supply curve will affect the equilibrium level of prices and output.

■ use the same graph to explain what kinds of shifts in the aggregate demand curve and the aggregate supply curve can give rise to a period of stagnation.

■ explain how an inflationary gap will self-destruct.

■ explain how a recessionary gap will self-destruct.

■ use the aggregate demand/aggregate supply diagram to show how increases in prices reduce the value of the multiplier.

Important Terms and Concepts

AGGREGATE SUPPLY CURVE

PRODUCTIVITY

EQUILIBRIUM OF REAL GDP AND THE PRICE LEVEL

INFLATIONARY GAP

SELF-CORRECTING MECHANISM

STAGFLATION

RECESSIONARY GAP

INFLATION AND THE MULTIPLIER

■   CHAPTER REVIEW

In Chapter 5 we first learned that for individual commodities equilibrium price and quantity are determined by the intersection of the relevant demand and supply curves. The same logic holds when analyzing the economy as a whole. The level of prices and aggregate output is determined by the intersection of the aggregate demand and aggregate supply curves. We have also learned how the aggregate demand curve can be derived from analyzing how changes in the price level affect the spending decisions that underlie the expenditure schedule. In this chapter we will derive the aggregate supply curve and use both curves to show how the price level and aggregate output are determined.

The aggregate supply curve is a schedule, showing for each possible price level, the total quantity of goods and services that all businesses are willing to supply during a specified period of time, holding all other factors influencing aggregate supply constant. You should note that the same logic applies here as to discussions of the supply decisions of individual firms. Businesses will adjust supply in pursuit of profits.

If prices rise while production costs per unit of output remain unchanged, we expect firms to

(1)   (increase/decrease) output. In fact, if prices stayed higher and production costs did not increase at all, there would be no limit to the increase in profits firms could derive from increases in output. However, even if the prices of inputs do not increase, production costs will eventually rise as firms try to expand output, putting a limit on the profitable increase in output. (Remember that in the short run the supply curve for an individual firm is the upward sloping portion of the firm's marginal cost curve.) The increase in output induced by an increase in the price level is a (movement along/shift in) the aggregate supply curve. Any change in production costs in the face of an otherwise unchanged price level— for example, an increase in energy prices imposed by a foreign supplier or an increase in money wages—will also affect profits and will lead to an adjustment in the quantity of goods and services that businesses are willing to supply. This time, however, the change in supply is a _____ _____ the aggregate supply curve. The aggregate supply curve would also shift following a change in productivity or in the available supplies of labor or capital. For example, as investment increases the stock of capital, the aggregate supply curve will shift to the (left/right).

Now, having derived both the aggregate demand curve and the aggregate supply curve, we are in a position to use both to determine the final equilibrium level of prices and aggregate output, or GDP. See, for example, Figure 28-1, where the equilibrium price level of 100 and the equilibrium level of GDP of $6,000 billion are given by the (intersection/slope) of the aggregate demand and supply curves. A higher price level, say, 110, implies (1) a lower quantity of aggregate demand as consumers respond to the loss of purchasing power of their money assets and net exports (increase/decrease) following the increase in domestic prices, and (2) a larger quantity of aggregate supply as

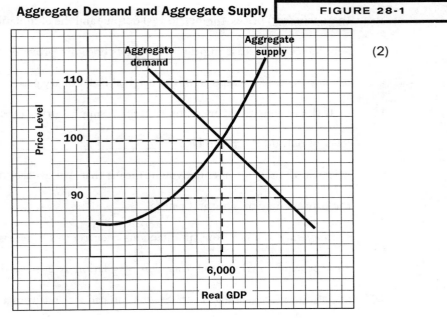

Aggregate Demand and Aggregate Supply   **FIGURE 28-1**

(2)

firms respond to higher prices. Clearly, more supply and less demand cannot be a point of equilibrium, since firms would experience continual (increases/decreases) in inventories. The result is likely to be reduced output and price reductions that move the economy back toward equilibrium. Similarly, a lower price level, such as 90, would induce analogous, although opposite, reactions.

Nothing in the analysis so far guarantees that the intersection of the aggregate demand and aggregate supply curves will be at the level of output corresponding to full employment. If the final equilibrium level of output is different from the full-employment level of output, the result is either a recessionary gap or an inflationary gap. Consider Figure 28-2, which shows a(n) _____ gap. The gap will eventually self-destruct as continuing increases in the price of inputs lead to shifts in the aggregate supply curve. As unemployment falls

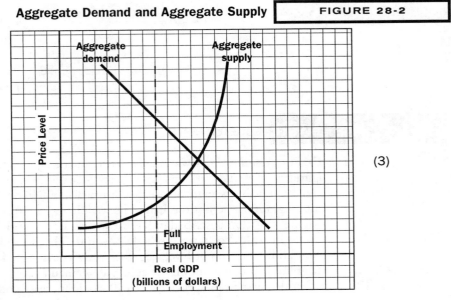

Aggregate Demand and Aggregate Supply   **FIGURE 28-2**

(3)

below frictional levels and material inputs become scarce, higher input prices will shift the aggregate supply curve (inward/outward) leading to a (movement along/shift in) the aggregate demand curve, (higher/lower) prices, (higher/lower) output, and the elimination of the inflationary gap. Note that the simultaneous increase in prices and wages does not prove that increasing wages cause inflation. Both are best seen as a symptom of the original inflationary gap.

If the aggregate demand and aggregate supply curves intersect to the left of the full-employment

(4)   level of output, there will be a _____ gap. The rigidity of wages and other input prices in the face of unemployment means that while a recessionary gap will eventually self-destruct the process may be slow and painful.

Stagflation refers to the simultaneous occurrence of increasing prices and increasing employment. The previous analysis suggests that stagflation is a natural result of the self-destruction of a(n)

(5)   (inflationary/recessionary) gap. Stagflation can also occur as a result of adverse shifts in the aggregate _____ curve.

■   **IMPORTANT TERMS AND CONCEPTS QUIZ**

Choose the best definition for each of the following terms.

1. _____ Aggregate supply curve

2. _____ Productivity

3. _____ Self-correcting mechanism

4. _____ Stagflation

a. Economy's way of restoring equilibrium through inflation or deflation.

b. Amount of a given input required to produce a unit of output.

c. Graph of total quantity of goods and services produced at each possible price level.

d. Inflation that occurs while the economy is growing slowly or in recession.

e. Amount of output produced per unit of input.

■   **BASIC EXERCISES**

1. This exercise first reviews the derivation of the aggregate demand curve and then uses both the aggregate demand and aggregate supply curves to determine the equilibrium level of income. Figure 28-3 shows an income-expenditure diagram in the top half and a price level–aggregate output diagram in the bottom half. The middle expenditure schedule in the top half duplicates the original situation described in Basic Exercise 1 of the previous chapter and assumes that the price level with this expenditure schedule is 100. The dashed line extending into the bottom figure shows how this output level, together with its associated price level, can be plotted in the lower diagram. It is one point on the aggregate demand curve.

   a. A decrease in the price level to 90 would increase consumption spending because a reduction in prices (decreases/increases) the purchasing power of consumer money assets and _____ net exports. The (movement along/shift in) the consumption function and the change in net exports shifts the expenditure schedule up. The new expenditure schedule, for a price level of 90, is shown in the top half of Figure 28-3. What is the equilibrium level of income in the income-expenditure diagram for a price level of 90?

b. Plot the combination of prices and output from part a in the lower diagram. This is a second point on the aggregate demand curve.

c. A price level of 110 would depress consumer spending and net exports, shifting both the consumption function and the expenditure schedule. Use the expenditure schedule for a price level of 110 to plot a third point on the aggregate demand curve.

d. Draw the aggregate demand curve by connecting the three points now plotted in the lower diagram.

e. Using the aggregate demand curve you have just derived and the aggregate supply curve that is already drawn, what is the equilibrium level of prices and real GDP?

Deriving the Aggregate Demand Curve

FIGURE 28-3

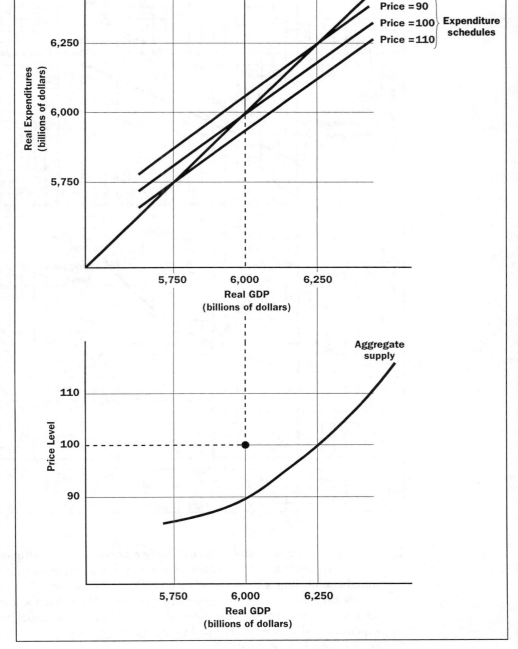

f. If the level of full-employment output were $6 trillion, would there be an inflationary gap or recessionary gap? How, if at all, might such a gap self-destruct and where would the price level and real GDP end up?

g. If the level of full-employment output were $6.125 trillion, would there be an inflationary gap or recessionary gap? How, if at all, might such a gap self-destruct and where would the price level and real GDP end up?

h. If the level of full-employment output were $6.250 trillion, would there be an inflationary or recessionary gap? How, if at all, might such a gap self-destruct and where would the price level and real GDP end up?

| FIGURE 28-4 | Adjustments Following a Shift in the Aggregate Demand Curve |

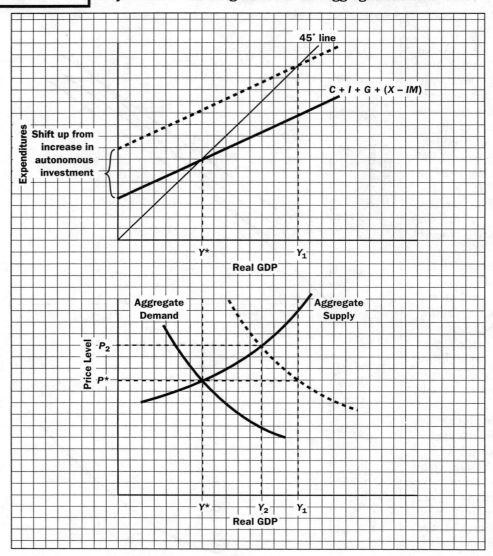

2. This exercise reviews the impact of higher prices on the multiplier. Consider Figure 28-4. The heavy lines show an initial expenditure schedule and the associated aggregate demand curve. The initial equilibrium is at a level of income Y^*, and price level P^*. The dashed expenditure schedule comes from an increase in investment spending. Note that the shift in the expenditure schedule leads to a shift in the aggregate demand curve. In fact, the initial new equilibrium on the income-expenditure diagram, Y_1, is equal to the (<u>horizontal/vertical</u>) shift of the aggregate demand curve in the lower half of the diagram.

   a. Is the combination Y_1, P^* the final equilibrium?

   b. If Y_1, P^* is not the final equilibrium, describe what will happen during the transition to the final equilibrium.

3. In Table 28-1, fill in the blanks as indicated to analyze the response to each change. In the first two columns use S or M for "shift in" or "movement along." In the last two columns use + or −.

TABLE 28-1

	Aggregate Demand Curve	Aggregate Supply Curve	Equilibrium Real GDP	Equilibrium Price Level
A reduction in business investment spending				
An increase in the price of many basic commodities used as inputs in the production of final goods and services				
An increase in the demand for exports caused by an economic boom abroad				
An increase in labor productivity due to a technological breakthrough				
An upward shift in the consumption function due to a stock market boom				
A large increase in energy prices				

SELF-TESTS FOR UNDERSTANDING ▪

TEST A

Circle the most appropriate answer.
1. The aggregate supply curve
   a. slopes down to the right.
   b. has a positive slope.
   c. slopes up to the left.
   d. has a negative slope.

2. The slope of the aggregate supply curve reflects the fact that
   a. inflation reduces the value of the oversimplified multiplier.
   b. the costs of important inputs, such as labor, are relatively fixed in the short run.
   c. the marginal propensity to consume is less than 1.0.
   d. recessionary gaps take a long time to self-destruct.

3. The aggregate supply curve will shift following changes in all but which of the following?
   a. The price level.
   b. Wage rates.
   c. Technology and productivity.
   d. Available supplies of factories and machines.

4. Which of the following will shift the aggregate supply curve outward?
   a. Lower prices.
   b. Higher wages.
   c. Higher energy prices.
   d. Improvements in technology that increase labor productivity.

5. The equilibrium price level and the equilibrium level of real GDP
   a. are determined by the intersection of the aggregate demand, and aggregate supply curves.
   b. will always occur at full employment.
   c. can be found in the income-expenditure diagram.
   d. do not change unless the aggregate demand curve shifts.

6. A change in the equilibrium price level
   a. will lead to a shift in the aggregate supply curve.
   b. will lead to a shift in the aggregate demand curve.
   c. reflects a shift in the aggregate demand curve and/or aggregate supply curve.
   d. will always lead to stagnation.

7. A higher price level will lead to which of the following? (There may be more than one correct answer.)
   a. A reduction in the purchasing power of consumers' money fixed assets.
   b. A downward shift in the consumption function.
   c. An increase in imports.
   d. A decrease in exports.
   e. A downward shift in the expenditure schedule.

8. An inflationary gap occurs
   a. when the equilibrium level of GDP exceeds potential GDP.
   b. whenever there is an upward shift in the expenditure schedule.
   c. whenever aggregate supply exceeds aggregate demand.
   d. during periods of high unemployment.

9. From an initial position of full employment, which one of the following will not lead to a recessionary gap?
   a. A shift in the aggregate supply curve in response to an increase in energy prices.
   b. A reduction in investment spending due to an increase in business taxes.
   c. A reduction in consumer spending due to an adverse shift in consumer expectations.
   d. An increase in exports that follows a business expansion in Europe.

10. Which of the following is not associated with the elimination of an inflationary gap?
    a. Rising prices.
    b. Falling output.
    c. Increased employment.
    d. Rising wages.

11. Which of the following is most likely to lead to an inflationary gap?
    a. An increase in government purchases of goods and services to fight a recession.
    b. An increase in exports that occurs when unemployment rates are high.
    c. A significant reduction in energy prices.
    d. Any increase in spending that shifts the aggregate demand curve to the right when GDP is at or beyond potential GDP.

12. In the face of a recessionary gap, the economy's self-correcting mechanism reflects the effects of
    a. weak labor markets.
    b. trade deficits.
    c. government deficits.
    d. an MPC that is less than 1.0.

13. Which of the following is most likely to lead to stagflation?
    a. An increase in aggregate demand that comes from an increase in government purchases of goods and services.
    b. An increase in exports that occurs when unemployment rates are high.
    c. A significant increase in energy prices.
    d. A technological breakthrough that lowers production costs.

14. Which of the following lead(s) to an increase in net exports? (There may be more than one correct answer.)
    a. Decrease in exports.
    b. Decrease in imports.
    c. Increase in imports.
    d. Increase in exports.

15. From an initial position of equilibrium, exports increase by $100 billion as both Japan and Europe experience business booms. This change will lead to which of the following? (There may be more than one correct answer.)
    a. An upward shift of the expenditure schedule.
    b. A shift to the right in the aggregate supply curve.
    c. A shift to the right in the aggregate demand curve.
    d. An increase in net exports.

16. At the new equilibrium following the increase in exports, American GDP will be _____ and the American price level will be _____.
    a. higher, lower
    b. lower, lower
    c. higher, higher
    d. lower, higher

17. The economy will experience increases in output with little inflation whenever
    a. the aggregate supply curve shifts to the left.
    b. the aggregate demand curve shifts to the right.
    c. both the aggregate demand and supply curves shift to the right in a similar fashion.
    d. the expenditure schedule becomes steeper.

18. Year-to-year changes in GDP and prices are probably best seen as the result of
    a. shifts in the aggregate demand curve that move the economy along an unchanged aggregate supply curve.
    b. shifts in the aggregate supply curve that move the economy along an unchanged aggregate demand curve.
    c. shifts in both the aggregate demand and aggregate supply curves.

19. Prices rise following an increase in autonomous spending whenever the
    a. marginal propensity to consume is less than 1.0.
    b. multiplier is greater than 1.0.
    c. aggregate demand curve has a negative slope.
    d. aggregate supply curve has a positive slope.

20. The aggregate demand curve–aggregate supply curve diagram shows that the multiplier will be smaller than suggested by the original shift of the expenditure schedule whenever
    a. the aggregate demand curve slopes down and to the right.
    b. the aggregate demand curve slopes up and to the right.
    c. the aggregate supply curve slopes up and to the right.
    d. the MPC is less than 1.0.

TEST B

Circle T or F for true or false.

T F 1. The aggregate supply curve shows for each possible price the total quantity of goods and services that the nation's businesses are willing to supply.

T F 2. The aggregate supply curve slopes upward because businesses will expand output as long as higher prices make expansion profitable.

T F 3. An increase in the capital stock from business investment will shift the aggregate supply curve to the right.

T F 4. The impact of unemployment on wages and prices is part of the process by which recessionary gaps self-destruct.

T F 5. If the aggregate supply curve shifts to the left, the result will be stagnation.

T F 6. The economy's self-correcting mechanisms insure that the aggregate demand and aggregate supply curves will always intersect at potential output.

T F 7. The final equilibrium level of prices and aggregate output is determined by the slope of the aggregate supply curve.

T F 8. A period of excessive aggregate demand is likely to be followed by a period of stagnation as the inflationary gap self-destructs.

T F 9. During the elimination of an inflationary gap, the real cause of inflation is excessive wage demands on the part of labor.

T F 10. Analysis of the aggregate supply curve shows that the multiplier derived from the income-expenditure diagram typically understates the final change in output.

■ **SUPPLEMENTARY EXERCISE**

The following equations are consistent with Basic Exercise 1.

$$T = 800$$
$$DI = Y - T$$
$$C = 740 + 0.8DI - 3.5P$$
$$I = 800$$
$$G = 850$$
$$X - IM = -50 - 0.5P$$
$$C + I + G + (X - IM) = Y \text{ (45-degree line)}$$

Aggregate supply curve

$$Y = 3,750 + 25P$$

T = taxes
DI = disposable income
C = consumption expenditures
I = investment expenditures
G = government purchases
X = exports
IM = imports
Y = GDP
P = price level

1. Use the consumption function along with the level of investment spending, government purchases, and net exports to determine an expression for the expenditure schedule. (Don't forget to substitute for disposable income and note that this expression will involve the variable P.)

2. Use the expenditure schedule and the equation for the 45-degree line to determine an expression for the aggregate demand curve.

3. Now use both the aggregate demand curve and the aggregate supply curve to determine the equilibrium level of prices and GDP.

4. Resolve the system on the assumption that investment expenditures decrease to $750.

ECONOMICS IN ACTION ■

HOW VARIABLE IS THE AGGREGATE SUPPLY CURVE?

What explains fluctuations in GDP—shifts in the aggregate demand curve or shifts in the aggregate supply curve? Keynesian analysis focuses on shifts in aggregate demand as the major source of fluctuations in output. In this view, the aggregate supply curve shifts out year by year more or less regularly and deviations from potential or full-employment output are the result of shifts in the aggregate demand curve that are greater or less than the shift in the aggregate supply curve. In recent years an alternative view has argued that the growth of potential output and the associated shifts in the aggregate supply curve may be less regular and more variable than had been suspected.

What difference does it make whether potential output grows smoothly or fluctuates from year to year? Estimates of potential output and the difference of actual output from potential are an important determinant of changes in fiscal and monetary policy. For example, when the economy is operating below potential, expansionary policies that increase aggregate demand can increase output and employment. If the aggregate supply curve is relatively flat, the increase in output may have little impact on prices. The magnitude of changes in fiscal and monetary policy to increase aggregate demand will be influenced by estimates of the shortfall from potential output.

But if GDP is low in part because of an adverse shift in the aggregate supply curve, then expansionary policy that ignores the decrease in potential output could turn out to be too expansionary, push the economy above potential, and create unwanted inflationary pressures. On the other hand, if GDP increased above traditional estimates of potential output because of a favorable shift in the aggregate supply curve, stabilization policy that tried to reduce aggregate demand because of a concern about possible inflationary pressures would unnecessarily increase unemployment.

Why is it so difficult to figure out how the aggregate supply curve is shifting? As economists John Boschen and Leonard Mills point out, potential GDP is not directly observable. Neither is the aggregate demand curve or the aggregate supply curve. The levels of output and prices that we observe give us information about where these curves intersect, but by themselves do not identify one curve or the other. In order to identify the aggregate supply curve one needs to use economic theory and make appropriate assumptions about factors that affect aggregate supply, just as we have done with regard to factors that affect aggregate demand. These theories of the aggregate supply curve are then tested by comparing implications of the models with data from the real world. Models of the aggregate supply curve are still in their infancy and estimates of the importance of supply-side factors in explaining fluctuations in output cover a wide range. A number of these estimates suggest that a third of the variation in output might be attributed to variability in the growth of potential GDP while others range as high as 50 to 70 percent.

1. What are the implications for stabilization policy if fluctuations in the aggregate supply curve account for 10 percent or 50 percent of the fluctuations in output?

SOURCES: John Boschen and Leonard Mills, "Monetary Policy with a New View of Potential GNP," *Business Review*, Federal Reserve Bank of Philadelphia (July/August 1990), pp. 3-10; and Satyajit Chatterjee, "Productivity Growth and the American Business Cycle," *Business Review*, Federal Reserve Bank of Philadelphia (September/October 1995), pp. 13–22.

STUDY QUESTIONS ■

1. Why is the aggregate supply curve drawn sloping upward to the right?

2. What factors influence the position of the aggregate supply curve?

3. What market forces move the economy to the equilibrium level of output and prices given by the intersection of the aggregate demand curve and aggregate supply curve?

4. Evaluate the following statement: "All periods of inflation are caused by excessive demands for high wages on the part of labor."

5. What is the process by which an inflationary gap self-destructs?

6. Is an adverse supply shock likely to give rise to an inflationary gap or a recessionary gap? Why?

7. What are some of the reasons the economy's self-correcting mechanisms might work slowly in the face of a recessionary gap?

8. What is meant by stagnation and when is it likely to occur?

9. How do considerations of aggregate supply affect the value of the multiplier?

MANAGING AGGREGATE DEMAND: FISCAL POLICY

LEARNING OBJECTIVES

After completing this chapter, you should be able to:

■ describe the process by which a change in government purchases of goods and services will lead to a shift in the aggregate demand curve.

■ describe the process by which a change in taxes will lead to a shift in the aggregate demand curve.

■ show on an income-expenditure diagram how a change from fixed to variable taxes affects the slope of the expenditure schedule.

■ explain why taxes that depend upon income (that is, variable taxes) reduce the value of the multiplier.

■ explain why the multiplier for a change in income taxes will be less than the multiplier for a change in government purchases of goods and services.

■ explain why economists treat government transfer payments like negative taxes, not like government purchases of goods and services.

■ describe the process by which a change in government transfer payments will lead to a shift in the aggregate demand curve.

- explain how automatic stabilizers help to reduce fluctuations in GDP.

- explain why active stabilization policy need not imply that government must get bigger and bigger.

- use the aggregate demand and supply diagram to show how supply-side tax cuts hope to reduce the impact on prices associated with stabilization policy to eliminate a recessionary gap.

- describe the kernel of truth in supply-side economics.

- discuss the reservations that most economists have in regard to supply-side economics.

■ CHAPTER REVIEW

The models of income determination in earlier chapters included a rather passive government. This chapter uses a more realistic model of taxes and provides a framework for considering how and when the government should vary spending and taxes. The government's plans for spending and taxes are

(1) called (fiscal/monetary) policy. The only trick is to understand how government spending and taxes affect the curves we have already derived, that is, how government spending and taxes affect the expenditure schedule, the aggregate demand curve, and the aggregate supply curve. After this, the analysis proceeds exactly as before: For a given price level, the equilibrium level of income on the income-expenditure diagram is determined by the intersection of the (consumption/expenditure) schedule and the 45-degree line. A change in prices will affect consumption spending and net exports. The different price levels and the associated equilibrium levels of income on the income-expenditure diagram can be combined to form the aggregate _____ curve. This curve together with the aggregate _____ curve will determine the final equilibrium for income and prices, just as before. A change in the government's fiscal policy will shift one or more of the curves and lead to new equilibrium values for income and prices.

There are three important ways government fiscal policy influences total spending in the economy:

1. The government purchases *goods* and *services*.

2. The government collects *taxes*, reducing the spending power of households and firms. Particular taxes may affect incentives for working, saving, investing, or spending.

3. The government gives *transfer payments* to some individuals, thereby increasing their purchasing power.

Government purchases of goods and services are a direct addition to total spending in the economy; that is, they shift the expenditure schedule (<u>up/down</u>) by the full amount of the purchases. Thus, if government spending increased by $1, the expenditure schedule would shift up by $_____. (An increase in autonomous investment spending or exports of $1 would also shift the expenditure schedule up by $_____.) Thus, changes in government spending shift the expenditure schedule in exactly the same way as other changes in autonomous spending and should have similar multiplier effects.

(2)

Government taxes (<u>are/are not</u>) a direct component of spending on currently produced goods and services. Personal income taxes affect consumption spending through their impact on disposable income. Following a decrease in personal income taxes, consumers' disposable income will be (<u>higher/lower</u>). The initial effect on consumption spending will depend in part on whether consumers view the tax change as permanent or temporary. The largest impact will come from a (<u>permanent/temporary</u>) tax cut. The change in consumption spending will be determined by the marginal propensity to consume which is (<u>less than/equal to/greater than</u>) 1.0. Thus, changes in personal income taxes affect spending, but indirectly through their effect on consumption expenditures. A change in corporate income taxes will change corporate profits after taxes, and is likely to affect _____ expenditures.

(3)

The third important function of the government regarding total spending in the economy is the magnitude of government transfer payments. These payments, like taxes, are not a direct element of total spending on goods and services. Also, like personal taxes, they affect total spending because they affect people's disposable _____ and thus their _____ expenditures. Remember that taxes are earned but not received while transfers are received but not earned. Thus in the models we will be working with, disposable income is equal to GDP (<u>minus/plus</u>) taxes (<u>minus/plus</u>) transfers, and transfers can be thought of as negative taxes.

(4)

An important feature of income taxes (and some transfer payments) is that they vary with GDP. Typically taxes go (<u>down/up</u>) as GDP goes up. If taxes change whenever income changes they are called _____ taxes. Taxes that do not change when GDP changes are called _____ taxes. Understanding the difference between fixed and variable taxes is important for understanding how to model changes in taxes on the income-expenditure diagram and for understanding how income taxes affect the value of the multiplier.

(5)

We have seen that the multiplier process arises because any autonomous increase in spending means higher income for those who supply the newly demanded goods. These higher incomes will lead to more consumption spending, and so on, and so on. This process continues to take place, but it is important to remember that each round of spending produces an increase in income *before* taxes. With variable taxes some of the increase in before-tax income goes to pay higher taxes, and after-tax income

(6) (or disposable income) will increase by (more/less). Thus, each induced round of consumption spending, responding to the increase in disposable income, will be (smaller/larger) than before.

To summarize, in an economy with income taxes (and transfer payments) that vary with income, each round in the multiplier process will be smaller than before, and thus the multiplier effect on income, from any increase in automatic spending, will be (smaller/larger) than before. The impact of income taxes on the multiplier is another important reason why our earlier formula for the multiplier, $1/(1 - \text{MPC})$, was oversimplified.

We can see these same results graphically on the income-expenditure diagram. Up to now we have assumed that taxes did not vary with income, that is, earlier models considered only fixed taxes. A $1 change in GDP meant a $1 increase in disposable income and led to an increase in consumption spending given by the MPC. Since in these models consumption spending was the only type of spending that changed when GDP changed, the slope of the expenditure schedule was equal to the

(7) _____. Now when we consider the impact of variable taxes, we see that a $1 increase in GDP leads to a(n) (smaller/equal/larger) increase in disposable income and a(n) _____ increase in consumption spending as compared with the case of fixed taxes. The result is a (flatter/steeper) expenditure schedule.

As we saw earlier, the multiplier can be derived from the slope of the expenditure schedule. A flatter expenditure schedule means a smaller multiplier. The slope of the expenditure schedule can be written as

$$\text{Slope of the Expenditure Schedule} = \frac{\Delta C}{\Delta \text{GDP}} + \frac{\Delta I}{\Delta \text{GDP}} + \frac{\Delta G}{\Delta \text{GDP}} + \frac{\Delta X}{\Delta \text{GDP}} - \frac{\Delta IM}{\Delta \text{GDP}}$$

Earlier we had assumed that all terms except $\frac{\Delta C}{\Delta \text{GDP}}$ were zero. If we continue to assume that these other terms are equal to zero, variable taxes means that $\frac{\Delta C}{\Delta \text{GDP}}$ is smaller than before. It is useful to note that

$$\frac{\Delta C}{\Delta \text{GDP}} = \frac{\Delta C}{\Delta DI} \frac{\Delta DI}{\Delta \text{GDP}}$$

The first term on the right-hand side of the equal sign is the marginal propensity to consume. With only fixed taxes, the second term will equal 1.0. If there are variable taxes, the second term is (greater than/equal to/less than) 1.0 and the slope of the expenditure schedule is less than the marginal propensity to consume.[1]   (8)

Modeling the impact of a change in taxes will depend upon whether the change is in the fixed or variable component of taxes. A reduction in fixed taxes would increase disposable income, and thus consumption, by the same amount at every level of GDP. Thus, it can be modeled as a parallel shift in the expenditure schedule. A change in variable taxes would be a change in the tax rate. A reduction in the tax rate means less of any increase in income goes for taxes, more ends up as disposable income, and a given change in GDP (i.e., national income) will mean a larger change in consumption spending. The result is that a change in variable taxes leads to a change in the slope of the expenditure schedule. Following a reduction in tax rates, the expenditure schedule would become (flatter/steeper).   (9)

Let us be more specific about how we can model a change in the fixed component of taxes. (Changes in transfer payments will have similar but opposite effects since transfer payments can be viewed as negative taxes.) We saw earlier that a $1 change in government purchases will shift the expenditure schedule by $1. Consider a permanent $1 reduction in the fixed component of income taxes. What is the magnitude of the initial shift of the expenditure schedule that initiates the multiplier process? At the initial equilibrium level of income, the reduction in income taxes will increase both disposable income and _____ spending. It is this initial impact on spending   (10) that determines the magnitude of the shift in the expenditure schedule. Our discussion of the consumption function showed that a $1 increase in disposable income will increase consumption spending by less than $1 because the _____ is (less than/equal to/greater than) 1.0. The result is that a $1 change in the fixed component of taxes shifts the expenditure schedule by (less/more) than a $1 change in government purchases. As a result, the multiplier associated with changes in income taxes will be (larger/smaller) than the multiplier associated with changes in government purchases.

---

[1]This analysis also helps us see how induced spending affects the slope of the expenditure schedule. For example, if investment spending increases when GDP increases, then $\Delta I/\Delta \text{GDP}$ will be greater than zero and the expenditure schedule will be steeper. If imports increase with increases in GDP, then $\Delta IM/\Delta \text{GDP}$ will be greater than zero and the slope of the expenditure schedule will be flatter.

We have now added government purchases of goods and services, taxes, and transfers to our model of income determination. Taken together, these variables are an important determinant of the equilibrium level of income. Changes in these variables, just like the autonomous changes we considered in earlier chapters, will have multiplier effects on the equilibrium level of GDP. Thus deliberate manipulation of these variables may help the government achieve its desired objectives for GDP and prices. Manipulation of government fiscal policy variables for GDP objectives is an example of stabilization policy. For example, if the government wants to increase GDP, it can decide to

(11) (increase/decrease) government purchases of goods and services, _____ personal taxes, _____ corporate taxes, or _____ transfer payments to individuals.

One of the reasons it is so difficult to agree on fiscal policy is that there are so many choices, all of which could have the same impact on national income, but very different impacts on other issues, such as the size of the public versus private sector, the burden of taxes between individuals and corporations, the composition of output between consumption and investment spending, and the amount of income redistribution through transfers to low-income families.

One might believe that if we could decide upon the amounts of government purchases, taxes, and transfers, effective fiscal policy would be simply a technical matter of choosing the right numbers so that the expenditure schedule would intersect the 45-degree line, and the aggregate demand curve would intersect the aggregate supply curve at full employment. In actuality, uncertainties about (1) private components of aggregate demand, (2) the precise size of the multiplier, (3) exactly what level of GDP is associated with full employment, (4) the time it takes for changes in fiscal policy to affect spending and (5) the slope of the aggregate supply curve all mean that fiscal policy will continue to be subject to much political give and take. One hopes that appropriate economic analysis will contribute to a more informed level of debate.

Changes in government spending or tax rates shift the aggregate demand curve directly, in the case of government purchases, and indirectly through impacts on private spending, in the case of taxes and transfer payments. Any shift in the aggregate demand curve, including changes in government spend-

(12) ing or taxes, affects both prices and output as we move along the aggregate _____ curve. Thus, expansionary fiscal policy, designed to increase GDP, is also likely to (increase/decrease)

prices. Supply-side policies attempt to minimize the impact on prices through changes in fiscal policy that shift the aggregate supply curve at the same time that they shift the aggregate demand curve.

Since 1980, there has been much attention given to supply-side tax cuts. Most economists have a number of reservations about the exaggerated claims of ardent supporters of supply-side tax cuts: Specific effects will depend on exactly which taxes are reduced; increases in aggregate supply are likely to take some time, while effects on aggregate demand will be much quicker. By themselves supply-side tax cuts are likely to lead to increased income inequality and to bigger, not smaller, government budget deficits. Do not let these serious objections to exaggerated claims blind you to the kernel of truth in supply-side economics: Marginal tax rates are important for decisions by individuals and firms. In particular situations, reductions in marginal tax rates can improve economic incentives.

IMPORTANT TERMS AND CONCEPTS QUIZ ■

Choose the best definition for each of the following terms.

1. _____ Fiscal policy

2. _____ Fixed taxes

3. _____ Variable taxes

4. _____ Government transfer payments

5. _____ Supply-side tax cuts

6. _____ Automatic stabilizers

a. Tax deductions that businesses may claim when they invest.

b. Money the government gives to individuals in the form of outright grants.

c. Taxes that do not change when GDP changes.

d. The government's plan for spending and taxes.

e. Tax policy designed to shift the aggregate supply curve to the right.

f. Taxes that change when GDP changes.

g. Features of the economy that reduce its sensitivity to shifts in demand.

BASIC EXERCISE ■

This exercise is designed to show how changes in government purchases and taxes will have multiplier effects on the equilibrium level of income and how these multipliers can be used to help determine appropriate fiscal policy. To simplify the numerical calculations, the exercise focuses on the shift in the expenditure schedule, holding prices constant. That is, we will consider how changes in fiscal policy shift the aggregate demand curve.

Table 29-1 has data on GDP, taxes, disposable income, consumption, investment, government spending, exports, and imports. This table is the same as Table 27-1 except that here taxes vary with income while in Table 27-1 they did not. Alternatively one could say that Table 29-1 considers an economy with variable taxes while Table 27-1 assumed that taxes were fixed taxes.

TABLE 29-1

Constant Prices

Income (Output) Y	Taxes T	Disposable Income DI	Consumption Spending C	Investment Spending I	Government Purchases G	Exports X	Imports IM	Total Spending C + I + G + (X − IM)
5,500	675.0	4,825.0	4,200	800	850	500	650	_____
5,750	737.5	5,012.5	4,350	800	850	500	650	_____
6,000	800.0	5,200.0	4,500	800	850	500	650	_____
6,250	862.5	5,387.5	4,650	800	850	500	650	_____
6,500	925.0	5,575.0	4,800	800	850	500	650	_____
6,750	987.5	5,762.5	4,950	800	850	500	650	_____
7,000	1,050.0	5,950.0	5,100	800	850	500	650	_____

1. Complete the column for total spending to verify that the initial equilibrium level of income is the same as you found in Table 27-1.

   Equilibrium level of GDP $ _____

2. Assume now that government purchases decrease by $200 to $650 as shown in Table 29-2. Following the decrease in government purchases, the new equilibrium level of income is $ _____.

TABLE 29-2

Constant Prices

Income (Output) Y	Taxes T	Disposable Income DI	Consumption Spending C	Investment Spending I	Government Purchases G	Exports X	Imports IM	Total Spending C + I + G + (X − IM)
5,500	675.0	4,825.0	4,200	800	650	500	650	_____
5,750	737.5	5,012.5	4,350	800	650	500	650	_____
6,000	800.0	5,200.0	4,500	800	650	500	650	_____
6,250	862.5	5,387.5	4,650	800	650	500	650	_____
6,500	925.0	5,575.0	4,800	800	650	500	650	_____
6,750	987.5	5,762.5	4,950	800	650	500	650	_____
7,000	1,050.0	5,950.0	5,100	800	650	500	650	_____

3. The multiplier for this decrease in government purchases is _____. (This multiplier can be computed by dividing the change in the equilibrium level of income by the change in government purchases.)

4. Now consider a subsequent across-the-board reduction in income taxes of $250. Table 29-3 shows the new relevant data for national income, taxes, disposable income, and consumption. The new equilibrium level of income after the reduction in taxes is $_____.

5. The multiplier for the across-the-board change in taxes is _____.

6. Why did it take a larger reduction in taxes to restore GDP to its initial level following the reduction in government purchases?

TABLE 29-3

Constant Prices

Income (Output) Y	Taxes T	Disposable Income DI	Consumption Spending C	Investment Spending I	Government Purchases G	Exports X	Imports IM	Total Spending C + I + G + (X − IM)
5,500	425.0	5,075.0	4,400	800	650	500	650	_____
5,750	487.5	5,262.6	4,550	800	650	500	650	_____
6,000	550.0	5,450.0	4,700	800	650	500	650	_____
6,250	612.5	5,637.5	4,850	800	650	500	650	_____
6,500	675.0	5,825.0	5,000	800	650	500	650	_____
6,750	737.5	6,012.5	5,150	800	650	500	650	_____
7,000	800.0	6,200.0	5,300	800	650	500	650	_____

7. Question 4 asked you to analyze the impact of a reduction in income taxes. Was this reduction in taxes self-financing? That is, was the increase in GDP stimulated by the reduction in taxes large enough so that on balance there was no decrease in government tax revenues? (Be sure to compare tax receipts at the equilibrium level of income in Table 29-2 with those at the equilibrium in Table 29-3.)

8. Now let us use the multipliers computed in questions 3 and 5 to figure out what changes in government purchases or taxes would be necessary to raise the equilibrium level of income from its initial value given in question 1 to its full-employment level of $6,250.

   Assuming no change in tax rates, the necessary increase in government purchases is $_____.

   Assuming no change in government purchases, the necessary reduction in taxes is $_____.

   (You can answer these questions by figuring out what appropriate change in government purchases or taxes, when multiplied by the relevant multiplier, will equal the desired change in income.) How would you choose between using changes in government purchases of goods and services on the one hand and reductions in taxes on the other?

9. What is the new equilibrium level of income if, from the initial equilibrium given in question 1, investment expenditures rather than government purchases fall by $200? (Now investment spending will be $600 while government purchases stay at $850. Create a new version of Table 29-1 if necessary.) What can one say about multipliers for autonomous changes in public versus private purchases of goods and services?

SELF-TESTS FOR UNDERSTANDING ∎

TEST A

Circle the most appropriate answer.

1. Fiscal policy involves decisions about all but which one of the following?
   a. Income tax rates.
   b. Eligibility rules for transfer payments.
   c. The money supply.
   d. Government purchases of goods and services.

2. The impact of transfer payments on disposable income suggests that an increase in transfer payments will have the same effect as
    a. an increase in taxes.
    b. an increase in government purchases of goods and services.
    c. a decrease in government purchases of goods and services.
    d. a decrease in taxes.

3. A simultaneous reduction in income taxes and transfer payments of $15 billion will leave aggregate disposable income
    a. lower than before the change.
    b. unchanged.
    c. higher than before the change.

4. Fixed taxes
    a. do not vary with GDP.
    b. increase whenever GDP increases.
    c. are the best way to model income taxes in the American economy.
    d. will be a constant proportion of GDP.

5. Variable taxes mean that the difference between GDP and disposable income will _____ as GDP increases.
    a. decrease
    b. stay the same
    c. increase

6. With fixed taxes and when other categories of aggregate demand—investment spending, net exports, government purchases—do not vary with GDP, the slope of the expenditure schedule will be
    a. less than the MPC.
    b. equal to the MPC.
    c. greater than the MPC.

7. With variable taxes and when other categories of aggregate demand—investment spending, net exports, government purchases—do not vary with GDP, the slope of the expenditure schedule will be
    a. less than the marginal propensity to consume.
    b. equal to the marginal propensity to consume.
    c. greater than the marginal propensity to consume.

8. The initial impact of a change in income taxes is on _____ and _____.
    a. imports, exports
    b. disposable income, investment
    c. GDP, consumption
    d. disposable income, consumption

9. A change in fixed taxes can be modeled as
    a. an increase in the marginal propensity to consume.
    b. a twist of the expenditure schedule.
    c. a parallel shift in the expenditure schedule.
    d. a decrease in the marginal propensity to consume.

10. Equal reductions in government purchases and taxes are likely to
    a. shift the expenditure schedule down.
    b. leave the expenditure schedule unchanged.
    c. shift the expenditure schedule up.

11. Equal increases in transfer payments and taxes are likely to
    a. reduce aggregate demand at all levels of GDP.
    b. have equal and offsetting impacts on aggregate demand for no net impact.
    c. increase aggregate demand at all levels of GDP.

12. If the basic expenditure multiplier is 2.0 and if the government wishes to decrease the level of GDP by $80 billion, what decrease in government purchases of goods and services would do the job?
    a. $20 billion.
    b. $40 billion.
    c. $80 billion.
    d. $160 billion.

13. Instead of decreasing government expenditures, the same objectives, in terms of reducing GDP, could also be achieved by
    a. reducing government transfer payments.
    b. reducing taxes.
    c. increasing both taxes and government transfer payments by equal amounts.
    d. reducing both taxes and government transfer payments by equal amounts.

14. If the basic expenditure multiplier is 2.0, a reduction in personal income taxes of $25 billion is likely to
    a. increase GDP by less than $50 billion.
    b. increase GDP by $50 billion.
    c. increase GDP by more than $50 billion.

15. A 10 percent reduction in income tax rates would
    a. lower the value of the basic expenditure multiplier.
    b. not affect the value of the basic expenditure multiplier.
    c. raise the value of the basic expenditure multiplier.

16. An increase in tax rates will lead to all but which one of the following?
    a. A decrease in the value of the multiplier.
    b. A movement along the aggregate demand curve.
    c. A reduction in the equilibrium level of GDP.
    d. A shift of the expenditure schedule.

17. Which of the following is not an example of an automatic stabilizer?
    a. Unemployment compensation.
    b. The corporate income tax.
    c. A special program to build more highways enacted to help combat a recession.
    d. Personal income taxes.

18. Political conservatives could still argue for active stabilization policy as long as the government agreed to _____ during periods of boom and _____ during recessions.
    a. increase taxes; increase government spending
    b. increase government spending; lower taxes
    c. lower government spending; lower taxes
    d. lower taxes; increase government spending

19. Supply-side tax cuts are designed to increase output without raising prices by shifting the
    a. expenditure schedule.
    b. aggregate demand curve.
    c. aggregate supply curve.
    d. 45-degree line.

20. Critics of supply-side tax cuts would agree with all but which one of the following?
    a. Supply-side tax cuts are likely to increase inequality in the distribution of income.
    b. Supply-side tax cuts will substantially reduce the rate of inflation.
    c. Supply-side tax cuts are likely to mean bigger deficits for the federal government.
    d. Supply-side tax cuts will have a larger initial impact on aggregate demand than on aggregate supply.

TEST B

Circle T or F for true or false.

T   F   1. An increase in income tax rates will increase the multiplier.

T   F   2. When taxes increase with increases in income, a $1 change in GDP will mean a smaller change in disposable income.

T   F   3. Income taxation reduces the value of the multiplier for changes in government purchases but does not affect the multiplier for changes in investment.

T   F   4. Since taxes are not a direct component of aggregate demand, changes in taxes do not have multiplier effects on income.

T   F   5. Changes in government purchases of goods and services and in government transfer payments to individuals are both changes in government spending and thus have the same multiplier effects on the equilibrium level of income.

T   F   6. A reduction in taxes matched by an equal reduction in government purchases of goods and services is likely to leave the expenditure schedule unchanged.

T   F   7. Active stabilization policy implies that the government must get bigger and bigger.

T   F   8. Automatic stabilizers reduce the sensitivity of the economy to shifts in aggregate demand.

T   F   9. Only the aggregate supply curve will shift following a supply-side tax cut that increases investment spending by firms.

T   F   10. There is general agreement among economists that supply-side tax cuts will increase output with little impact on prices.

APPENDIX: ALGEBRAIC TREATMENT OF FISCAL POLICY AND AGGREGATE DEMAND

■   BASIC EXERCISES

This exercise is meant to illustrate the material in the Appendix to Chapter 29. Just as in other chapters, we can use equations rather than graphs or tables to determine the equilibrium level of output and relevant multipliers. If we have done our work accurately, we should get the same answer regardless of whether we use graphs, tables, or algebra.

The following equations underlie the numerical example in the Basic Exercise.

$C = 340 + 0.8DI$
$T = -700 + 0.25Y$
$DI = Y - T$
$Y = C + I + G + (X - IM)$

1. What is the equilibrium level of income if investment spending is $800 billion, net exports are –$150 billion, and government purchases are $850 billion? Be sure that $C + I + G + (X - IM) = Y$.

2. Assume that both across-the-board taxes and government purchases decline by $50 billion so that government purchases are $800 billion and the tax equation is

$$T = -750 + 0.25Y$$

Is the equilibrium level of income unchanged following the balanced reduction in the size of the government? Why? What about the government deficit $(G - T)$?

3. Calculate the multiplier for each of the following:
   - change in investment spending
   - change in net exports
   - change in government purchases
   - change in taxes (that is, change in intercept of tax equation)

ECONOMICS IN ACTION ■

TAX CUTS OR COUPONS?

In early 1999 the Japanese economy was stuck in its worst recession since World War II. The Japanese unemployment rate, which over the previous 25 years had averaged one-third to one-fourth of that of the United States, was now about the same as in the United States. With interest rates close to zero, expansionary monetary policy to reduce interest rates had little ability to affect investment spending. In an effort to stimulate the economy, Prime Minister Keizo Obuchi's government tried to increase consumption spending. Rather than reducing taxes, the Japanese government distributed $6.7 billion of shopping coupons that consumers could use until August 1999 at which time they would become worthless.

Would these coupons lead to an increase in aggregate demand? Many observers were skeptical and expected little if any increase in aggregate demand. These skeptics argued that Japanese consumers would use the coupons and save an equivalent amount of cash for no net change in demand. Would consumers behave like Emiko Kawamura who said after receiving her coupons "I don't have to take so much out from my bank account this time." Or would they behave like Keiko Komine who planned to spend her coupons on a bookshelf for her six year old son and a skiing vacation?

Beyond questions about their macroeconomic affect, the coupons engendered widespread controversy because of regulations surrounding their distribution. When first proposed, everyone was to receive coupons, but in the end the distribution of coupons was limited to low income and disabled senior citizens and families with children under 15. Other regulations meant that consumers must normally use the coupons in their own neighborhood. In addition, local officials could decide what types of purchases coupons could be used for. In some communities this included gambling and nightclubs. In other communities purchases were more restricted. Some officials decided that coupons were immediately valuable at small shops but consumers would need to wait 40 days before coupons could be used at large department stores. All of these complications led Fuminori Komata, a thrift shop owner to wonder if this was a program to stimulate the economy or boost social welfare. Finally, even if all coupons were spent, $6.7 billion seems like a small amount when compared to Japanese GDP of $3.8 trillion.

1. In what ways is the distribution of coupons similar to a reduction in taxes or an increase in transfer payments? In what ways is it different?

2. Chapter 25 talked about distinguishing between permanent and temporary changes in taxes. Which is the most appropriate way to thik about the distribution of coupons?

3. Should all Japanese citizens have received coupons? What about restrictions on where coupons could be used and what products they could buy?

4. Were the coupons successful in helping the Japanese economy to recover?

SOURCE: "Japan Counts on Coupons to Boost Economy," *Los Angeles Times*, February 19, 1999. Sheryl WuDunn, "To Revive a Sick Economy, Japan Hands out Coupons," *The New York Times*, March 14, 1999

■ SUPPLEMENTARY EXERCISES

1. In his analysis of the impact of the 1964 tax cut, which reduced taxes on a permanent basis, Arthur Okun estimated that the MPC was 0.95.[2] At the same time, Okun estimated that the basic expenditure multiplier, applicable for any increase in autonomous spending, was only 2.73, not 20, which comes from the oversimplified formula of (1/(1 – MPC). How can such a large MPC be consistent with such a small multiplier?

2. The 1964 reduction in personal taxes was about $10 billion. Okun estimated that this tax reduction raised GDP by $25.9 billion. The ratio of the change in GDP to the change in taxes was only 2.59, not 2.73, the value of the basic expenditure multiplier. How can you account for this discrepancy?

   (*Hint:* In his analysis, Okun assumed prices did not change, so price effects on consumption expenditures are not part of the answer. You should think about whether the basic expenditure multiplier—the multiplier for a shift in the expenditure schedule—is the appropriate multiplier to apply directly to the change in taxes.)

3. What is it like to advise the President of the United States about economic policy? Martin S. Feldstein was chairman of the Council of Economic Advisers during the Reagan administration. You might enjoy reading his observations on the workings of the council and serving as chairman of the council in "The Council of Economic Advisers and Economic Advising in the United States" (*The Economic Journal*, September 1992, pp. 1223–1234).

■ STUDY QUESTIONS

1. How does the multiplier for a change in government spending compare to the multipliers in earlier chapters for changes in investment spending, net exports, and the autonomous component of consumption spending?

2. Consider a change from fixed to variable taxes. Does this change make the multiplier larger or smaller? Why?

3. Consider a change in taxes. How does one show the change in the expenditure schedule when the change in taxes is a change in fixed taxes? When it is a change in the tax rate(s) underlying variable taxes?

4. Why wouldn't equal increases in government purchases and taxes leave aggregate demand unchanged?

5. What is meant by the term automatic stabilizers? In what sense are they automatic? In what sense do they stabilize the economy?

---

[2]Arthur M. Okun, "Measuring the Impact of the 1964 Tax Cut," in W. W. Heller, ed., *Perspectives on Economic Growth* (New York: Vintage Books, 1968), pp. 25-49.

6. If you were charged with recommending changes in government purchases, taxes, and transfers to shift the aggregate demand curve to the right, what sorts of changes in each of these elements of fiscal policy would do the job?

7. How would you choose between the alternatives you proposed when answering question 6?

8. Why is designing fiscal policy to achieve full employment subject to such intense political debate rather than being a technical exercise best left to economists?

9. "Active stabilization policy—the deliberate use of fiscal policy to avoid recessions and inflation— must inevitably lead to bigger and bigger government." Do you agree or disagree? Why?

10. What are some examples of supply-side tax cuts? Explain how and why each of your examples is expected to affect the aggregate supply curve.

11. If supply-side tax cuts could increase the equilibrium level of output without increasing prices, they would be a superior instrument for short-run stabilization policy. Are supply-side tax cuts likely to work in this way? Why or why not? If not, what are supply-side tax cuts good for?

12. What would be necessary if tax cuts were to be self-financing? How likely are these conditions to be met in practice?

ECONOMICS ONLINE ■

Reports of the Congressional Budget Office analyzing the President's budget proposals, summarizing the economic and budget outlook, and reporting on special studies are published on a regular basis. They are available online at

http://www.cbo.gov/reports.html

MONEY AND THE BANKING SYSTEM

LEARNING OBJECTIVES

After completing this chapter, you should be able to:

■ explain the advantages of using money over barter.

■ distinguish between various functions of money. Which are unique to money? Which are shared with other assets?

■ list the desirable features of objects serving as money.

■ distinguish between commodity money and fiat money.

■ explain the differences between MI and M2 as measures of money.

■ describe the historical origins of fractional reserve banking and explain why the industry is so heavily regulated today.

■ explain how the banking system as a whole can create deposits, given an initial injection of bank reserves.

■ use the required reserve fraction to derive the oversimplified deposit creation multiplier.

■ explain why the deposit creation multiplier, based on the required reserve fraction, is oversimplified.

■ CHAPTER REVIEW

Whether it is the root of all evil or not, there is no argument that money has an important influence on the way our economy operates. The right amount of money can help to keep employment up and prices stable. Too much money may lead to excessive inflation; too little money may lead to excessive unemployment. This chapter is an introduction to money. What is it? Where did it come from? What role do banks play in the creation of money? The next chapter discusses how the government regulates the amount of money in the economy, and the chapter after that discusses the influence of money on economic activity.

It is possible that a society could be organized without money. If everyone were self-sufficient there would, by definition, be no trading between individuals and no need for money. If people concentrated their productive activities on what they did best and traded with each other to get goods they did not produce themselves, they might be able to get along without money. Direct trading of goods for

(1) goods, or goods for services, is called _____. For it to be successful there must be a double coincidence of wants. As societies become more complicated and people become ever more specialized, it is clear that barter becomes (<u>less difficult/more difficult</u>).

When a society uses a standard object for exchanging goods and services, a seller will provide goods or services to a buyer and receive the standard object as payment. The efficiency of such a system should be obvious. You no longer have to find someone who not only has what you want but also wants what you have. Anyone who has what you want will now do. Economists would call the standard object

(2) _____. If the object serving as money has intrinsic value, such as gold or jewelry, it is called _____ money. When objects serve as money it is useful that they are divisible, of uniform quality, durable, storable at little or no cost, and compact. Many commodity monies fail on one or more of these criteria. Today money has little intrinsic value and is called _____ money. Such money has value because everyone believes that everyone else will exchange goods and services for it. The bedrock for this foundation of faith is that the government will stand behind the money and limit its production.

When it comes to measuring the quantity of money, exactly where one draws the line is a bit unclear. We have defined money as a standard object used for exchanging goods and services. On this count, the sum of all coins and currency outside of banks plus the wide variety of checking accounts at banks and credit unions surely belongs in any measure of money. The measure that focuses on these items is known as _____. If one also includes savings accounts (because they can easily be (3) transferred into checking accounts), money market deposit accounts, and money market mutual funds, one is measuring _____.

Below are some data for December 1998.

Currency	$ 428.9 billion
Traveler's checks	7.9 billion
Checkable deposits	660.6 billion
Savings deposits including money market deposit accounts	2,364.9 billion
Money market mutual funds plus other deposit type securities	602.5 billion

SOURCE: H.6 Statistical Release, Board of Governors of the Federal Reserve System, March 11, 1999

How big is

M1? $ _____ billion   (4)

M2? $ _____ billion

Given the importance of bank deposits in all measures of money, it is important to understand how the banking system can create money. Banks subject to deposit reserve requirements must hold reserves that are at least as great as some stated percentage of their deposits. Reserves can be either cash in a bank's vaults or money that the bank has on deposit at its local Federal Reserve Bank. We will learn more about the Federal Reserve System in the next chapter. The stated percentage is the required reserve ratio. Thus, only some of the money used to open or to add to a bank deposit must be kept by the bank to meet reserve requirements. The rest can be used to make loans in the search for more profits. This system is known as fractional reserve banking.

The multiple creation of deposits is the counterpart to bank (lending/borrowing). Consider an indi- (5) vidual bank that is subject to a 10 percent reserve requirement. Following a new deposit of $1,000, the maximum amount of the new deposit that this bank could lend out and still meet the reserve requirement is $_____. As the proceeds of the loan are deposited in other banks, new deposits will be created. For the banking system as a whole, the maximum amount of loans that can be made, and thus the maximum amount of deposits that can be created following an increase in bank reserves, is limited by the _____ _____. The precise sequence of the multiple deposit creation process is illustrated in the Basic Exercise for this chapter.

Mathematical formulas have been devised to determine the maximum increase in deposits that can be created by the banking system following an increase in bank reserves:

(6) **Maximum increase in deposits = Initial increase in bank reserves × (1/_____)**

The increase in bank reserves may come from a deposit of cash. In this case, while deposits are up, cash outside banks is down, as some was deposited to start the process of multiple deposit creation. Thus, following a cash deposit, the maximum increase in the money supply will be (more/less) than the maximum increase in deposits.

The deposit creation formula is oversimplified for two reasons:

1. The formula assumes that the entire proceeds of each loan will eventually be redeposited in the banking system. If some of the proceeds of a loan do not get redeposited, then the deposit
(7) creation multiplier will be (larger/smaller).

2. The formula also assumes that every bank makes as large a loan as possible; that is, each bank is assumed to hold no _____ reserves. If banks do choose to hold such reserves, then the money creation formula would be (larger/smaller).

The discussion of the deposit creation multiplier showed how deposits can be created following an increase in bank reserves. The emphasis was on how a change in reserves leads to a change in deposits. One should not be surprised to learn that *total* deposits in all banks are similarly limited by *total* reserves. The cash deposit discussed in the text results in an increase in total reserves of the banking system. However, most increases in reserves at one bank are offset by a decrease in reserves at some other bank, with no change in reserves of the banking system as a whole. Consider Derek, who takes money out of his account at Bank A. Derek uses the money to buy a home computer, and the dealer deposits this money in her bank, Bank B. While Bank B experiences an increase in reserves, Bank A shows a decrease. The process of multiple deposit creation initiated at Bank B is offset by a process of
(8) multiple deposit _____ starting with Bank A. On net there is (some/no) increase in reserves and deposits for the banking system as a whole. The important factor for expanding deposits is new reserves available to the banking system. We will learn in the next chapter how the Federal Reserve is able to influence the volume of reserves available to the banking system.

IMPORTANT TERMS AND CONCEPTS QUIZ ▪

Choose the best definition for each of the following terms.

1. _____ Run on a bank
2. _____ Barter
3. _____ Unit of account
4. _____ Money
5. _____ Medium of exchange
6. _____ Store of value
7. _____ Commodity money
8. _____ Fiat money
9. _____ M1
10. _____ M2
11. _____ Near moneys
12. _____ Liquidity
13. _____ Fractional reserve banking
14. _____ Deposit insurance
15. _____ FDIC
16. _____ Required reserves
17. _____ Asset-
18. _____ Liability
19. _____ Balance sheet
20. _____ Net worth
21. _____ Deposit creation
22. _____ Excess reserves

a. Reserves in excess of the legal minimum.

b. Item an individual or firm owns.

c. Many depositors concurrently withdrawing cash from their accounts.

d. Item used to hold wealth from one point in time to another.

e. Ease with which an asset can be converted into cash.

f. System where bankers keep reserves equal to only a portion of total deposits.

g. Standard unit for quoting prices.

h. Value of all assets minus the value of all liabilities.

i. Amount of money balances the public will hold at a given price level.

j. System of exchange where people trade one good for another without using money.

k. Sum of coins, paper money, checkable deposits, money market mutual funds, and most savings account balances.

l. Accounting statement listing assets on the left-hand side and liabilities and net worth on the right-hand side.

m. Standard object used in exchanging goods and services.

n. Object, without value as commodity, which serves as money by government decree.

o. Liquid assets which are close substitutes for money.

p. System which guarantees depositors against loss if bank goes bankrupt.

q. Process by which banking system turns one dollar of reserves into several dollars of deposits.

r. Item an individual or firm owes.

s. Sum of coins, paper money, and checkable deposits.

t. Object used as a medium of exchange that also has substantial nonmonetary uses.

u. Minimum amount of reserves a bank must hold.

v. Government agency that insures depositors' checking and savings accounts.

■ BASIC EXERCISE

This exercise is designed to help you understand the multiple creation of bank deposits by working through a specific simplified example.

1. Column 1 of Table 30-1 is partly filled in for you to show the changes in the balance sheet of Bank A immediately following Janet's cash deposit of $10,000. At this point, bank deposits have increased by $ _____ and the stock of money in the economy—that is, bank deposits plus currency outside banks—is (higher/lower/unchanged). Assuming the required reserve fraction is 10 percent, fill in the last two rows of column 1, showing the initial changes in required and excess reserves.

| TABLE 30-1 | Balance Sheet Changes |

	(1) Bank A	(2) Bank A	(3) Bank B	(4) Bank B	(5) Bank C
Assets					
Reserves	$10,000	_____	_____	_____	_____
Loans	0	_____	_____	_____	_____
Liabilities					
Deposits	$10,000	_____	_____	_____	_____
Addendum					
Required reserves	_____	_____	_____	_____	_____
Excess reserves	_____	_____	_____	_____	_____

NOTE: Required reserve ratio is 10 percent.

2. Assume that Bank A responds to Janet's deposit by making as large a loan as it can to Earl, given the required reserve ratio. Now fill in column 2 to represent the changes in Bank A's balance sheet after the loan has been made and Earl has taken the proceeds of the loan in cash.

3. Earl uses the money from the loan to buy a car and the car dealer deposits this cash in Bank B. Fill in column 3 to represent the changes in Bank B's balance sheet following this cash deposit. At this point, total bank deposits have increased by $_____ and the stock of money in the economy has increased by $_____.

4. Assume now that Bank B also makes as large a loan as possible. Fill in column 4 to represent changes in Bank B's balance sheet after it makes the loan and this latest borrower takes the proceeds in cash.

5. Assume that the proceeds of this loan eventually get deposited in Bank C. Fill in column 5 to represent the changes in the balance sheet of Bank C following the increase in deposits. At this point total bank deposits have increased by $ _____ and the stock of money has increased by $_____.

6. Fill in the following sequence of increased deposits following the initial increase at Bank A, assuming that each bank makes the largest possible loan.

Increased deposits at Bank A $10,000

Increased deposits at Bank B _____

Increased deposits at Bank C _____

Increased deposits at Bank D _____

Increased deposits at Bank E _____

If you have not made any mistakes you will notice that each increase in deposit is less than the previous increase and can be expressed as $(1.0 - 0.1) \times$ (the previous increase in deposits).

Mathematically this is an infinite geometric progression with decreasing increments. If we carried the sum out far enough it would approach a limit given by $10,000 ÷ _____$, or $_____$. (You might try testing this result by using a computer to calculate the sum for a very large number of terms.) This specific numerical example illustrates the more general principle that the multiplier for the maximum increase in deposits following an increase in bank reserves is $1 ÷ _____ _____ _____$.

SELF-TESTS FOR UNDERSTANDING ■

TEST A

Circle the most appropriate answer.

1. Money serves all but which one of the following functions?
   a. Medium of exchange.
   b. Hedge against inflation.
   c. Unit of account.
   d. Store of value.

2. Which of the following is not an example of commodity money?
   a. Gold coins.
   b. Cigarettes.
   c. A $10 bill.
   d. Diamonds.

3. Where was paper money first used?
   a. China.
   b. Egypt.
   c. India.
   d. Italy.

4. Which of the following does not belong in M1?
   a. The coins in your pocket.
   b. Jodi's checking account.
   c. The cash in the vault at the bank downtown.
   d. The traveler's check that Heather has left over from last summer.

5. The difference between M2 and M1 includes which of the following? (There may be more than one correct answer.)
   a. Traveler's checks.
   b. Money market mutual fund balances.
   c. Marketable U.S. government debt.
   d. Savings deposits.

6. Liquidity is defined as the
   a. viscosity of financial assets.
   b. ease with which assets can be converted to money.
   c. net worth of a financial institution.
   d. ratio of liabilities to assets.

7. A bank's (or your) net worth is found by
    a. summing up all assets.
    b. adding total assets to total liabilities.
    c. subtracting total liabilities from total assets.
    d. dividing total assets by total liabilities.

8. Which of the following is not an asset for a bank?
    a. Excess reserves.
    b. Holdings of U.S. government securities.
    c. Checking account balances held by depositors.
    d. Mortgage loans made by the bank.

9. The key item that makes balance sheets balance is a bank's
    a. holdings of excess reserves.
    b. assets.
    c. required reserves.
    d. net worth.

10. If a bank holds more reserves than required, the difference is
    a. the bank's net worth.
    b. liquidity.
    c. solvency.
    d. excess reserves.

11. Banks could increase profits by
    a. holding more commodity money and less fiat money.
    b. reducing their liabilities.
    c. holding fewer excess reserves in order to make more loans.
    d. substituting M2 for M1.

12. If Damien deposits cash that he used to keep under his mattress in his checking account, the initial deposit will result in
    a. an increase in M1.
    b. a decrease in M2.
    c. an increase in the net worth of the banking system.
    d. no change in M1.

13. The most important government regulation of banks in terms of limiting the multiple creation of deposits is
    a. bank examinations and audits.
    b. limits on the kinds of assets that banks can buy.
    c. the required reserve ratio.
    d. requirements to disclose the volume of loans to bank officials.

14. If the minimum reserve requirement for all bank deposits is 5 percent, then the maximum multiple creation of deposits by the banking system as a whole following a cash deposit of $2,000 would be
    a. $(0.05) \times (\$2,000) = \$100$.
    b. $(1 + 0.05) \times (\$2,000) = \$2,100$.
    c. $(\$2,000) \div (1 - 0.05) = \$2,105$.
    d. $(\$2,000) \div (0.05) = \$40,000$.

15. The maximum increase in the money supply would be
    a. smaller than in question 14.
    b. larger than in question 14.
    c. the same as in question 14.
    (In fact, it would be $ _____.)

16. If the reserve requirement is 10 percent instead of 5 percent, then the maximum multiple creation of deposits would be
   a. smaller than in question 14.
   b. larger than in question 14.
   c. the same as in question 14.

17. If banks hold some of every increase in deposits in the form of excess reserves, then the amount of deposits actually created following a cash deposit would be
   a. less than that indicated in question 14.
   b. the same as that indicated in question 14.
   c. more than that indicated in question 14.

18. If the required reserve ratio is 20 percent and Rachel deposits $100 in cash in the First National Bank, the maximum increase in deposits by the banking system as a whole is
   a. 0.
   b. $20.
   c. $100.
   d. $500.

19. If the required reserve ratio is 20 percent and Sharon deposits $100 in the First National Bank by depositing a check from her mother written on the Second National Bank, the maximum increase in deposits by the banking system as a whole is
   a. 0.
   b. $20.
   c. $100.
   d. $500.

20. If a bank's total reserve holdings are $35 million and it has $12 million of excess reserves, then its required reserves are
   a. $12 million.
   b. $23 million.
   c. $35 million.
   d. $47 million.

TEST B

Circle T or F for true or false.

T F 1. A major advantage of the use of money rather than barter is that money avoids the problems of finding a "double coincidence of wants."

T F 2. Fiat money in the United States may be redeemed for gold from the U.S. Treasury.

T F 3. Many assets serve as a store of value but only money is also a medium of exchange.

T F 4. In periods with high rates of inflation, money is a good store of value.

T F 5. Banks could increase their profitability by holding higher levels of excess reserves.

T F 6. The existence of deposit insurance is an important reason for the dramatic decline in the number of bank failures.

T F 7. The oversimplified deposit creation multiplier of 1 divided by the required reserve ratio is an underestimate of the more appropriate, but more complicated, deposit multiplier.

T   F   8. Multiple deposit creation applies to increases in the money supply but reductions in the money supply can come about only through government taxation.

T   F   9. Required reserves are part of a bank's liabilities, whereas excess reserves are part of a bank's assets.

T   F   10. If a bank's liabilities exceed its assets, the bank is said to have negative net worth.

■ SUPPLEMENTARY EXERCISES

1.   If the required reserve ratio is 20 percent and banks want to hold 10 percent of any increase in deposits in the form of excess reserves and people want to hold $1 more in currency for every $10 increase in deposits, what is the eventual increase in deposits following a $1,000 cash deposit in the First National Bank? What is the eventual increase in the money supply?

2.   If M is the required reserve fraction, E is the ratio of excess reserves to deposits, and C is the ratio of currency to deposits, what is the formula that relates the change in deposits to a change in reserves?

■ ECONOMICS IN ACTION

THE REFORM OF DEPOSIT INSURANCE

As described in the text, the establishment of federal deposit insurance had a dramatic effect on the number of bank failures. Some critics argue that experience during the 1980s suggests that we may have had too much of a good thing. Economist Edward J. Kane has been especially critical of the actions of federal government officials, both elected and appointed, concerning deposit insurance. He was one of the first to describe the collapse of the Federal Savings and Loan Insurance Corporation (FSLIC), the deposit insurance agency for S&Ls, as resulting from a combination moral hazard and principal-agent problem.[1]

Moral hazard arose because deposit insurance provided an incentive for some S&Ls to engage in risky behavior. The period of high interest rates in the late 1970s and early 1980s had left these institutions with little or negative net worth. Owners of these institutions saw high-risk but potentially high-return loans as their only salvation. Insurance protected their depositors. Negative net worth meant that their own investment in the S&L had already been wiped out. They literally had nothing to lose by engaging in risky behavior.

Kane also charges that Congress and bank regulators (the agents) failed to act in the best interest of U.S. taxpayers (the principals). Kane charges that at critical points, and with the support and encouragement of key members of Congress, the FSLIC allowed bankrupt institutions to continue in business. Succumbing to lobbying pressures to focus on the original book value of assets rather than current market value allowed officials to pretend that bankrupt institutions were still solvent. The result was that problems were deferred as the cost of appropriate action increased. Opposition to increased federal spending and the impact on the deficit that would accompany the official closing of failed institutions further contributed to delay.

What is an appropriate stance for deposit insurance? There have been a large number of proposals. They include the mandatory use of market prices to value assets; mandatory and higher net worth requirements for financial institutions; automatic rules for closing insolvent institutions that remove the element of discretion on the part of regulators; deposit insurance premiums that vary with the riskiness of a bank's portfolio; and public notice of the results of bank examinations.

A number of observers have also argued that the present deposit insurance limit is so high that depositors have little incentive to concern themselves with the riskiness of a bank's portfolio. If a smaller

---

[1] *Moral hazard* refers to the tendency of insurance to make people less concerned with the risks associated with their behavior—after all its covered by insurance. Principal-agent relationships occur whenever one party, the principal, has to hire others, the agents, to act on the principal's behalf. An example would be stockholders who hire executives to manage corporations. It is often difficult for the principals to monitor the behavior of their agents to insure that the agents act to promote the principals' interests and not their (the agents') own.

amount, perhaps the first $40,000 or $50,000 of deposits, were insured and it was clear that deposits above this level had no insurance protection, depositors with large balances, especially businesses, would have a real incentive to pay attention to the riskiness of their bank's assets. According to this view, a bank that was imprudent would (and should) suffer a run on its deposits with little reason to expect that the run would spill over and harm sound banks.

1. What changes, if any, do you think there should be to the system of deposit insurance? Why? How far should the government go to protect depositors? How does one design a system of deposit insurance that addresses the problem of moral hazard?

You might want to consult the following:

Edward J. Kane, *The S&L Insurance Mess: How Did It Happen*, (Washington, D.C.: The Urban Institute Press, 1991).

Lawrence J. White, *The S&L Debacle*, (New York: Oxford University Press, 1991).

Ron J. Feldman and Arthur J. Rolnick, *Fixing FDICIA: A Plan to Address the Too-Big-To-Fail Problem*, (1997 Annual Report essay, Federal Reserve Bank of Minneapolis)

htpp://woodrow.mpls.frb.fed.us/pubs/ar/index.html

John H. Boyd and Arthur J. Rolnick, *A Case for Reforming Federal Deposit Insurance*, (1988 Annual Report essay, Federal Reserve Bank of Minneapolis)

htpp://woodrow.mpls.frb.fed.us/pubs/ar/index.html

STUDY QUESTIONS ■

1. What functions does money share with other assets and what functions are unique to money?

2. How does fiat money differ from commodity money? In particular, how do they compare with regard to the list of desirable characteristics discussed in the text?

3. Where would you draw the line if asked to come up with a measure of money for the American economy?

4. Rank the following in terms of their liquidity and justify your ranking: a 12-month savings certificate, the balance in your checking account, a corporate bond issued by Intel, some leftover traveler's checks from your most recent trip, a share of stock in du Pont, a $20 bill, a piece of lakeside vacation property.

5. What is full-bodied money? Is money in the United States today full-bodied? If not, where does its value come from?

6. If the government is going to insure deposits, it seems natural that it be allowed to examine a bank's books and put limits on some types of loans to control its risk. Alternatively, the need for deposit insurance could be eliminated if reserve requirements were set at 100 percent. What do you think would happen to bank service charges if reserve requirements were 100 percent? What other changes might you expect? In particular think about the incentive to create alternatives to bank deposits.

7. How can you tell when something is an asset or a liability?

8. As every banker wants her assets to exceed her liabilities, in what sense does a bank's balance sheet balance?

9. As the government controls the printing press, how can banks create money?

10. In what ways is the deposit creation multiplier, $1/m$, oversimplified? Does adjusting for these complications make the deposit creation multiplier larger or smaller?

ECONOMICS ONLINE

The Fed's latest release on the size of M1 and M2 can be found here.

http://www.bog.frb.fed.us/releases/H6/

MONETARY POLICY AND THE NATIONAL ECONOMY

LEARNING OBJECTIVES

After completing this chapter, you should be able to:

■ distinguish between the concepts "money" and "income."

■ analyze arguments in favor of and opposed to the independence of the Federal Reserve System.

■ draw and explain the logic behind both the supply-of-money schedule and the demand-for-money schedule.

■ analyze the impact of changes in the three major monetary policy instruments both in words and by using the demand-for- and supply-of-money schedules.

■ explain how bond prices and interest rates are related.

■ describe the impact of open market operations on bond prices and interest rates.

■ explain why the Fed's control of the stock of money is not exact.

■ describe how changes in monetary policy affect the expenditure schedule and the aggregate demand curve.

Important Terms and Concepts

CENTRAL BANK

FEDERAL RESERVE SYSTEM

FEDERAL OPEN MARKET COMMITTEE (FOMC)

INDEPENDENCE OF THE FED

OPEN MARKET OPERATIONS

BOND PRICES AND INTEREST RATES

CONTRACTION AND EXPANSION OF THE MONEY SUPPLY

FEDERAL RESERVE LENDING TO BANKS

RESERVE REQUIREMENTS

SUPPLY OF MONEY

DEMAND FOR MONEY

OPPORTUNITY COST

EQUILIBRIUM IN THE MONEY MARKET

MONETARY POLICY

WHY THE AGGREGATE DEMAND CURVE SLOPES DOWN

■ use the expenditure schedule along with the aggregate demand and supply curves to describe how changes in monetary policy affect the economy's macroeconomic equilibrium, that is, interest rates, investment spending, GDP, and prices.

■ explain how the impact of higher prices on the demand for money helps to explain why the aggregate demand curve has a negative slope.

■ CHAPTER REVIEW

In the preceding chapter we learned how deposits are created by the actions of banks. In this chapter we will see how actions taken by the Federal Reserve System can influence the stock of money and interest rates. Reserve requirements and the total amount of bank reserves are important keys to the Federal Reserve's control of bank deposits and the stock of money. We will also see how the equilibrium in the money market influences the economy's overall macroeconomic equilibrium. The emphasis in this chapter is on building models. In subsequent chapters we will use these models to understand policy issues.

(1)   The Federal Reserve System was established in _____ and is the nation's _____ bank. There are _____ district banks throughout the country, with headquarters in Washington, D.C. The people in charge in Washington are the seven members of the _____ of _____ of the Federal Reserve System. Major decisions about the stock of money are made by the FOMC, or the _____ _____ _____ Committee. Government spending and taxes are the nation's (fiscal/monetary) policy. Policy actions by the Federal Reserve constitute the nation's _____ policy.

We saw in the preceding chapter that the multiple creation of bank deposits is limited by the required reserve ratio and by the volume of bank reserves. Reserve requirements help to determine the deposit creation multiplier. The Fed's other two major policy instruments—open market operations and lending to banks—directly affect total bank reserves. We also saw that controlling reserve requirements and the volume of bank reserves does not allow for the precise control of the stock of money

(2)   because of possible changes in (excess/required) reserve holdings by banks and in currency holdings by the public. These slippages in the deposit creation formula are an important reason why the Federal Reserve's control over the stock of money, while strong and important, is not complete.

A reduction in reserve requirements does not change total bank reserves, but it will initially result

(3)   in a(n) (increase/decrease) in noninterest-earning excess reserves. Multiple deposit creation will take

place as banks try to put these nonearning excess reserves to work. Thus, a reduction in minimum reserve requirements should be associated with a (larger/smaller) volume of deposits and is an example of a(n) (expansionary/contractionary) change in monetary policy. An increase in reserve requirements will typically force banks to curtail lending in order to meet new, higher holdings of (excess/required) reserves. Such an increase would be an example of a _____ change in monetary policy.

Open market operations—the purchase and sale of government _____—represent   (4)
the most important and most commonly used instrument of monetary policy. Open market operations affect bank behavior by adding to or subtracting from the amount of bank reserves. The essence of an open market purchase is that the Fed creates bank reserves when it (buys/sells) a government security. The result is a(n) (increase/decrease) in noninterest-earning excess reserves, and the usual multiple deposit creation process is set in motion. An open market sale has exactly opposite effects. Payment to the Fed for government securities means a(n) (reduction/increase) in bank reserves and initiates a process of multiple deposit (creation/destruction).

Banks can add to their reserve holdings by borrowing directly from the Fed. Such borrowings might facilitate a multiple expansion of deposits or, more frequently, might forestall a multiple destruction of deposits. The Fed influences the volume of borrowing by changing the interest rate it charges banks. More bank borrowing would mean a (higher/lower) amount of bank reserves than oth-   (5)
erwise, and eventually a (higher/lower) volume of bank deposits. When banks borrow reserves from the Fed they must pay interest on these borrowings. In the United States the interest rate for these borrowings is called the _____ _____ .

Monetary policy decisions, affecting reserve requirements and the total volume of bank reserves, can be seen as putting an upper limit on the possible creation of bank deposits and hence on the stock of money. How much banks will want to exploit the potential to create deposits will be determined by the profitability of increased bank operations—more loans and more deposits. Higher interest rates on loans will induce banks to make (more/fewer) loans, hold (more/fewer) nonearning excess reserves,   (6)
and borrow (more/less) from the Fed (if they can). All of these actions will expand the volume of deposits and hence the stock of money. In brief, considering just banks, higher interest rates should be associated with a (larger/smaller) stock of money.

FIGURE 31-1

This behavior by banks is summarized in Figure 31-1, which shows an upward-sloping supply-of-money schedule. Movements along the schedule are related to the decisions of commercial banks as they respond to changes in interest rates. Shifts in the schedule come from changes in monetary policy. For example, an open market purchase increases the amount of bank reserves and shifts the money supply

(7)   schedule to the (<u>left/right</u>). Changes in other monetary policy variables will also shift the money supply schedule. To repeat, monetary policy decisions determine the position of the money supply schedule; they do not, by themselves, determine either the stock of money or the interest rate. The actual stock of money and the interest rate will be determined by the intersection of the supply-of-money schedule and the _____ -for-money schedule.

FIGURE 31-2

(8)

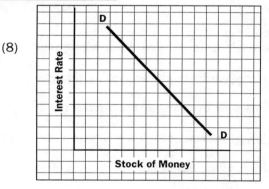

Figure 31-2 shows a demand schedule for money. The schedule has a negative slope because, as the interest rate rises, the demand for money (<u>increases/decreases</u>). The increase in interest rates means that the opportunity cost of holding money has (<u>increased/decreased</u>). If nominal GDP increases, that is, if real GDP or prices increase, the demand schedule will shift to the (<u>right/left</u>) as more transactions associated with a higher GDP will lead to a(n) (<u>increased/decreased</u>) demand for money at every interest rate. If nominal GDP decreases, the demand schedule will shift to the _____.

FIGURE 31-3

(9)

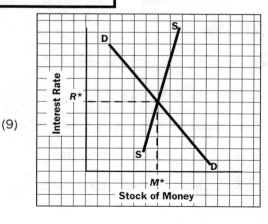

Equilibrium values for the stock of money and the rate of interest will be determined by the forces of both supply and demand. Graphically, the equilibrium can be represented by the _____ of the demand and supply curves, as in Figure 31-3. Changes in monetary policy will change the equilibrium values for both the stock of money and the rate of interest. An expansionary change in monetary policy would be represented by a shift of the (demand/supply) schedule to the (left/right), a(n) (increase/decrease) in the stock of money, and a(n) (increase/decrease) in the interest rate. A contractionary change in monetary policy would be represented by a shift of the supply schedule to the _____, a(n) _____ in the stock of money, and a(n) _____ in the interest rate.

With an understanding of how the demand and supply for money work together to determine interest rates, we are in a position to see how changes in monetary policy affect aggregate demand. Policy shifts in the (supply/demand)-of-money schedule will change interest rates as we move along the _____-for-money schedule. The change in interest rates will affect interest sensitive categories of demand, especially investment spending. Changes in investment spending lead to a (shift in/movement along) the expenditure schedule. The (shift in/movement along) the expenditure schedule will shift the aggregate (demand/supply) curve through the multiplier process. Overall macroeconomic equilibrium is reestablished at the new intersection of the aggregate demand curve and the aggregate supply curve. The division of effects, as between real output and prices, is determined by the slope of the aggregate _____ curve. This sequence of events is diagrammed at the end of this chapter in the text.[1]

(10)

The same reasoning helps us to understand two other important points:

WHY THE AGGREGATE DEMAND CURVE HAS A NEGATIVE SLOPE

Higher prices not only reduce the purchasing power of money fixed assets and affect the international price competitiveness of American goods, they also increase the transactions demand for money. With an unchanged supply-of-money schedule, the increase in the demand for money that comes with a higher price level will shift the demand-for-money schedule to the right, leading to an increase in interest rates and lower investment spending. Thus higher prices affect aggregate demand through their impact on investment as well as consumption and net exports.

---

[1]Expansionary monetary policy that lowers interest rates and increases investment spending will eventually affect the aggregate supply curve as investment projects are completed and add to the capital stock. We concentrate here on impacts on the aggregate demand curve as they are the most immediate.

WHY THE MULTIPLIER FORMULA 1/(1 − MPC) IS OVERSIMPLIFIED

Increases in nominal GDP from the multiplier process increase the transactions demand for money. Interest rates rise as the demand-for-money schedule moves along an unchanged supply-of-money schedule. The reduction in investment spending induced by the rise in interest rates is an important reason why the multiplier process of the income-expenditure diagram is oversimplified.

■ IMPORTANT TERMS AND CONCEPTS QUIZ

Choose the best definition for each of the following terms.

1. _____ Central bank

2. _____ Federal Reserve System

3. _____ Federal Open Market Committee

4. _____ Open market operations

5. _____ Reserve requirement

6. _____ Discount rate

7. _____ Opportunity cost

8. _____ Equilibrium in the money market

9. _____ Monetary policy

a. Forgone value of next-best alternative that is not chosen.

b. A bank for banks responsible for the conduct of monetary policy.

c. Branch of the U.S. Treasury responsible for minting coins.

d. Quantity of money and level of interest rate where money demand equals money supply.

e. Minimum amount of reserves a bank must hold.

f. Chief policymaking committee of the Federal Reserve System responsible for open market operations.

g. Actions Fed takes to affect money supply, interest rates, or both.

h. Central bank of the United States.

i. Interest rate Fed charges on loans to banks.

j. Fed's purchase or sale of government securities.

■ BASIC EXERCISES

1. **Instruments of Monetary Policy**

This exercise is designed to review the impact of various changes in monetary policy instruments.

a. Use Figure 31-4 to analyze the impact of an open market sale. The sale of a government security by the Fed results in a(n) (<u>increase/decrease</u>) in total bank reserves. This change in bank reserves can be represented as a shift of the supply-of-money schedule to the _____. (Be sure you can explain in words why the schedule shifts.) Draw a new supply-of-money schedule that represents the result of the open market sale. As a result of this (<u>expansionary/contractionary</u>) change in monetary policy, the equilibrium stock of money will (<u>fall/rise</u>) and interest rates will _____.

b. Use Figure 31-5 to analyze the impact of a reduction in minimum reserve requirements. The initial result of a reduction in minimum reserve requirements will be a(n) (increase/decrease) in excess reserves. The likely response by banks to this change in excess reserves will result in a process of multiple deposit (creation/destruction). In Figure 31-5 such a development can be represented as a shift of the supply-of-money schedule to the _____. Draw the new supply-of-money schedule. As a result of this _____ change in monetary policy, the equilibrium stock of money will _____ and interest rates will _____.

c. Use Figure 31-6 to analyze the impact of an increase in the discount rate. An increase in this rate will make banks (more/less) willing to borrow from the Fed. One expects that the volume of member bank borrowing will _____. The change in member bank borrowing is a direct change in bank reserves; so, as a result of the increase in the discount rate, total bank reserves will _____ and the supply-of-money schedule will shift to the _____. Draw the new supply-of-money schedule in Figure 31-6. As a result of this _____

FIGURE 31-4

FIGURE 31-5

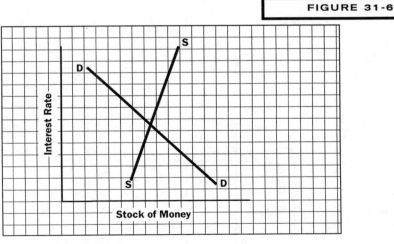

FIGURE 31-6

change in monetary policy, the equilibrium stock of money will _____ and interest rates will _____.

d. You should also be able to analyze the impact of each opposite change in monetary policy; that is, an open market purchase, an increase in minimum reserve requirements, and a decrease in the discount rate.

2. **Borrowing from the Fed**

Consider the data in Table 31-1 on interest rates and borrowings by depository institutions from the Federal Reserve. The federal funds rate is a market interest rate: it is the interest rate on overnight lending and borrowing or reserves between banks. Follow the instructions below to explore the influence of market interest rates on bank borrowings from the Fed.

a. The financial incentive to borrow from the Fed can be represented by the difference between the discount rate and market interest rates, represented here by the federal funds rate. Plot the data from the last two columns of Table 31-1, one point for each month, in the two-variable diagram in Figure 31-7. What does this data suggest is likely to happen to bank borrowings from the Fed if market interest rates increase while the discount rate remains unchanged?

TABLE 31-1

		Discount Rate (percent)	Federal Funds Rate (percent)	Fed Funds Rate minus Discount Rate (percent)	Borrowings from the Federal Reserve ($ millions)
Jan	1989	6.50	9.12	2.62	1,662
Feb	1989	6.59	9.36	2.77	1,487
Mar	1989	7.00	9.85	2.85	1,813
Apr	1989	7.00	9.84	2.84	2,289
May	1989	7.00	9.81	2.81	1,720
Jun	1989	7.00	9.53	2.53	1,490
Jul	1989	7.00	9.24	2.24	694
Aug	1989	7.00	8.99	1.99	675
Sep	1989	7.00	9.02	2.02	693
Oct	1989	7.00	8.84	1.84	555
Nov	1989	7.00	8.55	1.55	349
Dec	1989	7.00	8.45	1.45	265

SOURCE: *Economic Report of the President,* 1990, Tables C-69 and C-71.

FIGURE 31-7 Interest Rates and Borrowed Reserves

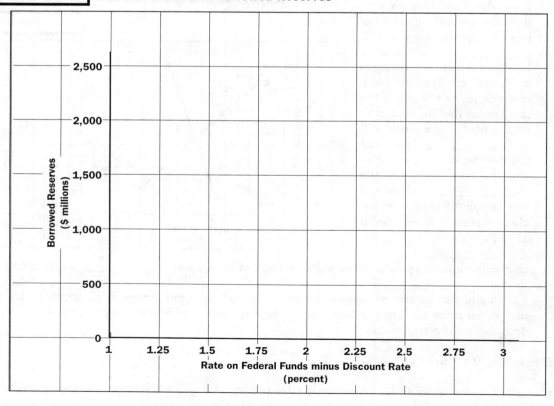

SELF-TESTS FOR UNDERSTANDING ■

TEST A

Circle the most appropriate answer.

1. The Federal Reserve is responsible for the conduct of
    a. environmental policy.
    b. fiscal policy.
    c. international economic policy.
    d. monetary policy.

2. The Federal Reserve is a bank for
    a. the Treasury.
    b. households.
    c. businesses.
    d. banks.

3. Which of the following is *not* an instrument of monetary policy?
    a. Open market operations.
    b. Lending to banks.
    c. Antitrust actions to promote competition in banking.
    d. Required reserve ratios.

4. Who has direct responsibility for open market operations?
    a. The Board of Governors.
    b. The Federal Open Market Committee.
    c. The president of the United States.
    d. The Banking Committee of the U.S. Senate.

5. Open market operations involve the Fed buying and selling
    a. stocks in American companies.
    b. U.S. government securities.
    c. gold.
    d. corporate bonds.

6. When making an open market purchase, the Fed gets the money to make the purchase from
    a. the Treasury.
    b. the Bureau of Printing and Engraving.
    c. cash in its vault.
    d. making a computer entry on its own books to credit the reserve account of the bank from which it purchases the security.

7. An open market purchase will lead to all but which one of the following?
    a. Supply-of-money schedule shifts to the right.
    b. Expenditure schedule shifts up.
    c. Multiplier increases.
    d. Aggregate demand curve shifts to the right.

8. An open market sale will result in all but which one of the following?
    a. decrease in the stock of money.
    b. increase in interest rates.
    c. lower investment spending.
    d. higher prices.

9. The immediate impact of a change in reserve requirements will be on the
    a. total volume of bank reserves.
    b. division of reserves (between required reserves and excess reserves).
    c. demand for money.
    d. discount rate.

10. An increase in reserve requirements will lead to all but which one of the following?
    a. An initial increase in required reserves.
    b. A reduction in the stock of money.
    c. An increase in interest rates.
    d. Higher investment spending.

11. A reduction in the discount rate will lead to all but which one of the following?
    a. An increased incentive for banks to borrow from the Fed.
    b. An expansion of bank reserves as banks borrow more.
    c. The money supply schedule shifts to the left.
    d. A reduction in interest rates.

12. Which of the following is not an example of expansionary monetary policy?
    a. An open market purchase.
    b. A reduction in reserve requirements.
    c. An increase in the interest rates charged on loans by the Fed to commercial banks.
    d. A reduction in the discount rate.

13. Which is the most frequently used instrument of monetary policy?
    a. Changes in the discount rate.
    b. Open market operations.
    c. Changes in reserve requirements.
    d. Stricter bank examinations.

14. Which of the following help to explain why the Fed does not have precise control of the money supply? (There may be more than one correct answer.)
    a. Banks may vary the amount of excess reserves they desire to hold.
    b. Open market operations can change the volume of bank reserves.
    c. Changes in the amount of currency as opposed to bank deposits that individuals and businesses want to hold.
    d. Changes in reserve requirements will affect the deposit creation multiplier.

15. Important determinants of the demand for money include all but which one of the following?
    a. The discount rate.
    b. The level of real output.
    c. Market interest rates.
    d. The price level.

16. A change in which of the following would lead to a shift in the demand-for-money schedule?
    a. Market interest rates.
    b. Reserve requirements.
    c. GDP.
    d. The discount rate.

17. The positive slope of the supply-of-money schedule indicates that
    a. at higher interest rates people will demand more money.
    b. banks are likely to respond to higher interest rates by holding fewer excess reserves.
    c. minimum reserve requirements increase directly with interest rates.
    d. the Fed is likely to engage in expansionary monetary policy actions as interest rates increase.

18. An increase in interest rates from 8 percent to 9 percent would be associated with _____ in the price of existing bonds.
    a. a decline
    b. no change
    c. an increase

19. Changes in interest rates resulting from changes in monetary policy are likely to affect investment spending and initially lead to a shift in the _____. (There may be more than one correct answer.)
    a. expenditure schedule
    b. aggregate supply curve
    c. consumption function
    d. aggregate demand curve

20. Knowing that an increase in the level of prices will increase the demand for money for transactions purposes helps to explain why
    a. the aggregate supply curve has a positive slope.
    b. the aggregate demand curve has a negative slope.
    c. equilibrium occurs at the intersection of the aggregate demand and aggregate supply curves.
    d. the multiplier response to a change in autonomous spending may be greater than 1.0.

TEST B

Circle T or F for true or false.

T   F   1. The independence of the Federal Reserve System is now so well established that it is beyond debate.

T   F   2. Most power in the Federal Reserve System is held by the 12 district Federal Reserve banks.

T   F   3. Monetary policy decisions by the Federal Reserve are subject to review by the president of the United States before being implemented.

T   F   4. An open market purchase by the Fed lowers interest rates without changing the stock of money.

T   F   5. A reduction in minimum reserve requirements is likely to lead to an increase in both the stock of money and the interest rate.

T   F   6. Changing the discount rate is the most frequently used instrument of monetary policy today.

T   F   7. Since many forms of money do not earn interest, people's demand for money is unaffected by changes in interest rates.

T   F   8. Higher interest rates would normally lead banks to reduce their holdings of excess reserves.

T   F   9. The impact of changes in monetary policy on interest-sensitive categories of demand affects GDP and prices as the economy moves along a given aggregate demand curve.

T   F   10. The impact of the price level on the demand for money, and hence interest rates, helps to explain why the aggregate demand curve has a negative slope.

■   **SUPPLEMENTARY EXERCISES**

1.   **An Algebraic Model of the Economy**

The following algebraic model builds on models from earlier chapters but this time includes explicit expressions for the demand for and supply of money. For simplicity the model assumes that the price level does not change. That is, it is equivalent to assuming that the aggregate supply curve is horizontal.

Consider an economy where consumption and investment spending are given by

$$C = 650 + 0.6DI$$

$$I = 1{,}710 - 30r$$

where r is the interest rate. In this economy, taxes are one-sixth of income and net exports are 100.
a.   If government purchases are 900 and r is 12 (that is, 12 percent), what is the equilibrium level of income?
b.   If the Fed lowers the interest rate to 8, what happens to the equilibrium level of income?
c.   The Fed can lower the interest rate by an appropriate increase in bank reserves; that is, an appropriate shift in the money supply schedule. But what is appropriate? Assume the demand for money is

$$M^D = 0.25Y - 10r$$

and the supply of money is

$$M^S = 5BR + 2.5r$$

where BR is the amount of bank reserves. If $BR = 270$, what is the equilibrium level of income? Of r? Of M?
d.   What increase in BR is necessary to reduce the interest rate to 8 and produce the increase in Y you found in question 2? What happens to M? (You might start by trying an increase in BR of 10 and figuring out what happens to Y and r. Then use these results to figure out how to get r to drop to 8.)

2.   **Bond Prices and Interest Rates**
a.   Consider a bond that pays $60 a year forever. If interest rates are 6 percent, such a bond should sell for $1,000 as ($60 ÷ $1,000) = .09. Assume now that interest rates fall to 4 percent. With bond payments of $60, what bond price offers investors a return of 4 percent? If interest rates rise to 10 percent, what must be the price of the bond paying $60 to offer investors a return of 10 percent?
b.   Bonds that pay only interest and never repay principal are called consols. Most bonds pay interest for a certain number of years and then repay the original borrowing or principal. Bond prices reflect the present value of those interest and principal payments as follows:

$$\text{Price} = \sum_{t=1}^{N} \frac{\text{INT}}{(1+r)^t} + \frac{\text{PRIN}}{(1+r)^N}$$

where INT = interest payments
   r = interest rate
   PRIN = principal
   N = maturity, number of years of interest payments (also number of years to principal payment)
   It will be easier to answer the following questions if you have access to a computer or sophisticated hand calculator.
   Verify that if INT = $60, PRIN = $1,000, N = 10, and r = .06, the price of the bond = $1,000.
   Calculate the price of the bond when r = .04 and when r = .10 while INT, PRIN, and N remain unchanged. These calculations show what would happen to the price of an existing

bond if interest rates change. Do your results confirm the negative correlation between bond prices and interest rates discussed in the text?

c.   Redo the calculations in questions b but for values of $N = 5$ and $N = 30$. Is the sensitivity of bond prices to a change in interest rates the same for all maturities?

3.   **Federal Open Market Committee**

The Federal Open Market Committee (FOMC) has 12 voting members: the seven members of the Board of Governors and five of the 12 district bank presidents. The president of the Federal Reserve Bank of New York is always a voting member of the FOMC. The remaining four votes rotate among the other 11 presidents. Presidents of nine banks share three votes. That is, each of these presidents is a voting member of the FOMC once every three years. Two bank presidents are voting members every other year. What banks do these two presidents represent?

ECONOMICS IN ACTION   ■

INDEPENDENCE OF THE FEDERAL RESERVE

In October 1993, Congressman Henry Gonzales (D-Texas), Chairman of the House Banking Committee, convened a series of committee hearings to consider issues related to the degree of independence of the Federal Reserve. Appointment procedures for presidents of the 12 district Federal Reserve Banks and the secrecy surrounding meetings of the Federal Open Market Committee (FOMC) were among the items of special concern to Congressman Gonzales.

With regard to the meetings of the FOMC, Congressman Gonzales proposed that decisions be disclosed within a week and that detailed transcripts and videotapes of each meeting be released within 60 days. He argued that his proposals would promote individual accountability and that "accurate information does not undermine markets. Partial information and leaked information undermine market efficiency."[2] Alan Greenspan, chairman of the Board of Governors, and the other federal representatives who appeared before the committee argued that videotaping would hinder free debate as individuals, concerned that their remarks might be misinterpreted and "cause unnecessary volatility in financial markets," would self-censor what they said. "Unconventional policy prescriptions and ruminations about the longer-term outlook for economic and financial market developments might never be surfaced . . . for fear of igniting a speculative reaction when the discussion was disclosed." Chairman Greenspan went on to argue that premature disclosure "could inhibit or even thwart" the ability of the FOMC to implement decisions. He was especially concerned that immediate disclosure would compromise the ability of the FOMC to implement "contingent plans—that is, if a given economic or financial event occurs, a particular policy action would ensue."[3]

Currently the president of each district bank is appointed by the district bank's Board of Directors, subject to the approval of the Board of Governors in Washington, D.C. District bank presidents serve as voting members of the FOMC on a rotating basis. Critics of the Federal Reserve argue that, in view of their membership on the FOMC and the importance of monetary policy, district bank presidents should be selected or reviewed by elected officials rather than appointed bodies. Options might include appointment by the President and/or confirmation by the Senate. Again Chairman Greenspan spoke against these changes, arguing that the current system represents a deliberate choice by the Congress to isolate decisions about monetary policy from political pressures. He argued that the Federal Reserve is accountable to the Congress and the public through reporting requirements and the daily scrutiny of the business and financial press. However, he warned that "if accountability is achieved by putting the conduct of monetary policy under the close influence of politicians subject to short-term election-cycle pressures, the resulting policy would likely prove disappointing over time. . . . The public-private and regional makeup of the Federal Reserve was chosen by Congress, in preference to a unitary public central bank, only after long and careful debate. The system was designed to avoid an excessive concentration of authority in federal hands and to ensure responsiveness to local needs ."[4]

[2] "Greenspan Warns Against Easing Fed's Secrecy," *The New York Times*, October 20, 1992.
[3] Testimony by Alan Greenspan, Chairman, Board of Governors of the Federal Reserve System, before the Committee on Banking, Finance and Urban Affairs, U.S. House of Representatives, October 13, 1993.
[4] Ibid.

1. When and in how much detail should decisions and minutes of the FOMC be released? Is Greenspan right when he argues that the advance announcement of contingent plans limits their effectiveness?

2. Who should select district bank presidents? Should voting membership on the FOMC be restricted to members of the Board of Governors and exclude district bank presidents?

STUDY QUESTIONS

1. What is the difference between money and income?

2. How much independence do you think is desirable for the Fed? Why?

3. What are the major instruments of monetary policy? Use a demand and supply diagram to show how changes in each instrument affect the stock of money and interest rates.

4. Open market operations are the most used instrument of monetary policy. Reserve requirements are changed only infrequently and the changes in the discount rate tend to be passive rather than active. What do you think explains the heavy reliance on open market operations rather than other instruments of monetary policy?

5. Why do interest rates and bond prices move inversely to each other?

6. Why can't the Fed control the stock of money to the penny?

7. Why does the supply-of-money schedule have a positive slope while the demand-for-money schedule has a negative slope?

8. What are the links by which changes in monetary policy affect spending and thus output, employment, and prices? Use an expenditure diagram and an aggregate demand–aggregate supply diagram to illustrate your answer.

9. "Recognizing that an increase in prices increases the demand for money for transactions purposes helps to explain why the aggregate demand curve has a negative slope." What is the logic behind this statement?

ECONOMICS ONLINE

The latest minutes of the Federal Open Market Committee are available here.

woodrow.mpls.frb.fed.us/info/policy/index.html

In the spring of 1999 all 12 district Federal Reserve banks were on-line with their own Web pages:

Atlanta	www.frbatlanta.org
Boston	www.std.com/frbbos
Chicago	www.frbchi.org
Cleveland	www.clev.frb.org
Dallas	www.dallasfed.org
Kansas City	www.kc.frb.org
Minneapolis	woodrow.mpls.frb.fed.us
New York	www.ny.frb.org
Philadelphia	www.phil.frb.org
Richmond	www.rich.frb.org
St. Louis	www.stls.frb.org
San Fransisco	www.frbsf.org
Board of Governors	www.bog.frb.fed.us

THE DEBATE OVER
MONETARY POLICY

LEARNING OBJECTIVES

After completing this chapter, you should be able to:

■ compute velocity given data on nominal income and
the stock of money.

■ describe the determinants of velocity.

■ explain the difference between the quantity theory and
the equation of exchange.

■ describe why the equation of exchange is not a theory
of income determination and why monetarists' use of
the same equation turns it into a theory of income
determination.

■ explain how investment spending and interest rates
interact to help determine how monetary policy works
in a Keynesian model of income determination.

■ explain how expansionary fiscal policy and related
increases in the demand for money, interest rates, and
velocity interact to determine how fiscal policy works in
a monetarist model.

■ distinguish between lags affecting fiscal policy and
those affecting monetary policy.

■ explain why the Fed does not have precise control over both *M* and *r*.

■ explain how and why the slope of the aggregate supply curve helps to determine the effectiveness of stabilization policy.

■ explain how long lags might mean that efforts to stabilize the economy could end up destabilizing it.

■ summarize the views of advocates and opponents of activist stabilization policy by the government.

■ CHAPTER REVIEW

This is one of the most important and most difficult of the macroeconomic chapters. While not much new material is introduced, the chapter summarizes and synthesizes many of the concepts presented in preceding chapters concerning the theory of income determination as it discusses a number of issues that policymakers must confront.

Earlier chapters presented an essentially Keynesian model of income determination. The monetarist viewpoint is a modern manifestation of an even older tradition known as the quantity theory of money. The concept of velocity is perhaps the most important tool associated with this approach. Velocity is the average number of times per year that a dollar changes hands to accomplish transac-

(1)   tions associated with GDP. Velocity is measured as nominal _____ divided by the stock of _____. Alternative measures of money, for example, M_1 and M_2, give rise to alternative measures of velocity, V_1 and V_2.

Related to the concept of velocity is something called the equation of exchange, which is simply another way of defining and calculating velocity. The equation of exchange says:

(2)   Money × velocity = _____.

In symbols, it is: _____ × _____ = _____ × _____.

Statisticians and national income accountants measure the stock of money and nominal GDP. Economists then calculate velocity by dividing nominal GDP by the stock of money. As a result, the equation of exchange is always true.

The quantity theory asserts that there is a close link between changes in nominal GDP and changes

(3)   in the stock of _____. This link comes about because the quantity theory assumes that velocity (does/does not) change very much. If velocity is constant, then a change in the money stock translates directly into a change in _____ _____. If velocity is 5 and the money stock increases by $20 billion, then nominal GDP will rise by $ _____ billion.

An analysis of the determinants of velocity as well as the study of historical data, suggest that one (should/should not) expect velocity to be constant. Velocity reflects how much money people hold to   (4) make transactions, which in turn reflects such institutional factors as the frequency of paychecks and the efficiency of moving funds between checking accounts and other assets, such as savings accounts. In the previous chapter we saw that the amount of money people want to hold, and hence velocity, is also affected by the interest rate as a measure of the _____ _____ of holding money. For example, an increase in expected inflation is likely to (decrease/increase) nominal interest rates and _____ the amount of money people want to hold.

Monetarism, like the quantity theory, starts with the equation of exchange. But rather than assuming that velocity does not change, monetarists try to predict how velocity will change. From a monetarist perspective, determinants of nominal GDP are broken down into implications for the stock of money and implications for _____. After accounting for appropriate changes, simple   (5) multiplication can be used to predict nominal GDP.

At first glance it may appear that a Keynesian approach to income determination cannot analyze changes in monetary policy whereas a monetarist approach ignores fiscal policy. Such a conclusion would be oversimplified and misleading. In formal theory the two viewpoints are closer than is commonly recognized. Keynesian theory implies that monetary policy can have important impacts on aggregate demand through its impact on interest rates and investment spending. An expansionary change in monetary policy will lead to a(n) (decline/increase) in interest rates. The change in interest rates will (increase/decrease) investment   (6) spending. As we have seen, an increase in investment spending shifts both the expenditure schedule and the aggregate demand curve. Putting all the pieces together we can see that expansionary monetary policy will tend to (increase/decrease) GDP. Restrictive monetary policy would work in exactly the opposite way.

Monetarists are able to analyze the impact of changes in fiscal policy as follows: Expansionary fiscal policy will be associated with (higher/lower) interest rates. As a result, velocity will (increase/decrease)   (7) and a monetarist would forecast a (higher/lower) value for nominal GDP. Neither alone nor together are Keynesian and monetarist theories sufficient to determine output and prices as both are theories of the (demand/supply) side of the economy and ignore the _____ side.

The impact of changes in fiscal policy on interest rates is not only important to a monetarist analysis of changes in fiscal policy. It is also one of the reasons why the multiplier formula of $1/(1 - MPC)$

is oversimplified; increases in autonomous spending will tend to increase interest rates which in turn induce partially offsetting changes in investment spending.[1]

The choice between monetary and fiscal policy is often influenced by how quickly changes in policy can occur and how long it takes for changes, once made, to affect the behavior of firms and consumers. In general, lags in formulating policy are shorter for (fiscal/monetary) policy, whereas spending responses of firms and households are typically shorter for _____ policy.

(8)

A major controversy in monetary policy is whether, when formulating monetary policy decisions, the Federal Reserve should pay greater attention to the money supply or to the interest rates. Imagine, for instance, that the Fed is happy with the stock of money and the interest rate given in Figure 32-1. Suddenly the demand-for-money schedule shifts to the right because of an increase in the demand for

FIGURE 32-1

(9)

money from some factor other than interest rates. Draw in the new schedule. If the Fed did nothing, then, as a result of this shift in the demand for money, the stock of money would be (higher/lower) and the interest rate would be _____. To maintain the original money supply, M^*, the Fed should shift the supply-of-money schedule to the _____; to maintain the same rate of interest, the Fed should shift the supply curve to the _____. It should be obvious that the Fed cannot do both at the same time.

Decisions to stick to original monetary targets are likely to mean greater changes in interest rates, while decisions to stabilize interest rates will mean greater changes in the stock of money. The appropriate choice will depend upon the state of the economy and the source of the unexpected changes in interest rates and the stock of money.

Stabilization policy affects the economy primarily by shifting the aggregate demand curve. The final result, however, in terms of changes in output and prices, also depends upon the slope of the aggregate supply curve. A flat aggregate supply curve means that shifts in the aggregate demand curve

[1] Other factors that mean the formula $1/(1 - MPC)$ is oversimplified include the change in imports that normally accompany a change in GDP, the effect of higher prices on consumption spending, net exports, and the demand for money when a shift in the aggregate demand curve leads to a movement along the aggregate supply curve, and income taxes that reduce the change in disposable income for a given change in GDP. In later chapters we will also see how the impact of changes in the exchange rate affect the multiplier.

will have large effects on (<u>output/price</u>) with only a small change in _____. On the other   (10)

hand, shifts of the aggregate demand curve will have big effects on prices without much change in out-

put if the aggregate supply curve is (<u>steep/flat</u>). While some argue that the aggregate supply curve is

flat and others that it is steep, an emerging consensus sees the slope of the aggregate supply curve as

depending upon the period of analysis. The aggregate supply curve is likely to be flatter in the

(<u>long/short</u>) run and steeper in the _____ run.

Some economists favor an activist-oriented approach to stabilization policy with significant latitude

for discretionary policy. Others favor less activism and a greater reliance on rules. Beyond views about

the slope of the aggregate supply curve, these differences also reflect differing political philosophies

and judgments concerning the importance of such factors as the speed of the economy's self-

correcting mechanisms, the length of various policy lags, the stability of the multiplier and velocity,

and the accuracy of economic forecasting.

It takes time before someone notices that the economy is not operating as hoped for and before the

appropriate part of the government can decide what policy measures should be adopted. Once a par-

ticular policy is decided upon, there may not be much impact on output and prices until the buying

habits of households and firms adjust to the new policy.

Because of lags, policy changes today are likely to have their greatest impact in the future. For pol-

icy to be effective economists must be able to anticipate future events. The more accurate the eco-

nomic forecasts, the more demanding the standards we can set for stabilization policy. At the present

time economic forecasts (<u>are/are not</u>) good enough for fine-tuning the economy.   (11)

Active use of fiscal policy to correct persistent and sustained deviations from potential output calls

for changes in government spending or taxes. The flexibility to use changes in spending, taxes and

monetary policy means that activist policy (<u>does/does not</u>) imply that government spending must take   (12)

an ever larger proportion of the economic pie.

■ IMPORTANT TERMS AND CONCEPTS QUIZ

Choose the best definition for each of the following terms.

1. _____ Quantity theory of money

2. _____ Velocity

3. _____ Equation of exchange

4. _____ Monetarism

a. Variables that normally turn down prior to recessions and turn up prior to expansions

b. Mode of analysis that uses the equation of exchange to organize and analyze macro-economic data.

c. Average number of times a dollar is spent in a year.

d. Formula that states that nominal GDP equals the product of money stock and velocity.

e. Theory of aggregate demand stating that nominal GDP is proportional to the money stock.

■ BASIC EXERCISES

1. This exercise is designed to give you practice computing and using velocity. Table 32-1 contains historical data for nominal GDP, M_1 and M_2.
   a. Use this data to compute V_1, velocity based on M_1; and V_2, velocity based on M_2.
   b. Assume you are a monetarist working for the Federal Reserve and are asked to predict nominal GDP one year in advance. Even if you knew the money supply, M, you would still need an estimate of V. One way to estimate velocity is to use data from the previous year. The idea is that, since you can't know velocity for, say, 1998 until you know nominal GDP and M_1 or M_2 for 1998, you might use velocity for 1997 to predict GDP for 1998. Table 32-2 assumes

TABLE 32-1

	Nominal GDP ($ billions)	M_1 ($ billions)	M_2 ($ billions)	V1	V2
1985	4,180.7	587.01	2,422.19	_____	_____
1986	4,422.2	666.46	2,618.96	_____	_____
1997	4,692.2	743.74	2,788.67	_____	_____
1988	5,049.6	774.98	2,938.84	_____	_____
1989	5,438.7	782.46	3,062.24	_____	_____
1990	5,743.8	811.10	3,229.92	_____	_____
1991	5,916.7	859.60	3,349.34	_____	_____
1992	6,244.4	966.25	3,413.72	_____	_____
1993	6,558.1	1,078.77	3,452.43	_____	_____
1994	6,947.0	1,145.34	3,500.10	_____	_____
1995	7,269.6	1,142.82	3,572.38	_____	_____
1996	7,661.6	1,106.13	3,745.60	_____	_____
1997	8,110.9	1,069.57	3,931.52	_____	_____
1998	8,511.0	1,079.45	4,222.02	_____	_____

SOURCE: GDP: *Economic Report of the President*, 1999, Tables B-1; M1 and M2: www.stls.frb.org/fred/data/monetary (April 25, 1999)

TABLE 32-2

	Actual M$_1$ ($ billions)	V$_1$ from Previous Year	Estimated Income ($ billions)	Actual Income ($ billions)	Estimated Income ($ billions)	V$_2$ from Previous Year	Actual M$_2$ ($ billions)
1986	666.46	_____	_____	4,422.2	_____	_____	2,618.96
1987	743.74	_____	_____	4,692.2	_____	_____	2,788.67
1988	774.98	_____	_____	5,049.6	_____	_____	2,938.84
1989	782.46	_____	_____	5,438.7	_____	_____	3,062.24
1990	811.10	_____	_____	5,743.8	_____	_____	3,229.92
1991	859.60	_____	_____	5,916.7	_____	_____	3,349.34
1992	966.25	_____	_____	6,244.4	_____	_____	3,413.72
1993	1,078.77	_____	_____	6,558.1	_____	_____	3,452.43
1994	1,145.34	_____	_____	6,947.0	_____	_____	3,500.10
1995	1,142.82	_____	_____	7,269.6	_____	_____	3,572.38
1996	1,106.13	_____	_____	7,661.6	_____	_____	3,745.60
1997	1,069.57	_____	_____	8,110.9	_____	_____	3,931.52
1998	1,079.45	_____	_____	8,511.0	_____	_____	4,222.02

that the Federal Reserve can control the money supply exactly. Use your numbers for velocity from the previous year to fill in the blank columns in Table 32-2 to predict income.

c. Which years show the largest prediction errors? Why?

2. For this exercise you are asked to assume the role of adviser to the Federal Reserve's Open Market Committee. Figure 32-2 uses the demand and supply for money to show the actual stock of money and the rate of interest when the committee last met. Assume that the economy was then at full employment with price stability. The next meeting of the Open Market Committee begins with a report detailing the unexpected increase in the stock of money and interest rates since the last meeting. What to do is not so obvious, however, as suggested by the following arguments offered by two different members of the committee:

Demand and Supply: Money

FIGURE 32-2

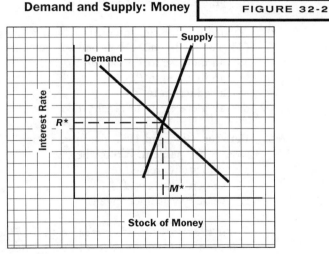

A: This report confirms my fear that aggregate demand is expanding too rapidly. We risk unnecessary inflation and should move to reduce aggregate demand by an appropriate change in monetary policy.

B: This report confirms my concern that there has been an increase in the demand for money that is unrelated to GDP. Businesses and individuals have been harmed buying esoteric and risky financial securities. As a result of these losses there has been a general increase in the demand for money. If we do not take appropriate action the increase in interest rates since our last meeting will reduce aggregate demand and threaten recession.

You are asked to use Figure 32-2 to illustrate what each speaker is arguing and what actions each are suggesting. For each speaker try to determine what curve has shifted and how. Each is arguing for a particular policy to shift the supply-of-money schedule. What is that shift and how is it consistent with each speaker's analysis? What is likely to happen if the Fed implements A's desired policy when B's analysis is correct? What is likely to happen if the Fed implements B's desired policy when A's analysis is correct?

■   **SELF-TESTS FOR UNDERSTANDING**

TEST A

Circle the most appropriate answer.

1. Velocity is measured by
    a. dividing the money stock by nominal GDP.
    b. computing the percentage change in nominal GDP from year to year.
    c. dividing nominal GDP by the stock of money.
    d. subtracting the rate of inflation from nominal interest rates.

2. The equation of exchange says that
    a. for every buyer there is a seller.
    b. $M \times V$ = nominal GDP.
    c. demand equals supply.
    d. P. T. Barnum was right when he said, "There is a sucker born every minute."

3. According to the equation of exchange, an increase in M may lead to
    (There may be more than one correct answer.)
    a. an increase in Y (real GDP).
    b. an increase in P.
    c. a reduction in V.
    d. an increase in nominal GDP.

4. According to the quantity theory, an increase in M will lead to _____.
    (There may be more than one correct answer.)
    a. an increase in Y (real GDP).
    b. an increase in P.
    c. a reduction in V.
    d. an increase in nominal GDP.

5. Between 1996 and 1997 the money supply (M_1) decreased by 3.3 percent and yet nominal GDP rose by 5.8 percent. It must be that
    a. velocity increased.
    b. velocity decreased.
    c. velocity was unchanged.

6. From 1985 to 1986 M_1 increased by 14.7 percent and V_1 declined from 6.89 to 6.35. It must be that nominal GDP increased by _____ percent.
    a. less than 14.7.
    b. exactly 14.7.
    c. more than 14.7.

7. The historical record shows
    a. that both V_1 and V_2 have been stable.
    b. continual decrease in V_2.
    c. continual increases in V_1.
    d. that V_2 has shown less variation than V_1.

8. Initially the stock of money is $600 billion and velocity is 5. If one can be sure that velocity will not change, what increase in M will be required to increase real GDP by $100 billion?
    a. $5 billion.
    b. $20 billion.
    c. $100 billion.
    d. insufficient information.

9. Which of the following developments is *not* likely to lead to an increase in velocity?
   a. An increase in the expected rate of inflation.
   b. A reduction in the required reserve ratio for banks.
   c. An increase in interest rates as a result of an expansionary change in fiscal policy.
   d. A widespread trend toward more frequent pay periods.

10. If expansionary fiscal policy increases interest rates, a monetarist would expect that nominal GDP would _____ even if there is no change in the stock of money.
    a. decrease
    b. be unaffected
    c. increase

11. Which of the following is not likely to increase nominal GDP according to a monetarist analysis of income determination?
    a. An open market purchase that increases the stock of money.
    b. An increase in government spending.
    c. A technological change in banking practices that increases velocity.
    d. An increase in income taxes.

12. Keynesian analysis argues that the change in interest rates that accompanies an open market purchase is likely to
    a. increase velocity.
    b. have no effect on velocity.
    c. reduce velocity.

13. Which of the following make the value of the multiplier less than $1/(1 - MPC)$?
    (There may be more than one correct answer.)
    a. The increase in interest rates that accompanies an increase in nominal GDP when the supply-of-money curve is constant.
    b. Income taxes.
    c. An increase in imports that normally accompanies an increase in GDP.
    d. Higher prices that reduce the purchasing power of money fixed assets and reduce net exports.

14. Which of the following is an example of a lag in policymaking as opposed to a lag in spending by firms and households?
    a. The construction of a new plant, induced by lower interest rates, cannot start for nine months, because it takes that long to prepare architectural drawings and contractors' bids.
    b. Congress takes five months to consider a presidential tax proposal.
    c. Through multiplier impacts, a $3 billion increase in defense spending eventually raises GDP by $5 billion.
    d. Refrigerator sales rise in the month following receipt of a $300 tax rebate.

15. Policy lags are probably shorter for _____ policy. Expenditure lags are probably shorter for _____ policy.
    a. fiscal; monetary
    b. monetary; fiscal
    c. fiscal; fiscal
    d. monetary; monetary

16. Assume that the stock of money and interest rates are both at levels desired by the Federal Reserve. Following a shift in the demand for money, the Fed can control _____.
    (There may be more than one correct answer.)
    a. M but not r.
    b. r but not M.
    c. both M and r.
    d. neither M nor r.

17. Stabilization policy will be effective in combating recession if the aggregate supply curve is _____ and effective in combating inflation if the aggregate supply curve is _____.
    a. flat; steep
    b. steep; flat
    c. flat; flat
    d. steep; steep

18. If the aggregate supply curve is relatively flat, then
    a. velocity will be constant.
    b. both monetary and fiscal policy will have relatively large effects on output without much effect on prices.
    c. a change in interest rates will have little impact on investment.
    d. monetary policy will be effective while fiscal policy will not.

19. The Federal Reserve cannot control both r and M because its policy actions affect
    a. the demand for money curve but not the supply of money curve.
    b. events in the short run but not the long run.
    c. investment spending but not consumption spending.
    d. the supply of money curve but not the demand for money curve.

20. Active stabilization policy
    a. must increase the size of government.
    b. will only be successful if the size of government declines.
    c. need not imply any tendency toward big government.
    d. will only mean larger and larger government deficits.

TEST B

Circle T or F for true or false.

T F 1. If the stock of money is $1 trillion and nominal GDP is $7 trillion, then velocity is 7.

T F 2. The quantity theory is not really a theory because velocity, by definition, is equal to the ratio of nominal GDP divided by the money stock.

T F 3. Monetarist and Keynesian theories are both incomplete in that they concentrate on demand and ignore the supply side of the economy.

T F 4. Expansionary monetary policy that increases the stock of money will only increase prices with no impact on real output.

T F 5. The lag between a change in fiscal policy and its effects on aggregate demand is probably shorter than the lag between a change in monetary policy and its effects on aggregate demand.

T F 6. The lag in adopting an appropriate policy is probably shorter for monetary policy than for fiscal policy.

T F 7. By simultaneously using open market operations and making changes in minimum reserve requirements, the Fed would be able to achieve any desired combination of the money stock and the interest rate.

T F 8. The shape of the aggregate supply curve is likely to be relatively flat in the short run and steeper in the long run.

T   F   9. If the aggregate supply curve is steep, then changes in fiscal and monetary policy will have major impacts on prices with little impact on output.

T   F   10. Long lags will help make for better stabilization policy because there is more time for a complete analysis of possible actions.

SUPPLEMENTARY EXERCISE ■

LEADING INDICATORS

Is the stock market a good leading indicator of overall economic conditions? Figure 32-3 shows stock prices over the postwar period. Using just Figure 32-3, make an estimate of how many recessions there have been since 1950. Try to date each one approximately. The National Bureau of Economic Research is the organization the dates business cycles. Check their web site www.nber.org to see how your business cycles compare with theirs. How many recessions does the NBER identify? How many did you identify? How many false indications of recession were there? What about the forecasting record of other leading indicators? What are the stock market and other leading indicators saying about a possible recession in the next 6 to 12 months?

In addition to the problem of false turning points, there are two other limitations to a purely mechanical use of leading indicators that you should be aware of:

a.   Most large declines in a leading indicator are the result of not one large decline, but rather a series of consecutive small declines. At the same time each series has so many ups and downs that most small declines are followed by a small increase. One needs some way of separating those small declines that signal the start of a major slump from those that are quickly reversed.

b.   A leading indicator that always changes direction a fixed amount of time before the economy does would be extremely useful. However, the length of time between movements in most leading indicators and the economy is quite variable.

Is the Stock Market a Good Leading Indicator?   **FIGURE 32-3**

ECONOMICS IN ACTION

WHAT TO DO?

What indicators should the Federal Reserve use when formulating monetary policy? General agreement exists that monetary policy should contribute to broad macroeconomic objectives—price stability, full employment, economic growth—although some would argue that greater weight should be placed on particular objectives, e.g., price stability or full employment. However, the Fed does not control the rate of inflation or the rate of unemployment. For that matter it does not even control interest rates or any measure of money precisely. It has strong influence over these latter variables, which in turn are important for things like GDP, employment, and prices. But strong influence is not precise control. A related problem is that observations on different macroeconomic variables are available at different times. Estimates of GDP come only every three months. Unemployment and inflation are measured monthly. Data on M_1 and M_2 are announced every week while interest rates are available at a moment's notice.

At times the Fed has put more emphasis on interest rates and at others on M_1, M_2, or bank reserves as indicators of monetary policy. The Humphrey-Hawkins Act requires that the Fed announce ranges it expects for the growth of money. When testifying before Congress in July of 1993, and reporting on growth ranges expected for 1994, Alan Greenspan, chairman of the Board of Governors of the Federal Reserve System, urged caution in interpreting the announced ranges.

> The historical relationships between money and income, and between money and the price level, have largely broken down, depriving the aggregates of much of their usefulness as guides to policy. At least for the time being, M_2 has been downgraded as a reliable indicator of financial conditions in the economy, and no single variable has yet been identified to take its place. . . . In the meantime, the process of probing a variety of data to ascertain underlying economic and financial conditions has become even more essential to formulating sound monetary policy. . . . In these circumstances it is especially prudent to focus on longer-term policy guides. One important guidepost is real interest rates, which have a key bearing on longer-run spending decisions and inflation prospects.

Greenspan emphasized what he called the equilibrium real rate of interest:

> . . . specifically the real rate level that, if maintained, would keep the economy at its production potential over time. . . . Real rates, of course, are not directly observable, but must be inferred from nominal interest rates and estimates of inflation expectations. The most important real rates for private spending decisions almost surely are the longer maturities. Moreover, the equilibrium rate structure responds to the ebb and flow of underlying forces affecting spending.

Greenspan concluded:

> While the guides we have for policy may have changed recently, our goals have not. As I have indicated many times to this Committee, the Federal Reserve seeks to foster maximum sustainable economic growth and rising standards of living. And in that endeavor, the most productive function the central bank can perform is to achieve and maintain price stability.

1. What indicators of monetary policy would you favor if you were a member of the Federal Open Market Committee?

2. When is it appropriate to emphasize measures of the stock of money and when is it appropriate to emphasize interest rates?

3. While one can observe nominal interest rates, how does one measure the equilibrium real rate of interest in a way that makes it operational for the conduct of monetary policy?

SOURCE: Testimony by Alan Greenspan, Chairman of the Board of Governors of the Federal Reserve System, before the Subcommittee on Economic Growth and Credit Formation of the Committee on Banking, Finance, and Urban Affairs, U.S. House of Representatives, July 20, 1993.

STUDY QUESTIONS ■

1. What is the difference between the equation of exchange, the quantity theory, and monetarism?

2. What do you think explains the different historical experience of V_1 and V_2?

3. How would a monetarist explain the impact of expansionary fiscal policy on GDP and prices?

4. Why can't one use monetarism to determine nominal GDP, Keynesian analysis to determine real GDP, and then compute the price level by dividing the one by the other?

5. What is the difference between policy lags and expenditure lags? Which are likely to be more important for fiscal policy? For monetary policy?

6. What's wrong with the following? "Long lags make for better policy as they provide more time for determining the best policy."

7. Why can't the Fed control both M and r?

8. Do you think monetary policy should focus on stabilizing interest rates or stabilizing the growth in the stock of money? Why?

9. Why are concerns about excessive levels of government spending not a legitimate reason to oppose active stabilization policy?

10. Do you favor a more or less activist stabilization policy? Why?

ECONOMICS ONLINE ■

The Fed's latest release on interest rates and the money supply can be found here.

www.bog.frb.fed.us/releases/

The Chicago and St. Louis Federal Reserve Banks offer electronic access to lots of historical monetary data. Their Web addresses are listed at the end of the previous chapter.

Professor Ted Bos, University of Alabama, Birmingham, has made much of this data available on his web site. You can use his web site to design your own graphs of this data.

www.economagic.com

BUDGET DEFICITS, MONETARY POLICY AND GROWTH

LEARNING OBJECTIVES

After completing this chapter, you should be able to:

■ explain how measures to balance the budget may unbalance the economy.

■ explain how appropriate fiscal policy depends on the strength of private demand and the conduct of monetary policy.

■ explain the difference between the government's budget deficit and the national debt.

■ discuss some facts about budget deficits and the national debt: When have budget deficits been largest? What has happened to the national debt as a proportion of GDP?

■ describe how the concept of structural deficits or surpluses differs from officially reported deficits or surpluses.

■ describe how traditional accounting procedures will overstate the interest component of government expenditures during a period of inflation.

■ distinguish between real and fallacious arguments about the burden of the national debt.

- describe the inflationary consequences of a budget deficit and explain why deficits will be more inflationary if they are monetized.

- evaluate arguments supporting the crowding-out and crowding-in properties of government deficit spending.

- explain how increased deficits can be associated with either higher or lower interest rates, higher or lower rates of inflation, and faster or slower growth in real output.

- explain the long run implications of changing the mix of monetary and fiscal policy while leaving GDP and prices unchanged.

- explain why most economists measure the true burden of deficits by their impact on the capital stock.

■ CHAPTER REVIEW

From 1980 to 1997 the federal government's budget deficits have been very much like the weather: everyone has been talking about them but no one seems able to do anything about them. In 1998 discussion shifted to the implications of budget surplus and now everyone had their own ideas of what should be done. By itself this chapter cannot make government deficits larger or smaller, but it can help to increase your understanding of the impacts of both government deficits and the national debt.

(1)   The government runs a deficit when its (spending/revenue) exceeds its _____. There is a surplus when _____ is greater than _____. The national debt measures the government's total indebtedness. The national debt will increase if the government budget shows a (deficit/surplus). The national debt will decrease if the government budget shows a _____.

What is appropriate deficit policy? Earlier chapters discussed the use of fiscal and monetary policy to strike an appropriate balance between aggregate demand and aggregate supply in order to choose between inflation and unemployment. Considerations of balanced budgets, per se, were absent from that discussion. The conclusion that budget policy should adapt to the requirements of the economy is shared by many economists. Note that this conclusion implies that appropriate fiscal policy depends upon the stance of monetary policy.

Some have advocated a policy of strict budget balance. There is good reason to expect that such a policy would balance the budget at the cost of unbalancing the economy. Consider an economy in an initial equilibrium at full employment with a balanced budget. An autonomous decline in private

(2)   spending would shift the expenditure schedule (down/up), resulting in a shift of the aggregate demand

schedule to the (right/left). In the absence of any further policy action the result would be a (decline/increase) in GDP. The change in GDP will also mean a(n) (decline/increase) in tax revenues. The government's budget will move from its initial position of balance to one of (deficit/surplus). At this point, deliberate policy actions to reestablish budget balance would call for either a(n) (decrease/increase) in taxes or a(n) (decrease/increase) in government spending. In either case the result would be an additional shift in the expenditure schedule and aggregate demand curve that would (accentuate/counteract) the original shift that was due to the autonomous decline in private spending.

The fact that tax revenues depend on the state of the economy is important to understanding many complicated issues about the impact of deficits. As seen above, it helps to explain why a policy of budget balancing can unbalance the economy in the face of changes in private spending. It helps to explain why deficits can sometimes be associated with a booming economy and at other times with a sagging economy. It also helps to explain interest in alternative measures of the deficit. The concept of structural deficits, or structural surpluses, is an attempt to control for the effects of the economy on the deficit. It does so by looking at spending and revenues at a specified high-employment level of income. Changes in tax revenues due to changes in GDP (will/will not) affect the actual deficit but (will/will not) affect the structural deficit. For this reason, many analysts prefer to use the structural deficit as a measure of the stance of fiscal policy.

(3)

Inflation, and especially the impact of inflation on interest rates, raises complicated measurement problems. As we learned earlier, during periods of inflation, increases in nominal interest rates that reflect expectations of future inflation may not imply any change in real interest rates. To the extent that nominal interest rates include such inflationary premiums, a portion of interest payments is not payment for the use of the purchasing power embodied in the original loan; rather it is a repayment of the purchasing power of the original loan balance itself. Careful inflation accounting adjusts nominal interest payments for their inflationary component.

Are deficits inflationary? The short answer is yes and the more complete answer asks for more details. If the alternative to any deficit is more taxation or less spending, then any deficit, whether the result of deliberate policy or of a reduction in autonomous spending, will mean a higher price level, a higher level of output, and less unemployment than the alternative of a balanced budget. Note that a deficit that arises when the economy slips into recession due to a decline in private spending is likely to be correlated with a reduction, not an increase, in interest rates and the rate of inflation.[1] An increase

(4)   in the structural deficit—that is, a deliberate (<u>increase/reduction</u>) in spending or _____ in taxes—would shift the aggregate demand curve to the right and increase both interest rates and prices. Exactly how much inflation would occur will depend upon the slope of the aggregate supply curve, whether the economy is close to or far away from full employment, and whether there is a simultaneous change in monetary policy that offsets the increase in the structural deficit.

A deficit that is associated with a deliberate reduction in taxes or increase in spending will increase output, prices, and interest rates as it shifts the aggregate demand curve to the right. Concerns about the impact of the deficit on interest rates may lead the Federal Reserve to increase the money supply. If the Federal Reserve acts to increase the stock of money by buying government securities, one says

(5)   it has _____ the deficit. Expansion of the money supply would imply a further expansionary shift in the aggregate demand curve and would mean even higher prices. Thus monetization of the deficit could lead to (<u>greater/less</u>) inflation. While a problem in some countries, monetization of the deficit has not been a problem in the United States.

Many feelings about the burden of the national debt may be as deeply ingrained and just as irrational as a Victorian's ideas about sex or a football coach's ideas about winning. Many fallacious arguments about the burden of the debt do, however, contain some elements of truth. Arguments about the burden of future interest payments or the cost of repaying the national debt are not relevant when considering debts held by domestic citizens but are relevant when considering debts held by

(6)   _____. To the extent that debt is held by domestic citizens, interest payments and debt repayments impose little burden on the nation as a whole; they are only transfers from taxpayers to bondholders, who may even be the same individuals. However, the impact on incentives from higher taxes to accomplish these transfers should not be ignored.

A real burden of the debt would arise from a deficit in a high-employment economy that crowded

(7)   out private (<u>consumption/investment</u>) spending and left a smaller capital stock to future generations. There will continue to be arguments as to whether U.S. deficits have entailed such a burden. Until 1980, the federal government's deficit had shown its largest increases during periods of _____

---

[1]This deficit arises as the aggregate demand curve shifts to the left. It is inflationary only in the sense that a move to balance the budget would mean a further shift of the aggregate demand curve to the left and a larger reduction in the rate of inflation.

and _____. Government deficits during periods of slack may actually result in a benefit rather than a burden if, as a result of increased demand, they lead to (<u>crowding-in/crowding-out</u>) rather than _____ _____. Major concerns about deficits during the late 1980s were that they occurred during a period of (<u>high/low</u>) employment and that they were thus likely to have led to crowding-_____.

Changes in the mix of fiscal and monetary policy may leave real GDP and the price level unaffected but there will be important effects on the budget deficit, the composition of output and economic growth. Consider an economy at full employment with a government budget that is in balance. A reduction in tax rates would shift the aggregate demand curve to the (<u>right/left</u>). The impact on aggregate demand could be offset by a move to (<u>restrictive/expansionary</u>) monetary policy. The net result would be no change in the aggregate demand curve and hence no change in real GDP or the price level. But that is not the end of the story. The reduction in tax rates will mean that the government is now running a (<u>deficit/surplus</u>). This change in the government budget together with the change in monetary policy will mean (<u>higher/lower</u>) interest rates and a _____ level of investment spending. Because of the change in investment spending, over time this economy is likely to grow (<u>faster/more slowly</u>).

(8)

IMPORTANT TERMS AND CONCEPTS QUIZ ■

Choose the best definition for each of the following terms.

1. _____ Budget deficit
2. _____ Budget surplus
3. _____ National debt
4. _____ Structural budget
5. _____ Inflation accounting
6. _____ Monetization of deficits
7. _____ Crowding-out
8. _____ Crowding-in

a. Amount by which governmental revenue exceeds spending.

b. Ratio of government debt to GDP.

c. State of budget under current fiscal policy if the economy was at full employment.

d. Amount by which government spending exceeds revenue.

e. Increase in private investment spending induced by increase in government spending.

f. Adjusting standard accounting procedures for changes in purchasing power.

g. Contraction of private investment spending induced by deficit spending.

h. Federal government's total indebtedness.

i. Purchases of government bonds by central bank to finance deficit.

■ BASIC EXERCISES

1. This exercise is designed to show how a rigid policy of balanced budgets may unbalance the economy. To simplify the calculations, the exercise assumes that prices do not change and thus focuses on the horizontal shift in the aggregate demand curve.

TABLE 33-1

Constant Prices

Income (Output) Y	Taxes T	Disposable Income DI	Consumption Spending C	Investment Spending I	Government Purchases G	Exports X	Imports IM	Total Spending C + I + G + (X − IM)
6,000	800.0	5,200.0	4,500	900	950	500	600	_____
6,250	862.5	5,387.5	4,650	900	950	500	625	_____
6,500	925.0	5,575.0	4,800	900	950	500	650	_____
6,750	987.5	5,762.5	4,950	900	950	500	675	_____
7,000	1,050.0	5,950.0	5,100	900	950	500	700	_____

a. Fill in the last column of Table 33-1 to determine the initial equilibrium level of income. The equilibrium level of income is $_____.

b. What is the deficit at the initial equilibrium level of income? _____

c. The high-employment level of income is $6,750. Is the structural budget in surplus or deficit? _____ What is the magnitude of the structural deficit/surplus? _____

d. Investment spending now declines by $125 billion. Use Table 33-2 to compute the new equilibrium level of income. What is the new equilibrium level of income? _____
How has the deficit changed, if at all? (increased/decreased) by _____
How has the structural deficit changed, if at all? (increased/decreased) by _____

e. If the government is committed to a balanced budget, would it raise or lower taxes to restore a balanced budget? _____ What would this change in taxes do to the equilibrium level of national income?

f. If the government decides to change government purchases to eliminate the deficit, would it raise or lower spending? _____ What would this change do to the equilibrium level of national income?

g. (Optional) How large a lump-sum change in taxes, that is, the same change at every level of income, would balance the budget? $_____ billion. The new equilibrium level of income would be $_____ billion.

h. (Optional) How large a change in government spending would balance the budget? $_____ billion. The new equilibrium level of income would be $_____ billion.

TABLE 33-2

Constant Prices

Income (Output) Y	Taxes T	Disposable Income DI	Consumption Spending C	Investment Spending I	Government Purchases G	Exports X	Imports IM	Total Spending C + I + G + (X − IM)
6,000	800.0	5,200.0	4,500	775	950	500	600	_____
6,250	862.5	5,387.5	4,650	775	950	500	625	_____
6,500	925.0	5,575.0	4,800	775	950	500	650	_____
6,750	987.5	5,762.5	4,950	775	950	500	675	_____
7,000	1,050.0	5,950.0	5,100	775	950	500	700	_____

2. This problem is meant to illustrate how the effects of changes in fiscal policy depend upon what happens to monetary policy. The solid lines in Figure 33-1 show an economy in an initial position of equilibrium at full employment with a balanced budget, low interest rates, and no trade deficit, i.e., exports equal imports. The dashed line shows the same economy following an increase in government spending. Assume the increase in G is equal to $100 billion.

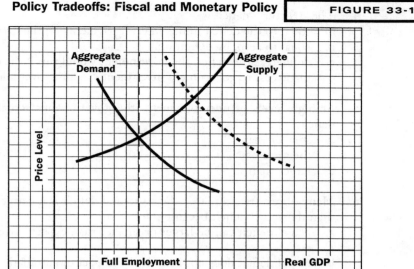

Policy Tradeoffs: Fiscal and Monetary Policy | **FIGURE 33-1**

   a. What is the increase in the structural deficit?

   b. If the only change is the increase in G, will the increase in the actual deficit be less than, equal to, or greater than the increase in the structural deficit? Why?
   c. Assume the monetary authority wants to avoid the inflation that would be associated with the increase in the structural deficit. Should the monetary authority engage in an open market purchase or sale? Why?
   d. Assume the monetary authority is successful in offsetting the expansionary impact of the increase in the structural deficit. That is, open market operations are successful in shifting the aggregate demand curve back to its initial position. Initially the economy was at full employment with no inflation, a balanced budget, low interest rates, and no trade deficit. Call this outcome Option A. Now the economy is again at full employment with no inflation, but with a structural deficit and high interest rates. Call this outcome Option B. What difference does it make whether the economy is at full employment under Option A or Option B?

SELF-TESTS FOR UNDERSTANDING ■

TEST A

Circle the most appropriate answer.

1. The federal government deficit is
   a. the excess of tax revenues over transfer payments.
   b. another term for political gridlock.
   c. total indebtedness of the government.
   d. the difference between government spending and the government's revenue for a given year.

2. The federal government runs a surplus when
   a. spending is greater than tax receipts.
   b. interest payments on the national debt are less than 5 percent.
   c. social security payments are balanced by social security taxes.
   d. revenues exceed spending.

3. The national debt is
   a. equal to the cumulation of past federal government deficits.
   b. another term for the federal government's deficit.
   c. what the U.S. government and private businesses owe foreigners.
   d. the excess of spending over revenue for a given year.

4. The structural deficit is
   a. equal to the deficit minus interest payments on the national debt.
   b. equal to zero, by definition.
   c. defined as the deficit the government would run if the economy were at full employment.
   d. the excess of government investment spending over allocations for these projects.

5. At high levels of unemployment, the government's actual deficit will be _____ the structural deficit.
   a. smaller than
   b. the same as
   c. larger than

6. Many observers argue that the structural deficit is a better measure of the stance of fiscal policy than the actual deficit because the
   a. actual deficit can be larger or smaller than expected if GDP is smaller or larger than expected.
   b. actual deficit does not include the impact of automatic stabilizers.
   c. structural deficit is based on real rather than nominal interest rates.
   d. structural deficit represents what the president proposes rather than what is enacted by Congress.

7. Until the 1980s, large government deficits were associated with periods of _____. (There may be more than one correct answer.)
   a. high inflation.
   b. war.
   c. recession.
   d. low unemployment.

8. In 1998 the federal government's budget was
   a. in deficit.
   b. in surplus.
   c. smaller than in 1983.
   d. in the red.

9. A decline in private investment spending will lead to all but which one of the following?
   a. A downward shift in the expenditure schedule.
   b. A decline in the equilibrium level of GDP.
   c. An increase in the government deficit or a reduction in the surplus.
   d. A decline in the structural budget deficit or surplus.

10. Rigid adherence to budget balancing will
    a. help the economy adjust to shifts in private spending.
    b. have little impact on business cycles.
    c. accentuate swings in GDP from autonomous changes in private spending.
    d. help maintain full employment.

11. If the Federal Reserve monetizes a budget deficit, there will be a(n)
    a. smaller inflationary impact.
    b. unchanged inflationary impact.
    c. larger inflationary impact.

12. The inflationary consequences of a budget deficit are likely to be greatest when
    a. the deficit is the result of a decline in private spending.
    b. the Fed conducts monetary policy to offset the impact of the deficit.
    c. the aggregate supply curve is flat.
    d. there is an increase in the structural deficit at a time of full employment.

13. Using real interest rates when measuring the deficit during a period of inflation would have what impact?
    a. It would make the deficit smaller.
    b. It would leave the deficit unchanged.
    c. It would make the deficit larger.

14. An increase in the deficit is likely to be correlated with which of the following? (There may be more than one correct answer.)
    a. Faster growth in GDP.
    b. Lower interest rates.
    c. A reduction in the rate of inflation.
    d. Higher interest rates.
    e. Greater inflation.
    f. A slowing of the rate of growth of GDP.

15. The macroeconomic impact of a reduction in government spending to reduce the deficit could be offset by
    a. an equal increase in taxes.
    b. an open market purchase.
    c. an equal reduction in taxes.
    d. an open market sale.

16. A deficit that follows a decline in private spending is likely to be associated with which of the following?
    a. Higher inflation.
    b. Lower interest rates.
    c. A reduction in unemployment.
    d. A reduction in the national debt.

17. Which of the following is a valid argument about the burden of the national debt for an economy whose debt is held entirely by its own citizens?
    a. Future generations will find interest payments a heavy burden.
    b. When the debt is due, future generations will be burdened with an enormous repayment.
    c. The debt will bankrupt future generations.
    d. If the deficits causing the debt reduced private investment spending, then future generations would be left with a smaller capital stock.

18. "Crowding-out" refers to
    a. increased population pressures and arguments for zero population growth.
    b. the effects of government deficits on private investment spending.
    c. what happens at the start of the New York City marathon.
    d. the impact of higher prices on the multiplier.

19. Crowding-out is likely to occur if _____. (There may be more than one correct answer.)
    a. the amount of private savings is unchanged.
    b. the economy is operating near full employment.
    c. the rate of unemployment is high.
    d. the aggregate supply curve is flat.

20. Crowding-in is more likely to occur when
    a. the economy is operating near full employment.
    b. prices are rising.
    c. the government lowers expenditures.
    d. there is substantial slack in the economy.

TEST B

Circle T or F for true or false.

T   F   1. A policy calling for continuous balance in the government's budget will help offset shifts in autonomous private demand.

T   F   2. A balanced high-employment budget is necessary if the equilibrium level of GDP is to equal the full-employment level of GDP.

T   F   3. Inflation accounting would increase the interest portion of government expenditures during periods of inflation.

T   F   4. Increases in the government's deficit are always associated with increases in interest rates.

T   F   5. The inflationary impact of any budget deficit depends on the conduct of monetary policy.

T   F   6. Government deficits between 1980 and 1997 mean that the ratio of national debt to GDP has never been higher than it is today.

T   F   7. Interest payments on the national debt, whether to domestic citizens or foreigners, are not really a burden on future generations.

T   F   8. A major limitation of the simple crowding-out argument is the assumption that the economy's total pool of savings is fixed.

T   F   9. Crowding-in is likely to occur when the economy is operating with slack employment, whereas crowding-out is likely to occur at full employment.

T   F   10. Government deficits may impose a real burden on future generations if, as a result of crowding-out, there is less private investment and a smaller capital stock in the future.

■   SUPPLEMENTARY EXERCISES

1. **Government Deficits and Interest Rates**

Between 1957 and 1958, the federal government's budget shifted from a surplus of $2.3 billion to a deficit of $10.3 billion. This was the largest deficit since World War II and in dollar terms was bigger than any deficit during the Great Depression. At the same time, interest rates declined. The rate on three-month Treasury bills declined from an average of 3.267 percent in 1957 to 1.839 percent in 1958. The rate on three- to five-year securities fell from 3.62 percent to 2.90 percent.

Between 1974 and 1975, the federal government's budget deficit increased from $11.6 billion to $69.4 billion. Interest rates again declined. The rate on three-month Treasury bills declined from 7.886 percent to 5.838 percent, while the rate on three- to five-year securities declined more modestly from 7.81 percent to 7.55 percent.

Between 1981 and 1982 the federal government deficit increased dramatically from $58.8 billion to $135.5 billion. Again, interest rates declined. The rate on three-month Treasury bills declined from 14.029 percent to 10.686 percent. Interest rates on longer term government securities also declined.

Between 1991 and 1992 the federal government's deficit went from $210.4 billion to $298 billion, the largest year-to-year increase to date. Interest rates on long-term government bonds declined from 7.86 percent to 7.01 percent while rates on short-term government borrowing declined almost two percentage points from 5.42 percent to 3.45 percent.

How do you explain the seemingly contradictory results that larger deficits are associated with lower, not higher, interest rates? Do these observations prove that larger deficits will always be associated with lower interest rates?

2. **Repudiate the National Debt?**

If the national debt is so onerous, we could solve the problem by simply repudiating the debt; that is, we would make no more interest or principal payments on the outstanding debt.

Imagine that in keeping with democratic principles such a proposition were put to American voters. Who do you think would vote pro and who would vote con? Which side would win? Would the outcome of the vote be different if the debt were held entirely by foreigners? By banks and other financial institutions? (The Treasury publishes data on who holds the national debt in the *Treasury Bulletin*. This data is also published in the annual *Economic Report of the President*. You might want to look at these data and consider what would happen to depositors, shareholders, and pensioners, both current and prospective, if the national debt held by banks, corporations, and pension funds was suddenly worthless.)

Repudiating the national debt might well limit future budget flexibility. What would be the likely consequences during periods of future recession? Inflation? War?

ECONOMICS IN ACTION ■

WHAT TO DO ABOUT SOCIAL SECURITY

There has been great concern about the long term viability of Social Security in the United States. For over 40 years, Social Security taxed workers to pay retirement benefits to eligible retirees. This system worked fine as long as there was a large number of workers relative to the number of retirees. As the ratio of retirees to workers increases, this pay-as-you-go strategy is increasingly less viable. In the mid-1980s, there was a significant increase in Social Security tax rates in order to build up a surplus in the Social Security trust funds that could be used to sustain benefits as the number of retirees continued to grow relative to the number of workers during the early parts of the twenty-first century.

In 1999 it was estimated that the Social Security trust funds would continue to increase until 2022 at which point Social Security taxes and interest on the trust fund balances would begin to fall short of outlays. According to these estimates, if current tax rates and benefit schedules remain unchanged, the trust funds themselves would be exhausted by 2034. If limited to tax collections, Social Security benefits could continue to be paid but would be smaller than before. Current benefit payments could be maintained if Social Security taxes were increased.

Some have argued for additional changes such as applying the Social Security tax to wages above the 1999 ceiling of $72,600, increasing the age of full benefits to mirror increases in life expectancy, and including Social Security payments in excess of already taxed employee contributions as part of taxable income. Others argue that a more radical restructuring of Social Security should be part of the solution.

Much of the recent discussion has focused on how and how much of Social Security revenues might be invested in stocks. At the moment all of the Social Security trust funds are invested in U.S. government bonds. Historically stocks have yielded a higher return that bonds. Some favor using Social Security taxes to establish mandatory retirement accounts that would be under the control of individual workers. Individuals would have wide discretion over how to invest these funds. This approach has been called privatization.

Critics of privatization are concerned that many individuals lack the sophistication to make the necessary investment decisions and that the competition for investment accounts would add significantly to the cost of managing these accounts, thereby reducing the return that workers would receive. They are also concerned about what would happen to individuals who make bad investment decisions. These critics favor individual accounts that would be managed in a collective manner by an independently established government agency. They point out that retirement accounts for members of Congress are currently organized in this manner. Proponents of privatization are concerned that the investments of such an agency would be too large a target to be independent of political control. Investment decisions might then come to represent powerful special interests and not the interests of future retirees.

What do you think should be done about Social Security and why?

Additional information about Social Security is available at the Social Security Administration web site

www.ssa.gov

Information from various advocacy groups for particular reforms are also available on the web. Try one of the popular search engines and search under Social Security.

SOURCE: David E. Rosenbaum, "On Social Security, The Good News Is Bad," *New York Times,* April 4, 1999; and Robert D. Reischauer, "The 75-year plan," *New York Times,* April 9, 1999

■ STUDY QUESTIONS

1. What is the difference between the government's deficit and its debt? What is the link between the two?

2. What does the historical record show about when the federal government has run large deficits?

3. Why are policies to stabilize the deficit likely to destabilize the economy?

4. When is a budget deficit appropriate and why? When is it inappropriate?

5. What does the historical record show about the ratio of federal government debt to GDP?

6. What is the difference between the structural deficit and the actual deficit? Which is usually larger and why? Which is a more accurate measure of the stance of fiscal policy?

7. Does an increase in the deficit always indicate a move to expansionary fiscal policy? Why?

8. Does an increase in the deficit always lead to higher interest rates and more inflation? Why?

9. Why do economists argue that foreign-held debt imposes more of a burden than government debt held by Americans?

10. What are the real burdens of the debt?

11. Since deficits are a result of fiscal policy decisions, why does the impact of deficits depend upon the conduct of monetary policy?

12. What is crowding-out and crowding-in? When is one more likely than the other and why?

■ ECONOMICS ONLINE

Find out more about the magnitude of the national debt and how you can own a part of it from the Bureau of the Public Debt in the U.S. Treasury Department.

www.publicdebt.treas.gov

THE PHILLIPS CURVE AND ECONOMIC GROWTH

LEARNING OBJECTIVES

After completing this chapter, you should be able to:

■ explain how prices can rise following either the rapid growth of aggregate demand or the sluggish growth of aggregate supply.

■ explain what the Phillips curve is and what it is not.

■ explain how the slope of the Phillips curve is related to the slope of the aggregate supply curve.

■ explain how the source of fluctuations in economic activity—whether predominantly from shifts of the aggregate demand curve or from shifts of the aggregate supply curve—will affect the shape of the Phillips curve.

■ explain why the economy's self-correcting mechanism means that the economy's true long-run choices lie along a vertical Phillips curve.

■ explain how the accuracy of expectations about inflation can affect the slope of both the aggregate supply curve and the Phillips curve.

■ discuss the implications of and evidence for the hypotheses of rational expectations.

■ explain how and why one's views on appropriate aggregate demand policy are likely to depend upon one's views on

■ the social costs of inflation vs. unemployment.

■ the slope of the short-run Phillips curve.

■ how quickly inflationary expectations adjust.

■ the efficiency of the economy's self-correcting mechanism.

■ discuss measures that have been advocated to reduce the natural rate of unemployment.

■ calculate how indexing would be applied to wages and interest rates, given the appropriate data on prices.

■ discuss the advantages and disadvantages of universal indexing.

■ CHAPTER REVIEW

This chapter discusses the hard choices that policymakers must make when deciding how to respond to inflation or unemployment. Previous chapters discussed how changes in various tools of fiscal and monetary policy can be used to influence aggregate demand. This chapter uses that material to study the policy implications for fighting unemployment and inflation.

Here, as in many other areas of life, one cannot have one's cake and eat it too. Actions taken to reduce unemployment will often lead to higher rates of inflation, while actions to reduce inflation will often lead to higher rates of unemployment. Economists can help to define the nature of this trade-off, examine the factors that are responsible for it, and clarify the implications of different choices, but they cannot tell anyone which choice to make. In a democratic society, this decision is left to the political process.

Any shift in the aggregate demand or aggregate supply curve, whether induced by policy or not, is likely to affect both prices and output. The nature of the association between changes in prices and changes in output will depend upon which curve shifts. If fluctuations in economic activity are predominantly the result of shifts in the aggregate demand curve, higher prices will be associated with

(1) (higher/lower) levels of output. The transition to higher prices is a period of inflation. A higher level of output means more employment and a lower level of unemployment. Hence, shifts in the aggregate demand curve imply that inflation and unemployment are (negatively/positively) correlated. That is, if you plotted the rate of unemployment on the horizontal axis and the rate of inflation on the vertical axis, the resulting curve, called the _____ curve, would have a (positive/negative) slope.

Data for the 1950s and 1960s was consistent with the view sketched above and seemed to imply that policymakers could choose between inflation and unemployment. In particular, it used to be thought that the Phillips curve implied that policymakers could permanently increase output beyond the level of full employment, or potential output, at the cost of only a small increase in the rate of inflation. Subsequent experience has shown that this view is (correct/incorrect). The Phillips curve represents (2) the statistical correlation between inflation and unemployment. It ignores the implications of the economy's self-correcting mechanisms.

As we have seen, output beyond the level of potential output results in a(n) (inflationary/recessionary) gap. The economy's self-correcting mechanism will shift the aggregate sup- (3) ply curve to reestablish long-run equilibrium at the _____ rate of unemployment. The economy's long-run choices lie along a _____ Phillips curve.

In the short run, shifts in the aggregate demand curve will move the economy up or down the short-run Phillips curve; but the economy's self-correcting mechanism implies that this trade-off is only temporary. How long this trade-off lasts depends upon the speed of the economy's self-correcting mechanism. Differing views about the relative costs of inflation and unemployment, the slope of the short-run Phillips curve, and the speed of the mechanism are an important part of differences in Keynesian and monetarist policy prescriptions.

Changes in money wages are an important determinant of shifts in the aggregate supply curve that lead an inflationary gap to self-destruct. It is the original increase in prices above wages that induces firms to expand output. As workers recognize that the purchasing power of their money wages has declined, the subsequent increases in wages to restore real wages will lead to shifts in the aggregate supply curve. Rather than always being a step behind, workers can try to protect their real wages by anticipating the increase in prices. In this case the expectation of higher prices will lead to higher wages and a shift in the aggregate supply curve in anticipation of inflation.[1] Compared with cases where the aggregate supply curve did not shift, a shift in the aggregate demand curve accompanied by an expectations-induced shift in the aggregate supply curve will have a (larger/smaller) impact on (4)

---

[1]The story of workers trying to protect themselves against inflation seems to imply that labor is responsible for inflation. When the economy is booming, workers will be concerned about inflation, but firms will willingly pay higher wages to attract workers in a tight labor market. The real cause of inflation is not workers or firms but rather excessive aggregate demand.

output and a _____ impact on prices. The result will be a (higher/lower) rate of inflation and the slope of the short-run Phillips curve will be (steeper/flatter).

Economists associated with the hypothesis of rational expectations have focused attention on the formation of expectations. While much remains to be learned, these economists argue that errors in predicting inflation should not be systematic. An implication of this view is that, except for random elements, both the aggregate supply curve and the short-run Phillips curve will be vertical. Not only is there no long-run trade-off between inflation and unemployment, but, according to this view, there is also no systematic short-run trade-off.

Others are less convinced that expectations are rational in the sense of no systematic errors. These economists believe that people tend to underpredict inflation when it is rising and overpredict it when it is falling. Long-term contracts also make it difficult to adjust to changing expectations of inflation. These economists argue that policy measures to shift the aggregate demand curve can affect output and employment in the short run. But remember that these short-run impacts are constrained by the

(5)   true long-run menu of choices which lie along a _____ Phillips curve.

Most economists believe that aggregate demand policy will affect employment and inflation in the short run and will also affect the place where the economy ends up on the long-run Phillips curve. Thus, to fight a recession rather than to wait for the economy's self-correcting mechanism will mean more employment in the short run and is likely to mean more inflation in the long run as compared to a status quo policy that waits on the economy's self-correcting mechanisms. (See Figure 34-14 in the text.) Whether one wants to use aggregate demand policy or wait for natural processes depends on one's assessment of the costs of inflation and unemployment, the slope of the short-run Phillips curve, the quickness with which inflationary expectations adjust, and the efficiency of the economy's self-correcting mechanisms.

A number of policies have been advocated in the hope that they will improve the inflation-unemployment trade-off. Increased efforts at education and job retraining are seen as efforts to reduce frictional unemployment and lower the natural rate of unemployment.

A number of individuals have argued that rather than trying to reduce the rate of inflation we should simply learn to live with it and rely on automatic adjustments of monetary payments to reflect changes in prices, a process known as indexing. Inflation linked automatic adjustment of tax brackets,

Social Security benefits, as well as other government transfer programs, and escalator clauses in wage contracts are examples of _____. A number of observers also advocate this mechanism for interest rates.   (6)

Indexing does seem to offer some relief from many of the social costs of inflation. As workers, firms, and lenders scramble to protect themselves against anticipated future increases in prices, current prices and interest rates will (increase/decrease) to reflect the expectation of inflation. If actual infla-   (7)
tion turns out to be greater or less than expected, there will be a redistribution of wealth that many feel is essentially arbitrary. Uncertainty over future prices may make individuals and businesses extremely reluctant to enter into long-term contracts. Indexing appears to offer relief from these problems. Labor contracts and other agreements could be written in real rather than nominal terms, and arbitrary redistributions would be avoided because money payments would reflect actual, not expected, inflation. At the same time, there is concern that learning to live with inflation may make the economy (more/less) inflation prone.

IMPORTANT TERMS AND CONCEPTS QUIZ ■

Choose the best definition for each of the following terms.

1. _____ Vertical Phillips curve

2. _____ Rational expectations

3. _____ Phillips curve

4. _____ Self-correcting mechanism

5. _____ Natural rate of unemployment

6. _____ Indexing

a. Graph depicting unemployment rate on horizontal axis and inflation rate on vertical axis.

b. Vertical line at the natural rate of unemployment.

c. Unemployment rate at full employment.

d. Vertical line at natural rate of inflation.

e. Forecasts which make optimal use of available and relevant data.

f. Adjustments of monetary payments whenever a specified price index changes.

g. The economy's way of curing inflationary and recessionary gaps via changes in the price level.

BASIC EXERCISE ■

This exercise is designed to illustrate the nature of the inflation-unemployment trade-off that policy-makers must face when planning aggregate demand policy.

1. Figure 34-1 shows an economy with a recessionary gap. Which of the following monetary and fiscal policies could be used to help eliminate this gap?

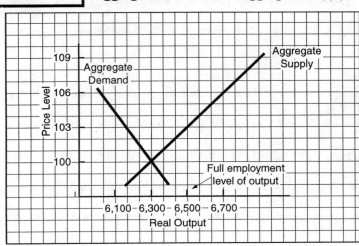

FIGURE 34-1   **Aggregate Demand and Aggregate Supply**

- open market (<u>purchase/sale</u>)

- (<u>increase/decrease</u>) of minimum reserve requirements

- (<u>increase/decrease</u>) in taxes

- (<u>increase/decrease</u>) in government transfer payments to individuals

- (<u>increase/decrease</u>) in government purchases of goods and services

2. Assume the full-employment level of income is $6,500 billion. Draw a new aggregate demand curve, representing one or more of the appropriate policies you identified in Question 1, that will restore full employment for this economy. Following a shift in the aggregate demand curve, prices will rise to _____.

3. Consider the following statement:

    "The increase in prices that resulted when we restored full employment was a small price to pay for the increased output. Why not try moving even farther along the aggregate supply curve? If we further stimulate the economy to lower unemployment we can increase output to, say, $6,700 billion and prices will only rise to 106. We can thus have a permanent increase in output of $200 billion every year in return for a one-time increase in prices of just under 3 percent. That's a pretty favorable trade-off." What is wrong with the reasoning of this argument?

4. Figure 34-2 shows an economy following an adverse shift in the aggregate supply curve. Equilibrium used to be an output of $6,500 and a price level of 103. Answer the following questions to see how stabilization policy that shifts the aggregate demand curve is constrained in efforts to offset the adverse impact of the shift in the aggregate supply curve.
    a. If there is to be no decline in employment, the government will need to implement (<u>expansionary/restrictive</u>) policies to shift the aggregate demand curve. The government could maintain employment, but at the cost of an increase in prices to _____.

    b. Alternatively, the government could avoid any increase in prices. Such a decision would require (<u>expansionary/restrictive</u>) policies and would result in a new equilibrium level of output of _____.

FIGURE 34-2   **Aggregate Demand and Aggregate Supply**

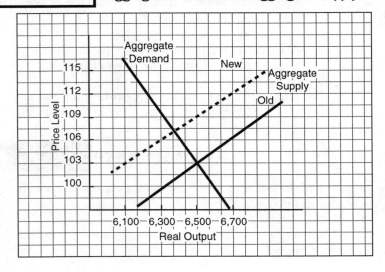

SELF-TESTS FOR UNDERSTANDING ■

Circle the most appropriate answer.

1. If fluctuations in economic activity are caused by shifts in the aggregate demand curve, then
   a. prices and output will be negatively correlated.
   b. the short-run Phillips curve will be vertical.
   c. the long-run Phillips curve will have a negative slope.
   d. the rates of inflation and unemployment will tend to be negatively correlated.

2. If fluctuations in economic activity are the result of shifts in the aggregate supply curve, then
   a. prices and output will be positively correlated.
   b. the short-run Phillips curve will have a negative slope.
   c. the long-run Phillips curve will be horizontal.
   d. the rate of inflation and rate of unemployment will tend to be positively correlated.

3. The Phillips curve
   a. is a statistical relationship between unemployment and inflation when economic fluctuations are dominated by changes in the growth of aggregate demand.
   b. is the set of long-term equilibrium relationships between the rate of unemployment and the rate of inflation.
   c. is the third turn at the Indianapolis 500 Speedway.
   d. shows how nominal interest rate changes when expectations of inflation change.

4. The economy's self-correcting mechanisms mean that in the long run the Phillips curve is likely to
   a. have a negative slope.
   b. have a positive slope.
   c. be horizontal.
   d. be vertical.

5. The long run Phillips curve will be vertical
   a. at the natural rate of inflation.
   b. at the point where real and nominal interest rates are equal.
   c. at the natural rate of unemployment.
   d. wherever the aggregate demand and aggregate supply curves intersect.

6. The positively sloped aggregate supply curve is drawn on the assumption that
   a. the cost of productive inputs remains unchanged in the short run as output changes.
   b. wages are fully indexed.
   c. the Phillips curve is never vertical.
   d. wage and price controls limit the impact of inflation.

7. An increase in wages, due either to inflation that has occurred in the past or inflation that is expected to occur in the future, can be modeled as
   a. an upward shift in the aggregate supply curve.
   b. an inward shift in the production possibilities frontier.
   c. a downward shift in the aggregate demand curve.
   d. a leftward shift in the long-run Phillips curve.

8. An increased emphasis on expectations of future inflation in wage settlements will lead to a ____ aggregate supply curve and a ____ Phillips curve.
   a. flatter; flatter
   b. flatter; steeper
   c. steeper; steeper
   d. steeper; flatter

9. Consider a shift to the right of the aggregate demand curve due to expansionary monetary and fiscal policy. Assume that the adoption of expansionary policies leads to expectations of inflation that induce a simultaneous shift in the aggregate supply curve. The resulting change in output will be _____ if there were no shift in the aggregate supply curve.
    a. smaller than
    b. the same as
    c. larger than

10. Under the same conditions as question 9, the resulting change in prices will be _____ if there were no shift in the aggregate supply curve.
    a. smaller than
    b. the same as
    c. larger than

11. Stabilization policy faces a trade-off between inflation and unemployment in the short run because changes in monetary and fiscal policy have their most immediate impact on the _____.
    a. aggregate supply curve
    b. Phillips curve
    c. production possibilities frontier
    d. aggregate demand curve

12. Which of the following are necessary for expectations to meet the economist's definition of rational expectations? (There may be more than one correct answer.)
    a. They are based on relevant and available information.
    b. They can only be made by economists and statisticians.
    c. There are no systematic errors.
    d. They are always correct.

13. A strong believer in rational expectations would be surprised by which one of the following occurrences?
    a. An announcement by the Fed that it will increase the rate of growth of the money supply leads to expectations of higher inflation.
    b. Plans to lower taxes give rise to expectations of higher prices.
    c. Plans to fight inflation by restrictive policy succeed in reducing the rate of inflation with no increase in unemployment.
    d. An examination of the record shows that people consistently underestimate the rate of inflation during periods when it is increasing.

14. The hypothesis of rational expectations implies that increases in output beyond the level of potential output can be produced
    a. by expected increases in prices.
    b. only by unexpected increases in prices.
    c. by any increase in prices whether expected or not.
    d. by preannounced increases in the money supply or reductions in taxes.

15. Which of the following is not a feasible alternative for aggregate demand policy following an adverse shift of the supply curve to the left?
    a. Do nothing and initially experience both higher prices and lower output.
    b. Avoid the reduction in output at the cost of even higher prices.
    c. Avoid the increase in prices at the cost of an even greater decline in output.
    d. Avoid both the reduction in output and increase in prices by using fiscal policy to shift the aggregate demand curve and monetary policy to shift the aggregate supply curve.

16. Restrictive monetary and fiscal policy adopted to reduce the rate of inflation will work quicker and have a smaller impact on unemployment when
    a. changes in inflationary expectations take a long time.
    b. the long-run Phillips curve is vertical.
    c. expectations of inflation adjust quickly to the change in macro policy.
    d. the natural rate of unemployment equals the natural rate of inflation.

17. Who is most likely to advocate government action to eliminate a recessionary gap? The economist who believes
    a. the short-run Phillips curve is quite steep.
    b. expectations of inflation will adjust rapidly to lower rates of inflation.
    c. we should pay any price to avoid higher inflation.
    d. the short-run Phillips curve is fairly flat.

18. If job retraining or other measures are successful in reducing the natural rate of unemployment,
    a. the long-run Phillips curve will shift to the left.
    b. the aggregate demand curve will become less steep.
    c. the short-run Phillips curve will become vertical.
    d. the natural rate of inflation will increase.

19. A general policy of indexing
    a. is an attempt to shift the aggregate supply curve downward and to the right.
    b. would help to balance the federal government's budget.
    c. is an attempt to ease the social cost of inflation.
    d. runs little risk of accelerating the rate of inflation.

20. Which of the following is an example of indexing?
    a. Tax penalties on firms that grant excessive wage increases.
    b. The adjustment of nominal interest rates in response to expectations of inflation.
    c. The average change in prices on the New York Stock Exchange.
    d. Increases in Social Security checks computed on the basis of changes in the consumer price index.

TEST B

Circle T or F for true or false.

T F 1. Inflation occurs only as a result of shifts in the aggregate demand curve.

T F 2. In contrast to expansionary monetary or fiscal policy, an autonomous increase in private spending will increase output without increasing prices.

T F 3. If fluctuations in economic activity are predominantly the result of shifts in the aggregate supply curve, the rate of unemployment and the rate of inflation will tend to be positively correlated.

T F 4. The economy's self-correcting mechanism implies that the only long-run policy choices for the economy lie along a vertical Phillips curve.

T F 5. The natural rate of unemployment is given by the position of the long-run Phillips curve.

T F 6. A belief that the economy's self-correcting mechanism works quickly is an argument in favor of activist demand-management policy.

T F 7. Expectations of inflation that lead to higher wages will be somewhat self-fulfilling as the increase in wages shifts the aggregate supply curve.

T   F   8. One can minimize the inflationary effects of fighting a recession by using fiscal policy rather than monetary policy.

T   F   9. Following an adverse shift in the aggregate supply curve, aggregate demand policies can stop the rise in prices with no increase in unemployment.

T   F   10. The economy's self-correcting mechanism means that, in the face of a recessionary gap, output and prices will eventually be the same with or without expansionary stabilization policy.

ECONOMICS IN ACTION

HOW NATURAL IS THE NATURAL RATE?

Writing in the *New York Times*, Michael Weinstein argues that the "relentless good news of the 1990s" has lead a number of economists to refine their views of the natural rate of unemployment. Based on estimates from the late 1980s or early 1990s, many would have expected that an unemployment rate of under 5 percent would have been accompanied by significant inflation. Instead, as the rate of unemployment fell from 7.5% in 1992 to under 4.5 percent in early 1999, the rate of inflation decreased rather than increased. Is there a clear and convincing answer as to why?

Economist Robert J. Gordon, believes that much of recent experience is related to good luck, fortuitous events that are unlikely to be as favorable over the long run. Falling food prices, reductions in the rate of increase of the cost of medical and cheap imports while reducing measured inflation are not likely to be factors that can continue forever. He is not optimistic the good news on inflation will continue.

On the other hand, economist Robert Hall argues that our good fortune reflects well executed monetary policy. He believes that the best policy for central bankers is "to set clear targets for inflation and stick by them . . . If the [Federal Reserve] convinces traders in financial markets that inflation will be low and steady, the economy will gravitate toward the lowest possible unemployment rate."

Should macroeconomic policy aim at lowering the rate of unemployment still further? Economists Lawrence Katz and Alan Kreuger argue that we may have reached bottom. The decline from 7.5 percent to under 4.5 percent has been easy as employers could hire from students, spouses and laid-off workers. Katz and Kreuger point to the increasing proportion of long-term unemployment and argue that many people who are currently unemployed will have a hard time meeting labor force needs as they may have obsolete skills and suffer from physical or mental limitations.

What do you think the value of the natural rate of unemployment is?

If you were responsible for macroeconomic policy, would you aim for still lower unemployment?

SOURCE: Michael M. Weinstein, "Unemployment's Natural Rate May Have a Mind of Its Own," *The New York Times*, April 22, 1999.

STUDY QUESTIONS

1. Why does the slope of the Phillips curve depend upon the source of macroeconomic fluctuations?

2. Does the Phillips curve offer macroeconomic policymakers a menu of choices between the rate of unemployment and inflation? Why?

3. What is meant by the statement that the economy's self-correcting mechanisms mean that in the long run the Phillips curve is vertical?

4. What is the natural rate of unemployment?

5. How does the expectation of future inflation and the expectations-related shifts in the aggregate supply curve affect the Phillips curve?

6. How can expectations of inflation be rational if they are not always correct?

7. What sort of policies might reduce the natural rate of unemployment?

8. Should wages and interest rates be fully indexed?

9. Should stabilization policy aim to reduce inflation to zero? Why?

10. Has the natural rate of unemployment changed in recent years? If so, why?

ECONOMICS ONLINE ■

The Livingston Survey, begun by Joseph Livingiston in 1946, summarizes the inflation forecasts of economists from industry, government, banking, and academia. The Livingston Survey along with other expectational data is available on-line from the Federal Reserve Bank of Philadelphia at

www.phil.frb.org/econ

The U.S. government now issues inflation indexed bonds. Find out more about inflation indexed bonds from Deloitte & Touche OnLine and from the Bureau of the Public Debt, U.S. Treasury.

www.dtonline.com/BONDS/CONTENTS.HTM

www.publicdebt.treas.gov/of/ofinflin.htm

INTERNATIONAL TRADE AND COMPARATIVE ADVANTAGE

LEARNING OBJECTIVES

After completing this chapter, you should be able to:

■ list the important factors that lead countries to trade with one another.

■ explain how voluntary trade, even if it does not increase total production, can be mutually beneficial to the trading partners.

■ explain in what ways international and intranational trade are similar and dissimilar.

■ distinguish between absolute and comparative advantage.

■ explain how absolute advantage and comparative advantage are related to the location and slope of a country's per capita production possibilities frontier.

■ explain how trade means that a country's consumption possibilities can exceed its production possibilities.

■ explain how world prices are relevant for determining a country's consumption possibilities.

■ explain how world prices are determined by the interaction of demand and supply curves for trading partners.

- use a pair of demand and supply diagrams to illustrate the impact of quotas and tariffs.

- contrast the efficiency and distribution effects of tariffs and quotas.

- analyze the arguments used to advocate trade restrictions.

- explain the role of adjustment assistance in a country favoring free trade.

- explain the fallacy in the "cheap foreign labor" argument.

■ CHAPTER REVIEW

The material in this chapter discusses the basic economic forces that influence the international division of labor in the production of goods and services along with the resulting pattern of international trade. Trade between cities or states within a single country is, in principle, no different than trade between nations. Economists and others spend more time studying international trade rather than intranational trade for several reasons: International trade involves more than one government with a resulting host of political concerns; it usually involves more than one currency; and the mobility of labor and capital between nations is typically more difficult than within nations.

Exchange rates—that is, the number of units of one country's currency that are changeable into another country's currency—are an important determinant of international trade and will be discussed in the next chapter. However, the real terms of trade—how many import goods a country can get indirectly through export production rather than through direct domestic production—are the important measure of the benefits of trade, and they are considered here in some detail.

Individual countries can try to meet the consumption needs of their citizens without trade by producing everything their populations need. Alternatively, they can specialize in the production of fewer commodities and trade for commodities they do not produce. Even if there were no differences between countries, specializing and trading would still make sense if there were important economies

(1) of _____ in production.

An important reason for trade is that differences in oil deposits, fertile soil, and other natural resources, as well as differences in labor inputs and productive capital, will affect the efficiency with

(2) which countries can produce different goods. It is the law of (absolute/comparative) advantage that then indicates where countries should concentrate their production to maximize the potential gains from trade.

Assume country A can produce 8,000 bushels of wheat if it produces one less car, while country B can produce only 7,000 bushels of wheat. For the same world production of cars, world production of wheat will increase if country (A/B) produced 10 fewer cars and country _____ produced 10 more (3) cars. (World wheat production would increase by _____ bushels.) In this case country A has a comparative advantage in the production of _____.[1]

Looking only at its own domestic production, the opportunity cost of one more car in country A is _____ bushels of wheat. Country B can produce one more car by giving up only _____ (4) bushels of wheat. Thus it should not be surprising if country B concentrates on the production of _____ and trades with country A, which concentrates on the production of _____.[2]

It is also important to realize that comparative advantage is not a static concept. The mix of industries that maximizes a country's comparative advantage is not something that can be determined once for all time. Rather, there will need to be continuing adjustments in response to innovations, both domestically and abroad, as well as competition from foreign producers. Countries that try to isolate themselves from foreign competition have usually ended up with stagnating industries and incomes.

As countries concentrate production on those goods in which they have a comparative advantage, equilibrium world prices and trade flows—that is, exports and imports—will be determined at the point where world _____ equals world _____. This price is not at the (5) intersection of domestic demand and supply curves; instead, it occurs at a point where the excess supply from (importing/exporting) countries (domestic supply minus domestic demand) equals the excess demand by _____ countries (domestic demand minus domestic supply).

Advanced courses in international trade show how prices derived under conditions of free trade will lead competitive profit-maximizing firms to exploit the comparative advantage of individual countries

---

[1] Note that we have said nothing so far about absolute advantage. For example, if it takes 500 labor hours to produce one car or 700 bushels of wheat in country B and 1,000 labor hours to produce 1 car or 8,000 bushels of wheat in country A, country B has an absolute advantage in the production of both goods while country A still has a comparative advantage in the production of wheat.

[2] Does the law of comparative advantage imply that all countries should specialize in the production of just a few commodities? No, it does not, for several reasons. One important reason is that production possibilities frontiers are likely to be curved rather than straight lines. The implication of the curved frontier is that the opportunity cost of cars in terms of wheat for country B will rise as B produces more cars. Simultaneously, the opportunity cost of cars in terms of wheat for country A will fall as A concentrates on wheat. In equilibrium, the opportunity cost, or slope of the production possibilities frontier, in both countries will be equal. At this point neither country has an incentive for further specialization. Exactly where this point will occur will be determined by world demand and supply for cars and wheat.

and help to achieve an efficient allocation of resources. Most countries do not have unrestricted free

(6)   trade. Rather, imports are often restricted by the use of _____ and _____,

and exports are often promoted through the use of export _____. Tariffs reduce the

quantity of imports by raising their _____ while quotas raise the price of imports by

restricting _____. Either a tariff or a quota could be used to achieve the same reduc-

tion in imports, but the choice between the two has other consequences.

(7)   Tariff revenues accrue directly to the _____ while the benefits of higher prices under

a quota are likely to accrue to private producers, both foreign and domestic. (The government might

be able to capture some of these profits by auctioning import licenses, but this is not usually done.)

Tariffs still require foreign suppliers to compete among themselves. This competition will favor the

(8)   survival of (<u>high/low</u>)-cost foreign suppliers. What about domestic firms? They (<u>do/do not</u>) have to

pay the tariff, so high-cost domestic suppliers (<u>can/cannot</u>) continue in business. Quotas are apt to be

distributed on almost any grounds except economic efficiency and thus have no automatic mechanism

that works in favor of low-cost foreign suppliers.

Why do countries impose tariffs and quotas? Many trade restrictions reflect the successful plead-

ings of high-cost domestic suppliers. Free trade and the associated reallocation of productive resources

in line with the law of comparative advantage would call for the elimination of these firms in their tra-

ditional lines of business. It is not surprising that managers and workers resist these changes. If every-

one is to benefit from the increased output opportunities offered by free trade, then a program of trade

(9)   _____ assistance will be necessary to help those most affected by the realignment of

productive activities.

(10)   Other traditional justifications for trade restriction include the national _____ argu-

ment and the _____ -industries argument. In both cases it is extremely difficult to sep-

arate firms with legitimate claims from those looking for a public handout. In recent years some have

argued that the threat of trade restrictions should be used in a strategic manner to convince others not

to impose restrictions.

Much of the free trade fuss in the United States is concerned about competing with low-cost for-

eign producers who pay workers lower wages. Concerns about wages need to be joined with measures

of productivity. A clear understanding of comparative advantages shows that the standard of living of workers in (<u>the exporting/the importing/both</u>) country(ies) can rise as a result of trade and specializa-   (11)

tion. While measures of absolute advantage are important when considering the standard of living

workers will enjoy, even countries with high wages can benefit from trade when high wages are asso-

ciated with high productivity and trade induces adjustments in the structure of worldwide production

consistent with the principle of _____ advantage.

IMPORTANT TERMS AND CONCEPTS QUIZ ■

Choose the most appropriate definition for each of the following terms.

1. _____ Imports

2. _____ Exports

3. _____ Specialization

4. _____ Absolute advantage

5. _____ Comparative advantage

6. _____ Mercantilism

7. _____ Tariff

8. _____ Quota

9. _____ Export subsidy

10. _____ Trade adjustment assistance

11. _____ Infant-industry argument

12. _____ Strategic trade policy

13. _____ Dumping

a. Maximum quantity that can be imported per unit of time.

b. Threats to implement protectionist policies designed to promote free trade.

c. Selling goods in a foreign market at higher prices than those charged at home.

d. Domestically produced goods sold abroad.

e. Selling goods in a foreign market at lower prices than those charged at home.

f. Tax on imports.

g. Decision by a country to emphasize production of particular commodities.

h. Provision of special aid to those workers and firms harmed by foreign competition.

i. Ability of one country to produce a good less inefficiently (relative to other goods) than another country.

j. Foreign-produced goods purchased domestically.

k. Tariff protection for new industries, giving them time to mature.

l. Payment by the government that enables domestic firms to lower prices to foreign buyers.

m. Ability of one country to produce a good using fewer resources than another country requires.

o. Doctrine arguing that exports are good while imports are bad.

■   **BASIC EXERCISES**

1.   This exercise is designed to review the law of comparative advantage.
   a.   Assume that the hours of labor shown below are the only input necessary to produce calcula-
        tors and backpacks in Canada and Japan.

	Calculators	Backpacks
Canada	4	5
Japan	2	3

Which country has an absolute advantage in the production of calculators? _____
Which country has an absolute advantage in the production of backpacks? _____
   b.   If labor in Canada is reallocated from the production of calculators to the production of back-
        packs, how many calculators must be given up in order to produce one more backpack?
        _____ What about Japan? How many calculators must it give up in order to produce
        one more backpack? _____ Which country has a comparative advantage in the pro-
        duction of backpacks? _____ Which country has a comparative advantage in the pro-
        duction of calculators? _____ According to the law of comparative advantage,
        _____ should concentrate on the production of backpacks while _____
        concentrates on the production of calculators.
   c.   Assume each country has 12 million hours of labor input that initially is evenly distributed in
        both countries between the production of backpacks and calculators: 6 million for each. Fill
        in the following table of outputs.

	Output of Calculators	Output of Backpacks
Canada	_____	_____
Japan	_____	_____
Total	_____	_____

   d.   Assume that Canada now reallocates 2.4 million labor hours away from the production of cal-
        culators and into backpacks. The change in Canadian calculator output is – _____. The
        change in Canadian backpack output is + _____.
   e.   What reallocation of labor in Japan is necessary to be sure that world output of calculators
        (Japan plus Canada) remains unchanged? _____ labor hours. What are the changes in
        Japanese output from this reallocation? The change in Japanese calculator output is +
        _____. The change in Japanese backpack output is – _____.
   f.   By assumption, the world output of calculators has not changed, but the net change in the
        world output of backpacks is a(n) (increase/decrease) of _____ backpacks.
   g.   Questions c through f showed how specialization according to the law of comparative advantage
        could increase the output of backpacks without decreasing the output of calculators. Adjustments
        in line with the law of comparative advantage could alternatively increase the output of both
        goods. Suppose Japan had reallocated 1,350,000 labor hours to the production of calculators. Fill
        in the following table and compare total outputs with your answers to question c.

Calculators

	Labor Input (millions of hours)	Output
Canada	3.60	_____
Japan	7.35	_____
Total		_____

Backpacks

	Labor input (millions of hours)	Output
Canada	8.40	_____
Japan	4.65	_____
Total		_____

h. Work through questions d and e again, but assume this time that the initial reallocation of 2.4 million labor hours in Canada is away from backpacks and to the production of calculators. Calculate the reallocation in Japan necessary to maintain world backpack output. What happens to the total output of calculators? Why?

i. Assume that the production of backpacks in Canada requires 6 hours rather than 5 hours. Work through the original output levels in question c and the reallocation of labor in questions d and e to see what now happens to total output of calculators and backpacks. Does your answer to question f differ from your original answer? Why?

2. This exercise is designed to give practice in analyzing the impact of quotas and tariffs. To simplify the analysis, the question assumes that the world is composed of only two countries, the United States and India.

   a. Figure 35-1 shows the demand and supply for shirts in the United States and India. Prices in India are expressed in terms of American dollars. In the absence of international trade, what are the domestic price and quantity of shirts in India and the United States?

	Price	Quantity
India	_____	_____
United States	_____	_____

Demand and Supply: Shirts   **FIGURE 35-1**

   b. Assume now that India and the United States are free to trade without restrictions. What is the world price of shirts? _____

   What happens to the production of shirts in India?

   What happens to the production of shirts in the United States?

   Who exports and who imports how many shirts?

   c. Assume that American producers are able to persuade the government to impose a quota limiting shirt imports to 200 million. Following imposition of the quota, what are prices and production in India and the United States?

	Price	Quantity
India	_____	_____
United States	_____	_____

   Compared to the free trade equilibrium described in b, shirt prices have increased in (India/the United States) and decreased in _____. The production of shirts has increased in _____ and decreased in _____.

    d. What tariff would have yielded the same results as the quota of 200 million shirts? _____.

    e. Discuss the reasons for choosing between a tariff and a quota.

3. This exercise offers another review of the law of comparative advantage.

Figure 35-2 shows the production possibilities frontier for Arcadia and Ricardia. For every computer they buy, citizens of each country want to consume 1,000 pounds of cheese. As a result production and consumption in each country takes place at the dot on the frontier. Some have argued that citizens in both countries could consume more of both goods if each country concentrated production on the good in which it has a comparative advantage and traded for the other good.

FIGURE 35-2   **Arcadia and Ricardia: PPFs**

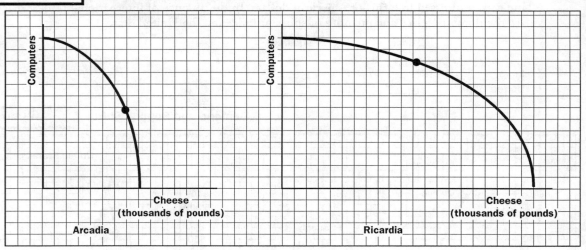

In order to construct a numerical example, assume that at the dot the slope of the PPF for Arcadia is –2 while the slope of the PPF for Ricardia is – 1/2. (Arcadia must give up two computers for an additional 1,000 pounds of cheese, while Ricardia can increase the production of cheese by 2,000 pounds at the cost of only one less computer.)

    a. Which country has a comparative advantage in the production of computers? _____

    b. Which country has a comparative advantage in the production of cheese? _____

    c. Construct a numerical example that shows how what changes in production and what pattern of trade would allow both countries to consume outside their PPF.

■ SELF-TESTS FOR UNDERSTANDING

TEST A

Circle the most appropriate answer.

1. Even if there were no differences in natural resources, climate, labor skills, etc., nations would still find it advantageous to specialize production and trade
    a. because of differences in absolute advantage.
    b. to take advantage of economies of scale.
    c. to take advantage of differences in national currencies.
    d. when inflation rates differ.

2. International trade is different from intranational trade because of
   a. political issues that arise from different governments.
   b. limitations of the ability of labor and capital to move between countries compared to their ability to move within countries.
   c. the use of different currencies.
   d. all of the above.

3. Economists argue that
   a. efficiency in international trade requires countries to produce those goods in which they have an absolute advantage.
   b. efficiency in international trade requires countries to produce those goods in which they have a comparative advantage.
   c. efficiency in international trade requires countries that have an absolute advantage in the production of all goods to become self-sufficient.
   d. countries with export surpluses will have a comparative advantage in the production of all goods.

4. Using per capita production possibilities frontiers showing the production of clothes on the vertical axis and cars on the horizontal axis, the absolute advantage in the production of clothes would be determined by comparing
   a. the slope of the per capita production possibilities frontiers.
   b. where the per capita production possibilities frontiers cut the horizontal axis.
   c. the area under the per capita production possibilities frontiers.
   d. where the per capita production possibilities frontiers cut the vertical axis.

5. Using per capita production possibilities frontiers described above, the comparative advantage in the production of clothes would be determined by comparing
   a. the slope of the per capita production possibilities frontiers.
   b. where the per capita production possibilities frontiers cut the horizontal axis.
   c. the area under the per capita production possibilities frontiers.
   d. where the per capita production possibilities frontiers cut the vertical axis.

6. Which of the following is an example of comparative advantage?
   a. Wages of textile workers are lower in India than in America.
   b. The slope of the production possibilities frontier between tomatoes and airplanes differs for Mexico and the United States.
   c. American workers must work an average of only 500 hours to purchase a car, while Russian workers must work 4,000 hours.
   d. In recent years Swedish income per capita has exceeded that of the United States.

7. Specialization and free trade consistent with the law of comparative advantage will enable
   a. increased world production of all traded goods.
   b. increases in the standard of living for workers in both exporting and importing countries.
   c. countries to consume at some point outside their production possibilities frontier.
   d. all of the above.

8. From a worldwide perspective, economic efficiency is enhanced if production and trade is organized according to the law of comparative advantage. Economic efficiency within a single country is enhanced if regional production and trade are organized according to
   a. absolute advantage.
   b. the political power of particular states or regions.
   c. which regions have the highest unemployment.
   d. comparative advantage.

9. If shoes can be produced with two hours of labor input in Italy and three hours of labor input in the United States, then it is correct to say that
    a. Italy has an absolute advantage in the production of shoes.
    b. Italy has a comparative advantage in the production of shoes.
    c. the United States has an absolute advantage in the production of shoes.
    d. the United States has a comparative advantage in the production of shoes.

10. Assuming that shoes are produced as in question 9 and shirts can be produced with four hours of labor in both countries, then it is correct to say that
    a. the United States has a comparative advantage in the production of shirts.
    b. Italy has a comparative advantage in the production of shirts.
    c. Italy has an absolute advantage in the production of shirts.
    d. the United States has an absolute advantage in the production of shirts.

11. Under free trade, world prices for exports and imports would be such that
    a. countries would specialize production along lines of absolute advantage.
    b. all countries would show a slight export surplus.
    c. the quantity supplied by exporters would just equal the quantity demanded by importers.
    d. every country would be self-sufficient in all goods.

12. All but which one of the following have been used to restrict trade?
    a. Export subsidies.
    b. Tariffs.
    c. Quotas.
    d. "Voluntary" export agreements.

13. A tariff affects trade by
    a. imposing a tax on imported goods.
    b. limiting the quantity of goods that can be imported.
    c. offering a subsidy to producers who export for foreign sales.
    d. the voluntary actions of foreign manufacturers to limit their exports.

14. A quota affects trade by
    a. imposing a tax on imported goods.
    b. limiting the quantity of goods that can be imported.
    c. offering a subsidy to producers who export for foreign sales.
    d. the voluntary action of foreign manufacturers to limit their exports.

15. Which of the following is an example of a tariff?
    a. Japanese car manufacturers agree to limit exports to the United States.
    b. U.S. law limits the imports of cotton shirts to 20 million.
    c. Television manufacturers outside Great Britain must pay a 10 percent duty on each set they ship to Great Britain.
    d. Foreign bicycle manufacturers receive a rebate of taxes from their own government for each bicycle they export.

16. One economic advantage of tariffs over quotas is that tariffs
    a. typically give preferential treatment to long-term suppliers.
    b. expose high-cost domestic producers to competition.
    c. force foreign suppliers to compete.
    d. help avoid destructive price wars.

17. The imposition of a tariff on steel will lead to all but which one of the following?
    a. A lower volume of steel imports.
    b. Higher domestic steel prices.
    c. Reduced domestic demand for steel.
    d. Reduced domestic production of steel as higher steel prices reduce demand.

18. The imposition of a quota on steel will lead to all but which one of the following?
    a. A lower volume of steel imports.
    b. Increased domestic production of steel.
    c. Lower domestic steel prices.
    d. Reduced domestic demand for steel.

19. A quota that limits the importation of foreign computer chips is likely to be in the interest of all but which of the following? (There may be more than one correct answer.)
    a. Domestic chip manufacturers.
    b. Domestic computer manufacturers.
    c. Labor employed domestically in the production of computer chips.
    d. Consumers interested in buying computers.

20. Which one of the following is a justification for fewer trade restrictions?
    a. Some industries would be so vital in times of war that we cannot rely on foreign suppliers.
    b. A temporary period of protection is necessary until an industry matures and is able to compete with foreign suppliers.
    c. Competition from foreign suppliers will help keep prices to consumers low.
    d. The threat of trade restrictions may prevent the adoption of restrictions by others.

TEST B

Circle T or F for true or false.

T   F   1. A country with an absolute advantage in producing all goods is better off being self-sufficient than engaging in trade.

T   F   2. Countries gain from trade only when it allows them to adjust productive resources to take advantage of economies of scale.

T   F   3. A country with an absolute advantage in the production of all goods should only export commodities.

T   F   4. The unequal distribution of natural resources among countries is one important reason why countries trade.

T   F   5. Which of two countries has a comparative advantage in the production of wine rather than cloth can be determined by comparing the slopes of the production possibilities frontiers of both countries.

T   F   6. It is possible for all countries to simultaneously expand exports and reduce imports.

T   F   7. A quota on shirts would reduce the volume of imported shirts by specifying the quantity of shirts that could be imported.

T   F   8. The infant-industry argument is used to justify protection for industries that are vital in times of war.

T   F   9. Dumping of goods by the United States on Japanese markets would necessarily harm Japanese consumers.

T   F   10. If foreign labor is paid less, foreign producers will always be able to undersell American producers.

■ SUPPLEMENTARY EXERCISES

1. Demand and supply for widgets in Baulmovia and Bilandia are as follows:

   Baulmovia
   Demand: $Q = 156 - 7P$
   Supply: $Q = -44 + 18P$

   Bilandia
   Demand: $Q = 320 - 10P$
   Supply: $Q = -20 + 10P$

   a. In the absence of trade, what are the price and quantity of widgets in Baulmovia? In Bilandia?
   b. With free trade what is the one common world price for widgets? Which country exports widgets? Which country imports widgets? What is the volume of exports and imports?
   c. Manufacturers in the importing country have convinced the government to impose a tariff on widget imports of $4.50 a widget. What will happen to trade and the price of widgets in the two countries?
   d. What quota would have the same impact on trade?
   e. What factors might lead one to prefer a tariff over a quota?

2. Ricardia is a small country that produces wine and cloth. The production possibilities frontier for Ricardia is

   $$W = 324 - C^2$$

   where W = millions of barrels of wine and C = millions of bolts of cloth.
   a. Use a piece of graph paper. Label the vertical axis "wine" and the horizontal axis "cloth." Draw the production possibilities frontier.
   b. Since Ricardia is a small country, it can export or import cloth or wine without affecting world prices. World prices are such that Ricardia can export one million barrels of wine for 750,000 bolts of cloth or it can export 750,000 bolts of cloth for one million barrels of wine. The government's chief economist argues that regardless of consumption preferences, Ricardia should produce 14.4 million bolts of cloth and 10.8 million barrels of wine. Do you agree? Why? (Hint: Consider what a graph of consumption possibilities looks like. For any production combination of wine and cloth, Ricardia's consumption possibilities are given by a negatively sloped straight line through the production point. The slope of the consumption possibilities line reflects world prices. A movement up the straight line to the left of the production point would imply exporting cloth in order to import and consume more wine. A movement down the straight line to the right would reflect exporting wine in order to import and consume more cloth. Exactly where Ricardia chooses to consume is a matter of preferences, but its choice is constrained by its consumption possibilities line, which in turn is determined by Ricardia's production choice and world prices for cloth and wine. Why does the production point 10.8 million barrels of wine and 14.4 million bolts of cloth offer the greatest consumption possibilities?)

■ ECONOMICS IN ACTION

TRADE, WAGES, AND JOBS

Why isn't it obvious to all economists that increasing competition with low-wage developing countries is destroying the American dream as jobs are being shipped out of the country? As suggested by the wording of the question, this is an issue that many people come to with preconceived ideas. The debate generates as much, if not more, political rhetoric than dispassionate analysis.

The question of the impact of trade on wages and jobs arose as the decline in demand for unskilled labor over the 1980s and 1990s occurred at the same time there was a significant increase in imports of light manufactured goods from developing countries. Was the one causing the other? As imports have risen from just over 5 percent of GDP in 1970 to about 14 percent in 1997, the proportion of imports that came from developing countries rose from 14 percent to almost 40 percent. According to various estimates, exports of light manufacturing goods from developing countries to western industrialized countries have grown from 5 percent of exports in 1955 to close to 60 percent.

Just because two events occur at the same time does not mean that one caused the other. Thus many economists are skeptical that changes in trade patterns explain all of the decline in wages for unskilled workers. These economists see the change in the relative wages of skilled and unskilled workers as the result of broader forces affecting the economy as a whole. The increasing sophistication of both factory and office jobs points to the importance of education and a skilled work force. On this view, moves to limit imports might do little to alleviate the plight of unskilled workers while imposing significant costs on the economy.

Why isn't it obvious that low-wage countries can undersell American workers and force down wages? Comparing wages is only part of the story. If higher paid workers are more productive, then costs may actually be lower in the high wage country. While there are differences across industries, American workers are, on average, more productive than workers in many other countries. Just because a country pays low wages does not mean that it can undersell products from high wage countries.

Some economists have estimated what would have happened to employment of unskilled workers if there had been no increase in imports. These studies typically find only small impacts on employment, impacts that are too small to explain the observed changes in wages. Why are these employment changes so small? Most unskilled workers are employed in retail trade and services, not manufacturing. It is also useful to remember that while total manufacturing output is 17 percent of GDP, total employment in manufacturing is now only about 15 percent of the American work force.

Had trade been the only factor explaining the job prospects of unskilled workers, many economists would have expected an increase in the use of unskilled workers in other sectors of the economy as firms in these sectors took advantage of declining wages to hire more unskilled workers. That there has been a decline, not an increase, in the use of unskilled labor in these other sectors of the economy suggests that broader forces are at work.

While analysis of the impact of trade on employment and wages is continuing and many issues are still in dispute, economist Richard Freeman spoke for many economists when in the summer of 1995 he said that no "smoking gun" has yet been identified. Freeman concluded, "My scorecard reads: trade matters, but it is neither all that matters nor the primary cause of observed changes."

1. What is your position on the question of the relation between trade and wages? Explain.

2. What do you see as America's current comparative advantage in international trade? How is it likely to change in the future, and what implications do these changes have for jobs and wages?

SOURCE: Richard B. Freeman, "Are Your Wages Set in Beijing?" *The Journal of Economic Perspectives,* Summer 1995, pp. 15–32. "Not So Absolutely Fabulous: By Themselves, Low Wages Do Not Guarantee Economic Success," *The Economist,* November 4, 1995, p. 86. Paul R. Krugman and Robert Z. Lawrence, "Trade, Jobs and Wages," *Scientific American,* April 1994, pp. 44–49. For a dissenting view see Adrian Wood, "How Trade Hurt Unskilled Workers," *The Journal of Economic Perspectives,* Summer 1995, pp. 57–80.

STUDY QUESTIONS ∎

1. Why do countries trade with each other? Why don't they try to be self-sufficient in the production of all goods?

2. What is the difference between absolute advantage and comparative advantage? (Use a per capita production possibilities frontier to illustrate your answer.)

3. Why do economists argue that a country with an absolute advantage in the production of all goods can still gain from trade if it specializes in a manner consistent with the law of comparative advantage? (Consider a two-good, two-country example.)

4. Why isn't it possible for all countries to improve their balance of trade by increasing exports and decreasing imports?

5. Why aren't a country's consumption possibilities limited by its production possibilities?

6. When considering a single commodity that is traded without tariffs or quotas, what are the two conditions that characterize equilibrium and determine world price and the location of production?

7. How are these conditions changed if the importing country imposes a tariff? A quota? (Use a demand-supply diagram to show an initial free trade equilibrium and how that equilibrium would be affected by a tariff or quota.)

8. It is often asserted that for every tariff there is a corresponding quota in the sense of having the same impact on prices and production. Is this statement correct and if so what difference(s) would one policy make over the other?

9. Since higher prices following the imposition of a tariff or a quota will reduce domestic demand, how can these policies ever be in the interest of domestic producers?

10. How do you evaluate the arguments supporting strategic trade policies?

11. What is the role of trade adjustment assistance and why do many think it a necessary element of a policy that favors free trade?

12. What is the infant-industry argument? Do you believe it is ever a compelling argument? Why?

13. Some industries argue for trade protection on the grounds of national defense. Do you believe this is ever a compelling argument? Why?

14. "In order to increase the consumption possibilities of Americans, the United States should never prohibit dumping by foreign manufacturers." Do you agree? Why?

15. Why isn't it obvious to many economists that the United States should enact tariffs to level the playing field and protect American workers from unfair competition from low-wage foreign workers?

■ ECONOMICS ONLINE

Data on American international trade is reported by several U.S. government offices.
U.S. Census Bureau

www.census.gov/ftp/pub/foreign-trade/www/

Office of Trade and Economic Analysis, International Trade Administration

www.ita.doc.gov/cgi-bin/otea_ctr?task=otea

Data on international accounts from the Bureau of Economic Analysis, U.S. Department of Commerce

www.bea.doc.gov/bea/di1.htm

Information on international trade from the World Trade Organization can be found through the WTO homepage.

www.wto.org

THE INTERNATIONAL MONETARY SYSTEM: ORDER OR DISORDER?

LEARNING OBJECTIVES

After completing this chapter, you should be able to:

■ identify the factors that help determine a country's exchange rate under a system of floating exchange rates.

■ explain why an appreciation of the dollar against any other currency is simultaneously a depreciation of that currency against the dollar.

■ distinguish between long-, medium-, and short-run factors that help determine the demand and supply of currencies.

■ use a demand and supply diagram to show how changes in GDP, inflation, or interest rates can lead to appreciation or depreciation of the dollar under a system of floating exchange rates.

■ show, on a supply-demand graph, how fixed exchange rates can lead to a balance of payments deficit or surplus.

■ explain the difference between the currency and capital accounts.

■ explain why, under the gold standard, countries lost control of their domestic money stock.

Important Terms and Concepts

INTERNATIONAL MONETARY SYSTEM

EXCHANGE RATE

APPRECIATION

DEPRECIATION

DEVALUATION

REVALUATION

SUPPLY OF AND DEMAND FOR FOREIGN EXCHANGE

FLOATING EXCHANGE RATES

PURCHASING-POWER PARITY THEORY

FIXED EXCHANGE RATES

BALANCE OF PAYMENTS DEFICIT AND SURPLUS

CURRENT ACCOUNT

CAPITAL ACCOUNT

GOLD STANDARD

BRETTON WOODS SYSTEM

INTERNATIONAL MONETARY FUND (IMF)

"DIRTY" OR "MANAGED" FLOAT

EURO

■ describe the options, other than changing the exchange rate, that were available under the Bretton Woods system to a country wanting to eliminate a balance of payments deficit or surplus.

■ explain why, under a system of fixed exchange rates, there was very little risk in speculating against an overvalued currency.

■ explain how speculators can reduce the uncertainty exporters and importers face under a system of floating exchange rates.

■ CHAPTER REVIEW

Meeting: President Richard M. Nixon and H. R. Haldeman, Oval Office, June 23, 1972 (10:04–11:39 A.M.)

Haldeman: Bums is concerned about speculation against the lira.

Nixon: Well, I don't give a (expletive deleted) about the lira . . . There ain't a vote in it.

SOURCE: Statement of Information: Appendix III, *Hearings before the Committee on the Judiciary,* House of Representatives, Ninety-third Congress, Second Session, May-June 1974, page 50.

Even American presidents now pay attention to exchange rates. So should you. Even if you are never president, exchange rates are important for all Americans. Consumers are affected by the price of imports, and jobs for workers can be affected by the price of exports and imports. This chapter discusses exchange rates, that is, the price of one currency in terms of another. The discussion in the text covers the economic factors that determine exchange rates, the implications of attempts by governments to fix exchange rates, and a review of recent history focusing on the evolution of the world's current mixed international monetary system.

Discussions of international monetary arrangements involve a whole new vocabulary of fixed and floating exchange rates, current and capital accounts, appreciating and depreciating currencies, and devaluations and revaluations. It may help you to keep the vocabulary straight if you remember that most of the analysis of international monetary arrangements is merely an application of the supply-demand analysis originally introduced in Chapter 5.

Find out how much it would cost, in American dollars, to buy one Canadian dollar. This figure is

(1)   the current _____ rate, expressed in American dollars. Many newspapers now publish exchange rates on a daily basis. A student in Canada could do the same thing and get a price for American dollars in terms of Canadian dollar. If you both call on the same day you should both get the same price (ignoring sales commissions).[1] If the American dollar price of one Canadian dollar increas-

---

[1]In the United States you might get a price of 68.5 cents for one Canadian dollar. The Canadian student would get a price of 1.46 Canadian dollar for one American dollar. If x is the American dollar price of one Canadian, then $1/x$ is the Canadian dollar price of one American dollar.

es, so that it takes more American dollars to buy one Canadian dollar, we say that the Canadian dollar has _____ relative to the American dollar. Alternatively, it will take (<u>fewer/more</u>) Canadian dollars to buy one American dollar and we would say that the American dollar has _____ relative to the Canadian dollar.

Under a system of floating exchange rates, exchange rates will be determined by market forces of _____ and _____ . Consider an example using two countries, Japan and the United States. The demand for Japanese yen has three major sources: (2)

(1)   the demand by Americans for Japanese exports, such as cars, cameras, and televisions;

(2)   the demand by Americans for Japanese financial assets, such as stocks and bonds; and

(3)   the demand by Americans for Japanese physical assets, such as factories and machines.

The supply of Japanese yen also has three sources: the demand by Japanese for American (<u>exports/imports</u>), American _____ assets, and American _____ assets. (Note that the demand and supply of yen has an interpretation in terms of the demand and supply of dollars. The demand for yen by Americans is simultaneously a _____ of dollars. Understanding this mirror-image aspect of exchange rates may help keep the vocabulary and analysis straight.)

Under a system of floating rates, the equilibrium exchange rate will be at a level where demand equals supply. A change in any factor that affects demand or supply will change the exchange rate. For example, a sudden increase in demand for British wool on the part of Americans would shift the (<u>demand/supply</u>) curve for pounds. The dollar price of pounds will (<u>increase/decrease</u>), a result economists call a(n) (<u>appreciation/depreciation</u>) of the pound in terms of the dollar. Conversely, a sudden increase in demand for California wines on the part of the English would shift the _____ curve of pounds and would mean a(n) (<u>appreciation/depreciation</u>) of the pound in terms of the dollar. A simultaneous boom in the United States and recession in England are likely to lead to a(n) _____ of the pound in terms of the dollar.   (3)

In the long run, the exchange rate between two currencies should reflect the prices of traded goods according to the theory of _____ _____ _____ .   (4)
In order that its goods remain competitive on world markets, a country with a very high rate of

inflation will see its exchange rate (<u>appreciate/depreciate</u>). In the medium run, a country that experiences an economic boom will find its imports rising and its exchange rate _____. In the short run, exchange rates will be affected by the movement of large pools of investment funds that are sensitive to international differences in interest rates. Restrictive monetary policy that increases interest rates will attract funds, (<u>appreciating/depreciating</u>) the exchange rate.

Governments may try to peg the exchange rate. In fact, from the end of World War II until 1973,

(5)   the world operated on a system of fixed exchange rates, established at the _____ Woods conference. At the time, it was thought that fixed exchange rates were necessary to stimulate the growth of international trade, so countries could reap the benefits of specialization according to the law of comparative advantage. Pegging an exchange rate is very similar to any other sort of price control and is subject to similar problems.

If, say, the Japanese government pegs the exchange rate at too high a level, the supply of Japanese

(6)   yen will exceed the demand for yen, and Japan will experience a balance of payments (<u>deficit/surplus</u>). If the government pegs the rate too low, then (<u>demand/supply</u>) will exceed _____ and the result will be a balance of payments _____. It is traditional to measure the demand and supply of currencies as either current or capital transactions. The current account includes private transactions for exports, imports, cross-border payments of interest, dividends, unilateral transfer, and gifts. The capital account includes private payments for financial investments and physical assets. Under a system of floating exchange rates we know that any current account deficit must be offset by a capital account _____ as total demand equals total supply. Adjustments in the _____ _____ insures the equality of the quantity demanded and supplied. Under a system of fixed exchange rates there may be an imbalance in private demand and supply requiring government intervention to maintain the exchange rate.

A government pegging its exchange rate and faced with a deficit will need to use its holdings of

(7)   international reserves, that is, foreign currencies, in order to (<u>buy/sell</u>) its own currency. A country faced with a surplus will need to supply its currency to satisfy the demand of foreigners offering their currencies. As a result, it will find its international reserves (<u>increasing/decreasing</u>).

Under fixed exchange rates, most of the pressure for adjustment is placed on countries experiencing a balance of payments (<u>deficit/surplus</u>). If nothing else, such a country will eventually run out of

(8)

international reserves. If a country does not want to change its exchange rate, other adjustment options include monetary and fiscal policies that (increase/decrease) interest rates, (increase/decrease) the rate of inflation, or induce a general (contraction/expansion) in the level of economic activity. Many of these adjustments occurred automatically under the gold standard as a balance of payments deficit led to an outflow of gold and an automatic (increase/reduction) in the stock of money.

A major weakness of the Bretton Woods system of fixed exchange rates was that deficit countries (liked/disliked) adjusting their domestic economies for balance of payments reasons rather than for   (9) domestic political and economic reasons. Another weakness was the special role accorded the U.S. dollar.

In recent years many of the world's major industrialized countries have operated under a mixed system of floating rates. Exchange rates are allowed to change on a daily basis in response to market forces. At the same time, many governments intervene by buying or selling currencies, hoping to influence the exchange rate to their advantage. Some have worried that floating exchange rates would be so volatile as to destroy world trade. However, market-determined prices need not be volatile, and importers and exporters can often relieve the business risk of changes in exchange rate by dealing with

_____.   (10)

The International Monetary Fund, or IMF, was established to oversee the fixed exchange rates established as part of the Bretton Woods agreement. Now the IMF provides loans to countries with significant balance of payments problems, although these loans usually come with significant restrictions and conditions. Some critics have argued that IMF conditions only help to insure that international investors from rich countries are protected while the contractionary macroeconomic policies bring hardship for local citizens.

In January 1999, 11 members of the European Union agreed to link their currencies at fixed exchange rates and, in 2002, are scheduled to replace their own currencies with the   (11)

_____.

■ IMPORTANT TERMS AND CONCEPTS QUIZ

Choose the best definition for each of the following terms.

1. _____ Exchange rate

2. _____ Appreciation

3. _____ Depreciation

4. _____ Devaluation

5. _____ Revaluation

6. _____ Floating exchange rates

7. _____ Purchasing-power parity theory

8. _____ Fixed exchange rates

9. _____ Balance of payments deficit

10. _____ Balance of payments surplus

11. _____ Current account

12. _____ Capital account

13. _____ Gold standard

14. _____ Bretton Woods system

15. _____ International Monetary Fund

16. _____ Dirty float

17. _____ Euro

a. Common currency used by 11 members of the European Union.

b. Price of one currency in terms of another.

c. Exchange rates determined in free market by supply and demand.

d. Increase in official value of a currency.

e. Value of currencies linked to the dollar whose value was linked to gold.

f. System where exchange rates change in response to market forces, but with intervention by central banks.

g. International agency that extends loans for infrastructure to developing countries.

h. Amount by which quantity supplied of a country's currency exceeds quantity demanded in a given year.

i. Balance of trade involving purchases and sales of assets.

j. International agency that monitors exchange rate policies of member countries.

k. Reduction in official value of a currency.

l. Balance of trade in goods and services plus cross-border payments for interest, dividends, gifts, and unilateral transfers.

m. System where currencies are defined in terms of gold.

n. Increase in the amount of foreign currency a unit of domestic currency can buy.

o. Exchange rates set by the government.

p. Amount by which quantity demanded of a country's currency exceeds quantity supplied.

q. Idea that exchange rates adjust to reflect differences in the prices of traded goods.

r. Drop in the amount of foreign currency a unit of domestic currency can buy.

BASIC EXERCISES ▪

1. Purchasing-Power Parity

This exercise is designed to illustrate the theory of purchasing-power parity.

Assume that the United States and France are the only suppliers of wine on the world market. Consumers of wine are indifferent between French and California wines and buy whichever is cheaper. Initially, the dollar-euro exchange rate is assumed to be $1.06 to the euro and California wine sells for $6.36 a bottle.

Ignoring transportation costs, the initial dollar price of French wines must be $6.36. Accordingly, we know that the initial franc price of French wine is 6 euros a bottle.

Assume now that inflation in the United States has raised the price of California wine to $10 a bottle, while inflation in France has raised the price of French wine to 8 euros. Based on this data, answer each of the following:

a. If the exchange rate is fixed at $1.06 to the euro, what is the new dollar price of French wine? $_____. What would happen to the sales of French and California wines? What happens to the American balance of payments?

b. If the dollar-euro exchange rate is free to adjust, what dollar price of a euro is necessary to equalize the dollar (or euro) price of both wines? _____ This change in the dollar price of a euro is a(n) (appreciation/depreciation) of the euro and a(n) _____ of the dollar.

c. Assuming that the change in the price of wine is typical of the change in other prices, who had had the higher rate of inflation? _____

d. From questions a and c, it is seen that the purchasing-power parity theory implies that under fixed exchange rates a currency with more inflation will experience a balance of payments (deficit/surplus).

e. From questions b and c, it is seen that the purchasing-power parity theory implies that under floating exchange rates a currency with more inflation will (appreciate/depreciate).

2. The Risks of Speculation Against Fixed Exchange Rates

Assume that in the fall of 1967 you are treasurer for a large multinational corporation with 10 million British pounds to invest. The fixed official exchange rate vis-à-vis the U.S. dollar has been $2.80. At this exchange rate Britain has been experiencing large and growing deficits in its balance of payments and has been financing this deficit by buying pounds with foreign currencies. Britain's holdings of foreign currencies are running low, and there is a general feeling that Britain will have to devalue the pound. Exactly how large the devaluation will be and exactly when it will occur are uncertain, but given the history of chronic deficits, there is absolutely no chance that the pound will be revalued.

Complete Table 36-1 to measure the risks of speculating against the pound. (Changing from pounds to dollars and back again will involve transactions costs. Table 36-1 abstracts from these costs, which are apt to be small.)

Results from Speculating Against the Pound | **TABLE 36-1**

	(1)	(2)	(3)
Initial holdings of pounds	£10,000,000	£10,000,000	£10,000,000
Current exchange rate	$2.80	$2.80	$2.80
Number of dollars if you sell pounds for dollars	_____	_____	_____
Possible new exchange rate	$2.80*	$2.60	$2.40
Number of pounds following reconversion to pounds after devaluation	_____	_____	_____

*This exchange rate assumes Britain takes other steps and does not devalue the pound.

What is the worst outcome?

As the talk of devaluation heats up, what are you apt to do? How will your actions affect the British balance of payments deficit and the pressures for devaluation?

3. **Determination of Exchange Rates**

This exercise is designed to contrast the impact of similar events under systems of fixed and floating exchange rates.

Assume that the world is divided into two countries, the United States and Japan. Table 36-2 lists a number of events. Fill in the squares in the table to analyze the impact of these events on (1) the dollar-yen exchange rate under a system of floating rates, and (2) the Japanese balance of payments under a system of fixed exchange rates. Assume that each event takes place from an initial equilibrium that under fixed exchange rates entails neither a deficit nor a surplus. Figure 36-1 illustrates such an equilibrium at an initial exchange rate of 110 yen per dollar.

| TABLE 36-2 | Dollar-Yen Exchange Rate/Balance of Payments |

| Event | Floating Rates | | | Fixed Rates |
	Shift in Demand Curve for Yen (left, right, no shift)	Shift in Supply Curve for Yen (left, right, no shift)	Appreciation or Depreciation of Yen	Change in Japanese Balance of Payments*
a. Federal Reserve policy raises interest rates in the United States.				
b. A change in tastes increases American demand for Japanese electronics.				
c. The U.S. economy enters a recession.				
d. Major labor strikes in Japan have resulted in a sudden increase in the (yen) price of Japanese goods.				
e. A terrible typhoon destroys the Japanese rice crop and increases the demand for American rice.				

*Appropriate answers would be deficit, surplus, or no change

| FIGURE 36-1 | Demand and Supply: Yen |

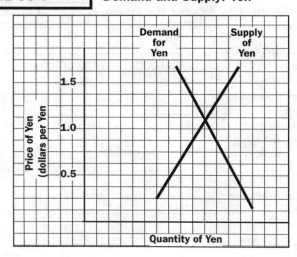

SELF-TESTS FOR UNDERSTANDING   ■

TEST A

Circle the most appropriate answer.

1. The exchange rate between the American dollar and the Mexican peso tells us
    a. how much gold each currency is worth.
    b. the dollar price of a peso and the peso price of a dollar.
    c. whether the Mexicans are running a balance of payments deficit.
    d. how many pounds each currency will purchase.

2. If an American can buy a Russian ruble for 4 cents, how many rubles must a Russian spend to buy a dollar?
    a. 0.4 rubles
    b. 4 rubles
    c. 25 rubles
    d. 40 rubles

3. If the euro appreciates relative to the British pound, then a euro will buy
    a. fewer pounds than before.
    b. the same number of pounds as before.
    c. more pounds than before.

4. If under a system of floating exchange rates the Mexican peso used to cost 30 cents and now costs 15 cents, one would say that _____. (There may be more than one correct answer.)
    a. the peso has appreciated relative to the dollar
    b. the peso has depreciated relative to the dollar
    c. the dollar has appreciated relative to the peso
    d. the dollar has depreciated relative to the peso

5. If it used to take 1 euro to buy one dollar and now it takes 1.05 euros, one would say that the _____. (There may be more than one correct answer.)
    a. euro has appreciated against the dollar
    b. dollar has appreciated against the euro
    c. dollar has depreciated against the euro
    d. euro has depreciated against the dollar

6. If the yen appreciates against the euro, then we know that the
    a. euro has appreciated against the dollar.
    b. dollar has also appreciated against the yen.
    c. euro has depreciated against the yen.
    d. yen has appreciated against the dollar.

7. Under a system of floating exchange rates, an increase in the demand for dollars by foreigners will cause a(n) _____ of the dollar.
    a. devaluation
    b. appreciation
    c. revaluation
    d. depreciation

8. Which of the following would cause an appreciation of the dollar? (There may be more than one correct answer.)
   a. An increase in American GDP.
   b. An increase in foreign GDP.
   c. A decrease in American interest rates.
   d. A decrease in foreign interest rates.
   e. An increase in inflation in the United States.
   f. An increase in inflation in the rest of the world.

9. Which of the following would cause a depreciation of the dollar?
   a. A decrease in American GDP.
   b. An increase in foreign GDP.
   c. An increase in American interest rates.
   d. A decrease in foreign interest rates.
   e. A decrease in inflation in the United States.
   f. A decrease in inflation in the rest of the world.

10. Under a system of floating exchange rates, which one of the following conditions will tend to depreciate the Japanese yen relative to the British pound?
    a. An economic boom in Britain.
    b. A higher level of inflation in Japan than in Britain.
    c. An increase in interest rates in Japan.
    d. A sudden increase in British demand for imports from Japan.

11. Which of the following would lead to an appreciation of the peso relative to the dollar?
    a. A recession in America.
    b. Less inflation in America than in Mexico.
    c. An increase in Mexican interest rates.
    d. A boom in Mexico.

12. An economic boom is likely to mean _____. (There may be more than one correct answer.)
    a. more imports
    b. a depreciation of a country's currency
    c. a balance of payments deficit under a system of floating exchange rates
    d. an appreciation of a country's currency

13. Purchasing-power parity theory says that
    a. only the volume of exports and imports determines exchange rates; interest rates have nothing to do with exchange rates.
    b. all countries are better off with a system of fixed exchange rates.
    c. adjustment of fixed exchange rates should be symmetrical between deficit and surplus countries.
    d. in the long run, exchange rates adjust to reflect differences in price levels between countries.

14. If inflation in United States is at an annual rate of 2 percent and inflation in the Brazil is at 8 percent, then the purchasing-power parity theory suggests that in the long run the dollar price of one Brazilian real will
    a. increase at an annual rate of 8 percent.
    b. decrease at an annual rate of 6 percent.
    c. increase at an annual rate of 6 percent.
    d. increase at an annual rate of 2 percent.

15. In question 14, one would say that the higher rate of inflation in the Brazil results in a(n)
    a. depreciation of the real relative to the dollar.
    b. appreciation of the real relative to the dollar.
    c. depreciation of the dollar relative to the real.
    d. cross-subsidy of the real by the dollar.

16. Assume that the real-dollar exchange rate is fixed, that Brazil and the United States are the only two countries in the world, and that inflation rates differ as described in question 14. Which country will have a balance of payments deficit?
    a. The United States.
    b. Brazil.

17. From an initial position of equilibrium under a system of fixed exchange rates, which of the following would lead to a balance of payments deficit? (There may be more than one correct answer.)
    a. A boom in the domestic economy.
    b. An increase in domestic interest rates.
    c. Domestic inflation in excess of inflation in the rest of the world.
    d. A devaluation by a country's major trading partner.

18. If the country of Zenon tries to fix its exchange rate at a level above that determined by demand and supply, it will likely _____. (There may be more than one correct answer.)
    a. run a balance of payments deficit
    b. run a balance of payments surplus
    c. find its exports being priced out of world markets
    d. see reduced interest by foreigners in investing in Zenon

19. Which one of the following policies would not help to eliminate a deficit under a system of fixed exchange rates?
    a. Monetary and fiscal policies to raise the level of unemployment.
    b. A devaluation of the exchange rate.
    c. Monetary and fiscal policies that increase the rate of inflation.
    d. A change in monetary policy that increases interest rates.

20. If it takes 12 cents to buy one Swedish kronor and $1.08 to buy one euro, then how many kronor should it take to buy one euro?
    a. $(.12 \div 1.08) = .111$
    b. $(1.08 \div .12) = 9$
    c. $(1.0 \div .12) = 8.333$
    d. $(1.0 \div 1.08) = .926$

TEST B

Circle T or F for true or false.

T F 1. If one dollar used to cost 140 yen and now costs 120 yen, the dollar has appreciated relative to the yen.

T F 2. A pure system of floating exchange rates requires government intervention—purchases and sales of its own currency—in order to work properly.

T F 3. Under a system of floating exchange rates, a sudden increase in the demand for U.S. exports will lead to appreciation of the dollar relative to other currencies.

T F 4. Under a system of fixed exchange rates, a sudden increase in American imports would increase the American balance of payments deficit (or reduce the size of the surplus).

T F 5. Purchasing-power parity is a theory of the long-run determination of exchange rates.

T F 6. Under a system of fixed exchange rates, a country that attempts to peg its exchange rate at an artificially low level will end up with a balance of payments surplus.

T   F   7. Today, world international monetary relations are based on the gold standard.

T   F   8. A major advantage of the gold standard was that countries could control their own domestic money stock.

T   F   9. The Bretton Woods gold-exchange system established a system of fixed exchange rates based on the convertibility of dollars into gold.

T   F   10. Under the Bretton Woods system of fixed exchange rates, both surplus and deficit countries felt the same pressure to correct any imbalance in their balance of payments.

■ SUPPLEMENTARY EXERCISE

WORLD TRADE UNDER FIXED AND FLEXIBLE EXCHANGE RATES

Some observers worried that the introduction of a system of floating exchange rates would have adverse effects on the volume of world trade, as exporters and importers would have trouble coping with short-run fluctuations in exchange rates. Look up data on the volume of international trade either in the Library or on the web. (You might try data from one of a variety of international organizations, including the World Trade Organization, the United Nations, the International Monetary Fund, or the World Bank.) What is the percentage change in the annual physical volume of trade since the establishment of the current mixed system of floating exchange rates in 1973? How does the growth in trade compare with growth in world output, that is, the sum of all countries' GDP?

■ ECONOMICS IN ACTION

HEDGING ONE'S INTERNATIONAL INVESTMENTS

The movement of exchange rates complicates the lives of companies and individual investors who by choice or necessity have to deal with international investments. Imagine that interest rates in Britain offer a better return than in the United States. Do you want to convert your dollars into pounds, invest in Britain, and then convert back to dollars? The higher interest return may look tempting, but any advantage of higher interest rates in Britain could be completely offset by an adverse movement in the dollar/pound exchange rate. For example, assume that a pound costs $1.60 when you invest to take advantage of a 10 percent interest rate in Britain compared to a 5 percent interest rate in the United States. What happens if at the end of the year, when you go to convert your pounds back into dollars, the pound has depreciated to $1.45 or appreciated to $1.75? As the example shows, changes in exchange rates can have a major impact on international investors and on the dollar value of international earnings of corporations.[2] Economists would say that these changes add to the variability and risk of international investments. If potential returns are sufficiently attractive, there is an incentive to learn how to manage the associated risk.

It is often argued that one should fully hedge international investments. That is, if you make an investment in Britain you should at the same time take other actions that lock-in the exchange rate you will use to convert your pounds back into dollars. While such actions mean you would not benefit from an appreciation of the pound, you would also avoid the loss that would accompany a depreciation. The use of futures markets—that is, dealing with speculators in foreign exchange—is one way to lock-in a particular exchange rate.

How important is it to hedge one's international investments? Economist Kenneth Froot argues that whether one should hedge international investments depends upon one's time horizon. Using almost 200 years' worth of data on exchange rates between the dollar and the pound along with investment returns

---

[2] Changes in exchange rates are not just an issue for a system of flexible exchange rates. The system of fixed rates under the Bretton Woods agreement included long periods of stable exchange rates marked by sudden and often large adjustments of official exchange rates. If one of those large changes occurred when you had made an international investment, you could be much worse or better off.

in the United States and the United Kingdom, Froot argues that hedging reduced the variance of international investments that were held for short horizons (e.g., one or two years) but that as one's investment horizon lengthened, there was less need to hedge international investments. How can this be?

Consider the following simple example. Assume that over longer time horizons, exchange rates tend toward levels defined by purchasing-power parity, real interest rates are the same in the United States and Britain, and nominal investment returns reflect any differences in inflation. If inflation is higher in Britain, then nominal interest rates in Britain should be higher than in the United States. Note that nominal interest rates in Britain are measured in terms of pounds while in the United States they are measured in terms of dollars. If exchange rates are determined by purchasing-power parity, the pound will depreciate at a rate that just offsets the difference in nominal interest rates. A U.S. investor would not be disadvantaged by the depreciation in the pound and would receive no benefit from dealing with speculators who would incorporate the difference in rates of inflation into the future exchange rates they offer investors. This view suggests that one should evaluate particular investments in the United States or Britain on their merits and that markets may work to minimize the risks associated with changes in the exchange rates if one is investing for the long term.[3]

How do businesses respond to the ups and downs of the dollar? A story in *The New York Times* talked about how Eastman Kodak and other companies deal with changes in exchange rates. These changes are of growing importance as American companies increase foreign operations. For example, by 1992 about 46 percent of Kodak's sales came from foreign countries. David Fiedler, director of foreign exchange for Kodak, reported that in the short term he uses financial hedges to protect against changes in exchange rates. Over the longer term he views questions of foreign exchange as a "business problem like any other business problem." That is, exchange rate risk is something that should be given careful consideration from the very beginning, when making decisions about markets, suppliers, and production sites. "Before 1988, Mr. Fiedler . . . often had to respond to currency swings within minutes after a phone call about foreign developments startled him from sleep. 'That's a real motivator to think of another way,' he said."

1. If you were to make a personal financial investment in a foreign stock market, in what market would you invest? How do you evaluate the exchange rate risks of your choice?

2. What strategies might business follow, other than financial hedges, to minimize the risks associated with international operations?

SOURCES: "Companies Learn to Live with Dollar's Volatility," *The New York Times,* August 31, 1992; Kenneth A. Froot, "Currency Hedging over Long Horizons," Working Paper No. 4355, National Bureau of Economic Research, May 1993.

STUDY QUESTIONS ■

1. If you know the dollar price of a euro, how can you figure out how many euros it takes to buy a dollar?

2. What is the difference between an appreciation and a depreciation of the dollar? Which is better for American tourists? For American exporters?

3. What factors would cause an appreciation of the dollar? What factors would cause a depreciation?

4. Is it possible for the dollar to appreciate against the pound and, at the same time, for the pound to appreciate against the dollar? Why?

5. What is meant by purchasing-power parity? How is it possible for exchange rates to vary from levels determined by purchasing-power parity?

6. How did the gold standard work to maintain fixed exchange rates?

---

[3] Froot's argument is controversial. Measures of the returns one might have received in the past are no guarantee of what one will receive in the future. Even if over the long term one need not worry about movements in exchange rates, an investment that does poorly in either country will have been a mistake.

7. What was the difference between the gold standard and the Bretton Woods system?

8. What is a balance of payments deficit? Is it possible to have an overall deficit under a system of floating exchange rates? Fixed exchange rates?

9. What is meant by the current account? The capital account? How are these measures related to a country's balance of payments?

10. Under a system of fixed exchange rates, what policies might a country adopt to eliminate a balance of payments deficit? Surplus?

11. Who bore most of the burden for adjustment under the Bretton Woods system, deficit or surplus countries? Why wasn't the burden of adjustment equal?

12. Under fixed exchange rates, balance of payment deficits reflect an overvalued exchange rate. The overvalued exchange rate increases the price of a country's exports. A devaluation would help to correct the balance of payments deficit by lowering the price of exports, increasing the demand for exports, and increasing employment in export industries. Yet most countries have resisted devaluation even when facing chronic deficits. What do you think explains this reluctance?

13. What steps might exporters and importers take to minimize the risk of currency fluctuations under a system of floating exchange rates?

14. Why is it said that under fixed exchange rates currency speculation was destabilizing, while under floating exchange rates it is likely to be stabilizing?

15. When would a country prefer a system of fixed exchange rates and when might it prefer a system of floating exchange rates?

16. What is meant by the term "dirty" or "managed" float?

17. What is the IMF and how effective have its policies been?

18. What are the advantages/disadvantages for Europe of adopting the euro?

■ ECONOMICS ONLINE

You can get up to the minute and historical information about exchange rates at a number of web sites. Current information is available at:

Federal Reserve Bank of New York:
www.ny.frb.org/pihome/mktrates/forex12.shtml

Bloomberg:
www.bloomberg.com/@@2TzongYA@s8JORCX/markets/cregion.html
CNN Financial: cnnfn.com/markets/currencies/

Historical information is available at:

Federal Reserve Bank of Chicago:
www.frbchi.org/econinfo/finance/for-exchange/welcome.html

Currency Converters allow you to pick any two currencies and a specific date. The converter will give you the exchange rate between those currencies on that date.

www.oanda.com/converter/classic

EXCHANGE RATES AND THE MACROECONOMY

LEARNING OBJECTIVES

After completing this chapter, you should be able to:

■ explain how an appreciation or depreciation in the exchange rate affects net exports.

■ show how an appreciation or depreciation of the exchange rate affects real GDP and the price of domestically produced goods by appropriate shifts of the aggregate demand and aggregate supply curves.

■ describe how changes in interest rates affect international capital flows and the exchange rate.

■ explain why the reaction of international capital flows to changes in interest rates works to offset the impact of changes in fiscal policy.

■ explain why the reaction of international capital flows to changes in interest rates works to enhance the impact of changes in monetary policy.

■ explain in what way government deficits and trade deficits are linked.

■ explain how a change in the mix of fiscal and monetary policy affects macroeconomic variables such as GDP, real interest rates, prices, the trade deficit, and the exchange rate.

Important Terms and Concepts

EXPORTS

IMPORTS

NET EXPORTS

CLOSED ECONOMY

OPEN ECONOMY

EXCHANGE RATE

APPRECIATION

DEPRECIATION

TRADE DEFICIT

INTERNATIONAL CAPITAL FLOWS

BUDGET DEFICITS AND TRADE DEFICITS

$(X - IM) = (S - I) - (G - T)$

■ evaluate the likely impact of proposals to reduce the U.S. trade deficit.

■   CHAPTER REVIEW

This chapter integrates the discussion of international trade and exchange rates of the preceding two chapters with the earlier discussions of income determination and fiscal and monetary policy. An econ-

(1) omy that did not trade with any other economy would be called a _____ economy. Today all industrial economies and most developing economies have extensive links with other economies through trade in goods and services and financial assets. Such economies are called _____ economies. These international linkages can affect important macroeconomic outcomes such as GDP and prices. While a complete and rigorous examination of these linkages is the stuff of more advanced courses in economics, we can use the model of income determination that we developed in earlier chapters to shed light on a number of important issues.

We start with a review of factors affecting the demand for exports and imports. As we saw earlier, the demand for exports and imports is influenced by income and prices. A decrease in foreign income

(2) will (decrease/increase) the demand for American exports and is an important reason why economic fluctuations abroad (are/are not) felt in the United States. Exports and imports are also influenced by changes in the exchange rate, as these changes alter the relative price of foreign and domestic goods. An appreciation of the dollar makes foreign goods (less/more) expensive. The result is likely to be a(n) (decrease/increase) in American imports and a(n) _____ in American exports. Putting these two effects together shows that an appreciation of the exchange rate will lead to a(n) (decrease/increase) in net exports, $(X - IM)$. Similar reasoning shows that a depreciation of the dollar will lead to a(n) _____ in exports, a(n) _____ in imports, and a(n) _____ in net exports.

A change in net exports that comes from a change in exchange rates is analogous to any other autonomous change in spending. It shifts the expenditure schedule and leads to a

(3) (movement along/shift in) the aggregate demand curve. More precisely, following an appreciation of the dollar, net exports decline, the expenditure schedule shifts (down/up), and the aggregate demand curve shifts to the (left/right). Opposite results follow from a depreciation of the dollar.

A change in exchange rates can also lead to a shift in the aggregate supply curve through its impact on the price of imported intermediate goods. An appreciation of the dollar makes imported inputs (less/more) expensive. This result can be modeled as a(n) (downward/upward) shift in the aggregate (4)

supply curve. A depreciation of the dollar makes imported inputs _____ expensive and

leads to a(n) _____ shift in the aggregate supply curve.

Once we understand the impact of a change in interest rates on international capital flows and on

the exchange rate, we will have all the pieces necessary to examine how fiscal and monetary policy

work in an open economy with flexible exchange rates. We saw in the previous chapter that an increase

in interest rates is apt to (decrease/increase) the demand by foreigners for American financial assets. (5)

This change in the demand for dollars should lead to a(n) (appreciation/depreciation) of the dollar.

Tracing through the impact of this capital-flow-induced change in the exchange rate is the key to

understanding how fiscal and monetary policy work in an open economy.

To review, consider a change in fiscal policy. A move to expansionary fiscal policy, say a(n)

(decrease/increase) in taxes, would shift the expenditure schedule (up/down) and shift the aggregate (6)

demand curve to the (right/left). With no changes in monetary policy (that is, no shift in the supply

of money schedule), there will be a(n) (decrease/no change/increase) in interest rates. If the exchange

rate did not change, this would be the end of our story. In a world of market determined flexible

exchange rates, the impact of higher interest rates on international capital flows will lead to a(n)

(appreciation/depreciation) in the exchange rate. This change in the exchange rate will shift the aggre-

gate demand curve to the (left/right) and shift the aggregate supply curve (down/up). The shift in the

aggregate demand curve, induced by the change in the exchange rate, works to (enhance/offset) the

original expansionary change in fiscal policy. The shift in the aggregate supply curve works to

(lower/raise) prices and to (increase/decrease) output. If the shift in the aggregate supply curve

induced by the change in exchange rates were large enough, it could offset the impact on output from

the exchange-rate-induced shift in the aggregate demand curve. Evidence suggests that the shift in the

aggregate supply curve is small and that, on net, the shifts in the two curves work to (enhance/offset)

the impact of expansionary fiscal policy on output.

A move to restrictive monetary policy can be analyzed in the same way. The initial effects will

include an increase in interest rates that leads to a(n) (appreciation/depreciation) of the exchange rate. (7)

The impact of the change in the exchange rate will (enhance/offset) the original restrictive change in

monetary policy.

Our equilibrium condition that $Y = C + I + G + (X - IM)$ can be manipulated to illustrate the important link between government budget deficits and trade deficits. Remembering that GDP equals disposable income plus net taxes and that disposable income equals consumption spending plus savings enables us to rewrite this equilibrium condition[1] as

$$(X - IM) = (S - I) - (G - T).$$

If the government runs a deficit—that is, if the government wants more output than it can command through taxes—then either private savings must exceed private investment, $(S - I)$, or additional output must be forthcoming from foreigners—that is, imports must exceed exports. As we have seen, in a world of flexible exchange rates, any deficit on the current account must be offset by a surplus on the capital account. Thus a trade deficit will be associated with a net capital inflow, that is, increased indebtedness to foreigners. It is changes in income, interest rates, exchange rates, and prices that enforce equilibrium and the link between budget deficits, trade deficits, and international capital flows.

Is the American trade deficit a problem? One's answer to this question depends upon whether capital inflows are a market response to extravagant spending requiring high interest rates in the United States to attract foreign capital or as the result of an autonomous increase in foreign demand for investment in the United States. The former suggests an economy spending beyond its means while the later suggests a strong economy in which people want to invest.

A number of suggestions have been made to reduce the trade deficit. Many argue that the United States should alter the mix of fiscal and monetary policy. According to this view, the increase in the

(8)   American trade deficit during the 1980s was the result of (<u>contractionary/expansionary</u>) fiscal policy and _____ monetary policy. Reversing these actions, that is, a move to _____ fiscal policy and _____ monetary policy, could work in reverse and lower the trade deficit as long as other factors, specifically the difference between domestic savings and investments, do not change. Rapid economic growth abroad would increase American (<u>exports/imports</u>). Protectionism would lower imports, but retaliation by foreign governments could (<u>lower/raise</u>) American exports with little change in net exports. One also needs to consider the impact

---

[1]Remember that on the income side GDP $= Y = DI + T = C + S + T$. Since both expressions equal GDP, we can set $C + S + T = C + I + G + (X - IM)$. Canceling C on both sides of the equal sign and rearranging terms yields the expression above. This condition can also be written as $G + I + X = S + T + IM$. In terms of the circular flow diagram we saw earlier, this formulation says that injections must equal leakages.

of protectionism on exchange rates. For any of these measures to work, the equilibrium condition described above, $G - T = (S - I) - (X - IM)$, shows us that any reduction in the trade deficit will require a combination of lower budget deficits, higher savings, or lower investment.

IMPORTANT TERMS AND CONCEPTS QUIZ ■

Choose the best definition for each of the following terms.

1. _____ Exports

2. _____ Imports

3. _____ Closed economy

4. _____ Open economy

5. _____ Trade deficit

a. Domestically produced goods sold abroad.

b. Graph depicting response of inflation to changes in the exchange rate.

c. Economy that trades with other economies.

d. Amount by which imports exceed exports.

e. Foreign-produced goods purchased domestically.

f. Economy that does not trade with other economies.

BASIC EXERCISES ■

This exercise is designed to review how the operation of fiscal and monetary policy is affected by interest-sensitive capital flows in an open economy.

1. Table 37-1 is designed to help you review the impact of changes in the exchange rate on various macroeconomic variables. First, complete the column for an appreciation of the exchange rate. Then complete the column for a depreciation of the exchange rate. In each cell indicate how each variable changes, i.e., increases or decreases, shifts left, right, up or down, as appropriate. Be sure you can explain why each variable shows the change you have indicated. If the change in GDP and the price level seems ambiguous, see if you can resolve the ambiguity by assuming, as in the text, that any shift in the aggregate demand curve is greater than the shift in the aggregate supply curve.

Monetary Policy in an Open Economy | TABLE 37-1

Macroeconomic Variable	Exchange Rate Appreciation	Exchange Rate Depreciation
Exports	_____	_____
Imports	_____	_____
Net Exports	_____	_____
Expenditure Schedule	_____	_____
Aggregate Demand Curve	_____	_____
Aggregate Supply Curve	_____	_____
Real GDP	_____	_____
Price Level	_____	_____

TABLE 37-2	Fiscal Policy in an Open Economy			
	Increase In G	Decrease In G	Open Market Sale	Open Market Purchase
Aggregate Demand Curve	Right	Left	Left	Right
Real GDP	Up	Down	Down	Up
Price Level	Up	Down	Down	Up
Interest Rate	_____	_____	_____	_____
Exchange Rate	_____	_____	_____	_____
Real GDP	_____	_____	_____	_____
Price Level	_____	_____	_____	_____
Overall Impact				
Real GDP	_____	_____	_____	_____
Price Level	_____	_____	_____	_____

FIGURE 37-1

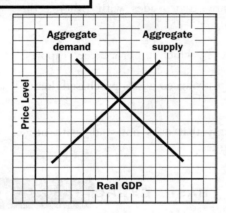

2. Table 37-2 is designed to analyze the impact on GDP and the price level of changes in fiscal and monetary policy. The completed upper portion of the table ignores any impact on exchange rates. Remembering that changes in interest rates are likely to influence the international investment of funds and hence the demand for dollars, complete Table 37-2 to determine whether capital flows offset or enhance these changes in monetary and fiscal policy. You should first specify the change in interest rates; determine how the exchange rate is affected; and consider the impact of the change in the exchange rate on GDP and prices. Finally, combine your results from the change in policy and the change in exchange rates to determine the overall impact. Figure 37-1 may be helpful when completing Table 37-2.

3. What general conclusion can you draw about the effectiveness of monetary and fiscal policy in a world of interest-sensitive capital flows and flexible exchange rates?

■   SELF-TESTS FOR UNDERSTANDING

TEST A

Circle the most appropriate answer.

1. An increase in foreign GDP is likely to lead to
   a. a decrease in our exports.
   b. little if any change in our exports.
   c. an increase in our exports.

2. An appreciation of the exchange rate will make
   a. both exports and imports cheaper.
   b. exports more expensive for foreigners but imports cheaper for domestic citizens.
   c. exports cheaper for foreigners but imports more expensive for domestic citizens.
   d. both exports and imports more expensive.

3. An appreciation of the exchange rate will lead to
   a. an increase in exports and imports.
   b. a decrease in exports and an increase in imports.
   c. an increase in exports and a decrease in imports.
   d. a decrease in both exports and imports.

4. An appreciation of the exchange rate will lead to _____ in net exports.
   a. a decrease
   b. no change
   c. an increase

5. A decrease in net exports will
   a. shift the aggregate demand curve to the left.
   b. have no impact on the aggregate demand curve.
   c. shift the aggregate demand curve to the right.

6. An appreciation of the exchange rate will
   a. shift the aggregate supply curve up.
   b. have no impact on the aggregate supply curve.
   c. shift the aggregate supply curve down.

7. Evidence suggests that when the exchange rate changes, shifts in the aggregate demand curve will _____ shifts in the aggregate supply curve.
   a. be smaller than
   b. just offset
   c. be larger than

8. On balance an appreciation of the exchange rate will tend to
   a. raise real GDP and raise the price of domestically produced goods.
   b. raise real GDP but lower the price of domestically produced goods.
   c. lower real GDP but raise the price of domestically produced goods.
   d. lower real GDP and lower the price of domestically produced goods.

9. A depreciation of the exchange rate tends to
   a. raise real GDP and raise the price of domestically produced goods.
   b. raise real GDP but lower the price of domestically produced goods.
   c. lower real GDP but raise the price of domestically produced goods.
   d. lower real GDP and lower the price of domestically produced goods.

10. Higher foreign interest rates are likely to be followed by _____. (There may be more than one correct answer.)
    a. an inflow of international capital
    b. an increase in foreign investments by domestic citizens, i.e., a capital outflow
    c. an appreciation of the exchange rate
    d. an increase in net exports

11. An increase in domestic interest rates should lead to which one of the following?
    a. Capital outflow.
    b. Appreciation of the dollar.
    c. Increase in exports.
    d. Upward shift in the expenditure schedule.

12. An appreciation in the dollar vis-à-vis other currencies should lead to all but which one of the following?
    a. A decrease in exports.
    b. An increase in imports.
    c. A shift of the aggregate demand curve to the right.
    d. A downward shift of the aggregate supply curve.

13. A move to expansionary fiscal policy will lead to all but which one of the following?
    a. An increase in interest rates.
    b. An appreciation of the dollar.
    c. A decrease in American imports.
    d. An increase in the American trade deficit.

14. A move to expansionary monetary policy will lead to all but which one of the following?
    a. A decrease in interest rates.
    b. An appreciation of the dollar.
    c. An upward shift in the expenditure schedule.
    d. An increase in inflationary pressures.

15. Taking account of interest-sensitive international capital flows means that in an open economy the impact of fiscal policy is
    a. smaller than in a closed economy.
    b. the same as in a closed economy.
    c. larger than in a closed economy.

16. Taking account of interest-sensitive international capital flows means that in an open economy the impact of monetary policy is
    a. smaller than in a closed economy.
    b. the same as in a closed economy.
    c. larger than in a closed economy.

17. In an open economy equilibrium requires that
    a. $IM - X = (S - I) + (G - T)$.
    b. $X - IM = (S - I) - (G - T)$.
    c. $X - IM = (I - S) - (G - T)$.
    d. $IM - X = (S - I) - (G - T)$.

18. If there is no change in the balance of domestic savings and investment, then any increase in the government deficit must be matched by _____. (There may be more than one correct answer.)
    a. an increase in the trade deficit
    b. a reduction in the equilibrium level of output
    c. a capital inflow
    d. a reduction in interest rates

19. Which one of the following would help to reduce the U.S. trade deficit?
    a. Higher government deficits.
    b. Increased domestic investment.
    c. Increased domestic savings.
    d. A decrease in exports.

20. An increase in the government deficit need not lead to an increase in the trade deficit if there is _____. (There may be more than one correct answer.)
    a. an increase in private saving
    b. a decrease in private investment
    c. an increase in consumption spending
    d. an increase in imports

TEST B

Circle T or F for true or false.

T   F   1. International trade means that an economic boom in the United States is likely to lead to recession in the rest of the world.

T F   2. A change in exports has no multiplier impacts.

T F   3. A shift in the expenditure schedule coming from an autonomous change in domestic investment spending would be expected to have no impact on a country's trade deficit.

T F   4. A depreciation in the exchange rate is inflationary.

T F   5. A depreciation in the exchange rate should help to reduce a country's trade deficit.

T F   6. Under floating exchange rates, a country with a trade surplus will also experience a capital outflow.

T F   7. Interest-sensitive international capital flows make monetary policy less effective.

T F   8. International capital flows are unaffected by changes in fiscal policy.

T F   9. Increased protectionism has been shown to be an effective tool for eliminating a trade deficit.

T F 10. The only way to reduce the trade deficit is by reducing the government's budget deficit.

ECONOMICS IN ACTION ■

SHOULD BRITAIN JOIN THE EURO?

The euro was launched in January 1999 when 11 members of the European Community (Austria, Belgium, Finland, France, Germany, Ireland, Italy, Luxembourg, the Netherlands, Portugal and Spain) agreed to fix the exchange rate between their individual currencies and the euro.

While national currencies will be in circulation until 2002, the euro will be used immediately for stock and bond trades, government borrowing and other financial transactions. In addition bank accounts and credit card transactions can be denominated in euros The inauguration of the euro also saw the creation of the European Central Bank which will decide monetary policy for euro nations.

Euro supporters see the establishment of the euro as an important step on the road to greater political integration across Europe. An immediate economic impact is the elimination of the need to deal in multiple currencies for trade within the euro zone. With national currencies there were often substantial price differences for the same goods in different countries. A single currency will make it more difficult to sustain these differences and will help to further the dream of a single common market for all of Europe. The result should be benefits for consumers and for firms who are nimble enough to take advantage of new opportunities. Euro optimists foresee a sustained economic boom.

At a macroeconomic level, euro supporters see the euro at the center of the development of a larger and more efficient capital market, one that might in time rival that of the United States. It is expected that the new European Central Bank will be an inflation hawk which would further increase the international attractiveness of the euro as a strong currency.

Others aren't so sure about the benefits of the euro for Europe. The United States has a single currency, dollars from New York trade for dollars from California at a fixed exchange rate of one to one. Part of the success of the American economy is a mobile labor force. When times are tough individual states cannot run their own monetary policy, but people do pick up and move to where there are better opportunities. A number of observers are skeptical that labor will be so mobile within Europe. Even if the currency is the same the language and culture may well be different.

Some American economists, most prominently Martin Feldstein, chairman of the Council of Economic Advisers under President Reagan, believe that the euro is likely to weaken European economies, not strengthen them. Feldstein argues that the decline in inflation in Europe over the past 20 years is the result of countries needing to match Germany's fiercely anti-inflation policies. Once inside the euro it will be harder for Germany to exercise this leadership when a number of other countries are facing unemployment rates of 10 percent or higher.

Feldstein is fearful that pressures to harmonize tax rates and other country specific policies that offer competitive advantages for exports may mean a highly regulated economy with inflexible rules and procedures. European monetary policy will be set according to European wide conditions while the euro eliminates the ability of countries to respond to country specific adverse shocks by easing their own monetary policy. All of these factors could mean weaker economies and increased tensions.

What has been the experience of the euro to date?

Britain did not join the euro initially but the Labour government has promised a referendum on the euro, probably in late 2001 or early 2002. Should Britain join the euro? Why?

SOURCES: "Martin Feldstein, "The Euro Risk," *Time*, January 25, 1999. "Euro brief: The Merits of One Money," *The Economist*, October 24, 1998.

STUDY QUESTIONS

1. What is the difference between an open and a closed economy?

2. How does an appreciation in the exchange rate affect net exports? What about a depreciation? Why?

3. How does a change in net exports, induced by a change in the exchange rate, affect the aggregate demand curve? The aggregate supply curve? Which effect is likely to be larger?

4. Does an increase in interest rates lead to an appreciation or depreciation of the exchange rate? Why?

5. Consider a move to contractionary fiscal policy that reduces aggregate demand. What is the likely impact on interest rates, international capital flows, the exchange rate, and net exports? Do these changes tend to enhance or offset the original change in fiscal policy?

6. Consider a move to expansionary monetary policy that increases aggregate demand. What is the likely impact on interest rates, international capital flows, the exchange rate, and net exports? Do these changes enhance or offset the original change in monetary policy?

7. What is the link between government deficits and trade deficits? Under what conditions does an increase in the government deficit lead to an increase in the trade deficit?

8. What is your evaluation of the cumulative impact of American trade deficits since 1980?

9. Some have argued for a change in the mix of fiscal and monetary policy—easier monetary policy and contractionary fiscal policy—as a way to reduce both government deficits and the trade deficit. Would these changes have the desired impact? Why?

10. Why isn't increased protectionism a sure-fire way to reduce the trade deficit?

11. Why didn't the large currency deprecations in Southeast Asia in 1997 and 1998 lead to expansions in output?

ECONOMICS ONLINE

The homepage for the Organization for Economic Co-operation and Development can be found at the address below. The OECD monitors economic trends and does comparative analysis for its 26 member countries.

www.oecd.org

Statistics Netherlands maintains a set of web links to statistical agencies for a number of countries. These links can be found at

www.cbs.nl/en/services/nsi-links.htm

What are current differences in interest rates in different countries? Bloomberg.com posts data for some of the world's largest economies at

www.bloomberg.com/markets/iyc.html

ANSWER KEY

CHAPTER 1
CHAPTER REVIEW
(1) information; value

IMPORTANT TERMS AND CONCEPTS QUIZ
1. f
2. j
3. b
4. e
5. g
6. a
7. c
8. i
9. d
10. k
11. h

BASIC EXERCISES
1. F
2. D
3. I
4. B
5. A
6. K
7. H
8. J
9. E
10. L
11. C
12. G

SELF-TESTS FOR UNDERSTANDING
Test A
1. a
2. c
3. b
4. c
5. a
6. d
7. c
8. a
9. c
10. b
11. d
12. b

Test B
1. F
2. F
3. T
4. T
5. F
6. F
7. F
8. F
9. F
10. F
11. F
12. F
13. F
14. F
15. F
16. F
17. F
18. F
19. F
20. F

CHAPTER 2
CHAPTER REVIEW
(1) horizontal; vertical; origin
(2) vertical; horizontal; constant; positive; up; negative; no
(3) ray; 45-degree
(4) tangent
(5) contour
(6) horizontal; vertical

IMPORTANT TERMS AND CONCEPTS QUIZ
1. f
2. g
3. q
4. m
5. r
6. o
7. k
8. p
9. t
10. b
11. c
12. j
13. e
14. i
15. n
16. u
17. h
18. d
19. l
20. s

BASIC EXERCISES
1. a. 300
   b. increase; 500
   c. decrease; 200
   d. −50
   e. Slope equals vertical change divided by horizontal change or the change in salary divided by the change in the quantity demanded. Information about the change in the number of new Ph.D. economists demanded as salary changes is given the reciprocal of the slope. For example, the demand curve implies that a $1,000 change in salary will reduce the quantity demand by about 8.
2. a. 4
   b. 5
   c. above
   d. non-economics
3. a. No, increases in aggregate consumption expenditures due to inflation or population do not increase individual purchasing power.
   b. 11.7 times; column 3: 1,839; 21,496
   c. 2.4 times; column 5: 7,930; 19,074
4. 18.13; 32.26; 25.79; 25.00; 27.03; 32.73; 26.52; 29.76; 30.99; 37.45; 36.64; 37.97; 35.83; 48.22; 21.25

5. The trend line from 1968 to 1983 seems to tell a similar story; but, just as in the 1960s, the trend line does not mean that appropriate macroeconomic policy cannot lower the rate of unemployment.

6. The graph in Figure 2-5a exaggerates the decrease in stock prices as it omits the origin. Figure 2-5b provides a more realistic picture.

SELF-TESTS FOR UNDERSTANDING: APPENDIX
Test A

1. b
2. b
3. c
4. d
5. a
6. a
7. c; a; b; d
8. A&E; C; B&D; none
9. d slope = vertical change/horizontal change = $(10-16)/(8-5) = -6/3 = -2$
10. c
11. b
12. b
13. b
14. d
15. c
16. a
17. d
18. a slope = 2/5 = 0.4
19. b
20. b

Test B

1. F
2. F
3. T
4. T
5. F
6. T
7. F
8. T
9. T
10. F

SUPPLEMENTARY EXERCISE
1992 dollars:

Public: 1,585; 1,194; 2,276; 2,900

Private: 6,566; 5,580; 11.995; 14,362

Proportion of per capita real income:

Public: 13.0%; 8.0%; 12.7%; 15.4%

Private: 53.8%; 37.3%; 67.2%;76.3%

CHAPTER 3
CHAPTER REVIEW

(1) domestic; product; GDP; productivity

(2) inputs; outputs; free; private

(3) open; closed; closed

(4) inflation; real; per capita

(5) recessions

(6) factors

(7) labor; 15 cents; service

(8) small

IMPORTANT TERMS AND CONCEPTS QUIZ

1. h
2. i
3. a
4. f
5. j
6. e
7. g
8. k
9. d
10. l
11. b

BASIC EXERCISES

1. 1960: 13.0%; 46.0%; 40.9%

   1998: 12.5%; 28.6%; 58.9%

2. 1960: 52.2%; 0.9%; 20.6%; 7.5%; 18.9%

3. Men: 42.6%; 64.4%; 82.0%; 93.2%; 89.2%; 68.1%; 16.5%

   Women: 41.9%; 62.6%; 73.0%; 76.3%; 77.1%; 76.2%; 51.2%; 8.6%

SELF-TESTS FOR UNDERSTANDING
Test A

1. a, d
2. c
3. b, c
4. d
5. a
6. d
7. b As it uses dollars of constant purchasing power, real GDP changes only if the volume of output changes.
8. c
9. d
10. c
11. d bread is the output
12. d
13. b
14. d
15. d Imports are goods produced abroad and bought in America.
16. a Exports are goods produced in America and sold in foreign countries.
17. c
18. a
19. c
20. a

Test B

1. T
2. F

3. F

4. F

5. T

6. T

7. F

8. F

9. F

10. T

CHAPTER 4
CHAPTER REVIEW

(1) scarce

(2) opportunity cost

(3) scarce; specialized; fewer; more; more; consumption

(4) slope

(5) increase; increasing; specialized

(6) inside; inefficient,

(7) will

IMPORTANT TERMS AND CONCEPTS QUIZ

1. g

2. i

3. n

4. r

5. m

6. j

7. a

8. s

9. f

10. q

11. p

12. b

13. e

14. l

15. h

16. d

17. u

18. o

19. k

20. t

BASIC EXERCISES

1. a. 560,000; 40,000; rises; 120,000; continue to rise; specialized

    b. Point A is not attainable; point B is attainable; point C is attainable; on and inside; on

    c. Point B is inefficient. You should be able to shade a small triangular area above and to the right of point B out to and including a small segment of the PPF.

2. a. Catskill, the economy that produces the greater amount of capital goods will have the greater shift. That is, next year the PPF for Catskill should lies outside that of Adirondack.

    b. An economist would measure the cost of economic growth by the differences in the output of consumption goods or 120,000 loaves of bread, 400,000 − 280,000.

SELF-TESTS FOR UNDERSTANDING
Test A

1. c

2. c

3. d

4. d

5. a

6. b

7. c

8. b

9. d

10. d

11. b

12. b   On the PPF, output of computers must decline by 500.

13. b   Borrowing money would enable firm to pay for additional resources.

14. a

15. b   Reflects economic growth.

16. c   More money helps a single firm buy resources. An economy's resources are given by its natural resources, population and capital.

17. c

18. a

19. b

20. d

Test B

1. F

2. F

3. T

4. T

5. F

6. F

7. T

8. T

9. F   Any economic unit with limited resources will need to make choices.

10. F   Dollar bills are not a factor of production.

SUPPLEMENTARY EXERCISES

3. a. 300,000 cars; 1,000 tanks

    c. yes, it bows out.

    d. $1/2C^*$, $1/2T^*$ should be on straight line connecting C^* and T^*. Combination is attainable, lies inside frontier; inefficient, not on frontier as frontier bows out.

    e. 6 cars; 30 cars; 120 cars

    f. opportunity cost = $(0.6)T$ cars; yes, opportunity cost increases as the production of tanks increases.

    g. new frontier lies everywhere outside the old frontier.

4. a. When $I = 1,600$ the sustainable level of $C = 10,292$.

    b. C drops by 400 to 9,892 and then rises to its new sustainable level of 10,574.

    c. The increase in consumption, 10,574 to 10,761, is less than in question b. Additional machines add to output but at a decreasing rate. This increase at a decreasing rate is an example of declining marginal productivity.

    d. There can be too much of a good thing. Additional machines increase total output, but with a constant labor force the increments to output are smaller and smaller. The additional machines also increase the amount of output that must be allocated to investment in order to offset the larger amount of depreciation because of the larger number of machines. With a large enough increase in the number of machines, the increase in investment needed to maintain machines requires all of the increase in output. Past this point, additional investment will actually lower the sustainable level of consumption. What is this critical point? $I = 3,655$, $M = 45,688$. More generally, it depends upon the size of L, exponents on L and M in equation (1) and the rate of depreciation. Ask your instructor for more details.

CHAPTER 5
CHAPTER REVIEW

(1) price; negative; more; movement along; shift in

(2) price; positive; more; shift in

(3) demand

(4) $300; 4,000; less; 6,000; 2,000; surplus; reduction; shortage; demanded; supplied; increase

(5) intersection; equilibrium

(6) demand; supply; movement along; supply; demand; demand

(7) maximum; minimum

(8) hard; auxiliary restrictions

(9) shortages; decrease

(10) high

IMPORTANT TERMS AND CONCEPTS QUIZ

1. k
2. e
3. g
4. c
5. i
6. q
7. o
8. p
9. n
10. h
11. f
12. m
13. d
14. j
15. b
16. a

BASIC EXERCISES

1. b. 40; 1,100

    c. increased; 50; increased; 1,200; less

    The impact of the change in price following the shift of the demand curve means that the change in the equilibrium quantity will be less than the horizontal shift in the demand curve.

    d. increase; decrease; 55; 1,100, less than

2. a. demand; right; rise; rise

    b. supply; right; fall; rise

    c. supply; left; rise; fall

    d. demand; left; fall; fall

3. a. 100; 100; neither, as ceiling exceeds equilibrium price

    b. 110; 80; shortage

    Price ceilings lead to shortages when they are less than the free market equilibrium price.

    c. 90; 120; surplus

    d. 100; 100; neither, as floor is less than equilibrium price

    Price floors lead to surpluses when they are greater than the free market equilibrium price.

SELF-TESTS FOR UNDERSTANDING
Test A

1. c
2. a
3. d
4. c
5. c
6. b
7. a
8. a   b, c, d, would shift the demand curve
9. d
10. b
11. c
12. a
13. b, d cotton cloth is an input; skirts, pants and blouses may be related outputs for clothing manufacturers.
14. b   The other changes are likely to affect equilibrium price and quantity by shifting the demand curve.
15. b
16. c
17. b
18. a
19. d

20. b

Test B

1. F   The law of supply and demand is an empirical regularity, not a Congressional statute.

2. T

3. T

4. F

5. F

6. T

7. T

8. F

9. F

10. F

11. T

12. F

13. T

14. F

15. F   The increase in price and quantity comes from the movement along the supply curve following the shift in the demand curve.

CHAPTER 6
CHAPTER REVIEW

(1) marginal; will; decrease

(2) consumer's; price; greater; increase

(3) greater; marginal; more; up; negative

(4) shift in; utility; inferior; fewer

(5) horizontal; negative

IMPORTANT TERMS AND CONCEPTS QUIZ

1. d
2. h
3. e
4. c
5. b
6. g
7. a

BASIC EXERCISES

1. a. 110; 100; 80; 70; 50; 30; 20

   b. 2; 4; 5

   c. Col. 3: 20; 30; 20; 0; –40; –100; –170; 2
   Col. 5: 50; 90; 110; 120; 110; 80; 40; 4
   Col. 7: 70; 130; 170; 200; 210; 200; 180; 5

   d. consumer's; quantities are the same

2. a. $18 ($63 – $45)

   b. $30 ($63 – 3 x $11)

   c. consumer surplus up by $4 ($15 – $11)

   d. 5

   e. $35 ($90 – 5 x $11)

   f. 6

SELF-TESTS FOR UNDERSTANDING
Test A

1. b
2. a
3. d
4. a   marginal utility = change in total utility = 300 – 200 = 100.
5. d
6. c   if MU > P then the difference between total utility and total spending will increase.
7. c
8. d
9. c
10. c
11. a
12. b
13. c
14. b
15. b
16. d
17. c
18. d

19. d

20. a, c

Test B

1. F
2. T
3. T
4. F
5. T
6. F
7. T
8. F   The label of inferior goods implies nothing about rationality. It refers to the impact of a change in income on the quantity demanded.
9. F
10. F

APPENDIX
APPENDIX REVIEW

(1) straight; negative; intercept; slope

(2) indifference; indifferent; are; never; negative

(3) in; more; substitution; decreases

(4) budget; indifference; highest; budget line

(5) budget line

IMPORTANT TERMS AND CONCEPTS QUIZ: APPENDIX

1. c
2. d
3. a
4. e

BASIC EXERCISE: APPENDIX

1. a. 40; 20

   b. 20; 10

   c. 3; 2

   e. equals the slope of the budget line

2. a. Z

Neither is an inferior good as point Z shows an increase in the quantity demanded for both following the increase in income.

   b. Y

SELF-TESTS FOR UNDERSTANDING: APPENDIX
Test A

1. c
2. c
3. d
4. c
5. b
6. d
7. c
8. b
9. b
10. c
11. d
12. b
13. a

Test B

1. F
2. T
3. F
4. F
5. F
6. T
7. F
8. F   Budget line shows commodity bundles consumer can buy. A single indifference curve shows bundles about which she is indifferent.
9. T
10. T   A doubling of money income and prices leaves the budget line unaffected.

SUPPLEMENTARY EXERCISE: APPENDIX

2. $F = (Y + 20P_C - 12P_F)/2P_F$

   $C = (Y - 20P_C + 12P_F)/2P_C$

   where P_F = price of food, P_C = price of clothing and Y = income. The demand curves come from solving the following two equations for F and C:

   Optimal purchases require that the marginal rate of substitution equals the ratio of market prices, or

   $(F + 12)/(C + 20) = P_C/P_F$

   The budget constraint requires that:

   $F \times P_F + C \times P_C = Y$

3. $F = 114$; $C = 43$
4. $F = 84$; $C = 44$
5. $F = 124$; $C = 48$; no

CHAPTER 7
CHAPTER REVIEW

(1) elasticity; demand
(2) zero; infinite; changes
(3) elastic; inelastic; unit elastic
(4) will not; 1.0
(5) greater; decrease; increase; less; increase; decrease
(6) cross
(7) complements; negative; increase; right
(8) substitutes; positive; decrease; left
(9) shift in

IMPORTANT TERMS AND CONCEPTS QUIZ

1. f
2. e
3. b
4. g
5. d
6. h
7. a
8. i

BASIC EXERCISES

1. b. 1.0
   c. 1.0
   d. 1.0

   Do not be fooled by appearances.

2. straight

   a. %Δ price: 10.53%; 11.76%; 13.33%; 15.38%

   %Δ quantity: −18.18%; −15.38%; −13.33%; −11.76%

   elasticity: 1.73; 1.31; 1.00; 0.76; decreases

   b. Total Revenue: $600,000; $648,000; $672,000; $672,000; $648,000.

   Total revenue increases (decreases) as price declines if the elasticity of demand is greater (less) than 1.0. Total revenue increases (decreases) as price increases if the elasticity of demand is less (greater) than 1.0.

SELF-TESTS FOR UNDERSTANDING
Test A

1. b   Slope is the reciprocal of the change in the quantity demanded divided by the change in price.
2. a
3. c
4. a
5. c
6. b
7. d
8. c
9. a
10. b
11. a
12. b

13. b

14. a

15. c

16. c

17. c

18. a

19. a

20. d

21. b

Test B

1. F   The ratio of changes = slope of demand curve, not price elasticity of demand

2. F

3. T

4. F   The statement is true for any demand curve with a negative slope, whether elastic or inelastic.

5. F   Inelastic means only that the absolute value of the percentage change in the quantity demanded is less than the percentage change in price.

6. T

7. F

8. T

9. F   They are substitutes.

10. T

11. T

12. F

13. F

14. F

APPENDIX
BASIC EXERCISES: APPENDIX

1. Not much; plotting historical data is an inappropriate way to estimate a demand curve.

2. a. 1996: $P = 22$; $Q = 380$

   1997: $P = 23$; $Q = 395$

   1998: $P = 24$; $Q = 410$

When only the demand curve shifts, the historical data on price and quantity trace out the supply curve. If you connect the three pairs of points, you should have a graph of the supply curve. Each point comes from the intersection of the demand curve for the specific year with the unchanging supply curve. In this case, the points of market equilibrium provide no information about the demand curve.

b. 1996: $P = 22.0$; $Q = 380$

1997: $P = 20.5$; $Q = 407.5$

1998: $P = 11.5$; $Q = 472.5$

With shifts in both demand and supply curves, the points of market equilibrium trace out neither curve. Try drawing the demand and supply curves for each year on the same diagram. As both curves shift, a line connecting the successive points of market equilibrium gives no information about either curve.

ECONOMICS IN ACTION

1. Elasticity of demand = $(3,570/1,997) \div (5.50/3.75) = 1.22$

   While the elasticity of demand is an indicator of the change in total revenue, a profit maximizing firm is interested in profits not revenues. Increased output may entail increased costs. In Mr. Grant's case, changing from first to second run movies dramatically cut the proportion of the ticket price claimed by movie distributors. The cut was so dramatic that net revenue before paying employees, utilities, etc., but after paying the admission tax and after paying the distributors, was unchanged at 61 cents a ticket.

2. a. If total revenue is to remain unchanged the price elasticity of demand would have to equal 1.0.

   b. Data on historical quanti-

ties is not a good way to measure demand. The relevant question is what would have been the demand for air travel in the summer of 1992 if fares had not been reduced. It is also relevant to note that some air travelers, those buying their tickets at the last minute, paid full fare and were not eligible for the discounted fares. At the same time it does appear that the fare war was a bonanza for travelers and not so good for airlines. A significant reduction in ticket prices appears to have induced only a modest increase in air travel.

CHAPTER 8
CHAPTER REVIEW

(1)   increase; physical; revenue

(2)   revenue; price

(3)   more; less; reduce; increase

(4)   reduce; less; more

(5)   production; increasing; decreasing; constant

(6)   short

(7)   output; total

(8)   long run; lower

(9)   is unchanged; less; fall; more; rises

IMPORTANT TERMS AND CONCEPTS QUIZ

1.   f

2.   g

3.   i

4.   e

5.   b

6.   l

7.   k

8.   d

9.   h

10. j

11. c

BASIC EXERCISES

1. 100 acres: increasing returns: 0 to 2 workers; decreasing returns: 2 to 4 workers; negative returns: 4 to 6 workers

2. 200 acres: increasing returns: 0 to 2 workers; decreasing returns: 2 to 5 workers; negative returns: 5 to 6 workers.

   300 acres: increasing returns: 0 to 2 workers; decreasing returns: 2 to 6 workers.

   The output-labor curve shifts up as land increases.

3. 100: 1; 3; 2; 1; –1; –2

   200: 2; 4; 3.5; 2.5; 1; –1

   300; 3; 4.5; 3.5; 3; 2; 1

4. Marginal returns to land generally decline.

5. increasing; increasing; constant; increasing; decreasing

6. $10,000; $20,000; $17,500; $12,500; $5,000; –$5,000

   Hire 4 workers: $28,000 = (12,000 x $5) – ($8,000 x 4)

   Hire 5 workers: (13,000 x $5) – ($8,000 x 5) = $25,000

   Hire 3 workers: (9,500 x $5) – ($8,000 x 3) = $23,500

SELF-TESTS FOR UNDERSTANDING
Test A

1. d

2. c

3. d

4. b

5. d

6. b   Marginal physical product starts to decline after the second worker.

7. a

8. c

9. d   Marginal costs reflect variable costs, not fixed costs

10. a

11. b

12. a

13. a   A change in the price of output may change where a firm wants to produce, but does not shift its cost curves.

14. d

15. c

16. c

17. b

18. d

19. b

20. d

21. a

Test B

1. F

2. T

3. F

4. F

5. T

6. F

7. F

8. F

9. T

10. F

APPENDIX
APPENDIX REVIEW

(1) production indifference; more

(2) negative; will; diminishing marginal; do not

(3) straight; horizontal

(4) lowest; less; more

(5) expansion

IMPORTANT TERMS AND CONCEPTS QUIZ:
APPENDIX

1. c

2. d

3. a

BASIC EXERCISE:
APPENDIX

1. 200; 2; 100; 3. Total costs are constant along a single budget line. Total costs are greater along higher budget lines.

2. $80

SELF-TESTS FOR UNDERSTANDING:
APPENDIX
Test A

1. d

2. b   The least costly input combination is where the slope of the production indifference curve = the ratio of input prices.

3. c

4. c

5. c

6. b

7. c

8. d   Total cost will double, but the least costly input combination does not change as the slope of the budget line is unchanged.

9. d   Production indifference curves are determined by the production function, not input prices.

Test B

1. F   Output is constant along a production indifference curve.

2. T

3. T

4. F   An increase in the price of the input measured on the vertical axis makes the budget line flatter.

5. F   A change in the price of one input typically changes the optimal use of all inputs.

6. F   A change in output prices may induce a movement along the expansion path but it does not shift the production indif-

ference curves or the slope of the budget line. Thus it does not change the cost minimizing input combination for a given level of output.

7. T

SUPPLEMENTARY EXERCISES

2. For labor: $MPP_L/P_L = (M/L)^{1/2}/12$.

   For machines: $MPP_M/P_M = (L/M)^{1/2}/48$.

   Set the two expressions equal and solve for L in terms of M. When the price of labor hours is 12 and the price of machine hours is 48, the least costly combination of inputs requires that $L = 4M$.

   From the production function

   $W = L^{1/2} M^{1/2}$

   Knowing that for the least-cost combination of inputs $L = 4M$, the equation can be rewritten as $500,000 = M^{1/2} (4M)^{1/2}$

   $500,000 = (4M^2)^{1/2} = 2M$

   $M = 250,000$ machine hours

   $L = 1,000,000$ labor hours

3. a. Total output $= 500\sqrt{L}$

   b. MPP of labor $= 250/\sqrt{L}$; the MPP of labor is the slope of the total product curve.

   c. For this production function, MPP of labor declines continuously, but is never negative.

   d. 1,085,069.45 labor hours; (Find the quantity of labor such that the MRP of labor is equal to the price of labor. $(250/\sqrt{L}) \times 50 = 12$.)

   Output = 520,833.33 widgets.

4. For this production function, the expansion path is a straight line.

5. Constant: $(2M)^{1/2} (2L)^{1/2} = 2M^{1/2}L^{1/2} = 2W$. A doubling of inputs doubles output.

CHAPTER 9

CHAPTER REVIEW

(1) average; marginal

(2) marginal; marginal; profits; revenue; cost

(3) total

(4) marginal; marginal; positive; zero; equals

IMPORTANT TERMS AND CONCEPTS QUIZ

1. i
2. g
3. f
4. e
5. a
6. j
7. b
8. k
9. c
10. h

BASIC EXERCISES

1. a. Total Profits: 1,500; 3,600; 5,200; 6,300; 6,600; 6,100; 5,000; 3,400; 1,300; −1,300; 5 widgets

   b. Marginal Revenue: 3,500; 3,100; 2,700; 2,300; 1,900; 1,500; 1,100; 700; 300; −100 Marginal Cost: 2,000; 1,000; 1,100; 1,200; 1,600; 2,000; 2,200; 2,300; 2,400; 2,500, 5 widgets. The 5th widget adds 300 to profit: Increasing output to 6 widgets would lower profit by 500.

   c. profit; does not; does not; the difference between average revenue and average cost is greatest when output = 2. expanding output as long as MR > MC increases profits, but expanding output further, even if AR > AC, will reduce total profits.

   d. In the top panel of Fig 8-1, the total cost curve shifts up by $3,000. In the middle

panel, the total profit curve measures the difference between the two curves in the top panel; following the increase in fixed costs, the total profit curve shifts down by $3,000. In the bottom panel, neither curve shifts. The marginal revenue curve measures the slope of the total revenue curve and the marginal cost curve measures the slope of the total cost curve. Even though the total cost curve shifted up, there is no change in its slope.

2. is not; horizontal; vertical; horizontal

SELF-TESTS FOR UNDERSTANDING
Test A

1. b
2. c
3. c
4. d
5. b
6. a
7. b If marginal cost were zero or negative, total cost would be constant or decline.
8. d
9. d
10. a Review Basic Exercise 2.
11. c
12. c
13. b
14. c
15. c
16. a
17. b
18. b
19. a Zero accounting profits leave nothing to cover the opportunity cost of owner supplied inputs.

20. d

Test B

1. F

2. F

3. F

4. F   Review Basic Exercise 2

5. T

6. T

7. T

8. F

9. F   A firm is making profits if AR > AC but should increase output only if MR > MC.

10. F

APPENDIX

1. Data on Heather's batting is consistent with Rule 3 and Rule 4. Note that from game 3 to 4 Heather's daily batting average actually increased, from .250 to .333 and yet her season batting average declined from .417 to .400. Even though her performance for the 4th game was better than for the 3rd, it was still below her overall average. As a result, and consistent with Rule 4, her season batting average declined.

2. b. The marginal profit curve should equal zero where total profits are maximized.

   c. The marginal cost curve should go through the minimum of the average cost curve.

SUPPLEMENTARY EXERCISES

1. a. $16,000

   b. AC = 16,000/Q + 120 – .4Q + .002Q^2

   MC = 120 –.8Q + .006Q^2

   c. It should.

   d. MR = 300 – .5Q

   f. Q = 200

g. Find the positive value of Q such that MC = MR; 120 –.8Q + .006Q^2 = 300 –.5Q
   Q = 200

h. P = $250; TR = $50,000; TC = $40,000; total profits = $10,000

j. AC = 20,000/Q + 120 –.4Q + .0002Q^2 No change in profit maximizing level of output as the change in fixed costs does not change either marginal cost or marginal revenue; total profits = $6,000

2. a. Set MC = MR.

   Marginal cost: when P_L = 12 and P_M = 48, the least cost combination of inputs uses four hours of labor input for each hour of machine time. (See supplementary exercise 2 in Chapter 7.) To produce one widget, a firm would use two hours of labor with a half-hour of machine time for a total cost of $48. As the production function exhibits constant returns to scale, average and marginal cost are equal at $48 per widget.

   W = 2,500,000 – 25,000 P_W

   Total Revenue = 100 W –.00004 W^2

   MR = 100 – .00008 W

   To find the profit maximizing level of output set MC = MR.

   48 = 100 – .00008 W

   W = 650,000

   L = 1,300,000

   M = 325,000

   P_W = $74

   b. Output: W = $(200,000)^{1/2}L^{1/2}$

   Labor Input: $L = W^2/200,000$

   Total (labor) cost = $12W^2/200,000$

   Marginal (labor) cost = $24W/200,000$

=.00012W

MR = 100 – .00008 W

Set MC = MR

.00012W = 100 – .0008 W

.0002 W = 100

W = 500,000

L = 1,250,000

P_W = $80.

3. We know that profit maximizing firms set MR = MC and MC = MR > 0. If MR > 0, total revenue increases if quantity increases and total revenue decreases if quantity decreases. That is the price elasticity of demand for a profit maximizing firm is > 1.

CHAPTER 10
CHAPTER REVIEW

(1) Many; Identical; Easy; Perfect; do not; zero

(2) horizontal; marginal

(3) marginal; losses; variable; marginal cost; variable

(4) horizontal; demand; supply

(5) loss; two; better; opportunity; economic; accounting

(6) profits; (shaded rectangle should go from the y axis to a quantity of 1450 and from 20 to 15.30, the difference between the market price and the firm's average cost when producing 1450 units of output); enter; right; fall; $15.00 (minimum long run average cost; see the Basic Exercise); long-run average

IMPORTANT TERMS AND CONCEPTS QUIZ

1. g

2. m

3. c

4. n

5. a

6. k

7. f

8. j

9. b

10. i

11. l

12. h

13. d

BASIC EXERCISE

1. 1,400; $5,544 = (P – AC)Q$; $5,310; $5,330

2. 1,200; –$4,380 = $(P – AC)Q$; –$4,550; –$4,532; –$10,140 (fixed costs)

3. 0; price does not cover average variable cost.

4. Firm's short-run supply curve is the portion of its marginal cost curve above average variable cost.

5. While under perfect competition marginal revenue equals price, one also needs to consider how a change in output affects costs. That is, the relevant comparison is with marginal cost, not average cost.

6. $15.00; 1300 widgets

SELF-TESTS FOR UNDERSTANDING
Test A

1. b

2. c

3. a

4. d   A horizontal demand curve is perfectly elastic.

5. c   In this case MR = AR = price

6. c

7. b

8. c

9. b

10. b   Zero accounting profits implies negative economic profits

11. c

12. d

13. d

14. b

15. c

16. c

17. b

18. d

19. c   Firms will expand output until MC = P.

20. d

Test B

1. F

2. F   If P > MC firm should expand output. If P < MC firm should reduce output.

3. F

4. F   Maybe in the short run if P > AC, but not in the long run.

5. F

6. F   If P > AC, a firm can increase profits by expanding output only if MC < P.

7. F

8. T

9. F

10. F

SUPPLEMENTARY EXERCISES

1. a. Average Cost = $10,140/Q + .00001Q^2 – .02Q + 16.3$

    b. Average variable cost = $.00001Q^2 – .02Q + 16.3$

    c. Marginal cost = $.00003Q^2 – .04Q + 16.3$

3. To find the minimum of either average cost curve sets its derivative equal to zero.

    For AC, $Q = 1,300$; AC = 15.00; at $Q = 1,300$, MC = 15.00

    For AVC, $Q = 1,000$; AVC = 6.30; at $Q = 1,000$, MC = 6.30

4. Supply = 0 if $P < 6.30$

Supply = $(.04 + \sqrt{-.000356 + .00012P})/.00006$ if $P \geq 6.30$

CHAPTER 11
CHAPTER REVIEW

(1) are not

(2) selecting; planning; distribution

(3) was not; efficient

(4) efficient; decreasing

(5) utility; cost

(6) increase; cost; greater; is not; equals

(7) price; marginal cost; price; price

(8) utility; cost; equals

(9) input; output

IMPORTANT TERMS AND CONCEPTS QUIZ

1. c

2. f

3. a

4. e

5. g

6. b

BASIC EXERCISE

1. $25; $15

2. $10; more

3. decrease; $3; fewer

4. $18

SELF-TESTS FOR UNDERSTANDING
Test A

1. d   Conditions for efficiency say nothing about necessities and luxuries. Prices will depend upon consumer preferences and production costs.

2. b

3. d

4. c

5. d   The location of the PPF reflects available resources and technology.

6. c

7. b

8. c

9. b

10. b

11. c

12. a

13. b Increased production typically increases marginal cost, while increased consumption typically lowers marginal utility.

14. c

15. b Imposing Leon's preferences would be equivalent to imposing those of a central planner.

16. c

Test B

1. T

2. F

3. F

4. T

5. F

6. F

7. T

8. T

9. F

10. T

SUPPLEMENTARY EXERCISES

1. a. No

    b. increase; 1; increase; 2; inefficient

    c. All consumers respond to the same set of prices and consume so that marginal utility equals price,

2. a. 120; 1200; 160; 800; +40; +400. Note that this reallocation of inputs should work to move the ratio of marginal physical products in the production of corn and tomatoes toward equality.

    b. In competitive markets, profit maximizing firms adjust the use of inputs until the ratio of marginal physical products is equal to the ratio of input prices. By adjusting to common prices, the ratio of marginal physical products is equated across alternative uses.

CHAPTER 12
CHAPTER REVIEW

(1) one; no

(2) natural; barriers; entry

(3) negative; lower; decrease

(4) marginal; marginal; price; is not

(5) average; less; below; above

(6) demand; greater; less; less; will not; higher; lower

(7) price; price; marginal revenue; less; greater than

(8) down

(9) will not; does not; maker

IMPORTANT TERMS AND CONCEPTS QUIZ

1. e

2. a

3. h

4. b

5. f

6. d

BASIC EXERCISES

1. a. Total cost: $84,816; $90,441; $96,516; $103,041; $110,016

    14

    b. Marginal revenue: $6,900; $6,500; $6,100; $5,700

    Marginal cost: $5,625; $6,075; $6,525; $6,975

    revenue; cost; 14

    c. 9,100

    d. 30,884

    f. Total revenue: $114,000; $120,900; $127,400; $133,500; $139,200

    Marginal revenue: $6,900; $6,500; $6,100; $5,700

    Total cost: $96,816; $103,441; $110,516; $118,041; $126,016

    Marginal cost: $6,625; $7,075; $7,525; $7,975

    13 widgets; $9,300;

    g. $13,000; $200; If Mario increased his price by $1,000, the decline in sales would be so great that MR > MC.

    h. $17,459

    i. No change in output = 14 widgets; no change in price = $9,100; profits down $13,000 to $17,884. No change in pollution as output is unchanged. The differences between questions f and i reflect the differences between the effects of a change in marginal and fixed costs. Note that in Question f marginal cost changed as the tax was imposed on each widget produced. In Question i marginal cost is unchanged as the pollution charge is independent of the number of widgets produced.

2. a. Total Revenue: $2,400,000; $3,093,750; $3,675,000; $4,143,750; $4,500,000; $4,743,750; $4,875,000; $4,893,750

    Marginal Revenue: $37; $31; $25; $19; $13; $7; $1

    Price $33; Output 143,750; Profits $806,250

    b. Centerville: Total Revenue: $480,000; $1,125,000; $1,680,000; $2,145,000;

$2,520,000; $2,805,000;
$3,000,000; $3,105,000

Marginal Revenue: $43;
$37; $31; $25; $19; $13; $7

Price $30; Quantity
100,000

Middletown: Total
Revenue: $1,920,000;
$1,968,750; $1,995,000;
$1,998,750; $1,980,000;
$1,938,750; $1,875,000;
$1,788,750

Marginal Revenue: $13, $7;
$1; –$5; –$11; –$17, –$23

Price $45; Quantity 43,750

Profits: $1,031,250

c. Middletown; Centerville

SELF-TESTS FOR UNDERSTANDING
Test A

1. d
2. c
3. b
4. d
5. c
6. c
7. a
8. c Rule 4 in the Appendix to Chapter 9.
9. a
10. d
11. c
12. c
13. c
14. b
15. b
16. c
17. b An increase in fixed costs would increase average cost but leave the marginal cost curve unchanged.
18. c
19. b Profit maximizing level of

output is determined where marginal cost equals marginal revenue. A change in fixed cost will not change marginal revenue or marginal cost and will not change the profit maximizing level of output.

20. a See question 2 in the Supplementary Exercises.

Test B

1. F
2. T
3. F
4. F Monopolist would face the downward sloping market demand curve.
5. T
6. F As compared to the competitive situation, price is up and quantity is down.
7. T
8. F Even if price exceeds average cost, profits will decline if marginal revenue is less than marginal cost.
9. F
10. F

SUPPLEMENTARY EXERCISES

1. a. Total revenue = $11,900Q - 200Q^2$

        Marginal revenue = $11,900 - 400Q$

        Average cost = $225Q + 52,416/Q$

        Marginal cost = $450Q$

    c. $11,900 - 400Q = 450Q$; $850Q = 11,900$; $Q = 14$

    d. Per-unit charge:

        $TC = 52,416 + 225Q^2 + 1,000Q$

        $AC = 225Q + 52,416/Q + 1,000$

        $MC = 450Q + 1,000$

        Fixed charge:

$TC = 65,416 + 225Q^2$

$AC = 225Q + 65,416/Q$

$MC = 450Q$

Note that the addition of a fixed cost element does not change marginal cost.

2. If a monopolist is originally producing where demand is inelastic, then an increase in market price will increase profits. The increase in price reduces costs as quantity declines and increases revenue as the percentage decline in the quantity sold is more than offset by the percentage increase in price. Thus the initial point could not have been a point of profit maximization. Similar reasoning rules out b, the case of unit elastic demand, as a point of profit maximization. Again profits increase as the reduction in quantity from an increase in price reduces costs while revenue is unchanged from the assumption of unit elasticity of demand.

CHAPTER 13
CHAPTER REVIEW

(1) monopolistic; negative; marginal revenue; marginal cost; zero; entry; average

(2) oligopoly; cartel; price leadership

(3) zero; lower; larger

(4) will; will not; marginal; cost

(5) payoff; strategy; maximin; Nash; reputation; credible

(6) entry; exit; opportunity cost; capital

IMPORTANT TERMS AND CONCEPTS QUIZ

1. g
2. c
3. m
4. a
5. i

6. n

7. k

8. e

9. p

10. h

11. l

12. o

13. j

14. f

15. d

BASIC EXERCISES

1. a. Profit-maximizing level of output = 1,000 meals

   b. Marginal revenue: $2,200; $1,400; $600; –$200

      Marginal cost: $998; $1,000; $996; $1,000

      Profit-maximizing level of output = 1,000 meals

      MC is less than MR at less than 1,000 meals

      MC exceeds MR at more than 1,000 meals

      See also the Supplementary Exercise to this chapter.

2. a. 1,000; $200; Marginal revenue exceeds marginal cost up to 1,000 sets and is less than marginal cost beyond 1,000 sets.

   b. No change in price or quantity. It is the kink in the demand curve that gives rise to the discontinuity in marginal revenue. Fluctuations of marginal cost within this discontinuity have no impact on the profit maximizing level of output or price.

   c. Marginal cost would have to rise above $150 a set.

   d. Marginal cost would have to fall below $50 a set.

SELF-TESTS FOR UNDERSTANDING
Test A

1. b

2. c

3. a

4. b

5. a

6. b

7. c

8. b

9. d

10. b

11. d

12. c

13. c

14. b

15. c

16. c

17. d

18. c

19. b

20. a

Test B

1. T

2. T

3. F

4. F

5. F

6. T

7. T

8. F

9. T

10. F

SUPPLEMENTARY EXERCISES

1. Total Revenue = $25Q - Q^2/100$

   Marginal Revenue = $25 - Q/50$

   Average Cost = $10,000/Q + 5$

   Marginal Cost = 5

   Profit-maximizing level of output:

   $25 - Q/50 = 5; Q = 1000$

2. TR = $80Q - .005Q^2$

   AR = $80 - .005Q$

   MR = $80 - .01Q$

   AC = $.00000015625Q^2 - .003125Q + 40.625$

   MC = $.00000046875Q^2 - .00625Q + 40.625$

   a. Set MR = MC

      $Q = 6,000; P = 60$; profits = 135,000

   b. Set MR = 0

      $Q = 8,000; P = 40$; profits = 115,000

   c. yes

CHAPTER 14
CHAPTER REVIEW

(1) opportunity

(2) marginal cost; marginal utility; on

(3) little

(4) externalities; detrimental; beneficial

(5) higher; higher

(6) private; inefficient; much; less

(7) depletability; excludability; public

(8) difficult; rider

(9) zero; zero

(10) does not; less

(11) irreversible

(12) limited

IMPORTANT TERMS AND CONCEPTS QUIZ

1. q

2. h

3. e

4. b

5. n

6. j

7. f

8. k

9. p

10. 1

11. c

12. i

13. d

14. o

15. g

16. m

BASIC EXERCISE

1. Col. 1: $2,640,000; $11; $2,112,000; $10.56

2. Col. 2: 120; $2,640,000; $11; 100; $2,200,000; $11; cost of producing widgets unchanged; cost per hour of police service up 4.17 percent.

3. Col. 3: 80; $2,640,000; $11; 100; $3,300,000; $16.50; cost of producing widgets unchanged; cost per hour of police service up 50 percent over 10 years.

SELF-TESTS FOR UNDERSTANDING

Test A

1. c

2. c   Chapter 4 showed that production inside the PPF is inefficient.

3. d

4. c

5. d   (and possibly b)

6. d

7. a

8. a

9. a

10. c

11. d

12. c

---

13. b   When busy with a patient, a doctor is unavailable to others; nonpaying patients can be excluded.

14. b

15. b   The adjustment of nominal interest rates during periods of inflation is not an argument that private markets make inappropriate decisions about savings and investment.

16. d

17. b   It is easier to introduce labor saving innovations into the production of TVs than in the other examples were labor requirements may be more or less fixed.

18. a

19. c

20. b

Test B

1. F

2. F

3. T

4. F

5. F

6. F

7. T

8. T

9. T

10. F

SUPPLEMENTARY EXERCISES

1. b. Widgets:

    $MP(L) = 22.61$

    $AP(L) = 45.23$

    Recitals:

    $MP(L) = 50$

    $AP(L) = 50$

    c. Widgets:

    $MP(L) = 25.63$

    $AP(L) = 51.26$

Recitals:

$MP(L) = 50$

$AP(L) = 50$

Productivity of widget workers is up 13.3 percent. No increase in the productivity of musicians.

d. Opportunity cost of recitals has risen 13.3 percent from .45 widgets to .51 widgets.

PPF: Recitals = $50[40,000 - W^2/(3600K)]$

e. Except for when all labor is allocated to playing recitals, the new production possibilities frontier is outside the original frontier.

CHAPTER 15
CHAPTER REVIEW

(1) 20

(2) innovation

(3) cost

(4) entry

(5) cumulative

(6) trading; licensing

(7) higher; lower

IMPORTANT TERMS AND CONCEPTS QUIZ

1. d

2. b

3. c

4. j

5. k

6. g

7. i

8. f

9. a

10. h

BASIC EXERCISES

$31,000; $51,047; $83,849; $137,393; $224,584

Note that although the growth rate increases by the same one-half of one percent, the difference in GDP per capita gets bigger and bigger.

SELF-TESTS FOR UNDERSTANDING
Test A

1. c
2. c
3. b
4. d
5. c
6. b, d
7. b
8. b
9. d
10. a
11. d
12. c
13. d
14. b
15. d
16. c
17. c
18. b
19. d
20. b

Test B

1. F
2. F
3. T
4. T
5. T
6. F
7. F
8. T
9. T
10. T

CHAPTER 16
CHAPTER REVIEW

(1) proprietorship; partnership; corporation; limited

(2) stock; bonds; plowback (or retained earnings)

(3) are not; more; bonds; meet bond payments

(4) falls; loss; increase

(5) diversification; program; takeover

(6) are not; riskiness

(7) higher; lower; insurance

(8) random walk; today

IMPORTANT TERMS AND CONCEPTS QUIZ

1. e
2. j
3. l
4. n
5. b
6. o
7. k
8. d
9. m
10. h
11. g
12. q
13. i
14. p
15. c
16. a

BASIC EXERCISES

1. a. 16%; 10%; 6.25%; 4%

   b. $40; no; the price of the stock adjusts so that the dividend yield offers a return that is competitive with other options.

   c. Stock price will fall to $25; stock price will rise to $64.

   d. At the previous price of $40; a dividend of $8 offers a 20 percent return, twice that available on corporate bonds. The increased demand for XYZ stock will increase its price now.

   e. $80; $80 stock price and $8 dividend imply a 10 percent return.

2. The return on the diversified portfolio will be an average of the returns on individual stocks. The diversified portfolio misses the big gainers but minimizes the impact of the worst performers.

   The portfolio as a whole would have yielded a 28.98% return. The numbers below represent the gross return on a $10,000 investment in each stock. The dollar return on a $1,000 investment would be one tenth as large. The percentage rate of return would be the same in either case.

   AT&T: $13,215.90; 32.16%

   Boeing: $7,124.39; -28.76%

   Cendant; $5,618.18; -43.82%

   Citigroup: $9,757.31; -2.43%

   General Electric: $12.976.68; 29.77%

   IBM: $17,958.90; 79.59%

   Iomega: $5,879.40; –41.21%

   Lucent: 27,607.51; 176.18%

   Micron: $19,493.98; 94.94%

   Walt Disney: $9,345.55; –6.55%

SELF-TESTS FOR UNDERSTANDING
Test A

1. b
2. a
3. b
4. b
5. a
6. c
7. d
8. c

9. b

10. d

11. a

12. a

13. b   Changes in the price of outstanding shares mean gains or losses for current stockholders.

14. c

15. c

16. e

17. a

18. b   Speculators succeed when they buy low (excess supply) and sell high (excess demand).

19. d

20. c

Test B

1. T

2. T

3. F

4. F

5. F

6. F

7. F

8. F

9. F

10. F

SUPPLEMENTARY EXERCISES

1. The prices of bonds for all companies are likely to move together in response to changes in economy-wide interest rates. Stock prices are more heavily influenced by the fortunes and misfortunes of individual companies. As a result, changes in share prices are more likely to differ across companies.

CHAPTER 17
CHAPTER REVIEW

(1)   productivity; revenue

(2)   negative; more; positive; higher; below

(3)   discounting; fewer; lower

(4)   is not

(5)   all; no

(6)   most; part; is

(7)   higher; equal; low

(8)   increase; increase; more

(9)   greater; greater; innovation; greater

IMPORTANT TERMS AND CONCEPTS QUIZ

1. g

2. c

3. j

4. m

5. d

6. e

7. n

8. h

9. k

10. o

11. i

12. a

13. p

14. f

15. l

BASIC EXERCISE

1. Economic profit = Net revenue – opportunity cost of labor – cost of other inputs; Economic profit = $400 – ($8 × 40) – $30 = $400 – $350 = $50.

2. $30; The rent for the sunny plot should reflect the difference in the cost of production as compared to the marginal plot.

3. If the owner of the sunny plot tried charging a rent that exceeded the $30 difference in production costs, Darlene would make a greater profit by growing her flowers on the marginal plot. With a rent of $30 for the sunny plot she would be indifferent about using either plot.

SELF-TESTS FOR UNDERSTANDING
Test A

1. d

2. a

3. c

4. b   The increase in the price of widgets shifts the curves of marginal revenue product and hence the demand curves for inputs to the right.

5. c

6. c

7. a

8. c

9. d

10. d

11. a

12. b

13. c

14. a

15. c

16. b

17. b

18. b

19. c

20. a

Test B

1. F

2. T

3. T

4. T

5. F

6. T

7. F

8. F

9. T

10. F

IMPORTANT TERMS AND CONCEPTS QUIZ: APPENDIX

1. a

BASIC EXERCISES: APPENDIX

1. a. $4,000; $1,818.18; $2,066.12; $3,884.30; –$115.70

    b. cost; no

    c. $4,000; $1,904.76; $2,267.57; $4,172.33; $172.33

    d. present value of returns; yes

    e. 5 percent: $200; $4,200; $2,200; $110; $2,310. 10 percent: $400; $4,400; $2,400; $240; $2,640

    f. 5 percent: $1,800; $90; $4,390; $190 10 percent: $1,600; $160; $4,260; –$140

2. The contest sponsors could meet their payments to Mr. Calhoun by investing a smaller sum in 1993 and using both the initial investment along with the interest earnings to make the necessary future payments. Present value calculations show how much must be invested today to fund the future payments. Assuming the first payment was made right away, the sponsors need to invest a sum sufficient to fund 19 future payments of $50,000, or

$$\sum_{t=1}^{19} \frac{\$50,000}{(1 + i)^t}$$

If the interest rate was 6.5%, the present value of the 19 future payments was only $557,906. Including the first payment to Mr. Calhoun brings the total cost of $1,000,000 to $607,906. A higher interest rate would mean higher interest earnings and result in a lower present value, while a lower interest rate would mean a higher present value and require a larger initial investment by the contest sponsors.

CHAPTER 18

CHAPTER REVIEW

(1) leisure; more; decrease; income

(2) more; substitution; increases; offset; position; income

(3) demand; higher

(4) does; do not

(5) minimum

(6) Taft-Hartley

(7) monopolist; demand; right

(8) monopsonist; wages; lower; higher; two; bilateral

(9) collective bargaining; mediation; arbitration; mediator; arbitrator

IMPORTANT TERMS AND CONCEPTS QUIZ

1. c

2. h

3. l

4. b

5. d

6. p

7. f

8. k

9. m

10. a

11. j

12. e

13. n

14. o

15. i

BASIC EXERCISES

1. 60; 55; 50; 45; 40; 35; 30; 25; 20; 15

2. $2,400; $2,200; $2,000; $1,800; $1,600; $1,400; $1,200; $1,000; $800; $600

3. 7

4. Total profits with 7 workers: $4,900 = (315 × $40) – (7 × $1,100)

   Total profits with 6 workers: $4,800 = (285 × $40) – (6 × $1,100)

   Total profits with 8 workers: $4,800 = (340 × $40) – (8 × $1,100)

5. $1,000; 800; 8; $5,600; if 7 workers, profits also = $5,600 as MRP = wage for eighth worker.

6. a. $1,800

    b. 900 workers

    c. $1,400 and 600 workers, or $1,200 and 700 workers

SELF-TESTS FOR UNDERSTANDING
Test A

1. d

2. a   More workers shift the supply of labor to the right

3. b

4. d

5. b

6. c

7. c

8. b

9. b

10. a   For a competitive firm, MRP = $P \times$ MPP

11. d

12. b   the marginal physical product of labor (MPP_L) derives from the production function for schmoos. The increase in the price of schmoos shifts the

curve of MRP and leads to a movement along the MPP_L schedule.

13. c

14. a

15. c.

16. c

17. a

18. d

19. b

20. c; a; d; e; b; f

Test B

1. T

2. T

3. F

4. F   A change in wages leads to a movement along the supply curve.

5. F

6. F   A union is a monopolist, the sole supplier of labor. A monopsonist is the sole buyer of something.

7. F   Bilateral monopoly.

8. F

9. F

10. T

SUPPLEMENTARY EXERCISES

a. $1,000; 8

b. greater

   Total labor cost: $300; $800; $1,500; $2,400; $3,500; $4,800; $6,300; $8,000; $9,900; $12,000

   Marginal labor cost: $300; $500; $700; $900; $1,100; $1,300; $1,500; $1,700; $1,900; $2,100

d. 6 workers

e. $800

f. $6,600 = $40 x 285 – 6 x $800.

g. Both wages and employ-

ment would increase. Tony would hire 7 workers at $1,100 a month. The "high" minimum wage increases employment because Tony is a monopsonist. The minimum wage changes Tony's marginal cost of labor schedule.

h. No. If the union had more than 7 workers, it might want a lower wage to increase employment. If the union had 7 or fewer workers, it might be able to extract a higher wage by bargaining for some of Tony's profits.

CHAPTER 19
CHAPTER REVIEW

(1)   16,400; absolute; relative

(2)   Lorenz; zero; 45-degree; below; equality; inequality

(3)   47.2%; 4.2%

(4)   efficiency

(5)   decrease

(6)   decrease; break-even; negative; small

(7)   different; are not; overstate

(8)   employers

IMPORTANT TERMS AND CONCEPTS QUIZ

1. a

2. c

3. i

4. g

5. b

6. e

7. f

8. h

BASIC EXERCISES

1.   13,000; 13,494; 16,723; 14,723; 16,037; 17,138; 17,340; 19,930; 20,961; 25,963; 29,758

3.   Col. 4: 494; 3,229; -2,000; 1,314; 1,101; 202; 2,590; 1,031; 5,002; 3,794

Col. 5: 106; 3,970; 2,001; 286; 1,499; 98; 3,010; 2,269; 3,893; 1,111

Col. 6: 17.6; 55.2; 200,055.2; 17.9; 57.7; 32.7; 53.8; 68.8; 43.8; 22.7;

The marginal tax rates in column 6 should be equivalent to the slopes of the line segments you graphed in Figure 19-1.

SELF-TESTS FOR UNDERSTANDING
Test A

1. d

2. c

3. b

4. a

5. b

6. c

7. d   Even in the absence of economic discrimination, incomes will differ.

8. a   See also Supplementary Exercise.

9. c

10. b

11. b

12. d   Breakeven level = guarantee level ÷ tax rate

13. c   With a 50 percent tax rate, earnings of $8,000 reduce negative tax payments by $4,000 to $4,000, for a total income of $12,000.

14. c   Breakeven level = guarantee level ÷ tax rate

15. a   Reducing the tax rates raises costs which can only be offset by a reduction in the minimum guarantee.

16. a, d

17. a

18. a   Differences in schooling might reflect voluntary decisions or discrimination in access to schooling.

19. d

20. b

Test B

1. T   In principle, growth can push all incomes past an absolute standard. Relative standards will usually increase with economic growth.

2. F

3. F

4. T

5. F

6. F

7. F

8. F

9. T

10. F

CHAPTER 20
CHAPTER REVIEW

(1) less; innovation

(2) increasing; reduction; increase

(3) scale; scope; is not; bottleneck; below; above

(4) high

(5) decline; less; losses; demand

(6) reduces; inefficiency; efficiency

(7) Sherman

(8) Clayton; price discrimination; tying; interlocking directorates; reason; is not

(9) predatory pricing; is not; variable

(10) concentration; little

(11) merger; horizontal

IMPORTANT TERMS AND CONCEPTS QUIZ

1. c

2. k

3. n

4. l

5. o

6. i

7. p

8. a

9. b

10. j

11. m

12. e

13. g

14. d

15. q

16. f

BASIC EXERCISES

1. a. *Q*: 60; 90; 120; 150

    AC: 26.25¢; 22.5¢;20.625¢;19.5¢

    MC: 15.0¢;15.0¢; 15.0¢; 15.0¢

    b. $6.75 million loss at all levels of output.

    c. No; fixed costs are never covered.

2. a. Assuming that average variable cost is used as the indicator of predatory pricing, any price at or above 75¢ a pound would protect Michelle.

    b. The admonition to shut down if price drops below average variable cost assumes that the acts of shutting down and restarting are themselves costless. If, in contrast, it is costly to shutdown and then restart production lines, a firm might continue with production for a short period of time even if price is less than average variable cost to avoid the costs of shutting down and restarting. In the case of predatory pricing, a firm would deliberately accept losses for a short period of time, if it gave the firm monopoly power and the ability to earn economic profits in the future sufficient to overcome the losses incurred while driving out rivals. Thus a price below average variable cost might be an indication of predatory pricing, but it might also be a rational response to changing market conditions and by itself is likely to be insufficient evidence of predatory pricing.

SELF-TESTS FOR UNDERSTANDING
Test A

1. FCC = c

    FERC = g

    Fed. Res. = a

    SEC = f

2. b

3. d

4. c

5. b

6. a

7. c

8. d

9. c

10. b

11. b

12. d

13. c

14. a

15. c

16. d

17. a

18. c

19. c

20. d

Test B

1. F

2. F

3. F

4. F

5. T

6. T

7. F

8. F

9. F

10. F

CHAPTER REVIEW

(1) direct; indirect; personal income; payroll; corporate

(2) average; marginal; progressive; proportional; regressive

(3) payroll; regressive; do not; zero

(4) sales; property; federalism

(5) equity; horizontal; vertical; vertical; benefits; benefits

(6) burden; greater; excess burden; does not; smallest

(7) higher; lower; smaller

(8) incidence; flypaper; shifting

(9) demand; supply; inelastic; workers; firms

IMPORTANT TERMS AND CONCEPTS QUIZ

1. b

2. p

3. i

4. n

5. r

6. g

7. s

8 k

9. a

10. m

11. h

12. t

13. o

14. c

15. d

16. q

17. e

18. j

19. l

BASIC EXERCISES

2. $42; 50 million

3. $46; 44 million

4. $4; it is less than increase in tax.

5. All are likely to decline.

7. The first demand curve.

8. $50; 48 million; Figure 20-3; Figure 20-3; consumers

SELF-TESTS FOR UNDERSTANDING
Test A

1. b

2. c

3. d

4. c

5. d

6. c

7. c

8. d As long as the marginal tax rate exceeds the average rate the average rate will continue to increase whether the marginal rate increases or decreases. Consider Table 21-1 in the text and Rule 4 in the Appendix to Chapter 6.

9. c, 750 Increase in taxes = 0.15 × $5,000,

10. c Average rate increases as income rises.

11. b

12. b

13. c

14. c

15. c

16. b

17. a Zero price elasticity of demand means a vertical demand curve. Any increase in price from the sales tax induces no change in behavior.

18. d

19. a

20. a

Test B

1. F

2. T

3. T

4. T

5. T

6. F

7. F

8. T

9. F

10. F

SUPPLEMENTARY EXERCISE

1. Taxes: 0; $1,000; $3,000; $5,000; $15,000; $35,000

   Average Tax Rate: 0; 0.033; 0.075; 0.10; 0.15; 0.175

   Marginal Tax Rate: 0.20; 0.20; 0.20; 0.20; 0.20

2. b. Revenue = $T \times Q$

   Harris:

   Revenue = $25.608\ T - 2.95\ T^2$

   T = $4.34 maximizes revenue; revenue = $55.57 billion
   Grossman: Revenue = $27.5184T - 10.91\ T^2$

   T = $1.26 maximizes revenue;

   revenue = $17.35 billion

   c. Harris: ΔQ = 1.475; elasticity = .275

      Grossman: ΔQ = 5.455; elasticity = 1.107 When demand is more elastic, every increase in the tax leads to a larger reduction in the quantity demanded. As a result the revenue maximizing tax is lower.

Harris did not solve for the revenue maximizing tax. Rather he analyzed the impact of $2 increase in cigarette taxes and estimated a net increase in revenue of $28 billion. The approximation to the Harris demand curve for this exercise shows a gross increase in revenue of $37.56 billion following a $2 tax increase.

d. When the supply curve is infinitely elastic (horizontal), consumers pay all of any increase in taxes. If the supply curve were perfectly inelastic (vertical), then producers would pay all of any increase in taxes and there would be no change in the quantity demanded regardless of the elasticity of demand. If the supply curve has a positive slope, that is if the elasticity of supply is not infinite or zero, then the incidence of any increase in taxes will be divided between consumers and producers depending upon the elasticities of demand and supply.

CHAPTER 22
CHAPTER REVIEW
(1) externality; decrease; taxes

(2) controls

(3) inefficient; more

(4) marginal

(5) can never; price

(6) interest; increasing

(7) interest

(8) discourage; incentive; encourage; incentive; encouraging

IMPORTANT TERMS AND CONCEPTS QUIZ
1. d

2. f

3. b

4. e

5. g

6. a

BASIC EXERCISES
a. 15 cents; 10 million

b. falls; rises; no change in short run, declines in long run; shifts up by 5 cents; short run—declines; long run—no change or falls to zero, i.e., some firms leave industry; declines as industry output declines in short- and long-run.

c. Since the tax is per bag, not per unit of pollution, the pollution control equipment will not reduce a firm's pollution tax.

d. No. Since the equipment is only 75 percent effective, the total cost of using the equipment (4 cents plus the 1.25 cent emission tax per bag) is greater than the tax of 5 cents per bag.

e. Less than 3.75 cents; more than 5.33 cents

f. Price rises and industry output declines as at least some high-cost firms leave the industry.

2. Energy: 19.6; 19.3; 19.2; 19.0; 18.6; 18.2; 18.2; 17.9; 17.3; 17.0; 16.5; 15.7; 15.3; 14.7; 14.4; 13.9; 13.5; 13.6; 13.7; 13.4; 13.7; 13.8; 13.7; 13.7; 13.5; 13.4; 13.4; 13.0

Energy use rose during the late 1960s as the relative price of energy fell. The rise in energy prices following 1973 led to a significant decline in energy consumption per dollar of GDP. Energy consumption per thousand dollars of GDP has continued to decline throughout the 1980s even as relative energy prices have fallen. Patterns of energy consumption per thousand dollars of GDP up to 1981 could be interpreted as a movement along a demand curve in response to changes in relative price. The introduction of energy conservation practices, e.g., home insulation, energy-efficient machines and cars meant that one would not expect energy consumption to return to earlier levels even as relative energy prices declined. Changes in the structure of the economy, i.e., the increasing importance of services as compared to manufacturing, is also likely to reduce the demand for energy. Energy prices are now as low or lower than they were in the late 1960s and yet energy use is dramatically lower.

SELF-TESTS FOR UNDERSTANDING
Test A

1. b

2. e

3. b

4. d

5. b

6. a

7. b

8. b

9. b

10. a

11. d   Firms have an incentive to reduce pollution as long as it is cheaper to continue to reduce pollution than to pay the pollution charges.

12. c

13. b

14. d

15. a   Others are either supply responses or reflect a shift in the demand curve.

16. c

17. a

18. c

19. c See Basic Exercise 2.

20. d

Test B

1. F

2. F

3. F

4. F An increase in price from the imposition of an excise tax will reduce demand and hence the quantity of output and pollution as we move along the demand curve.

5. F The Principle of Increasing Costs suggests that reducing pollution to zero would be prohibitively expensive. The Law of Conservation of Matter and Energy suggests a society could not reduce pollution to zero even if it wanted to.

6. F

7. F

8. F

9. T

10. T

SUPPLEMENTARY EXERCISE

1. MC = 15.

   $MR = 65 - .05Q$; $P = 65 - .025Q$; $TR = 65Q - .025Q^2$.

   Set MC = MR to solve for profit maximizing output: $15 = 65 - .05Q$; $Q = 1,000$; $P = 40$ cents; Profit = 25 cents on each of 1,000 million bags or $250 million.

2. If price rises by 5 cents, quantity demanded will decline to 800 million bags. At price of 45 cents, profit is 25 cents a bag or $200 million. Set MC = MR to determine profit maximizing level of output: $20 = 65 - .05Q$; $Q = 900$; $P = 42.5$ cents ; profits 22.5 cents a bag or $202.5 million.

3. Long-run equilibrium price equals minimum average cost = 15 cents. Market quantity = 2,000 million bags; 200 firms producing 10 million bags each.

4. Short run: For representative firm AC = $.4(Q - 10)^2 + 20$.

   $TC = .4Q^3 - 8Q^2 + 60Q$.

   $MC = 1.2Q^2 - 16Q + 60$.

   As each firm supplies 1/200 of the market, we can find the short-run profit maximizing position of each firm by setting MC equal to price.

   $MC = 65 - .025(Q \times 200)$, or

   $1.2Q^2 - 16Q + 60 = 65 - 5Q$.

   The mathematics of solving this equation for Q are a bit cumbersome. Rounding off, firm output = 9.6 million bags; industry output = 1,920 million bags; and price = 17 cents. Note that price is now less than average cost.

   Long run: Some firms leave in response to short-run losses. Long-run equilibrium occurs where remaining firms produce at minimum average cost.

   Price = 20 cents; market demand = 1,800; each of 180 firms produce 10 million bags.

   The conditions in this problem—marginal cost for the monopolist equal to the minimum average cost of competitive firms, new firms can operate with the same cost curves, i.e., the long run industry supply curve is horizontal and the same demand curve under either market structure—imply the following: 1) by restricting output, the monopolist creates less pollution than the perfectly competitive industry; 2) the monopolist is unable to pass on the full extent of the pollution tax; and 3) in long-run equilibrium under perfect competition, consumers pay all of the pollution tax.

ECONOMICS IN ACTION

1. Simon won the original bet and received a check for $567.07 from Ehrlich. You can read about the bet in John Tierney's article "Betting the Planet," *New York Times Magazine*, December 2, 1990.

   You can check recent trends in commodity prices by consulting *The Knight-Ridder CRB Commodity Yearbook*, an annual publication of the Commodity Research Bureau, published by John Wiley.

CHAPTER 23
CHAPTER REVIEW

(1) microeconomics; macroeconomics

(2) price; quantity; domestic product

(3) inflation; deflation; recessions; higher; higher; left; decrease; stagnation

(4) money; final; excludes; includes; are not

(5) nominal; real; real; nominal; real

(6) is not; increase; decreasing; larger; lower

(7) up; depends; risen

(8) inflation; stabilization; recessions; inflation

IMPORTANT TERMS AND CONCEPTS QUIZ

1. p

2. h

4. i

4. m

5. o

6. q

7. l

8. b

9. n

10. d

11. j

12. g

13. k

14. c

15. f

16. e

BASIC EXERCISES

1. a. c; d

    b. b; yes, 1929–1933

    c. a

    d. c

2. a. shift aggregate demand curve to left

    b. shift aggregate demand curve to right

    c. Real GDP will fall as aggregate demand curve is shifted to the left; prices will rise as aggregate demand curve is shifted to the right.

3. a. col (3): $600; $300; $225; $1,125 col (6): $868; $416; $297; $1,581

    b. 40.5 percent

    c. $620; $320; $247.50; $1,187.50

    d. 5.56 percent

    e. The increase in real GDP is less than the increase in nominal GDP as the increase in nominal GDP includes both the increase in production and the increase in prices. The increase in real GDP is the better measure of the change in output. It is a weighted average of the increases in the output of hamburgers, shakes, and fries. The weights sum to one and reflect the relative importance of each good in GDP during the base year, 1998, in this example.

SELF-TESTS FOR UNDERSTANDING
Test A

1. b
2. d
3. a
4. c
5. a
6. b
7. a
8. a
9. c
10. d
11. d
12. b
13. a
14. d
15. d
16. b
17. d
18. c
19. b
20. c

Test B

1. F
2. T
3. F   Not if the increase comes from a increase in prices.
4. T
5. F   If aggregate demand curve shifts to the left, prices will fall.
6. F
7. F
8. T
9. T
10. F

ECONOMICS IN ACTION

1. The NBER committee dated the business cycle peak in July 1990 and the trough in March 1991.

CHAPTER 24
CHAPTER REVIEW

(1) more; more; demand; supply; out; right; increase

(2) is; 200

(3) potential; actual GDP

(4) discouraged; decrease; understate; understate; overstate

(5) frictional; cyclical; structural

(6) frictional; increased; lower

(7) cannot; partial; some

(8) real; the same; as; were unchanged

(9) different; less; more

(10) higher; nominal; real

(11) will; be unchanged; small; large; nominal

(12) usury; nominal; real; nominal; real

IMPORTANT TERMS AND CONCEPTS QUIZ

1. r
2. c
3. g
4. e
5. q
6. b
7. h
8. j
9. n
10. i
11. d
12. p
13. m
14. o
15. l
16. f
17. a

BASIC EXERCISES

1. a. $27.34

   b. $35.94

   c. No, labor productivity still increases but at a slower rate.

   d. Real GDP per capita starts out at $11,635 = [13.71 × (40 × 52) × .408] and ends up at $31,426 = [35.94 × (34.6 × 52) × .486].

   The numbers in this problem were chosen to reflect American experience over the period 1948 to 1998. The numbers for labor productivity are estimates of real GDP per hour worked. Over that period of time there was a steady decline in the average number of hours worked per week of about 0.5% per year. While there was little change in the proportion of the population that was employed over the first 25 years, there has been a substantial increase since 1973. This increase reflects the dramatic increase in the labor force participation of women and the change in the age structure of the population as the baby boom generation went to work.

2. a. $250,000; $5,250,000; $4,772,727; $5,750,000; $5,227,273. Borrowers gain at expense of lenders.

   b. $775,000; $5,775,000; $5,250,000; $5,225,000; $4,750,000. Both are treated equally.

   c. $1,000,000; $6,000,000; $5,454,545; $5,000,000; $4,545,455. Lenders gain at expense of borrowers.

3. a. 1.7; 1.21; –3.18; –5.03; 0.41; 1.70; –1.81; –2.04; –3.00; –0.52; 5.98; 9.05; 5.11; 6.21; 5.53; 6.57; 1.47; 2.77; 4.39; 1.62; 3.95; 1.48; 1.01; 0.91; 4.64; 2.01; 3.77; 3.93

   c. When actual inflation turns out to be much greater than expected, the difference between nominal interest rates that were set at the beginning of the period and the actual rate of inflation may be negative.

   d. While the nominal rate was highest in December 1977, the actual real rate from December 1977 to December 1978 was negative as inflation turned out to be even higher.

SELF-TESTS FOR UNDERSTANDING
Test A

1. d

2. a

3. c

4. b, a, d, c

5. a, b, d

6. a

7. c

8. b

9. b

10. b

11. c

12. b

13. b

14. a

15. b

16. d

17. c

18. a Nominal return after taxes = 6%. Real return after taxes ≈ 2%

19. a

20. c

Test B

1. F

2. F

3. F Reduced hours, loss of overtime, and involuntary part-time reduce income for individuals counted as employed.

4. F

5. F

6. F

7. F

8. F

9. F

10. T

APPENDIX
IMPORTANT TERMS AND CONCEPTS QUIZ: APPENDIX

1. b

2. d

3. a Don't forget to multiply by 100.

4. c

5. f

BASIC EXERCISES: APPENDIX

1. a. 2,500; 400

   b. $16,500 = 2,500 × $2.36 + 400 × $26.50

   c. 110 = (16,500/15,000) × 100

   e. 10 percent

   f. $15,771 ($1,990); 5.1 percent

2. 1997 index, using 1998 base, 91.1. 1998 base implies inflation of 9.8 percent. The slightly lower rate of inflation reflects a larger weight on more slowly rising clothing prices when using the 1998 expenditure pattern.

SUPPLEMENTARY EXERCISE

1. a and b. Insufficient information; for example, the value of the price index for Canada for 1997 shows how 1997 Canadian prices compare to Canadian prices in 1982–1984, not how Canadian prices compare to those in other countries.

c. Inflation within a country can be measured by the percentage change in that country's price index. Italy had the most inflation; Germany had the least inflation.

CHAPTER 25
CHAPTER REVIEW

(1) demand; consumption; investment; government; exports; imports; net exports

(2) before; taxes; transfer

(3) more; movement along; shift in

(4) C; I; G; X; IM; less; decrease

(5) increase; marginal; larger; more; smaller

IMPORTANT TERMS AND CONCEPTS QUIZ

1. g
2. d
3. h
4. c
5. k
6. l
7. b
8. n
9. a
10. i
11. e
12. m
13. j

BASIC EXERCISES

1. a. consumption spending; disposable income; .75;.75;.75;.75

b. .9; .825; .8; .7875; .78

e. slope of consumption function

f. rays become less steep, that is their slope decreases. For a straight line consumption function with a positive Y intercept and MPC < 1.0, the APC will be greater than the MC although the difference will get smaller as income increases.

2. a. $9,000; $39,000; $4,800,000

b. .78; .9

c. $12,750; $35,250; $4,800,000

d. In this example, MPC is the same for the rich and poor. The rich reduce their consumption by the same amount that the poor increase their consumption.

3. $C = 1,500 + .75\ DI$

4. a. Estimated MPC = 0.55/0.50 = 1.1

b. The estimate in a is greater than the slope of the consumption function. It overestimates the MPC because it includes the effect of the shift of the consumption function.

SELF-TESTS FOR UNDERSTANDING
Test A

1. b
2. b
3. d
4. b Circular flow diagram shows spending on newly produced goods and services.
5. b
6. d
7. c
8. a
9. c
10. b
11. d
12. a
13. b
14. c $\Delta C = MPC \times \Delta DI$
15. c $MPC = \Delta C/\Delta DI$
16. c Δ taxes $= -\Delta DI = \Delta C/MPC$
17. a $MPC = \Delta C/\Delta DI$.

For 14, 15, 16, and 17, remember:

$MPC = \Delta C/\Delta DI$. Each question gives you two numbers; you must use those two and the expression for MPC to solve for the third.

18. d
19. d
20. c Changes in withholding affect the timing of when taxes are paid but do not change what taxpayers owe.

Test B

1. F
2. F
3. F
4. T
5. T
6. T
7. F
8. T
9. T
10. T

APPENDIX
APPENDIX REVIEW

(1) final; produced

(2) exports; imports; produced

(3) income, do not; net national; depreciation

(4) value added

IMPORTANT TERMS AND CONCEPTS QUIZ: APPENDIX

1. a

2. e

3. b

4. c

BASIC EXERCISES: APPENDIX

1. a. $2,200

   b. $1,700

   c. $1,700; wages = $1,200; profits $500

   d. $500

   e. $1,200 ($1,700 - $500)

   f. $1,700

   g. $1,700

   h. $1,700

2. a. $1,000; $2,100; $1,600; $4,700

   b. 0; $1,500; $3,200; $4,700 (Sales for final use for firm C includes the $200 addition to inventories.

SELF-TESTS FOR UNDERSTANDING: APPENDIX

Test A

1. c

2. c

3. b

4. c

5. a   This year's GDP only includes goods produced this year.

6. d

7. d   Computers shipped to Japan are exports.

8. b   Used equipment represents production in some prior year.

9. c   Social Security payments are transfers.

10. d

11. b

12. d

13. c

14. c

15. a

16. d

17. c

18. c

19. c

20. b

Test B

1. F

2. T

3. F

4. F   No effect on GDP. Value added by GM up. Value added by suppliers down.

5. F

6. T

7. F   It's depreciation.

8. F

9. F

10. T   These are alternative ways to measure national income.

SUPPLEMENTARY EXERCISE

1. MPC = $50/\sqrt{DI}$; MPC declines as income rises. Thus consumption spending rises following redistribution from rich to poor as increase in consumption by poor is greater than decline in consumption by rich.

   S = $DI - 100\sqrt{DI}$; MPS = $1 - 50/\sqrt{DI}$

   APC = $100/\sqrt{DI}$; APS = $1 - 100/\sqrt{DI}$

   MPC + MPS = 1.0; APC + APS = 1.0

CHAPTER 26
CHAPTER REVIEW

(1) increase; increasing; decrease

(2) equal to

(3) exports; imports

(4) horizontal; vertical; intersection

(5) less; reduce; increase; less; downward; lower; increase; increase; higher

(6) price level

(7) less; recessionary; inflationary

IMPORTANT TERMS AND CONCEPTS QUIZ

1. d

2. l

3. f

4. b

5. g

6. j

7. a

8. i

9. e

10. c

11. k

BASIC EXERCISES

1. e. $6,200

   f. 5,900; 6,000; 6,100; 6,200; 6,300

   g. Spending would be greater than output, inventories would decline, firms would increase output.

   h. inflationary gap, $200; recessionary gap, $300

   i. Expenditure schedule shifts up; $6,400; $4,700

2. b. $6,000

   c. $6,400

   d. aggregate demand curve

   c. negative

3. Following increase in investment spending new aggregate demand curve should lie to the right of the aggregate demand curve in question 2.

SELF-TESTS FOR UNDERSTANDING
Test A

1. b
2. c
3. a
4. a   Net exports = $X - IM$; IM up when GDP up.
5. c
6. c
7. a, c, d, e, g
8. c
9. a
10. c
11. d
12. c
13. a
14. b
15. c
16. a
17. a
18. c
19. b
20. a, b, c The lower price level increases consumption spending and net exports leading to a shift in the expenditure schedule and a movement along the aggregate demand curve

Test B

1   F
2. T
3. F
4. F
5. T
6. F
7. T
8. F
9. F
10. T

APPENDIX

1. $C = 1,850 + .5 (Y - T) = 1,500 + .5Y$
2. $C + I + G + (X - IM) = 3,100 + .5Y$
3. $Y = 3,100 + .5Y = 6,200$

CHAPTER 27
CHAPTER REVIEW

(1)   more than; autonomous; induced
(2)   MPC
(3)   consumption spending
(4)   income; MPC
(5)   smaller; inflation; trade; income; financial
(6)   do not; supply; autonomous; shift in; horizontal

IMPORTANT TERMS AND CONCEPTS QUIZ

1.   d
2.   a
3.   e
4.   b

BASIC EXERCISES

1.   a.   Total spending: 5,600; 5,800; 6,000; 6,200; 6,400; 6,600; 6,800; equilibrium: 6,000

     b.   Total spending: 5,700; 5,900; 6,100; 6,300; 6,500; 6,700; 6,900; equilibrium = 6,500

     c.   500

     d.   5; equilibrium level; income; autonomous spending

     e. $.8 = \Delta C/\Delta DI = 200/250$

     f. $1/(1 - 0.8) = 1/(0.2) = 5$

     g.   slope expenditure schedule = 200/250 = 0.8. For this example, the slope of the expenditure schedule = MPC. See Appendix B for a different example.

2.   a.   Total spending: 5,800; 6,000; 6,200; 6,400; 6,600; 6,800; 7,000; equilibrium = 7,000

     b.   500

     c.   5; it is the same as the investment spending multiplier.

3.   less; autonomous

     a.   Total spending: 5,750; 5,950; 6,150; 6,350; 6,550; 6,750; 6,950; equilibrium = 6,750

     b.   –250

     c.   fall

     d. $5 = -250/-50$

     e.   the same

     f.   It ignores effects of inflation, taxes, the financial system, and international trade.

SELF-TESTS FOR UNDERSTANDING
Test A

1.   c
2.   b
3.   d
4.   c
5.   a; c; e; g
6.   c
7.   b
8.   e
9.   c
10.   c   If MPC is larger, 1/(1-MPC) is also larger as the denominator in the multiplier expression is smaller.
11.   b   See comment to 10.
12.   b
13.   b; d Japanese imports from the United States are America exports to Japan.
14.   c   300/100 = 3.
15.   d   An autonomous increase in imports shifts the expenditure schedule down.

16. b

17. c

18. a

19. b

20. b

Test B

1. F
2. F
3. T
4. T
5. T
6. F
7. F
8. F
9. F
10. T

<hr>

APPENDIX A
BASIC EXERCISES: APPENDIX A

1. $Y = a + b(Y - T) + I + G + X - IM$

$Y - bY = a - bT + I + G + X - IM$

$Y = (a - bT + I + G + X - IM) / (1 - b)$

Multiplier = $1/(1 - b)$

2. $\Delta Y = [1/(1 - b)] \Delta a$

$\Delta Y = [1/(1 - b)] \Delta I$

$\Delta Y = [1/(1 - b)] \Delta G$

$\Delta Y = [1/(1 - b)] \Delta X$

$\Delta Y = [-1/(1 - b)] \Delta IM$

<hr>

APPENDIX B
BASIC EXERCISES: APPENDIX B

1. Total spending: 5,625; 5,812.5; 6,000; 6,187.5; 6,375; 6,562.5; 6,750; equilibrium = 6,000

2. Total spending: 5,750; 5937.5; 6,125; 6,312.5; 6,500; 6,787.5; 6,875; equilibrium = 6,500

3. multiplier = 500/125 = 4

4. The multiplier is smaller because imports increase with income. The slope of the expenditure schedule = 187.5/250 = 0.75. Multiplier = 1/(l - 0.75) = 1/0.25 = 4. Alternatively, the marginal propensity to import = 0.05. Multiplier = 1/(1 - MPC + MPImport) = 1/(l - 0.8 + 0.05) = 1/(0.25) = 4.

SUPPLEMENTARY EXERCISES: APPENDIX B

1. It ignores the multiplier.

3. b. Model should show change in income of 500 for multiplier of 5 = 1/(l - MPC).

c. They should all give the same result in terms of the multiplier.

d. Larger MPC will mean larger multiplier; smaller MPC means smaller multiplier.

e. Now multiplier should be 4 = 1(1 - .8 + .05).

<hr>

CHAPTER 28
CHAPTER REVIEW

(1) increase; movement along; shift in; right

(2) intersection; decrease; increases

(3) inflationary; inward; movement along; higher; lower

(4) recessionary

(5) inflationary; supply

IMPORTANT TERMS AND CONCEPTS QUIZ

1. c
2. e
3. a
4. d

BASIC EXERCISES

1. a. increases; increase; shift in; $6,250

e. 95; $6,125

f. Inflationary gap; increasing wages and other business costs would shift the aggregate supply curve up; 100 and $6,000

g. no gaps

h. recessionary gap; elimination of gap likely to be very slow; 90; $6,250

2. horizontal

a. no

b. At P^* aggregate demand would exceed aggregate supply. Prices would rise. The increase in prices would mean a movement along the dashed aggregate demand curve to the equilibrium, (Y_2, P_2), given by the intersection of the dashed aggregate demand curve and the solid aggregate supply curve.

The increase in investment spending, which shifted the expenditure schedule and gave rise to the dashed aggregate demand curve, will lead to an increase in prices as part of the broader multiplier process, reducing net exports and the purchasing power of money-fixed assets. The reduction in net exports and the shift in the consumption function means a downward shift in the expenditure schedule (not drawn) that partially offsets the expansionary impact of the original increase in investment spending and reconciles equilibrium in the income-expenditure diagram with that of the aggregate demand-aggregate supply diagram. That is, to complete the analysis one would need to draw a third expenditure schedule between the solid and dashed ones already shown in Figure 28-4. We know from the equilibrium determined in the aggregate demand-aggregate supply diagram that this final expenditure schedule will intersect the 45-degree line at a real GDP level of Y_2.

3. s, m, -, -; m, s, -, +; s, m, +, +; m, s, +; -; s, m, +, +; m, s, -, +

SELF-TESTS FOR UNDERSTANDING
Test A

1. b

2. b

3. a Change in the price level leads to a movement along the aggregate supply curve

4. d

5. a

6. c Remember the definition of equilibrium in Ch. 5.

7. a, b, c, d, e

8. a

9. d The increase in exports shifts the aggregate demand curve to the right.

10. c

11. d An increase in G when there is a recessionary gap need not result in an inflationary gap.

12. a

13. c

14. b, d Net exports = $X - IM$

15. a, c, d The increase in net exports leads to shifts on the demand side.

16. c A shift in the aggregate demand curve leads to a movement along the aggregate supply curve.

17. c Fig. 28-4 shows a shift in the aggregate demand curve. Draw a new aggregate supply curve with a similar shift.

18. c

19. d

20. c

Test B

1. T

2. T

3. T

4. T

5. T

6. F While there is a tendency to move toward full employment or potential output, there is nothing that requires the aggregate demand and supply to always intersect there.

7. F Equilibrium is determined by intersection of both curves.

8. T

9. F

10. F

SUPPLEMENTARY EXERCISES

1. $C + I + G + (X - IM) = 1,700 + .8Y - 5P$

2. $P = 340 - .04Y$ *or* $Y = 8,500 - 25P$

3. $P = 95; Y = 6,125; C = 4,572.5; I = 800; G = 850; X - IM = -97.5$

4. $P = 90; Y = 6,000; C = 4495; I = 750; G = 850; X - IM = -95$

   New expenditure schedule:

   $C + I + G + (X - IM) = 1,650 + .8Y - 5P$

   New aggregate demand curve:

   $P = 330 - .04Y$

CHAPTER 29
CHAPTER REVIEW

(1) fiscal; expenditure; demand; supply

(2) up; 1; 1

(3) are not; higher; permanent; less than; investment

(4) income; consumption; minus; plus

(5) up; variable; fixed

(6) less; smaller

(7) smaller

(8) MPC; smaller; smaller; flatter

(9) less than

(10) steeper

(11) consumption; MPC; less than; less; smaller

(12) increase; decrease; decrease; increase

(13) supply; increase

IMPORTANT TERMS AND CONCEPTS QUIZ

1. d

2. c

3. f

4. b

5. e

6. g

BASIC EXERCISES

1. Total spending: 5,700; 5,850; 6,000; 6,150; 6,300; 6,450; 6,600; equilibrium = 6,000

2. Total spending: 5,500; 5,650; 5,800; 5,950; 6,100; 6,250; 6,400; equilibrium = 5,500

3. 2.5 = 500/200

4. Total spending: 5,700; 5,850; 6,000; 6,150; 6,300; 6,450; 6,600; equilibrium = 6,000

5. 2.0 = 500/250

6. The multiplier for a change in taxes is less than the multiplier for a change in government purchases.

7. No. The increase in GDP from the multiplier process increased tax revenues by $125, an amount less than the reduction in taxes that initiated the multiplier process.

8. 100 = 250/2.5; 125 = 250/2.0

9. 5,500; the multipliers are the same.

SELF-TESTS FOR UNDERSTANDING
Test A

1. c   Money supply is monetary policy decision.

2. d

3. b

4. a

5. c

6. b   With fixed taxes $\Delta DI = \Delta$ GDP and in this case only C changes as GDP changes.

7. a   With variable taxes Δ DI $<$ Δ GDP leading to a smaller change in C when GDP changes then in question 6.

8. d

9. c

10. a

11. b   These changes leave disposable income unchanged. See question 3, Test A.

12. b   Since ΔGDP = $\Delta G \times$ multiplier; $\Delta G = \Delta$GDP/multiplier.

13. a   A reduction in transfer payments reduces disposable income and aggregate demand.

14. a

15. c   A reduction in income tax rates makes the expenditure schedule steeper and increases the value of the multiplier.

16. b   A change in any variable affecting demand except price will lead to a shift in the aggregate demand curve.

17. c

18. c

19. c

20. b

Test B

1. F   See comment to question 15, Test A.

2. T

3. F   Multiplier applies to any change in autonomous spending, i.e. any vertical shift in expenditure schedule.

4. F

5. F

6. F

7. F

8. T

9. F

10. F

SUPPLEMENTARY EXERCISES

1. Income taxes are an important reason why Okun's multiplier is less than the oversimplified formula.

2. The multiplier for a change in taxes is less than the multiplier for changes in autonomous spending.

APPENDIX
BASIC EXERCISE: APPENDIX

1. Y = 340 + 0.8 [Y - (-700 + 0.25Y)] + 800 + 850 - 150

   Y = [340 + 560 + 800 + 850 - 150]/[1 - 0.8 (1 - 0.25)]

   Y = 6,000

2. No; Y declines by 25 to $5,975; tax and spending multipliers differ. Deficit increases from 50 to 56.25

3. Multipliers:

   $\Delta I = 2.5$; $\Delta Y/ \Delta I = 1/(1-b(1-t))$

   $\Delta G = 2.5$; $\Delta Y/\Delta G = 1/(1-b(1-t))$

   $\Delta(X - IM) = 2.5$; $\Delta Y/\Delta(X - IM)$

   $= 1/(1-b(1-t))$

   $\Delta T_0 = -2.0$ (change in intercept)

   $\Delta Y/\Delta T_0 = -b/(1-b(1-t))$

   $b = .8$; $t = .25$

CHAPTER 30
CHAPTER REVIEW

(1) barter; more difficult

(2) money; commodity; fiat

(3) M1; M2

(4) 1,097.4; 4,064.8

(5) lending; 900; reserve requirement

(6) 1/(reserve requirement); less

(7) smaller; excess; smaller

(8) contraction; no

IMPORTANT TERMS AND CONCEPTS QUIZ

1. c

2. j

3. g

4. m

5. m

6. d

7. t

8. n

9. s

10. k

11. o

12. e

13. f

14. p

15. v

16. u

17. b

18. r

19. l

20. h

21. q

22. a

BASIC EXERCISES

1. $10,000; unchanged; col. 1: $1,000; $9,000

2. col. 2: $1,000; $9,000; $10,000; $1,000; 0

3. col. 3: $9,000; 0; $9,000; $900; $8,100; $19,000; $9,000

4. col. 4: $900; $8,100; $9,000; $900; 0

5. col. 5: $8,100; 0; $8,100; $810; $7,290; $27,100; $17,100

6. B: $9,000; C: $8,100; D: $7,290; E: $6,561; 0.1; $100,000; required reserve ratio.

SELF-TESTS FOR UNDERSTANDING
Test A

1. b

2. c

3. a

4. c   M1 includes cash in circulation. Vault cash is included in a bank's reserves.

5. b, d

6. b

7. c

8. c

9. d

10. d

11. c

12. d   The increase in deposits offsets the reduction in cash in circulation.

13. c

14. d

15. a   38,000; net increase in money supply = deposit expansion - cash deposit.

16. a

17. a

18. d $100 \div (0.2) = 500$

19. a   Interbank claims lead to offsetting chains of deposit creation and destruction.

20. b   total reserves = required + excess.

Test B

1. T

2. F

3. T

4. F

5. F

6. T

7. F

8. F

9. F

10. T

SUPPLEMENTARY EXERCISES

1. 2,500; 1,500

2. Change in deposits = $[1/(M + E + C)] \times$ (change in reserves)

CHAPTER 31
CHAPTER REVIEW

(1) 1914; central; 12; Board; Governors; Federal Open Market; fiscal; monetary

(2) excess

(3) increase; larger; expansionary; required; contractionary

(4) securities; buys; increase; reduction; destruction

(5) higher; higher; discount rate

(6) more; fewer; more; larger

(7) right; demand

(8) decreases; increased; right; increased; left

(9) intersection; supply; right; increase; decrease; left; decrease; increase

(10) supply; demand; shift in; shift in; demand; supply

IMPORTANT TERMS AND CONCEPTS QUIZ

1. b

2. h

3. f

4. j

5. e

6. i

7. a

8. d

9. g

BASIC EXERCISES

1. a. decrease; left; contractionary; fall; rise

   b. increase; creation; right; expansionary; rise; fall

   c. less; decline; decline; left; contractionary; fall; rise

2. a. The scatter of points has a positive slope suggesting that an increase in the difference between the federal funds rate and the discount rate is associated with a larger volume of bank borrowing from the Fed.

SELF-TESTS FOR UNDERSTANDING
Test A

1. d

2. d

3. c

4. b

5. b

6. d

7. c   Multiplier is determined by slope of expenditure schedule (e.g., MPC and tax rates) along with the slope of aggregate supply curve.

8. d   Shift of aggregate demand curve to left should reduce inflation, that is make prices lower than they otherwise would be.

9. b

10. d   Higher interest rates reduce investment spending

11. c   Money supply schedule shifts to the right.

12. c

13. b

14. a, c

15. a   Discount rate affects banks' willingness to borrow reserves.

16. c   A change in interest rates leads to a movement along the demand for money schedule.

17. b

18. a

19. a, d It takes time for an increase in investment to affect the aggregate supply curve.
     p.

20. b

Test B

1. F

2. F

3. F

4. F

5. F   Reduction in reserve requirement shifts money supply schedule to the right, increasing M and decreasing R.

6. F

7. F   Interest rates affect the opportunity cost of holding money.

8. T

9. F   Changes in monetary policy lead to shifts in the aggregate demand curve.

10. T

SUPPLEMENTARY EXERCISES

1. a. $Y = 6,000$; $C = 3,650$; $I = 1,350$; $G = 900$; $X - IM = 100$

    b. Y increases to 6,240; $C = 3,710$; $I = 1,470$; $G = 900$; $X - IM = 100$

    c. In this model, equilibrium in the income-expenditure diagram depends on the rate of interest. The expenditure schedule is as follows:

    $C + I + G + (X - IM)$

    $= 650 + .6(5/6) Y + 1,710 - 30r + 900 + 100$

    $= 3,360 - 30r + .5Y$

The 45-degree line is $C + I + G + (X - IM) = Y$. Solving these two equations for one expression in Y and r yields

$Y = 6,720 - 60r$

Setting the demand for money equal to supply of money yields a second expression in Y and r.

$Y = 20BR + 50r.$

When $BR = 270$, $Y = 6,000$, and $r = 12$, $M = 1,380$. The value of M can be found from either the demand for money equation or the supply of money equation.

    d. Changing bank reserve shifts the second equation for Y and r. A little experimentation should show that bank reserves of 292 will yield an interest rate of 8 and a money stock of 1,480.

2. a. $1,500; $600

    b. $1,220.80; $698.87

CHAPTER 32
CHAPTER REVIEW

(1) GDP; money

(2) nominal GDP; M; V; P; Y

(3) money; does not; nominal GDP; 100

(4) should not; opportunity cost; increase; decrease

(5) velocity

(6) decline; increase; increase

(7) higher; increase; higher; demand; supply

(8) monetary; fiscal

(9) higher; higher; left; right

(10) output; prices; steep; short; long

(11) are not

(12) does not

IMPORTANT TERMS AND CONCEPTS QUIZ

1. e

2. c

3. d

4. b

BASIC EXERCISES

1. a. V1: 7.12; 6.64 6.31; 6.52; 6.95; 7.08; 6.88; 6.46; 6.08; 6.07; 6.36; 6.93; 7.58; 7.88

    V_2:1.73; 1.69 1.68; 1.72; 1.78; 1.78; 1.77; 1.83; 1.90; 1.98;2.03; 2.05; 2.06; 2.02

    b. Col. 3: 4,746.5; 4,935.0; 4,889.4; 5,098.3; 5,637.8; 6,086.6; 6,651.6; 6,971.6; 6,962.8; 6,931.7; 7,036.2; 7,408.4; 8,185.8

    Col. 5: 4,520.3; 4,708.8; 4,945.0; 5,261.6; 5,736.5; 5,956.2; 6,030.4; 6,315.2; 6,648.7; 7,090.5; 7,622.1; 8,041.9; 8,710.2

    c. Errors are highest when velocity changes. The greater variation in V_1 leads to larger prediction errors based on M_1.

2. Each speaker is arguing that the demand for money has shifted to the right. In both cases the shift is consistent with the reported increase in M and r.

    Speaker A is arguing that the shift in the demand for money derives from an autonomous shift in the aggregate demand curve to the right. According to A, it is the increase in nominal GDP that has shifted the demand for money schedule. A shift of the money supply curve to the left, i.e., an open market sale, would increase interest rates even further, inducing an offsetting shift of the aggregate demand curve to the left. With a bit of luck, the policy induced shift of the aggregate demand curve to the left would offset the autonomous shift in the aggregate demand curve to the right, and there would be no inflation.

Speaker B is arguing that there has been an autonomous increase in the demand for money, that is an increase that is unrelated to any change in nominal GDP. If there is no offsetting increase in the supply of money schedule, interest rates will rise, inducing a shift of the aggregate demand curve to the left. In this case the appropriate action would be to shift the money supply curve to the right and hold interest rates constant to avoid inducing a shift in the aggregate demand curve.

The appropriate policy response, whether to focus on M or r, depends upon the origins of the shift in the demand for money.

SELF-TESTS FOR UNDERSTANDING
Test A

1. c

2. b

3. a, b, c, d The increase in nominal GDP may reflect an increase in *Y, P,* or both.

4. a, b, d

5. a

6. a   The reduction in *V* means that the percentage increase in *P* times *Y* must be less than the percentage increase in *M.*

7. d

8. d   If *V* is unchanged, an increase in *M* will increase nominal GDP but without more information one cannot be sure how much of the increase will in terms of real output and how much will be in terms of prices.

9. b   This change should lower interest rates and reduce velocity.

10. c

11. d   Increase in taxes would lower nominal GDP.

12. c

13. a, b, c, d

14. b

15. b

16. a, b

17. a

18. b

19. d

20. c

Test B

1. T

2. F

3. T

4. F   Fig. 32-5 and Fig. 32-6 in the text.

5. T

6. T

7. F

8. T

9. T

10. F

CHAPTER 33
CHAPTER REVIEW

(1)   spending; revenue; revenue; spending; deficit; surplus

(2)   down; left; decline; decline; deficit; increase; decrease; accentuate

(3)   will; will not

(4)   increase; reduction

(5)   monetized; greater

(6)   foreigners

(7)   investment; recession; war; crowding in; crowding out; high; out

(8)   right; restrictive; deficit; higher; lower; more slowly

IMPORTANT TERMS AND CONCEPTS QUIZ

1. d

2. a

3. h

4. c

5. f

6. i

7. g

8. e

BASIC EXERCISES

1. a. Total spending: 6,250; 6,375; 6,500; 6,625; 6,750; equilibrium = 6,500

   b. -25

   c. surplus; 37.5

   d. Total spending: 6,125; 6,250; 6,375; 6,500; 6,625; equilibrium = 6,250; actual deficit increases to 87.5; structural surplus is unchanged at 37.5.

   e. raise; lower equilibrium level of income.

   f. lower; lower equilibrium level of income.

   g. 146; 6,016.7

   h. -175; 5,900

Note: Figuring out the correct answers to g and h is a bit tricky. With regard to g, increasing the fixed component of taxes by 87.5 would eliminate the deficit if Y did not change. However, the increase in fixed taxes will reduce Y and result in a smaller net increase in taxes. Letting FT stand for the fixed component of taxes, one can find the necessary increase in fixed taxes by solving the following two equations:

ΔDeficit = ΔFT - 0.25 ΔY

$\Delta Y = \Delta FT$ [MPC/(0.5)].

The first equation shows how the deficit changes when the

fixed component of taxes and Y change. The second shows how Y changes when the fixed component of taxes changes. The number 0.25 measures the responsiveness of taxes to income, and the expression [MPC/(0.5)] is the multiplier for a change in fixed taxes in this model. Setting the change in the deficit equal to –87.5, one can solve for the necessary change in fixed taxes and the associated change in Y. A similar approach provides the answer to question h, but note that in the equation for ΔY one must use the multiplier for a change in government spending, not the multiplier for a change in fixed taxes:

Δ Deficit = ΔG - 0.25 ΔY

$\Delta Y = \Delta G$ [1/(0.5)].

2. a. $100 billion

   b. The increase in GDP increases tax receipts so the increase in the actual deficit will be less than the increase in the structural deficit.

   c. An open market sale would increase interest rates, reduce investment spending and shift the aggregate demand curve to the left, offsetting the shift to the right from the increase in the structural deficit.

   d. Under Option B there is more public spending, but less private investment. In a few chapters we will also see that, with flexible exchange rates, higher interest rates are likely to mean a currency appreciation, a reduction in net exports, and an increase in the trade deficit. When choosing between Option A and Option B, one would want to compare the benefits from higher public spending against the

impacts on investment and the trade deficit.

SELF-TESTS FOR UNDERSTANDING
Test A

1. d

2. d

3. a

4. c   Note that if revenues at full employment exceed spending, then the result is a structural surplus.

5. c

6. a

7. b, c

8. b

9. d

10. c

11. c   Monetization means a further rightward shift of the aggregate demand curve.

12. d

13. a

14. a, b, c, d, e, f   It all depends on why the deficit increased

15. b   A reduction in taxes would not reduce the deficit. An increase in taxes would reduce the deficit but would not offset the shift in the aggregate demand curve.

16. b   When a deficit arises because the aggregate demand curve shifts to the left, the decline in GDP shifts the demand for money curve to the left, lowering interest rates.

17. d

18. b

19. a, b

20. d

Test B

1. F

2. F   Depending upon the strength of private demand, a

deficit or surplus may be required to insure that aggregate demand and supply curves intersect at full employment.

3. F

4. F   See answer to question 16, Test A

5. T

6. F

7. F

8. T

9. T

10. T

SUPPLEMENTARY EXERCISES

1. It is important to distinguish between deficits during periods of recession and deficits from deliberate increases in G or reductions in T. All of the examples come from periods when the economy was falling into recession.

CHAPTER 34
CHAPTER REVIEW

(1) higher; negatively; Phillips; negative

(2) incorrect

(3) inflationary; natural (or full-employment); vertical

(4) smaller; larger; higher; steeper

(5) vertical

(6) indexing

(7) increase; more

IMPORTANT TERMS AND CONCEPTS QUIZ

1. b

2. e

3. a

4. g

5. c

6. f

BASIC EXERCISE

1. purchase; decrease; decrease; increase; increase

2. 103

3. The aggregate supply curve will continue to shift up as long as output exceeds full-employment level of output.

4. a. expansionary; 109

   b. restrictive; 6,100

SELF-TESTS FOR UNDERSTANDING
Test A

1. d

2. d

3. a

4. d

5. c

6. a

7. a The aggregate supply curve shifts up when the cost of any input increases.

8. c

9. a

10. c

11. d

12. a, c

13. d

14. b

15. d Changes in both fiscal and monetary policy shift in the aggregate demand curve.

16. c

17. d

18. a

19. c

20. d

Test B

1. F

2. F Any shift in the aggregate demand curve, from whatever source, will affect prices.

3. T

4. T

5. T

6. F

7. T

8. F Both monetary and fiscal policy shift the aggregate demand curve along the aggregate supply curve with similar effects on prices.

9. F See comments to question 15, Test A, and question 3, Basic Exercise.

10. F

CHAPTER 35
CHAPTER REVIEW

(1) scale

(2) comparative

(3) A; B; 10000; wheat

(4) 8000; 7000; cars; wheat

(5) demand; supply; exporting, importing

(6) tariffs; quotas; subsidies; price; quantity

(7) government

(8) low; do not; can

(9) adjustment

(10) defense; infant

(11) both; comparative

IMPORTANT TERMS AND CONCEPT QUIZ

1. j

2. d

3. g

4. m

5. i

6. o

7. f

8. a

9. l

10. h

11. k

12. b

13. e

BASIC EXERCISES

1. a. Japan; Japan

   b. 1.25; 1.5; Canada; Japan; Canada; Japan

   c. Calculators: 1,500,000; 3,000,000; 4,500,000

   Backpacks: 1,200,000; 2,000,000; 3,200,000

   d. 600,000; 480,000

   e. 1,200,000 hours; 600,000 calculators; 400,000 backpacks

   f. increase; 80,000

   g. Calculators: 900,000; 3,675,000; 4,575,000

   Backpacks: 1,680,000; 1,550,000; 3,230,000

   The output of both calculators and backpacks has increased as compared to the initial situation in Question c.

   h. Canadian backpack output would fall to 720,000. Japan would need to reallocate 1,440,000 labor hours. Total calculator output would fall to 4,380,000. This reallocation is not in line with the principle of comparative advantage. The opportunity cost of backpacks in terms of calculators is greater in Japan than in Canada.

   i. There will be no change in total world output. Neither country has a comparative advantage. The opportunity cost of increased calculator or backpack production is the same in both countries.

2. a. India: $10; 1,000 United States: $40; 600

   b. $20; production in India increases to 1200; production in United States decreases to 400; India exports, United States imports 400 shirts.

c. United States: price = $30; production = 500; imports = 200

India: price = $15; production = 1100; exports = 200

United States; India; United States; India; decreased

d. Tariff of $15

3. a. Arcadia

b. Ricardia

c. Arcadia should increase the production of computers and export computers to Ricardia which should increase the production of cheese and export cheese to Arcadia. The following table is a particular example that is illustrates how by changing production in line with the principle of comparative advantage and then trading, both countries can consume outside their PPF.

	Computers	Cheese
Arcadia	+ 4	− 3
Ricardia	− 2	+ 4
World	+ 2	+ 1

If Arcadia and Ricardia trade one computer for 1,167 pounds of cheese, both countries will be able to consume outside their PPF. Arcadia exports up 3 computers for 3,500 pounds of cheese while Ricardia imports 3 computers for 3,500 pounds of cheese. Both countries end up with 1 more computer and an additional 500 pounds of cheese as compared to their pre-trade situation.

SELF-TESTS FOR UNDERSTANDING
Test A

1. b

2. d

3. b

4. d

5. a

6. b

7. d

8. d

9. a

10. a

11. c

12. a   Export subsidies increase the volume of trade.

13. a

14. b

15. c

16. c

17. d   Although domestic demand declines, a tariff induces a greater decline in foreign imports, allowing for an increase in domestic production.

18. c   Quota will increase price paid by domestic citizens.

19. b, d Higher prices hurt the users of computer chips—computer manufacturers and consumers.

20. c

Test B

1. F

2. F

3. F   Trade should reflect comparative not absolute advantage.

4. T   Differences in natural resources are one source of differences in comparative advantage.

5. T

6. F   As world exports must equal world imports, it is not possible for all countries to increase exports without increasing

imports.

7. T

8. F

9. F

10. F

SUPPLEMENTARY EXERCISES

1. a. Baulmovia: 8,100; Bilandia: 17,150

b. 12; Baulmovia; Bilandia; 100

c. Baulmovia: price = 10;

Bilandia: price = 14.5;

Trade = 50.

d. 50

e. Tariff revenues accrue to the government. Tariffs do not protect high-cost foreign producers.

2. Production of 14.4 million bolts of cloth and 10.8 million barrels of wine allows Ricardia to choose from the outermost consumption possibilities line. Note that to be on the outermost consumption possibilities line Ricardia must choose to produce at the point where the slope of the production possibilities frontier equals the ratio of world prices.

CHAPTER 36
CHAPTER REVIEW

(1) exchange; appreciated; fewer; depreciated

(2) demand; supply; exports; financial; physical; supply

(3) demand; increase; appreciation; supply; depreciation; appreciation

(4) purchasing power parity; depreciate; depreciating; appreciating

(5) Bretton

(6) deficit; demand; supply; surplus; surplus; exchange rate

(7)   buy; increasing

(8)   deficit; increase; decrease; contraction; reduction

(9)   disliked

(10)   speculators

(11)   euro

IMPORTANT TERMS AND CONCEPTS QUIZ

1.   b

2.   n

3.   r

4.   k

5.   d

6.   c

7.   q

8.   o

9.   h

10.   p

11.   l

12.   i

13.   m

14.   e

15.   j

16.   f

17.   a

BASIC EXERCISES

1.   a. $8.48. Sales of French wine would increase. Sales of California wines would decrease. The U.S. balance of payments would show a deficit.

    b. $1.25; appreciation; depreciation

    c.   United States (57 percent vs. 33 percent)

    d.   deficit

    e.   depreciate

2.   Col. 1: $28,000,000; £10,000,000

    Col. 2: $28,000,000; £10,769,231

Col. 3: $28,000,000; £11,666,667

If there is no devaluation, you are out only the transactions costs. If the pound is devalued, you stand to make a handsome profit. As the prospect of devaluation increases, there is a greater incentive to sell your pounds before their price falls. Your efforts to sell pounds, along with similar actions by others, will only increase the pressure for devaluation.

On November 18, 1967, the pound was devalued from $2.80 to $2.40.

3.   a.   The demand curve may shift to the left if some Americans now find Japanese investments less attractive. The supply curve shifts to the right as Japanese investors are attracted by higher U.S. interest rates. With floating rates, the Yen depreciates. With fixed rates, a deficit results.

    b.   The demand curve shifts to the right. There is no shift in the supply curve. With floating rates, the yen appreciates. With fixed rates, a surplus results.

    c.   The demand curve shifts to the left as Americans import less. The supply curve shifts to the right if a recession leads to lower dollar prices of U.S. exports. With floating rates, the yen depreciates. With fixed rates, a deficit results.

    d.   The demand curve shifts to the left. The supply curve might shift to the right if Japanese citizens import more. With floating rates, the yen depreciates. With fixed rates, a deficit results.

    e.   The supply curve shifts to the right as the increase in

the price of Japanese rice leads Japanese citizens to increase their demand for American rice. With floating rates the yen depreciates. With fixed rates, a deficit results.

SELF-TESTS FOR UNDERSTANDING
Test A

1.   b

2.   c

3.   c

4.   b, c

5.   a, c

6.   c

7.   b

8.   b, d, f   These factors should increase the demand for American goods or financial assets and, hence, the demand for American dollars.

9.   f should increase the supply of dollars as Americans increase their demand for foreign goods. b, c, d, and e should increase the demand for dollars. a should reduce the supply of dollars. f

10.   b

11.   c

12.   a, b

13.   d

14.   b   A 6 percent appreciation of the dollar is necessary to equalize the purchasing power of dollars and reals.

15.   a

16.   b   Higher inflation in the Brazil increases supply of reals as Brazilians demand less expensive American goods resulting in U.S. surplus and Brazilian deficit.

17.   a, c, d   All should shift the supply of domestic currency to the right.

18. a, c, d   At the overvalued exchange rate, demand for Zenon currency would be less than under a system of floating exchange rates.

19. c

20. b   Exchange rates should adjust so that, except for transactions costs, direct conversion between kronor and euros costs neither more nor less than first converting into dollars and then into kronor or euros.

Test B

1. F   An appreciating currency buys more units of foreign currency; a depreciating currency buys fewer units of foreign currency;.

2. F   A pure system of floating exchange rates involves no government intervention by definition.

3. T

4. T   An increase in imports would mean an increase in the supply of dollars by Americans. The shift in the supply schedule for dollars would increase a deficit or reduce any surplus.

5. T

6. T

7. F

8. F

9. T

10. F   Deficit countries were under greater pressure to make adjustments.

CHAPTER 37
CHAPTER REVIEW

(1) closed; open

(2) decrease; are; less; increase; decrease; decrease; increase; decrease; increase

(3) shift in; down; left

(4) less; downward; more; upward

(5) increase; appreciation

(6) decrease; up; right; increase; appreciation; left; down; offset; lower; increase; offset

(7) appreciation; enhance

(8) expansionary; contractionary; contractionary; expansionary; exports; lower

IMPORTANT TERMS AND CONCEPTS QUIZ

1. a
2. e
3. f
4. c
5. d

BASIC EXERCISES

1. Appreciation: Exports decrease; Imports increase; Net exports decrease; Expenditure Schedule shifts down; Aggregate Demand Curve shifts to the left; Aggregate Supply Curve shifts down; Real GDP decreases; Price level decreases.

Depreciation: Exports increase; Imports decrease; Net exports increase; Expenditure Schedule shifts up; Aggregate Demand Curve shifts to the right; Aggregate Supply Curve shifts up; Real GDP increases; Price level increases.

2. Increase in G: Interest rate increases; Exchange rate appreciates; GDP and price level down, which work to offset the initial impact of the increase in G.

Decrease in G: Interest rate decreases; Exchange rate depreciates; GDP and price level up, which work to offset the initial impact of the decrease in G.

Open Market Sale: Interest rate increases; Exchange rate appreciates; GDP and price level down, which work to enhance the initial impact of the open

market sale.

Open Market Purchase: Interest rate decreases; Exchange rate depreciates; GDP and price level increase, which work to enhance the initial impact of the open market purchase.

3. The impact of monetary policy is enhanced. The impact of fiscal policy is diminished.

SELF-TESTS FOR UNDERSTANDING
Test A

1. c
2. b
3. b
4. a
5. a
6. c
7. c
8. d
9. a
10. b, d   The capital outflow will tend to depreciate the exchange rate which leads to an increase in net exports.
11. b
12. c   The decrease in exports following an appreciation of the dollar shifts the aggregate demand curve to the left.
13. c
14. b   The reduction in interest rates from the move to expansionary monetary policy leads to a capital outflow and a depreciation of the dollar.
15. a
16. c
17. b
18. a, c
19. c
20. a, b

Test B

1. F

2. F   A change in exports, whether from a change in foreign GDP or a change in the exchange rate, is modeled as an autonomous change in spending with multiplier effects similar to those of any other autonomous change.

3. F   Autonomous shifts in investment spending affect interest rates, exchange rates, net exports, and the trade deficit in a manner analogous to changes in fiscal policy.

4. T

5. T

6. T

7. F

8. F

9. F

10. F